YOU CAN'T SAY BOOBS ON SUNDAY

The Second Collection of the Syndicated Cartoon
Stone Soup

by
Jan Eliot

Cheers!
Jan Eliot

FOUR PANEL PRESS
Eugene, Oregon

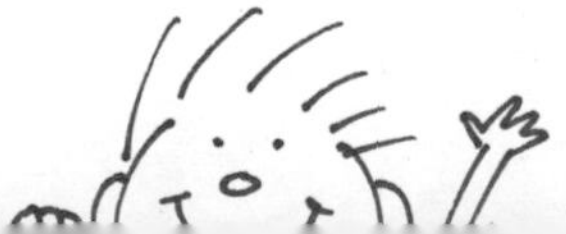

Published by Four Panel Press, P.O. Box 50032, Eugene, OR 97405.

Stone Soup is distributed internationally by Universal Press Syndicate.

ISBN 0-9674102-0-7

Library of Congress Catalog Card Number: 99-65947

A portion of the profits from this book will go to alleviate hunger through our local food bank, Food for Lane County.

For Mary Petty, Helen Hokinson, Dale Messick, Nicole Hollander, Claire Bretecher, Lynn Johnston, and all the other talented women cartoonists who've inspired and encouraged me.

You Can't Say BOOBS On Sunday

When I first became syndicated, my friends thought my new association sounded slightly reminiscent of a relationship with the Mafia. But in fact, my syndicate, Universal Press, has no ties to the mob that I know of, and is essentially my agent, or business partner. They devote themselves to marketing, selling and distributing my work, so that I can devote myself to the job of trying to be funny on a daily basis (which is easier on some days than others). It's a wonderful arrangement.

I also have an editor at the syndicate who tries to make sure I use appropriate commas, appropriate language, and am appropriately funny. She doesn't try to control the direction of my strip. She simply tries to be helpful, insightful, and will generously talk to me in the middle of her own busy day when I have been alone in the studio just a bit too long. Rarely does she censor an idea.

And yet the day came when she called to tell me a particular Sunday strip I'd written would not fly. "Because," as she put it, "you can't say boobs on Sunday."

You can, however, say boobs Monday through Saturday. Apparently comic strip readers are less sensitive during the week. But on Sunday, newspaper editors like to picture Grandma, Grandpa, Dad, and the kids reading the marvelous Sunday Funnies in front of the fire while mom cooks pot roast in the kitchen. Nobody in this setting wants to open up that most wholesome part of the Sunday paper and see—*gasp*— the word BOOBS big as life. Or so I am told.

So I sent in a substitute strip. Mom, Dad, Grandma, and the kids are safe for now. I won't say boobs in the Sunday funnies. But nobody said I couldn't put it in the title of my book.

The Making of *Stone Soup*

People often ask me how I became a cartoonist. The truth is I spent 16 years trying to break into the funny pages. During 10 of those years I was the single mom of two daughters. I was broke a lot, and much of the material for *Stone Soup* comes from those trying and inspirational days, when there was too much life and too little time, money or patience. What got me through? A few good laughs.

I had a good friend, Cynthia, who thought that I was funny. When I was looking for a creative outlet to relieve the boredom of my working life, she suggested cartooning. It was cheap as art forms go, which fit my budget, and relatively quick to complete, which fit my hectic life. When I discovered what a great outlet for my frustrations it was, I was thoroughly hooked. Like most cartoonists I had to keep my "day job" (everything from car sales to graphic design) while I improved my craft and sought syndication. It was a long road, and many times I thought I was crazy to keep trying. The strip saw three incarnations, I spent years being published in tiny papers and newsletters, years doing a weekly feature in two local papers, years earning less than $70 a month as a cartoonist. But in 1994, Universal Press Syndicate decided I was good enough to gamble on, and in 1995 we launched *Stone Soup* in 26 papers. Against all advice, I quit my day job. I was finally, officially, a syndicated cartoonist. It was a dream come true, and I have never been happier.

The characters in Stone Soup come from my life. I have a friend named Wally (though many across the United States have claimed to be him) and a friend named Val. Holly and Alix are not really my two daughters, but rather an amalgamation of my girls and myself as a child. As a matter of fact, all the characters are a bit me and a bit my friends and acquaintances, and many of the situations are stolen from the lives of the people around me. I hope they'll forgive me.

Incidentally, we took the name *Stone Soup* from an old fairy tale. It essentially means "something from nothing." My mother often referred to this when opening our seemingly empty fridge. "There's nothing to eat," I'd say. "Sure there is," she'd counter, "we'll make Stone Soup." Somehow a casserole would appear on the dinner table in an hour, with slightly mysterious contents she'd refuse to reveal.

My daughters thought that this perfectly represented the life we'd led — a life where we often made do, where we had too few resources but somehow, with the help of family and friends, still got by just fine. Something from nothing: *Stone Soup*.

Enjoy! *Jan Eliot*

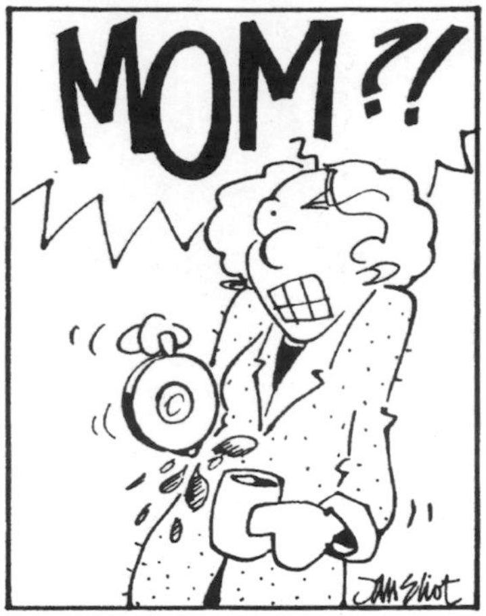
MOM?!

Who's Who, and Why, in *Stone Soup*

VAL

Valerie Stone is a widow in her late 30s. Her husband died when her daughters, Holly and Alix, were quite young. She is a middle-income professional, mature and somewhat serious, who bears much of the financial burden for her extended family. Besides her own two daughters, Val shares her home with her economically strapped sister (who has a 2-year-old son), her mother and a yappy little dog — creating a household filled with controlled chaos.

Val's deceased husband was the love of her life, and between the pressures of a full-time job and raising her daughters she's had little interest in romance. Recently, however, a chance encounter with a motorcycle cop has added a little excitement to her life.

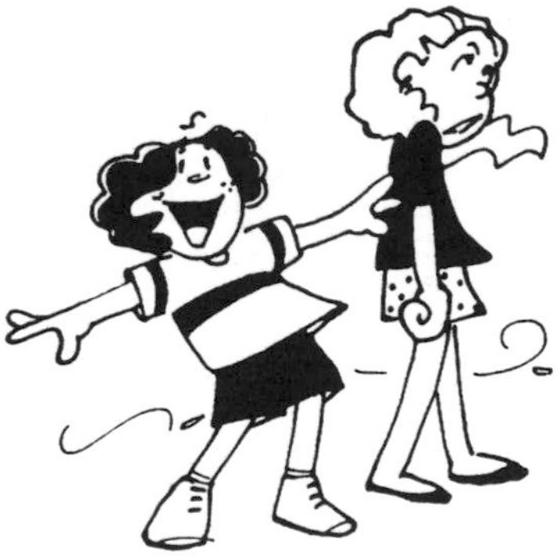

HOLLY and ALIX

These are Val's darling daughters. They are 13 and 10. Young Alix is still in elementary school, in the midst of a blissfully naïve childhood and full of tomboy energy. She is mystified by her sister Holly's middle-school histrionics. Holly, like many girls her age, is full of angst, self-absorbed, and obeys most of the rules most of the time — if it's convenient. Holly and Alix share a room, fight, shout, compete for attention, and generally make their family's life interesting.

JOAN

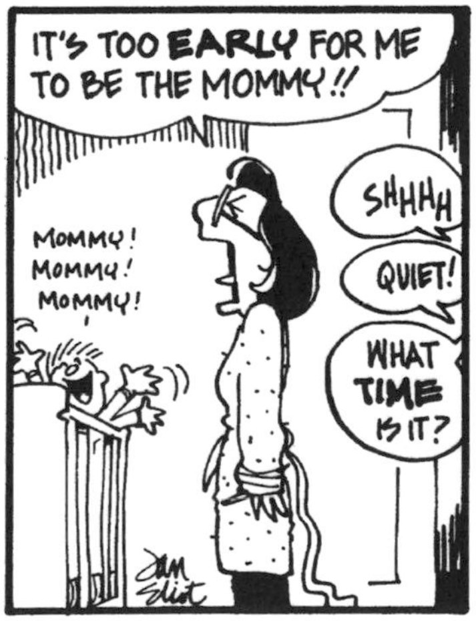
IT'S TOO EARLY FOR ME TO BE THE MOMMY!!
MOMMY! MOMMY! MOMMY!
SHHHH
QUIET!
WHAT TIME IS IT?

Joan is Val's younger sister. She has a 2-year-old son named Max, and has lived with Val ever since her husband Leon went out for milk — and never returned. Rumor has it that the convenience store he visited is in the Virgin Islands. With a young son and fewer career options than her sister Val, Joan struggles to make ends meet. She works at home as a free-lance copywriter.

Since her arrival, Joan has been the object of the affections of Wally, the nice guy next door. Unfortunately, she has for much of her life been attracted to the wrong kind of guy (remember Leon?), and has found Wally a little too "nice." However, after a three-year on-again, off-again relationship, things are looking up.

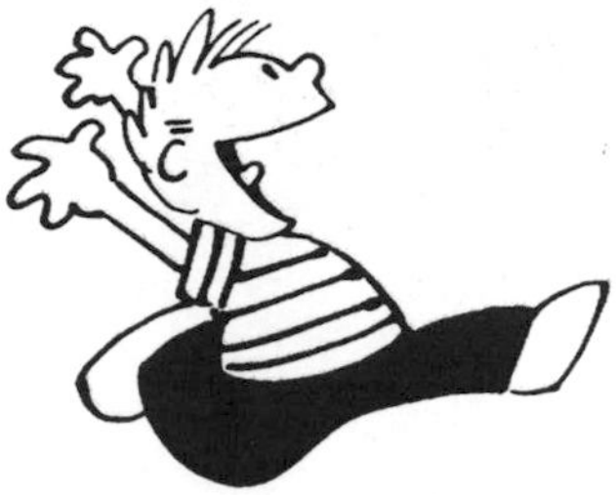

MAX

Joan's 2-year-old has two emotions: He's either thrilled with life or totally miserable. He can move between these emotions at a moment's notice, with little warning. He's a sprightly bundle of energy that is nearly always darting around his mother's feet. He idolizes Wally and the dog.

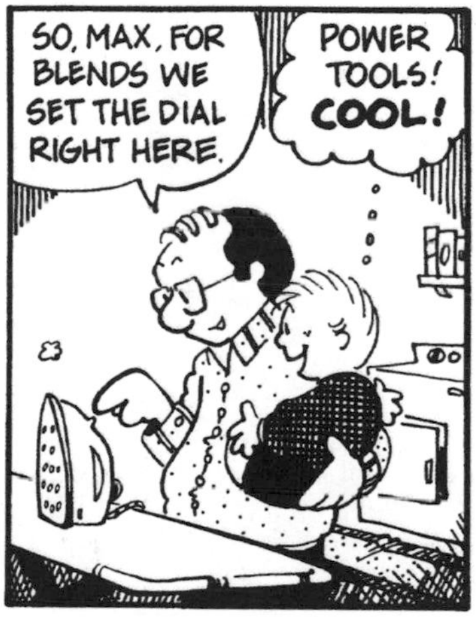

SO, MAX, FOR BLENDS WE SET THE DIAL RIGHT HERE.
POWER TOOLS! COOL!

WALLY

Wally is the epitome of a swell guy. He lives across the fence from the Stone family, steering clear of their chaos and helping out when he can. He's in his 30s, sells insurance, is a little bit schlumpy and balding. He dearly loves Max and Joan, and loves getting to be "dad." Recently his 15-year-old nephew has come to live with him for a while... and it remains to be seen how smoothly this arrangement will go.

GRAMMA

Val and Joan's mother lives upstairs. She is not the usual warm and fuzzy grandmother, but rather pragmatic and sometimes stern. She has no patience for new-age child-rearing techniques, baby-sits on a limited basis, and is always happy to express her opinion, whether it's asked for or not. She has no romance in her life at the moment, but her fans have been lobbying heavily.

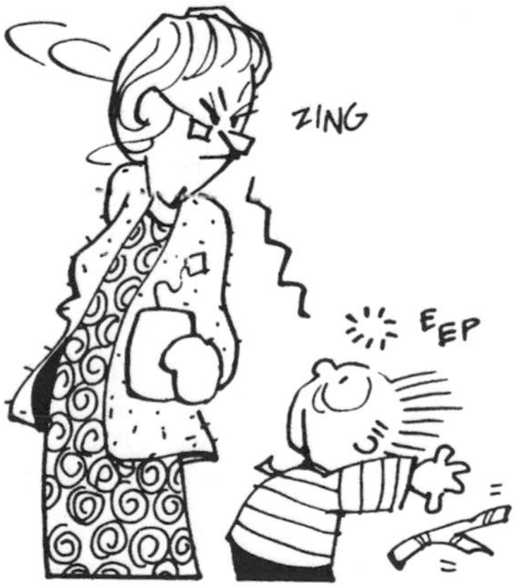

ZING
EEP

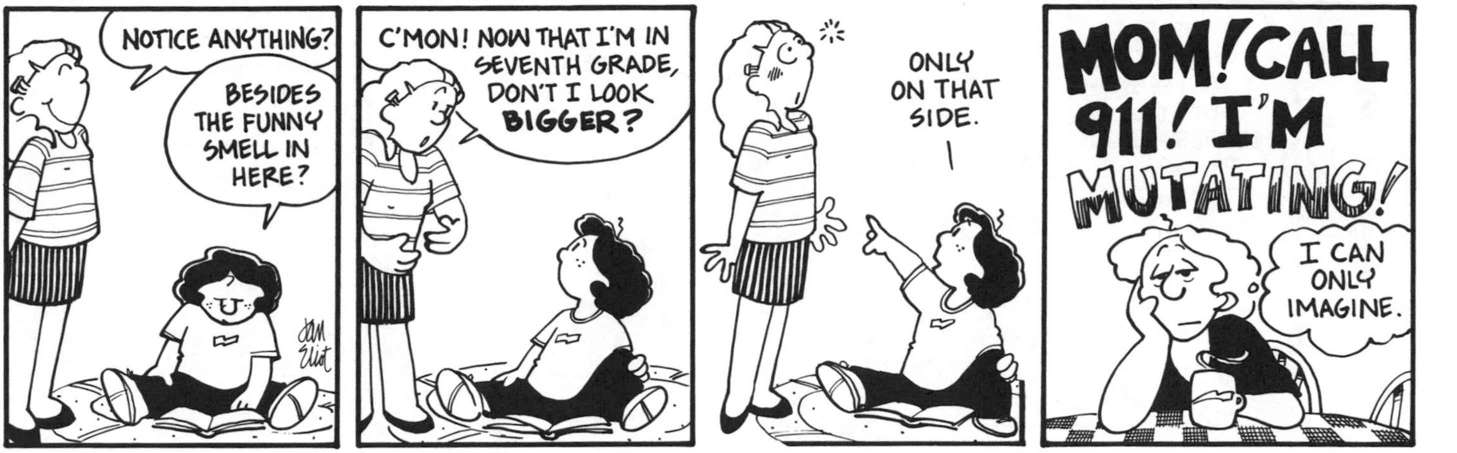
NOTICE ANYTHING?
BESIDES THE FUNNY SMELL IN HERE?
C'MON! NOW THAT I'M IN SEVENTH GRADE, DON'T I LOOK **BIGGER**?
ONLY ON THAT SIDE.
MOM! CALL 911! I'M MUTATING!
I CAN ONLY IMAGINE.

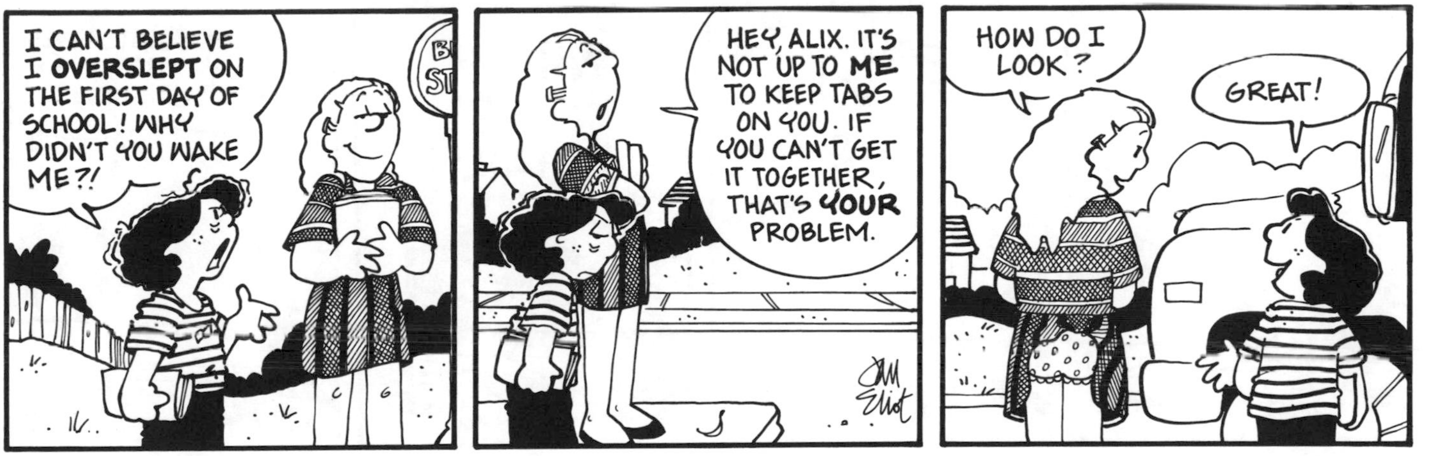
I CAN'T BELIEVE I **OVERSLEPT** ON THE FIRST DAY OF SCHOOL! WHY DIDN'T YOU WAKE ME?!
HEY, ALIX. IT'S NOT UP TO **ME** TO KEEP TABS ON YOU. IF YOU CAN'T GET IT TOGETHER, THAT'S **YOUR** PROBLEM.
HOW DO I LOOK?
GREAT!

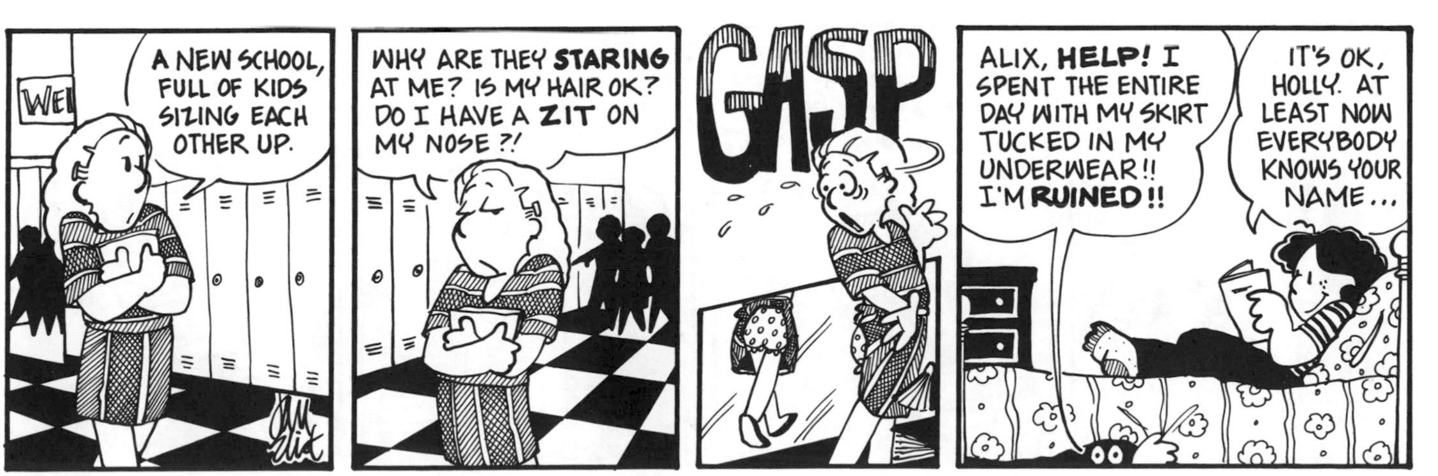
A NEW SCHOOL, FULL OF KIDS SIZING EACH OTHER UP.
WHY ARE THEY **STARING** AT ME? IS MY HAIR OK? DO I HAVE A **ZIT** ON MY NOSE?!
GASP
ALIX, **HELP!** I SPENT THE ENTIRE DAY WITH MY SKIRT TUCKED IN MY UNDERWEAR!! I'M **RUINED**!!
IT'S OK, HOLLY. AT LEAST NOW EVERYBODY KNOWS YOUR NAME...

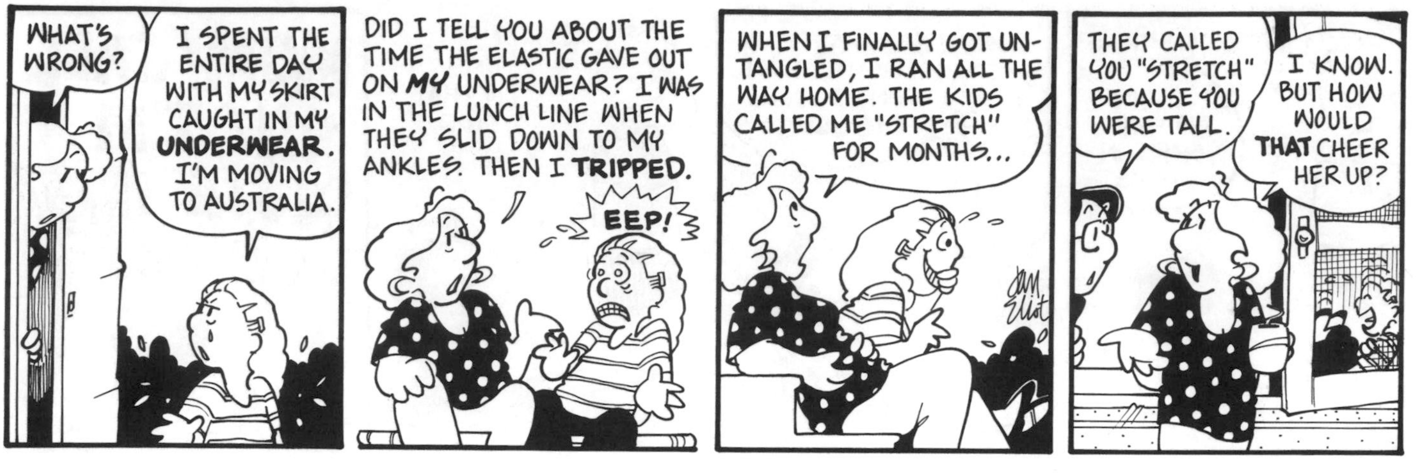
WHAT'S WRONG?
I SPENT THE ENTIRE DAY WITH MY SKIRT CAUGHT IN MY UNDERWEAR. I'M MOVING TO AUSTRALIA.
DID I TELL YOU ABOUT THE TIME THE ELASTIC GAVE OUT ON MY UNDERWEAR? I WAS IN THE LUNCH LINE WHEN THEY SLID DOWN TO MY ANKLES. THEN I TRIPPED.
EEP!
WHEN I FINALLY GOT UNTANGLED, I RAN ALL THE WAY HOME. THE KIDS CALLED ME "STRETCH" FOR MONTHS...
THEY CALLED YOU "STRETCH" BECAUSE YOU WERE TALL.
I KNOW. BUT HOW WOULD THAT CHEER HER UP?

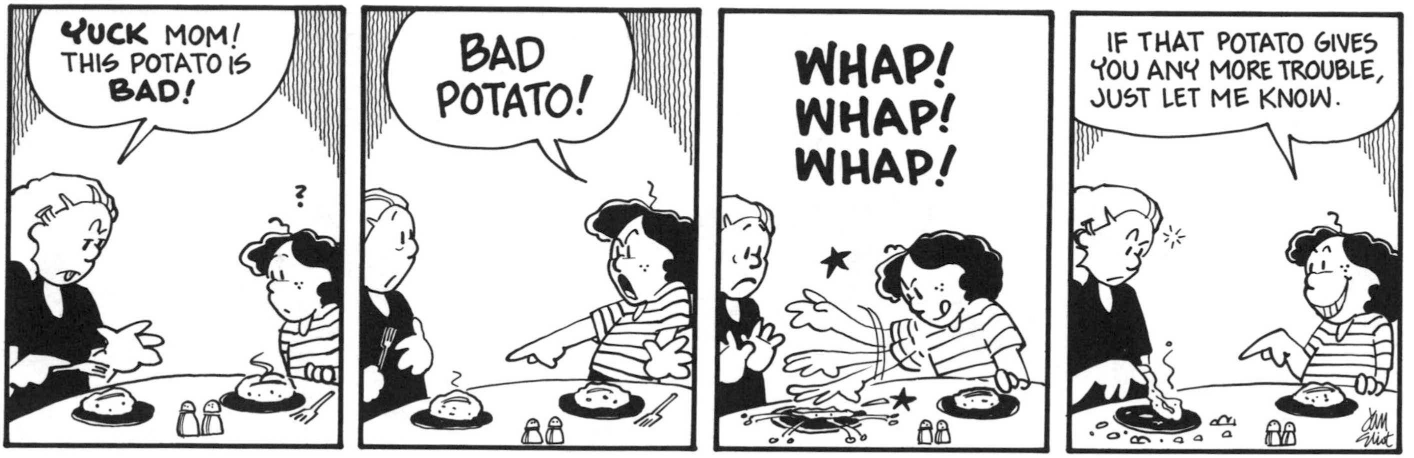
YUCK MOM! THIS POTATO IS BAD!
BAD POTATO!
WHAP! WHAP! WHAP!
IF THAT POTATO GIVES YOU ANY MORE TROUBLE, JUST LET ME KNOW.

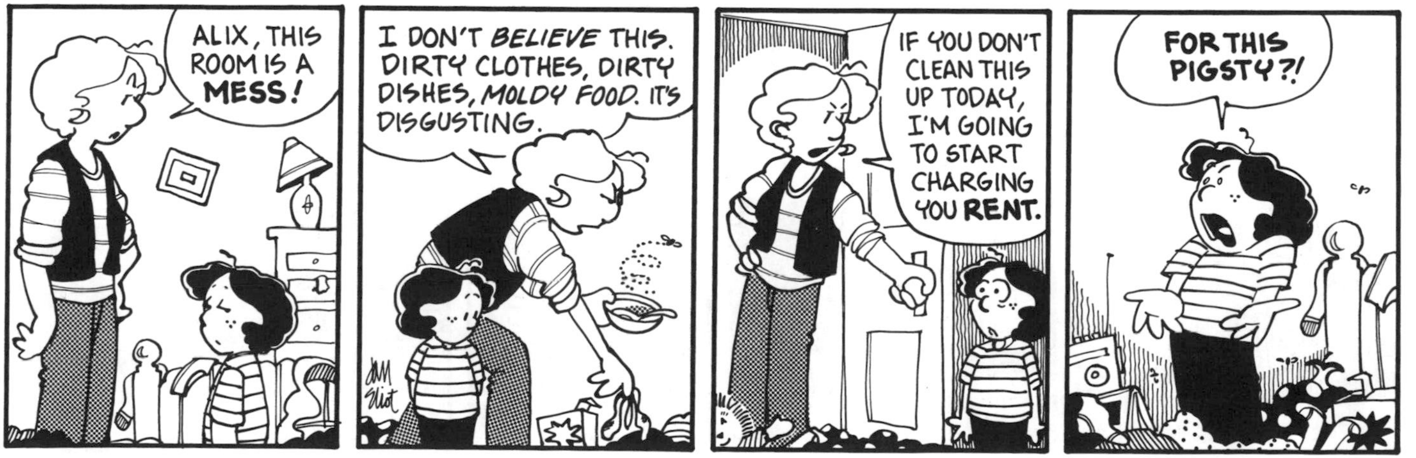
ALIX, THIS ROOM IS A MESS!
I DON'T BELIEVE THIS. DIRTY CLOTHES, DIRTY DISHES, MOLDY FOOD. IT'S DISGUSTING.
IF YOU DON'T CLEAN THIS UP TODAY, I'M GOING TO START CHARGING YOU RENT.
FOR THIS PIGSTY?!

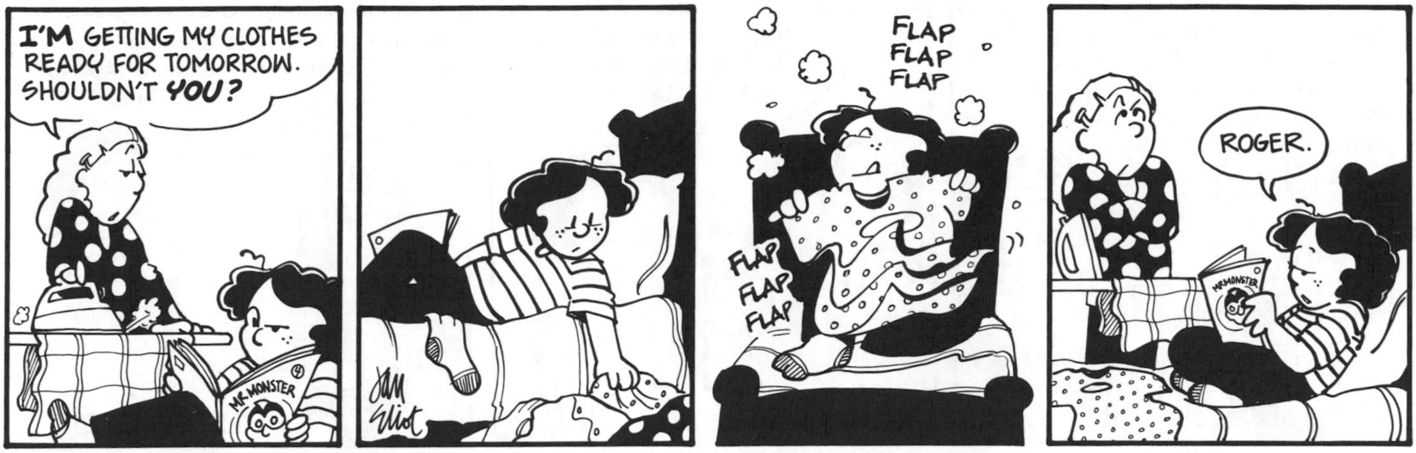
I'M GETTING MY CLOTHES READY FOR TOMORROW. SHOULDN'T YOU?
MR. MONSTER
FLAP FLAP FLAP
FLAP FLAP FLAP
ROGER.

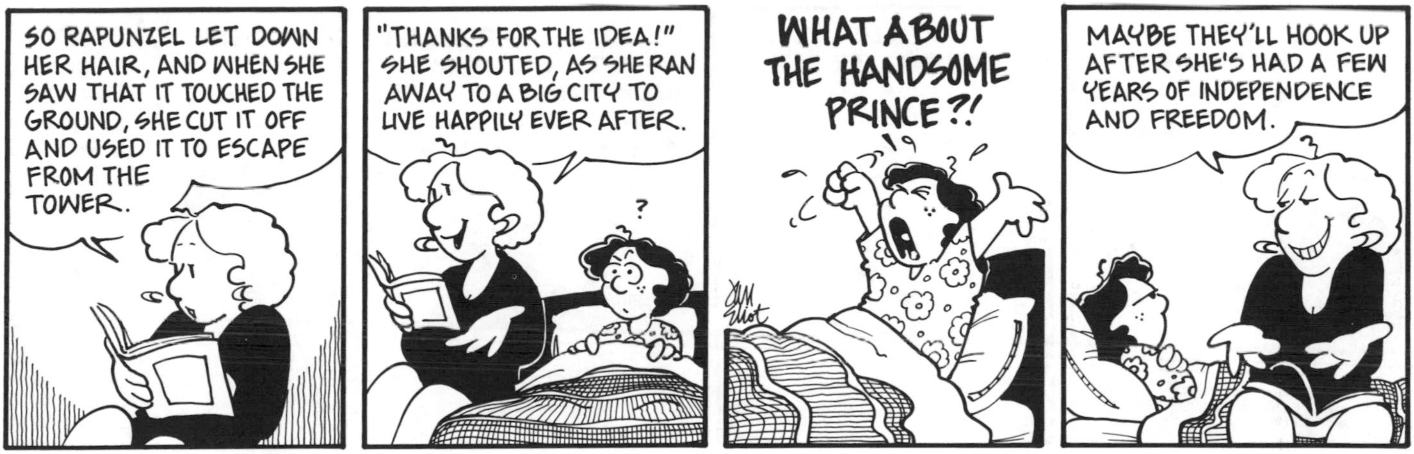
SO RAPUNZEL LET DOWN HER HAIR, AND WHEN SHE SAW THAT IT TOUCHED THE GROUND, SHE CUT IT OFF AND USED IT TO ESCAPE FROM THE TOWER.
"THANKS FOR THE IDEA!" SHE SHOUTED, AS SHE RAN AWAY TO A BIG CITY TO LIVE HAPPILY EVER AFTER.
WHAT ABOUT THE HANDSOME PRINCE?!
MAYBE THEY'LL HOOK UP AFTER SHE'S HAD A FEW YEARS OF INDEPENDENCE AND FREEDOM.

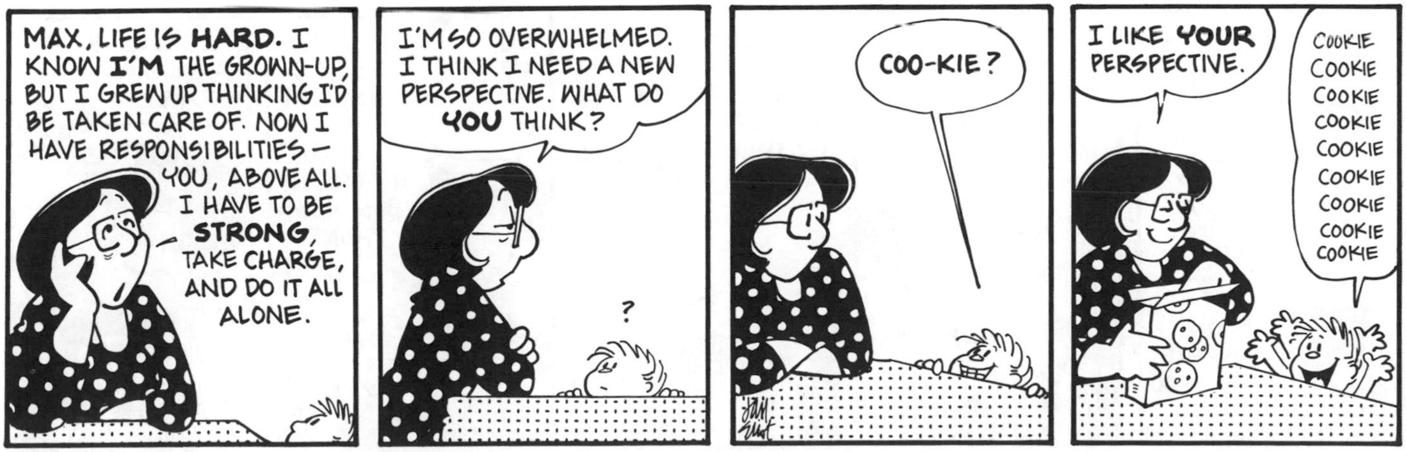
MAX, LIFE IS HARD. I KNOW I'M THE GROWN-UP, BUT I GREW UP THINKING I'D BE TAKEN CARE OF. NOW I HAVE RESPONSIBILITIES — YOU, ABOVE ALL. I HAVE TO BE STRONG, TAKE CHARGE, AND DO IT ALL ALONE.
I'M SO OVERWHELMED. I THINK I NEED A NEW PERSPECTIVE. WHAT DO YOU THINK?
?
COO-KIE?
I LIKE YOUR PERSPECTIVE.
COOKIE COOKIE COOKIE COOKIE COOKIE COOKIE COOKIE COOKIE COOKIE

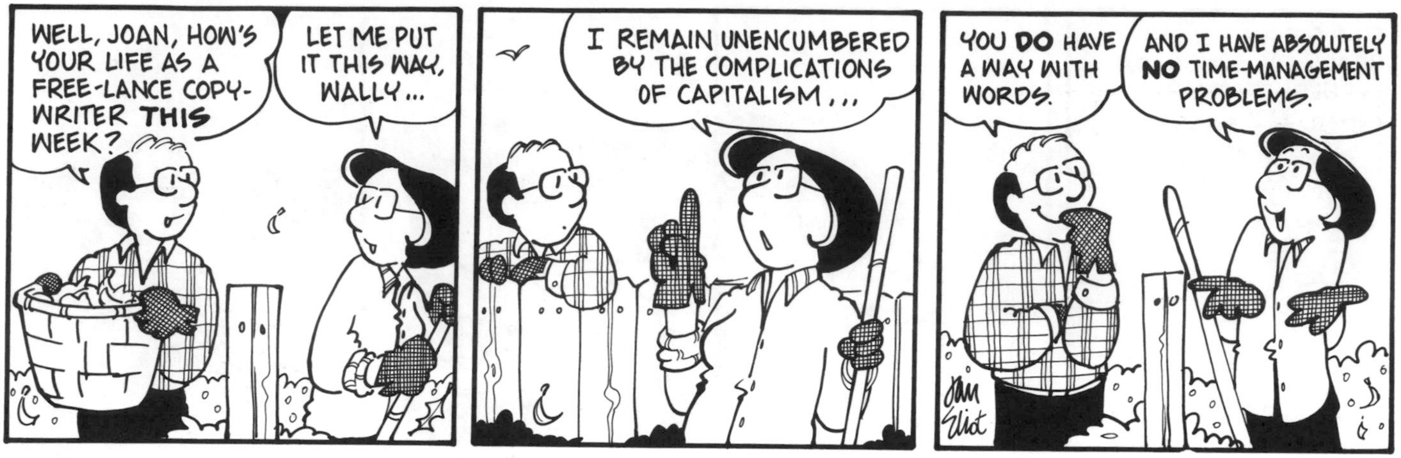
WELL, JOAN, HOW'S YOUR LIFE AS A FREE-LANCE COPY-WRITER THIS WEEK?
LET ME PUT IT THIS WAY, WALLY...
I REMAIN UNENCUMBERED BY THE COMPLICATIONS OF CAPITALISM...
YOU DO HAVE A WAY WITH WORDS.
AND I HAVE ABSOLUTELY NO TIME-MANAGEMENT PROBLEMS.
Jan Eliot

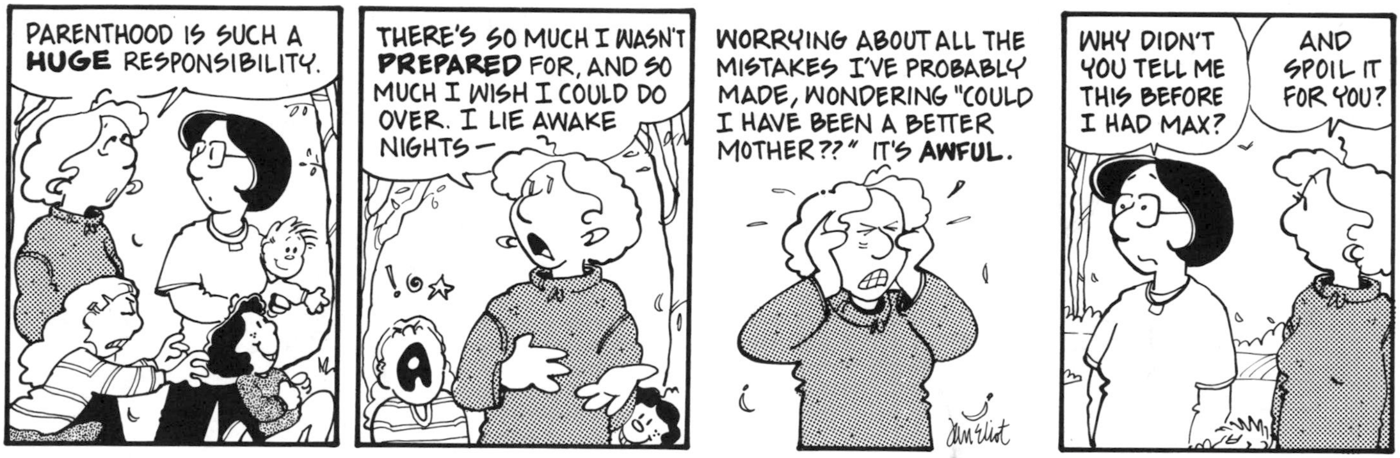
PARENTHOOD IS SUCH A HUGE RESPONSIBILITY.
THERE'S SO MUCH I WASN'T PREPARED FOR, AND SO MUCH I WISH I COULD DO OVER. I LIE AWAKE NIGHTS—
WORRYING ABOUT ALL THE MISTAKES I'VE PROBABLY MADE, WONDERING "COULD I HAVE BEEN A BETTER MOTHER??" IT'S AWFUL.
WHY DIDN'T YOU TELL ME THIS BEFORE I HAD MAX?
AND SPOIL IT FOR YOU?
Jan Eliot

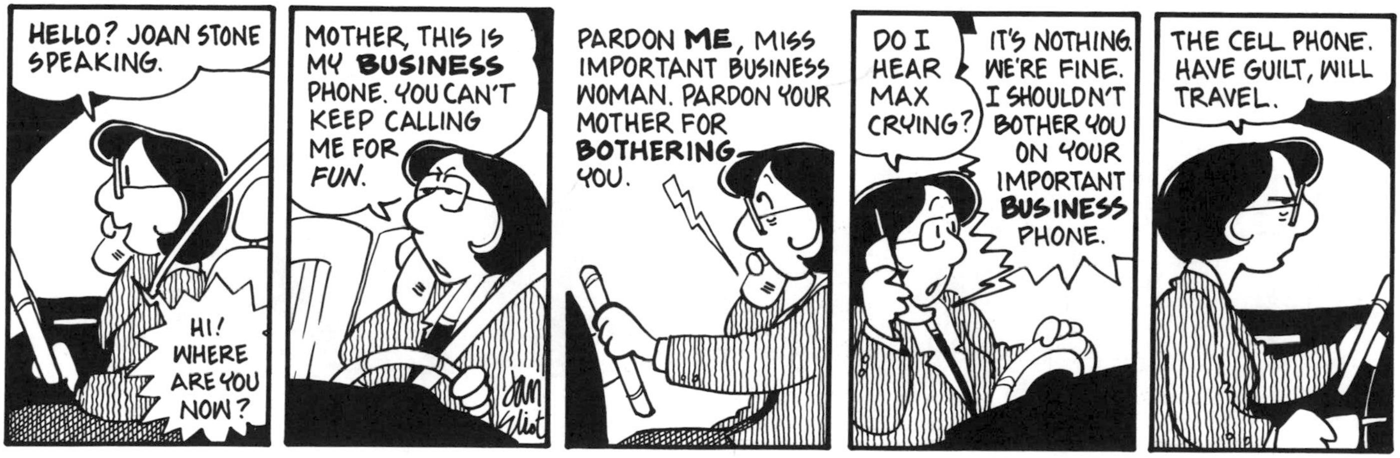
HELLO? JOAN STONE SPEAKING.
HI! WHERE ARE YOU NOW?
MOTHER, THIS IS MY BUSINESS PHONE. YOU CAN'T KEEP CALLING ME FOR FUN.
Jan Eliot
PARDON ME, MISS IMPORTANT BUSINESS WOMAN. PARDON YOUR MOTHER FOR BOTHERING YOU.
DO I HEAR MAX CRYING?
IT'S NOTHING. WE'RE FINE. I SHOULDN'T BOTHER YOU ON YOUR IMPORTANT BUSINESS PHONE.
THE CELL PHONE. HAVE GUILT, WILL TRAVEL.

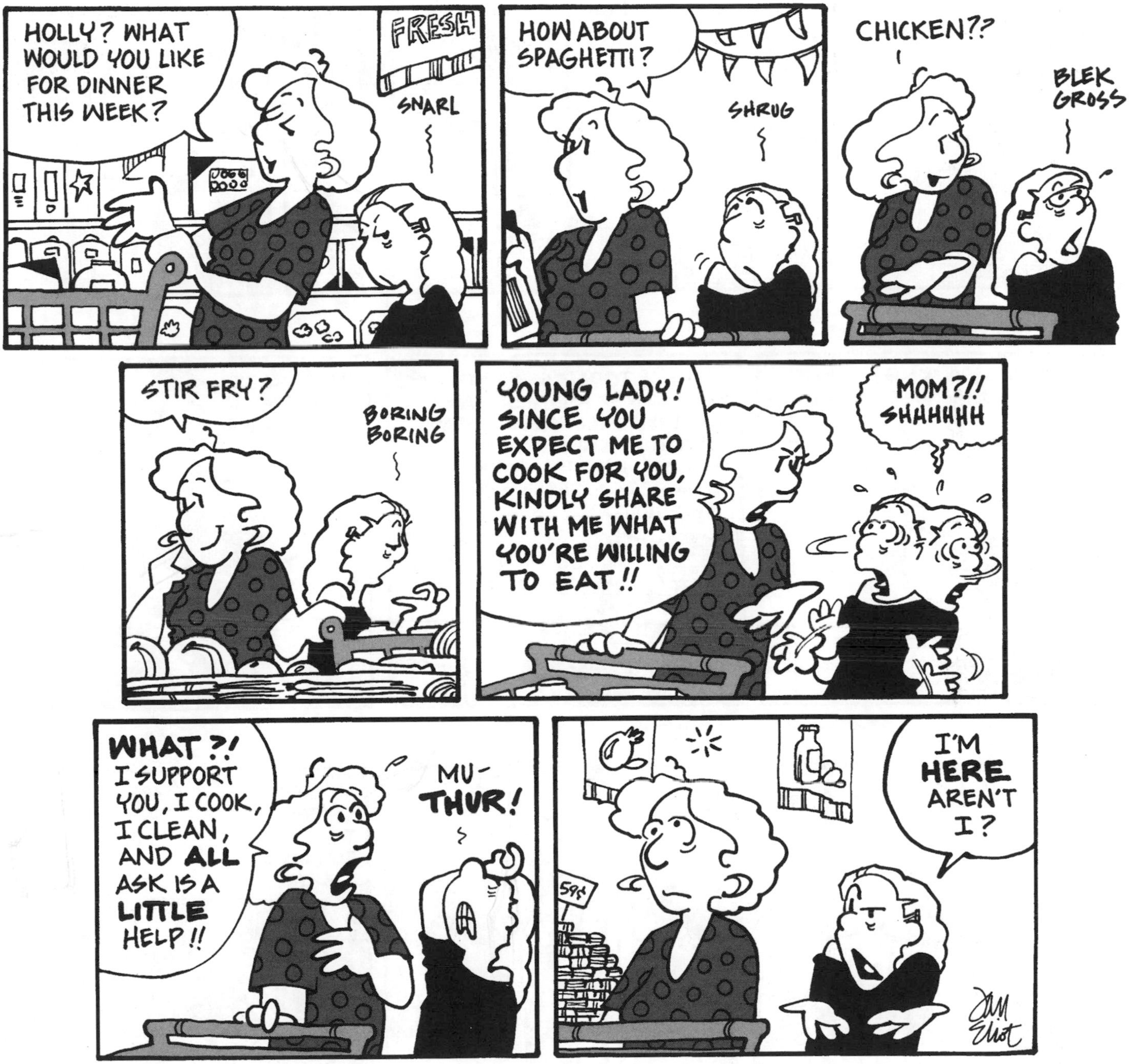
HOLLY? WHAT WOULD YOU LIKE FOR DINNER THIS WEEK?
FRESH
SNARL
HOW ABOUT SPAGHETTI?
SHRUG
CHICKEN??
BLEK GROSS
STIR FRY?
BORING BORING
YOUNG LADY! SINCE YOU EXPECT ME TO COOK FOR YOU, KINDLY SHARE WITH ME WHAT YOU'RE WILLING TO EAT!!
MOM?!! SHHHHHH
WHAT?! I SUPPORT YOU, I COOK, I CLEAN, AND ALL I ASK IS A LITTLE HELP!!
MU-THUR!
59¢
I'M HERE AREN'T I?

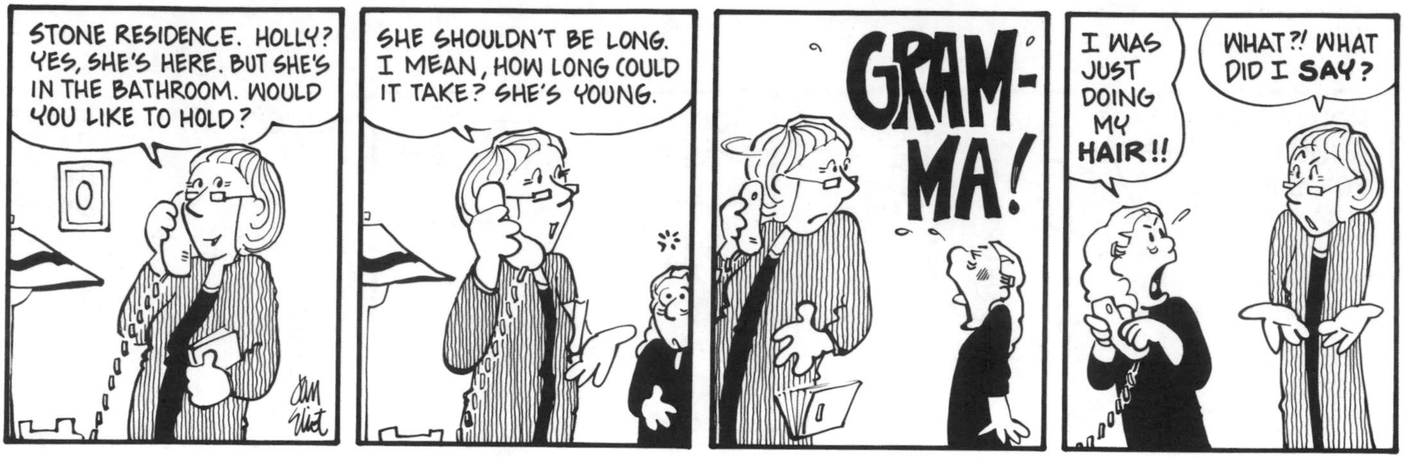
STONE RESIDENCE. HOLLY? YES, SHE'S HERE. BUT SHE'S IN THE BATHROOM. WOULD YOU LIKE TO HOLD?
SHE SHOULDN'T BE LONG. I MEAN, HOW LONG COULD IT TAKE? SHE'S YOUNG.
GRAM-MA!
I WAS JUST DOING MY HAIR!!
WHAT?! WHAT DID I SAY?

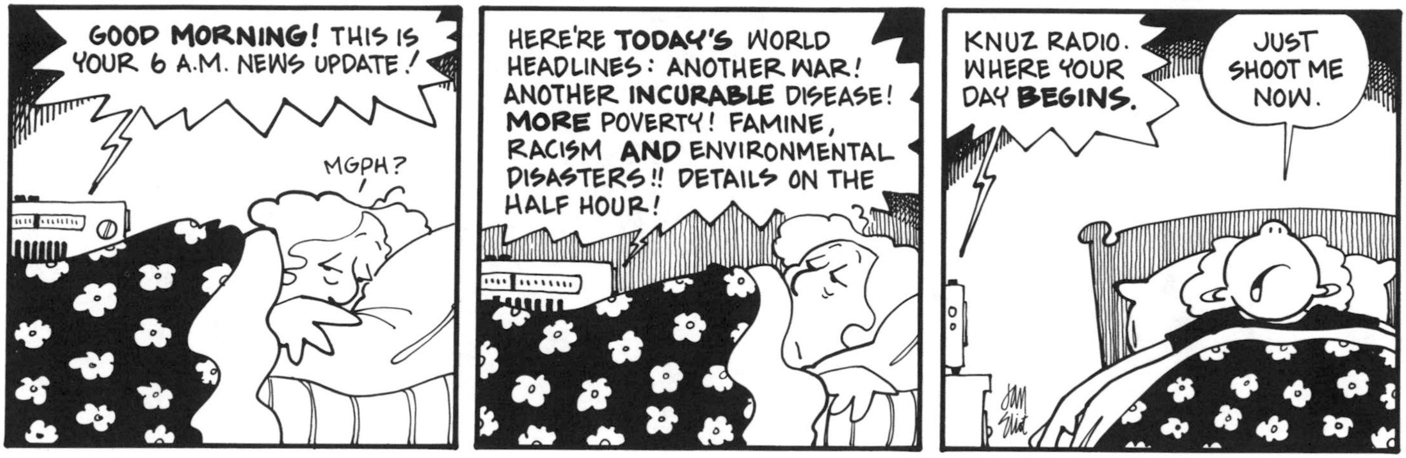
GOOD MORNING! THIS IS YOUR 6 A.M. NEWS UPDATE!
MGPH?
HERE'RE TODAY'S WORLD HEADLINES: ANOTHER WAR! ANOTHER INCURABLE DISEASE! MORE POVERTY! FAMINE, RACISM AND ENVIRONMENTAL DISASTERS!! DETAILS ON THE HALF HOUR!
KNUZ RADIO. WHERE YOUR DAY BEGINS.
JUST SHOOT ME NOW.

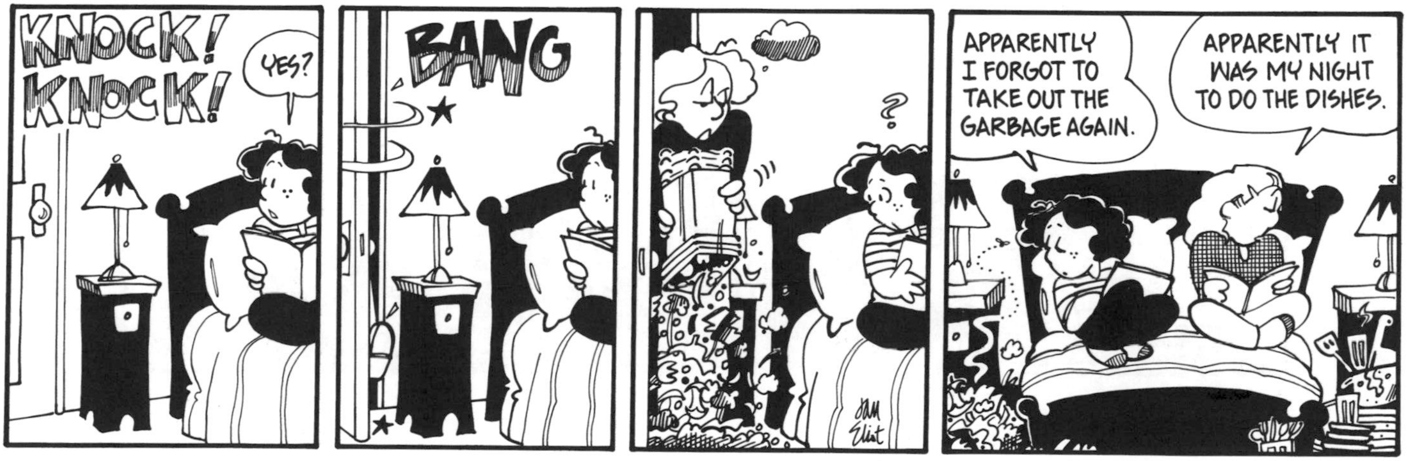
KNOCK! KNOCK!
YES?
BANG
?
APPARENTLY I FORGOT TO TAKE OUT THE GARBAGE AGAIN.
APPARENTLY IT WAS MY NIGHT TO DO THE DISHES.

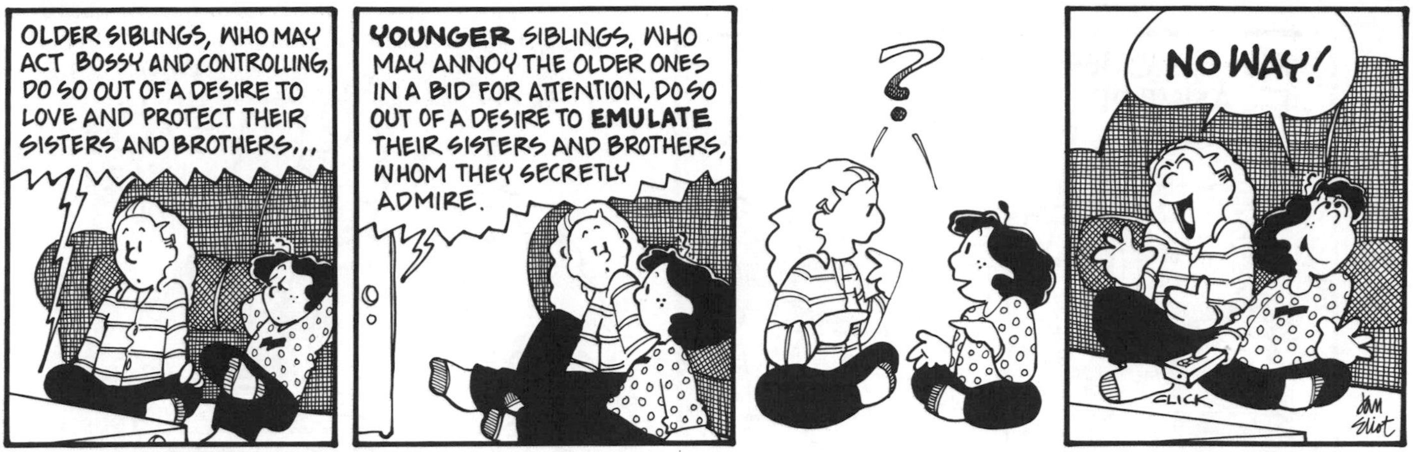
OLDER SIBLINGS, WHO MAY ACT BOSSY AND CONTROLLING, DO SO OUT OF A DESIRE TO LOVE AND PROTECT THEIR SISTERS AND BROTHERS...
YOUNGER SIBLINGS, WHO MAY ANNOY THE OLDER ONES IN A BID FOR ATTENTION, DO SO OUT OF A DESIRE TO **EMULATE** THEIR SISTERS AND BROTHERS, WHOM THEY SECRETLY ADMIRE.
?
NO WAY!
CLICK

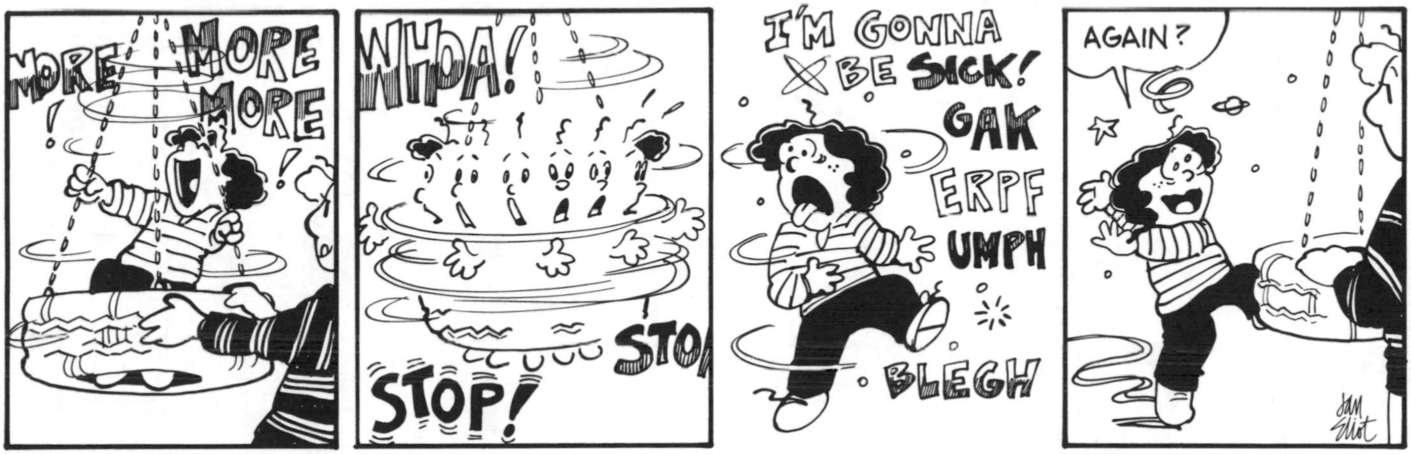
MORE MORE MORE
WHOA!
STOP!
STO
I'M GONNA BE SICK!
GAK
ERPF
UMPH
BLEGH
AGAIN?

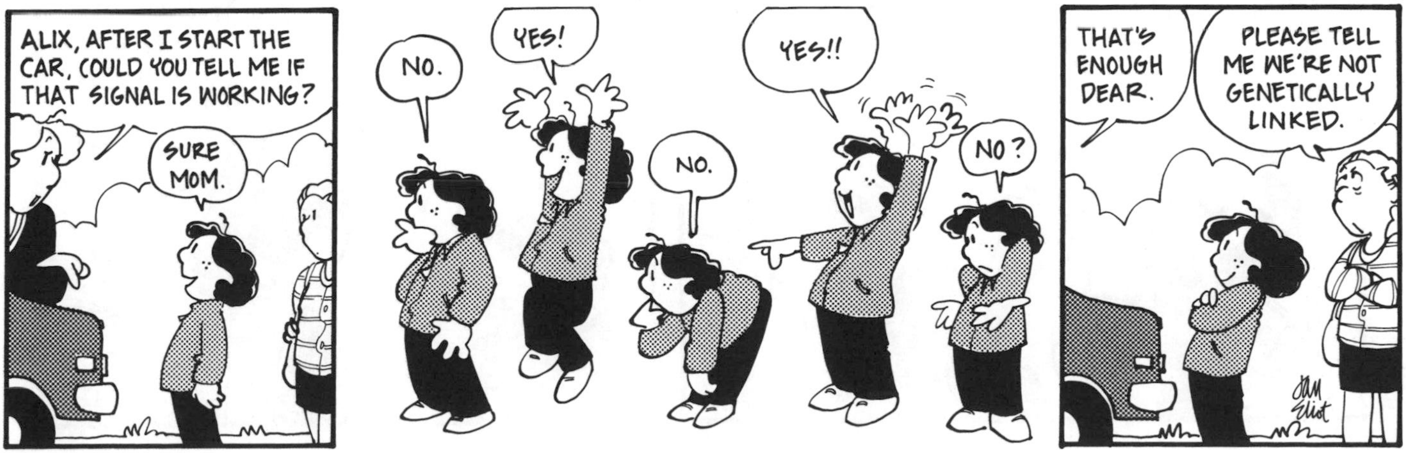
ALIX, AFTER I START THE CAR, COULD YOU TELL ME IF THAT SIGNAL IS WORKING?
SURE MOM.
NO.
YES!
NO.
YES!!
NO?
THAT'S ENOUGH DEAR.
PLEASE TELL ME WE'RE NOT GENETICALLY LINKED.

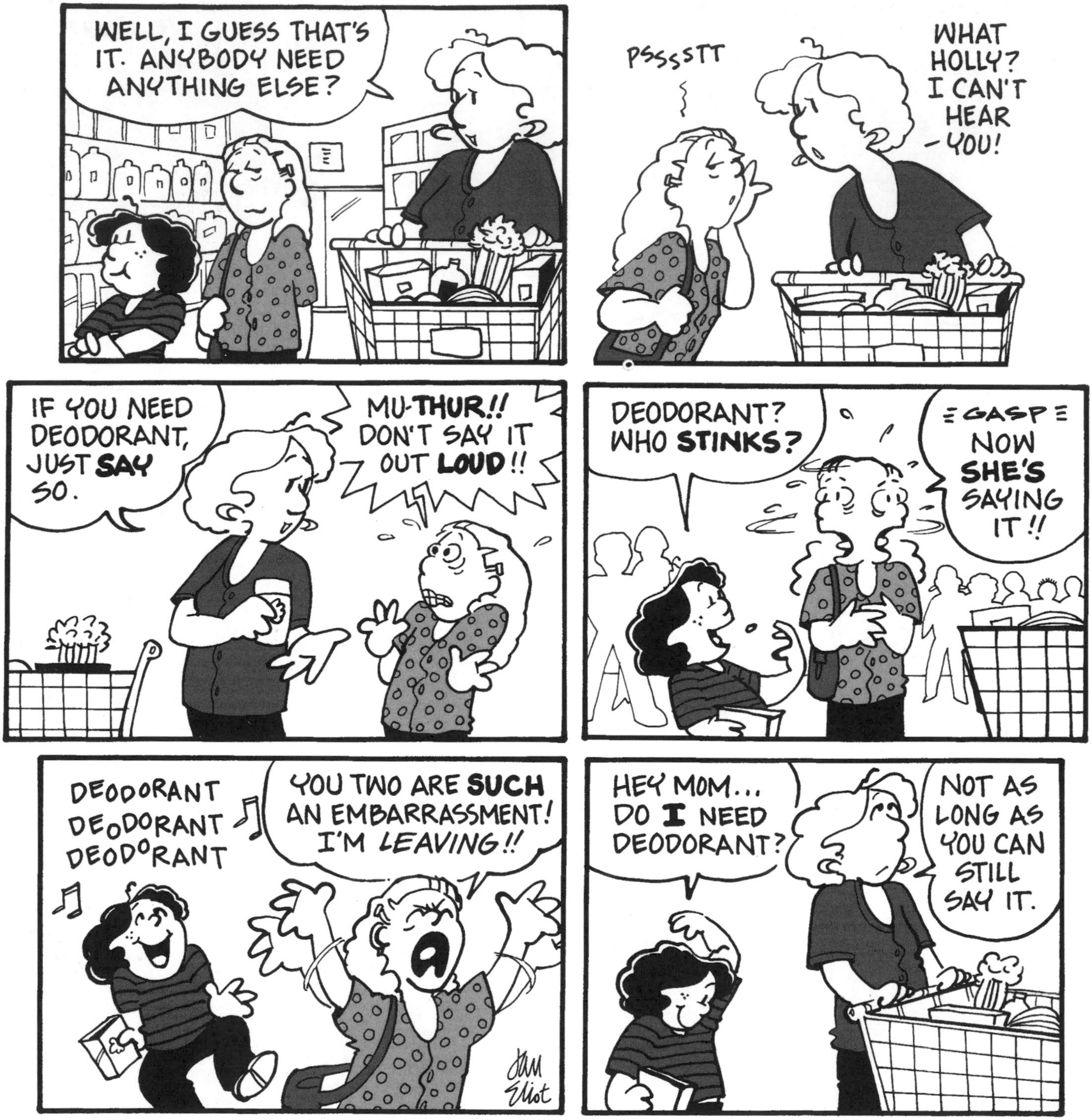
WELL, I GUESS THAT'S IT. ANYBODY NEED ANYTHING ELSE?
PSSSSTT
WHAT HOLLY? I CAN'T HEAR YOU!
IF YOU NEED DEODORANT, JUST SAY SO.
MU-THUR!! DON'T SAY IT OUT LOUD!!
DEODORANT? WHO STINKS?
GASP
NOW SHE'S SAYING IT!!
DEODORANT DEODORANT DEODORANT
YOU TWO ARE SUCH AN EMBARRASSMENT! I'M LEAVING!!
Jan Eliot
HEY MOM... DO I NEED DEODORANT?
NOT AS LONG AS YOU CAN STILL SAY IT.

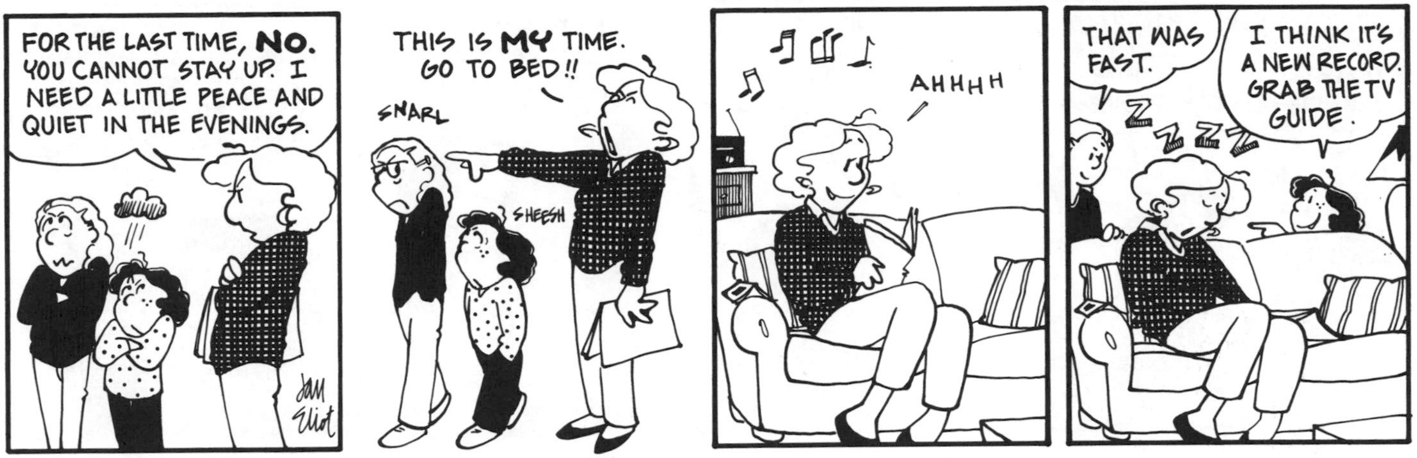
FOR THE LAST TIME, NO. YOU CANNOT STAY UP. I NEED A LITTLE PEACE AND QUIET IN THE EVENINGS.
THIS IS MY TIME. GO TO BED!!
SNARL
SHEESH
AHHHH
THAT WAS FAST.
I THINK IT'S A NEW RECORD. GRAB THE TV GUIDE.

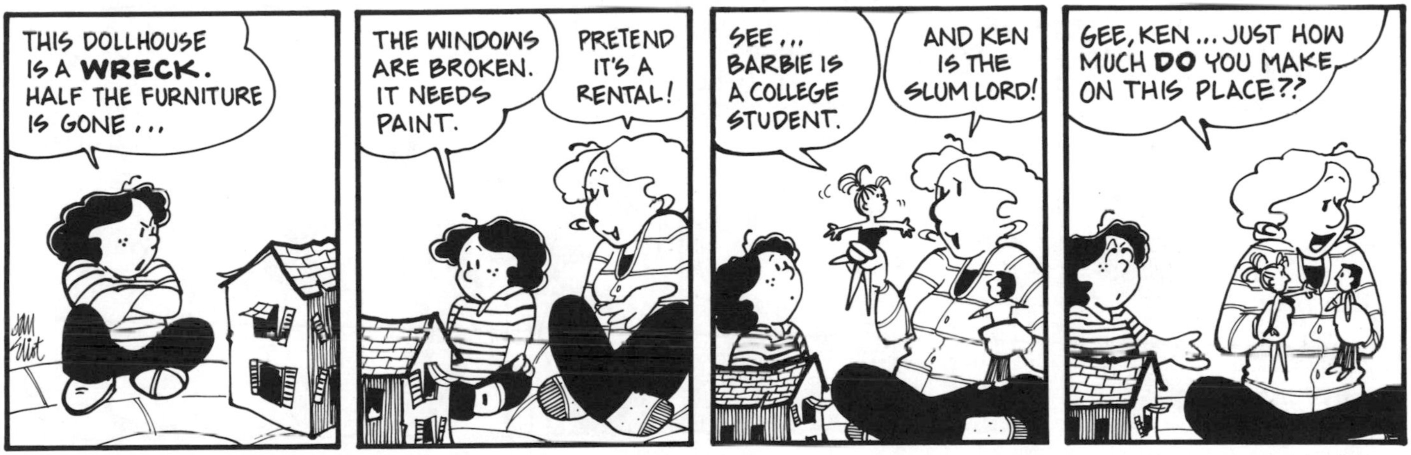
THIS DOLLHOUSE IS A WRECK. HALF THE FURNITURE IS GONE...
THE WINDOWS ARE BROKEN. IT NEEDS PAINT.
PRETEND IT'S A RENTAL!
SEE... BARBIE IS A COLLEGE STUDENT.
AND KEN IS THE SLUM LORD!
GEE, KEN... JUST HOW MUCH DO YOU MAKE ON THIS PLACE??

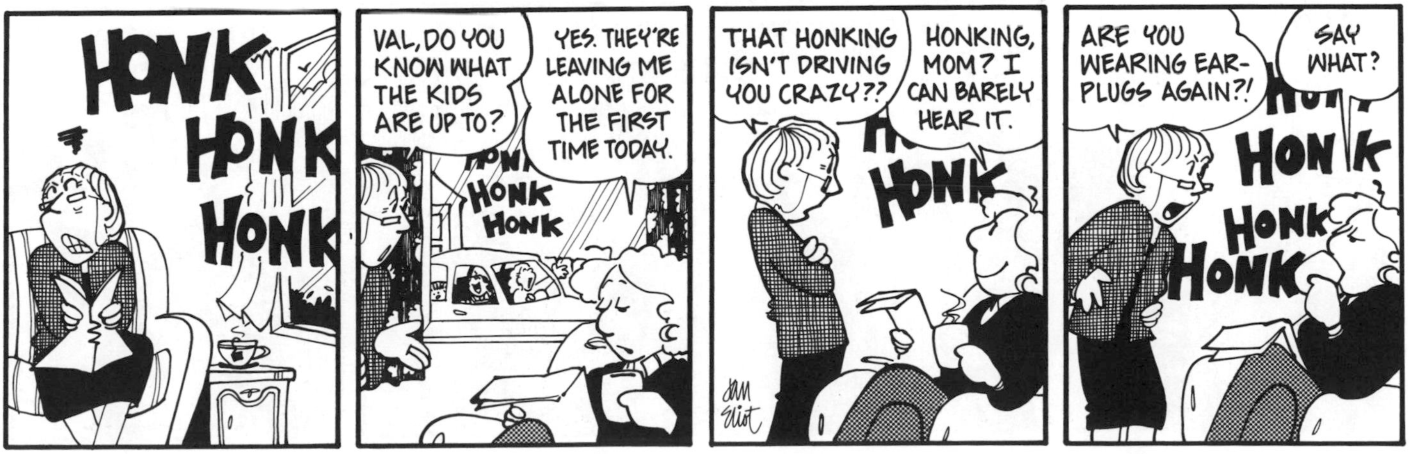
HONK
HONK
HONK
VAL, DO YOU KNOW WHAT THE KIDS ARE UP TO?
YES. THEY'RE LEAVING ME ALONE FOR THE FIRST TIME TODAY.
HONK
HONK
THAT HONKING ISN'T DRIVING YOU CRAZY??
HONKING, MOM? I CAN BARELY HEAR IT.
HONK
ARE YOU WEARING EAR-PLUGS AGAIN?!
SAY WHAT?
HONK
HONK
HONK

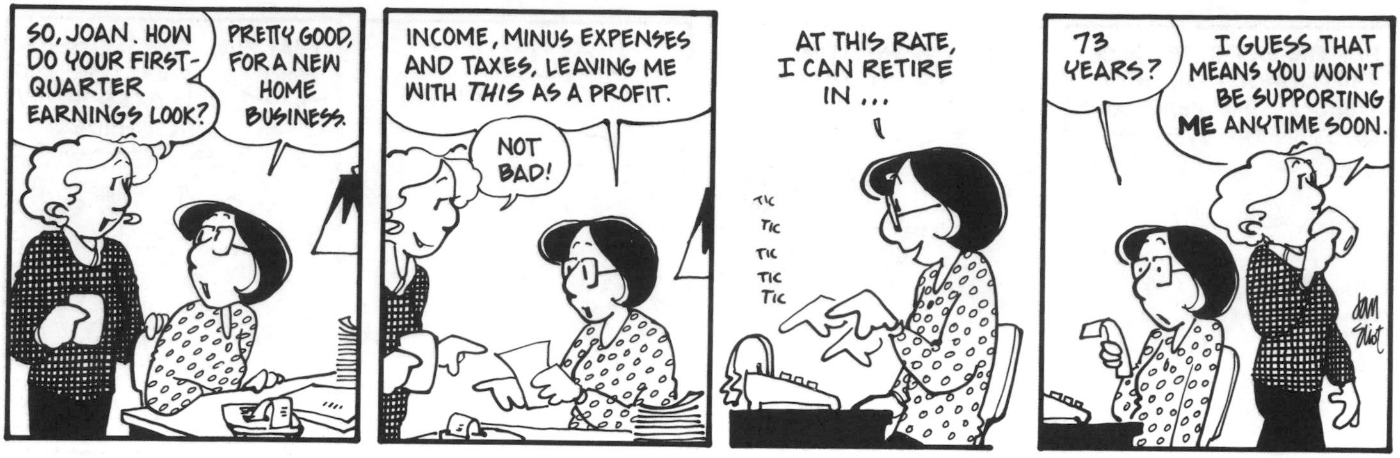
SO, JOAN. HOW DO YOUR FIRST-QUARTER EARNINGS LOOK?
PRETTY GOOD, FOR A NEW HOME BUSINESS.
INCOME, MINUS EXPENSES AND TAXES, LEAVING ME WITH *THIS* AS A PROFIT.
NOT BAD!
AT THIS RATE, I CAN RETIRE IN ...
TIC TIC TIC TIC TIC
73 YEARS?
I GUESS THAT MEANS YOU WON'T BE SUPPORTING **ME** ANYTIME SOON.

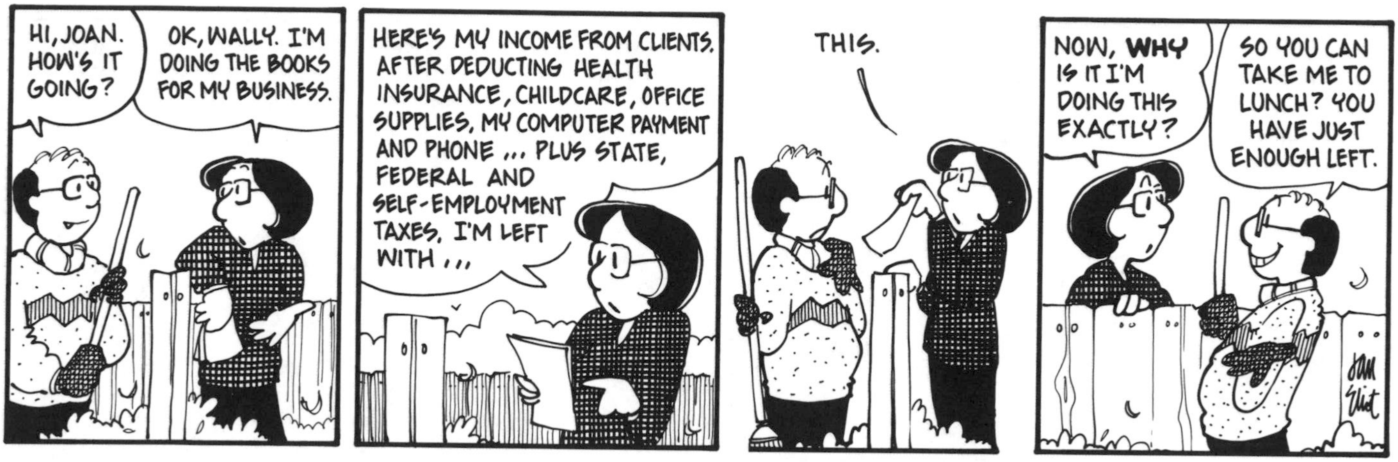
HI, JOAN. HOW'S IT GOING?
OK, WALLY. I'M DOING THE BOOKS FOR MY BUSINESS.
HERE'S MY INCOME FROM CLIENTS. AFTER DEDUCTING HEALTH INSURANCE, CHILDCARE, OFFICE SUPPLIES, MY COMPUTER PAYMENT AND PHONE ... PLUS STATE, FEDERAL AND SELF-EMPLOYMENT TAXES, I'M LEFT WITH ...
THIS.
NOW, **WHY** IS IT I'M DOING THIS EXACTLY?
SO YOU CAN TAKE ME TO LUNCH? YOU HAVE JUST ENOUGH LEFT.

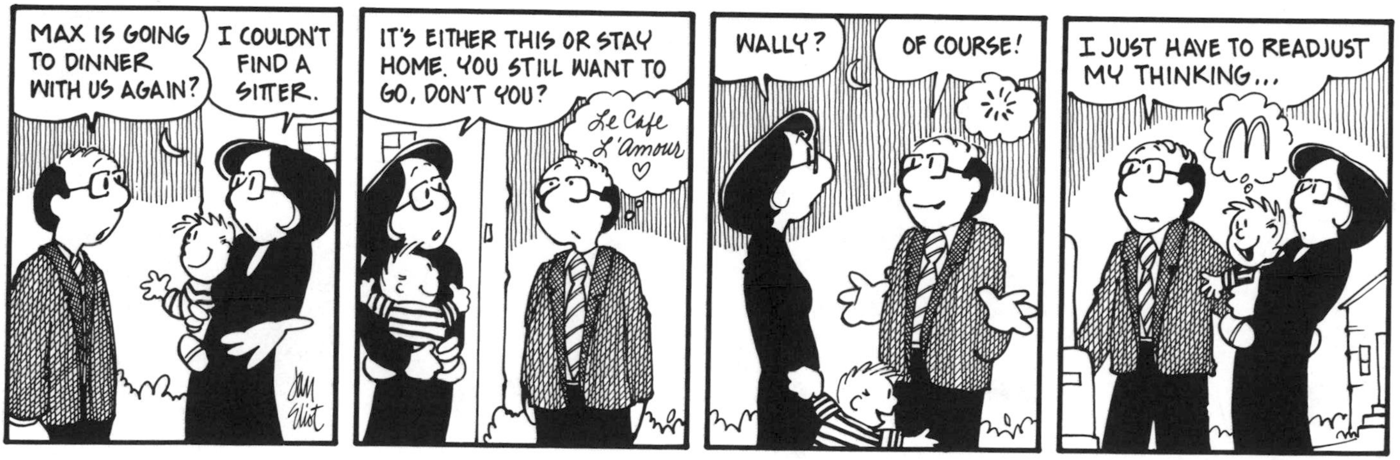
MAX IS GOING TO DINNER WITH US AGAIN?
I COULDN'T FIND A SITTER.
IT'S EITHER THIS OR STAY HOME. YOU STILL WANT TO GO, DON'T YOU?
Le Cafe L'Amour
WALLY?
OF COURSE!
I JUST HAVE TO READJUST MY THINKING...

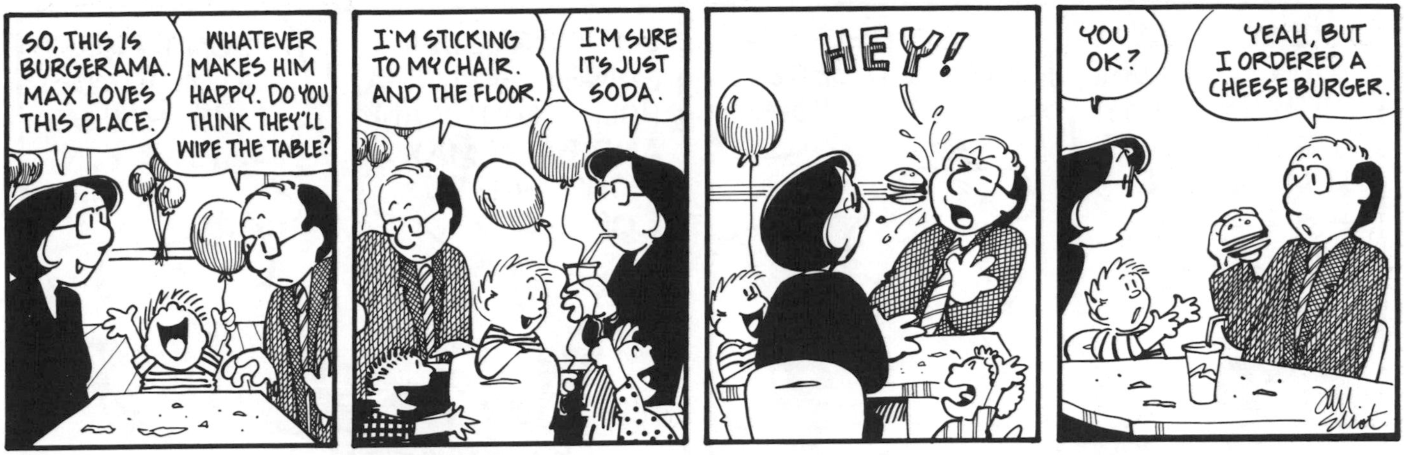
SO, THIS IS BURGERAMA. MAX LOVES THIS PLACE.
WHATEVER MAKES HIM HAPPY. DO YOU THINK THEY'LL WIPE THE TABLE?
I'M STICKING TO MY CHAIR. AND THE FLOOR.
I'M SURE IT'S JUST SODA.
HEY!
YOU OK?
YEAH, BUT I ORDERED A CHEESE BURGER.

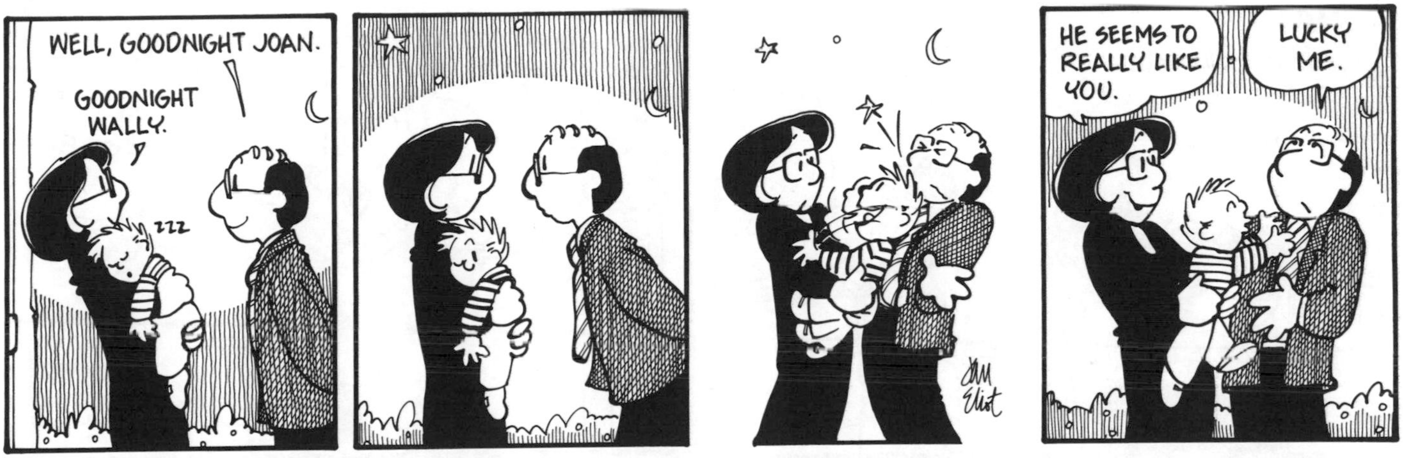
WELL, GOODNIGHT JOAN.
GOODNIGHT WALLY.
ZZZ
HE SEEMS TO REALLY LIKE YOU.
LUCKY ME.

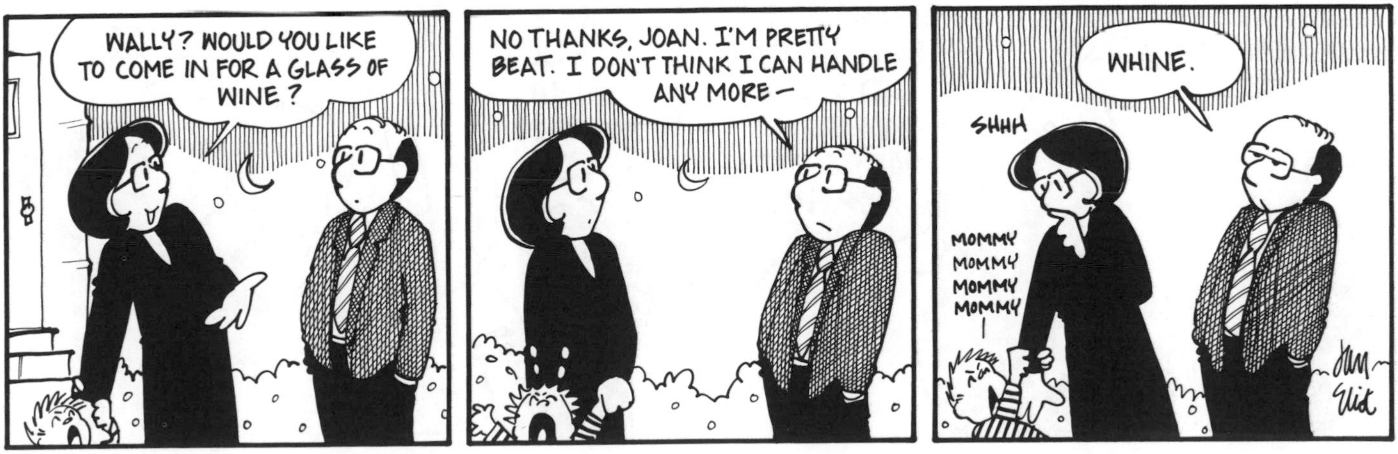
WALLY? WOULD YOU LIKE TO COME IN FOR A GLASS OF WINE?
NO THANKS, JOAN. I'M PRETTY BEAT. I DON'T THINK I CAN HANDLE ANY MORE –
WHINE.
SHHH
MOMMY MOMMY MOMMY MOMMY

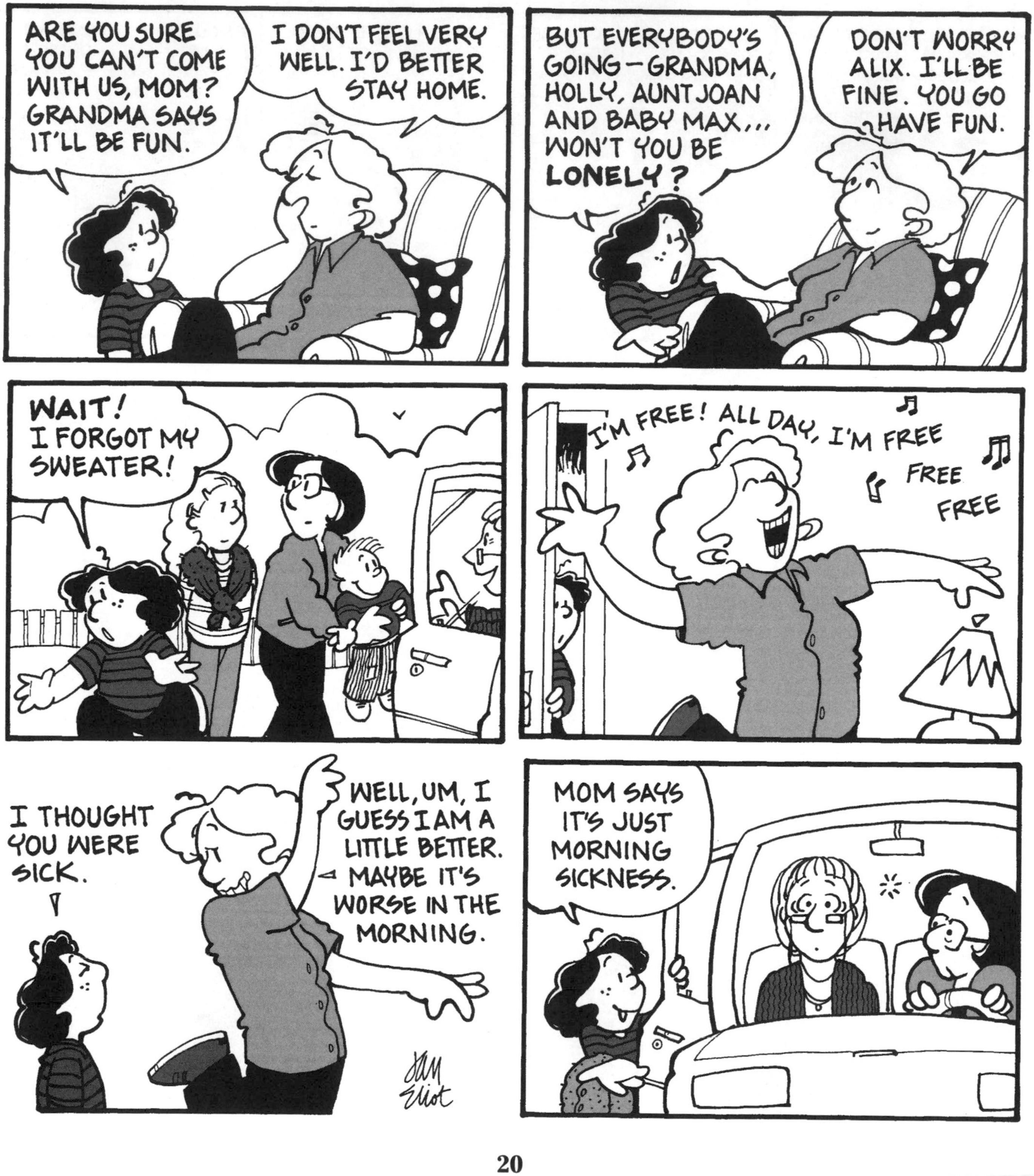
ARE YOU SURE YOU CAN'T COME WITH US, MOM? GRANDMA SAYS IT'LL BE FUN.
I DON'T FEEL VERY WELL. I'D BETTER STAY HOME.
BUT EVERYBODY'S GOING – GRANDMA, HOLLY, AUNT JOAN AND BABY MAX,... WON'T YOU BE **LONELY**?
DON'T WORRY ALIX. I'LL BE FINE. YOU GO HAVE FUN.
WAIT! I FORGOT MY SWEATER!
I'M FREE! ALL DAY, I'M FREE
FREE
FREE
I THOUGHT YOU WERE SICK.
WELL, UM, I GUESS I AM A LITTLE BETTER. MAYBE IT'S WORSE IN THE MORNING.
MOM SAYS IT'S JUST MORNING SICKNESS.
JAN Eliot

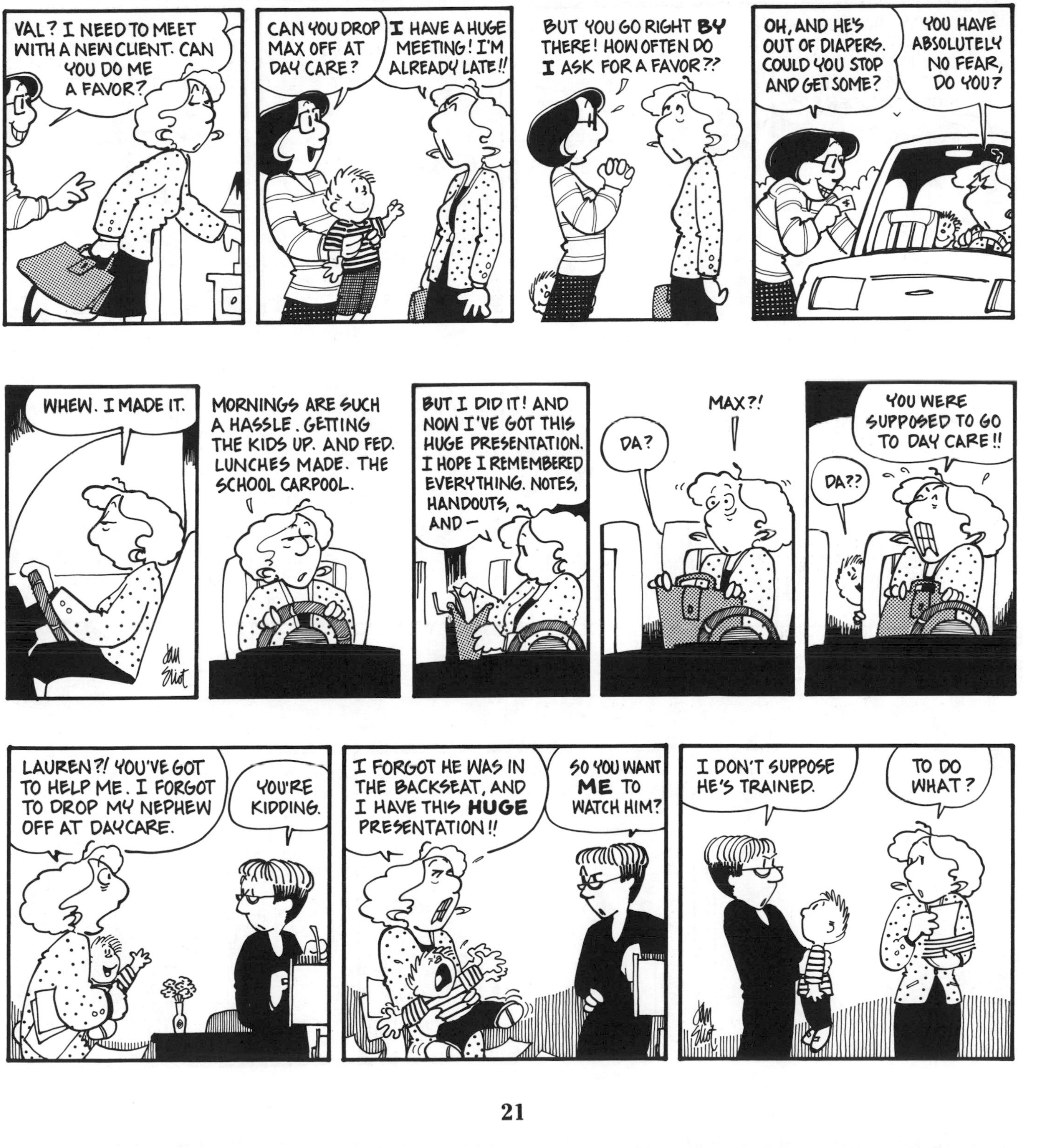

VAL? I NEED TO MEET WITH A NEW CLIENT. CAN YOU DO ME A FAVOR?
CAN YOU DROP MAX OFF AT DAY CARE?
I HAVE A HUGE MEETING! I'M ALREADY LATE!!
BUT YOU GO RIGHT BY THERE! HOW OFTEN DO I ASK FOR A FAVOR??
OH, AND HE'S OUT OF DIAPERS. COULD YOU STOP AND GET SOME?
YOU HAVE ABSOLUTELY NO FEAR, DO YOU?
WHEW. I MADE IT.
MORNINGS ARE SUCH A HASSLE. GETTING THE KIDS UP. AND FED. LUNCHES MADE. THE SCHOOL CARPOOL.
BUT I DID IT! AND NOW I'VE GOT THIS HUGE PRESENTATION. I HOPE I REMEMBERED EVERYTHING. NOTES, HANDOUTS, AND—
DA?
MAX?!
DA??
YOU WERE SUPPOSED TO GO TO DAY CARE!!
LAUREN?! YOU'VE GOT TO HELP ME. I FORGOT TO DROP MY NEPHEW OFF AT DAYCARE.
YOU'RE KIDDING.
I FORGOT HE WAS IN THE BACKSEAT, AND I HAVE THIS HUGE PRESENTATION!!
SO YOU WANT ME TO WATCH HIM?
I DON'T SUPPOSE HE'S TRAINED.
TO DO WHAT?

VAL, I KNOW YOU'RE GETTING READY FOR YOUR MEETING, AND I'M HAPPY TO WATCH MAX, BUT DOES HE HAVE ANY MORE **DIAPERS**?

TIC TIC TIC TIC

I WAS SUPPOSED TO STOP AND GET SOME...

MAYBE IF WE CALLED MAINTENANCE...

HEY **ED**! C'MERE! YOU GOTTA HEAR **THIS** ONE!!

THIS MORNING, I'VE PREPARED A REPORT ON...

WAA AA

AGENDA

THE RECOMMENDATION THAT THE COMPANY BUILD A...

WAAA

DAY CARE CENTER...

HE WANTS **YOU**.

WAAAAA

ON SITE.

DO YOU HAVE ANY STATISTICS, OR ARE WE SIMPLY GOING TO RELY ON VISUAL AIDS?

WAAAAA

CAN YOU BELIEVE IT? I HEARD SOMEBODY BROUGHT A **KID** TO WORK!

I MEAN, GET *REAL*! IS THIS A SERIOUS WORK ENVIRONMENT OR *NOT*? **SOME** OF US CONSIDER OURSELVES PROFESSIONALS.

HEY BRAD! WANNA GET IN ON THE FOOTBALL POOL? WE'RE BETTING ON THE COMBINED BUST SIZE OF THIS YEAR'S DALLAS CHEERLEADER SQUAD.

I'M THERE, MAN.

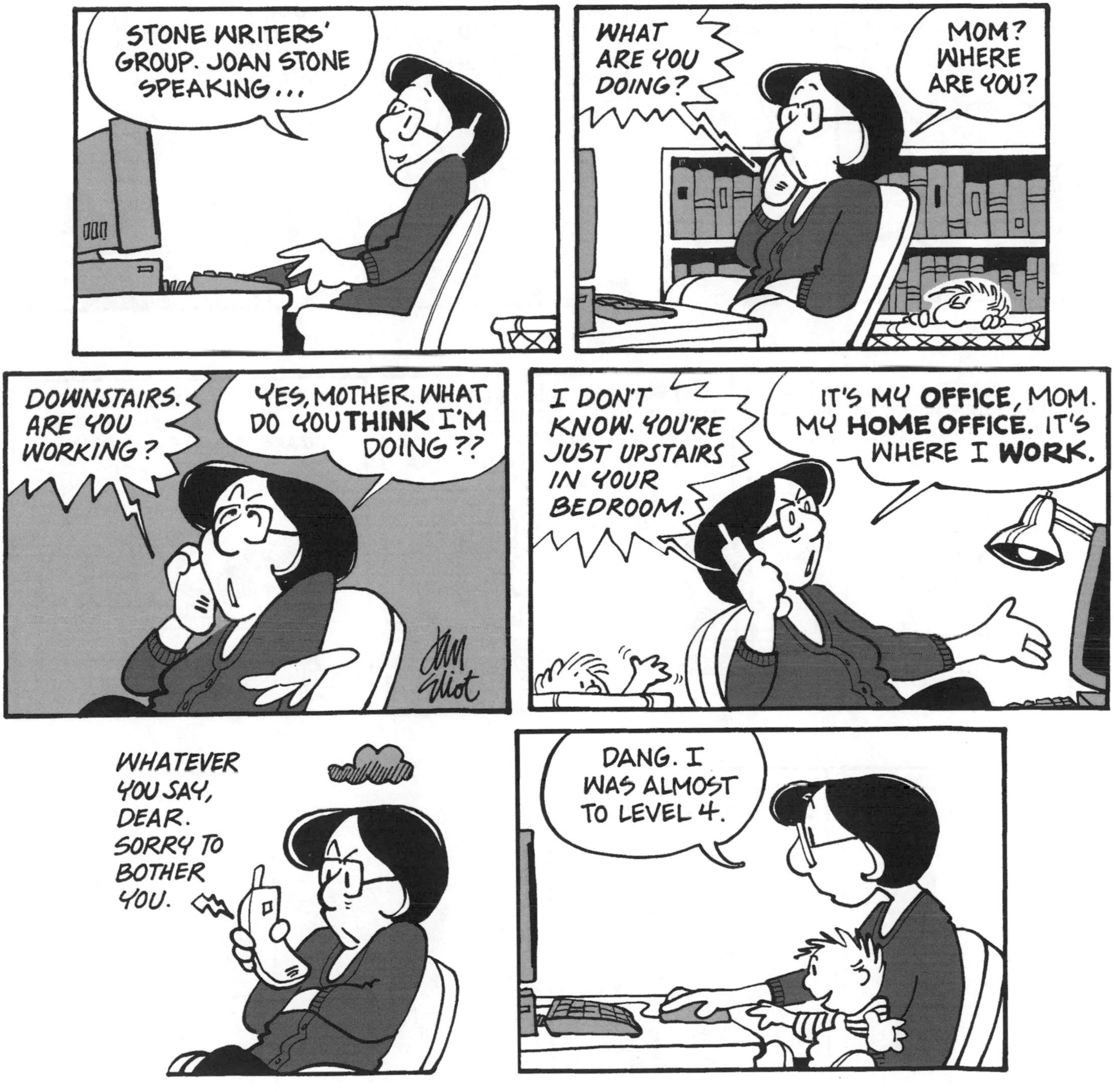

STONE WRITERS' GROUP. JOAN STONE SPEAKING...
WHAT ARE YOU DOING?
MOM? WHERE ARE YOU?
DOWNSTAIRS. ARE YOU WORKING?
YES, MOTHER. WHAT DO YOU THINK I'M DOING??
I DON'T KNOW. YOU'RE JUST UPSTAIRS IN YOUR BEDROOM.
IT'S MY OFFICE, MOM. MY HOME OFFICE. IT'S WHERE I WORK.
WHATEVER YOU SAY, DEAR. SORRY TO BOTHER YOU.
DANG. I WAS ALMOST TO LEVEL 4.

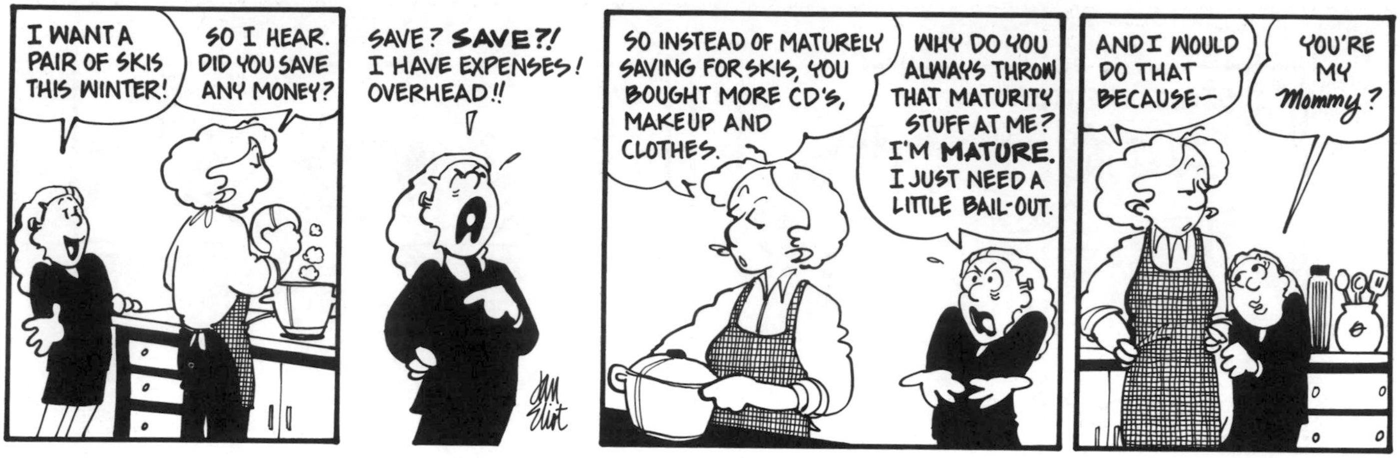
I WANT A PAIR OF SKIS THIS WINTER!
SO I HEAR. DID YOU SAVE ANY MONEY?
SAVE? **SAVE?!** I HAVE EXPENSES! OVERHEAD!!
SO INSTEAD OF MATURELY SAVING FOR SKIS, YOU BOUGHT MORE CD'S, MAKEUP AND CLOTHES.
WHY DO YOU ALWAYS THROW THAT MATURITY STUFF AT ME? I'M **MATURE.** I JUST NEED A LITTLE BAIL-OUT.
AND I WOULD DO THAT BECAUSE—
YOU'RE MY *Mommy*?

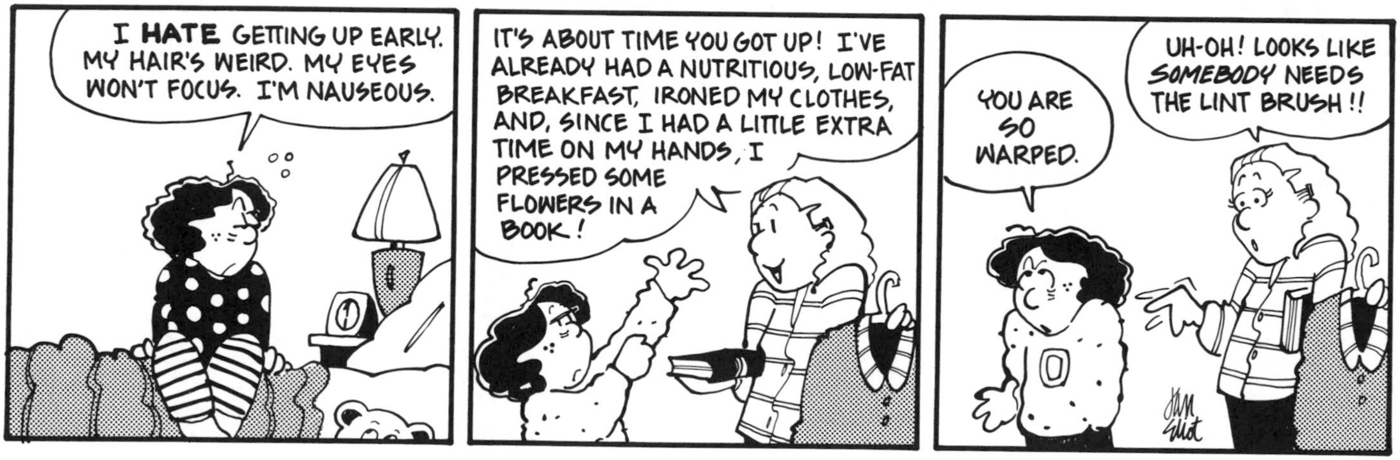
I **HATE** GETTING UP EARLY. MY HAIR'S WEIRD. MY EYES WON'T FOCUS. I'M NAUSEOUS.
IT'S ABOUT TIME YOU GOT UP! I'VE ALREADY HAD A NUTRITIOUS, LOW-FAT BREAKFAST, IRONED MY CLOTHES, AND, SINCE I HAD A LITTLE EXTRA TIME ON MY HANDS, I PRESSED SOME FLOWERS IN A BOOK!
YOU ARE SO WARPED.
UH-OH! LOOKS LIKE *SOMEBODY* NEEDS THE LINT BRUSH!!

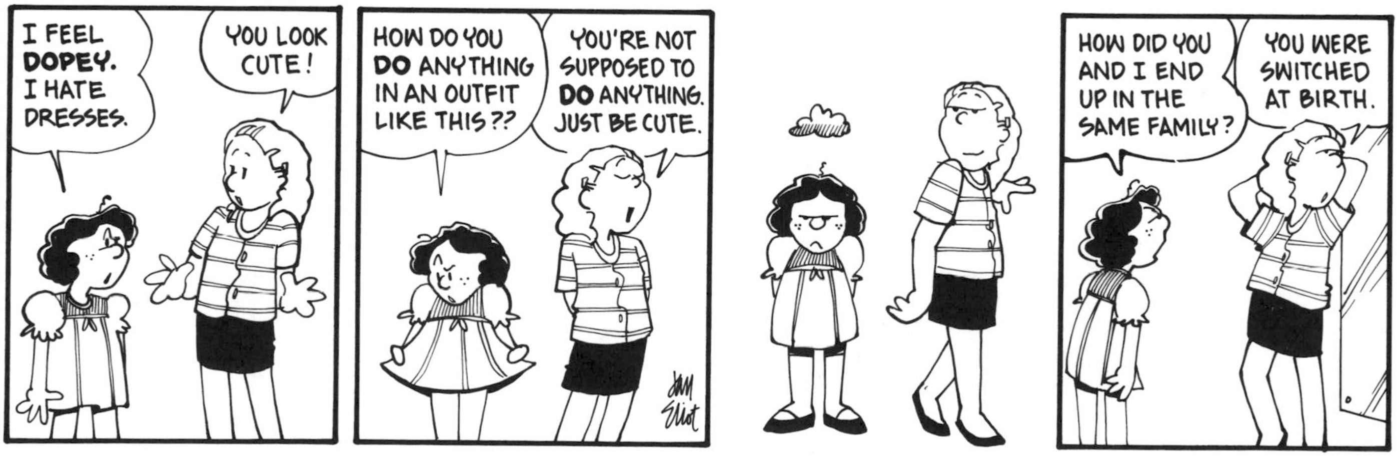
I FEEL **DOPEY.** I HATE DRESSES.
YOU LOOK CUTE!
HOW DO YOU **DO** ANYTHING IN AN OUTFIT LIKE THIS??
YOU'RE NOT SUPPOSED TO **DO** ANYTHING. JUST BE CUTE.
HOW DID YOU AND I END UP IN THE SAME FAMILY?
YOU WERE SWITCHED AT BIRTH.

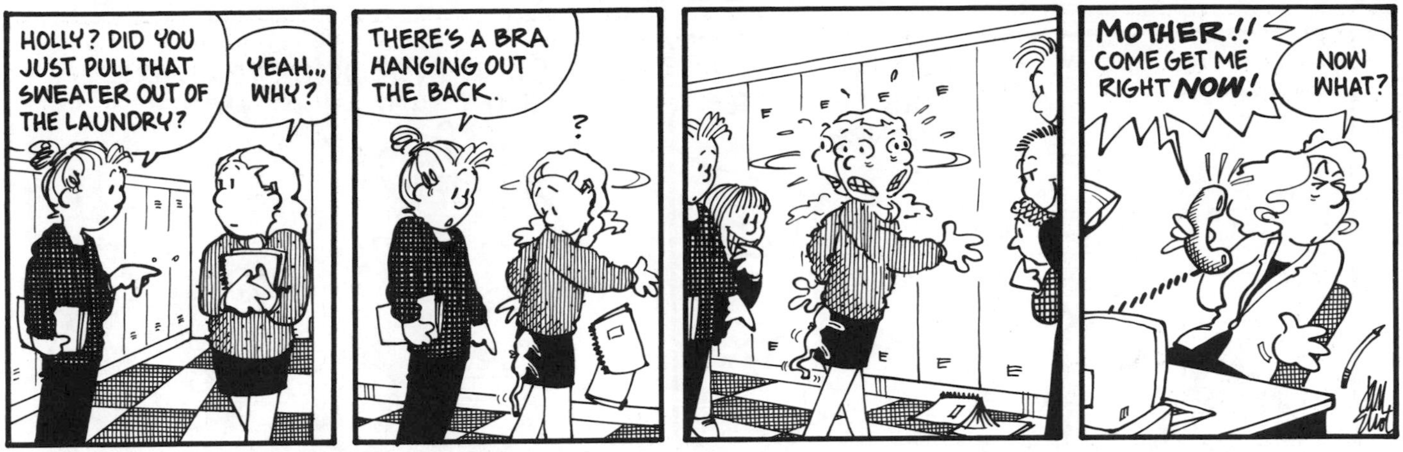
HOLLY? DID YOU JUST PULL THAT SWEATER OUT OF THE LAUNDRY?
YEAH... WHY?
THERE'S A BRA HANGING OUT THE BACK.
?
MOTHER!! COME GET ME RIGHT NOW!
NOW WHAT?

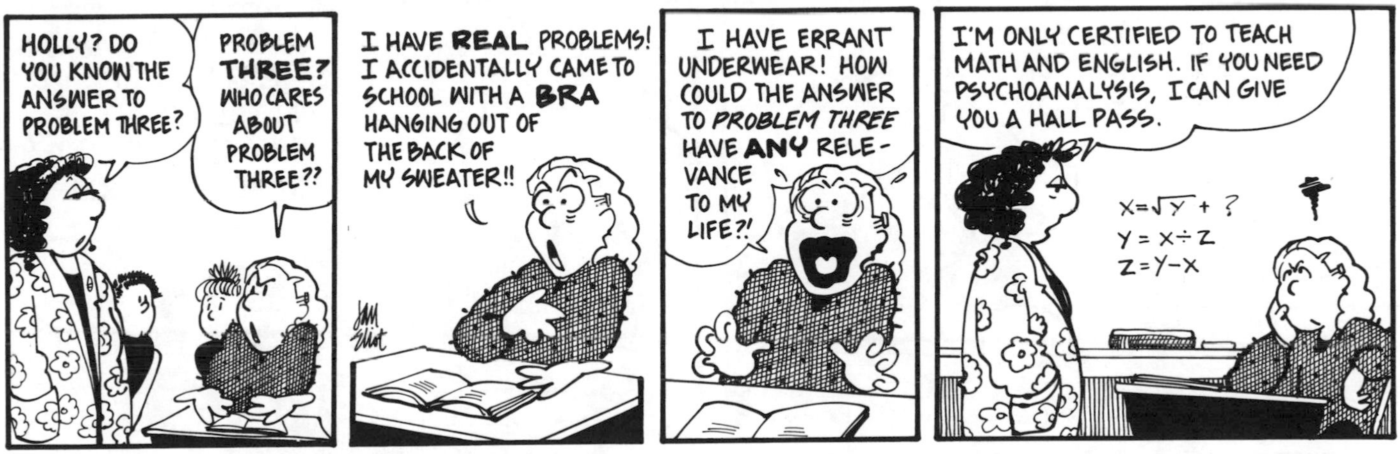
HOLLY? DO YOU KNOW THE ANSWER TO PROBLEM THREE?
PROBLEM THREE? WHO CARES ABOUT PROBLEM THREE??
I HAVE REAL PROBLEMS! I ACCIDENTALLY CAME TO SCHOOL WITH A BRA HANGING OUT OF THE BACK OF MY SWEATER!!
I HAVE ERRANT UNDERWEAR! HOW COULD THE ANSWER TO PROBLEM THREE HAVE ANY RELE-VANCE TO MY LIFE?!
I'M ONLY CERTIFIED TO TEACH MATH AND ENGLISH. IF YOU NEED PSYCHOANALYSIS, I CAN GIVE YOU A HALL PASS.
X=√Y + ?
Y = X÷Z
Z=Y−X

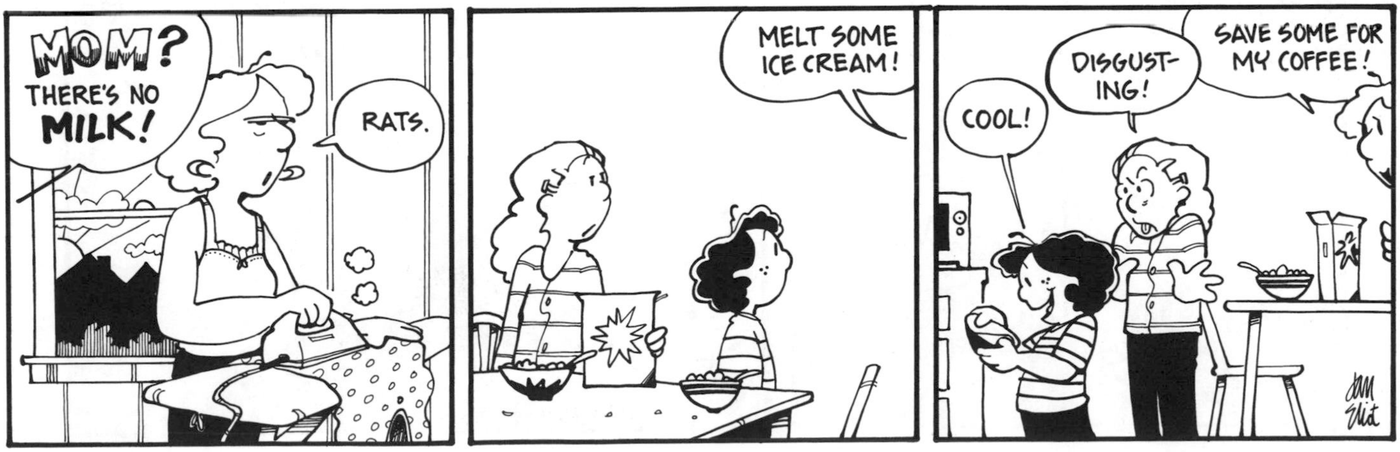
MOM? THERE'S NO MILK!
RATS.
MELT SOME ICE CREAM!
COOL!
DISGUST-ING!
SAVE SOME FOR MY COFFEE!

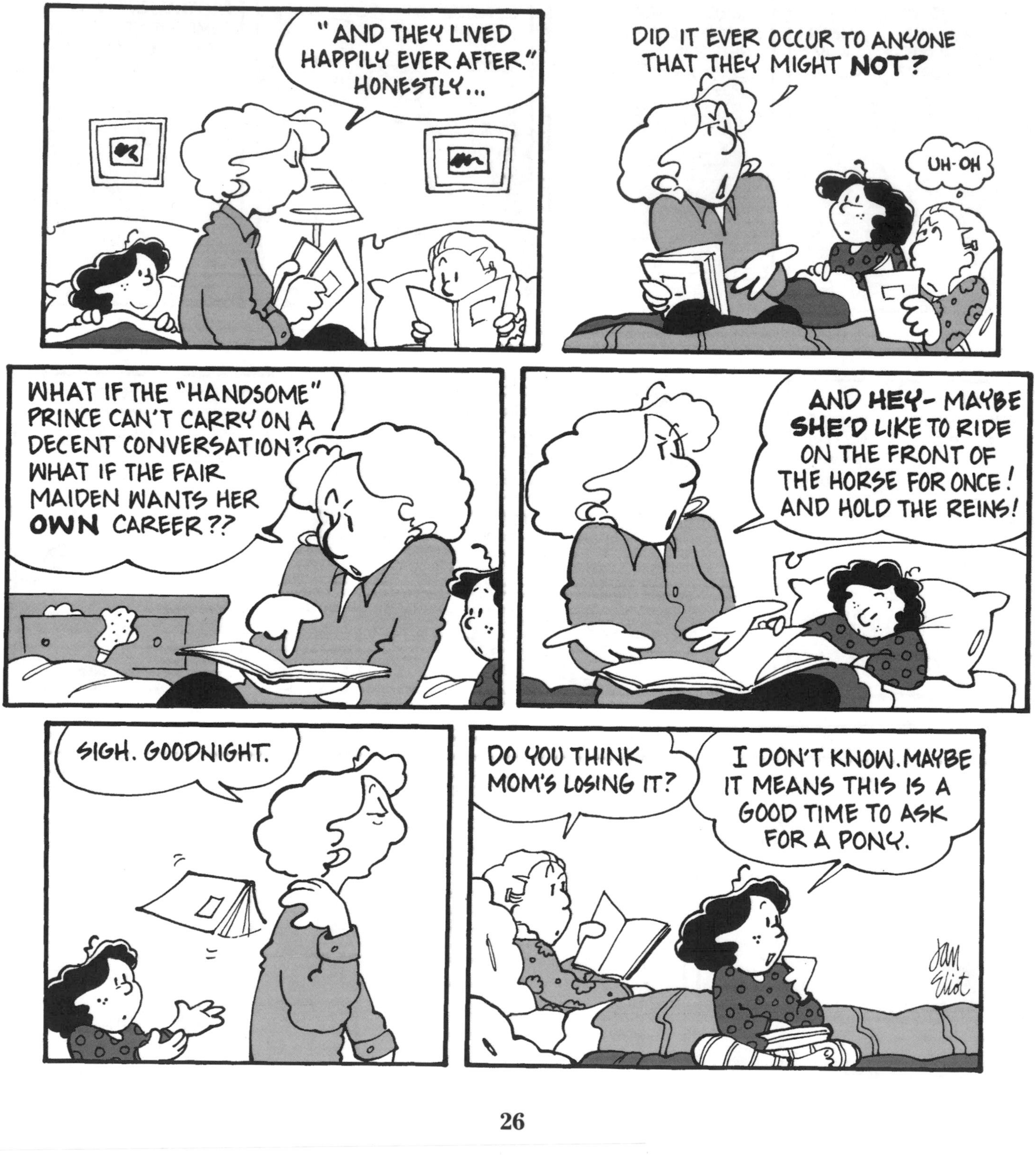
"AND THEY LIVED HAPPILY EVER AFTER." HONESTLY...
DID IT EVER OCCUR TO ANYONE THAT THEY MIGHT **NOT?**
UH-OH
WHAT IF THE "HANDSOME" PRINCE CAN'T CARRY ON A DECENT CONVERSATION? WHAT IF THE FAIR MAIDEN WANTS HER **OWN** CAREER??
AND **HEY**- MAYBE **SHE'D** LIKE TO RIDE ON THE FRONT OF THE HORSE FOR ONCE! AND HOLD THE REINS!
SIGH. GOODNIGHT.
DO YOU THINK MOM'S LOSING IT?
I DON'T KNOW. MAYBE IT MEANS THIS IS A GOOD TIME TO ASK FOR A PONY.
Jan Eliot

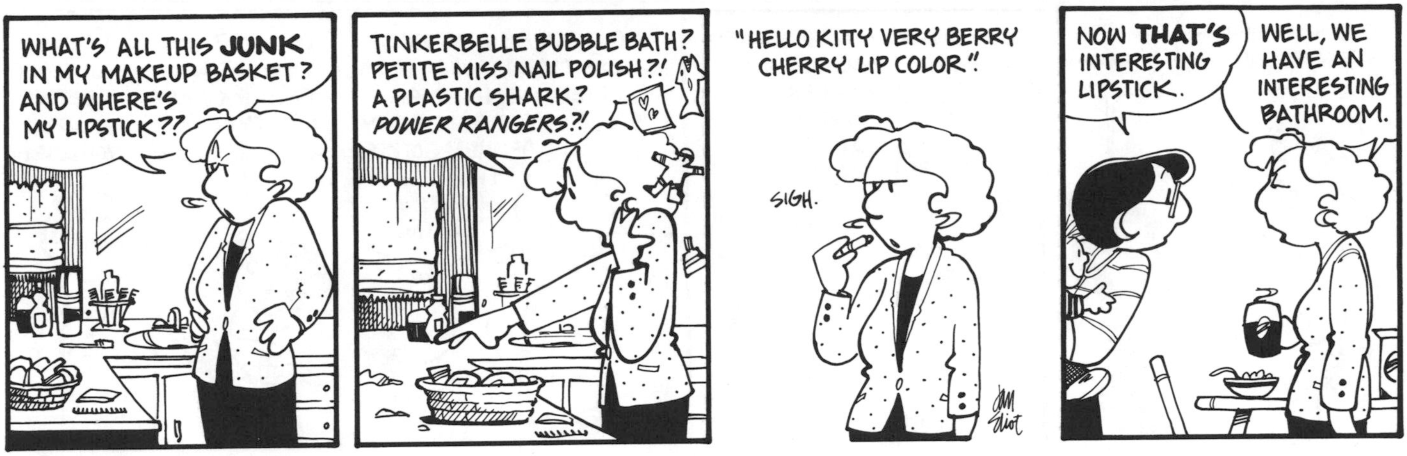
WHAT'S ALL THIS JUNK IN MY MAKEUP BASKET? AND WHERE'S MY LIPSTICK??
TINKERBELLE BUBBLE BATH? PETITE MISS NAIL POLISH?! A PLASTIC SHARK? POWER RANGERS?!
"HELLO KITTY VERY BERRY CHERRY LIP COLOR."
SIGH.
NOW THAT'S INTERESTING LIPSTICK.
WELL, WE HAVE AN INTERESTING BATHROOM.

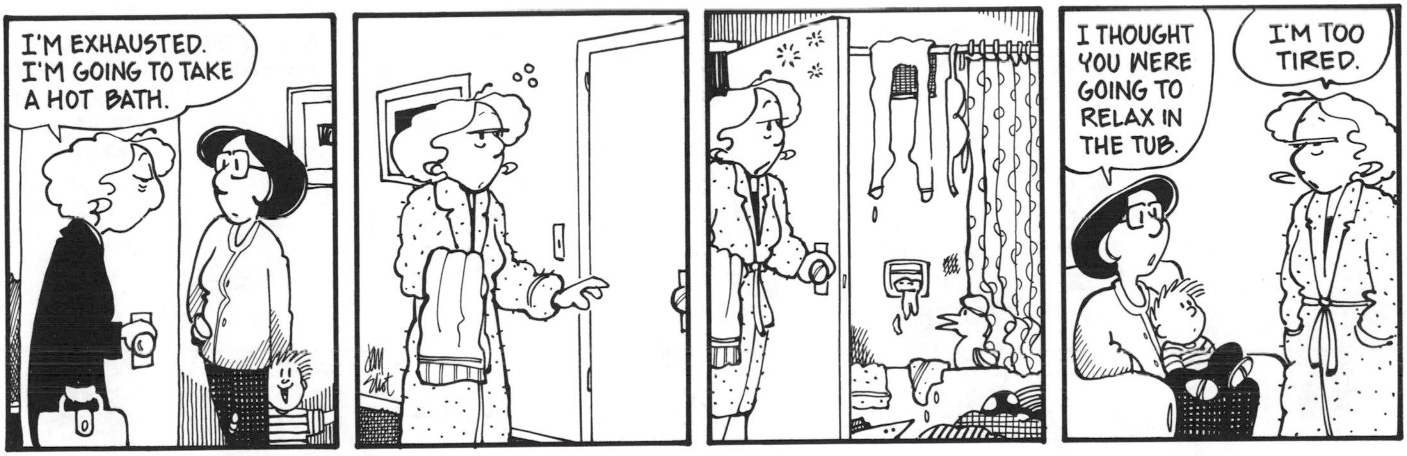
I'M EXHAUSTED. I'M GOING TO TAKE A HOT BATH.
I THOUGHT YOU WERE GOING TO RELAX IN THE TUB.
I'M TOO TIRED.

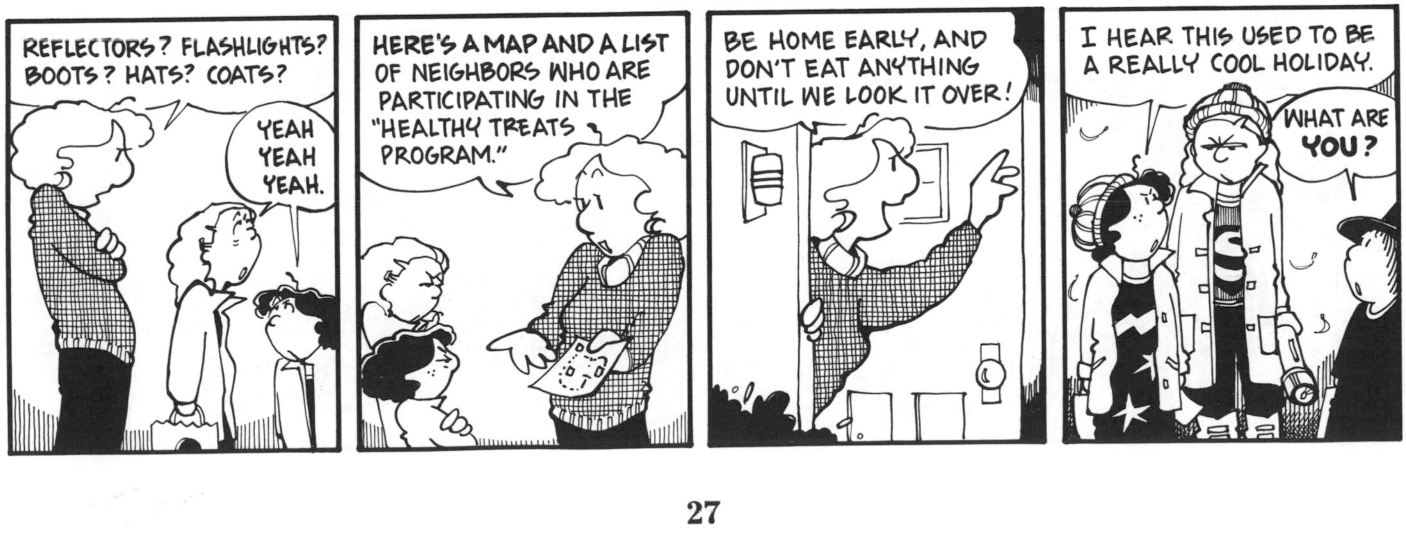
REFLECTORS? FLASHLIGHTS? BOOTS? HATS? COATS?
YEAH YEAH YEAH.
HERE'S A MAP AND A LIST OF NEIGHBORS WHO ARE PARTICIPATING IN THE "HEALTHY TREATS PROGRAM."
BE HOME EARLY, AND DON'T EAT ANYTHING UNTIL WE LOOK IT OVER!
I HEAR THIS USED TO BE A REALLY COOL HOLIDAY.
WHAT ARE YOU?

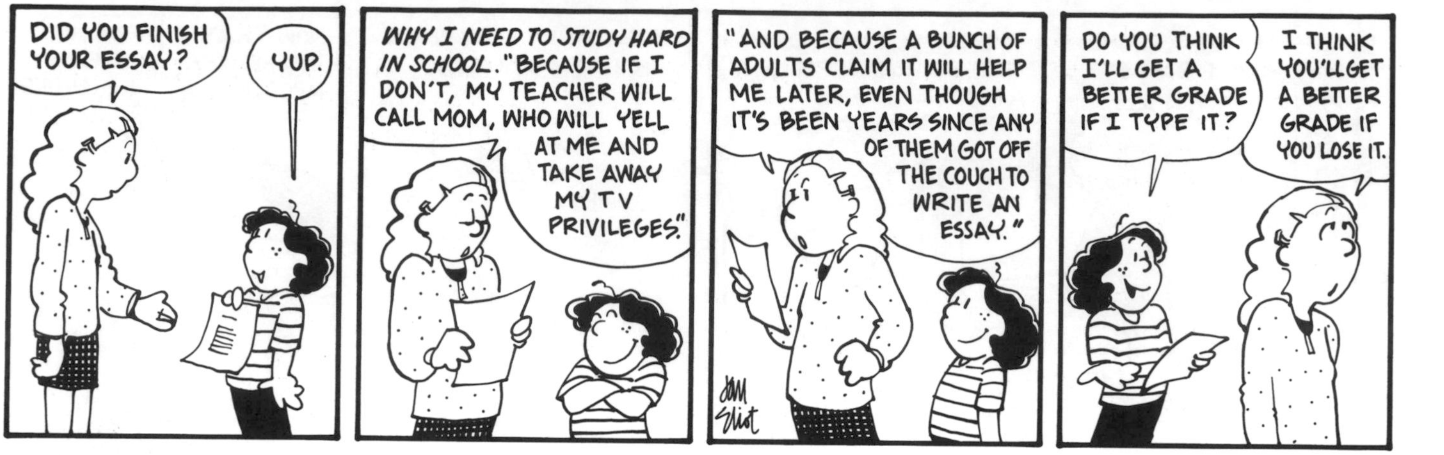
DID YOU FINISH YOUR ESSAY?
YUP.
WHY I NEED TO STUDY HARD IN SCHOOL. "BECAUSE IF I DON'T, MY TEACHER WILL CALL MOM, WHO WILL YELL AT ME AND TAKE AWAY MY TV PRIVILEGES."
"AND BECAUSE A BUNCH OF ADULTS CLAIM IT WILL HELP ME LATER, EVEN THOUGH IT'S BEEN YEARS SINCE ANY OF THEM GOT OFF THE COUCH TO WRITE AN ESSAY."
DO YOU THINK I'LL GET A BETTER GRADE IF I TYPE IT?
I THINK YOU'LL GET A BETTER GRADE IF YOU LOSE IT.

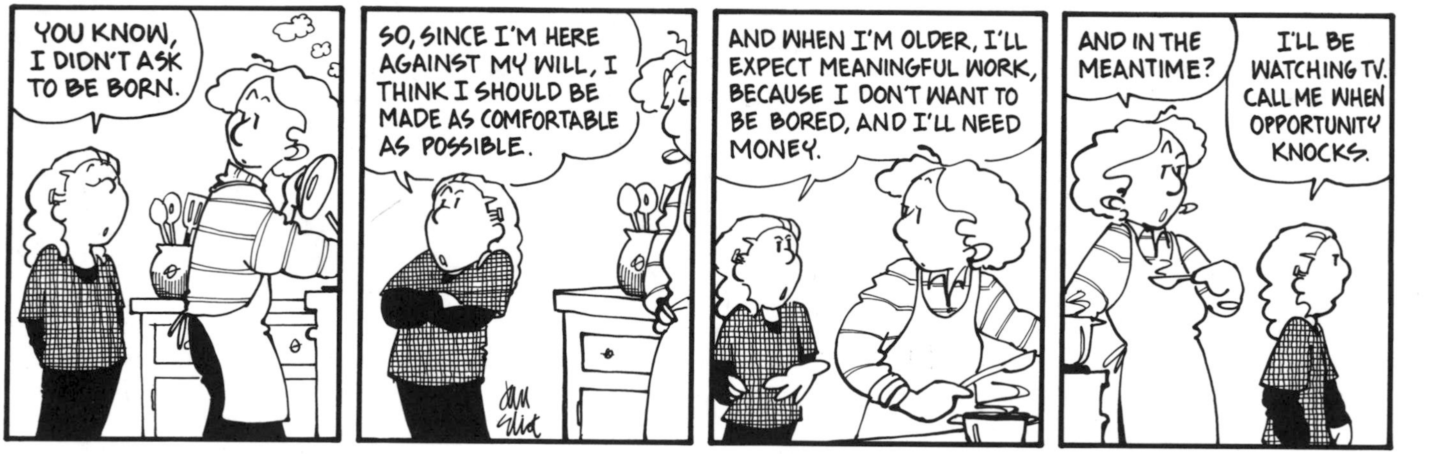
YOU KNOW, I DIDN'T ASK TO BE BORN.
SO, SINCE I'M HERE AGAINST MY WILL, I THINK I SHOULD BE MADE AS COMFORTABLE AS POSSIBLE.
AND WHEN I'M OLDER, I'LL EXPECT MEANINGFUL WORK, BECAUSE I DON'T WANT TO BE BORED, AND I'LL NEED MONEY.
AND IN THE MEANTIME?
I'LL BE WATCHING TV. CALL ME WHEN OPPORTUNITY KNOCKS.

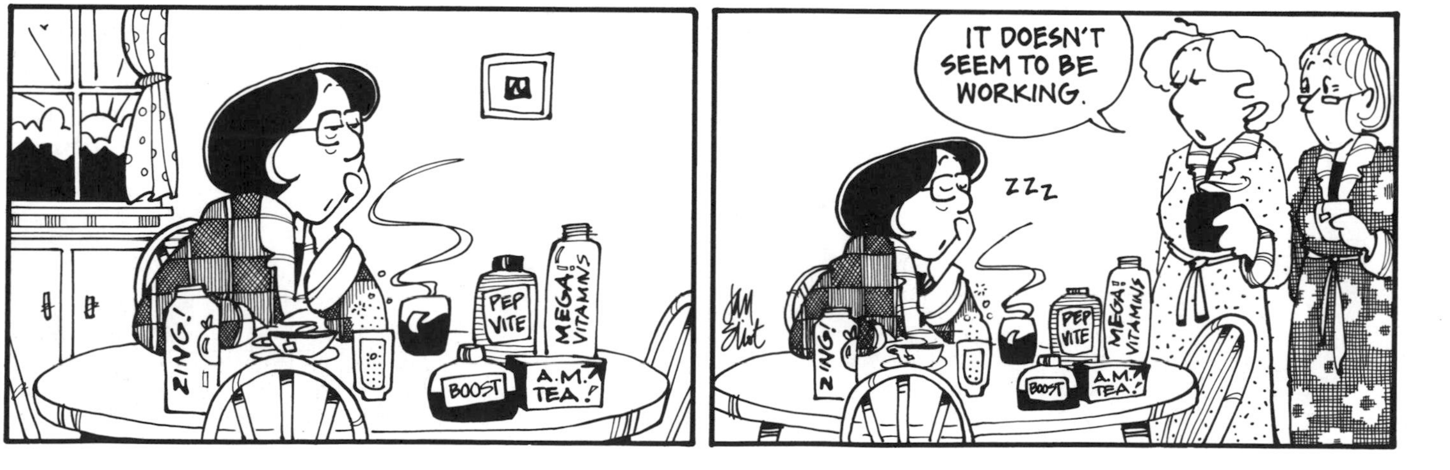
ZING!
PEP VITE
MEGA! VITAMINS
BOOST
A.M. TEA!
IT DOESN'T SEEM TO BE WORKING.
ZZZ

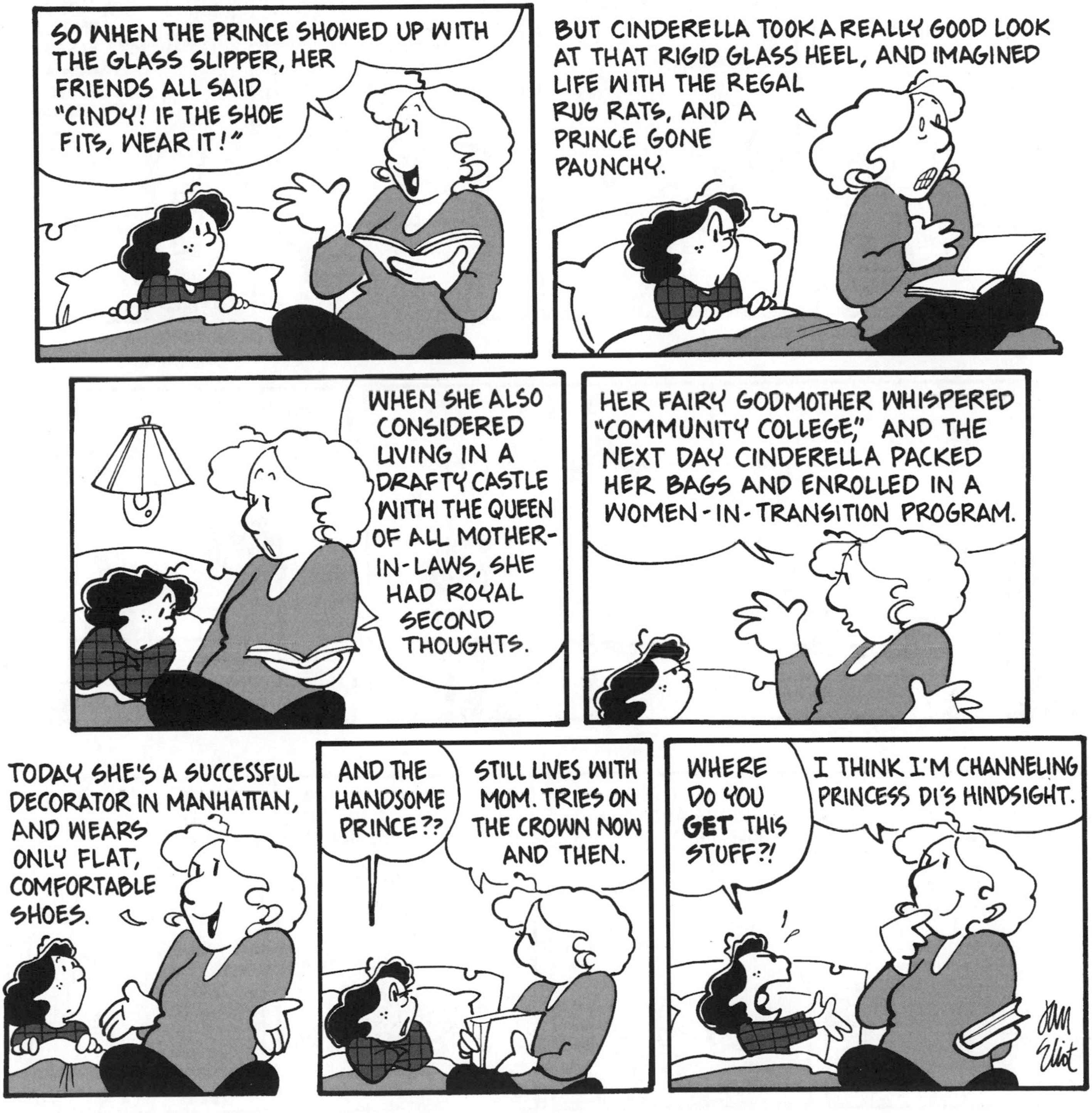
SO WHEN THE PRINCE SHOWED UP WITH THE GLASS SLIPPER, HER FRIENDS ALL SAID "CINDY! IF THE SHOE FITS, WEAR IT!"
BUT CINDERELLA TOOK A REALLY GOOD LOOK AT THAT RIGID GLASS HEEL, AND IMAGINED LIFE WITH THE REGAL RUG RATS, AND A PRINCE GONE PAUNCHY.
WHEN SHE ALSO CONSIDERED LIVING IN A DRAFTY CASTLE WITH THE QUEEN OF ALL MOTHER-IN-LAWS, SHE HAD ROYAL SECOND THOUGHTS.
HER FAIRY GODMOTHER WHISPERED "COMMUNITY COLLEGE," AND THE NEXT DAY CINDERELLA PACKED HER BAGS AND ENROLLED IN A WOMEN-IN-TRANSITION PROGRAM.
TODAY SHE'S A SUCCESSFUL DECORATOR IN MANHATTAN, AND WEARS ONLY FLAT, COMFORTABLE SHOES.
AND THE HANDSOME PRINCE??
STILL LIVES WITH MOM. TRIES ON THE CROWN NOW AND THEN.
WHERE DO YOU GET THIS STUFF?!
I THINK I'M CHANNELING PRINCESS DI'S HINDSIGHT.
Jan Eliot

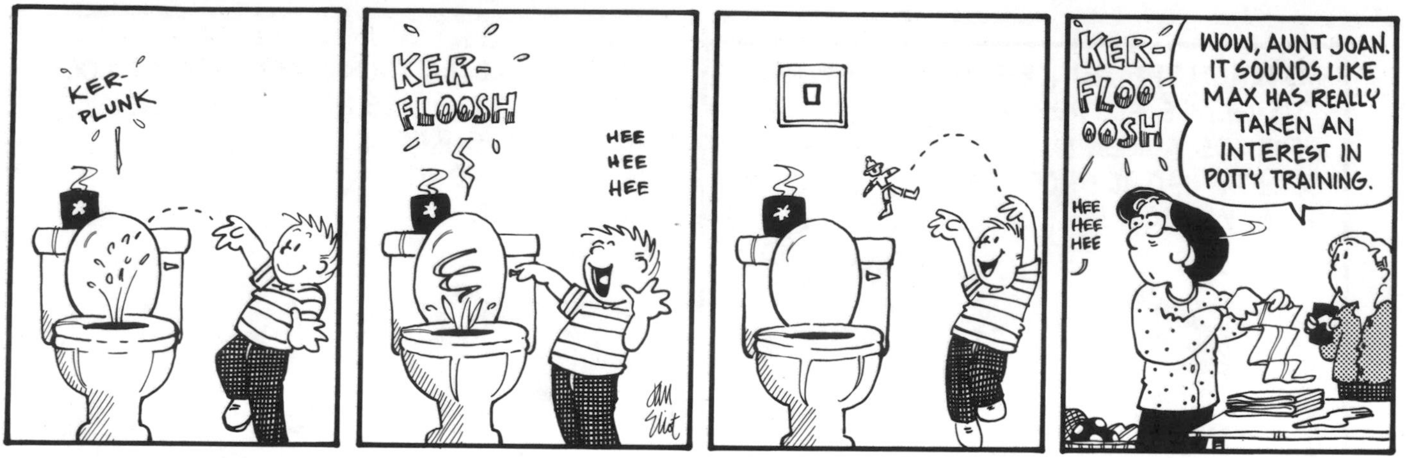
KER-
PLUNK
KER-
FLOOSH
HEE
HEE
HEE
KER-
FLOO
OOSH
HEE
HEE
HEE
WOW, AUNT JOAN. IT SOUNDS LIKE MAX HAS REALLY TAKEN AN INTEREST IN POTTY TRAINING.

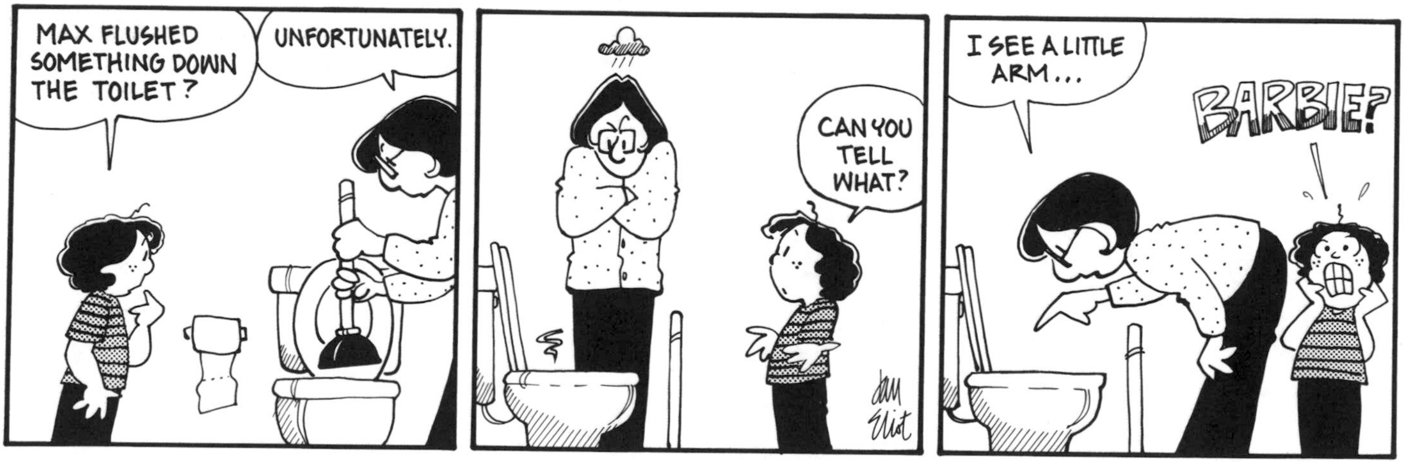
MAX FLUSHED SOMETHING DOWN THE TOILET?
UNFORTUNATELY.
CAN YOU TELL WHAT?
I SEE A LITTLE ARM...
BARBIE?

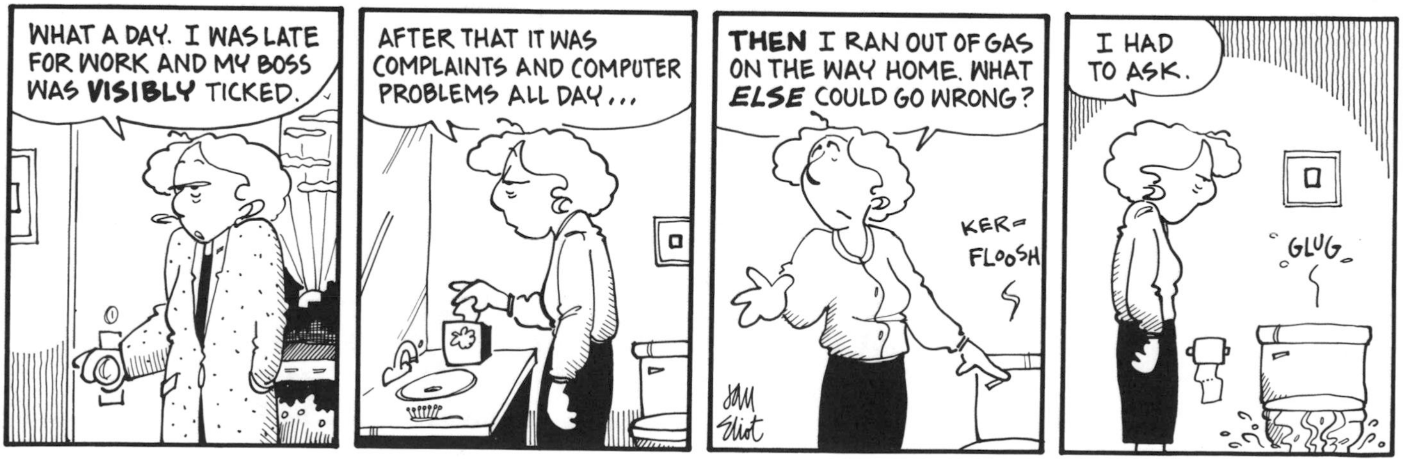
WHAT A DAY. I WAS LATE FOR WORK AND MY BOSS WAS VISIBLY TICKED.
AFTER THAT IT WAS COMPLAINTS AND COMPUTER PROBLEMS ALL DAY...
THEN I RAN OUT OF GAS ON THE WAY HOME. WHAT ELSE COULD GO WRONG?
KER-
FLOOSH
I HAD TO ASK.
GLUG

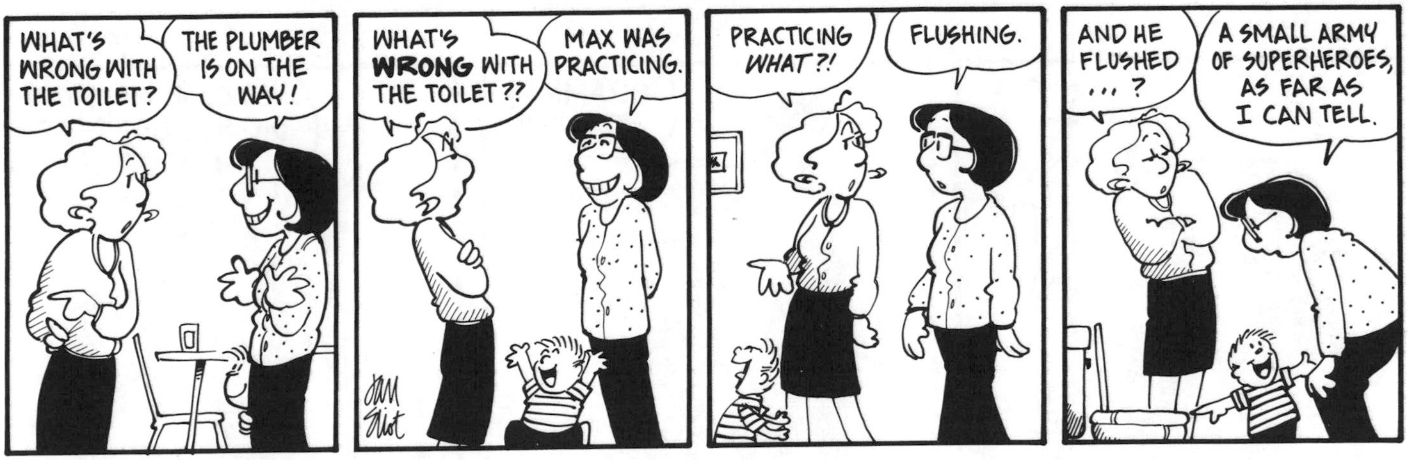
WHAT'S WRONG WITH THE TOILET?
THE PLUMBER IS ON THE WAY!
WHAT'S **WRONG** WITH THE TOILET??
MAX WAS PRACTICING.
PRACTICING *WHAT?!*
FLUSHING.
AND HE FLUSHED ...?
A SMALL ARMY OF SUPERHEROES, AS FAR AS I CAN TELL.

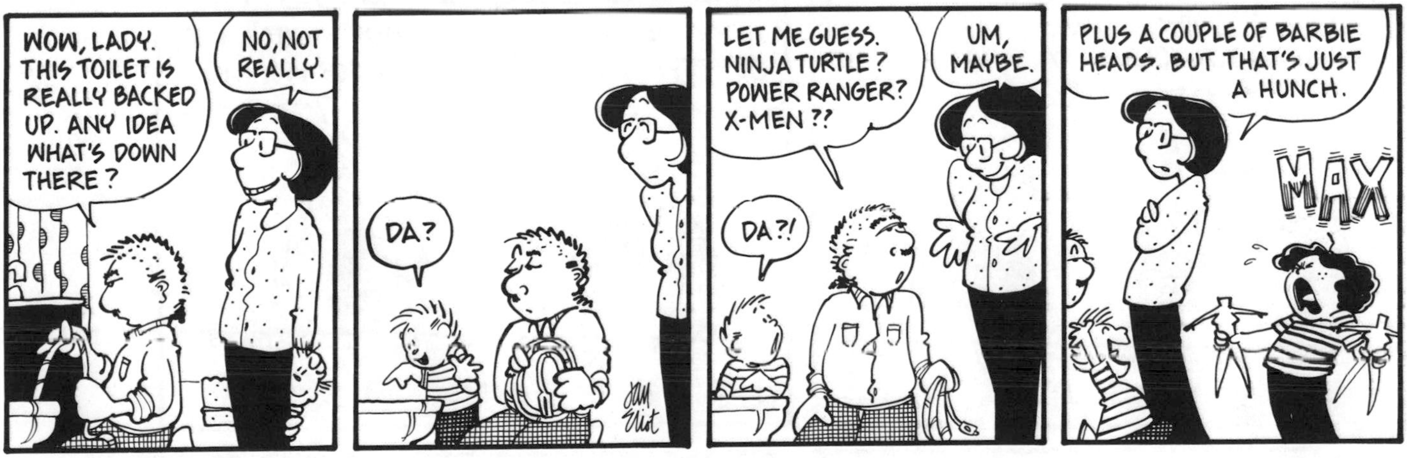
WOW, LADY. THIS TOILET IS REALLY BACKED UP. ANY IDEA WHAT'S DOWN THERE?
NO, NOT REALLY.
DA?
LET ME GUESS. NINJA TURTLE? POWER RANGER? X-MEN??
UM, MAYBE.
DA?!
PLUS A COUPLE OF BARBIE HEADS. BUT THAT'S JUST A HUNCH.
MAX

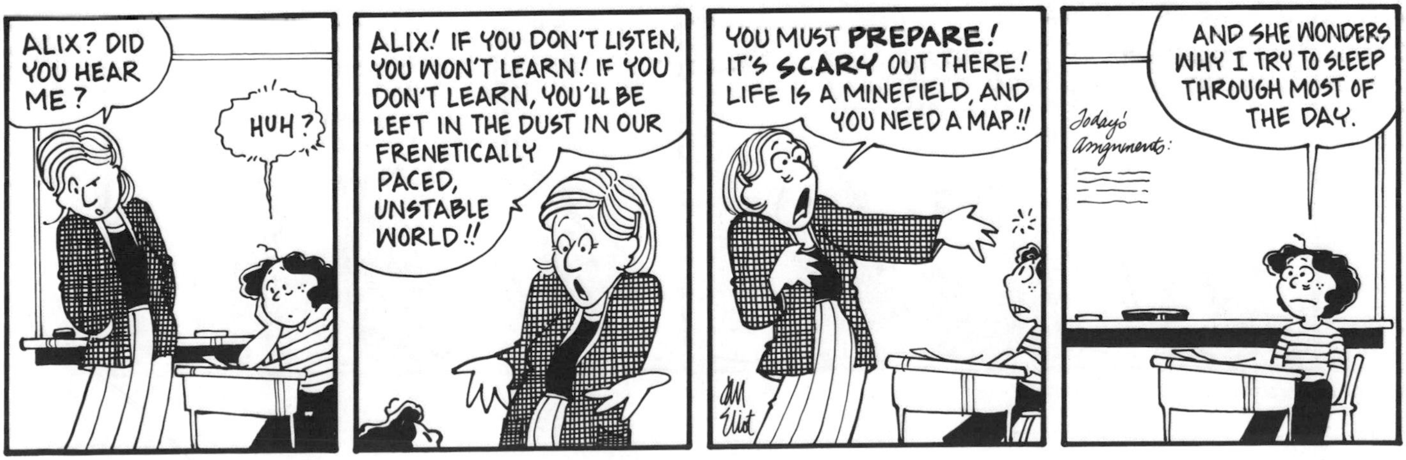
ALIX? DID YOU HEAR ME?
HUH?
ALIX! IF YOU DON'T LISTEN, YOU WON'T LEARN! IF YOU DON'T LEARN, YOU'LL BE LEFT IN THE DUST IN OUR FRENETICALLY PACED, UNSTABLE WORLD!!
YOU MUST **PREPARE**! IT'S **SCARY** OUT THERE! LIFE IS A MINEFIELD, AND YOU NEED A MAP!!
Today's Assignments:
AND SHE WONDERS WHY I TRY TO SLEEP THROUGH MOST OF THE DAY.

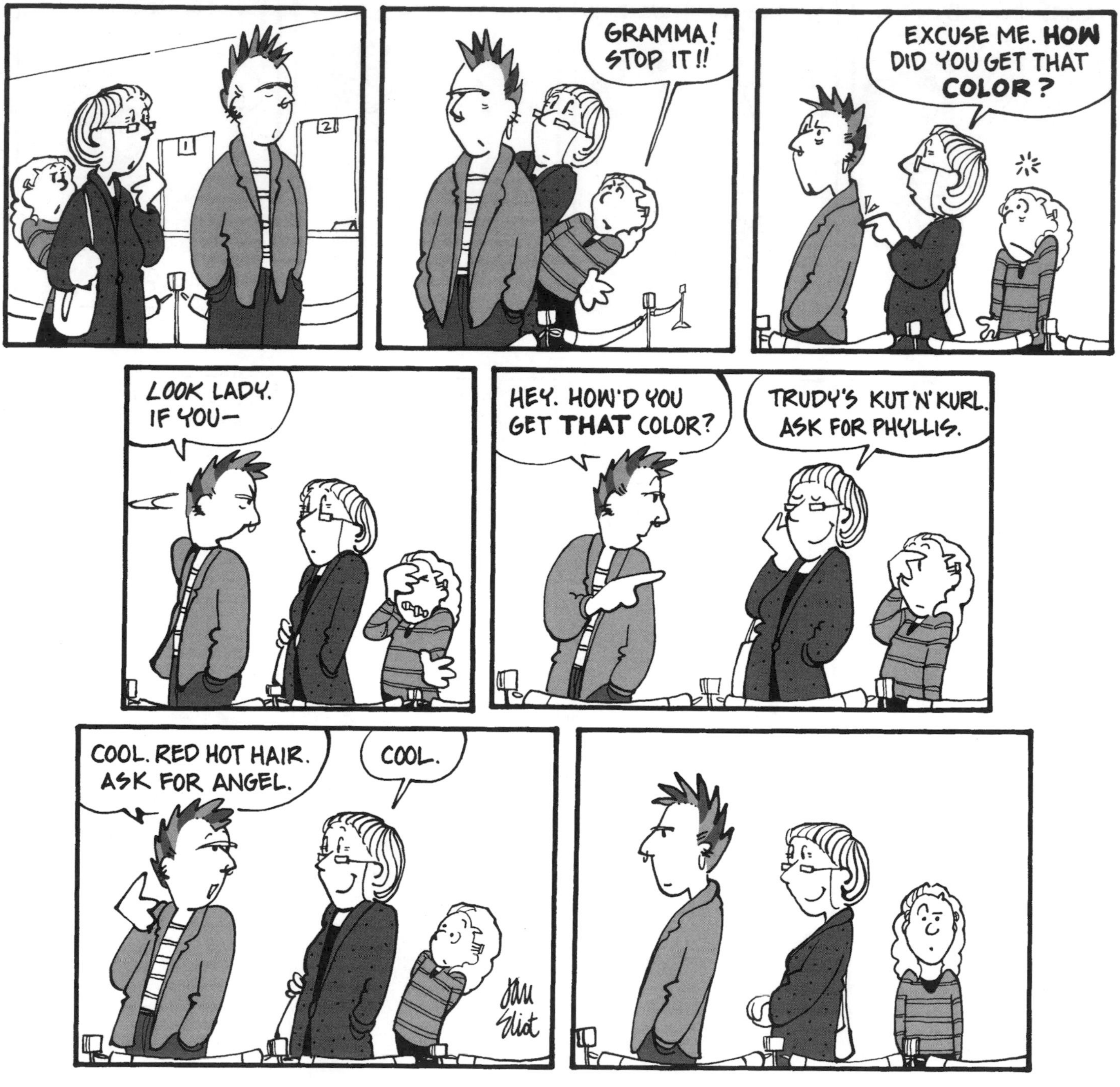
GRAMMA! STOP IT!!
EXCUSE ME. HOW DID YOU GET THAT COLOR?
LOOK LADY. IF YOU—
HEY. HOW'D YOU GET THAT COLOR?
TRUDY'S KUT 'N' KURL. ASK FOR PHYLLIS.
COOL. RED HOT HAIR. ASK FOR ANGEL.
COOL.

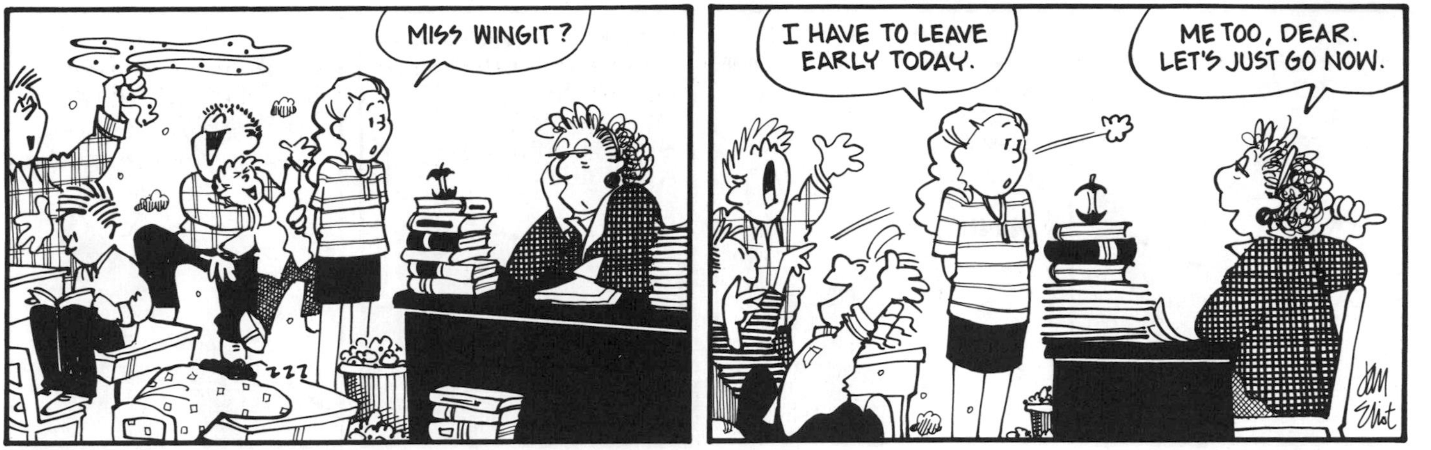
MISS WINGIT?
I HAVE TO LEAVE EARLY TODAY.
ME TOO, DEAR. LET'S JUST GO NOW.

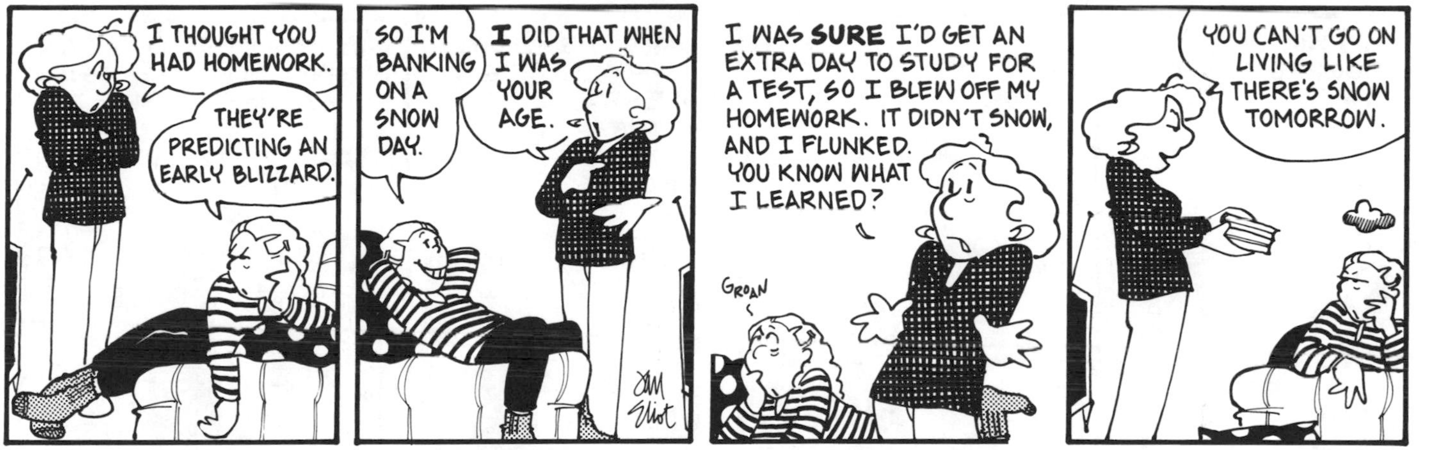
I THOUGHT YOU HAD HOMEWORK.
THEY'RE PREDICTING AN EARLY BLIZZARD.
SO I'M BANKING ON A SNOW DAY.
I DID THAT WHEN I WAS YOUR AGE.
I WAS SURE I'D GET AN EXTRA DAY TO STUDY FOR A TEST, SO I BLEW OFF MY HOMEWORK. IT DIDN'T SNOW, AND I FLUNKED. YOU KNOW WHAT I LEARNED?
GROAN
YOU CAN'T GO ON LIVING LIKE THERE'S SNOW TOMORROW.

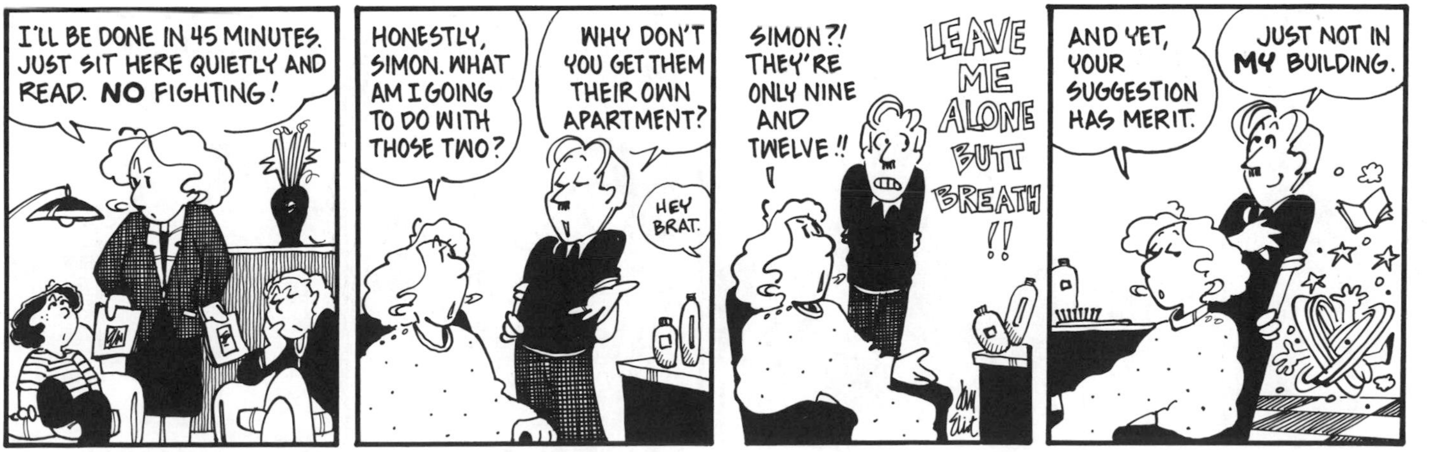
I'LL BE DONE IN 45 MINUTES. JUST SIT HERE QUIETLY AND READ. NO FIGHTING!
HONESTLY, SIMON. WHAT AM I GOING TO DO WITH THOSE TWO?
WHY DON'T YOU GET THEM THEIR OWN APARTMENT?
HEY BRAT.
SIMON?! THEY'RE ONLY NINE AND TWELVE!!
LEAVE ME ALONE BUTT BREATH !!
AND YET, YOUR SUGGESTION HAS MERIT.
JUST NOT IN MY BUILDING.

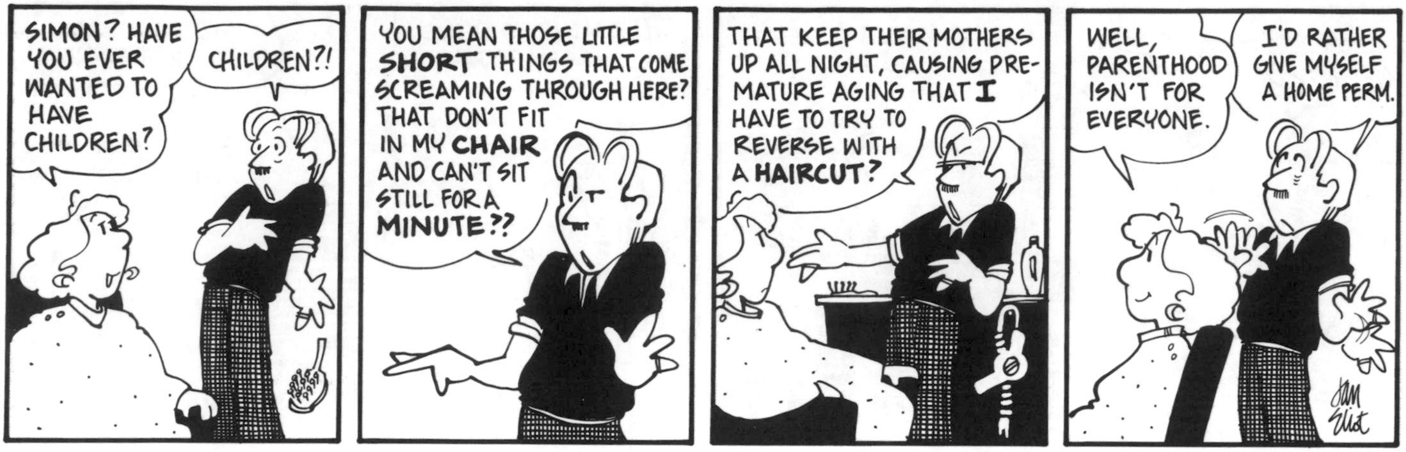
SIMON? HAVE YOU EVER WANTED TO HAVE CHILDREN?
CHILDREN?!
YOU MEAN THOSE LITTLE SHORT THINGS THAT COME SCREAMING THROUGH HERE? THAT DON'T FIT IN MY CHAIR AND CAN'T SIT STILL FOR A MINUTE??
THAT KEEP THEIR MOTHERS UP ALL NIGHT, CAUSING PRE-MATURE AGING THAT I HAVE TO TRY TO REVERSE WITH A HAIRCUT?
WELL, PARENTHOOD ISN'T FOR EVERYONE.
I'D RATHER GIVE MYSELF A HOME PERM.

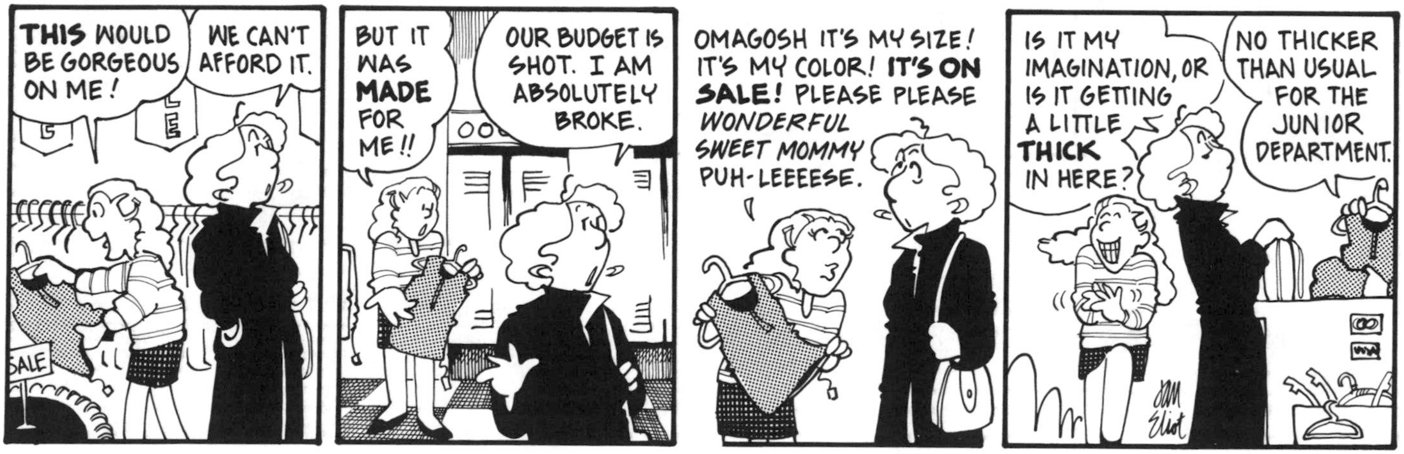
THIS WOULD BE GORGEOUS ON ME!
WE CAN'T AFFORD IT.
SALE
BUT IT WAS MADE FOR ME!!
OUR BUDGET IS SHOT. I AM ABSOLUTELY BROKE.
OMAGOSH IT'S MY SIZE! IT'S MY COLOR! IT'S ON SALE! PLEASE PLEASE WONDERFUL SWEET MOMMY PUH-LEEEESE.
IS IT MY IMAGINATION, OR IS IT GETTING A LITTLE THICK IN HERE?
NO THICKER THAN USUAL FOR THE JUNIOR DEPARTMENT.

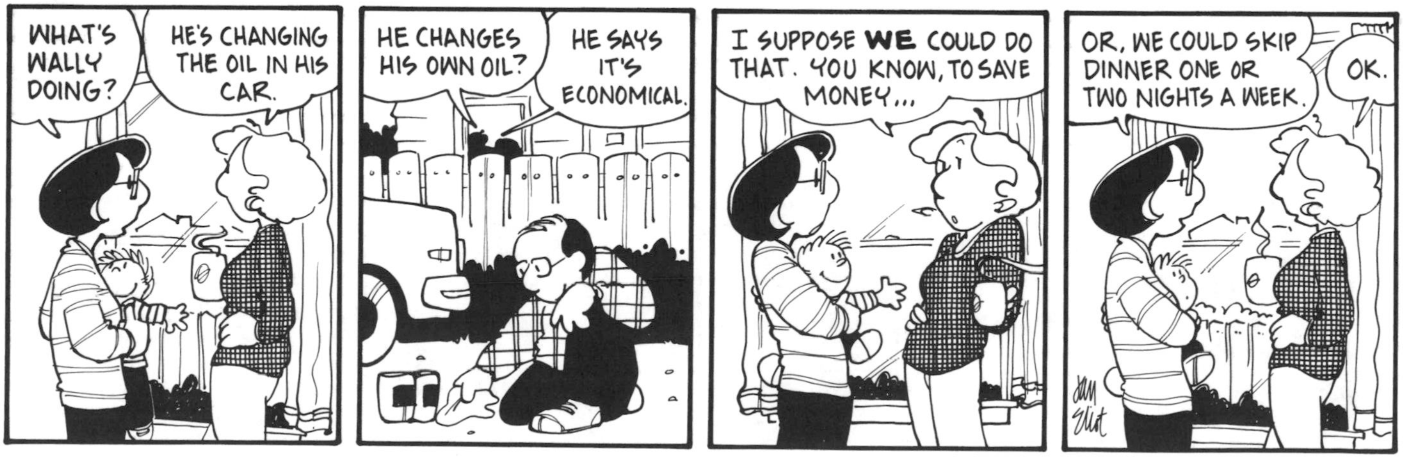
WHAT'S WALLY DOING?
HE'S CHANGING THE OIL IN HIS CAR.
HE CHANGES HIS OWN OIL?
HE SAYS IT'S ECONOMICAL.
I SUPPOSE WE COULD DO THAT. YOU KNOW, TO SAVE MONEY...
OR, WE COULD SKIP DINNER ONE OR TWO NIGHTS A WEEK.
OK.

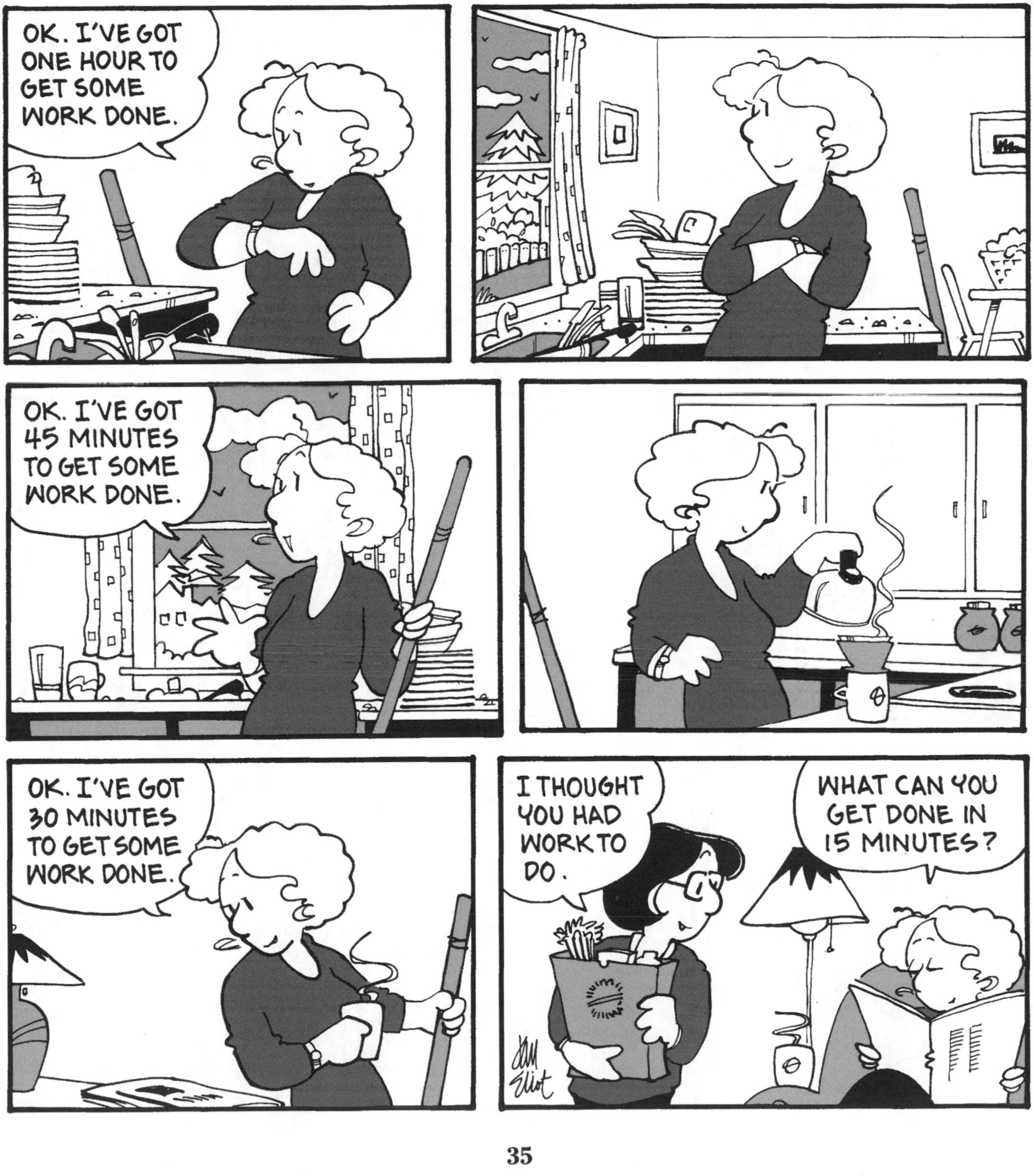
OK. I'VE GOT ONE HOUR TO GET SOME WORK DONE.
OK. I'VE GOT 45 MINUTES TO GET SOME WORK DONE.
OK. I'VE GOT 30 MINUTES TO GET SOME WORK DONE.
I THOUGHT YOU HAD WORK TO DO.
WHAT CAN YOU GET DONE IN 15 MINUTES?

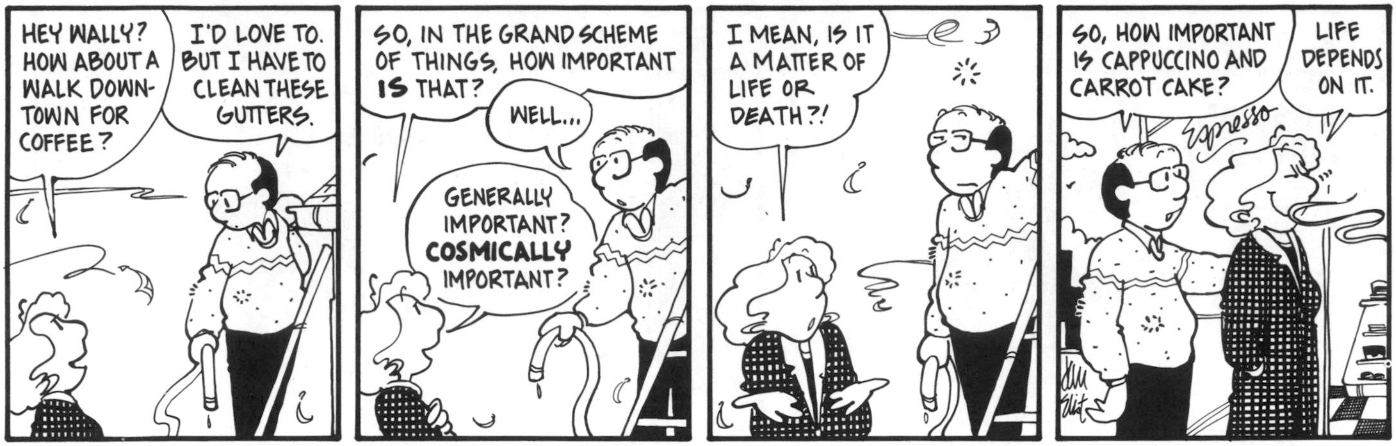
HEY WALLY? HOW ABOUT A WALK DOWN-TOWN FOR COFFEE?
I'D LOVE TO. BUT I HAVE TO CLEAN THESE GUTTERS.
SO, IN THE GRAND SCHEME OF THINGS, HOW IMPORTANT IS THAT?
WELL...
GENERALLY IMPORTANT? COSMICALLY IMPORTANT?
I MEAN, IS IT A MATTER OF LIFE OR DEATH?!
SO, HOW IMPORTANT IS CAPPUCCINO AND CARROT CAKE?
LIFE DEPENDS ON IT.
Espresso

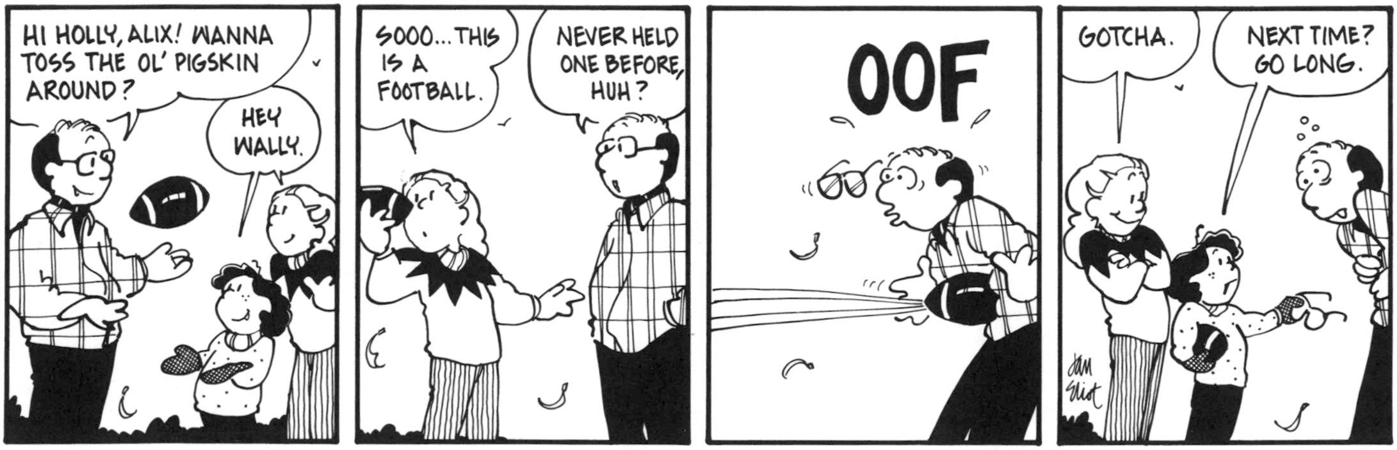
HI HOLLY, ALIX! WANNA TOSS THE OL' PIGSKIN AROUND?
HEY WALLY.
SOOO... THIS IS A FOOTBALL.
NEVER HELD ONE BEFORE, HUH?
OOF
GOTCHA.
NEXT TIME? GO LONG.

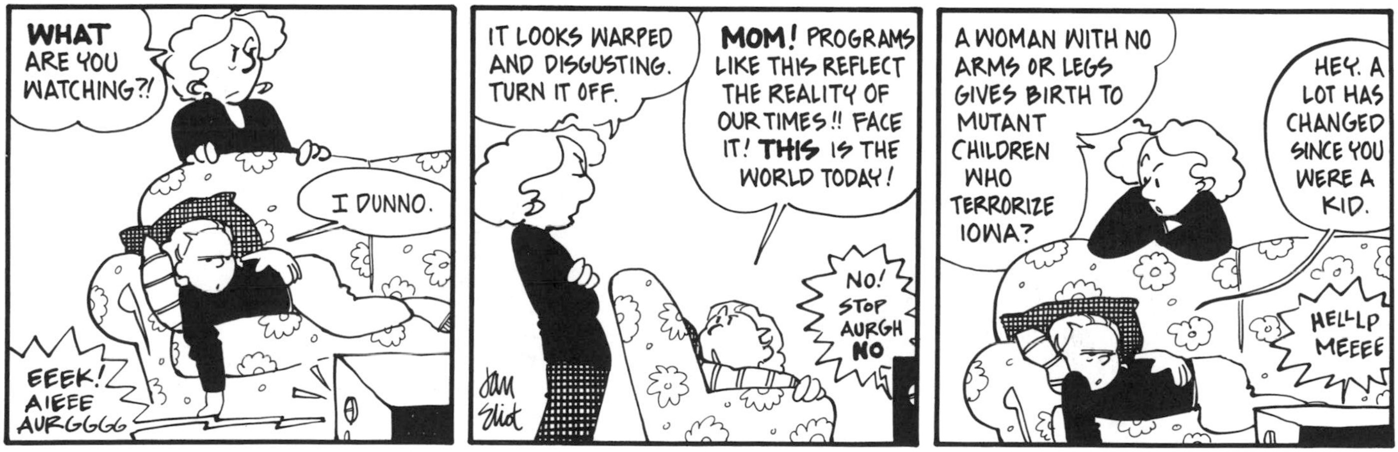
WHAT ARE YOU WATCHING?!
I DUNNO.
EEEK! AIEEE AURGGGG
IT LOOKS WARPED AND DISGUSTING. TURN IT OFF.
MOM! PROGRAMS LIKE THIS REFLECT THE REALITY OF OUR TIMES!! FACE IT! THIS IS THE WORLD TODAY!
NO! STOP AURGH NO
A WOMAN WITH NO ARMS OR LEGS GIVES BIRTH TO MUTANT CHILDREN WHO TERRORIZE IOWA?
HEY. A LOT HAS CHANGED SINCE YOU WERE A KID.
HELLLP MEEEE

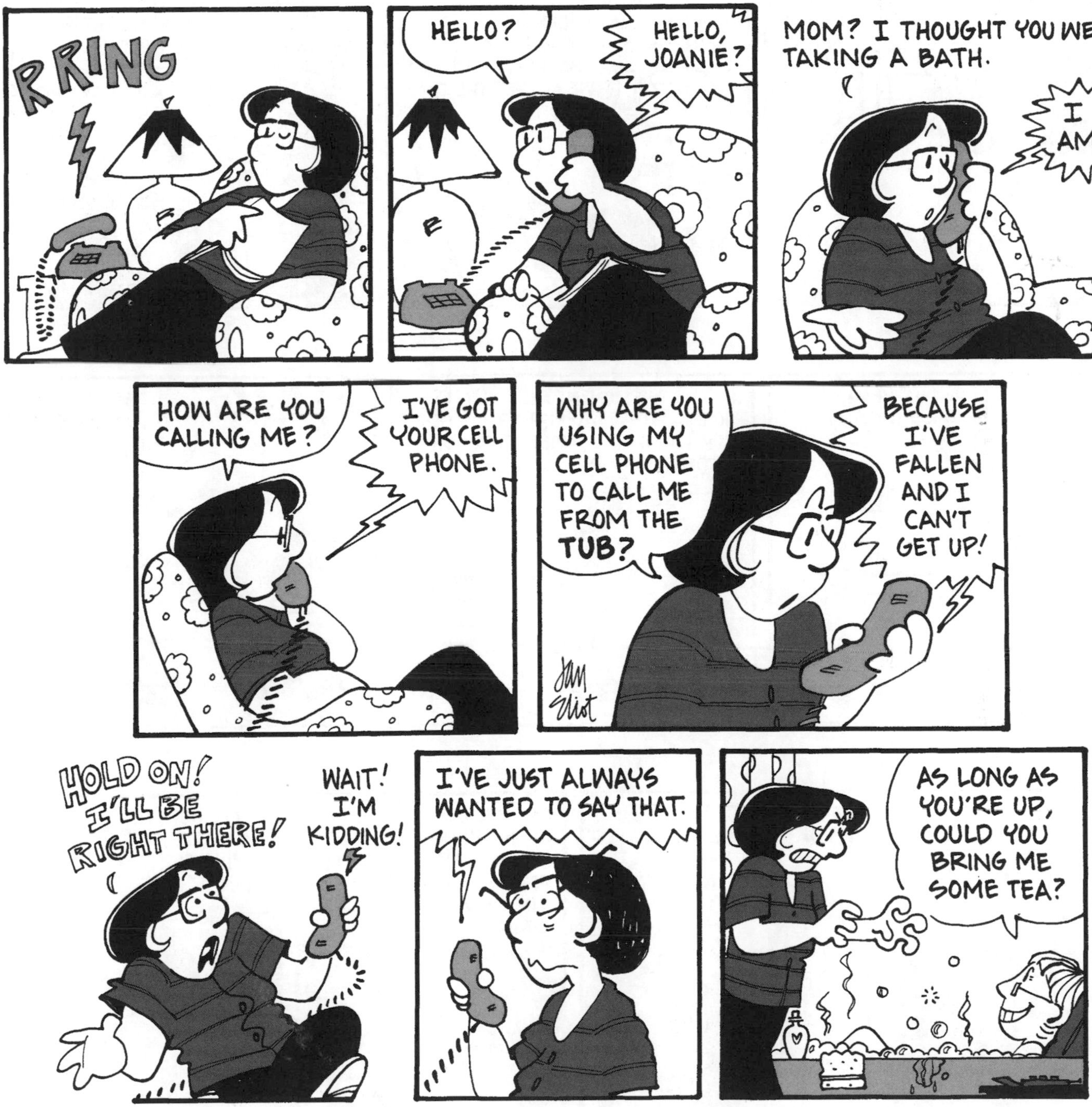
RRING
HELLO?
HELLO, JOANIE?
MOM? I THOUGHT YOU WERE TAKING A BATH.
I AM.
HOW ARE YOU CALLING ME?
I'VE GOT YOUR CELL PHONE.
WHY ARE YOU USING MY CELL PHONE TO CALL ME FROM THE TUB?
BECAUSE I'VE FALLEN AND I CAN'T GET UP!
HOLD ON! I'LL BE RIGHT THERE!
WAIT! I'M KIDDING!
I'VE JUST ALWAYS WANTED TO SAY THAT.
AS LONG AS YOU'RE UP, COULD YOU BRING ME SOME TEA?

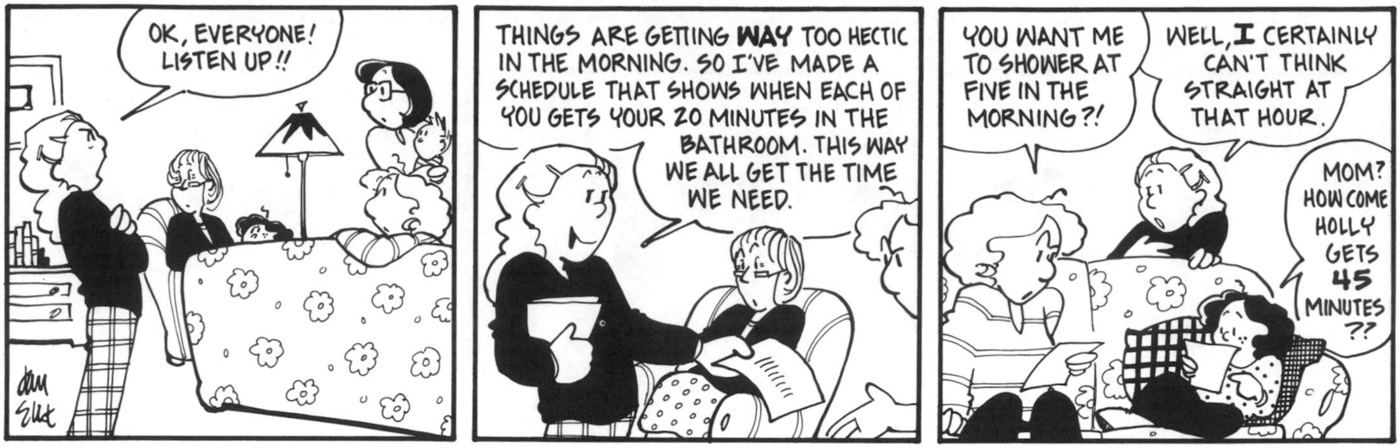
OK, EVERYONE! LISTEN UP!!
THINGS ARE GETTING **WAY** TOO HECTIC IN THE MORNING. SO I'VE MADE A SCHEDULE THAT SHOWS WHEN EACH OF YOU GETS YOUR 20 MINUTES IN THE BATHROOM. THIS WAY WE ALL GET THE TIME WE NEED.
YOU WANT ME TO SHOWER AT FIVE IN THE MORNING?!
WELL, **I** CERTAINLY CAN'T THINK STRAIGHT AT THAT HOUR.
MOM? HOW COME HOLLY GETS **45** MINUTES??

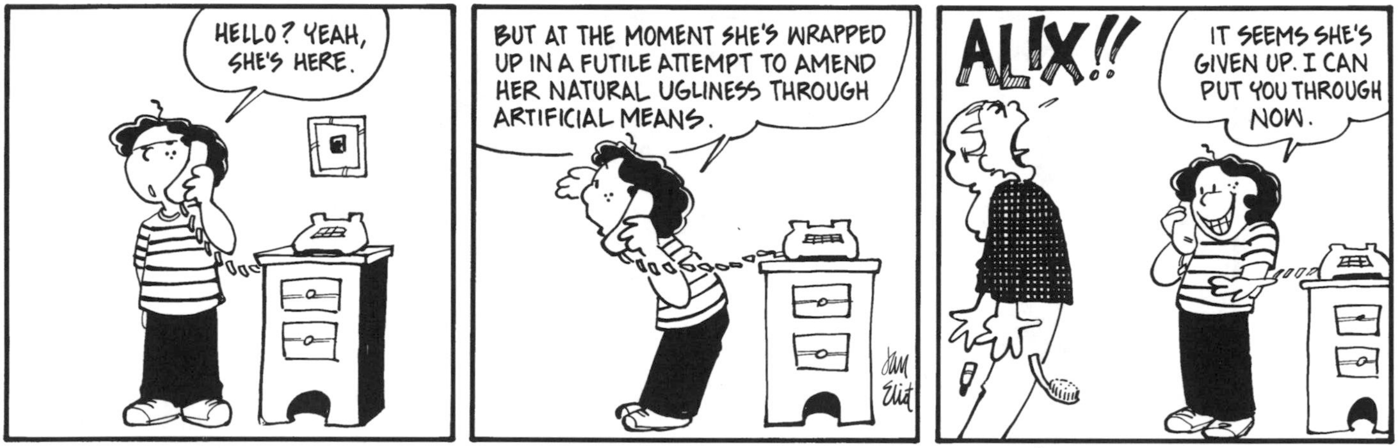
HELLO? YEAH, SHE'S HERE.
BUT AT THE MOMENT SHE'S WRAPPED UP IN A FUTILE ATTEMPT TO AMEND HER NATURAL UGLINESS THROUGH ARTIFICIAL MEANS.
ALIX!!
IT SEEMS SHE'S GIVEN UP. I CAN PUT YOU THROUGH NOW.

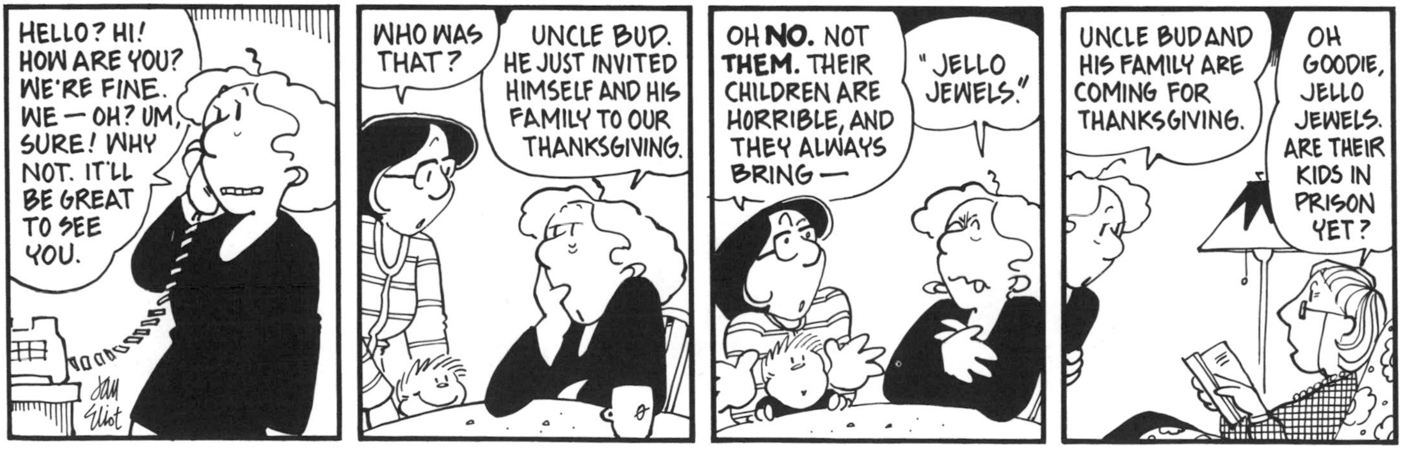
HELLO? HI! HOW ARE YOU? WE'RE FINE. WE — OH? UM, SURE! WHY NOT. IT'LL BE GREAT TO SEE YOU.
WHO WAS THAT?
UNCLE BUD. HE JUST INVITED HIMSELF AND HIS FAMILY TO OUR THANKSGIVING.
OH **NO.** NOT **THEM.** THEIR CHILDREN ARE HORRIBLE, AND THEY ALWAYS BRING —
"JELLO JEWELS."
UNCLE BUD AND HIS FAMILY ARE COMING FOR THANKSGIVING.
OH GOODIE, JELLO JEWELS. ARE THEIR KIDS IN PRISON YET?

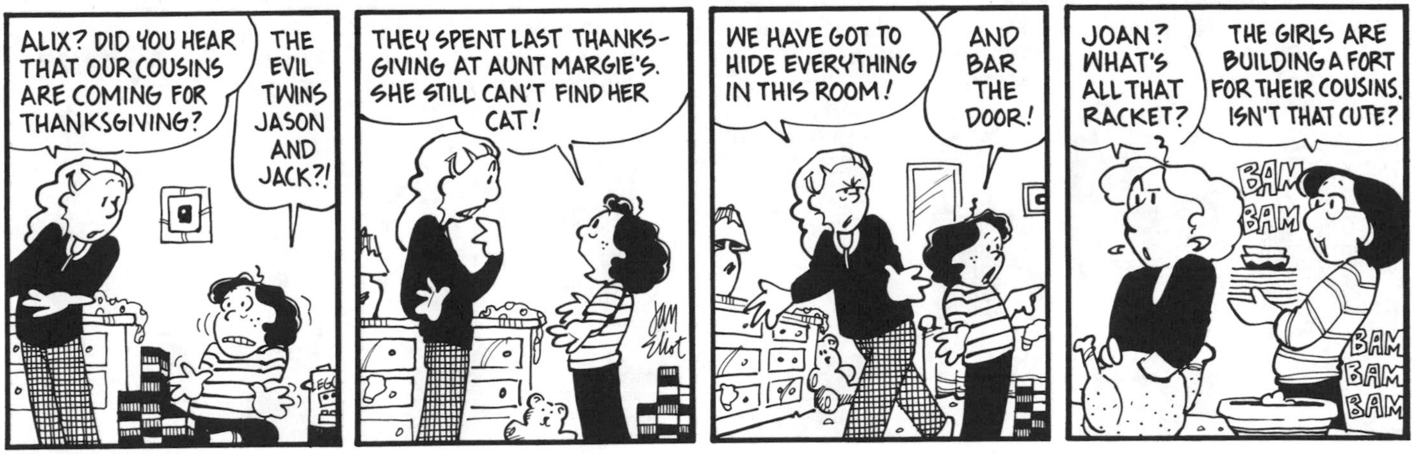
ALIX? DID YOU HEAR THAT OUR COUSINS ARE COMING FOR THANKSGIVING?
THE EVIL TWINS JASON AND JACK?!
THEY SPENT LAST THANKSGIVING AT AUNT MARGIE'S. SHE STILL CAN'T FIND HER CAT!
WE HAVE GOT TO HIDE EVERYTHING IN THIS ROOM!
AND BAR THE DOOR!
JOAN? WHAT'S ALL THAT RACKET?
THE GIRLS ARE BUILDING A FORT FOR THEIR COUSINS. ISN'T THAT CUTE?
BAM BAM
BAM BAM BAM

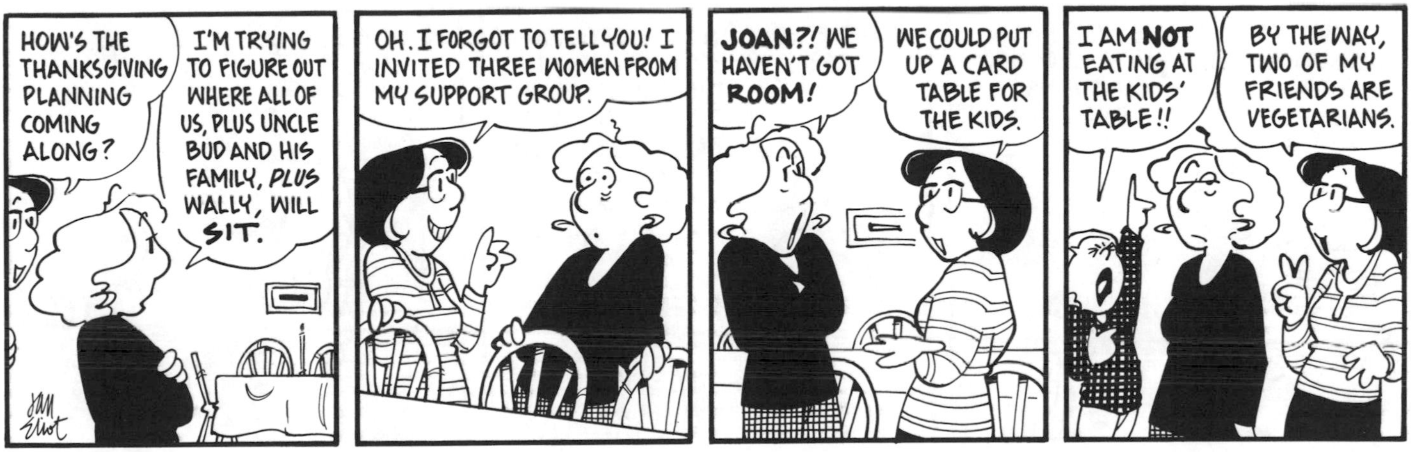
HOW'S THE THANKSGIVING PLANNING COMING ALONG?
I'M TRYING TO FIGURE OUT WHERE ALL OF US, PLUS UNCLE BUD AND HIS FAMILY, *PLUS* WALLY, WILL **SIT**.
OH. I FORGOT TO TELL YOU! I INVITED THREE WOMEN FROM MY SUPPORT GROUP.
JOAN?! WE HAVEN'T GOT **ROOM**!
WE COULD PUT UP A CARD TABLE FOR THE KIDS.
I AM **NOT** EATING AT THE KIDS' TABLE!!
BY THE WAY, TWO OF MY FRIENDS ARE VEGETARIANS.

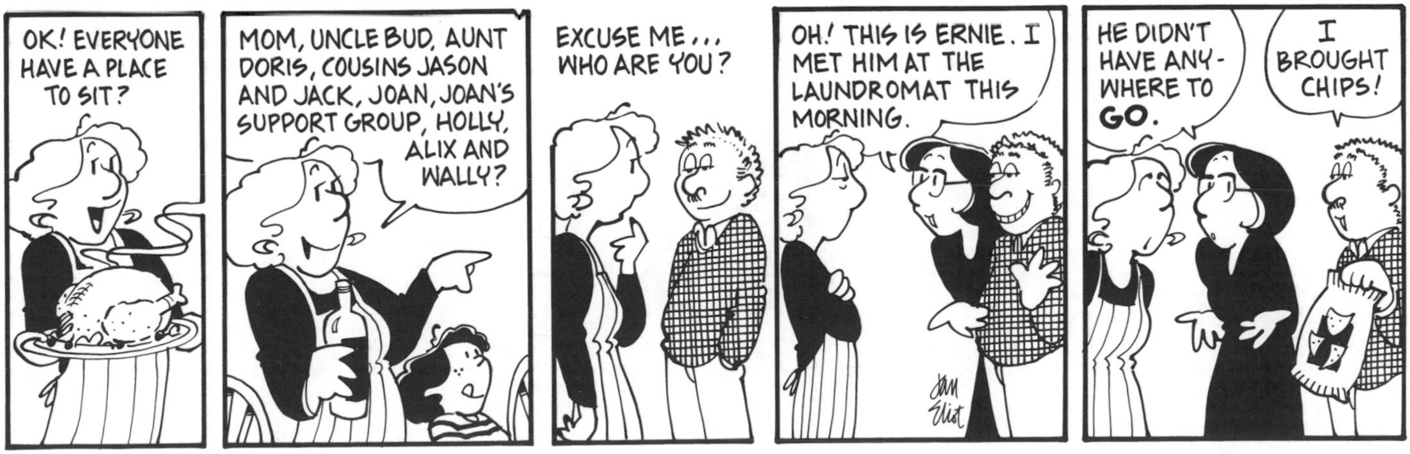
OK! EVERYONE HAVE A PLACE TO SIT?
MOM, UNCLE BUD, AUNT DORIS, COUSINS JASON AND JACK, JOAN, JOAN'S SUPPORT GROUP, HOLLY, ALIX AND WALLY?
EXCUSE ME... WHO ARE YOU?
OH! THIS IS ERNIE. I MET HIM AT THE LAUNDROMAT THIS MORNING.
HE DIDN'T HAVE ANYWHERE TO **GO**.
I BROUGHT CHIPS!

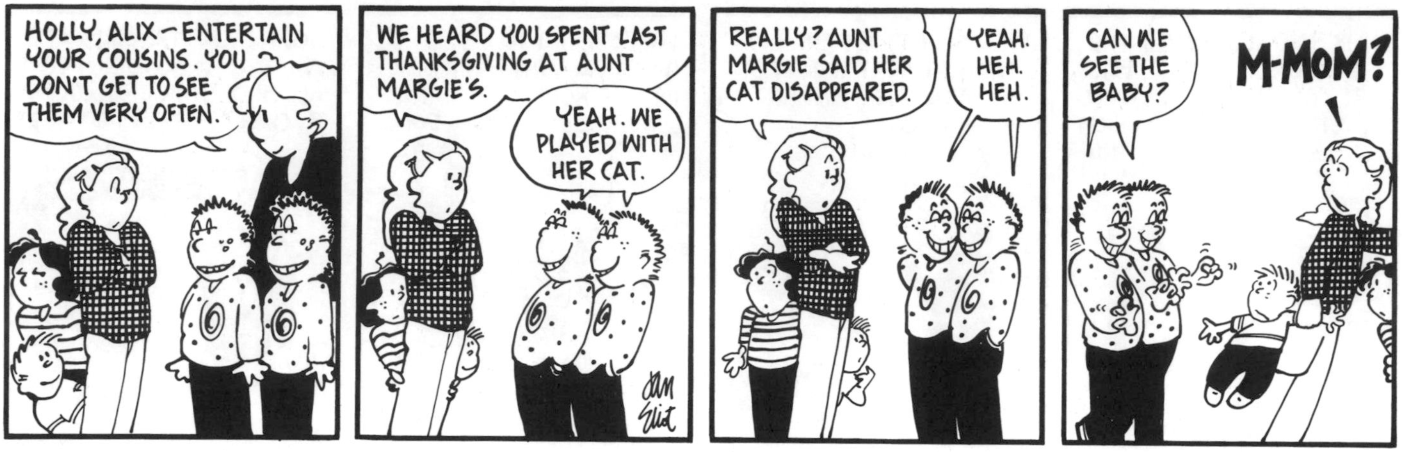
HOLLY, ALIX – ENTERTAIN YOUR COUSINS. YOU DON'T GET TO SEE THEM VERY OFTEN.
WE HEARD YOU SPENT LAST THANKSGIVING AT AUNT MARGIE'S.
YEAH. WE PLAYED WITH HER CAT.
REALLY? AUNT MARGIE SAID HER CAT DISAPPEARED.
YEAH. HEH. HEH.
CAN WE SEE THE BABY?
M-MOM?

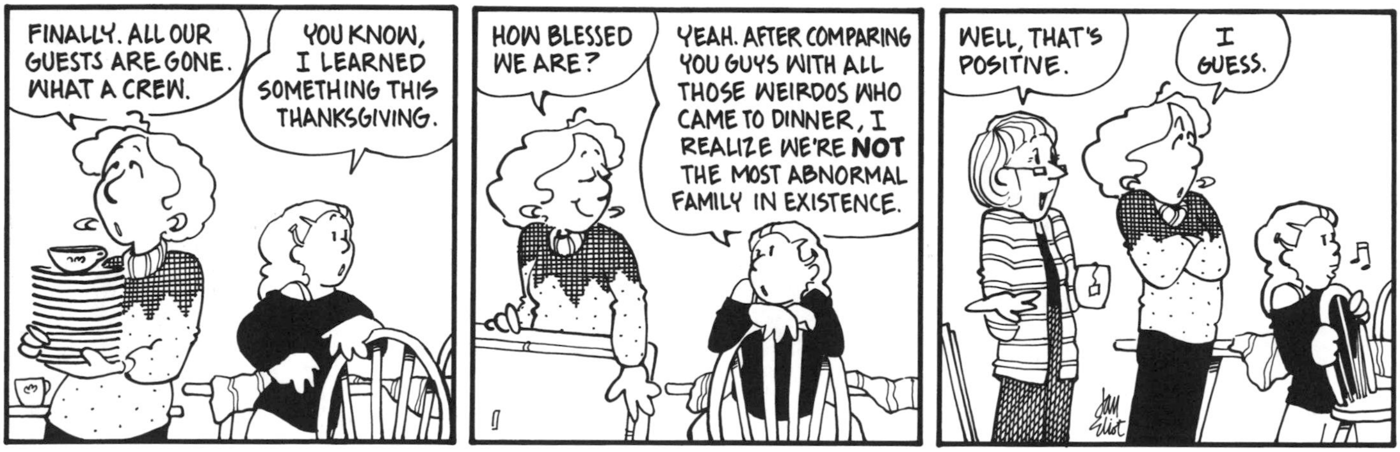
FINALLY. ALL OUR GUESTS ARE GONE. WHAT A CREW.
YOU KNOW, I LEARNED SOMETHING THIS THANKSGIVING.
HOW BLESSED WE ARE?
YEAH. AFTER COMPARING YOU GUYS WITH ALL THOSE WEIRDOS WHO CAME TO DINNER, I REALIZE WE'RE **NOT** THE MOST ABNORMAL FAMILY IN EXISTENCE.
WELL, THAT'S POSITIVE.
I GUESS.

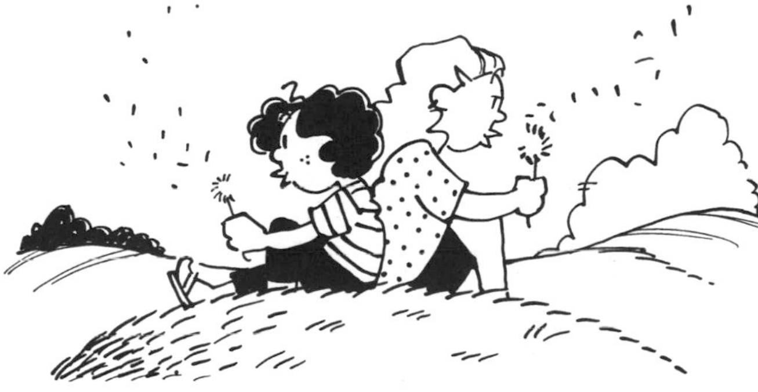

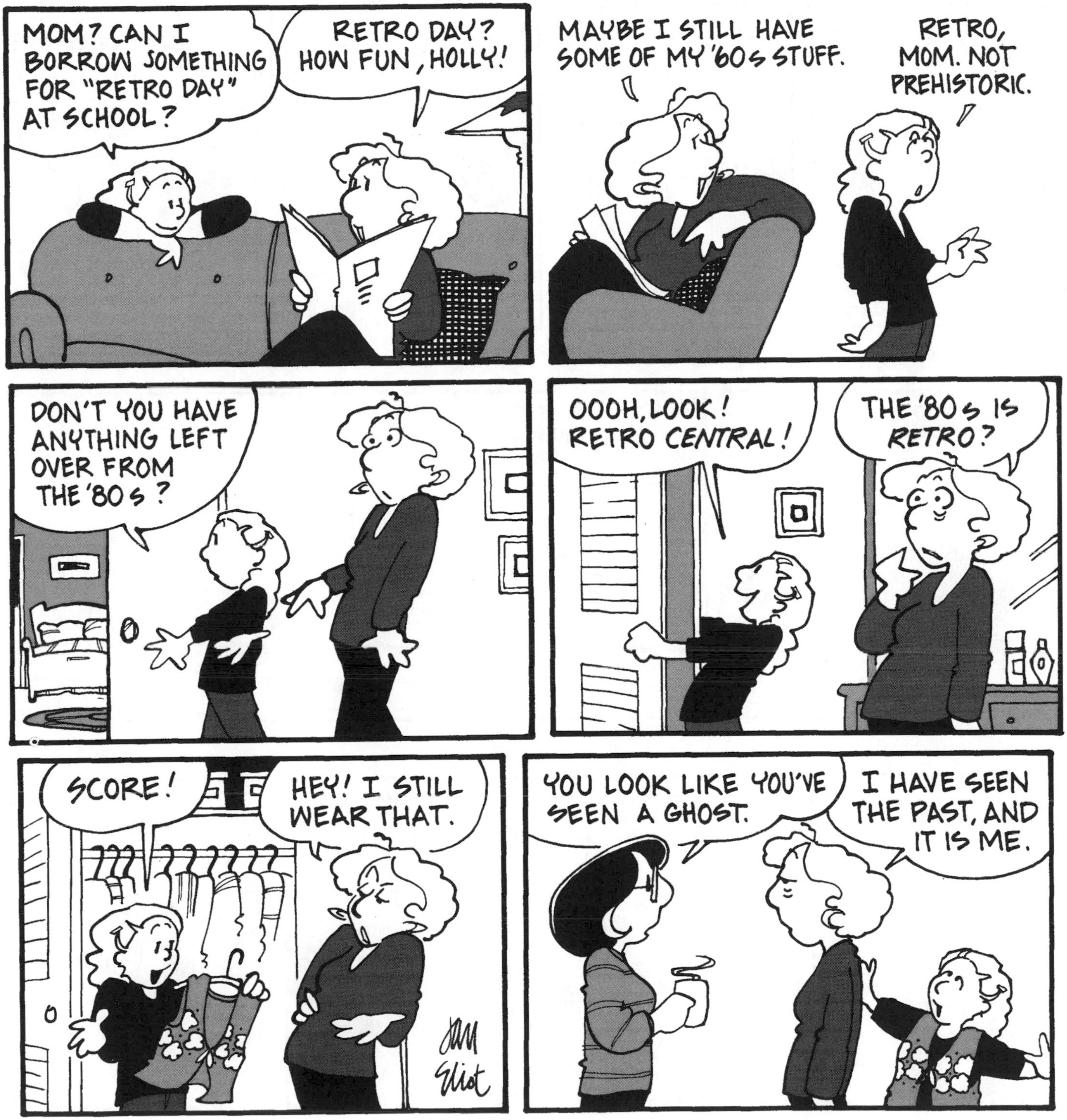
MOM? CAN I BORROW SOMETHING FOR "RETRO DAY" AT SCHOOL?
RETRO DAY? HOW FUN, HOLLY!
MAYBE I STILL HAVE SOME OF MY '60s STUFF.
RETRO, MOM. NOT PREHISTORIC.
DON'T YOU HAVE ANYTHING LEFT OVER FROM THE '80s?
OOOH, LOOK! RETRO CENTRAL!
THE '80s IS RETRO?
SCORE!
HEY! I STILL WEAR THAT.
YOU LOOK LIKE YOU'VE SEEN A GHOST.
I HAVE SEEN THE PAST, AND IT IS ME.

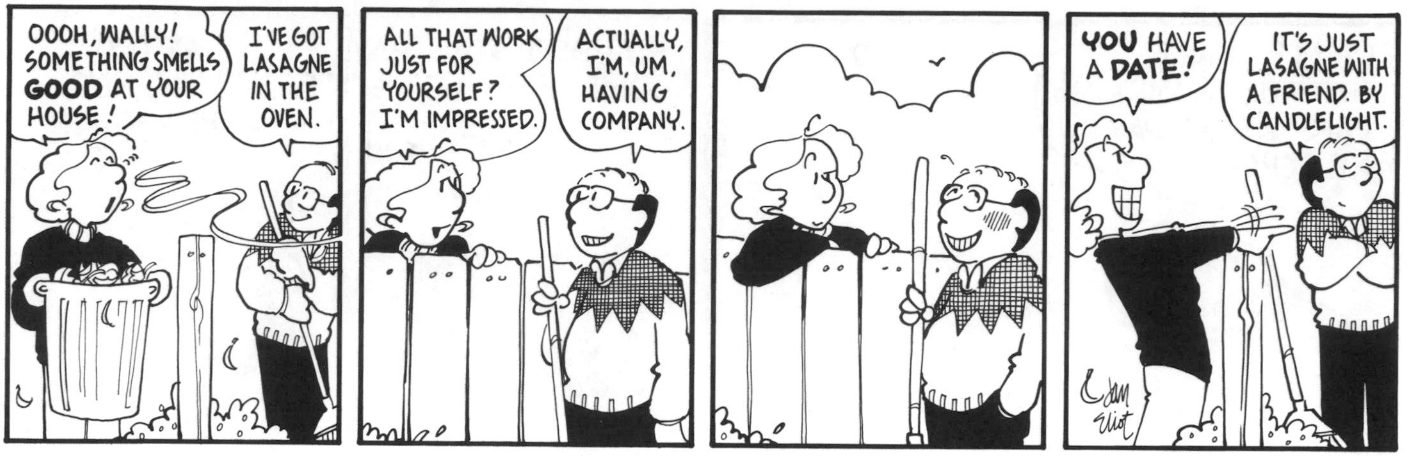
OOOH, WALLY! SOMETHING SMELLS **GOOD** AT YOUR HOUSE!
I'VE GOT LASAGNE IN THE OVEN.
ALL THAT WORK JUST FOR YOURSELF? I'M IMPRESSED.
ACTUALLY, I'M, UM, HAVING COMPANY.
YOU HAVE A **DATE**!
IT'S JUST LASAGNE WITH A FRIEND. BY CANDLELIGHT.

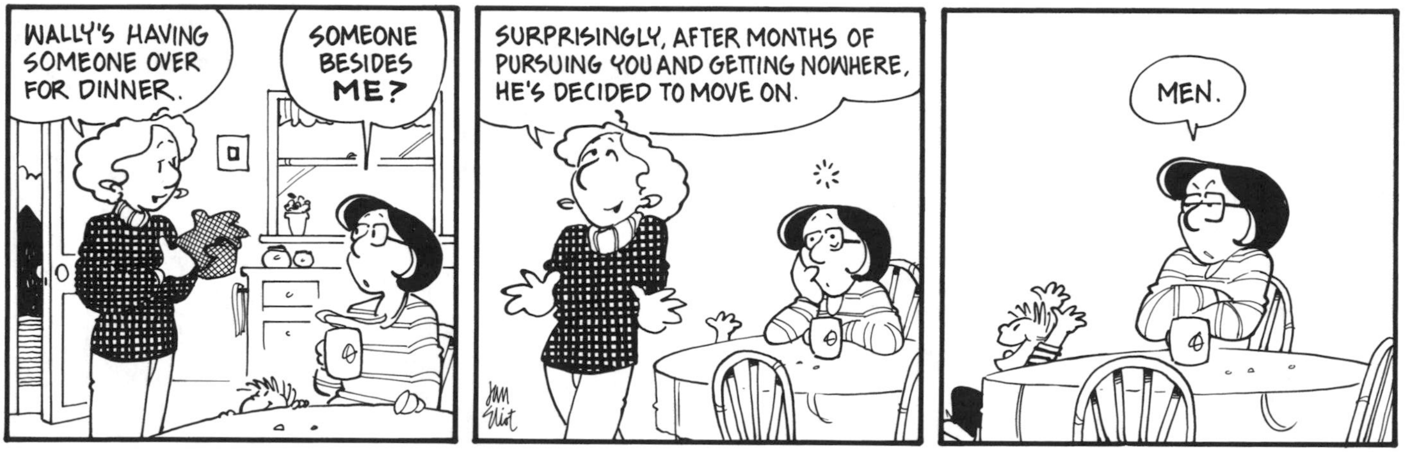
WALLY'S HAVING SOMEONE OVER FOR DINNER.
SOMEONE BESIDES **ME?**
SURPRISINGLY, AFTER MONTHS OF PURSUING YOU AND GETTING NOWHERE, HE'S DECIDED TO MOVE ON.
MEN.

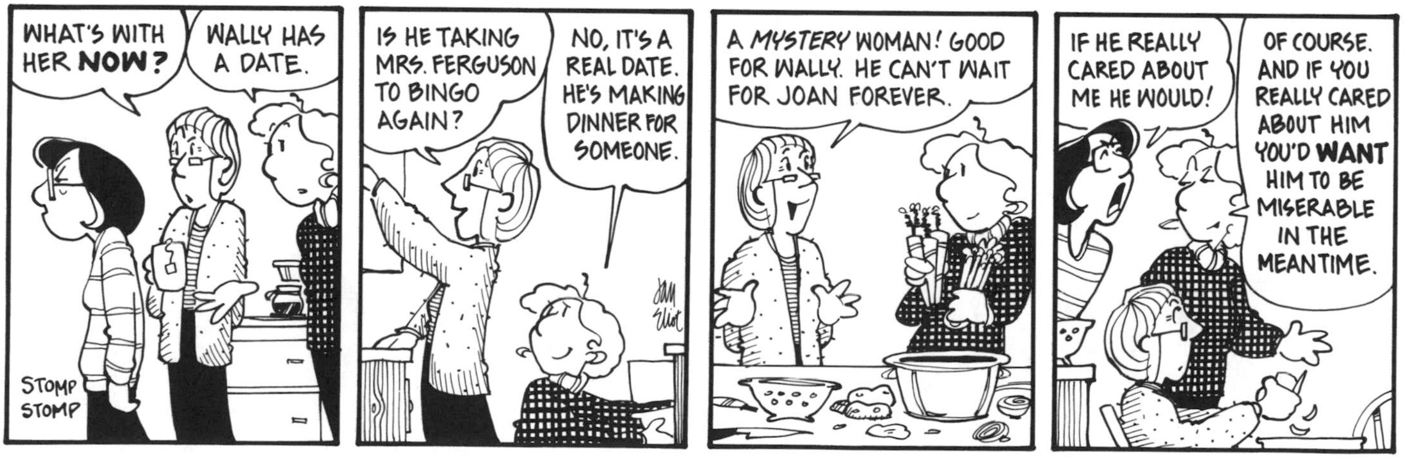
WHAT'S WITH HER **NOW?**
WALLY HAS A DATE.
STOMP STOMP
IS HE TAKING MRS. FERGUSON TO BINGO AGAIN?
NO, IT'S A REAL DATE. HE'S MAKING DINNER FOR SOMEONE.
A *MYSTERY* WOMAN! GOOD FOR WALLY. HE CAN'T WAIT FOR JOAN FOREVER.
IF HE REALLY CARED ABOUT ME HE WOULD!
OF COURSE. AND IF YOU REALLY CARED ABOUT HIM YOU'D **WANT** HIM TO BE MISERABLE IN THE MEANTIME.

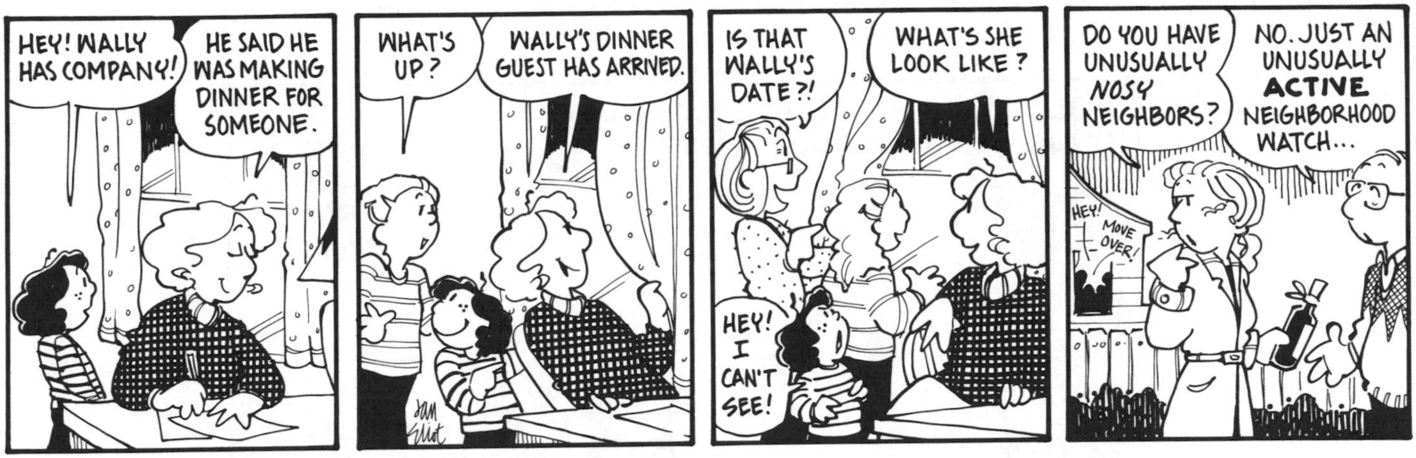
HEY! WALLY HAS COMPANY!
HE SAID HE WAS MAKING DINNER FOR SOMEONE.
WHAT'S UP?
WALLY'S DINNER GUEST HAS ARRIVED.
IS THAT WALLY'S DATE?!
WHAT'S SHE LOOK LIKE?
HEY! I CAN'T SEE!
DO YOU HAVE UNUSUALLY *NOSY* NEIGHBORS?
NO. JUST AN UNUSUALLY **ACTIVE** NEIGHBORHOOD WATCH...
HEY!
MOVE OVER!

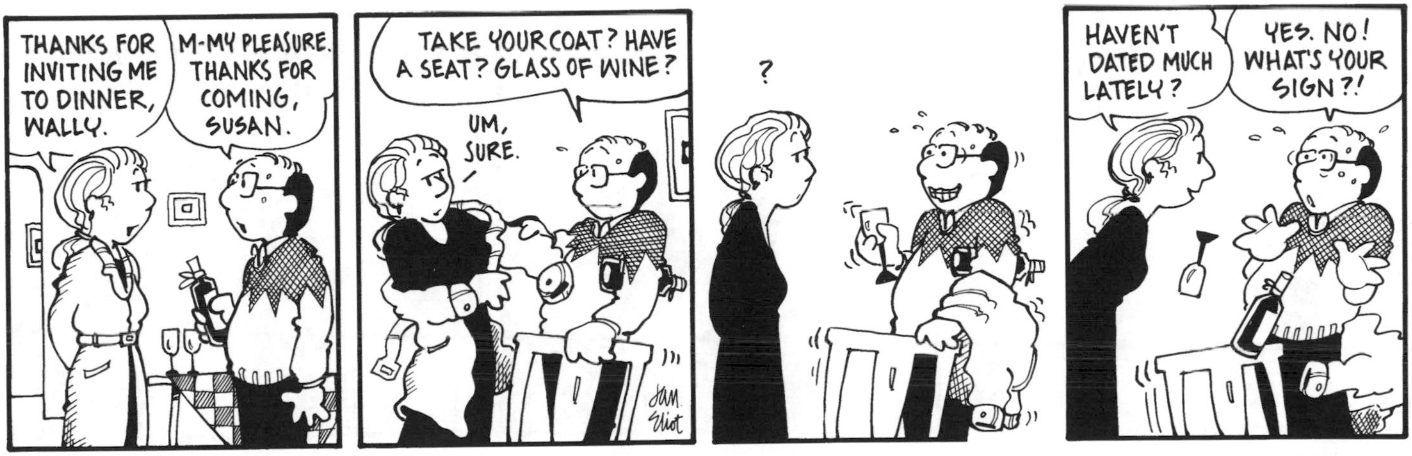
THANKS FOR INVITING ME TO DINNER, WALLY.
M-MY PLEASURE. THANKS FOR COMING, SUSAN.
TAKE YOUR COAT? HAVE A SEAT? GLASS OF WINE?
UM, SURE.
?
HAVEN'T DATED MUCH LATELY?
YES. NO! WHAT'S YOUR SIGN?!

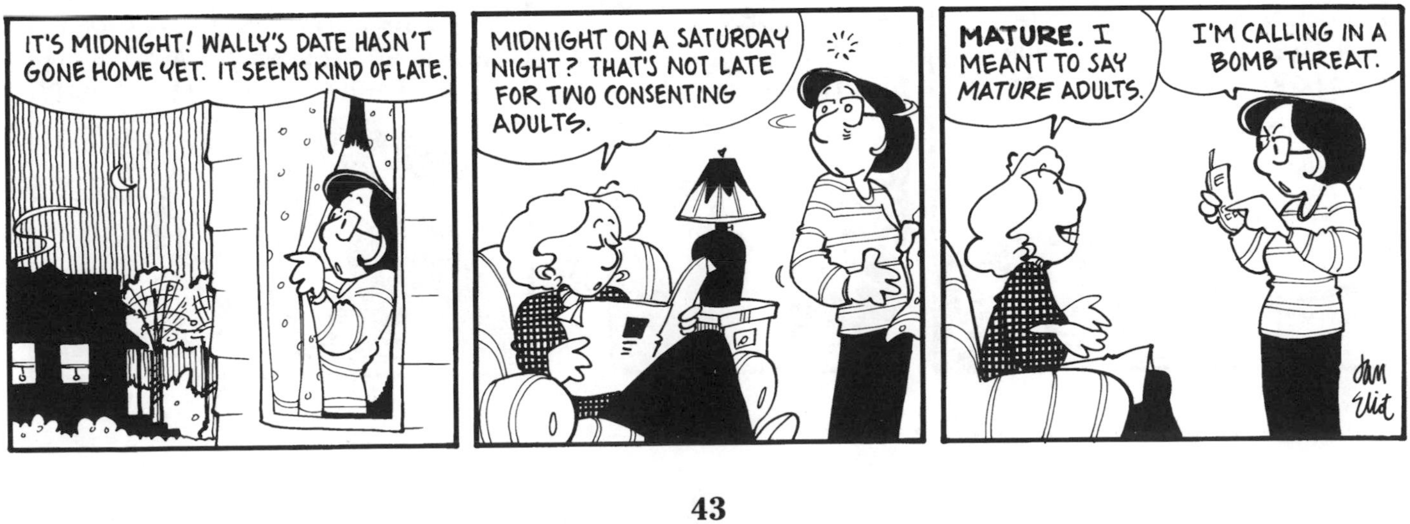
IT'S MIDNIGHT! WALLY'S DATE HASN'T GONE HOME YET. IT SEEMS KIND OF LATE.
MIDNIGHT ON A SATURDAY NIGHT? THAT'S NOT LATE FOR TWO CONSENTING ADULTS.
MATURE. I MEANT TO SAY *MATURE* ADULTS.
I'M CALLING IN A BOMB THREAT.

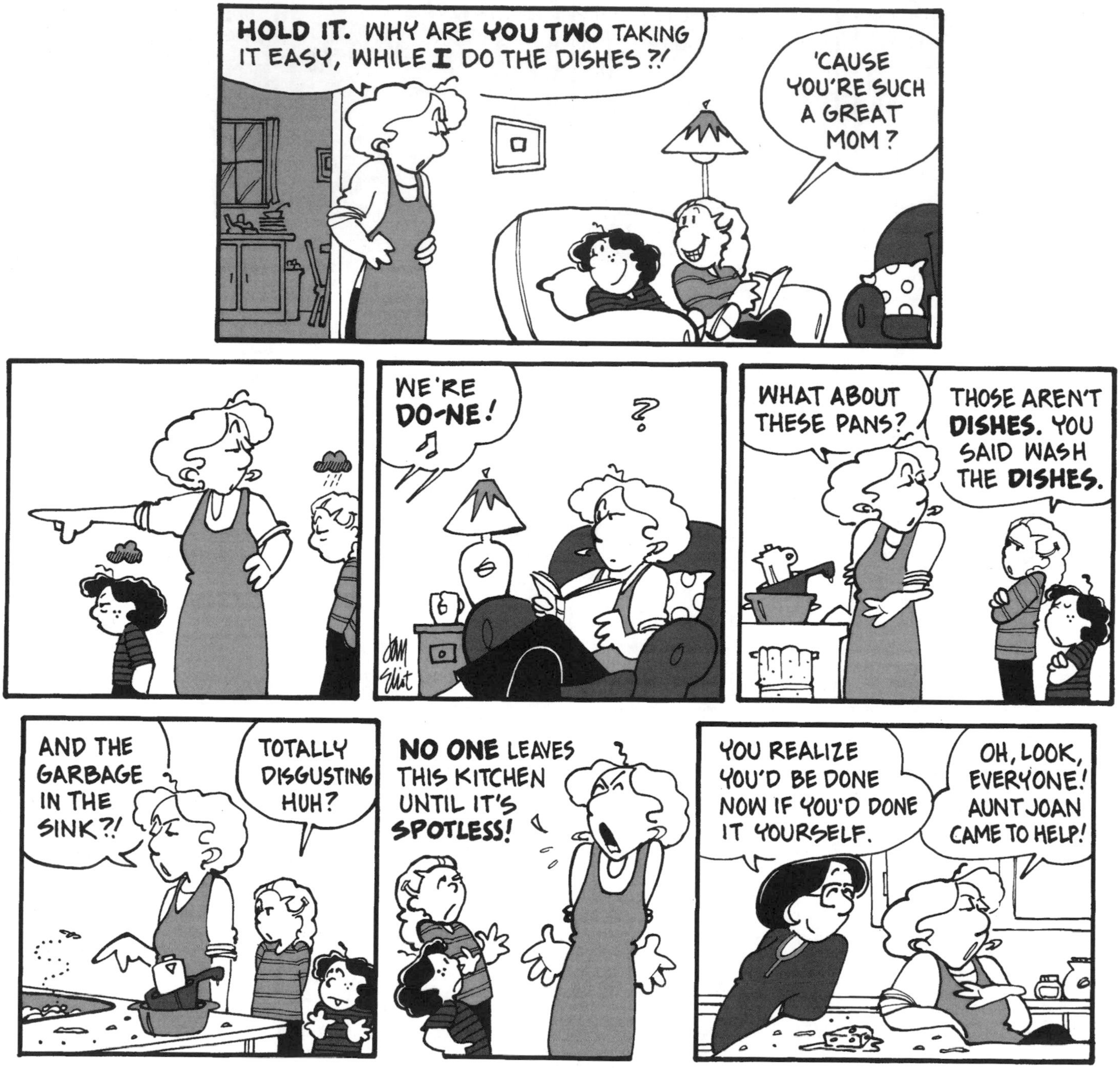

HOLD IT. WHY ARE YOU TWO TAKING IT EASY, WHILE I DO THE DISHES ?!
'CAUSE YOU'RE SUCH A GREAT MOM ?
WE'RE DO-NE!
?
WHAT ABOUT THESE PANS?
THOSE AREN'T DISHES. YOU SAID WASH THE DISHES.
AND THE GARBAGE IN THE SINK ?!
TOTALLY DISGUSTING HUH?
NO ONE LEAVES THIS KITCHEN UNTIL IT'S SPOTLESS!
YOU REALIZE YOU'D BE DONE NOW IF YOU'D DONE IT YOURSELF.
OH, LOOK, EVERYONE! AUNT JOAN CAME TO HELP!

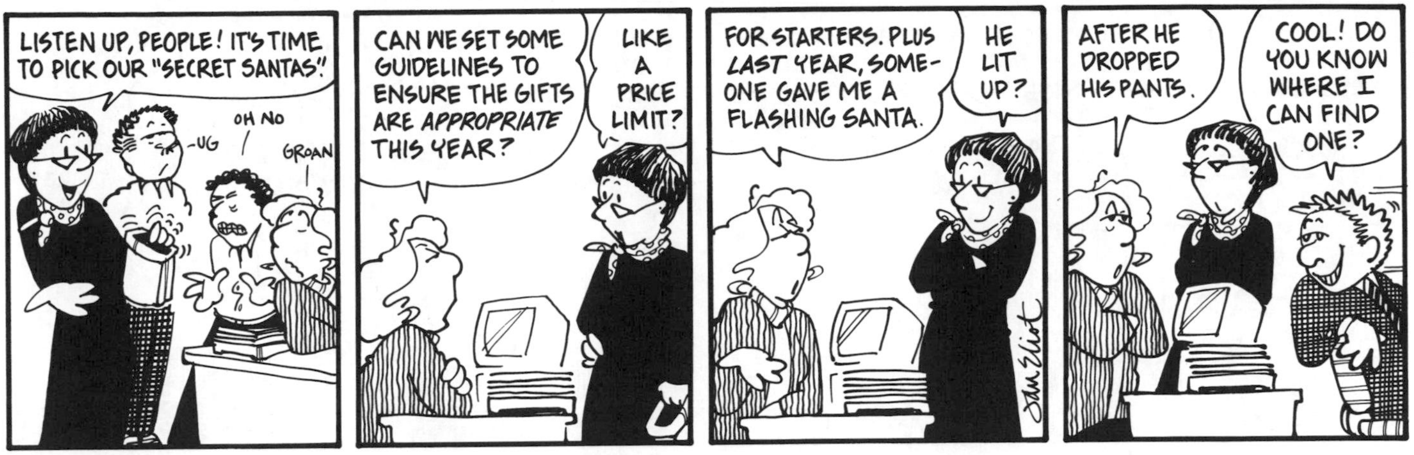
LISTEN UP, PEOPLE! IT'S TIME TO PICK OUR "SECRET SANTAS."
-UG
OH NO
GROAN
CAN WE SET SOME GUIDELINES TO ENSURE THE GIFTS ARE *APPROPRIATE* THIS YEAR?
LIKE A PRICE LIMIT?
FOR STARTERS. PLUS *LAST* YEAR, SOMEONE GAVE ME A FLASHING SANTA.
HE LIT UP?
AFTER HE DROPPED HIS PANTS.
COOL! DO YOU KNOW WHERE I CAN FIND ONE?

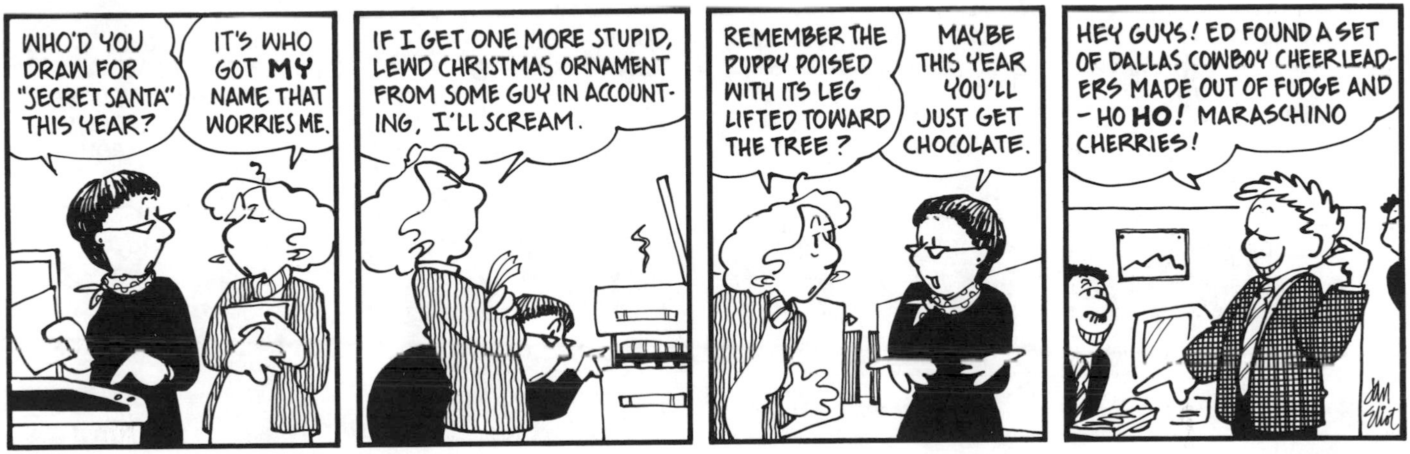
WHO'D YOU DRAW FOR "SECRET SANTA" THIS YEAR?
IT'S WHO GOT **MY** NAME THAT WORRIES ME.
IF I GET ONE MORE STUPID, LEWD CHRISTMAS ORNAMENT FROM SOME GUY IN ACCOUNTING, I'LL SCREAM.
REMEMBER THE PUPPY POISED WITH ITS LEG LIFTED TOWARD THE TREE?
MAYBE THIS YEAR YOU'LL JUST GET CHOCOLATE.
HEY GUYS! ED FOUND A SET OF DALLAS COWBOY CHEERLEADERS MADE OUT OF FUDGE AND - HO **HO!** MARASCHINO CHERRIES!

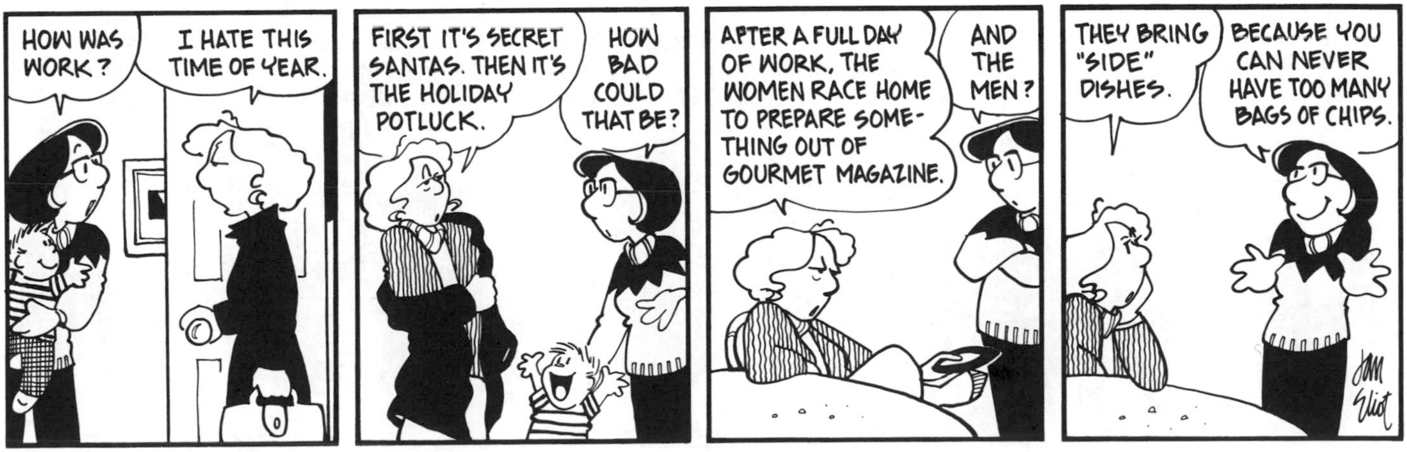
HOW WAS WORK?
I HATE THIS TIME OF YEAR.
FIRST IT'S SECRET SANTAS. THEN IT'S THE HOLIDAY POTLUCK.
HOW BAD COULD THAT BE?
AFTER A FULL DAY OF WORK, THE WOMEN RACE HOME TO PREPARE SOMETHING OUT OF GOURMET MAGAZINE.
AND THE MEN?
THEY BRING "SIDE" DISHES.
BECAUSE YOU CAN NEVER HAVE TOO MANY BAGS OF CHIPS.

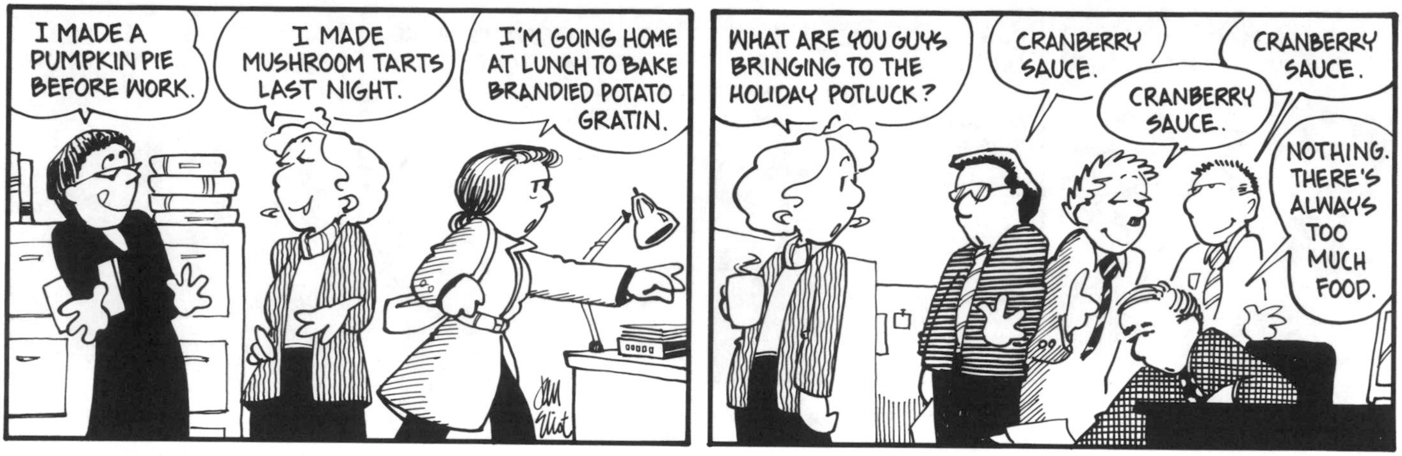
I MADE A PUMPKIN PIE BEFORE WORK.
I MADE MUSHROOM TARTS LAST NIGHT.
I'M GOING HOME AT LUNCH TO BAKE BRANDIED POTATO GRATIN.
WHAT ARE YOU GUYS BRINGING TO THE HOLIDAY POTLUCK?
CRANBERRY SAUCE.
CRANBERRY SAUCE.
CRANBERRY SAUCE.
NOTHING. THERE'S ALWAYS TOO MUCH FOOD.

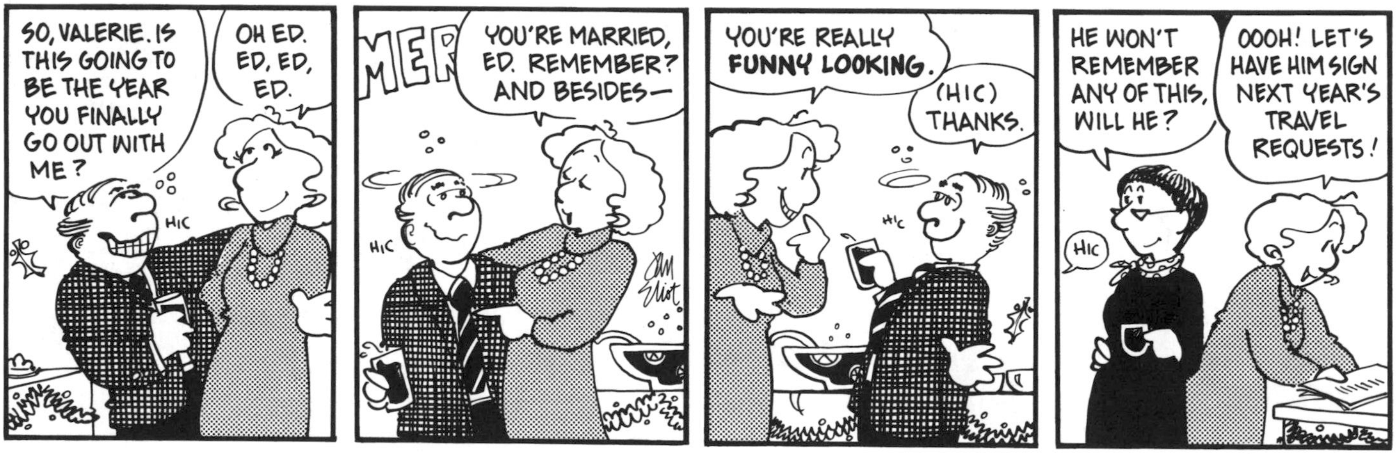
SO, VALERIE. IS THIS GOING TO BE THE YEAR YOU FINALLY GO OUT WITH ME?
HIC
OH ED. ED, ED, ED.
HIC
YOU'RE MARRIED, ED. REMEMBER? AND BESIDES—
YOU'RE REALLY **FUNNY LOOKING**.
HIC
(HIC) THANKS.
HE WON'T REMEMBER ANY OF THIS, WILL HE?
HIC
OOOH! LET'S HAVE HIM SIGN NEXT YEAR'S TRAVEL REQUESTS!

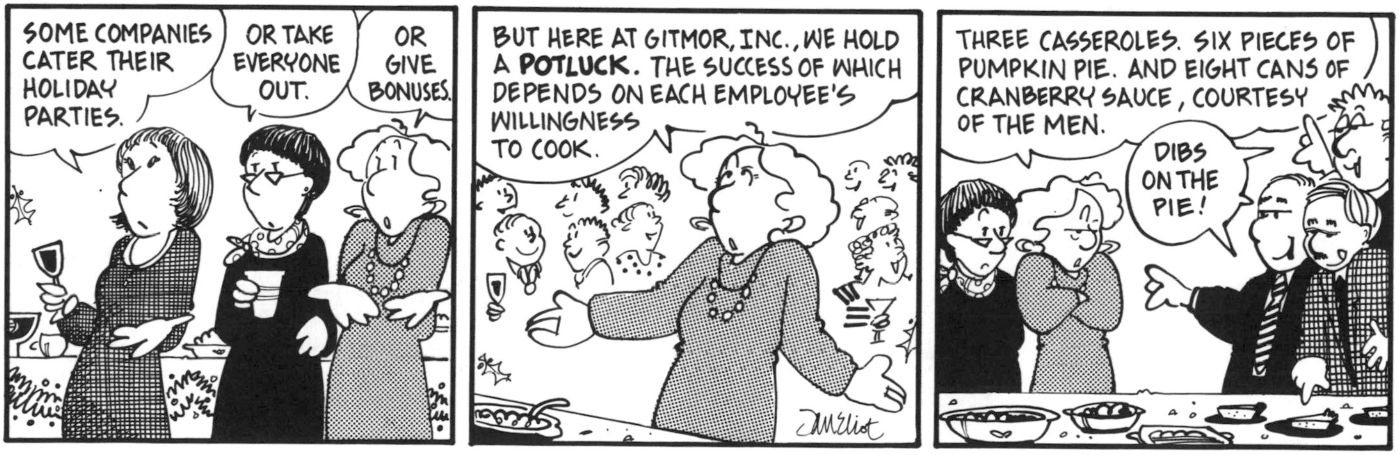
SOME COMPANIES CATER THEIR HOLIDAY PARTIES.
OR TAKE EVERYONE OUT.
OR GIVE BONUSES.
BUT HERE AT GITMOR, INC., WE HOLD A **POTLUCK**. THE SUCCESS OF WHICH DEPENDS ON EACH EMPLOYEE'S WILLINGNESS TO COOK.
THREE CASSEROLES. SIX PIECES OF PUMPKIN PIE. AND EIGHT CANS OF CRANBERRY SAUCE, COURTESY OF THE MEN.
DIBS ON THE PIE!

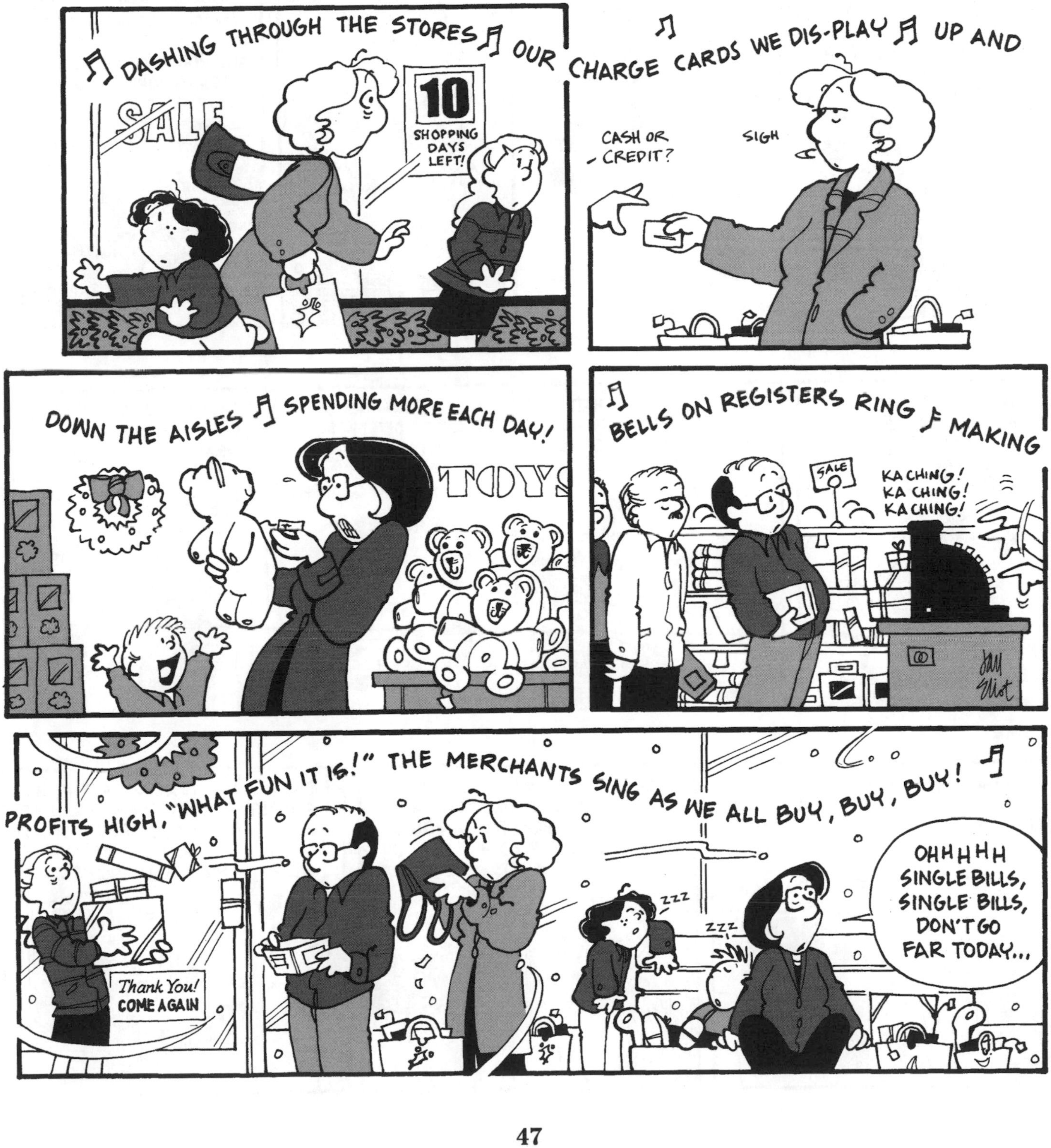
DASHING THROUGH THE STORES
SALE
10 SHOPPING DAYS LEFT!
OUR CHARGE CARDS WE DIS-PLAY
CASH OR CREDIT?
SIGH
UP AND DOWN THE AISLES
SPENDING MORE EACH DAY!
TOYS
BELLS ON REGISTERS RING
MAKING
SALE
KA CHING! KA CHING! KA CHING!
PROFITS HIGH, "WHAT FUN IT IS!" THE MERCHANTS SING AS WE ALL BUY, BUY, BUY!
Thank You! COME AGAIN
ZZZ
ZZZ
OHHHHH SINGLE BILLS, SINGLE BILLS, DON'T GO FAR TODAY...

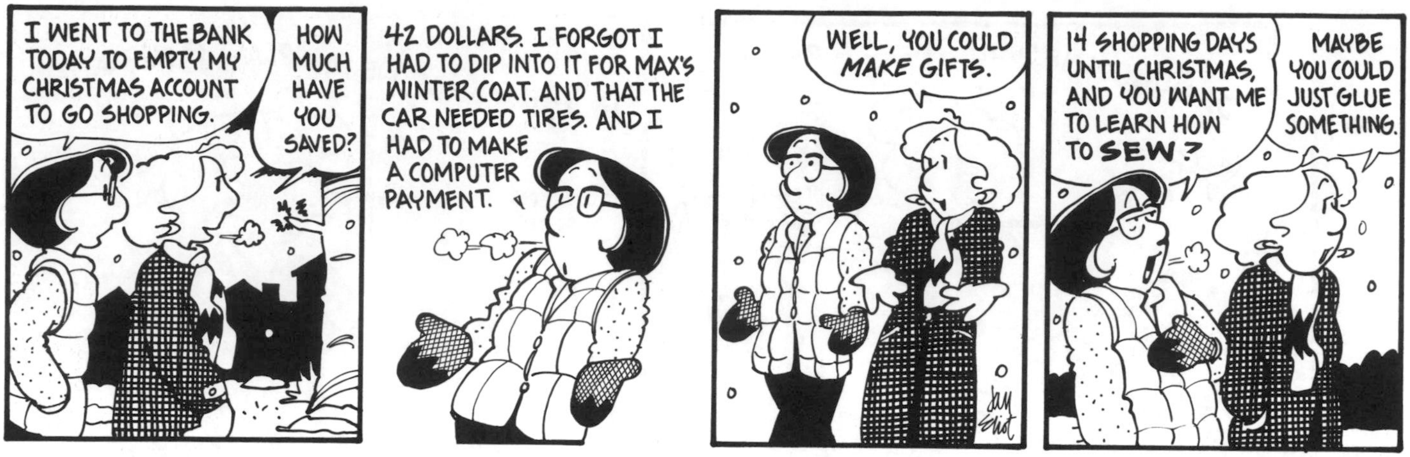
I WENT TO THE BANK TODAY TO EMPTY MY CHRISTMAS ACCOUNT TO GO SHOPPING.
HOW MUCH HAVE YOU SAVED?
42 DOLLARS. I FORGOT I HAD TO DIP INTO IT FOR MAX'S WINTER COAT. AND THAT THE CAR NEEDED TIRES. AND I HAD TO MAKE A COMPUTER PAYMENT.
WELL, YOU COULD MAKE GIFTS.
14 SHOPPING DAYS UNTIL CHRISTMAS, AND YOU WANT ME TO LEARN HOW TO SEW?
MAYBE YOU COULD JUST GLUE SOMETHING.

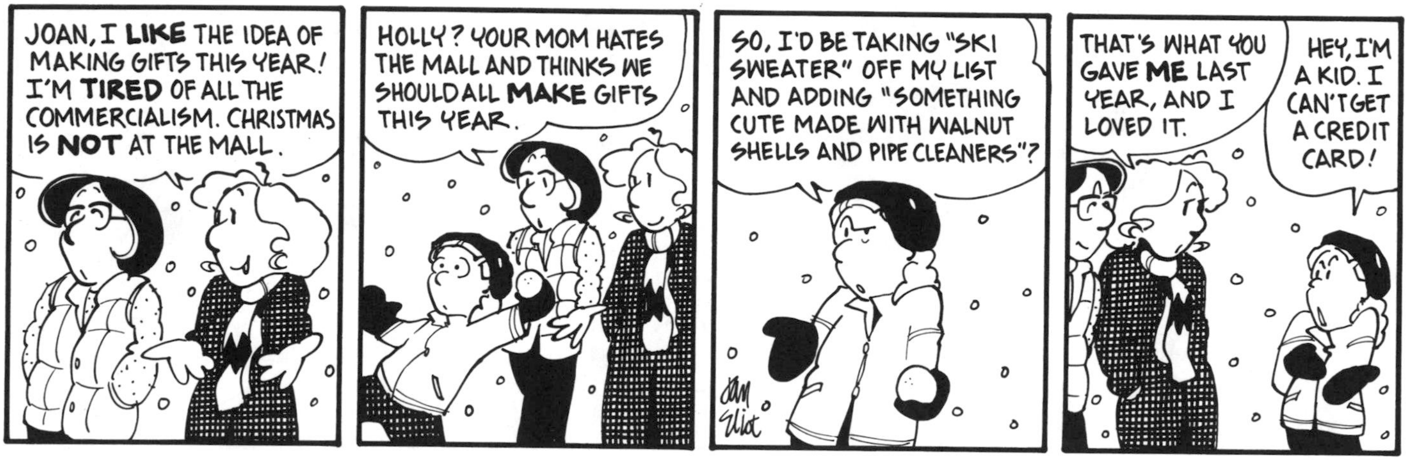
JOAN, I LIKE THE IDEA OF MAKING GIFTS THIS YEAR! I'M TIRED OF ALL THE COMMERCIALISM. CHRISTMAS IS NOT AT THE MALL.
HOLLY? YOUR MOM HATES THE MALL AND THINKS WE SHOULD ALL MAKE GIFTS THIS YEAR.
SO, I'D BE TAKING "SKI SWEATER" OFF MY LIST AND ADDING "SOMETHING CUTE MADE WITH WALNUT SHELLS AND PIPE CLEANERS"?
THAT'S WHAT YOU GAVE ME LAST YEAR, AND I LOVED IT.
HEY, I'M A KID. I CAN'T GET A CREDIT CARD!

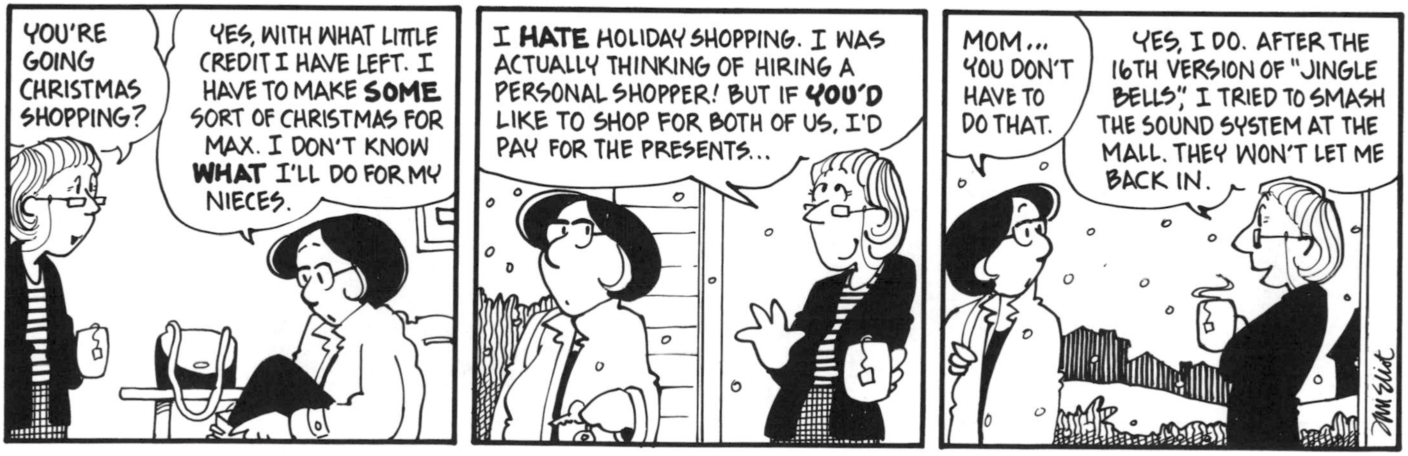
YOU'RE GOING CHRISTMAS SHOPPING?
YES, WITH WHAT LITTLE CREDIT I HAVE LEFT. I HAVE TO MAKE SOME SORT OF CHRISTMAS FOR MAX. I DON'T KNOW WHAT I'LL DO FOR MY NIECES.
I HATE HOLIDAY SHOPPING. I WAS ACTUALLY THINKING OF HIRING A PERSONAL SHOPPER! BUT IF YOU'D LIKE TO SHOP FOR BOTH OF US, I'D PAY FOR THE PRESENTS...
MOM... YOU DON'T HAVE TO DO THAT.
YES, I DO. AFTER THE 16TH VERSION OF "JINGLE BELLS", I TRIED TO SMASH THE SOUND SYSTEM AT THE MALL. THEY WON'T LET ME BACK IN.

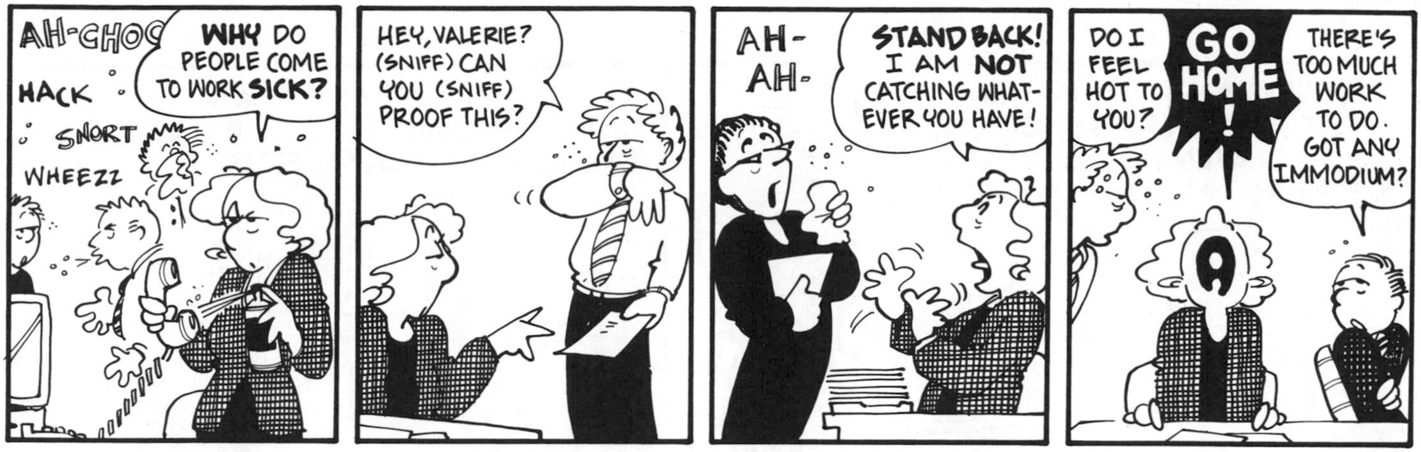
AH-CHOO
HACK
SNORT
WHEEZZ
WHY DO PEOPLE COME TO WORK SICK?
HEY, VALERIE? (SNIFF) CAN YOU (SNIFF) PROOF THIS?
AH-AH-
STAND BACK! I AM NOT CATCHING WHAT-EVER YOU HAVE!
DO I FEEL HOT TO YOU?
GO HOME!
THERE'S TOO MUCH WORK TO DO. GOT ANY IMMODIUM?

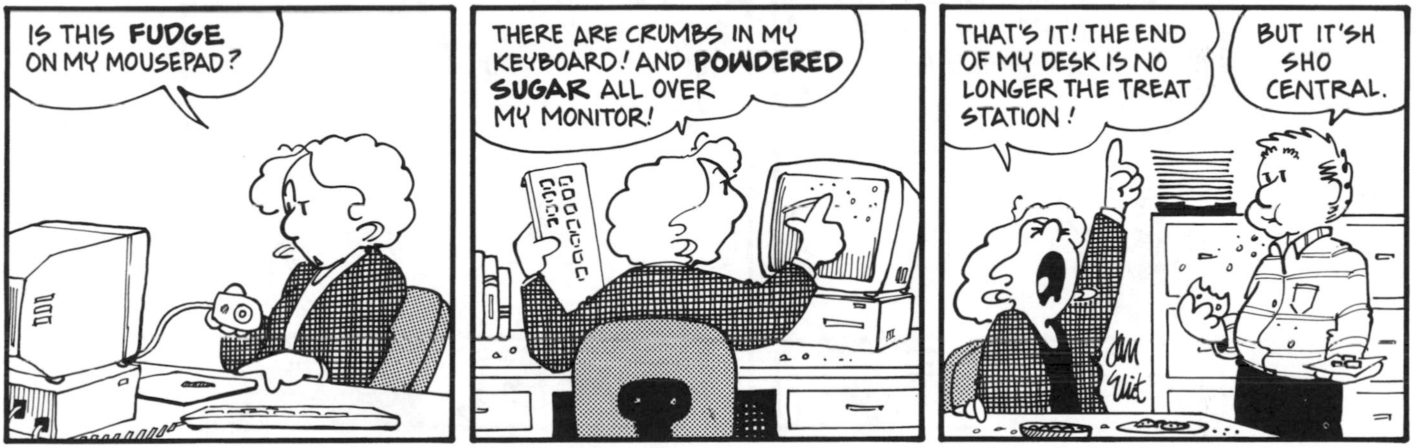
IS THIS FUDGE ON MY MOUSEPAD?
THERE ARE CRUMBS IN MY KEYBOARD! AND POWDERED SUGAR ALL OVER MY MONITOR!
THAT'S IT! THE END OF MY DESK IS NO LONGER THE TREAT STATION!
BUT IT'SH SHO CENTRAL.

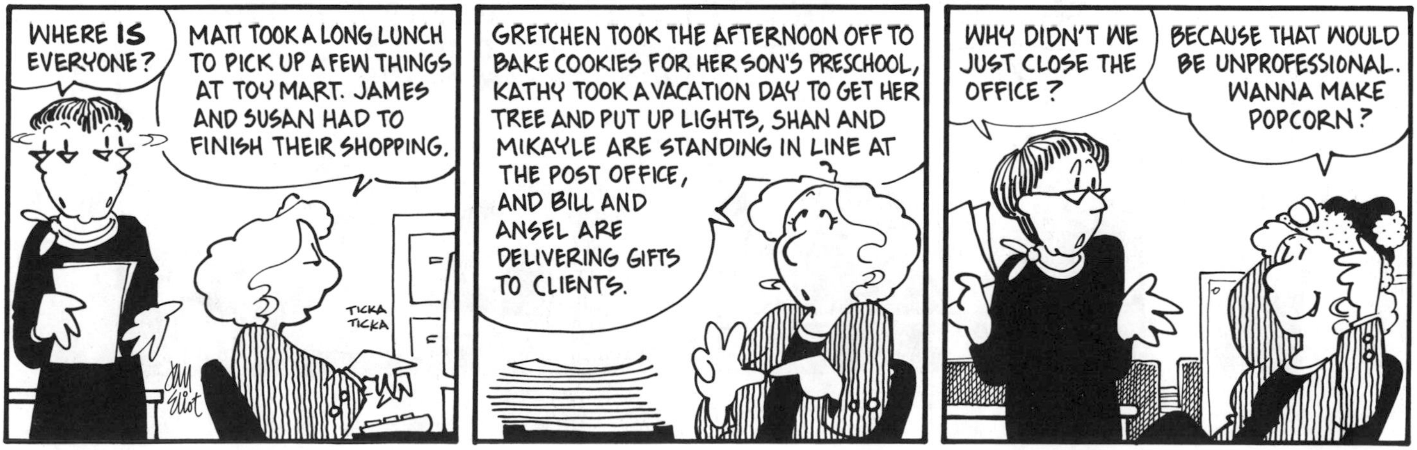
WHERE IS EVERYONE?
MATT TOOK A LONG LUNCH TO PICK UP A FEW THINGS AT TOY MART. JAMES AND SUSAN HAD TO FINISH THEIR SHOPPING.
TICKA TICKA
GRETCHEN TOOK THE AFTERNOON OFF TO BAKE COOKIES FOR HER SON'S PRESCHOOL, KATHY TOOK A VACATION DAY TO GET HER TREE AND PUT UP LIGHTS, SHAN AND MIKAYLE ARE STANDING IN LINE AT THE POST OFFICE, AND BILL AND ANSEL ARE DELIVERING GIFTS TO CLIENTS.
WHY DIDN'T WE JUST CLOSE THE OFFICE?
BECAUSE THAT WOULD BE UNPROFESSIONAL. WANNA MAKE POPCORN?

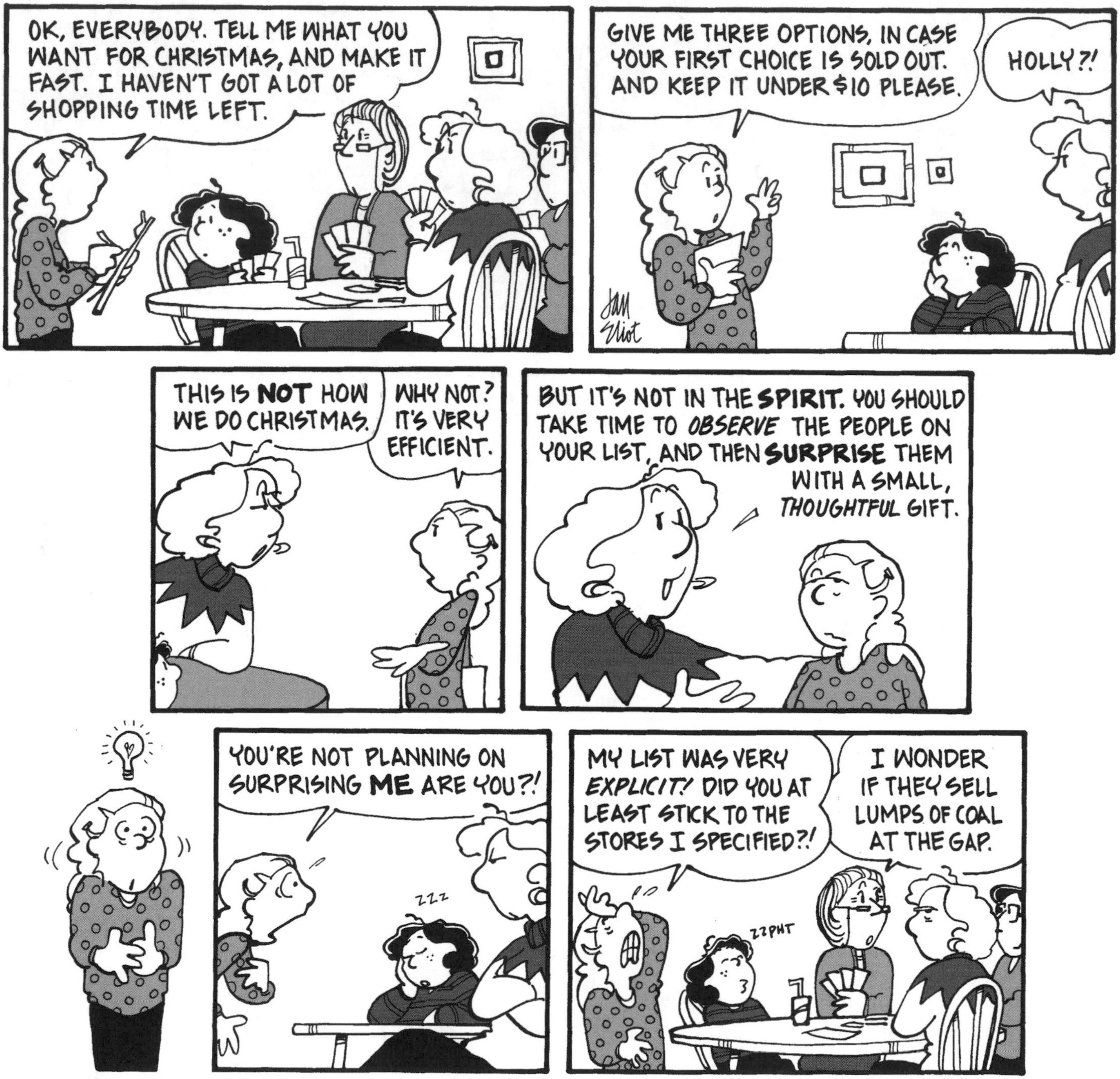
OK, EVERYBODY. TELL ME WHAT YOU WANT FOR CHRISTMAS, AND MAKE IT FAST. I HAVEN'T GOT A LOT OF SHOPPING TIME LEFT.
GIVE ME THREE OPTIONS, IN CASE YOUR FIRST CHOICE IS SOLD OUT. AND KEEP IT UNDER $10 PLEASE.
HOLLY?!
THIS IS **NOT** HOW WE DO CHRISTMAS.
WHY NOT? IT'S VERY EFFICIENT.
BUT IT'S NOT IN THE **SPIRIT.** YOU SHOULD TAKE TIME TO *OBSERVE* THE PEOPLE ON YOUR LIST, AND THEN **SURPRISE** THEM WITH A SMALL, *THOUGHTFUL* GIFT.
YOU'RE NOT PLANNING ON SURPRISING **ME** ARE YOU?!
ZZZ
MY LIST WAS VERY *EXPLICIT!* DID YOU AT LEAST STICK TO THE STORES I SPECIFIED?!
I WONDER IF THEY SELL LUMPS OF COAL AT THE GAP.
ZZPHT

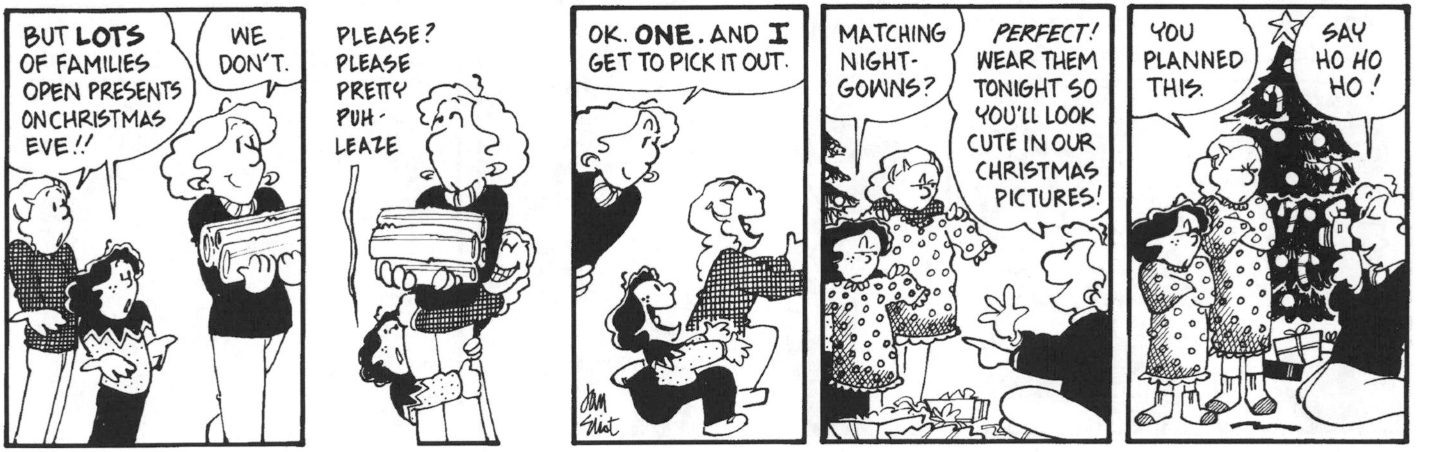
BUT LOTS OF FAMILIES OPEN PRESENTS ON CHRISTMAS EVE!!
WE DON'T.
PLEASE? PLEASE PRETTY PUH-LEAZE
OK. ONE. AND I GET TO PICK IT OUT.
MATCHING NIGHT-GOWNS?
PERFECT! WEAR THEM TONIGHT SO YOU'LL LOOK CUTE IN OUR CHRISTMAS PICTURES!
YOU PLANNED THIS.
SAY HO HO HO!

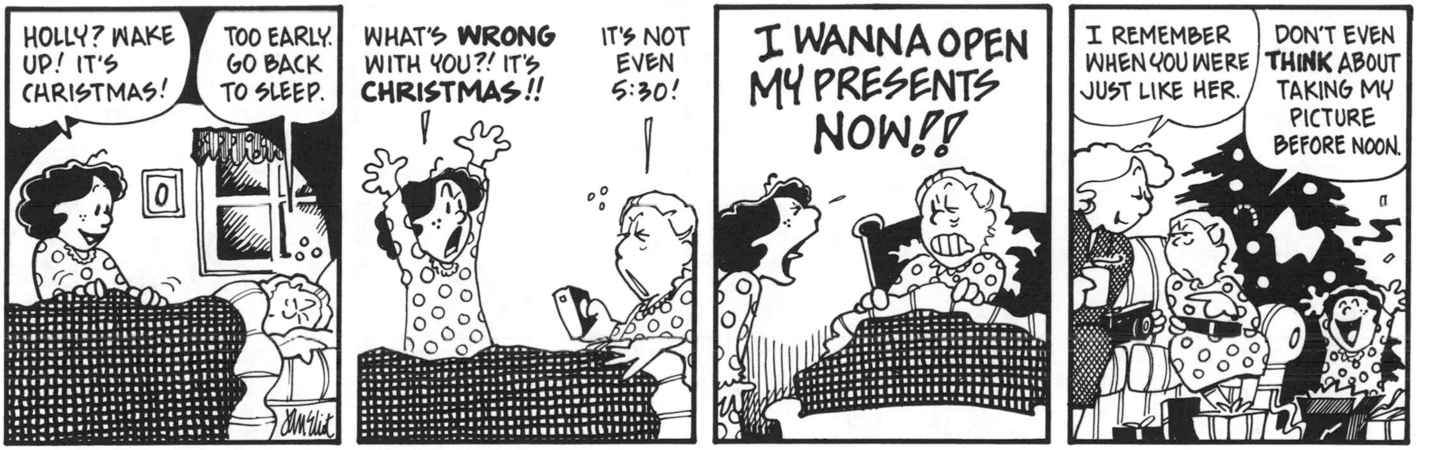
HOLLY? WAKE UP! IT'S CHRISTMAS!
TOO EARLY. GO BACK TO SLEEP.
WHAT'S WRONG WITH YOU?! IT'S CHRISTMAS!!
IT'S NOT EVEN 5:30!
I WANNA OPEN MY PRESENTS NOW!!
I REMEMBER WHEN YOU WERE JUST LIKE HER.
DON'T EVEN THINK ABOUT TAKING MY PICTURE BEFORE NOON.

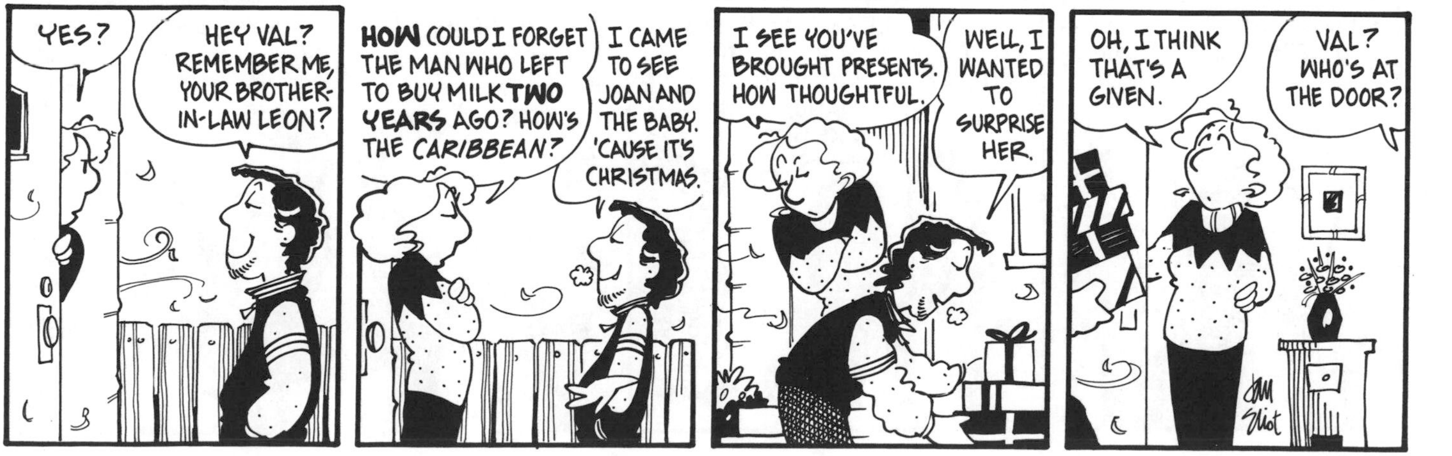
YES?
HEY VAL? REMEMBER ME, YOUR BROTHER-IN-LAW LEON?
HOW COULD I FORGET THE MAN WHO LEFT TO BUY MILK TWO YEARS AGO? HOW'S THE CARIBBEAN?
I CAME TO SEE JOAN AND THE BABY. 'CAUSE IT'S CHRISTMAS.
I SEE YOU'VE BROUGHT PRESENTS. HOW THOUGHTFUL.
WELL, I WANTED TO SURPRISE HER.
OH, I THINK THAT'S A GIVEN.
VAL? WHO'S AT THE DOOR?

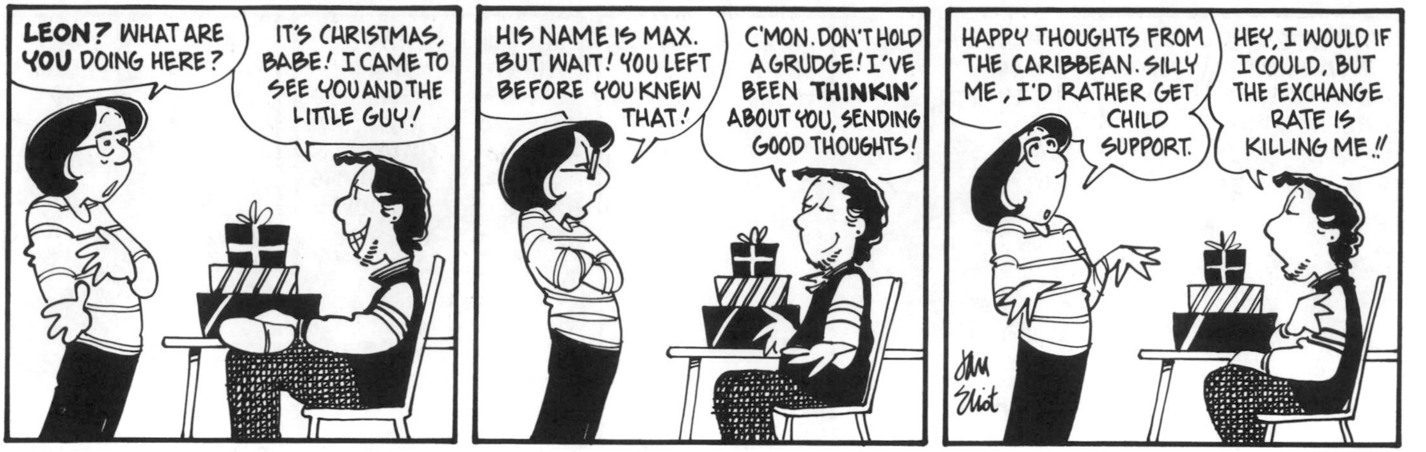
LEON? WHAT ARE YOU DOING HERE?
IT'S CHRISTMAS, BABE! I CAME TO SEE YOU AND THE LITTLE GUY!
HIS NAME IS MAX. BUT WAIT! YOU LEFT BEFORE YOU KNEW THAT!
C'MON. DON'T HOLD A GRUDGE! I'VE BEEN THINKIN' ABOUT YOU, SENDING GOOD THOUGHTS!
HAPPY THOUGHTS FROM THE CARIBBEAN. SILLY ME, I'D RATHER GET CHILD SUPPORT.
HEY, I WOULD IF I COULD, BUT THE EXCHANGE RATE IS KILLING ME!!

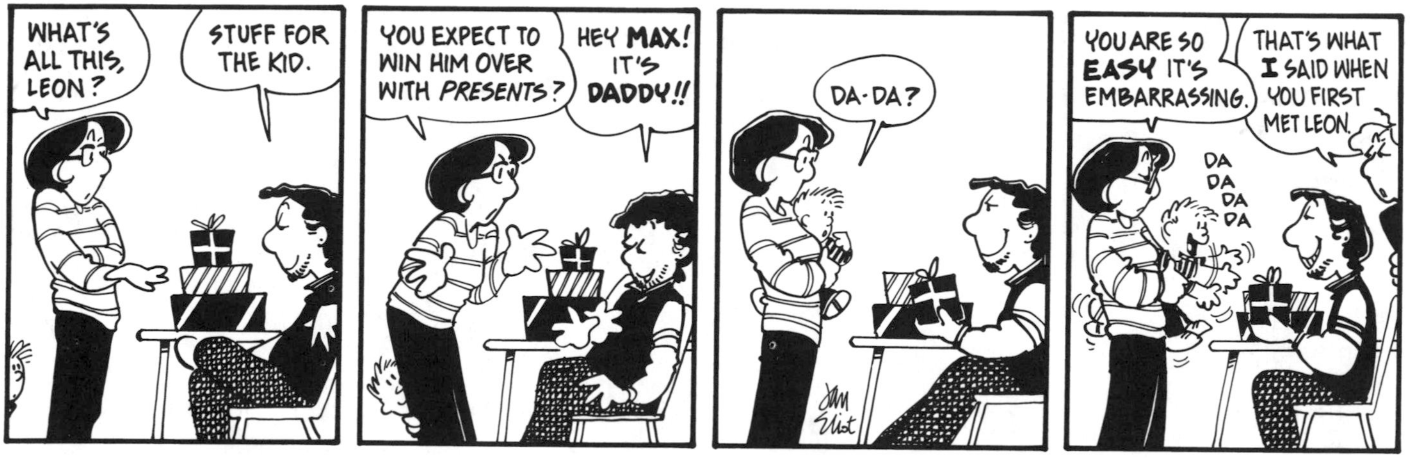
WHAT'S ALL THIS, LEON?
STUFF FOR THE KID.
YOU EXPECT TO WIN HIM OVER WITH PRESENTS?
HEY MAX! IT'S DADDY!!
DA-DA?
YOU ARE SO EASY IT'S EMBARRASSING.
DA DA DA DA
THAT'S WHAT I SAID WHEN YOU FIRST MET LEON.

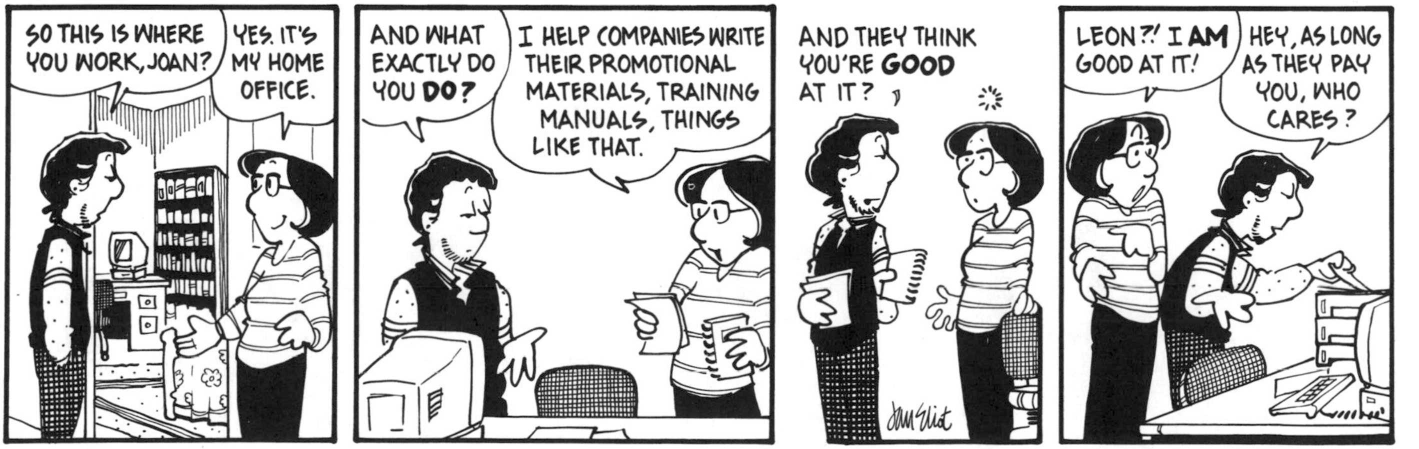
SO THIS IS WHERE YOU WORK, JOAN?
YES. IT'S MY HOME OFFICE.
AND WHAT EXACTLY DO YOU DO?
I HELP COMPANIES WRITE THEIR PROMOTIONAL MATERIALS, TRAINING MANUALS, THINGS LIKE THAT.
AND THEY THINK YOU'RE GOOD AT IT?
LEON?! I AM GOOD AT IT!
HEY, AS LONG AS THEY PAY YOU, WHO CARES?

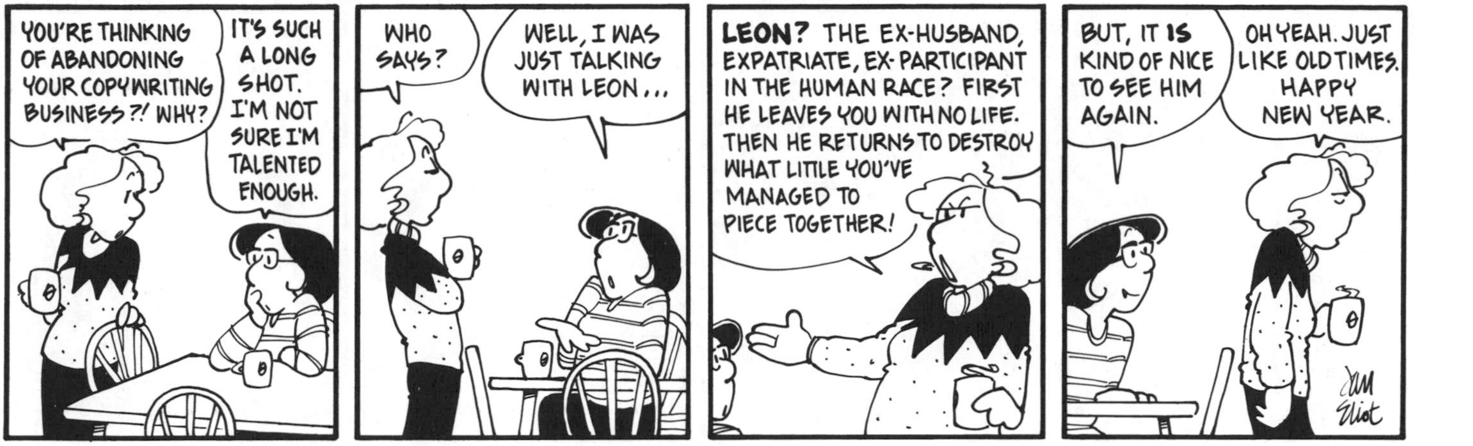
YOU'RE THINKING OF ABANDONING YOUR COPYWRITING BUSINESS?! WHY?
IT'S SUCH A LONG SHOT. I'M NOT SURE I'M TALENTED ENOUGH.
WHO SAYS?
WELL, I WAS JUST TALKING WITH LEON...
LEON? THE EX-HUSBAND, EXPATRIATE, EX-PARTICIPANT IN THE HUMAN RACE? FIRST HE LEAVES YOU WITH NO LIFE. THEN HE RETURNS TO DESTROY WHAT LITTLE YOU'VE MANAGED TO PIECE TOGETHER!
BUT, IT IS KIND OF NICE TO SEE HIM AGAIN.
OH YEAH. JUST LIKE OLD TIMES. HAPPY NEW YEAR.
JAN Eliot

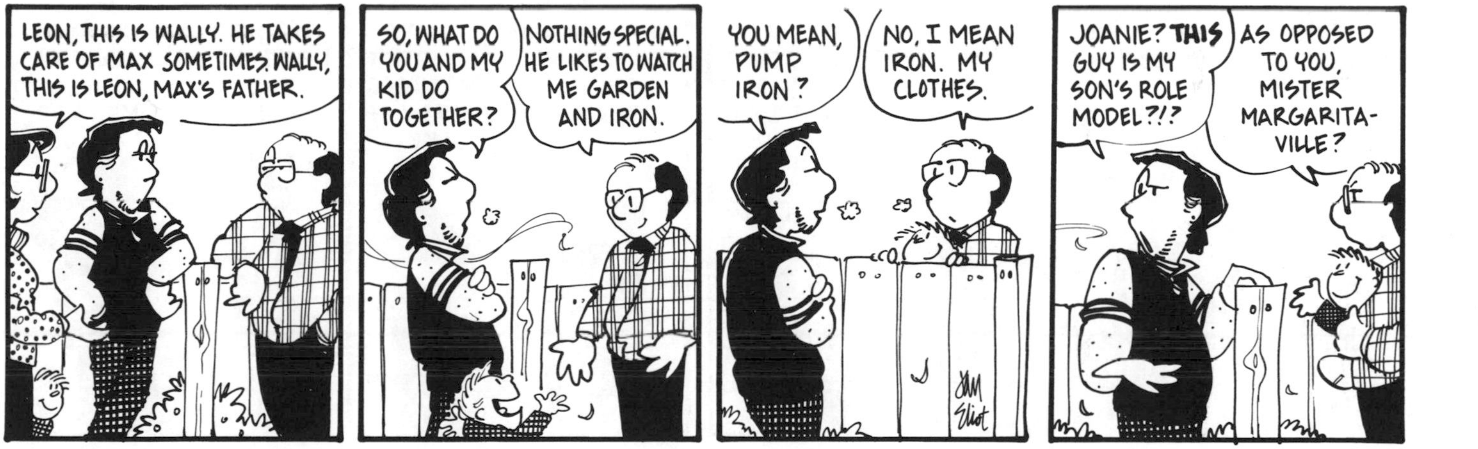
LEON, THIS IS WALLY. HE TAKES CARE OF MAX SOMETIMES. WALLY, THIS IS LEON, MAX'S FATHER.
SO, WHAT DO YOU AND MY KID DO TOGETHER?
NOTHING SPECIAL. HE LIKES TO WATCH ME GARDEN AND IRON.
YOU MEAN, PUMP IRON?
NO, I MEAN IRON. MY CLOTHES.
JAN Eliot
JOANIE? THIS GUY IS MY SON'S ROLE MODEL?!?
AS OPPOSED TO YOU, MISTER MARGARITA-VILLE?

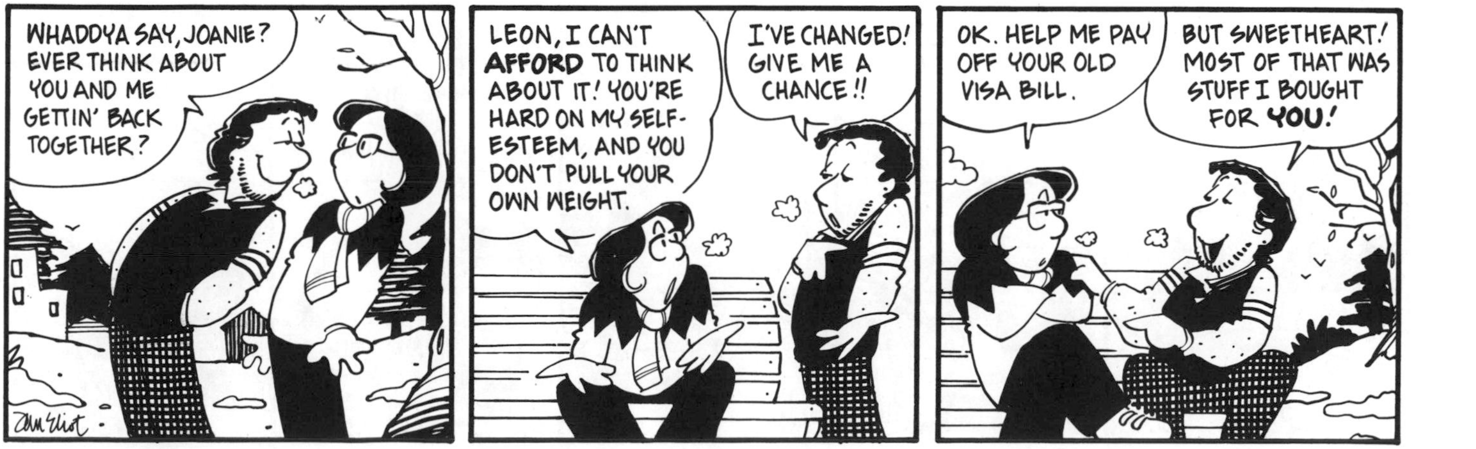
WHADDYA SAY, JOANIE? EVER THINK ABOUT YOU AND ME GETTIN' BACK TOGETHER?
JAN Eliot
LEON, I CAN'T AFFORD TO THINK ABOUT IT! YOU'RE HARD ON MY SELF-ESTEEM, AND YOU DON'T PULL YOUR OWN WEIGHT.
I'VE CHANGED! GIVE ME A CHANCE!!
OK. HELP ME PAY OFF YOUR OLD VISA BILL.
BUT SWEETHEART! MOST OF THAT WAS STUFF I BOUGHT FOR YOU!

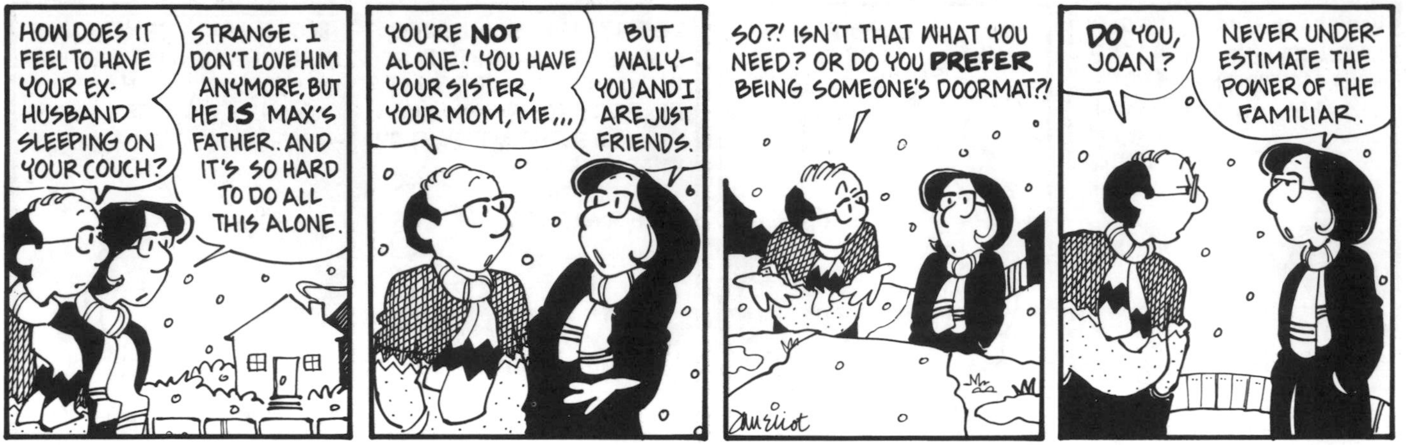
HOW DOES IT FEEL TO HAVE YOUR EX-HUSBAND SLEEPING ON YOUR COUCH?
STRANGE. I DON'T LOVE HIM ANYMORE, BUT HE IS MAX'S FATHER. AND IT'S SO HARD TO DO ALL THIS ALONE.
YOU'RE NOT ALONE! YOU HAVE YOUR SISTER, YOUR MOM, ME,..
BUT WALLY-YOU AND I ARE JUST FRIENDS.
SO?! ISN'T THAT WHAT YOU NEED? OR DO YOU PREFER BEING SOMEONE'S DOORMAT?!
DO YOU, JOAN?
NEVER UNDER-ESTIMATE THE POWER OF THE FAMILIAR.

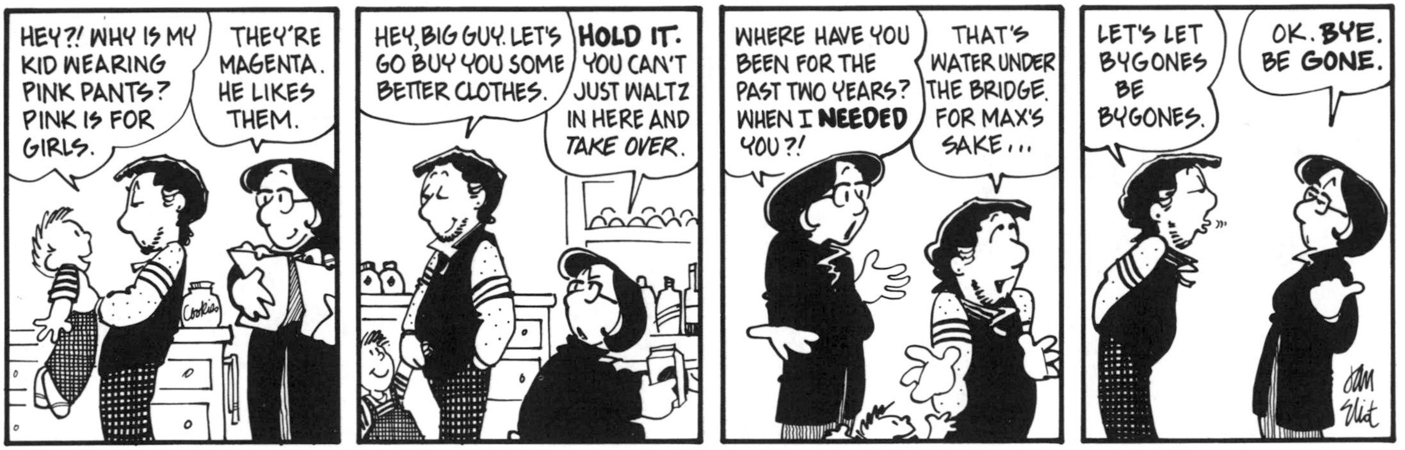
HEY?! WHY IS MY KID WEARING PINK PANTS? PINK IS FOR GIRLS.
THEY'RE MAGENTA. HE LIKES THEM.
HEY, BIG GUY. LET'S GO BUY YOU SOME BETTER CLOTHES.
HOLD IT. YOU CAN'T JUST WALTZ IN HERE AND TAKE OVER.
WHERE HAVE YOU BEEN FOR THE PAST TWO YEARS? WHEN I NEEDED YOU?!
THAT'S WATER UNDER THE BRIDGE. FOR MAX'S SAKE...
LET'S LET BYGONES BE BYGONES.
OK. BYE. BE GONE.

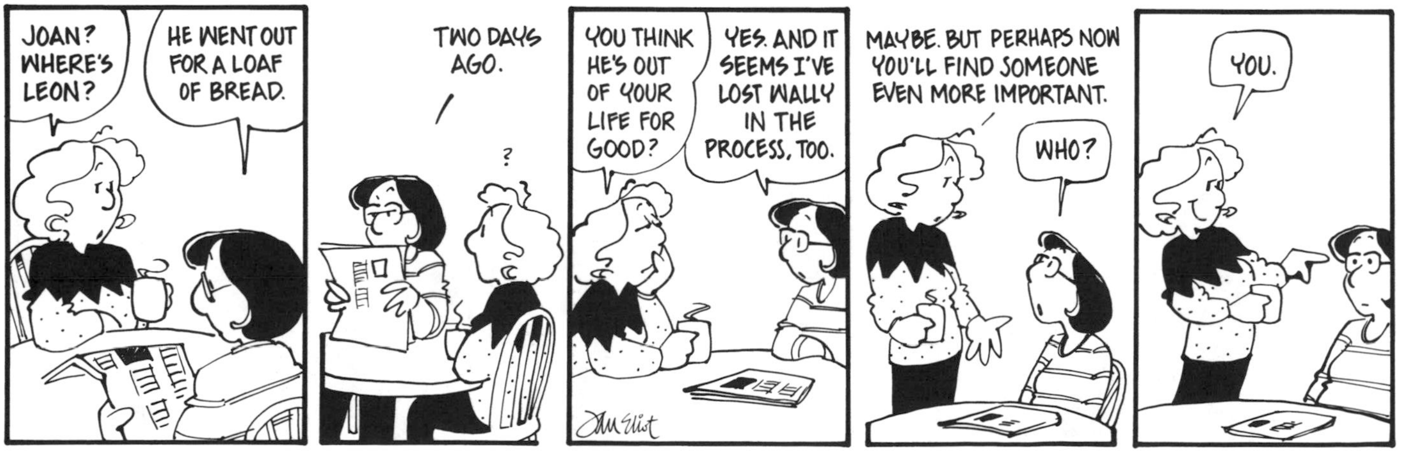
JOAN? WHERE'S LEON?
HE WENT OUT FOR A LOAF OF BREAD.
TWO DAYS AGO.
?
YOU THINK HE'S OUT OF YOUR LIFE FOR GOOD?
YES. AND IT SEEMS I'VE LOST WALLY IN THE PROCESS, TOO.
MAYBE. BUT PERHAPS NOW YOU'LL FIND SOMEONE EVEN MORE IMPORTANT.
WHO?
YOU.

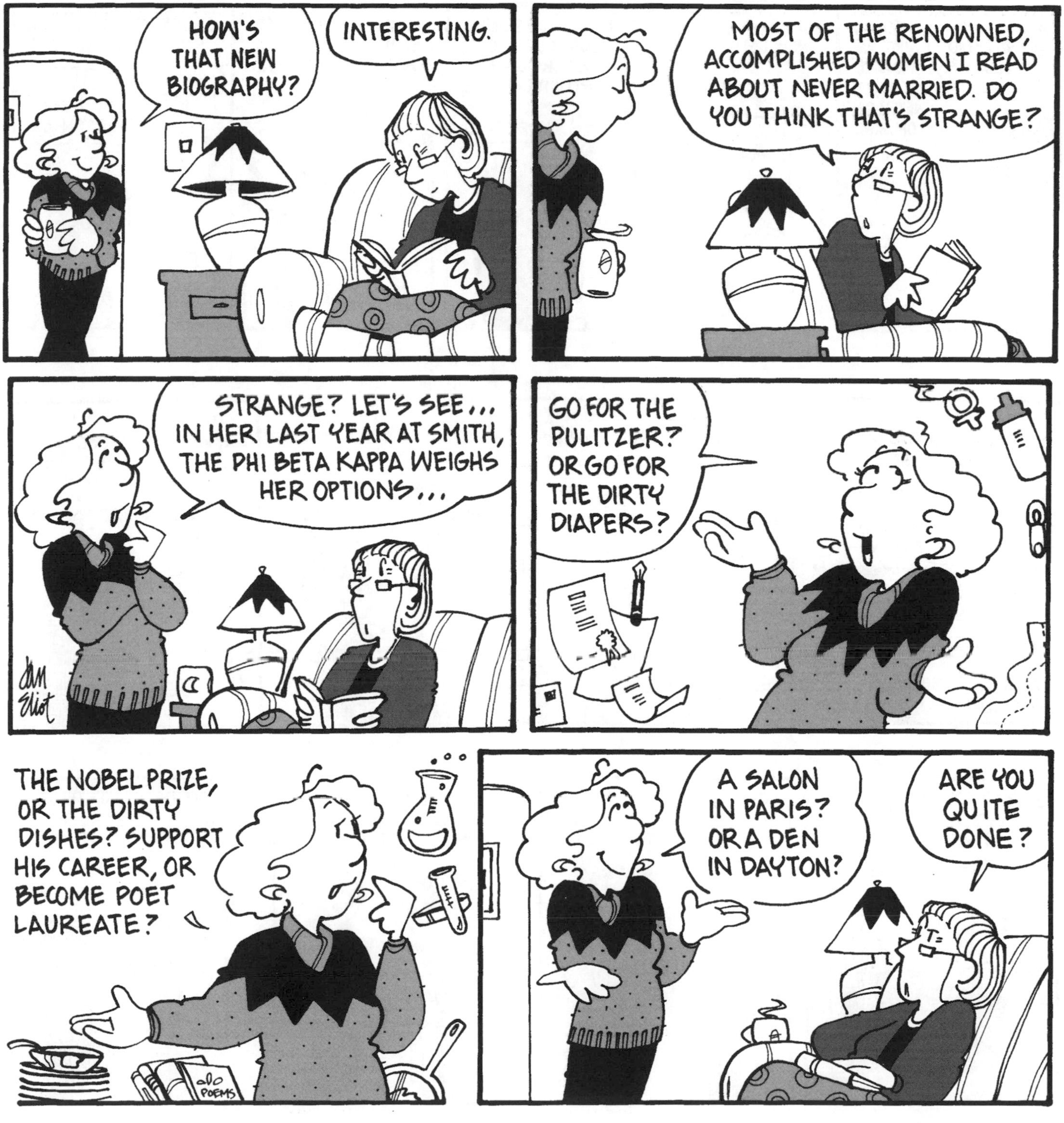
HOW'S THAT NEW BIOGRAPHY?
INTERESTING.
MOST OF THE RENOWNED, ACCOMPLISHED WOMEN I READ ABOUT NEVER MARRIED. DO YOU THINK THAT'S STRANGE?
STRANGE? LET'S SEE... IN HER LAST YEAR AT SMITH, THE PHI BETA KAPPA WEIGHS HER OPTIONS...
GO FOR THE PULITZER? OR GO FOR THE DIRTY DIAPERS?
THE NOBEL PRIZE, OR THE DIRTY DISHES? SUPPORT HIS CAREER, OR BECOME POET LAUREATE?
POEMS
A SALON IN PARIS? OR A DEN IN DAYTON?
ARE YOU QUITE DONE?

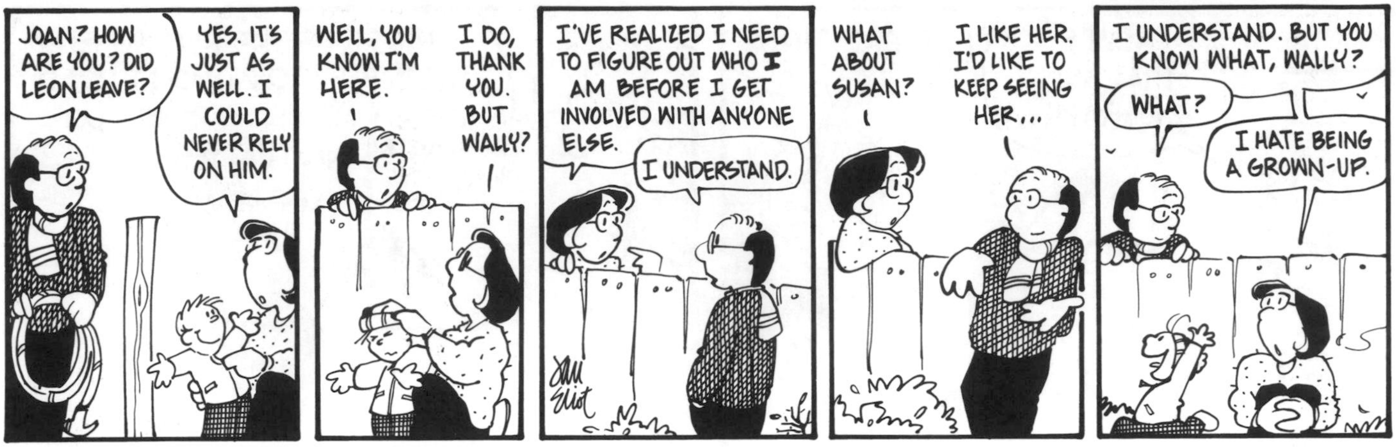
JOAN? HOW ARE YOU? DID LEON LEAVE?
YES. IT'S JUST AS WELL. I COULD NEVER RELY ON HIM.
WELL, YOU KNOW I'M HERE.
I DO, THANK YOU. BUT WALLY?
I'VE REALIZED I NEED TO FIGURE OUT WHO **I** AM BEFORE I GET INVOLVED WITH ANYONE ELSE.
I UNDERSTAND.
WHAT ABOUT SUSAN?
I LIKE HER. I'D LIKE TO KEEP SEEING HER...
I UNDERSTAND. BUT YOU KNOW WHAT, WALLY?
WHAT?
I HATE BEING A GROWN-UP.

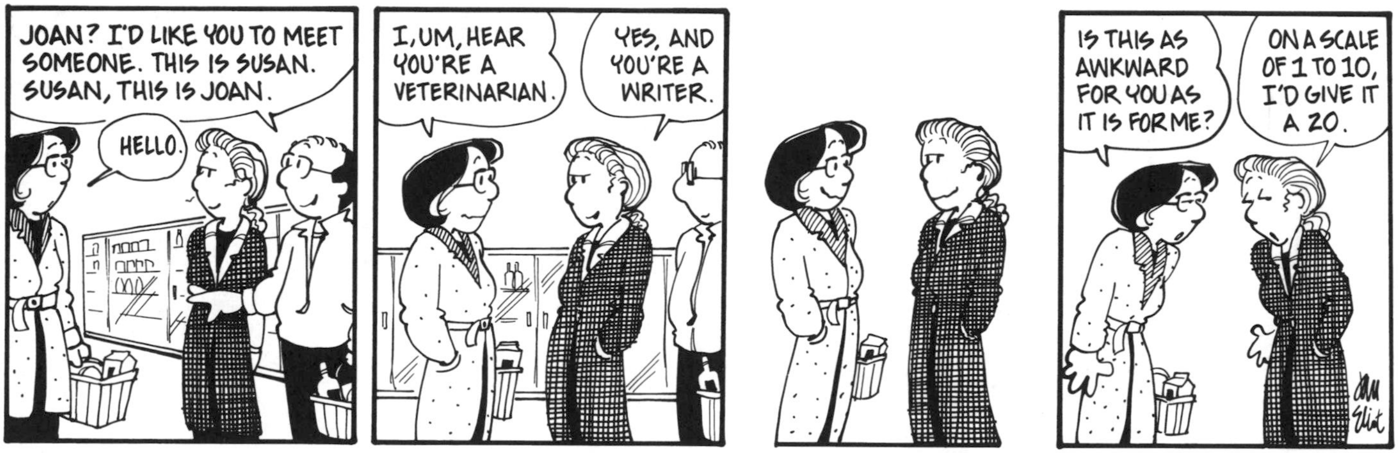
JOAN? I'D LIKE YOU TO MEET SOMEONE. THIS IS SUSAN. SUSAN, THIS IS JOAN.
HELLO.
I, UM, HEAR YOU'RE A VETERINARIAN.
YES, AND YOU'RE A WRITER.
IS THIS AS AWKWARD FOR YOU AS IT IS FOR ME?
ON A SCALE OF 1 TO 10, I'D GIVE IT A 20.

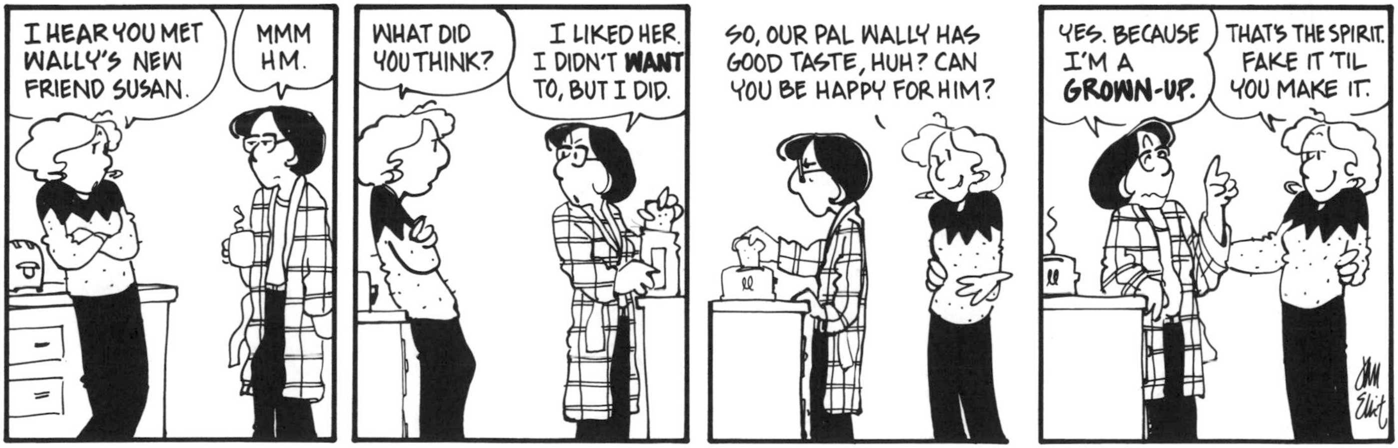
I HEAR YOU MET WALLY'S NEW FRIEND SUSAN.
MMM HM.
WHAT DID YOU THINK?
I LIKED HER. I DIDN'T **WANT** TO, BUT I DID.
SO, OUR PAL WALLY HAS GOOD TASTE, HUH? CAN YOU BE HAPPY FOR HIM?
YES. BECAUSE I'M A **GROWN-UP.**
THAT'S THE SPIRIT. FAKE IT 'TIL YOU MAKE IT.

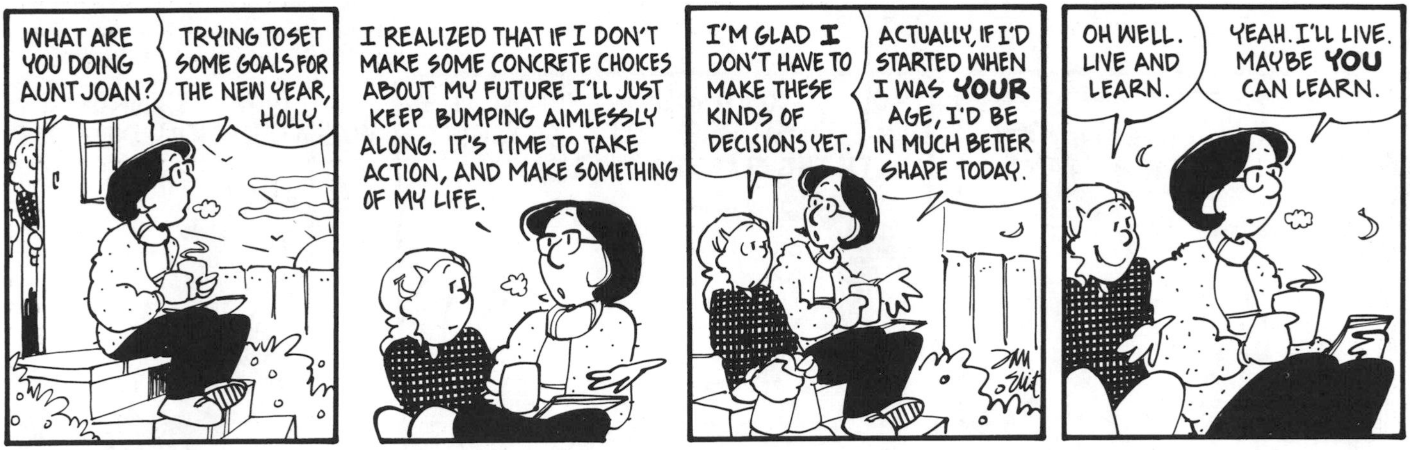
WHAT ARE YOU DOING AUNT JOAN?
TRYING TO SET SOME GOALS FOR THE NEW YEAR, HOLLY.
I REALIZED THAT IF I DON'T MAKE SOME CONCRETE CHOICES ABOUT MY FUTURE I'LL JUST KEEP BUMPING AIMLESSLY ALONG. IT'S TIME TO TAKE ACTION, AND MAKE SOMETHING OF MY LIFE.
I'M GLAD I DON'T HAVE TO MAKE THESE KINDS OF DECISIONS YET.
ACTUALLY, IF I'D STARTED WHEN I WAS YOUR AGE, I'D BE IN MUCH BETTER SHAPE TODAY.
OH WELL. LIVE AND LEARN.
YEAH. I'LL LIVE. MAYBE YOU CAN LEARN.

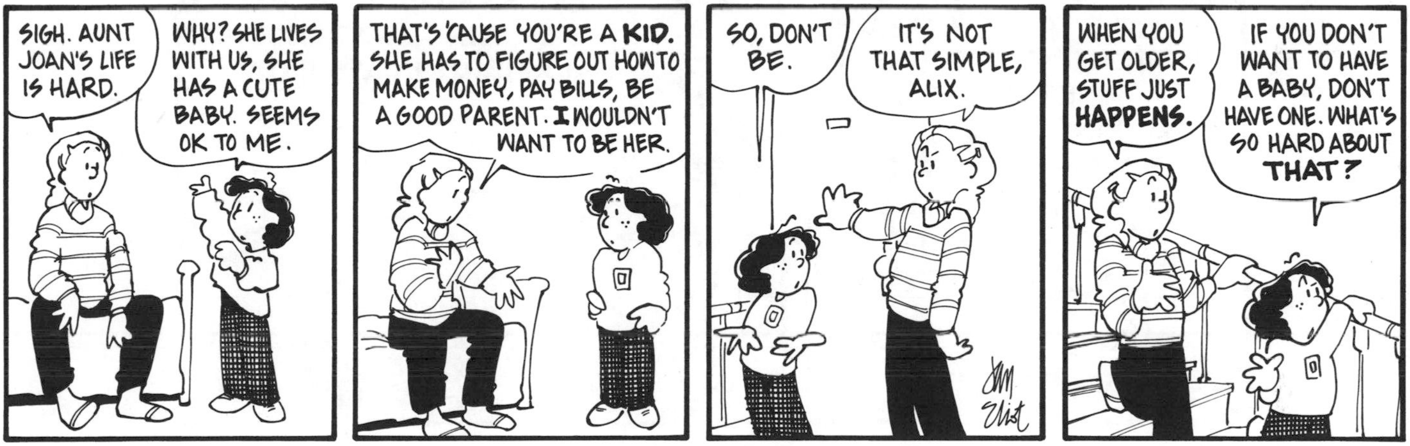
SIGH. AUNT JOAN'S LIFE IS HARD.
WHY? SHE LIVES WITH US, SHE HAS A CUTE BABY. SEEMS OK TO ME.
THAT'S 'CAUSE YOU'RE A KID. SHE HAS TO FIGURE OUT HOW TO MAKE MONEY, PAY BILLS, BE A GOOD PARENT. I WOULDN'T WANT TO BE HER.
SO, DON'T BE.
IT'S NOT THAT SIMPLE, ALIX.
WHEN YOU GET OLDER, STUFF JUST HAPPENS.
IF YOU DON'T WANT TO HAVE A BABY, DON'T HAVE ONE. WHAT'S SO HARD ABOUT THAT?

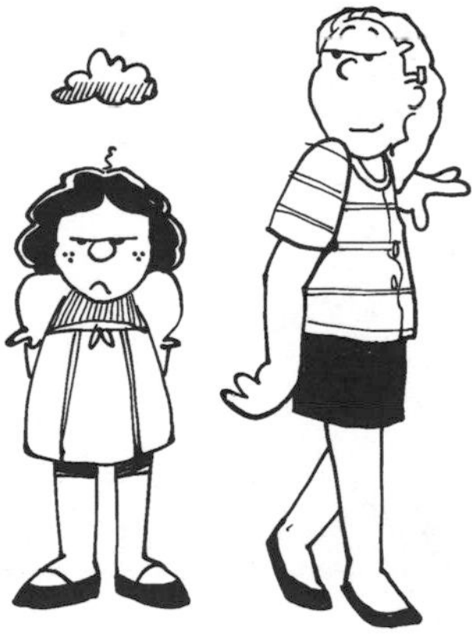

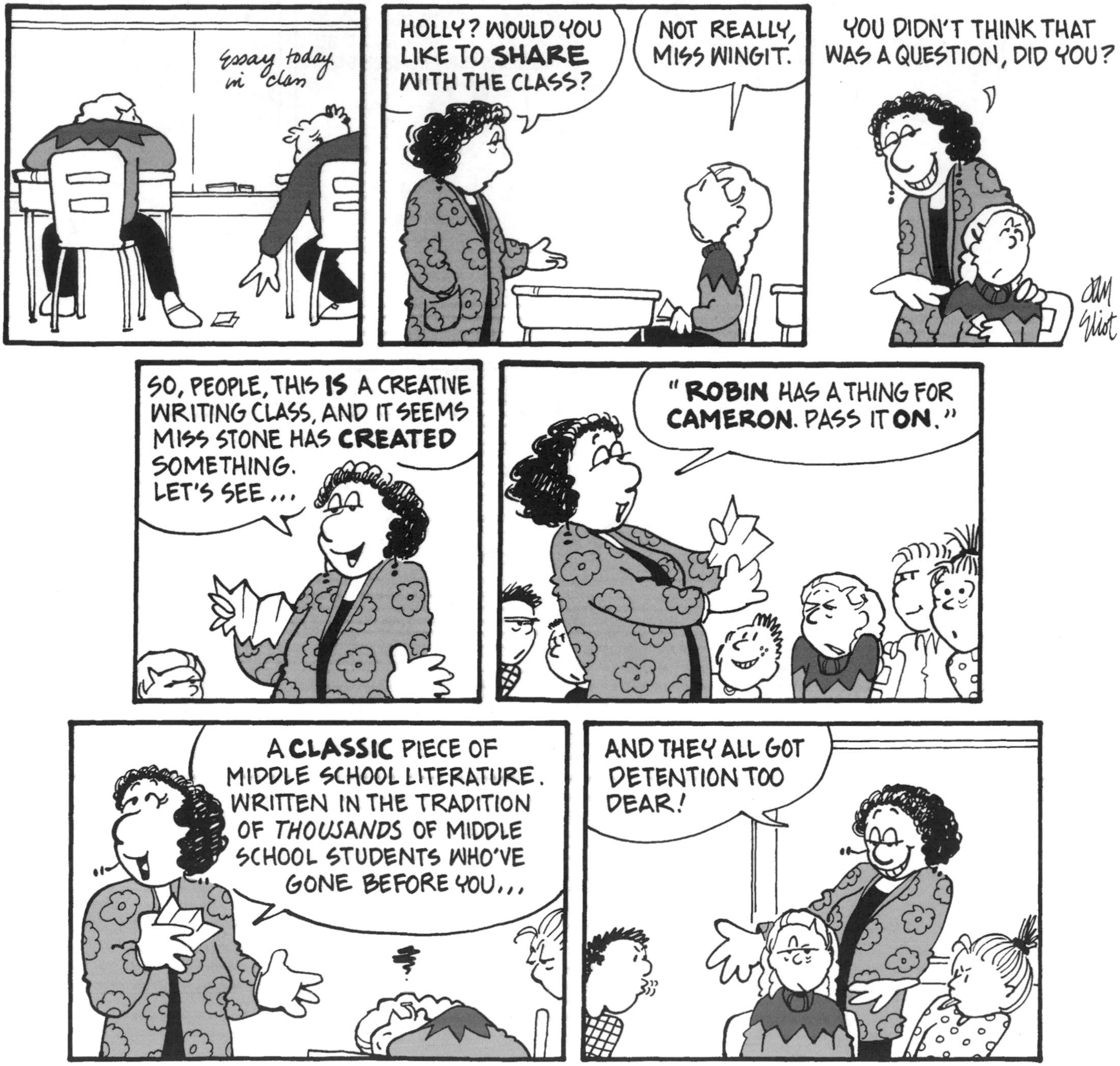
Essay today in class
HOLLY? WOULD YOU LIKE TO SHARE WITH THE CLASS?
NOT REALLY, MISS WINGIT.
YOU DIDN'T THINK THAT WAS A QUESTION, DID YOU?
SO, PEOPLE, THIS IS A CREATIVE WRITING CLASS, AND IT SEEMS MISS STONE HAS CREATED SOMETHING. LET'S SEE...
"ROBIN HAS A THING FOR CAMERON. PASS IT ON."
A CLASSIC PIECE OF MIDDLE SCHOOL LITERATURE. WRITTEN IN THE TRADITION OF THOUSANDS OF MIDDLE SCHOOL STUDENTS WHO'VE GONE BEFORE YOU...
AND THEY ALL GOT DETENTION TOO DEAR!

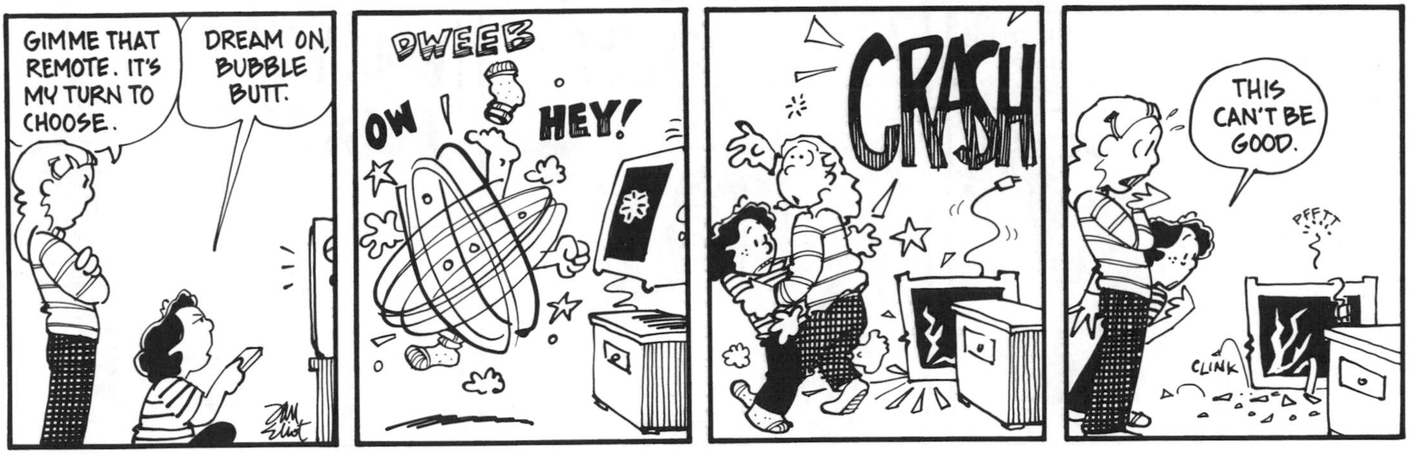
GIMME THAT REMOTE. IT'S MY TURN TO CHOOSE.
DREAM ON, BUBBLE BUTT.
DWEEB
OW
HEY!
CRASH
THIS CAN'T BE GOOD.
PFFTT
CLINK

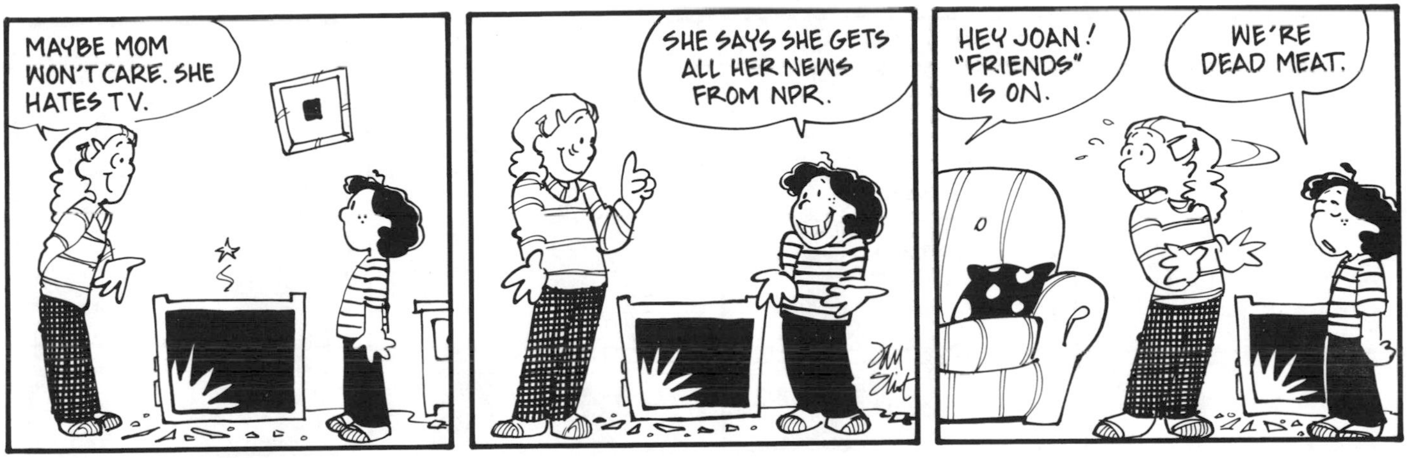
MAYBE MOM WON'T CARE. SHE HATES T.V.
SHE SAYS SHE GETS ALL HER NEWS FROM NPR.
HEY JOAN! "FRIENDS" IS ON.
WE'RE DEAD MEAT.

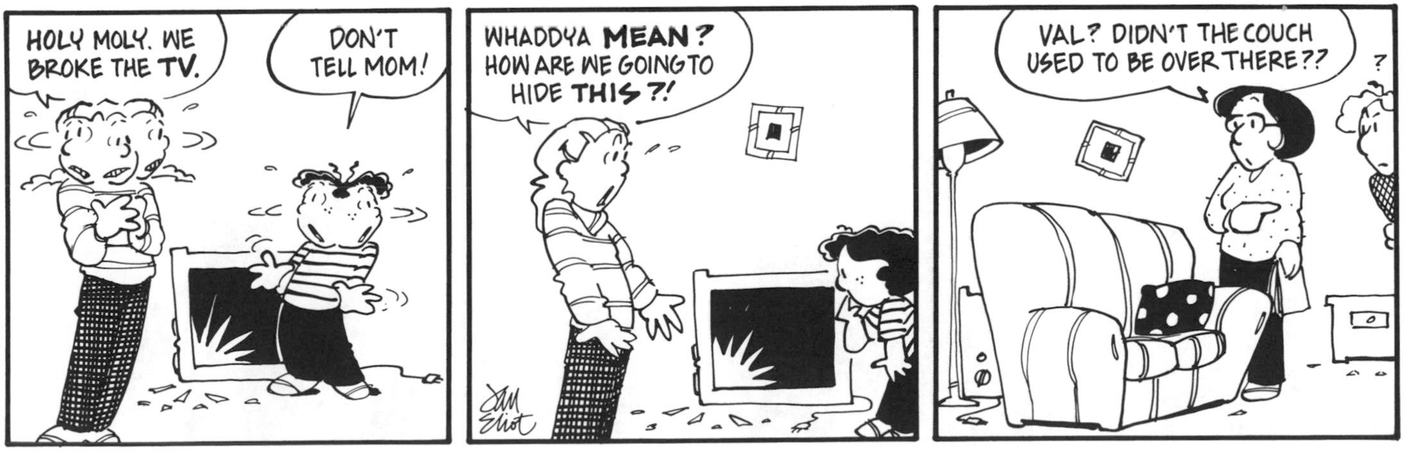
HOLY MOLY. WE BROKE THE TV.
DON'T TELL MOM!
WHADDYA MEAN? HOW ARE WE GOING TO HIDE THIS?!
VAL? DIDN'T THE COUCH USED TO BE OVER THERE??
?

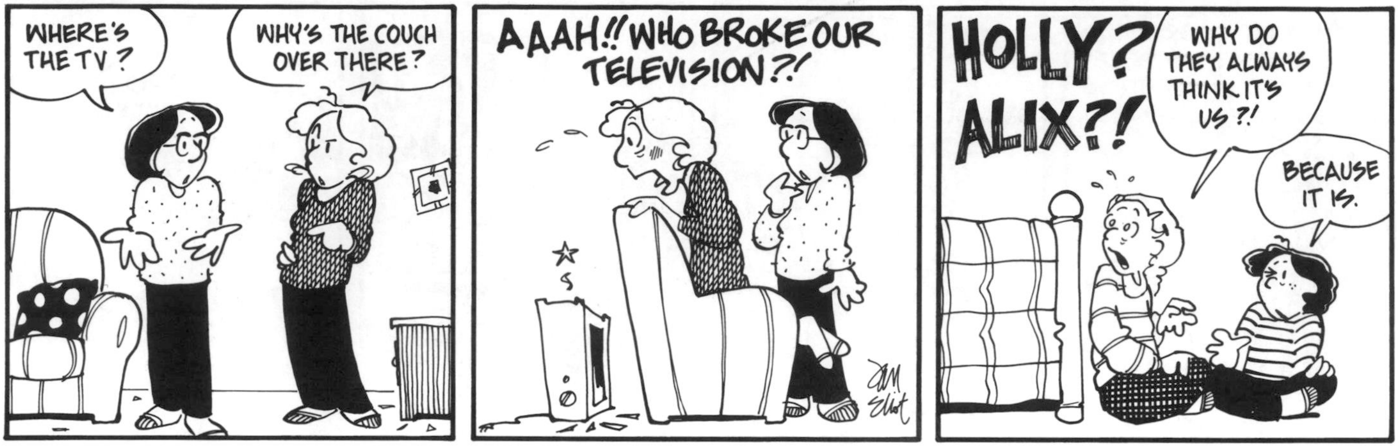
WHERE'S THE TV?
WHY'S THE COUCH OVER THERE?
AAAH!! WHO BROKE OUR TELEVISION?!
HOLLY? ALIX?!
WHY DO THEY ALWAYS THINK IT'S US?!
BECAUSE IT IS.

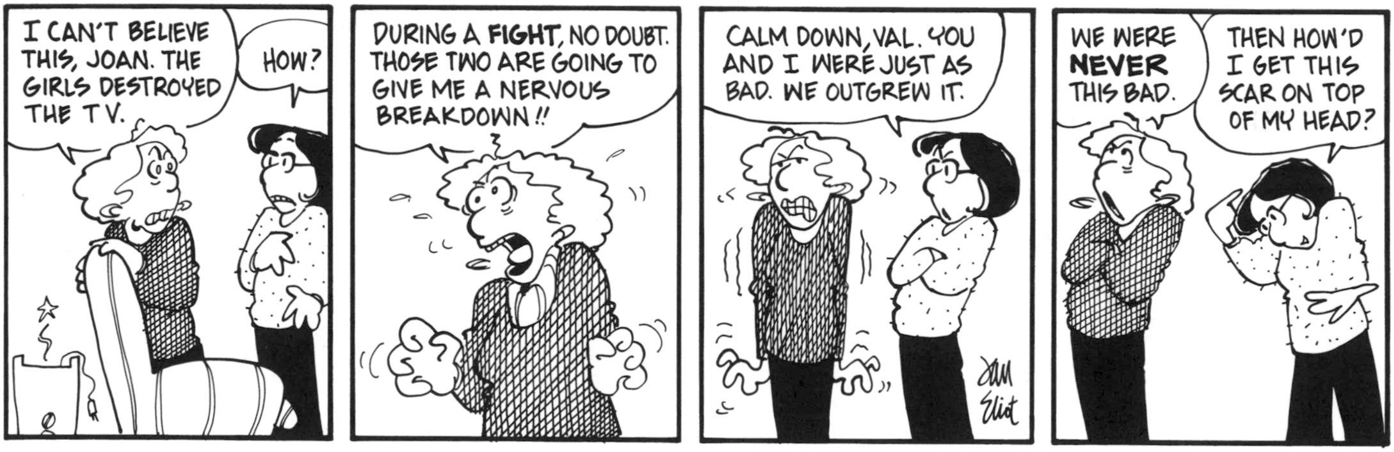
I CAN'T BELIEVE THIS, JOAN. THE GIRLS DESTROYED THE TV.
HOW?
DURING A **FIGHT**, NO DOUBT. THOSE TWO ARE GOING TO GIVE ME A NERVOUS BREAKDOWN!!
CALM DOWN, VAL. YOU AND I WERE JUST AS BAD. WE OUTGREW IT.
WE WERE **NEVER** THIS BAD.
THEN HOW'D I GET THIS SCAR ON TOP OF MY HEAD?

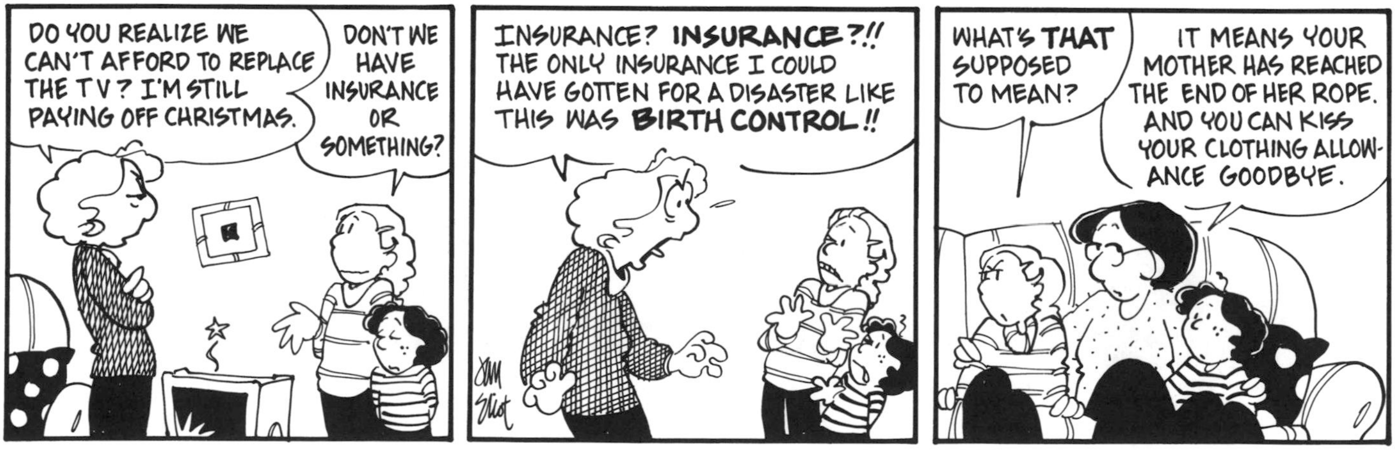
DO YOU REALIZE WE CAN'T AFFORD TO REPLACE THE TV? I'M STILL PAYING OFF CHRISTMAS.
DON'T WE HAVE INSURANCE OR SOMETHING?
INSURANCE? **INSURANCE?!!** THE ONLY INSURANCE I COULD HAVE GOTTEN FOR A DISASTER LIKE THIS WAS **BIRTH CONTROL!!**
WHAT'S **THAT** SUPPOSED TO MEAN?
IT MEANS YOUR MOTHER HAS REACHED THE END OF HER ROPE. AND YOU CAN KISS YOUR CLOTHING ALLOW-ANCE GOODBYE.

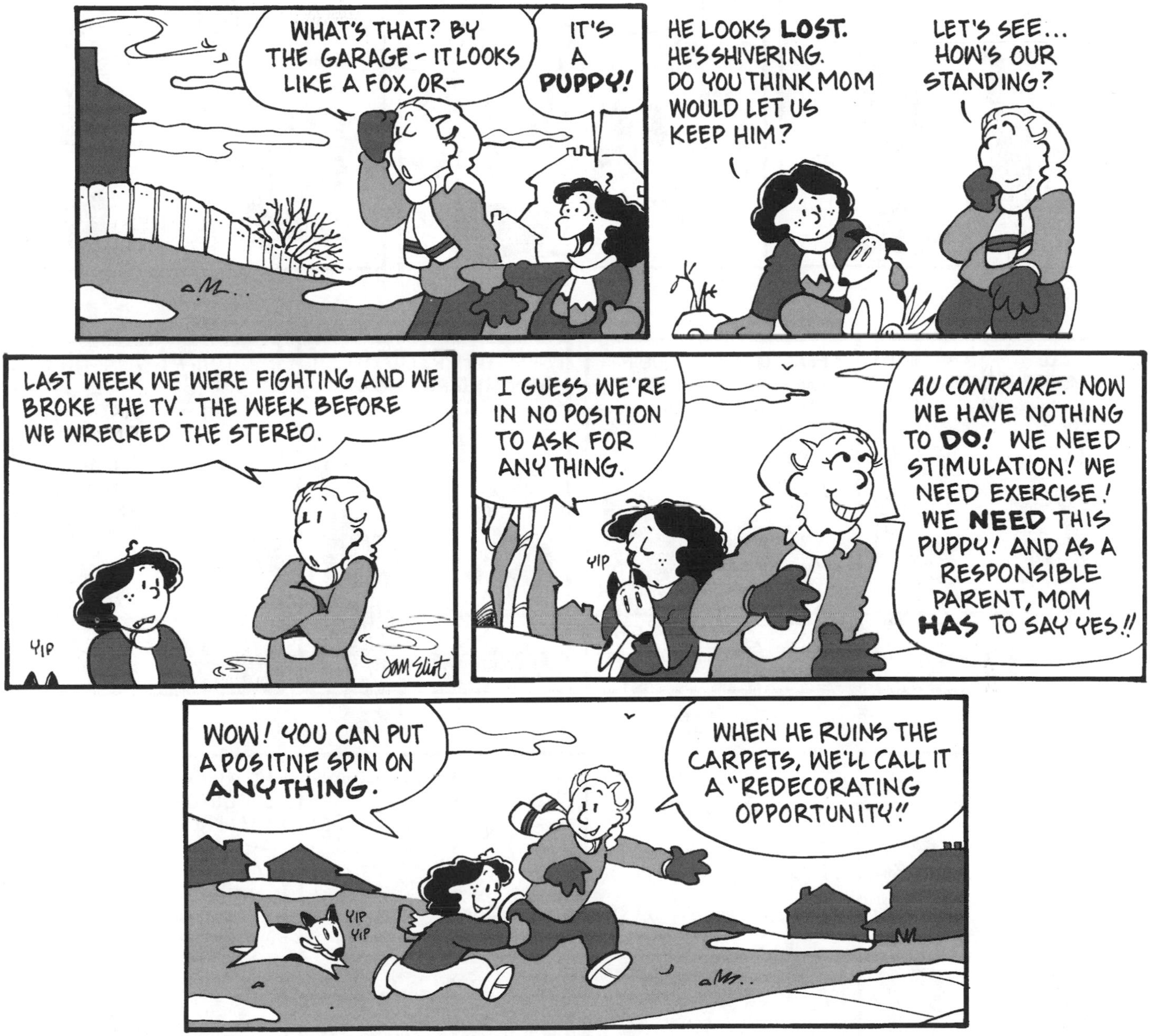
WHAT'S THAT? BY THE GARAGE - IT LOOKS LIKE A FOX, OR—
IT'S A **PUPPY!**
HE LOOKS **LOST.** HE'S SHIVERING. DO YOU THINK MOM WOULD LET US KEEP HIM?
LET'S SEE... HOW'S OUR STANDING?
LAST WEEK WE WERE FIGHTING AND WE BROKE THE TV. THE WEEK BEFORE WE WRECKED THE STEREO.
YIP
I GUESS WE'RE IN NO POSITION TO ASK FOR ANYTHING.
YIP
AU CONTRAIRE. NOW WE HAVE NOTHING TO **DO!** WE NEED STIMULATION! WE NEED EXERCISE! WE **NEED** THIS PUPPY! AND AS A RESPONSIBLE PARENT, MOM **HAS** TO SAY YES!!
WOW! YOU CAN PUT A POSITIVE SPIN ON **ANYTHING.**
WHEN HE RUINS THE CARPETS, WE'LL CALL IT A "REDECORATING OPPORTUNITY!"
YIP YIP

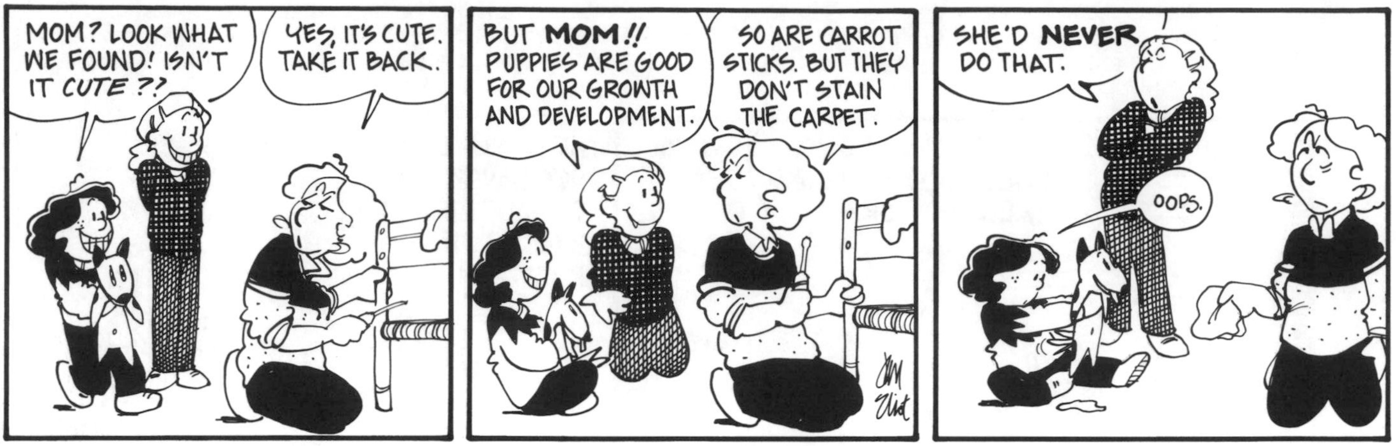
MOM? LOOK WHAT WE FOUND! ISN'T IT *CUTE* ?!
YES, IT'S CUTE. TAKE IT BACK.
BUT **MOM**!! PUPPIES ARE GOOD FOR OUR GROWTH AND DEVELOPMENT.
SO ARE CARROT STICKS. BUT THEY DON'T STAIN THE CARPET.
SHE'D **NEVER** DO THAT.
OOPS.

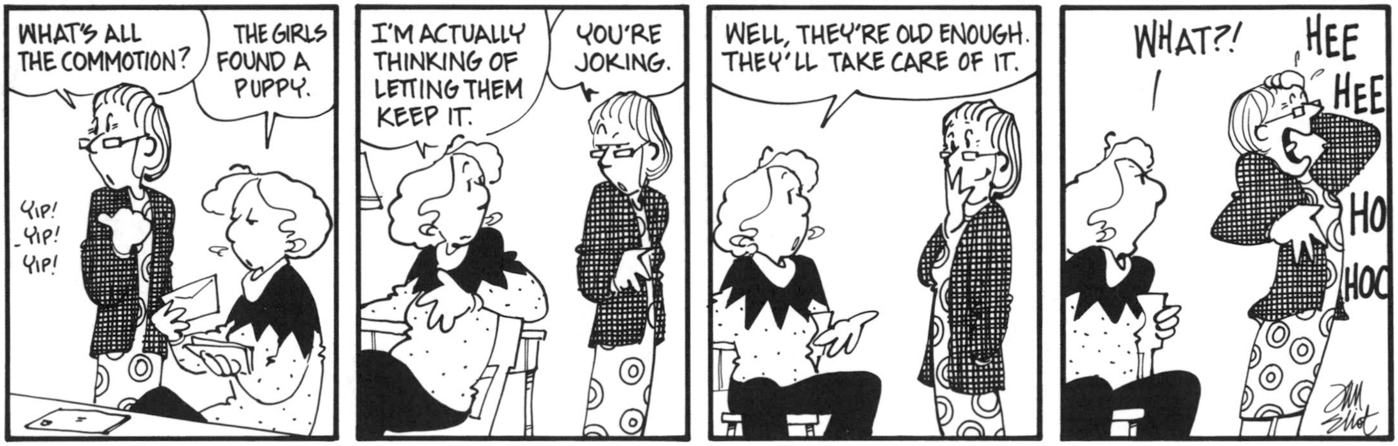
WHAT'S ALL THE COMMOTION?
THE GIRLS FOUND A PUPPY.
YIP! YIP! YIP!
I'M ACTUALLY THINKING OF LETTING THEM KEEP IT.
YOU'RE JOKING.
WELL, THEY'RE OLD ENOUGH. THEY'LL TAKE CARE OF IT.
WHAT?!
HEE HEE HO HO

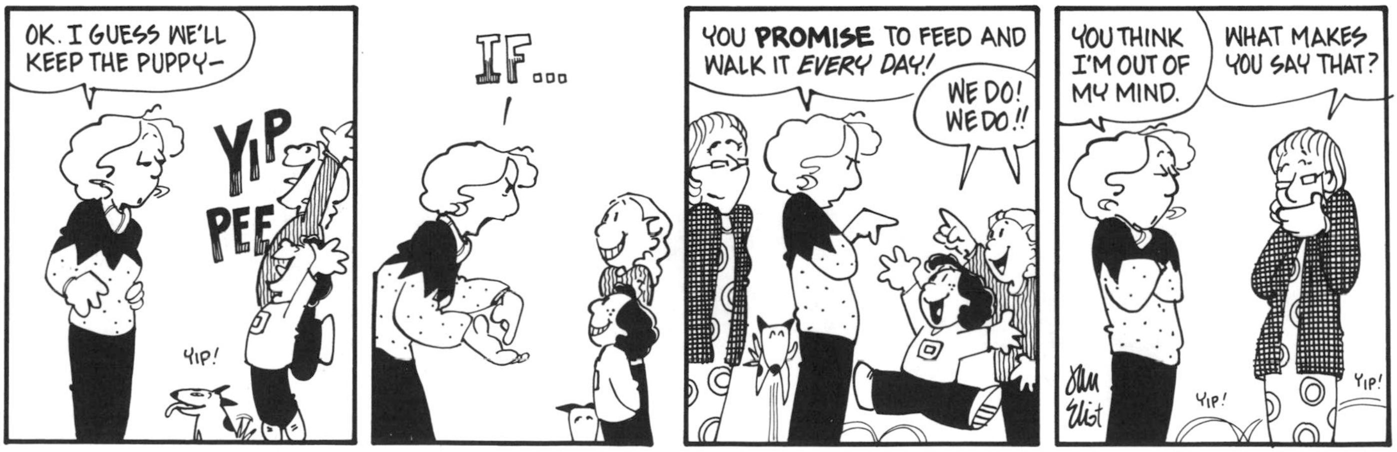
OK. I GUESS WE'LL KEEP THE PUPPY—
YIP PEE
YIP!
IF...
YOU **PROMISE** TO FEED AND WALK IT *EVERY DAY!*
WE DO! WE DO!!
YOU THINK I'M OUT OF MY MIND.
WHAT MAKES YOU SAY THAT?
YIP!
YIP!

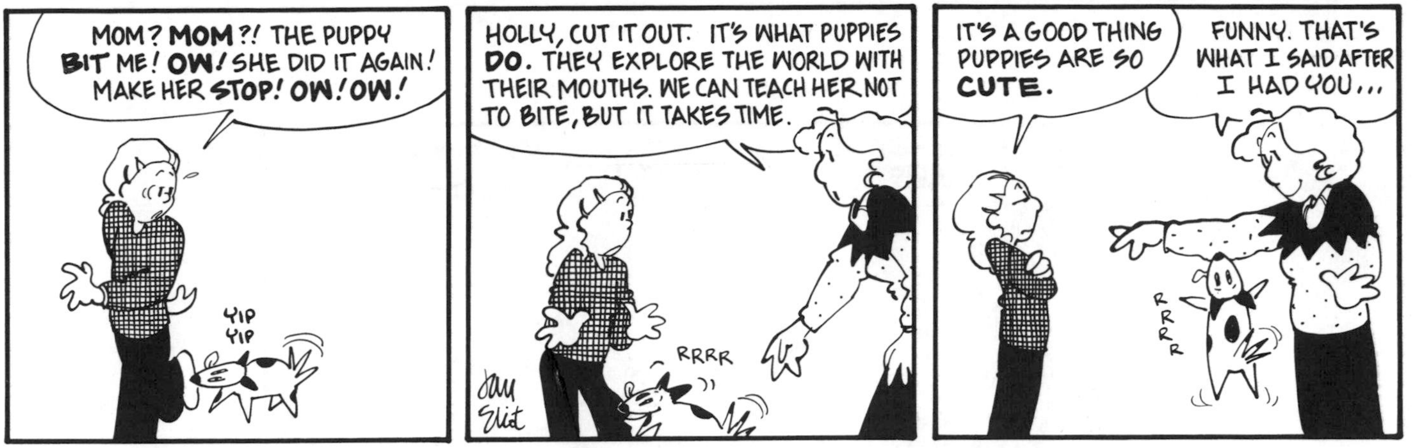
MOM? MOM?! THE PUPPY BIT ME! OW! SHE DID IT AGAIN! MAKE HER STOP! OW! OW!
YIP YIP
HOLLY, CUT IT OUT. IT'S WHAT PUPPIES DO. THEY EXPLORE THE WORLD WITH THEIR MOUTHS. WE CAN TEACH HER NOT TO BITE, BUT IT TAKES TIME.
RRRR
IT'S A GOOD THING PUPPIES ARE SO CUTE.
FUNNY. THAT'S WHAT I SAID AFTER I HAD YOU...
RRRR

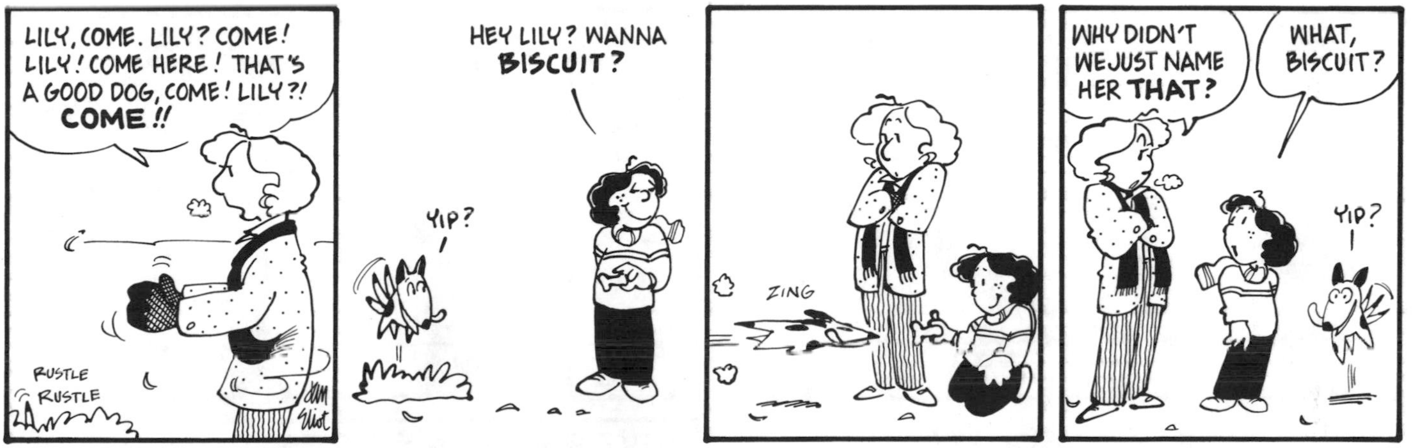
LILY, COME. LILY? COME! LILY! COME HERE! THAT'S A GOOD DOG, COME! LILY?! COME!!
RUSTLE RUSTLE
HEY LILY? WANNA BISCUIT?
YIP?
ZING
WHY DIDN'T WE JUST NAME HER THAT?
WHAT, BISCUIT?
YIP?

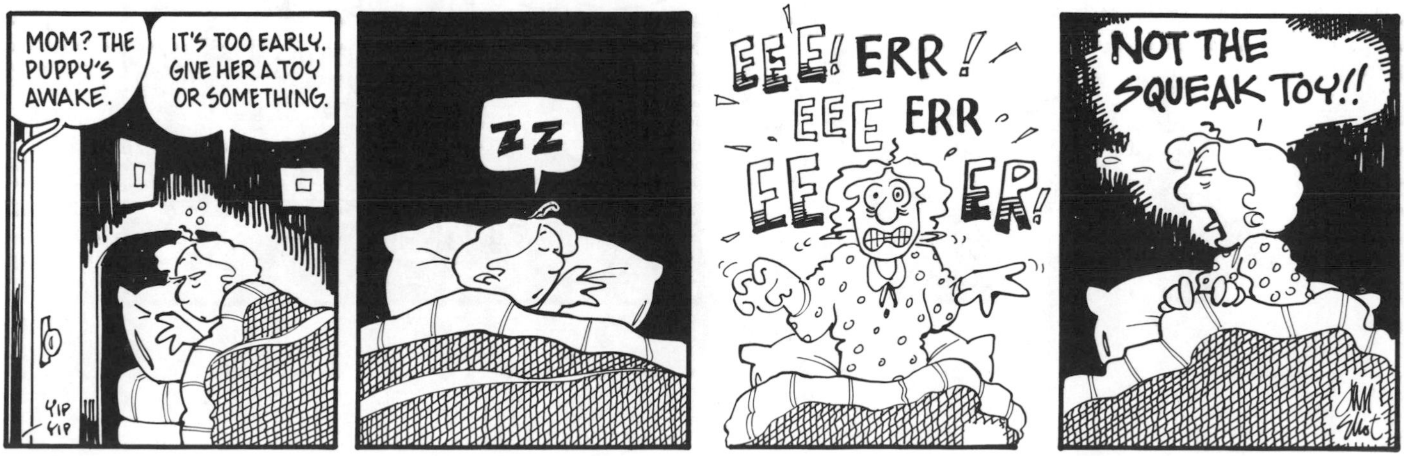
MOM? THE PUPPY'S AWAKE.
IT'S TOO EARLY. GIVE HER A TOY OR SOMETHING.
YIP YIP
ZZ
EEE! ERR! EEE ERR EE ER!
NOT THE SQUEAK TOY!!

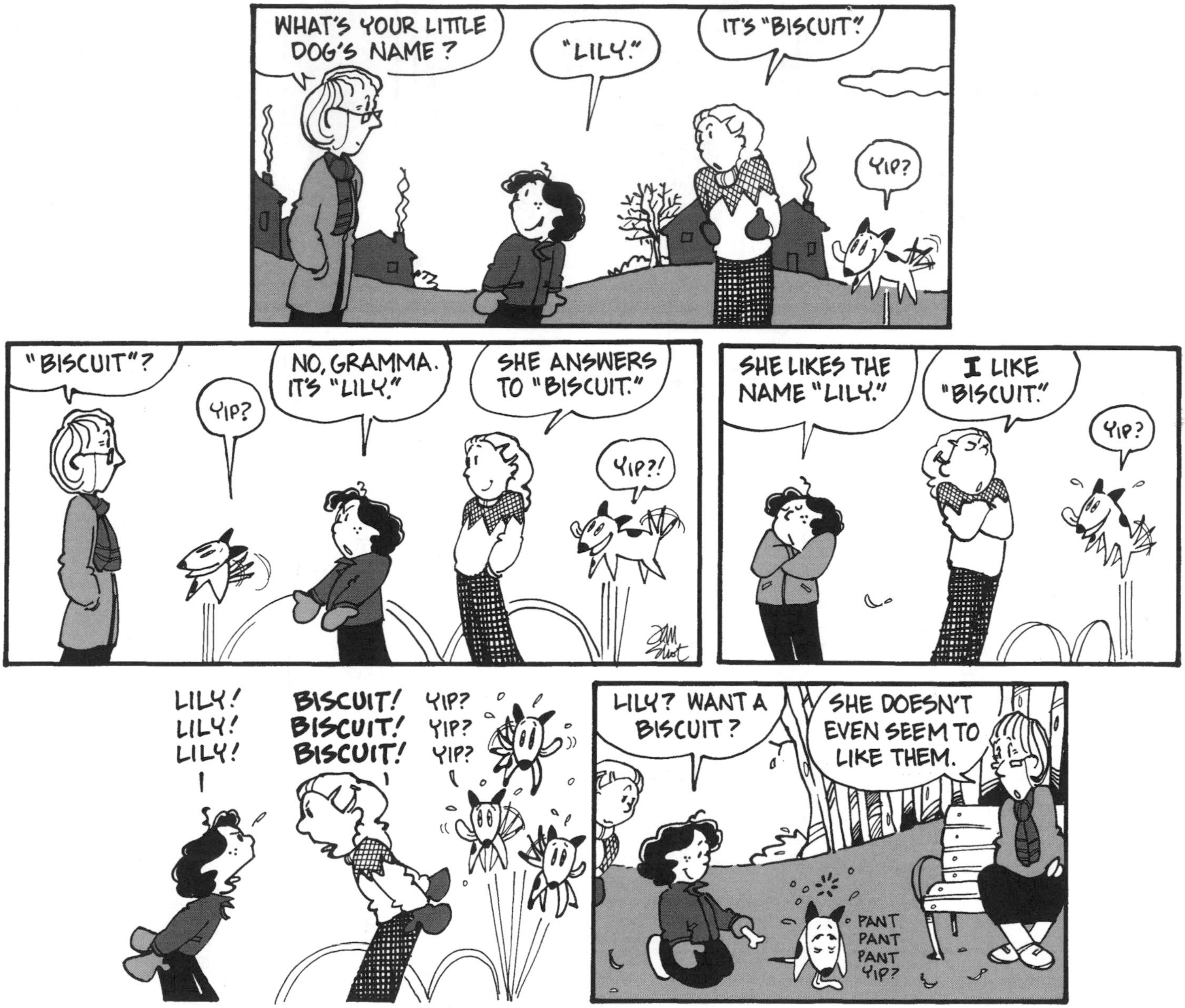
WHAT'S YOUR LITTLE DOG'S NAME?
"LILY."
IT'S "BISCUIT."
YIP?
"BISCUIT"?
YIP?
NO, GRAMMA. IT'S "LILY."
SHE ANSWERS TO "BISCUIT."
YIP?!
SHE LIKES THE NAME "LILY."
I LIKE "BISCUIT."
YIP?
LILY! LILY! LILY!
BISCUIT! BISCUIT! BISCUIT!
YIP? YIP? YIP?
LILY? WANT A BISCUIT?
SHE DOESN'T EVEN SEEM TO LIKE THEM.
PANT PANT PANT YIP?

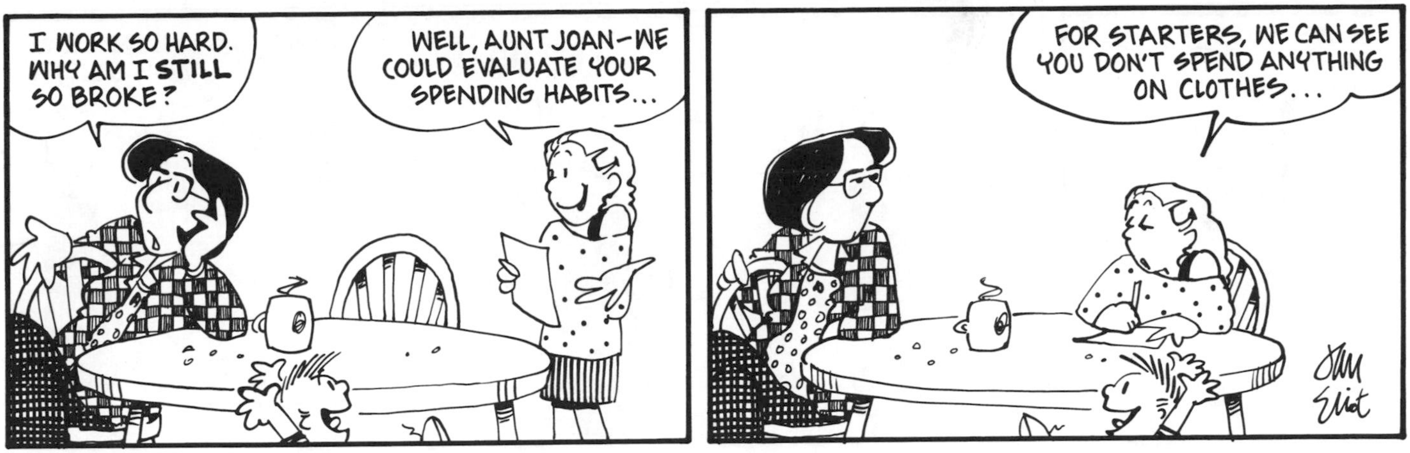
I WORK SO HARD. WHY AM I STILL SO BROKE?
WELL, AUNT JOAN—WE COULD EVALUATE YOUR SPENDING HABITS...
FOR STARTERS, WE CAN SEE YOU DON'T SPEND ANYTHING ON CLOTHES...

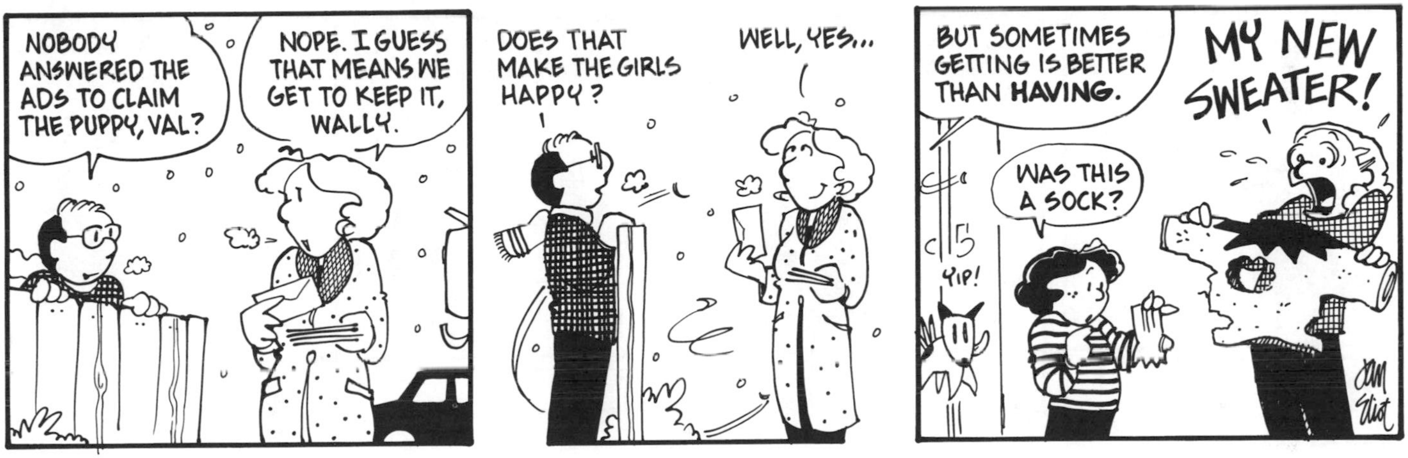
NOBODY ANSWERED THE ADS TO CLAIM THE PUPPY, VAL?
NOPE. I GUESS THAT MEANS WE GET TO KEEP IT, WALLY.
DOES THAT MAKE THE GIRLS HAPPY?
WELL, YES...
BUT SOMETIMES GETTING IS BETTER THAN HAVING.
MY NEW SWEATER!
WAS THIS A SOCK?
YIP!

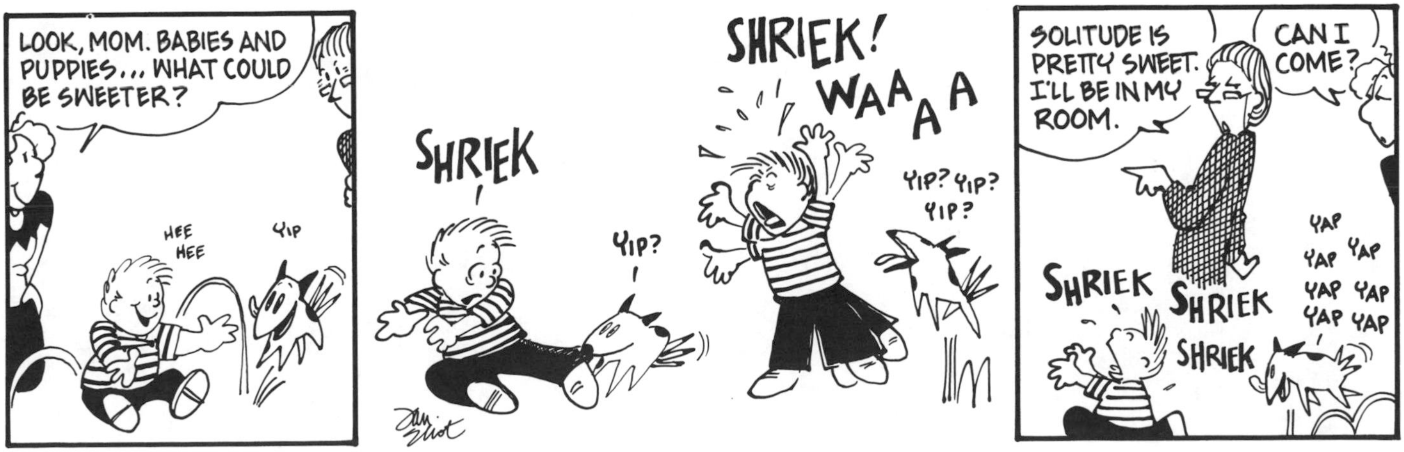
LOOK, MOM. BABIES AND PUPPIES... WHAT COULD BE SWEETER?
HEE HEE
YIP
SHRIEK
YIP?
SHRIEK!
WAAAA
YIP? YIP? YIP?
SOLITUDE IS PRETTY SWEET. I'LL BE IN MY ROOM.
CAN I COME?
YAP YAP YAP YAP YAP YAP YAP
SHRIEK SHRIEK SHRIEK

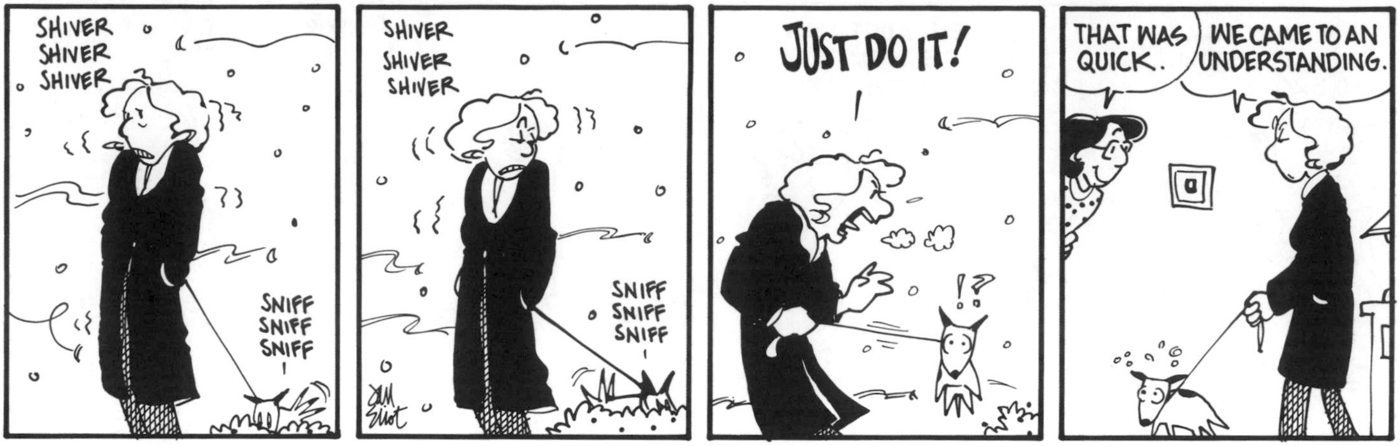
SHIVER
SHIVER
SHIVER
SNIFF
SNIFF
SNIFF
SHIVER
SHIVER
SHIVER
SNIFF
SNIFF
SNIFF
JUST DO IT!
!?
THAT WAS QUICK.
WE CAME TO AN UNDERSTANDING.

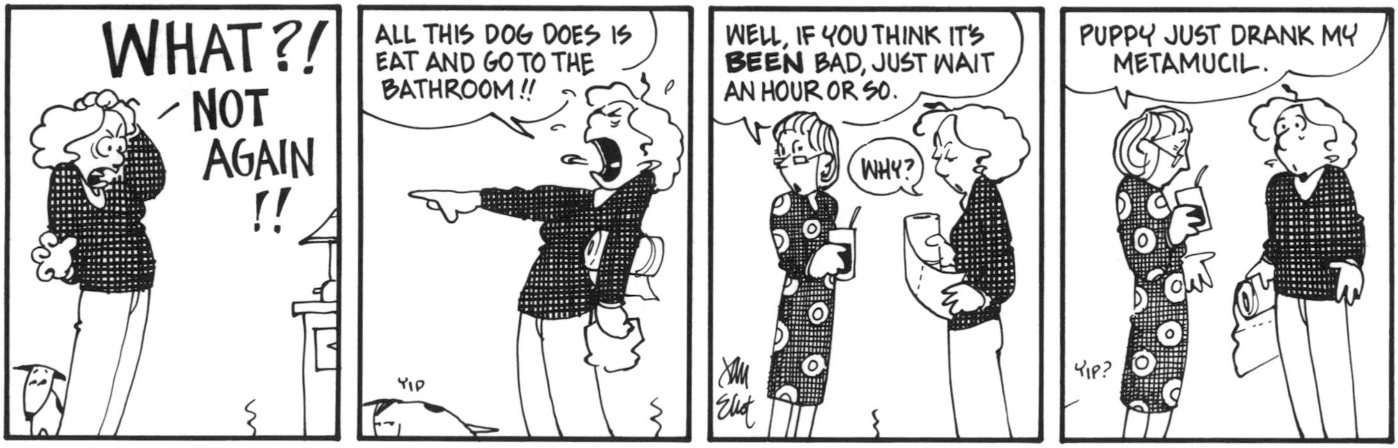
WHAT?!
NOT AGAIN !!
ALL THIS DOG DOES IS EAT AND GO TO THE BATHROOM!!
YIP
WELL, IF YOU THINK IT'S **BEEN** BAD, JUST WAIT AN HOUR OR SO.
WHY?
PUPPY JUST DRANK MY METAMUCIL.
YIP?

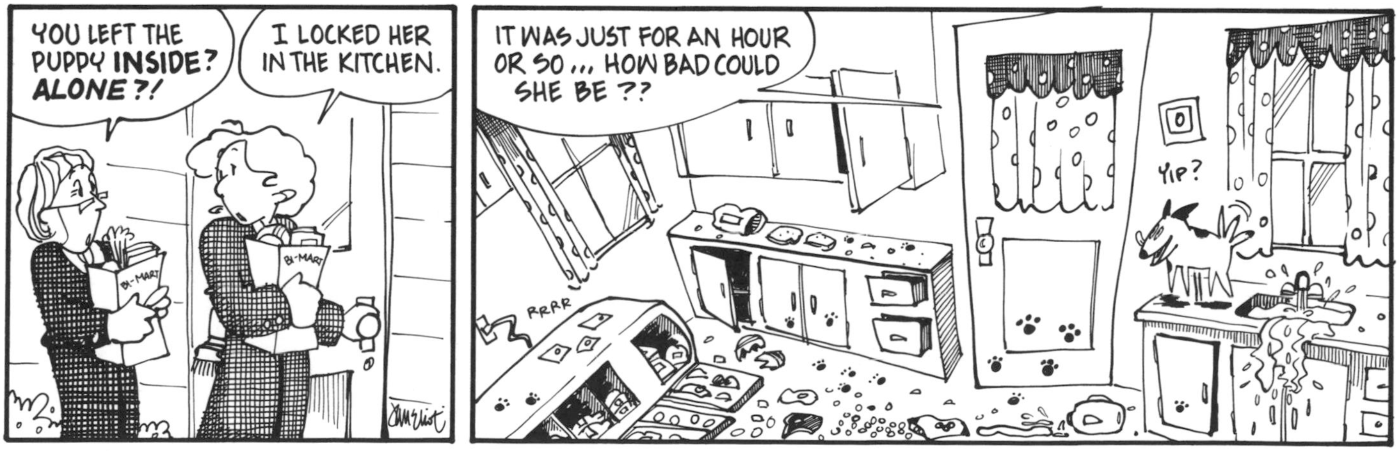
YOU LEFT THE PUPPY **INSIDE**? **ALONE**?!
I LOCKED HER IN THE KITCHEN.
BI-MART
BI-MART
IT WAS JUST FOR AN HOUR OR SO ... HOW BAD COULD SHE BE ??
RRRR
YIP?

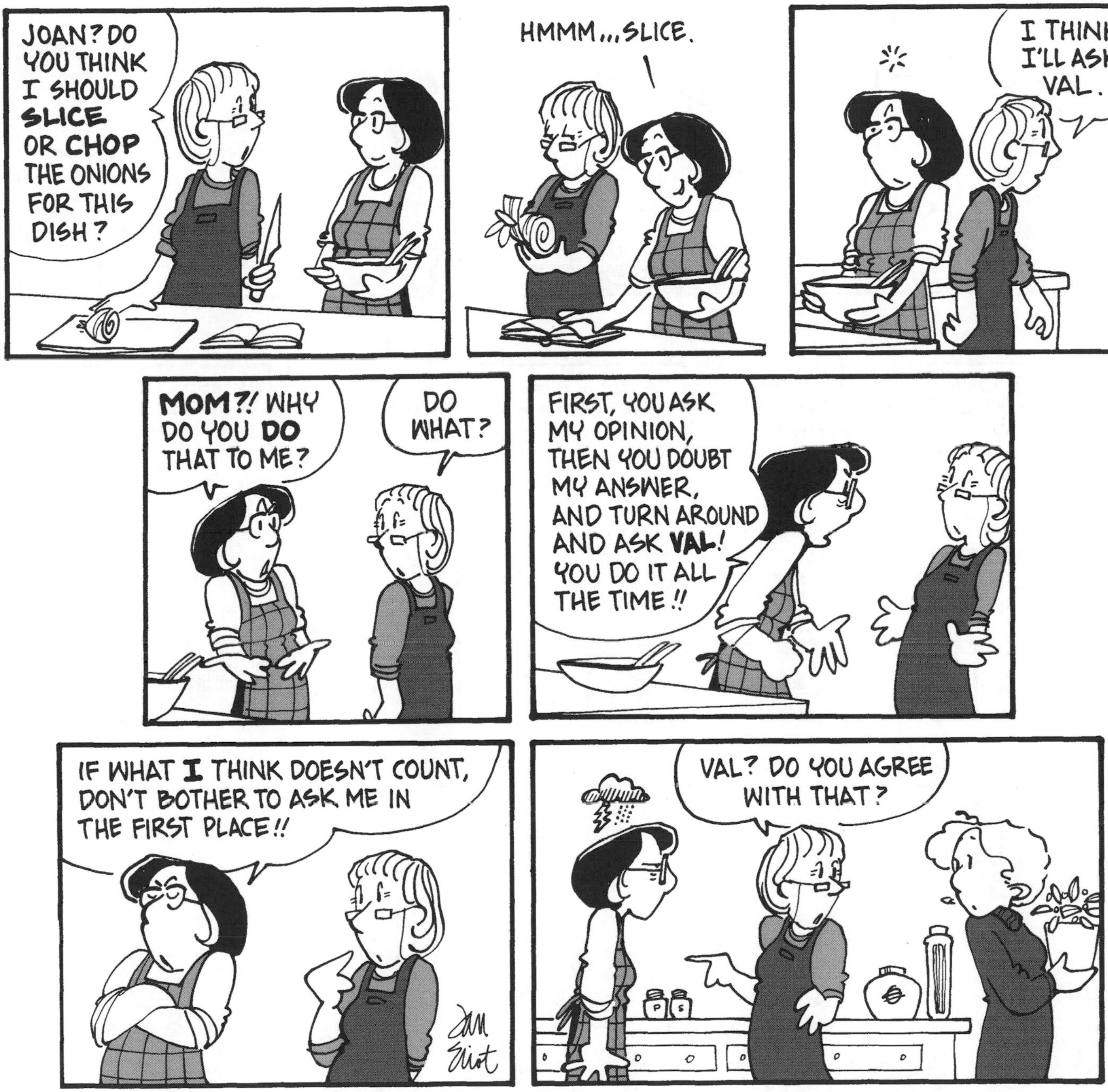

JOAN? DO YOU THINK I SHOULD **SLICE** OR **CHOP** THE ONIONS FOR THIS DISH?
HMMM... SLICE.
I THINK I'LL ASK VAL.
MOM?! WHY DO YOU **DO** THAT TO ME?
DO WHAT?
FIRST, YOU ASK MY OPINION, THEN YOU DOUBT MY ANSWER, AND TURN AROUND AND ASK **VAL**! YOU DO IT ALL THE TIME!!
IF WHAT **I** THINK DOESN'T COUNT, DON'T BOTHER TO ASK ME IN THE FIRST PLACE!!
VAL? DO YOU AGREE WITH THAT?

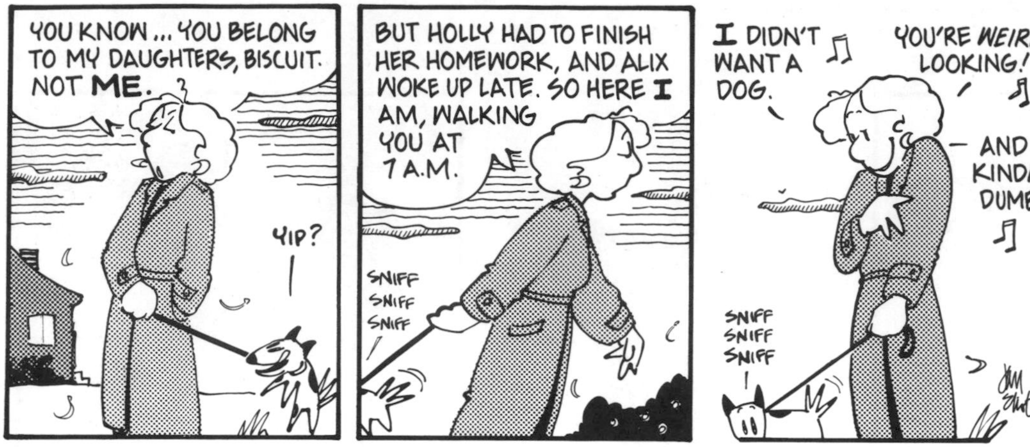
YOU KNOW ... YOU BELONG TO MY DAUGHTERS, BISCUIT. NOT **ME**.
YIP?
BUT HOLLY HAD TO FINISH HER HOMEWORK, AND ALIX WOKE UP LATE. SO HERE **I** AM, WALKING YOU AT 7 A.M.
SNIFF SNIFF SNIFF
I DIDN'T WANT A DOG.
YOU'RE *WEIRD* LOOKING!
AND KINDA DUMB.
SNIFF SNIFF SNIFF
AS LONG AS YOU **SOUND** HAPPY, DOGS DON'T CARE ***WHAT*** YOU SAY.
HEL-**LO** LITTLE PEA BRAIN!
YIP YIP YIP

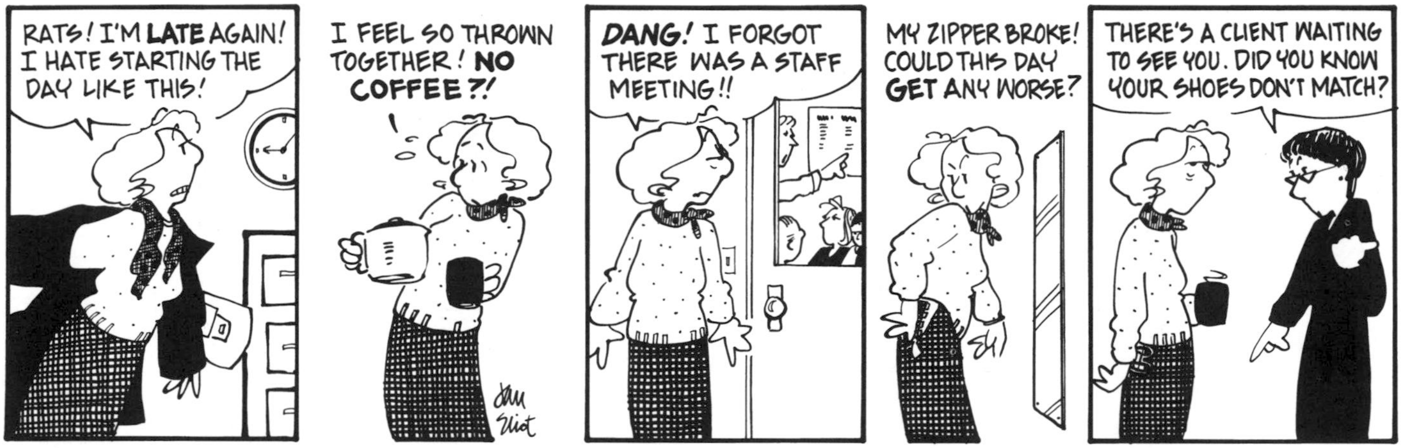
RATS! I'M **LATE** AGAIN! I HATE STARTING THE DAY LIKE THIS!
I FEEL SO THROWN TOGETHER! **NO COFFEE?!**
DANG! I FORGOT THERE WAS A STAFF MEETING!!
MY ZIPPER BROKE! COULD THIS DAY **GET** ANY WORSE?
THERE'S A CLIENT WAITING TO SEE YOU. DID YOU KNOW YOUR SHOES DON'T MATCH?

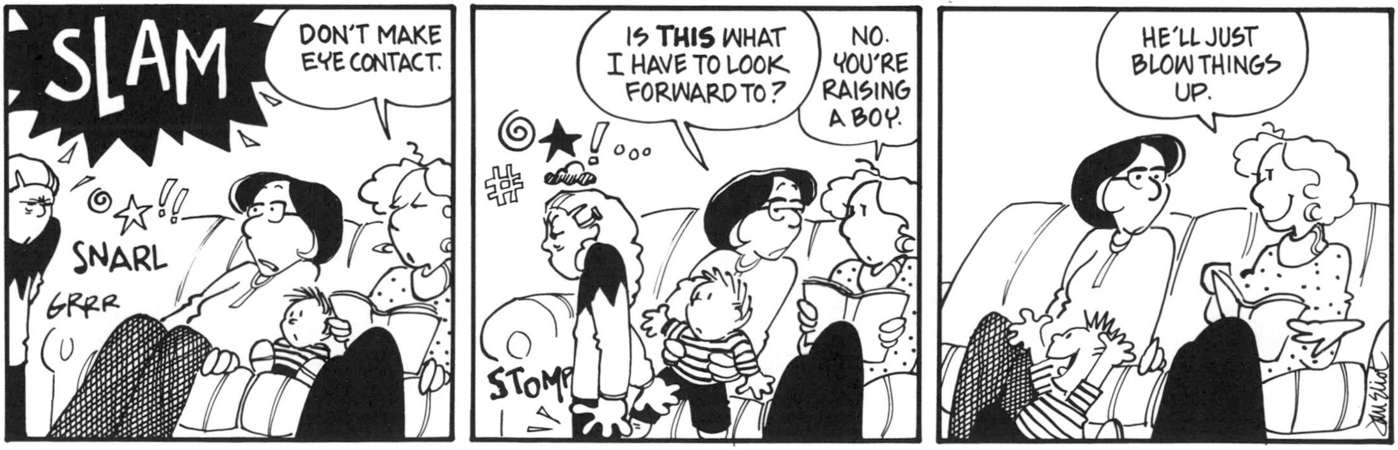
SLAM
DON'T MAKE EYE CONTACT.
SNARL
GRRR
IS **THIS** WHAT I HAVE TO LOOK FORWARD TO?
NO. YOU'RE RAISING A BOY.
STOMP
HE'LL JUST BLOW THINGS UP.

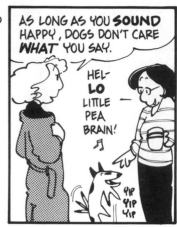

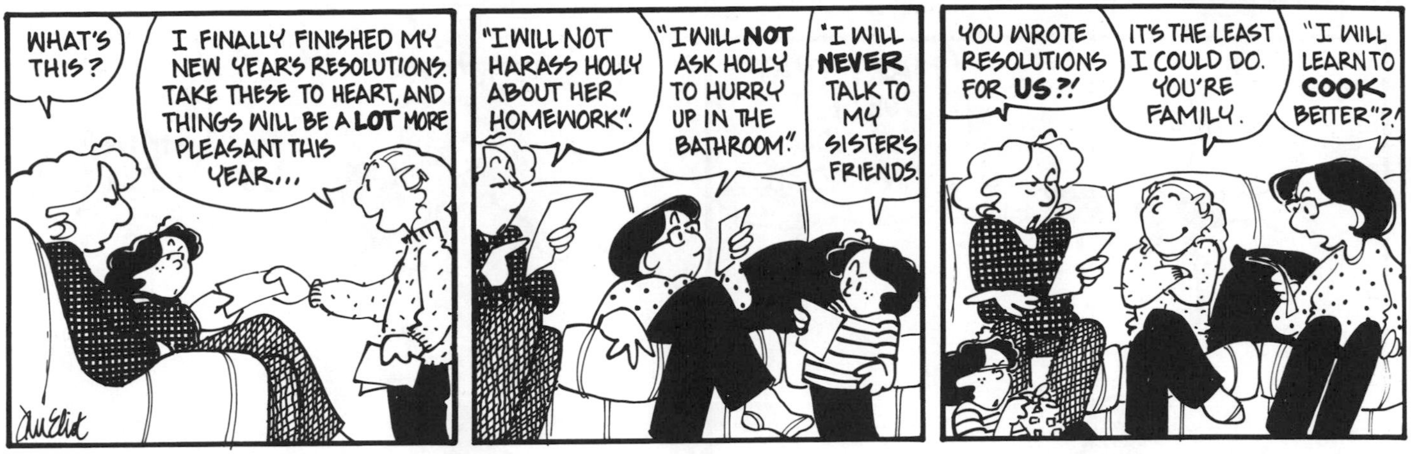
WHAT'S THIS?
I FINALLY FINISHED MY NEW YEAR'S RESOLUTIONS. TAKE THESE TO HEART, AND THINGS WILL BE A **LOT** MORE PLEASANT THIS YEAR...
"I WILL NOT HARASS HOLLY ABOUT HER HOMEWORK."
"I WILL **NOT** ASK HOLLY TO HURRY UP IN THE BATHROOM."
"I WILL **NEVER** TALK TO MY SISTER'S FRIENDS.
YOU WROTE RESOLUTIONS FOR **US**?!
IT'S THE LEAST I COULD DO. YOU'RE FAMILY.
"I WILL LEARN TO **COOK** BETTER"?!

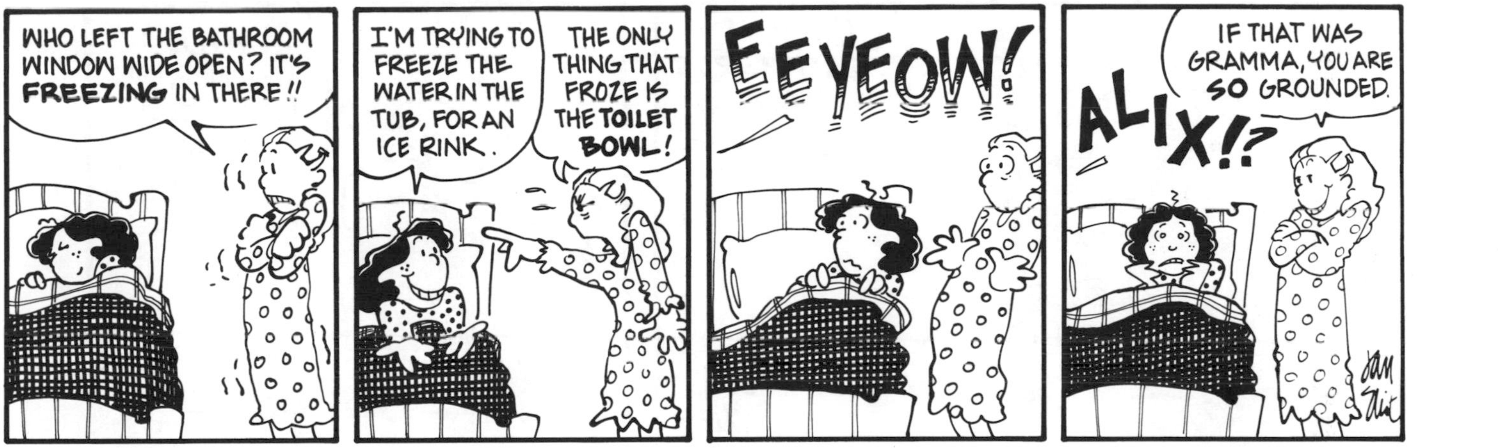
WHO LEFT THE BATHROOM WINDOW WIDE OPEN? IT'S **FREEZING** IN THERE!!
I'M TRYING TO FREEZE THE WATER IN THE TUB, FOR AN ICE RINK.
THE ONLY THING THAT FROZE IS THE **TOILET BOWL**!
EEYEOW!
ALIX!?
IF THAT WAS GRAMMA, YOU ARE **SO** GROUNDED.

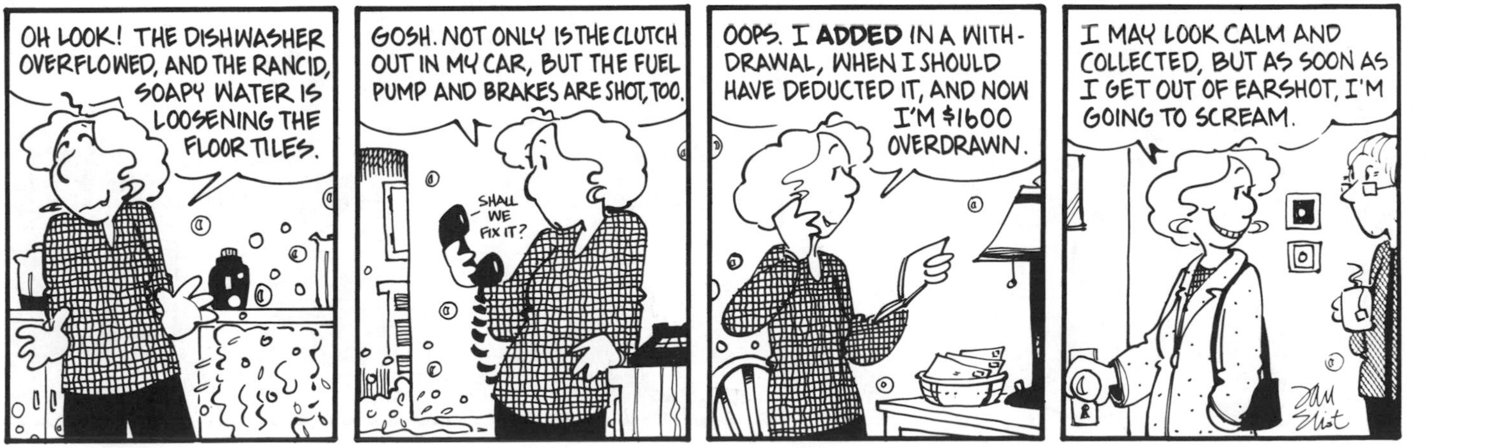
OH LOOK! THE DISHWASHER OVERFLOWED, AND THE RANCID, SOAPY WATER IS LOOSENING THE FLOOR TILES.
GOSH. NOT ONLY IS THE CLUTCH OUT IN MY CAR, BUT THE FUEL PUMP AND BRAKES ARE SHOT, TOO.
SHALL WE FIX IT?
OOPS. I **ADDED** IN A WITHDRAWAL, WHEN I SHOULD HAVE DEDUCTED IT, AND NOW I'M $1600 OVERDRAWN.
I MAY LOOK CALM AND COLLECTED, BUT AS SOON AS I GET OUT OF EARSHOT, I'M GOING TO SCREAM.

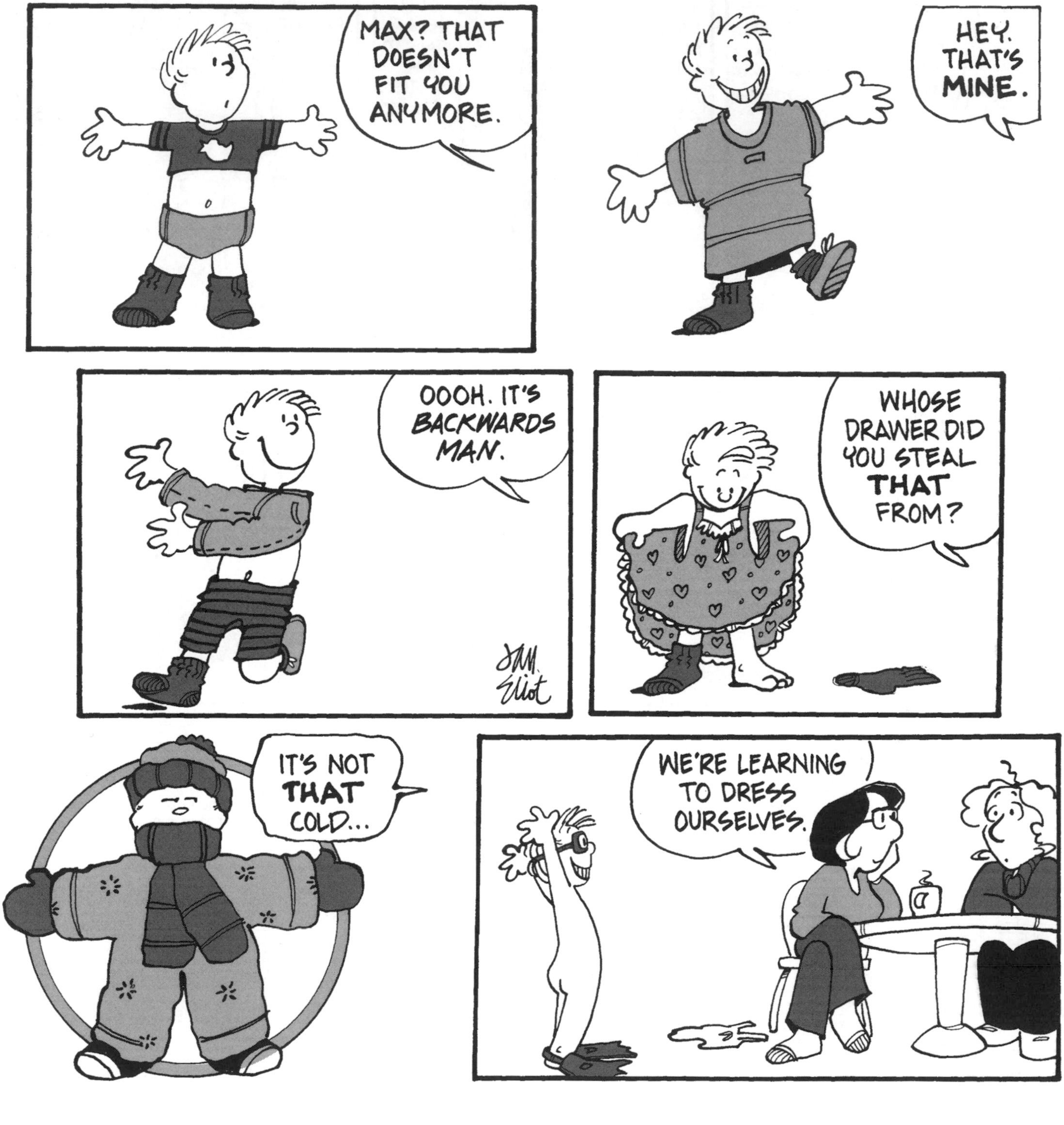
MAX? THAT DOESN'T FIT YOU ANYMORE.
HEY. THAT'S **MINE**.
OOOH. IT'S *BACKWARDS MAN*.
WHOSE DRAWER DID YOU STEAL **THAT** FROM?
IT'S NOT **THAT** COLD...
WE'RE LEARNING TO DRESS OURSELVES.

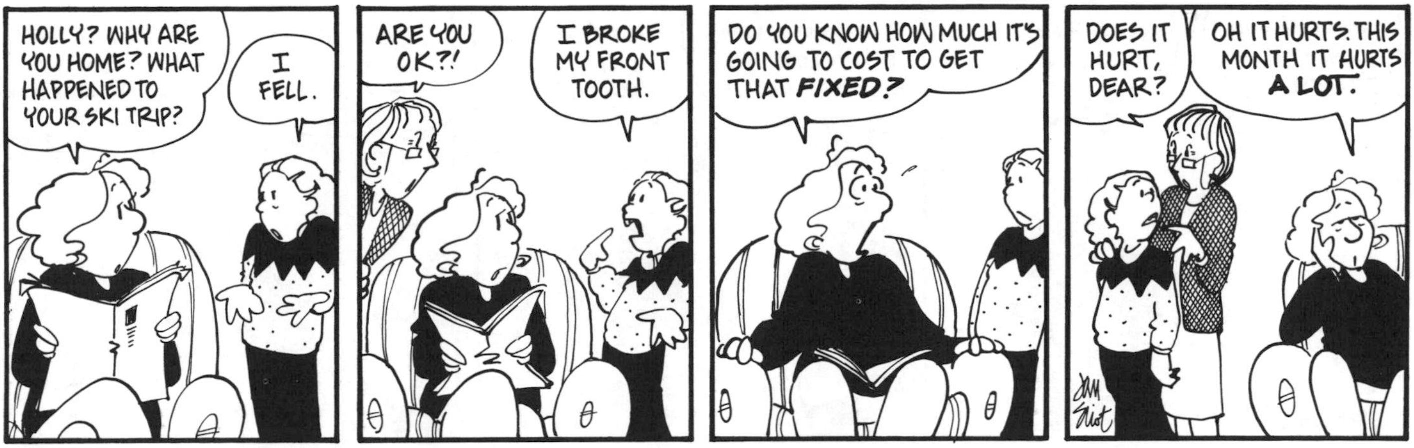
HOLLY? WHY ARE YOU HOME? WHAT HAPPENED TO YOUR SKI TRIP?
I FELL.
ARE YOU OK?!
I BROKE MY FRONT TOOTH.
DO YOU KNOW HOW MUCH IT'S GOING TO COST TO GET THAT FIXED?
DOES IT HURT, DEAR?
OH IT HURTS. THIS MONTH IT HURTS A LOT.

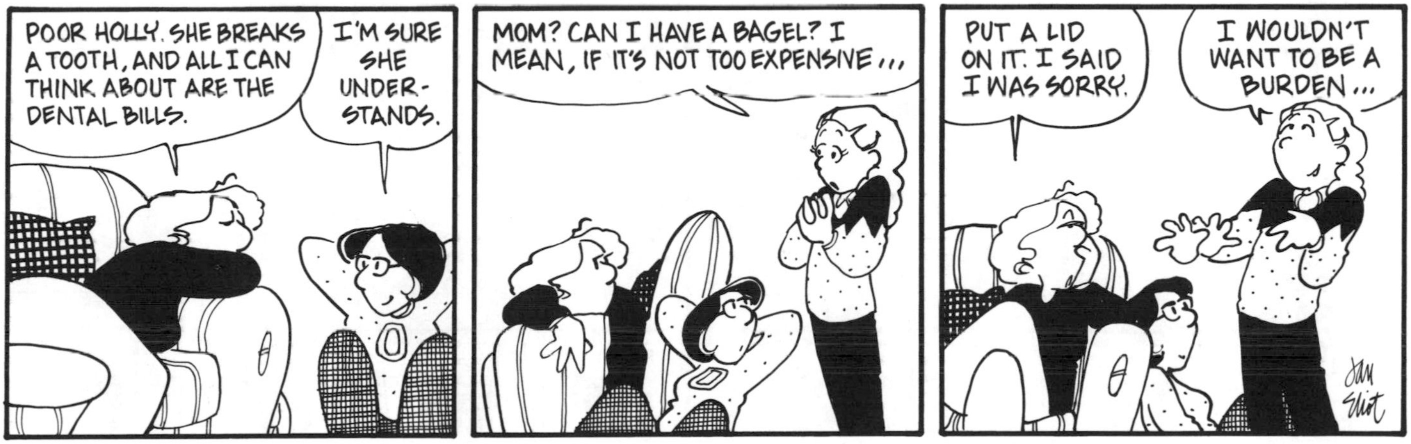
POOR HOLLY. SHE BREAKS A TOOTH, AND ALL I CAN THINK ABOUT ARE THE DENTAL BILLS.
I'M SURE SHE UNDER-STANDS.
MOM? CAN I HAVE A BAGEL? I MEAN, IF IT'S NOT TOO EXPENSIVE...
PUT A LID ON IT. I SAID I WAS SORRY.
I WOULDN'T WANT TO BE A BURDEN...

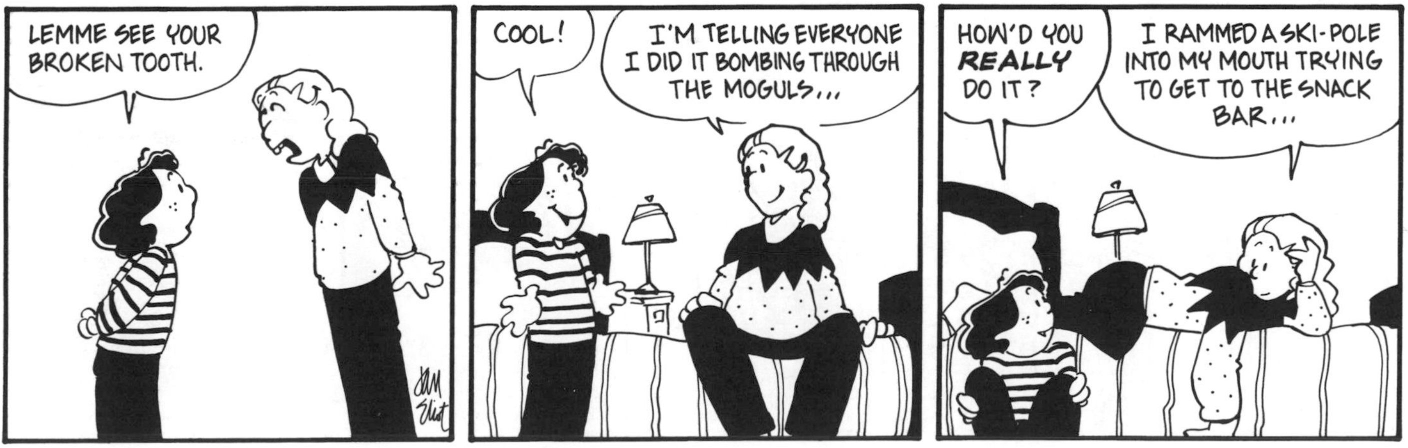
LEMME SEE YOUR BROKEN TOOTH.
COOL!
I'M TELLING EVERYONE I DID IT BOMBING THROUGH THE MOGULS...
HOW'D YOU REALLY DO IT?
I RAMMED A SKI-POLE INTO MY MOUTH TRYING TO GET TO THE SNACK BAR...

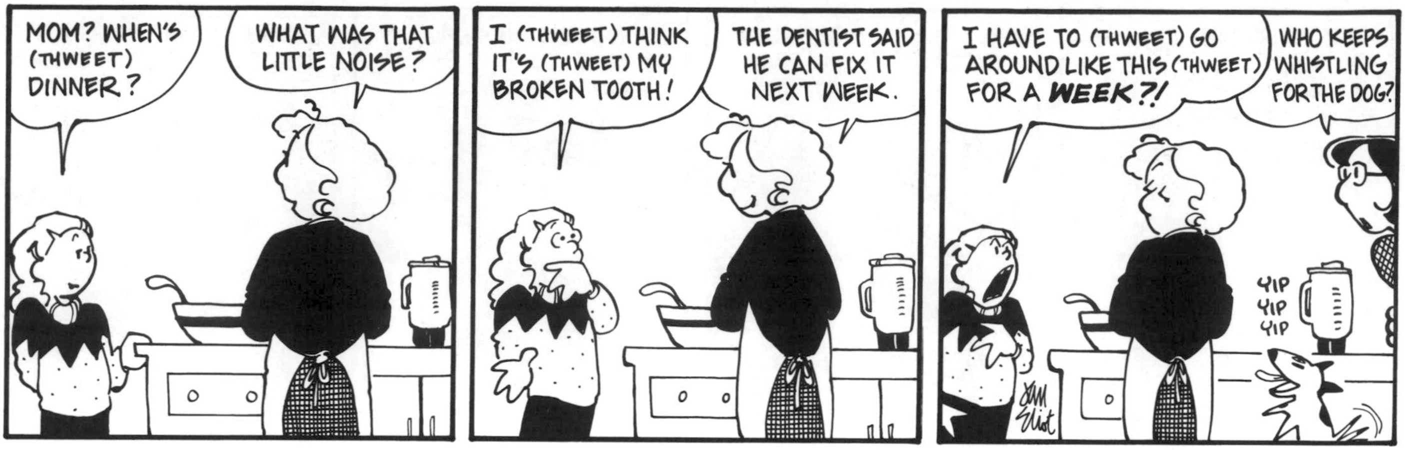
MOM? WHEN'S (THWEET) DINNER?
WHAT WAS THAT LITTLE NOISE?
I (THWEET) THINK IT'S (THWEET) MY BROKEN TOOTH!
THE DENTIST SAID HE CAN FIX IT NEXT WEEK.
I HAVE TO (THWEET) GO AROUND LIKE THIS (THWEET) FOR A **WEEK?!**
WHO KEEPS WHISTLING FOR THE DOG?
YIP YIP YIP

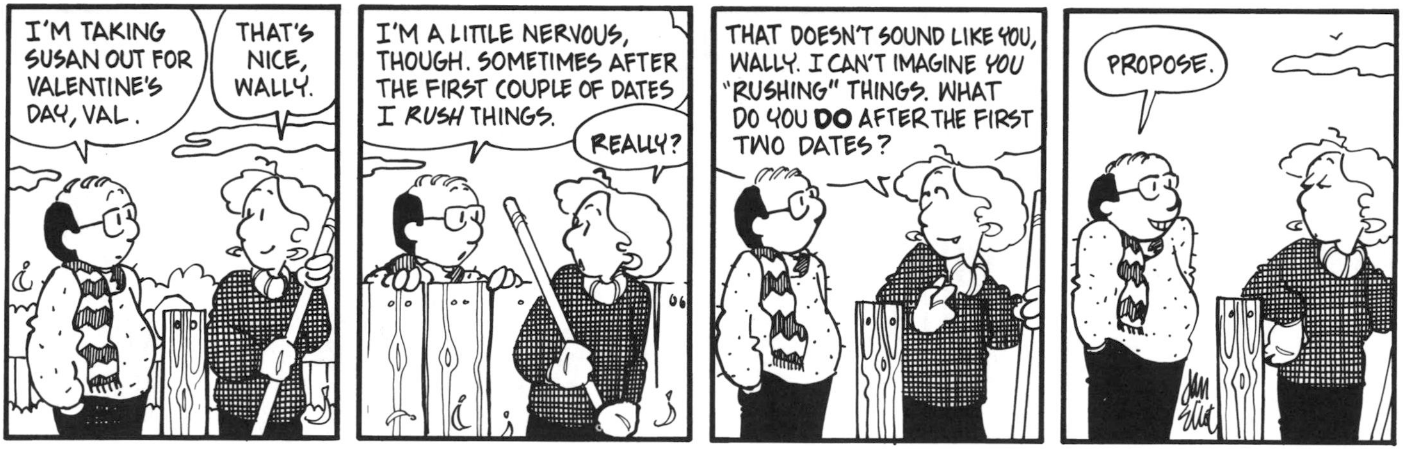
I'M TAKING SUSAN OUT FOR VALENTINE'S DAY, VAL.
THAT'S NICE, WALLY.
I'M A LITTLE NERVOUS, THOUGH. SOMETIMES AFTER THE FIRST COUPLE OF DATES I *RUSH* THINGS.
REALLY?
THAT DOESN'T SOUND LIKE YOU, WALLY. I CAN'T IMAGINE *YOU* "RUSHING" THINGS. WHAT DO YOU **DO** AFTER THE FIRST TWO DATES?
PROPOSE.

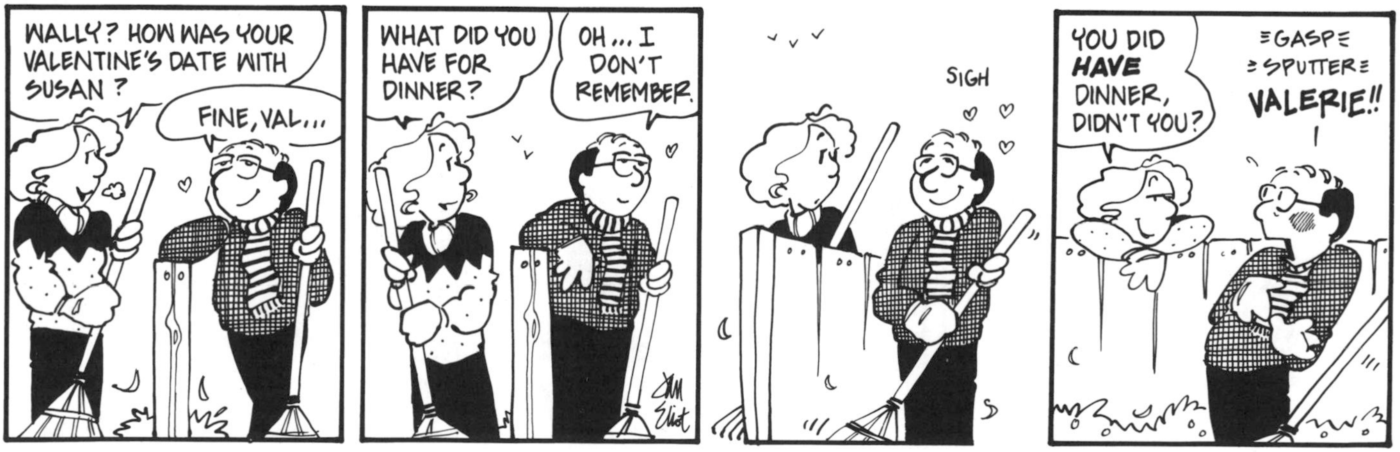
WALLY? HOW WAS YOUR VALENTINE'S DATE WITH SUSAN?
FINE, VAL...
WHAT DID YOU HAVE FOR DINNER?
OH... I DON'T REMEMBER.
SIGH
YOU DID **HAVE** DINNER, DIDN'T YOU?
GASP
SPUTTER
VALERIE!!

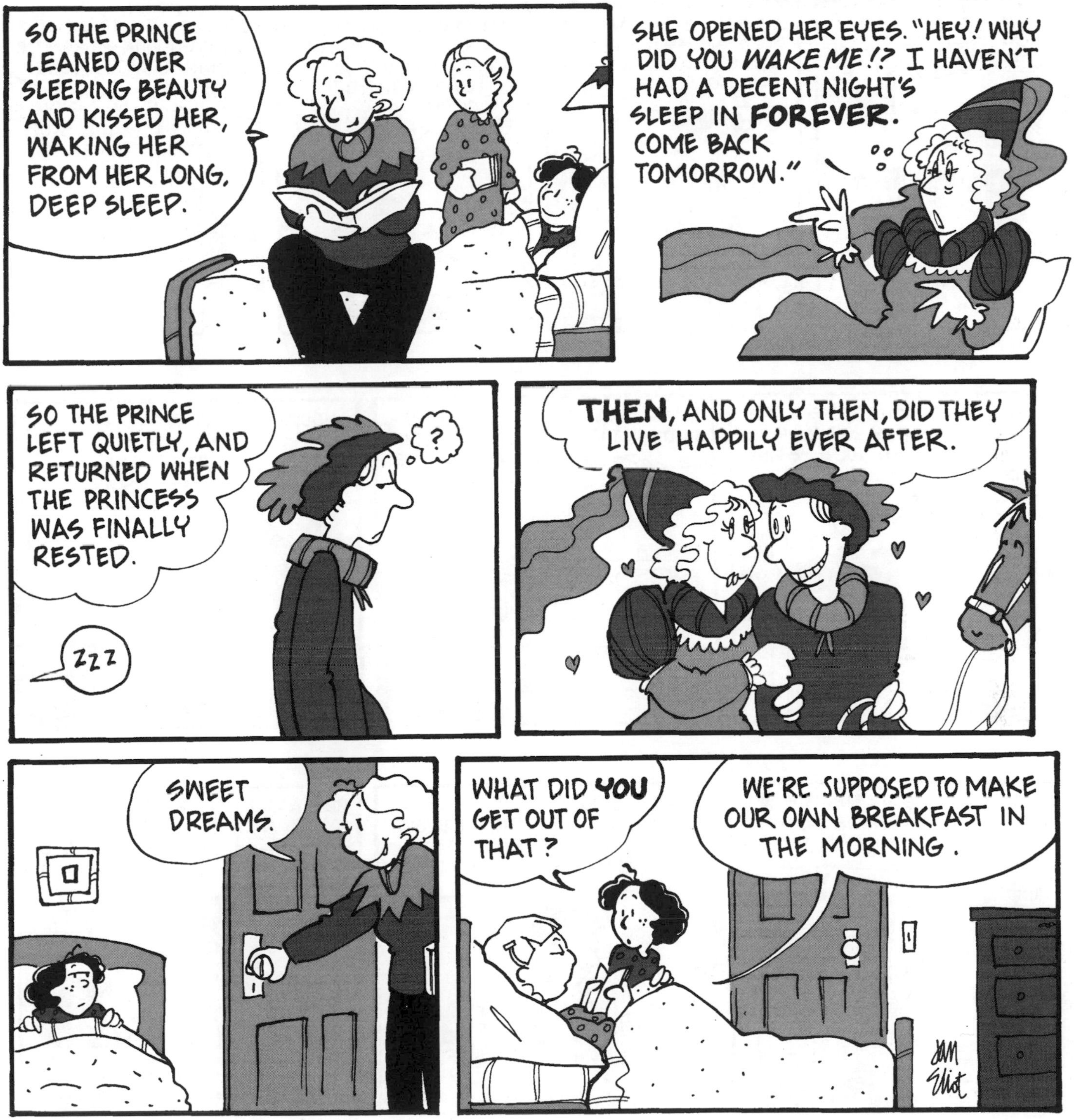
SO THE PRINCE LEANED OVER SLEEPING BEAUTY AND KISSED HER, WAKING HER FROM HER LONG, DEEP SLEEP.
SHE OPENED HER EYES. "HEY! WHY DID YOU WAKE ME!? I HAVEN'T HAD A DECENT NIGHT'S SLEEP IN FOREVER. COME BACK TOMORROW."
SO THE PRINCE LEFT QUIETLY, AND RETURNED WHEN THE PRINCESS WAS FINALLY RESTED.
?
ZZZ
THEN, AND ONLY THEN, DID THEY LIVE HAPPILY EVER AFTER.
SWEET DREAMS.
WHAT DID YOU GET OUT OF THAT?
WE'RE SUPPOSED TO MAKE OUR OWN BREAKFAST IN THE MORNING.
JAN ELIOT

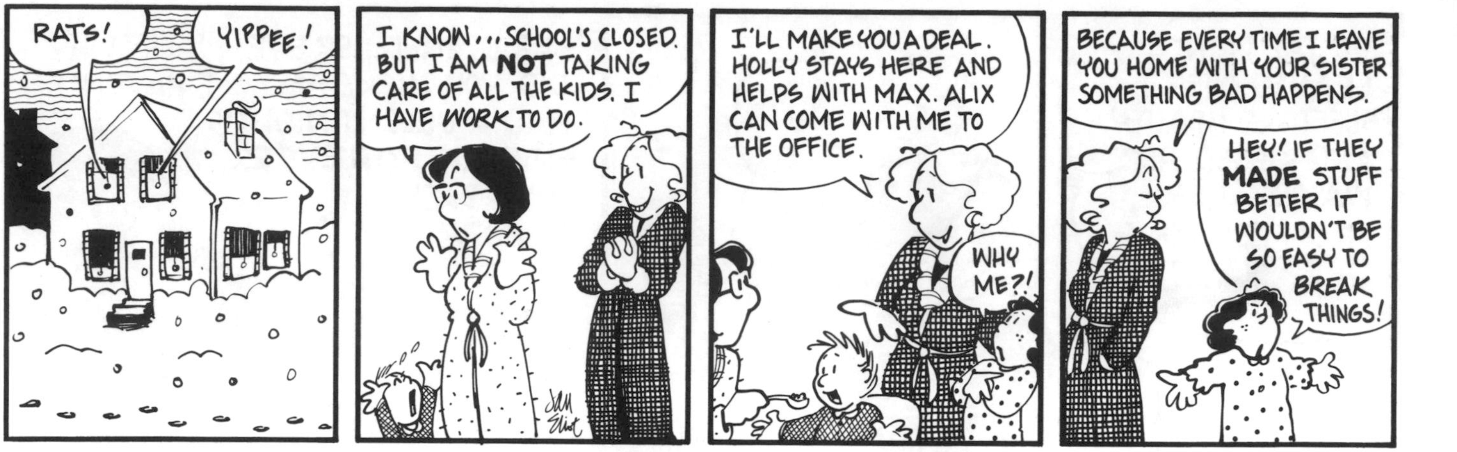
RATS!
YIPPEE!
I KNOW... SCHOOL'S CLOSED. BUT I AM NOT TAKING CARE OF ALL THE KIDS. I HAVE WORK TO DO.
I'LL MAKE YOU A DEAL. HOLLY STAYS HERE AND HELPS WITH MAX. ALIX CAN COME WITH ME TO THE OFFICE.
WHY ME?!
BECAUSE EVERY TIME I LEAVE YOU HOME WITH YOUR SISTER SOMETHING BAD HAPPENS.
HEY! IF THEY MADE STUFF BETTER IT WOULDN'T BE SO EASY TO BREAK THINGS!

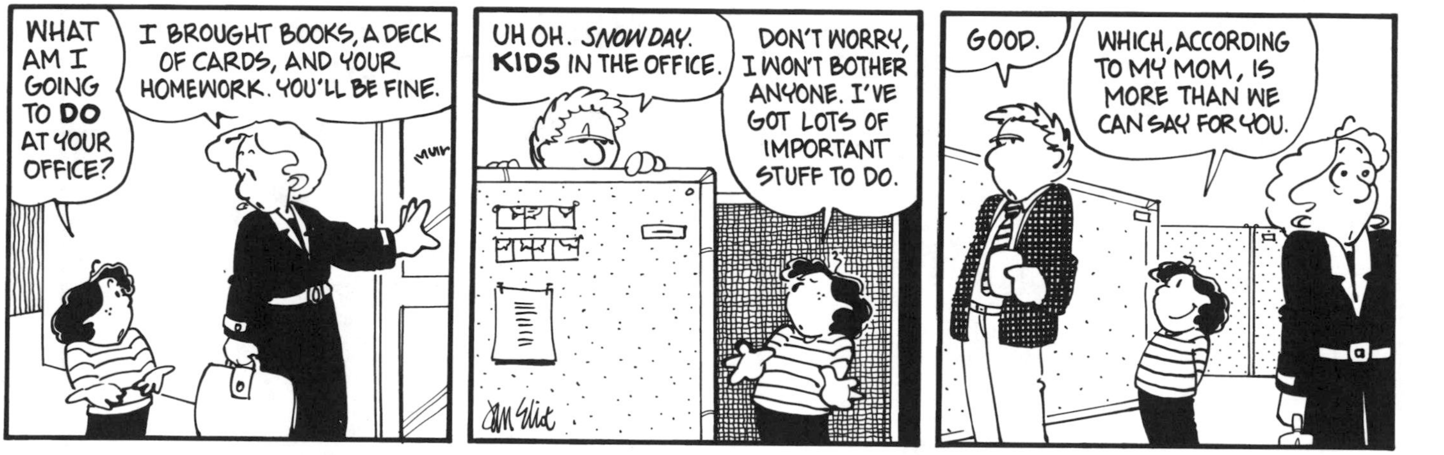
WHAT AM I GOING TO DO AT YOUR OFFICE?
I BROUGHT BOOKS, A DECK OF CARDS, AND YOUR HOMEWORK. YOU'LL BE FINE.
UH OH. SNOW DAY. KIDS IN THE OFFICE.
DON'T WORRY, I WON'T BOTHER ANYONE. I'VE GOT LOTS OF IMPORTANT STUFF TO DO.
GOOD.
WHICH, ACCORDING TO MY MOM, IS MORE THAN WE CAN SAY FOR YOU.

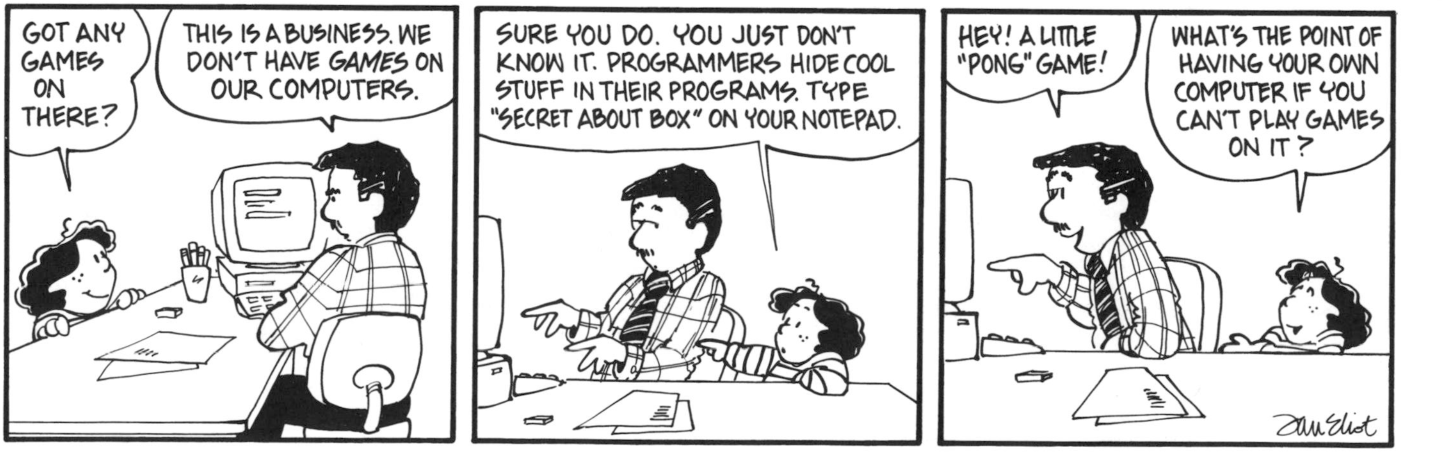
GOT ANY GAMES ON THERE?
THIS IS A BUSINESS. WE DON'T HAVE GAMES ON OUR COMPUTERS.
SURE YOU DO. YOU JUST DON'T KNOW IT. PROGRAMMERS HIDE COOL STUFF IN THEIR PROGRAMS. TYPE "SECRET ABOUT BOX" ON YOUR NOTEPAD.
HEY! A LITTLE "PONG" GAME!
WHAT'S THE POINT OF HAVING YOUR OWN COMPUTER IF YOU CAN'T PLAY GAMES ON IT?

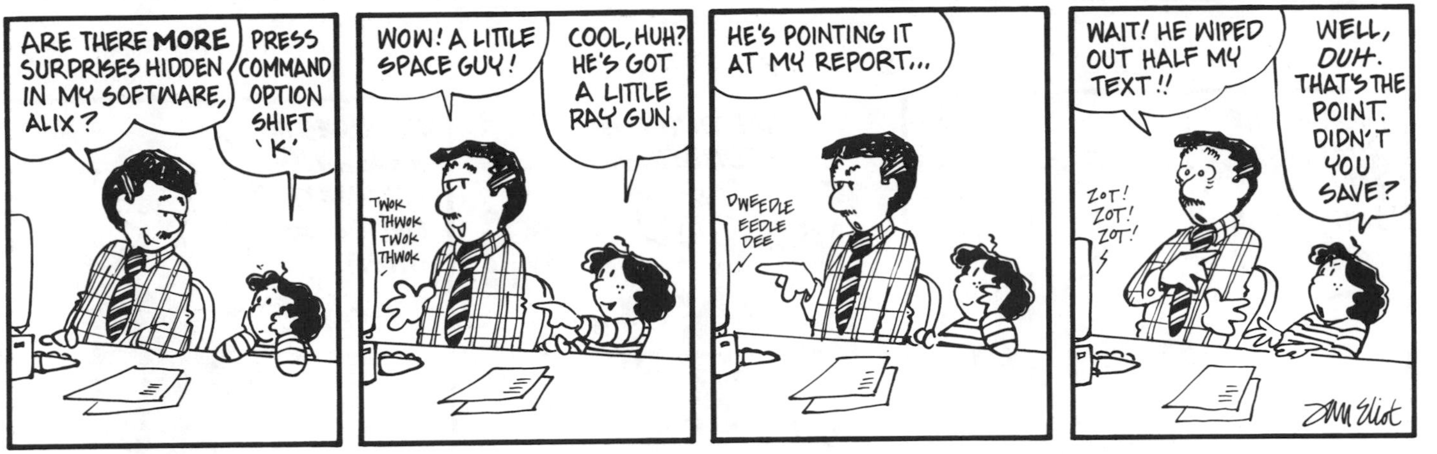
ARE THERE **MORE** SURPRISES HIDDEN IN MY SOFTWARE, ALIX?
PRESS COMMAND OPTION SHIFT 'K'
WOW! A LITTLE SPACE GUY!
COOL, HUH? HE'S GOT A LITTLE RAY GUN.
TWOK THWOK TWOK THWOK
HE'S POINTING IT AT MY REPORT...
DWEEDLE EEDLE DEE
WAIT! HE WIPED OUT HALF MY TEXT!!
WELL, *DUH*. THAT'S THE POINT. DIDN'T YOU SAVE?
ZOT! ZOT! ZOT!
Jan Eliot

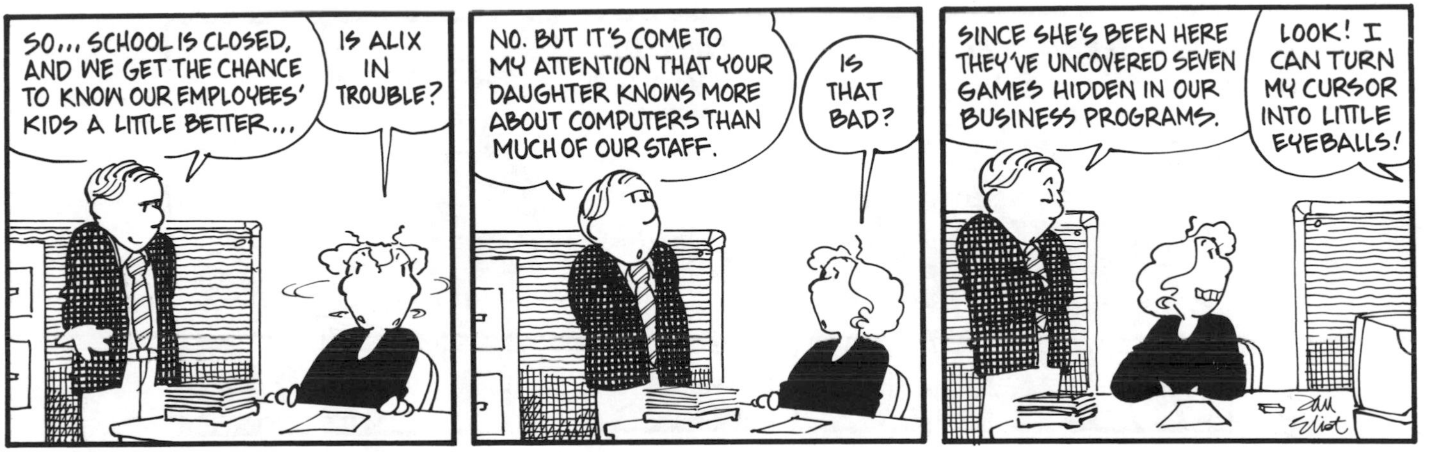
SO... SCHOOL IS CLOSED, AND WE GET THE CHANCE TO KNOW OUR EMPLOYEES' KIDS A LITTLE BETTER...
IS ALIX IN TROUBLE?
NO. BUT IT'S COME TO MY ATTENTION THAT YOUR DAUGHTER KNOWS MORE ABOUT COMPUTERS THAN MUCH OF OUR STAFF.
IS THAT BAD?
SINCE SHE'S BEEN HERE THEY'VE UNCOVERED SEVEN GAMES HIDDEN IN OUR BUSINESS PROGRAMS.
LOOK! I CAN TURN MY CURSOR INTO LITTLE EYEBALLS!
Jan Eliot

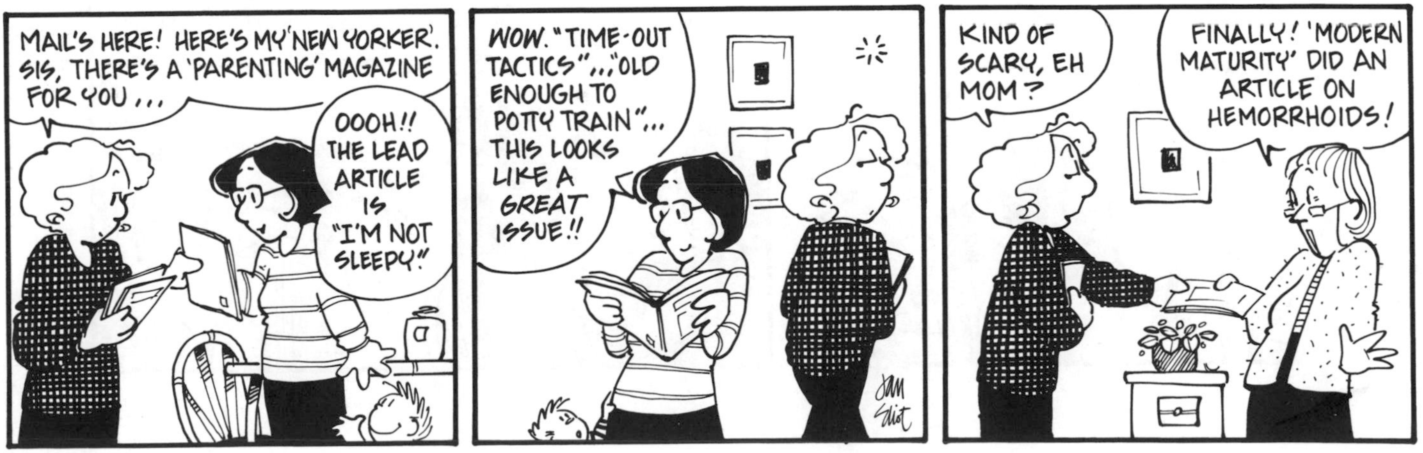
MAIL'S HERE! HERE'S MY 'NEW YORKER'. SIS, THERE'S A 'PARENTING' MAGAZINE FOR YOU...
OOOH!! THE LEAD ARTICLE IS "I'M NOT SLEEPY!"
WOW. "TIME-OUT TACTICS"..."OLD ENOUGH TO POTTY TRAIN"... THIS LOOKS LIKE A *GREAT* ISSUE!!
Jan Eliot
KIND OF SCARY, EH MOM?
FINALLY! 'MODERN MATURITY' DID AN ARTICLE ON HEMORRHOIDS!

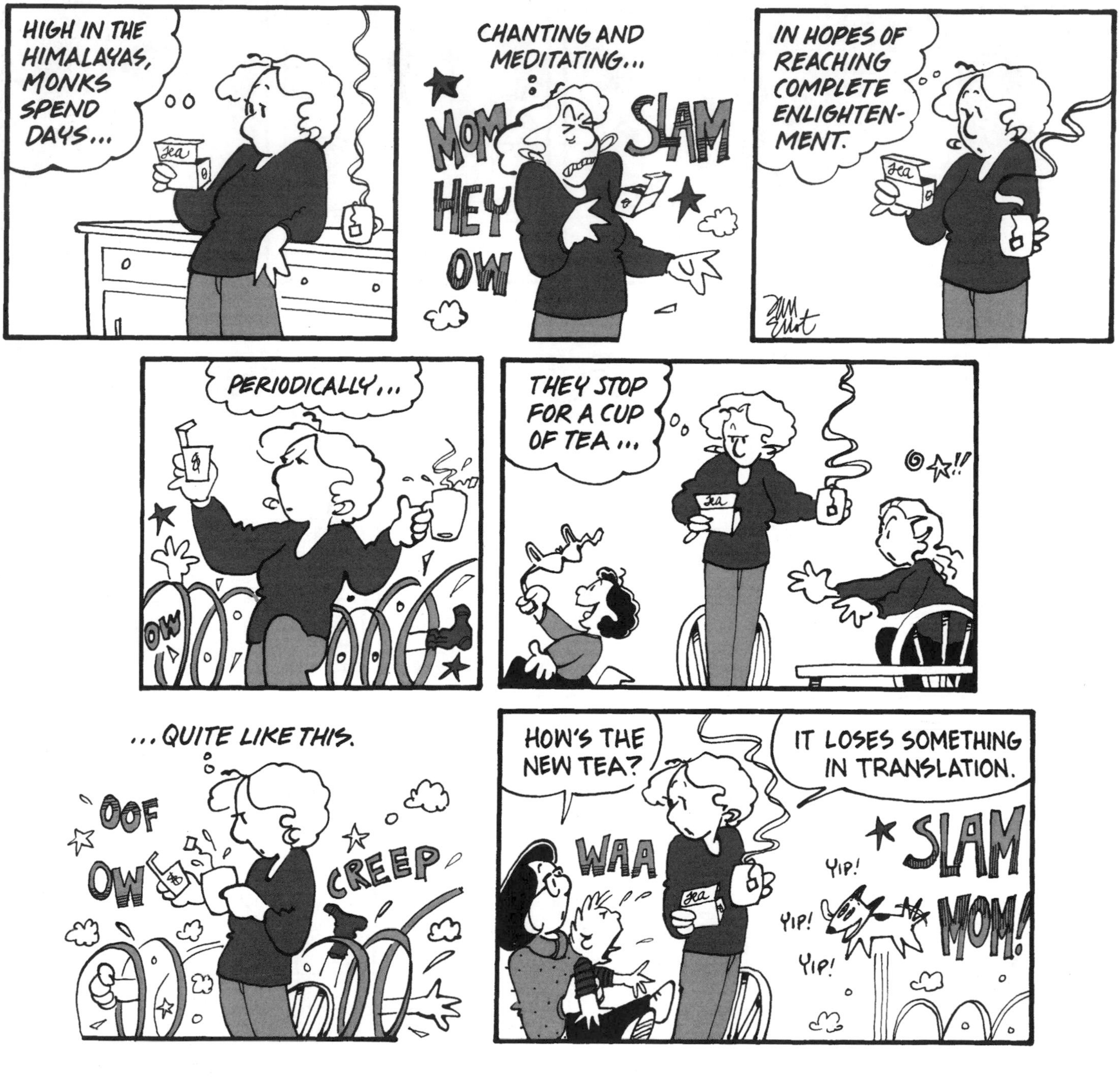
HIGH IN THE HIMALAYAS, MONKS SPEND DAYS...
CHANTING AND MEDITATING...
MOM
HEY
OW
SLAM
IN HOPES OF REACHING COMPLETE ENLIGHTEN-MENT.
PERIODICALLY...
OW
THEY STOP FOR A CUP OF TEA...
...QUITE LIKE THIS.
OOF
OW
CREEP
HOW'S THE NEW TEA?
IT LOSES SOMETHING IN TRANSLATION.
WAA
SLAM
YIP!
YIP!
YIP!
MOM!

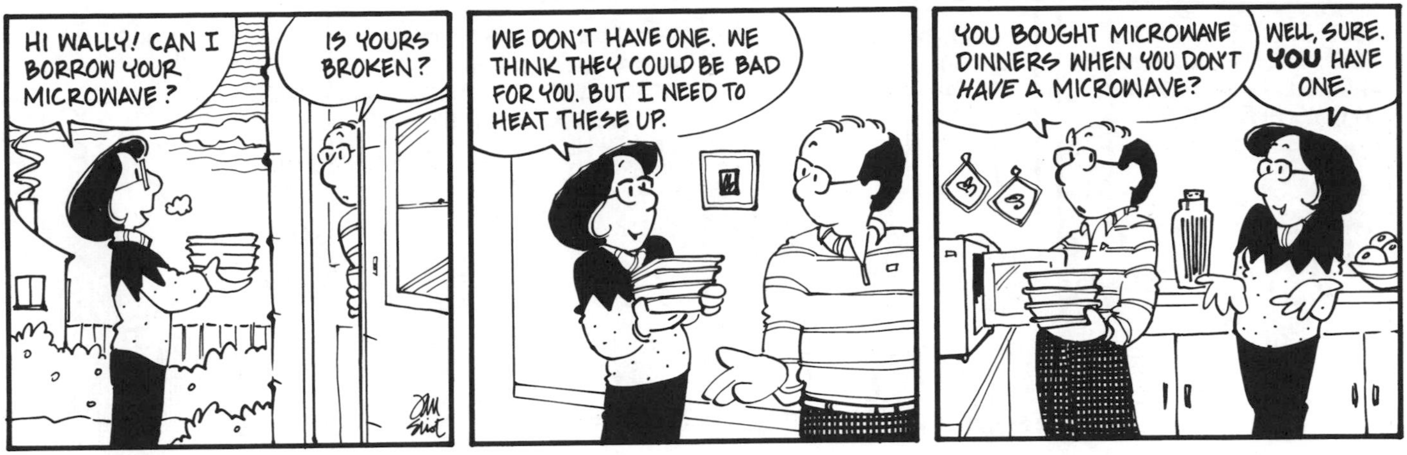
HI WALLY! CAN I BORROW YOUR MICROWAVE?
IS YOURS BROKEN?
WE DON'T HAVE ONE. WE THINK THEY COULD BE BAD FOR YOU. BUT I NEED TO HEAT THESE UP.
YOU BOUGHT MICROWAVE DINNERS WHEN YOU DON'T *HAVE* A MICROWAVE?
WELL, SURE. **YOU** HAVE ONE.

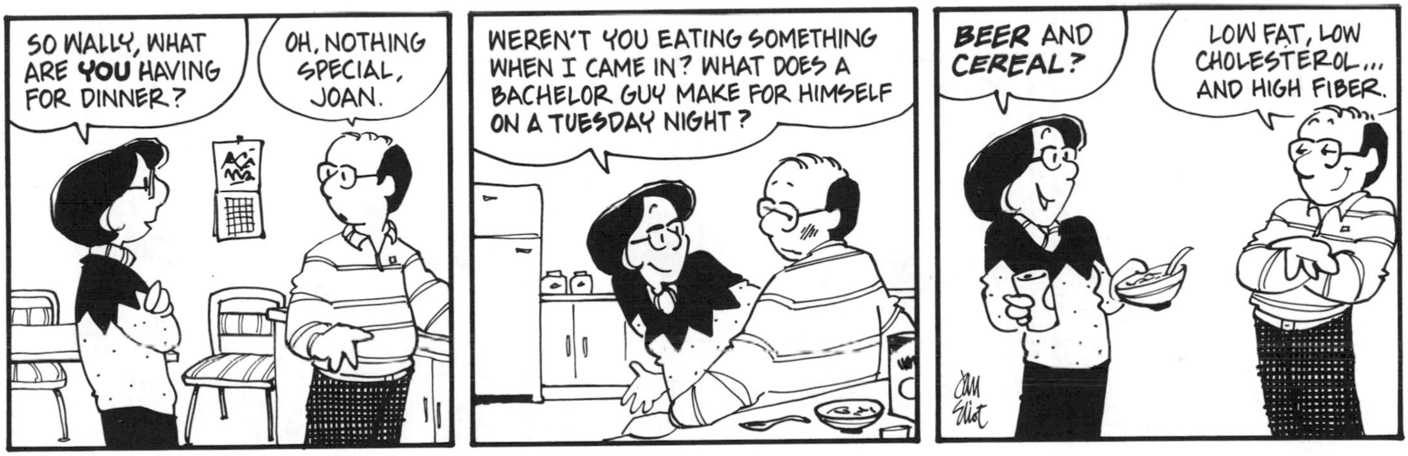
SO WALLY, WHAT ARE **YOU** HAVING FOR DINNER?
OH, NOTHING SPECIAL, JOAN.
WEREN'T YOU EATING SOMETHING WHEN I CAME IN? WHAT DOES A BACHELOR GUY MAKE FOR HIMSELF ON A TUESDAY NIGHT?
BEER AND **CEREAL?**
LOW FAT, LOW CHOLESTEROL... AND HIGH FIBER.

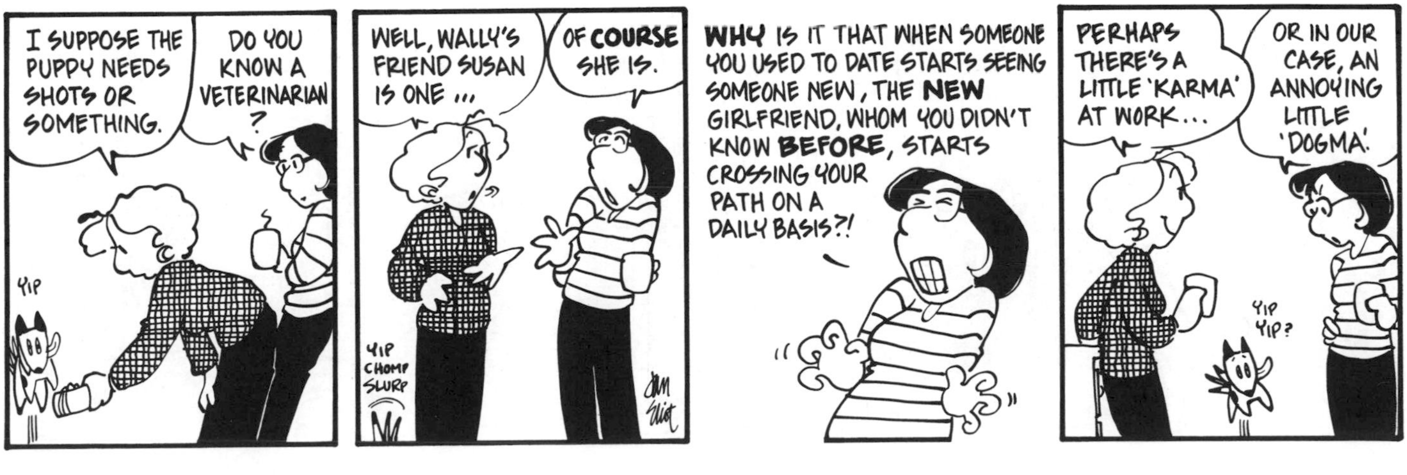
I SUPPOSE THE PUPPY NEEDS SHOTS OR SOMETHING.
DO YOU KNOW A VETERINARIAN?
YIP
WELL, WALLY'S FRIEND SUSAN IS ONE...
OF **COURSE** SHE IS.
YIP CHOMP SLURP
WHY IS IT THAT WHEN SOMEONE YOU USED TO DATE STARTS SEEING SOMEONE NEW, THE **NEW** GIRLFRIEND, WHOM YOU DIDN'T KNOW **BEFORE**, STARTS CROSSING YOUR PATH ON A DAILY BASIS?!
PERHAPS THERE'S A LITTLE 'KARMA' AT WORK...
OR IN OUR CASE, AN ANNOYING LITTLE 'DOGMA'.
YIP YIP?

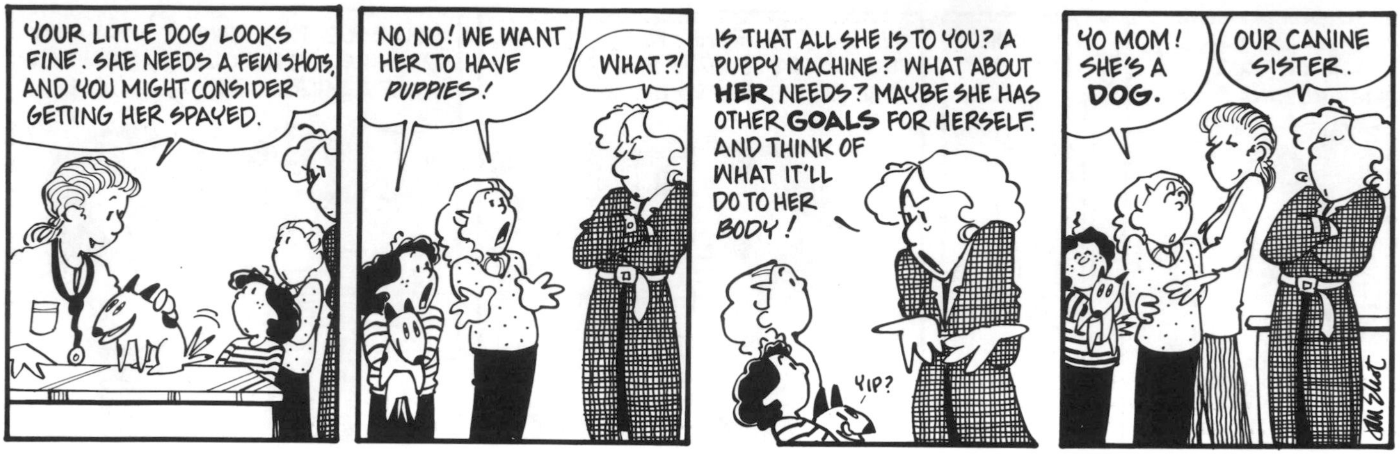
YOUR LITTLE DOG LOOKS FINE. SHE NEEDS A FEW SHOTS, AND YOU MIGHT CONSIDER GETTING HER SPAYED.
NO NO! WE WANT HER TO HAVE *PUPPIES*!
WHAT?!
IS THAT ALL SHE IS TO YOU? A PUPPY MACHINE? WHAT ABOUT **HER** NEEDS? MAYBE SHE HAS OTHER **GOALS** FOR HERSELF. AND THINK OF WHAT IT'LL DO TO HER *BODY*!
YIP?
YO MOM! SHE'S A **DOG**.
OUR CANINE SISTER.

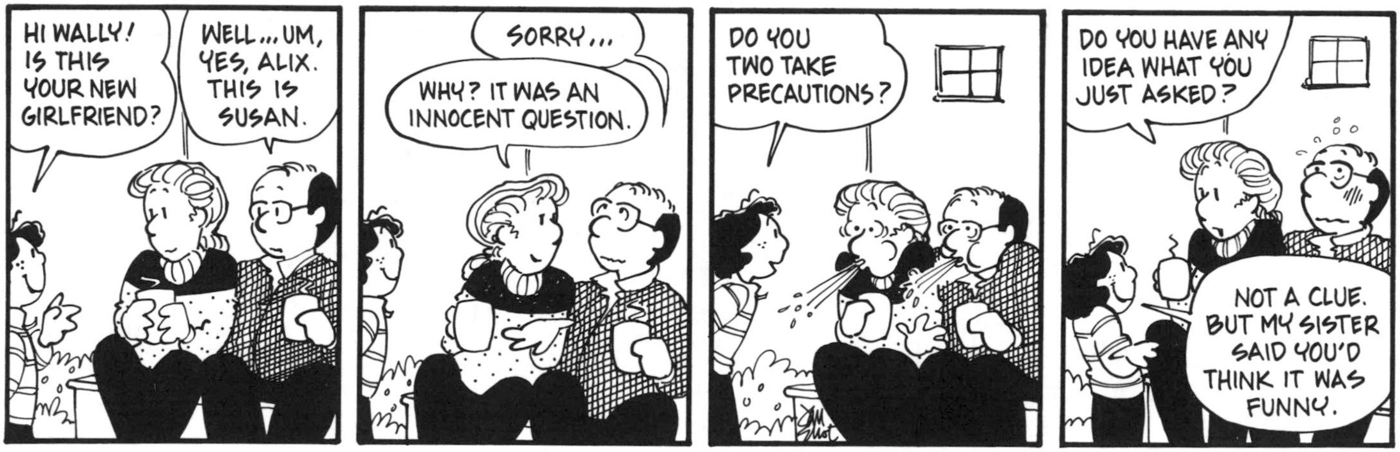
HI WALLY! IS THIS YOUR NEW GIRLFRIEND?
WELL... UM, YES, ALIX. THIS IS SUSAN.
SORRY...
WHY? IT WAS AN INNOCENT QUESTION.
DO YOU TWO TAKE PRECAUTIONS?
DO YOU HAVE ANY IDEA WHAT YOU JUST ASKED?
NOT A CLUE. BUT MY SISTER SAID YOU'D THINK IT WAS FUNNY.

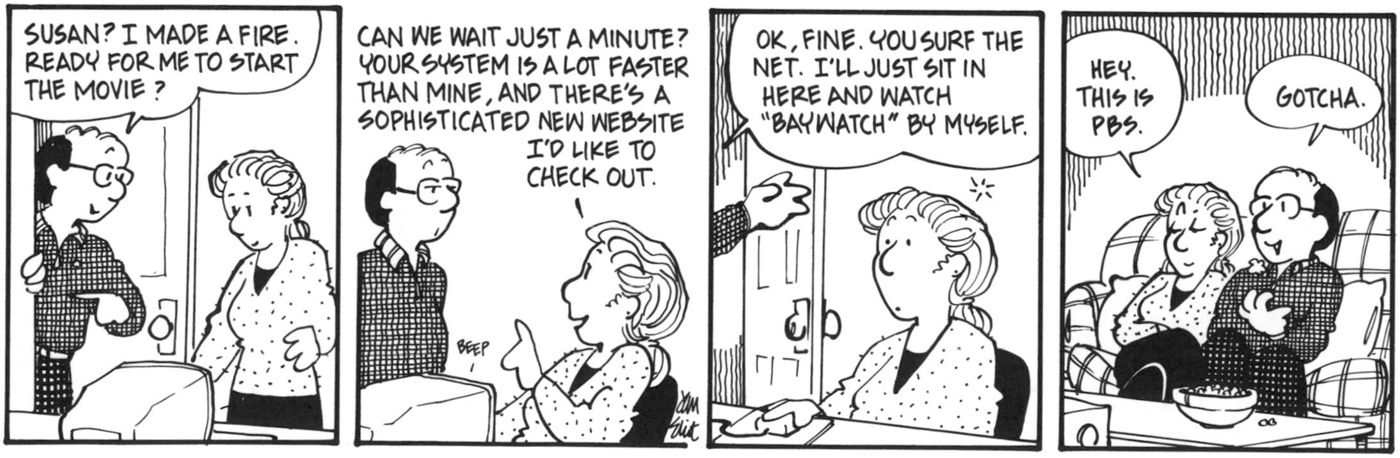
SUSAN? I MADE A FIRE. READY FOR ME TO START THE MOVIE?
CAN WE WAIT JUST A MINUTE? YOUR SYSTEM IS A LOT FASTER THAN MINE, AND THERE'S A SOPHISTICATED NEW WEBSITE I'D LIKE TO CHECK OUT.
BEEP
OK, FINE. YOU SURF THE NET. I'LL JUST SIT IN HERE AND WATCH "BAYWATCH" BY MYSELF.
HEY. THIS IS PBS.
GOTCHA.

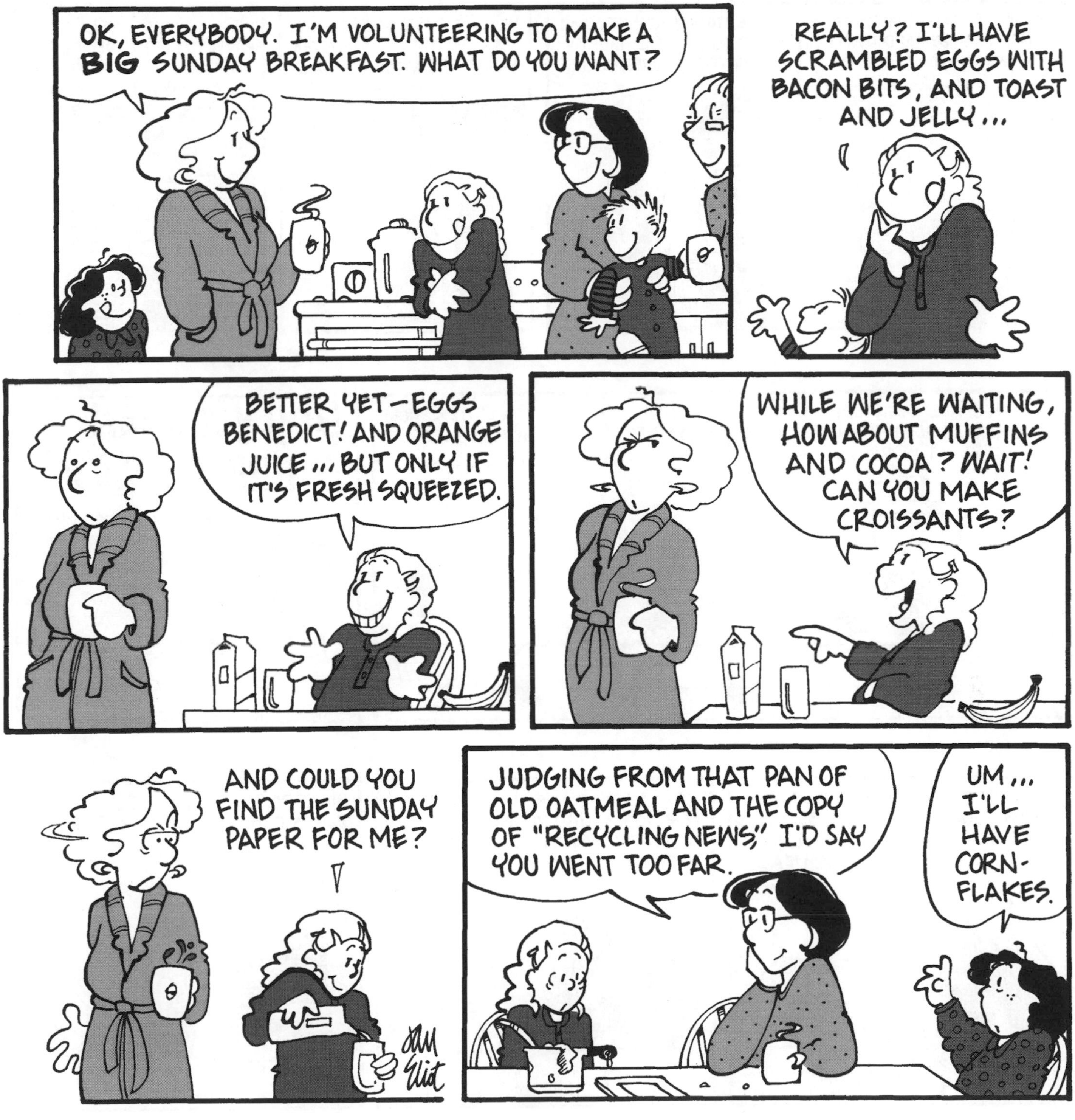
OK, EVERYBODY. I'M VOLUNTEERING TO MAKE A BIG SUNDAY BREAKFAST. WHAT DO YOU WANT?
REALLY? I'LL HAVE SCRAMBLED EGGS WITH BACON BITS, AND TOAST AND JELLY...
BETTER YET–EGGS BENEDICT! AND ORANGE JUICE... BUT ONLY IF IT'S FRESH SQUEEZED.
WHILE WE'RE WAITING, HOW ABOUT MUFFINS AND COCOA? WAIT! CAN YOU MAKE CROISSANTS?
AND COULD YOU FIND THE SUNDAY PAPER FOR ME?
JUDGING FROM THAT PAN OF OLD OATMEAL AND THE COPY OF "RECYCLING NEWS," I'D SAY YOU WENT TOO FAR.
UM... I'LL HAVE CORN-FLAKES.

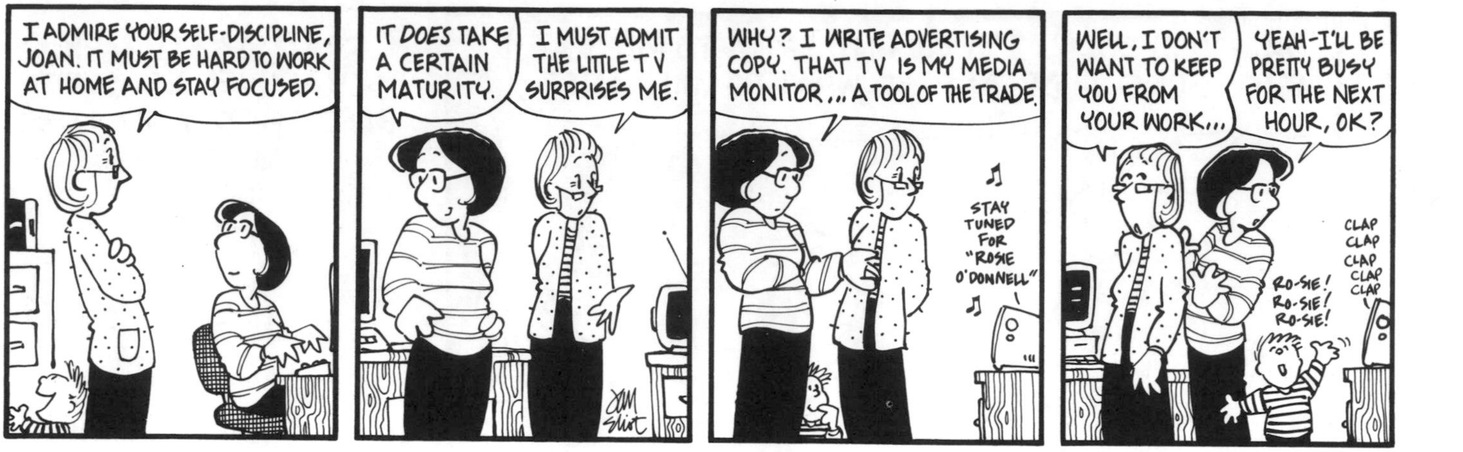
I ADMIRE YOUR SELF-DISCIPLINE, JOAN. IT MUST BE HARD TO WORK AT HOME AND STAY FOCUSED.
IT DOES TAKE A CERTAIN MATURITY.
I MUST ADMIT THE LITTLE TV SURPRISES ME.
WHY? I WRITE ADVERTISING COPY. THAT TV IS MY MEDIA MONITOR ... A TOOL OF THE TRADE.
STAY TUNED FOR "ROSIE O'DONNELL"
WELL, I DON'T WANT TO KEEP YOU FROM YOUR WORK...
YEAH-I'LL BE PRETTY BUSY FOR THE NEXT HOUR, OK?
RO-SIE! RO-SIE! RO-SIE!
CLAP CLAP CLAP CLAP CLAP

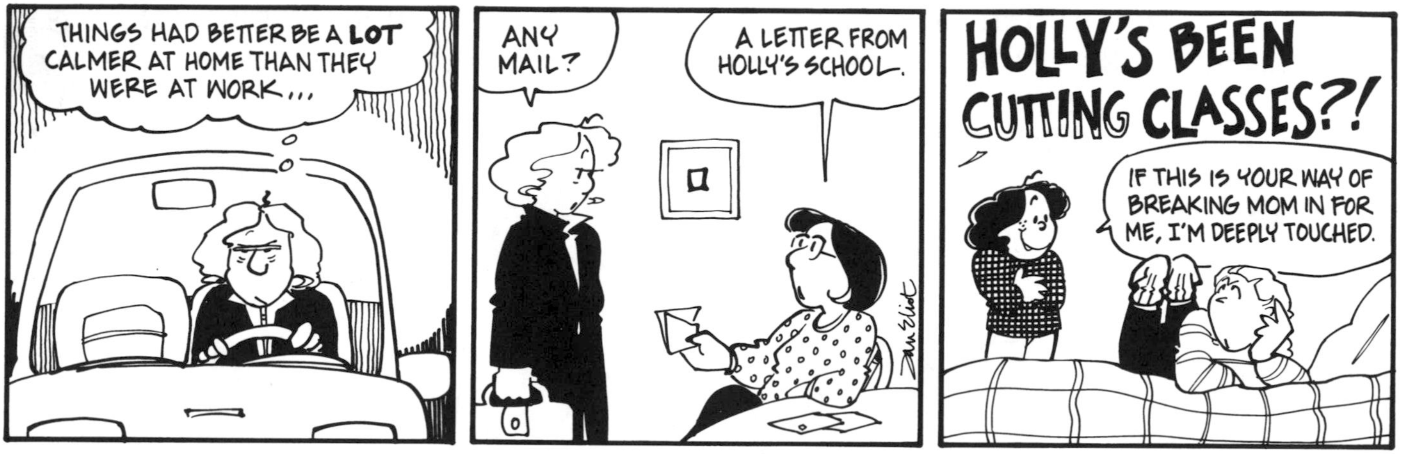
THINGS HAD BETTER BE A LOT CALMER AT HOME THAN THEY WERE AT WORK...
ANY MAIL?
A LETTER FROM HOLLY'S SCHOOL.
HOLLY'S BEEN CUTTING CLASSES?!
IF THIS IS YOUR WAY OF BREAKING MOM IN FOR ME, I'M DEEPLY TOUCHED.

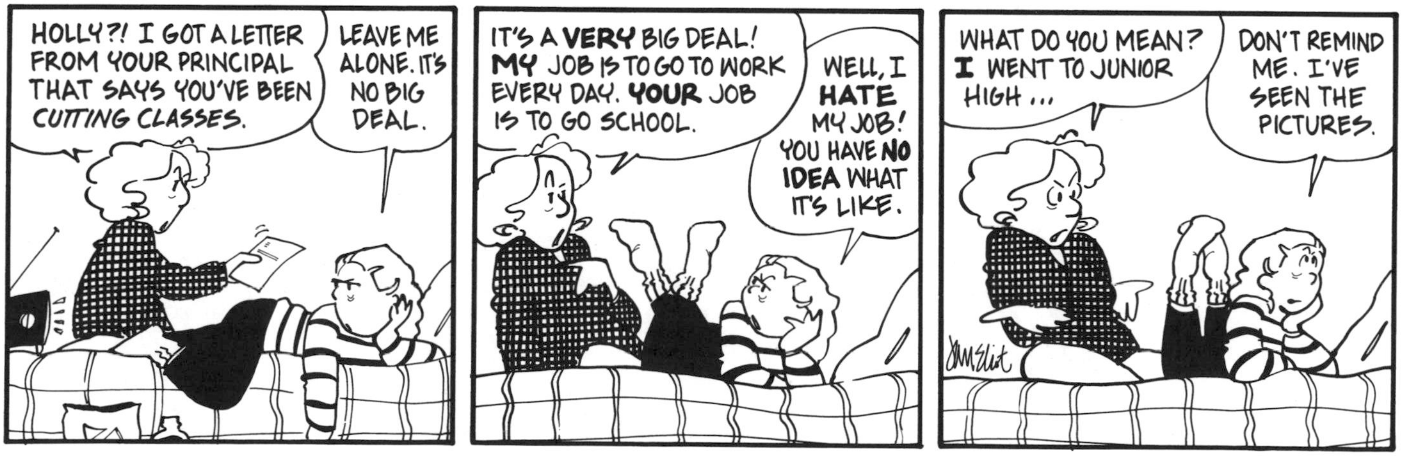
HOLLY?! I GOT A LETTER FROM YOUR PRINCIPAL THAT SAYS YOU'VE BEEN CUTTING CLASSES.
LEAVE ME ALONE. IT'S NO BIG DEAL.
IT'S A VERY BIG DEAL! MY JOB IS TO GO TO WORK EVERY DAY. YOUR JOB IS TO GO SCHOOL.
WELL, I HATE MY JOB! YOU HAVE NO IDEA WHAT IT'S LIKE.
WHAT DO YOU MEAN? I WENT TO JUNIOR HIGH ...
DON'T REMIND ME. I'VE SEEN THE PICTURES.

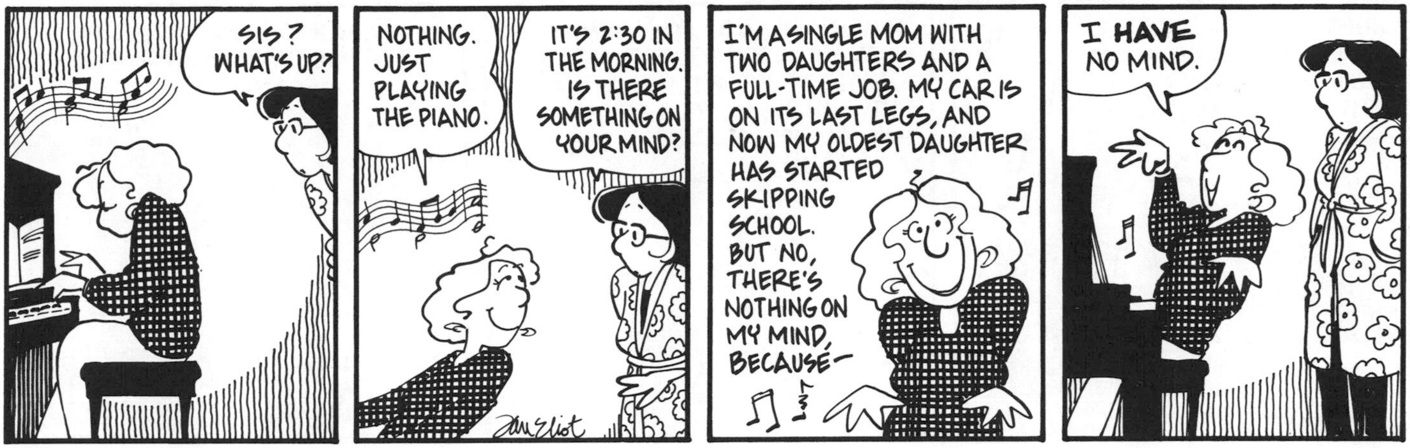
SIS? WHAT'S UP?
NOTHING. JUST PLAYING THE PIANO.
IT'S 2:30 IN THE MORNING. IS THERE SOMETHING ON YOUR MIND?
I'M A SINGLE MOM WITH TWO DAUGHTERS AND A FULL-TIME JOB. MY CAR IS ON ITS LAST LEGS, AND NOW MY OLDEST DAUGHTER HAS STARTED SKIPPING SCHOOL. BUT NO, THERE'S NOTHING ON MY MIND, BECAUSE–
I **HAVE** NO MIND.

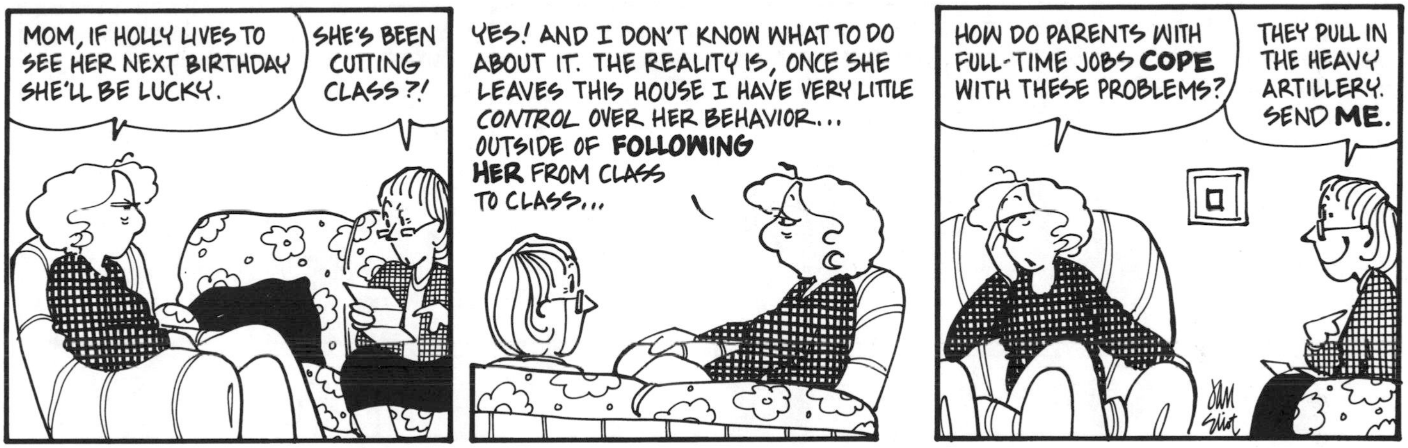
MOM, IF HOLLY LIVES TO SEE HER NEXT BIRTHDAY SHE'LL BE LUCKY.
SHE'S BEEN CUTTING CLASS?!
YES! AND I DON'T KNOW WHAT TO DO ABOUT IT. THE REALITY IS, ONCE SHE LEAVES THIS HOUSE I HAVE VERY LITTLE *CONTROL* OVER HER BEHAVIOR... OUTSIDE OF **FOLLOWING HER** FROM CLASS TO CLASS...
HOW DO PARENTS WITH FULL-TIME JOBS **COPE** WITH THESE PROBLEMS?
THEY PULL IN THE HEAVY ARTILLERY. SEND **ME.**

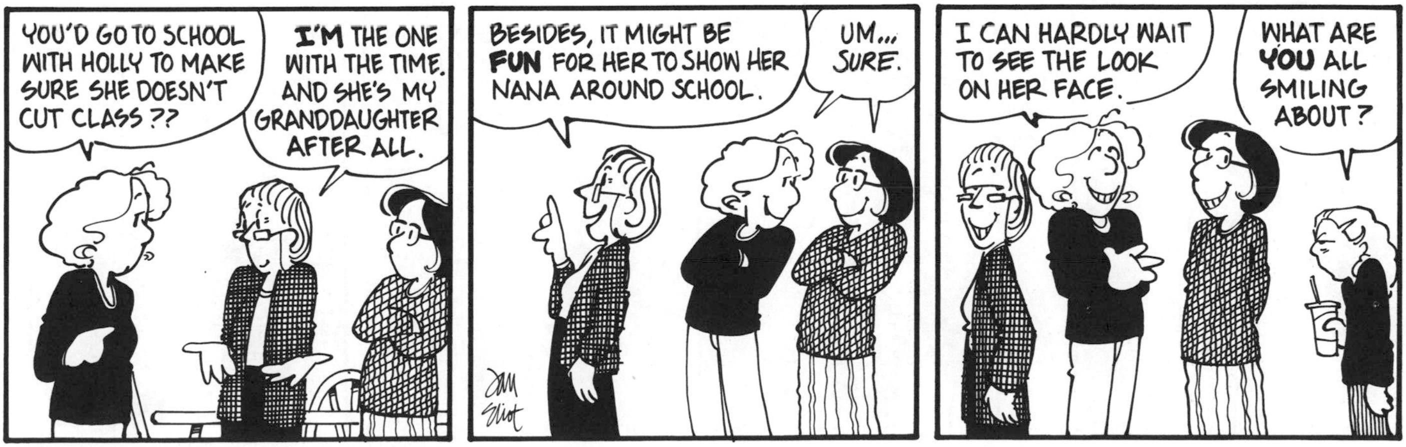
YOU'D GO TO SCHOOL WITH HOLLY TO MAKE SURE SHE DOESN'T CUT CLASS??
I'M THE ONE WITH THE TIME. AND SHE'S MY GRANDDAUGHTER AFTER ALL.
BESIDES, IT MIGHT BE **FUN** FOR HER TO SHOW HER NANA AROUND SCHOOL.
UM... *SURE.*
I CAN HARDLY WAIT TO SEE THE LOOK ON HER FACE.
WHAT ARE **YOU** ALL SMILING ABOUT?

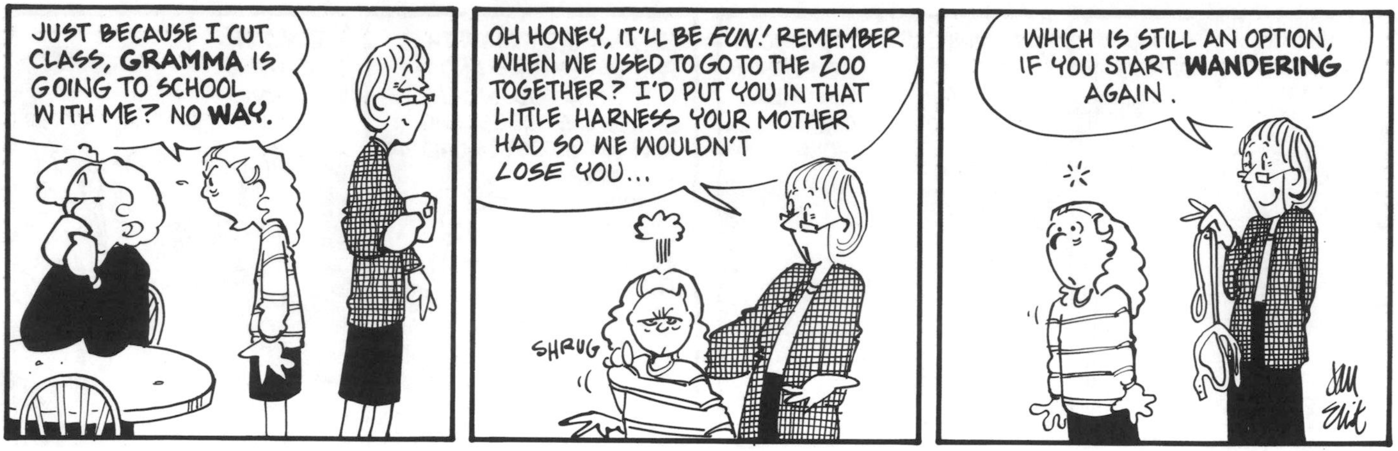
JUST BECAUSE I CUT CLASS, **GRAMMA** IS GOING TO SCHOOL WITH ME? NO **WAY**.
OH HONEY, IT'LL BE *FUN*! REMEMBER WHEN WE USED TO GO TO THE ZOO TOGETHER? I'D PUT YOU IN THAT LITTLE HARNESS YOUR MOTHER HAD SO WE WOULDN'T *LOSE* YOU...
SHRUG
WHICH IS STILL AN OPTION, IF YOU START **WANDERING** AGAIN.

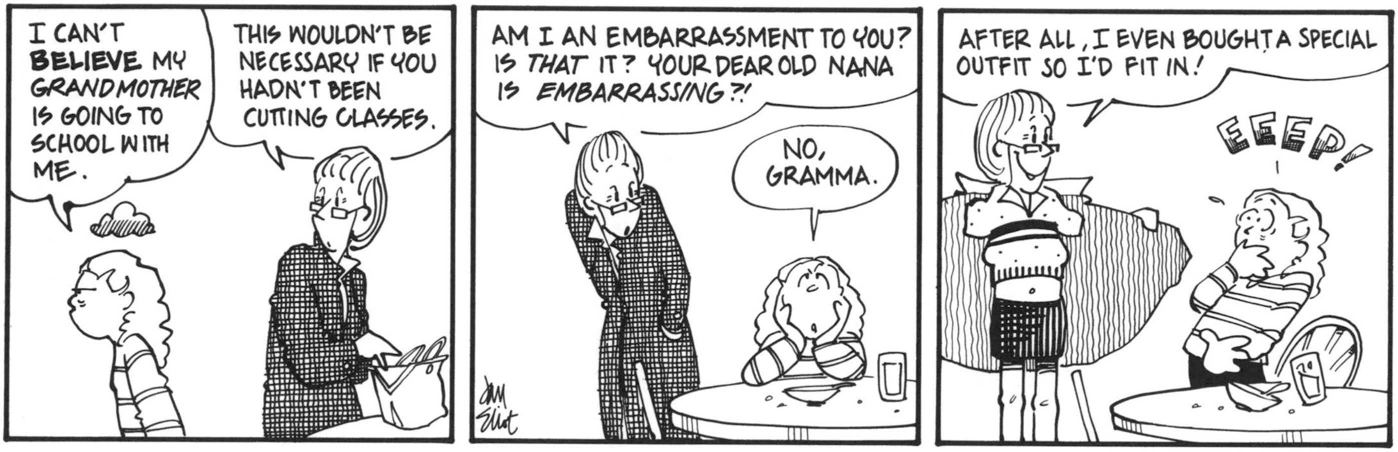
I CAN'T **BELIEVE** MY *GRANDMOTHER* IS GOING TO SCHOOL WITH ME.
THIS WOULDN'T BE NECESSARY IF YOU HADN'T BEEN CUTTING CLASSES.
AM I AN EMBARRASSMENT TO YOU? IS *THAT* IT? YOUR DEAR OLD NANA IS *EMBARRASSING*?!
NO, GRAMMA.
AFTER ALL, I EVEN BOUGHT A SPECIAL OUTFIT SO I'D FIT IN!
EEEP!

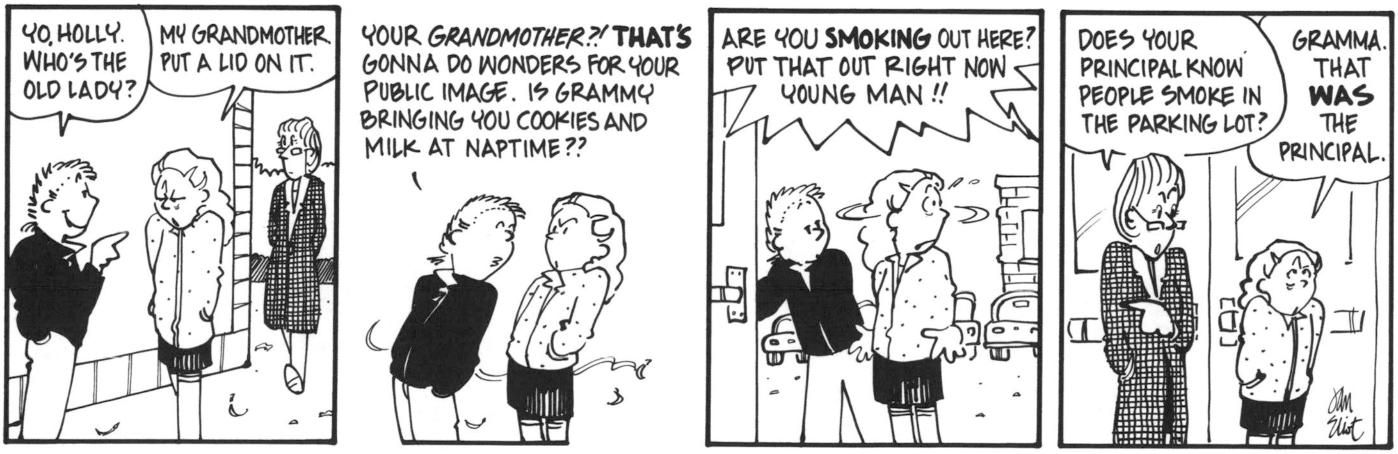
YO, HOLLY. WHO'S THE OLD LADY?
MY GRANDMOTHER. PUT A LID ON IT.
YOUR *GRANDMOTHER*?! **THAT'S** GONNA DO WONDERS FOR YOUR PUBLIC IMAGE. IS GRAMMY BRINGING YOU COOKIES AND MILK AT NAPTIME??
ARE YOU **SMOKING** OUT HERE? PUT THAT OUT RIGHT NOW YOUNG MAN!!
DOES YOUR PRINCIPAL KNOW PEOPLE SMOKE IN THE PARKING LOT?
GRAMMA. THAT **WAS** THE PRINCIPAL.

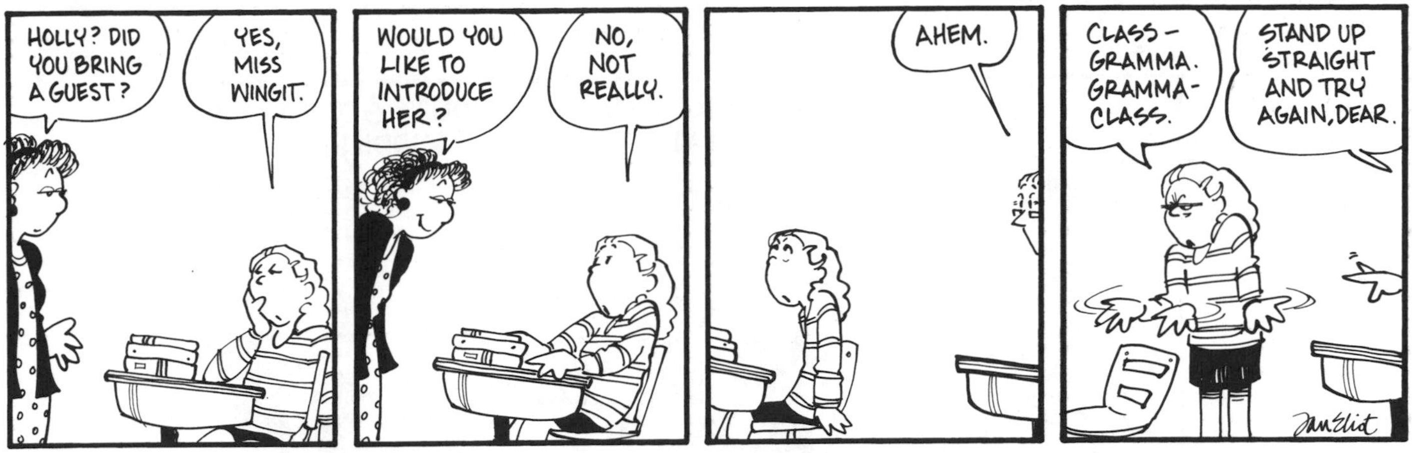
HOLLY? DID YOU BRING A GUEST?
YES, MISS WINGIT.
WOULD YOU LIKE TO INTRODUCE HER?
NO, NOT REALLY.
AHEM.
CLASS - GRAMMA. GRAMMA - CLASS.
STAND UP STRAIGHT AND TRY AGAIN, DEAR.

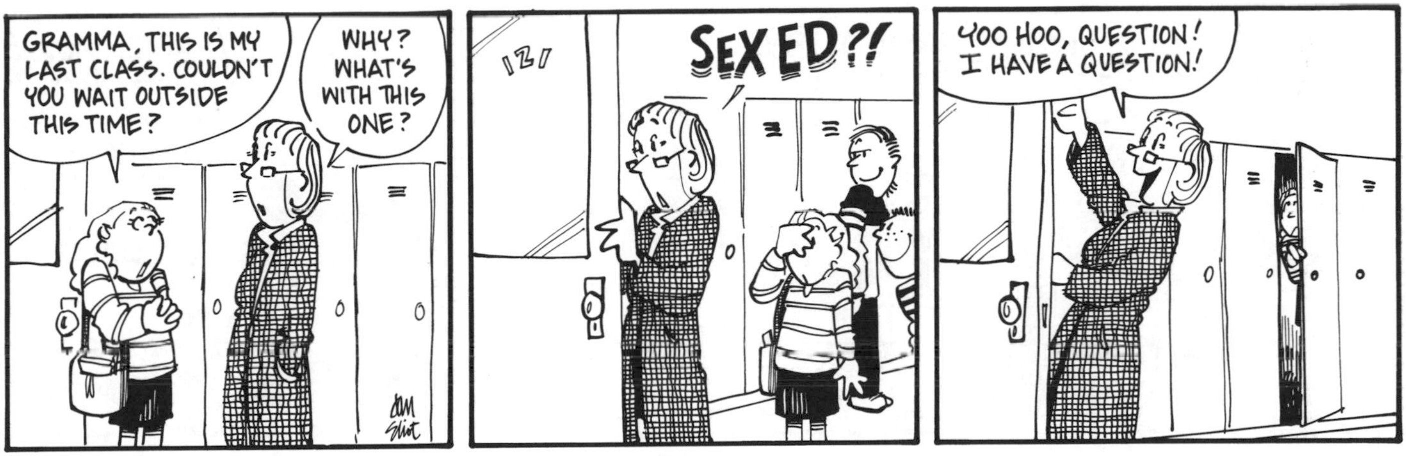
GRAMMA, THIS IS MY LAST CLASS. COULDN'T YOU WAIT OUTSIDE THIS TIME?
WHY? WHAT'S WITH THIS ONE?
SEX ED?!
YOO HOO, QUESTION! I HAVE A QUESTION!

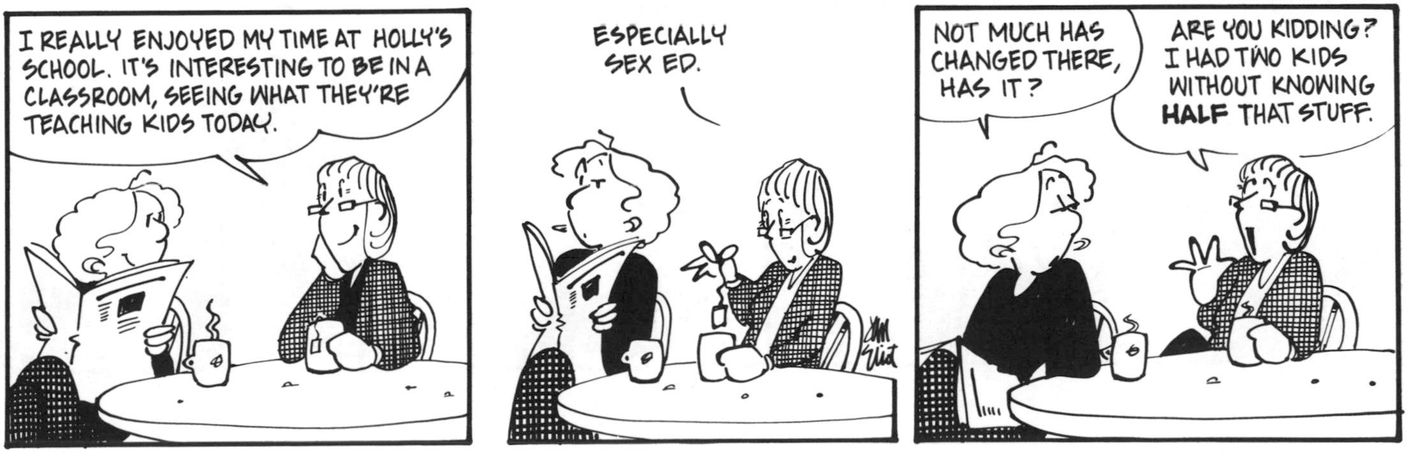
I REALLY ENJOYED MY TIME AT HOLLY'S SCHOOL. IT'S INTERESTING TO BE IN A CLASSROOM, SEEING WHAT THEY'RE TEACHING KIDS TODAY.
ESPECIALLY SEX ED.
NOT MUCH HAS CHANGED THERE, HAS IT?
ARE YOU KIDDING? I HAD TWO KIDS WITHOUT KNOWING HALF THAT STUFF.

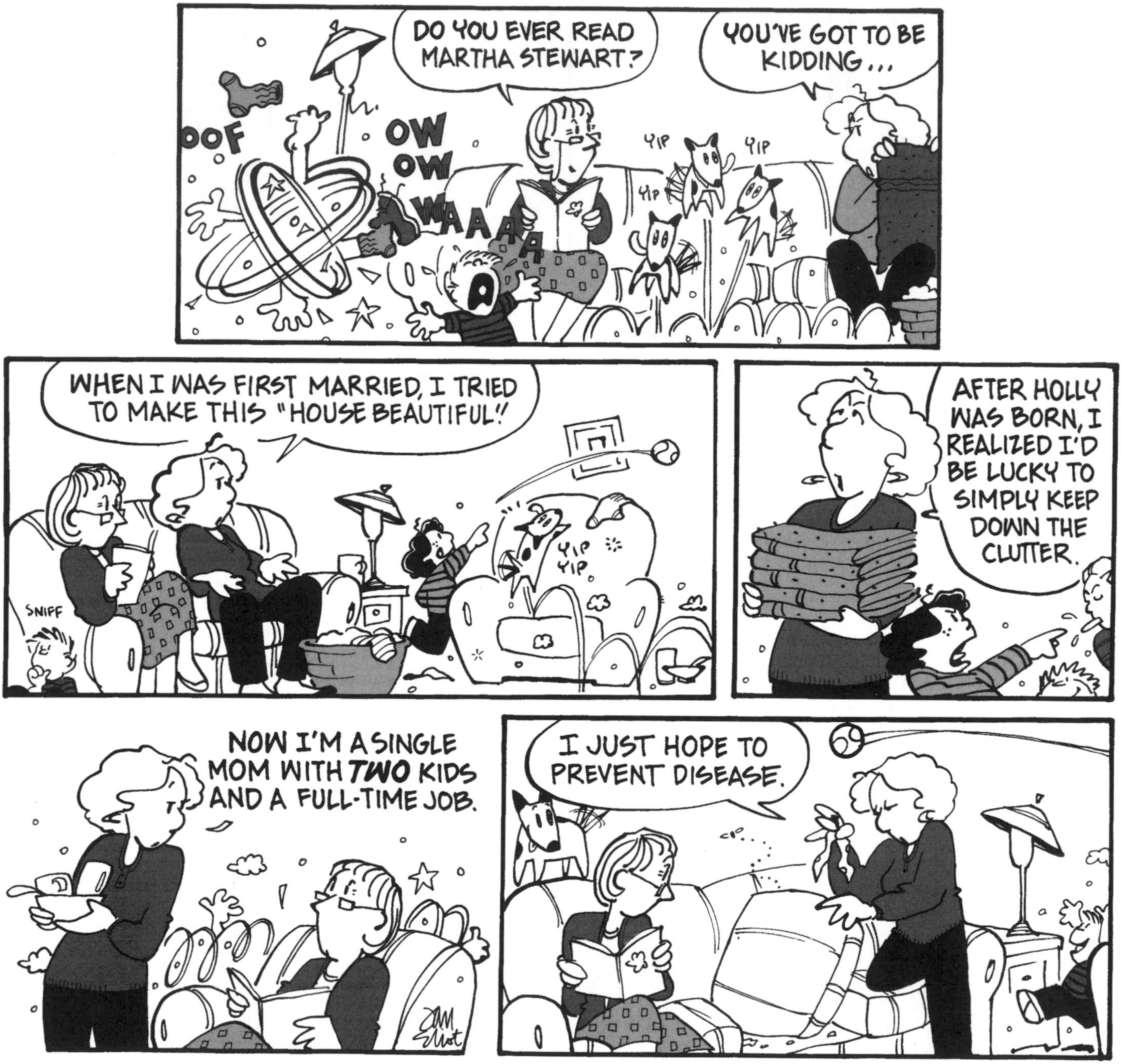
DO YOU EVER READ MARTHA STEWART?
YOU'VE GOT TO BE KIDDING...
OOF
OW
OW
WAAAAA
YIP
YIP
YIP
WHEN I WAS FIRST MARRIED, I TRIED TO MAKE THIS "HOUSE BEAUTIFUL."
SNIFF
YIP
YIP
AFTER HOLLY WAS BORN, I REALIZED I'D BE LUCKY TO SIMPLY KEEP DOWN THE CLUTTER.
NOW I'M A SINGLE MOM WITH TWO KIDS AND A FULL-TIME JOB.
I JUST HOPE TO PREVENT DISEASE.

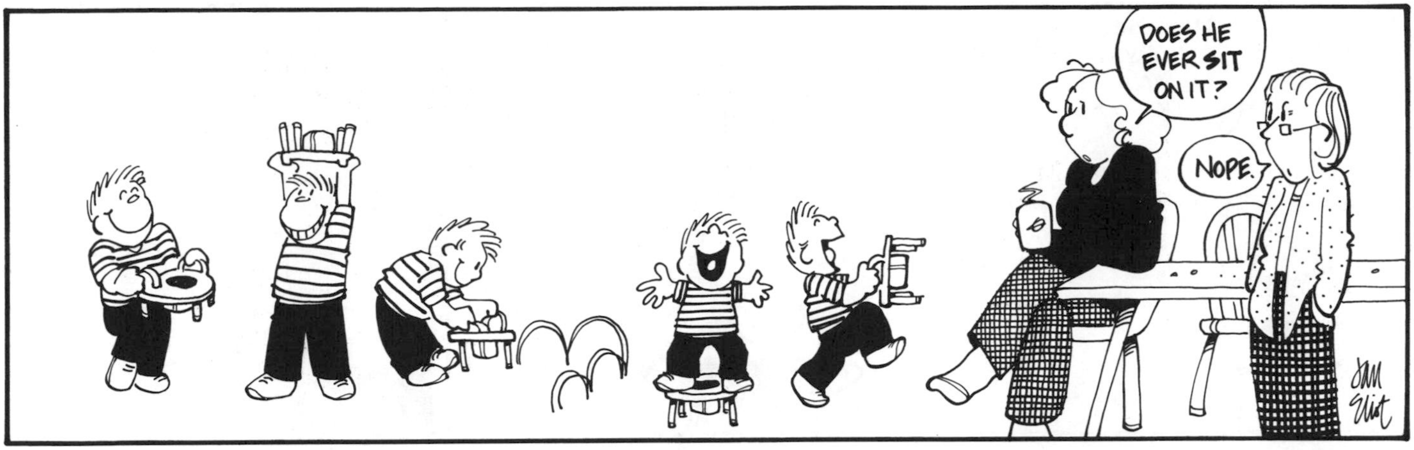
DOES HE EVER SIT ON IT?
NOPE.

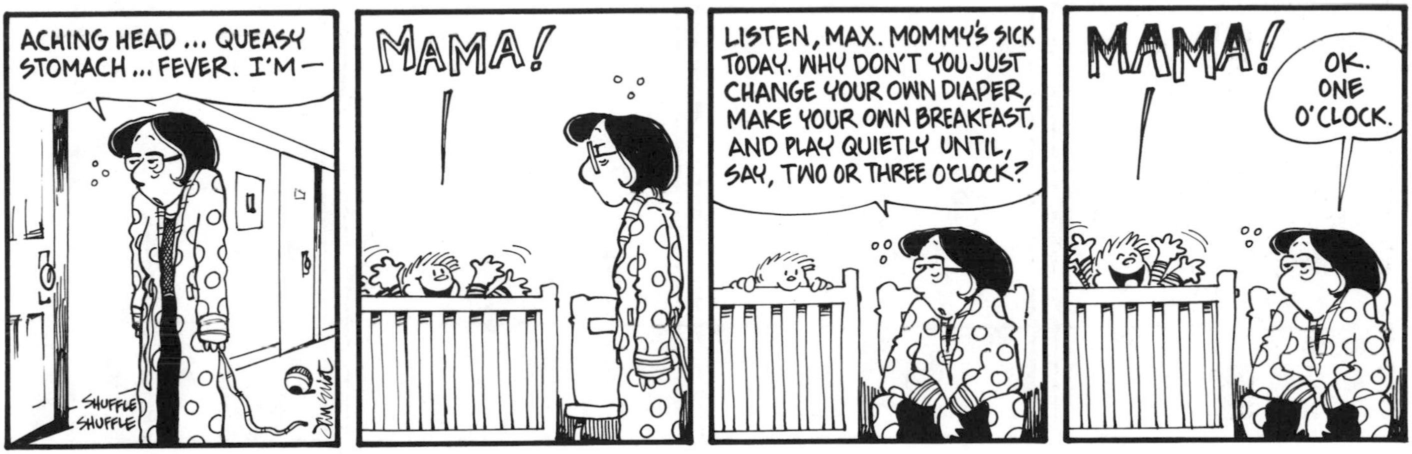
ACHING HEAD ... QUEASY STOMACH ... FEVER. I'M—
SHUFFLE SHUFFLE
MAMA!
LISTEN, MAX. MOMMY'S SICK TODAY. WHY DON'T YOU JUST CHANGE YOUR OWN DIAPER, MAKE YOUR OWN BREAKFAST, AND PLAY QUIETLY UNTIL, SAY, TWO OR THREE O'CLOCK?
MAMA!
OK. ONE O'CLOCK.

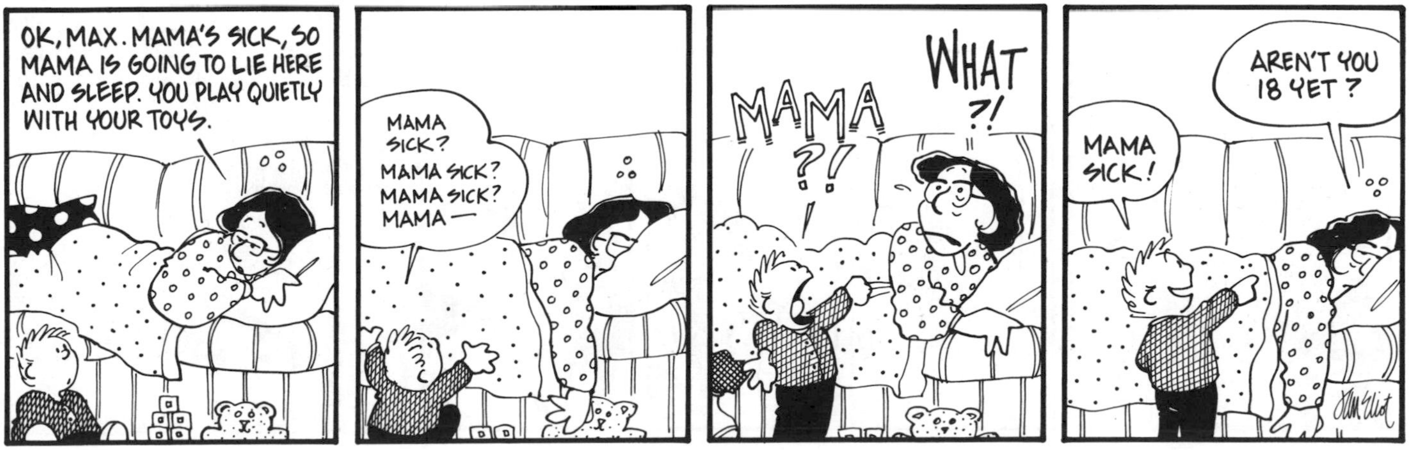
OK, MAX. MAMA'S SICK, SO MAMA IS GOING TO LIE HERE AND SLEEP. YOU PLAY QUIETLY WITH YOUR TOYS.
MAMA SICK? MAMA SICK? MAMA SICK? MAMA—
MAMA ?!
WHAT ?!
MAMA SICK!
AREN'T YOU 18 YET?

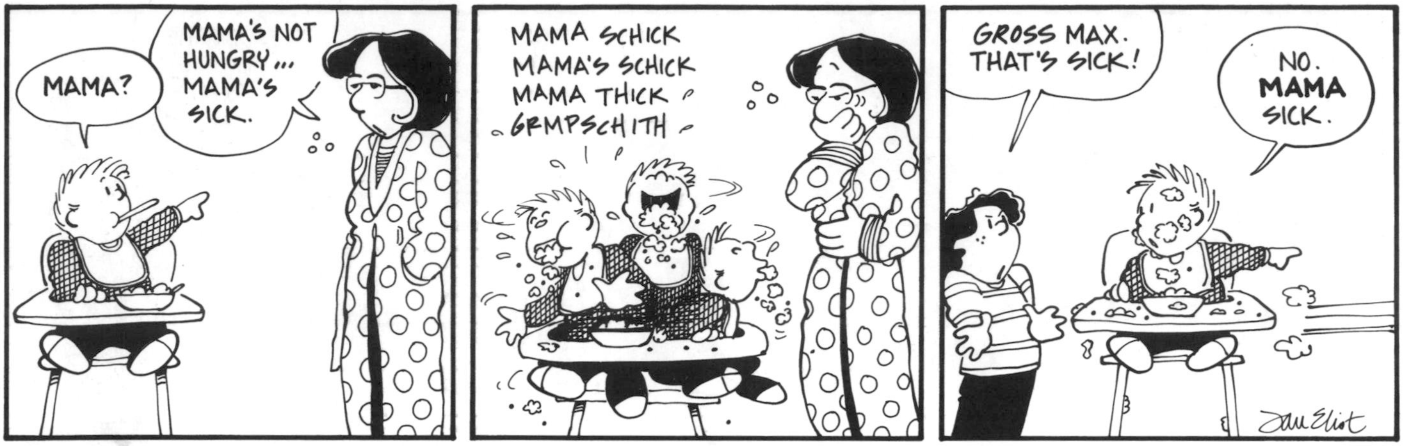
MAMA?
MAMA'S NOT HUNGRY... MAMA'S SICK.
MAMA SCHICK MAMA'S SCHICK MAMA THICK GRMPSCHITH
GROSS MAX. THAT'S SICK!
NO. MAMA SICK.

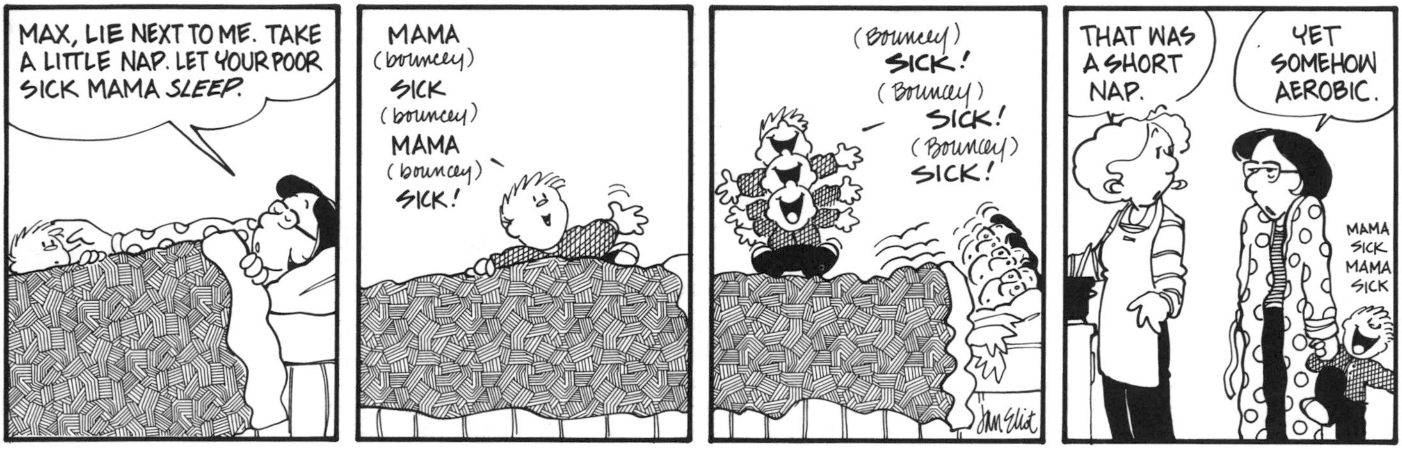
MAX, LIE NEXT TO ME. TAKE A LITTLE NAP. LET YOUR POOR SICK MAMA SLEEP.
MAMA (bouncey) SICK (bouncey) MAMA (bouncey) SICK!
(Bouncey) SICK! (Bouncey) SICK! (Bouncey) SICK!
THAT WAS A SHORT NAP.
YET SOMEHOW AEROBIC.
MAMA SICK MAMA SICK

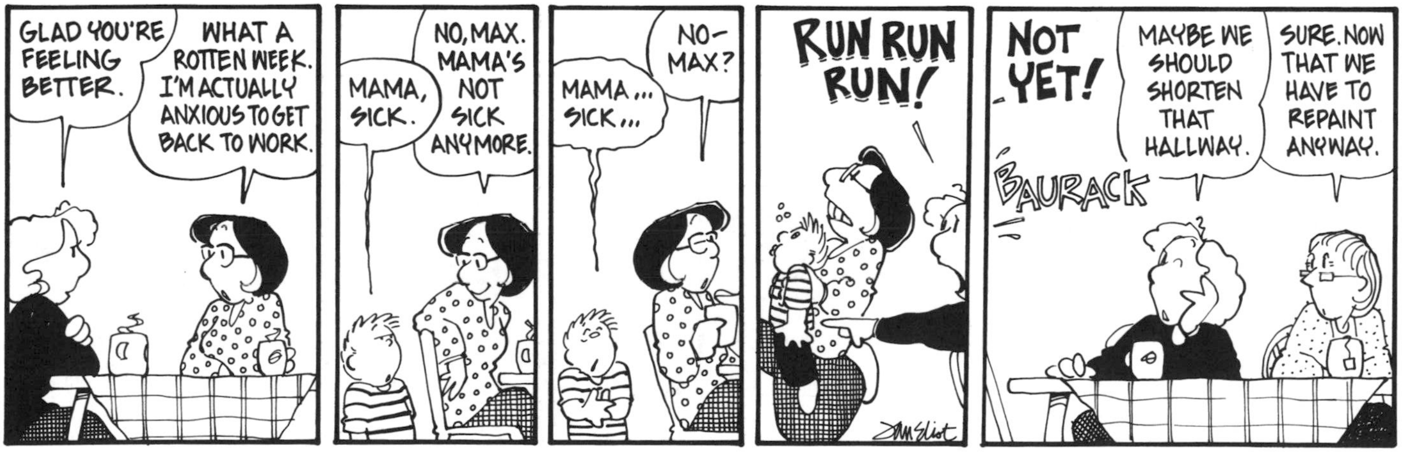
GLAD YOU'RE FEELING BETTER.
WHAT A ROTTEN WEEK. I'M ACTUALLY ANXIOUS TO GET BACK TO WORK.
MAMA, SICK.
NO, MAX. MAMA'S NOT SICK ANYMORE.
MAMA... SICK...
NO-MAX?
RUN RUN RUN!
NOT YET!
BAURACK
MAYBE WE SHOULD SHORTEN THAT HALLWAY.
SURE. NOW THAT WE HAVE TO REPAINT ANYWAY.

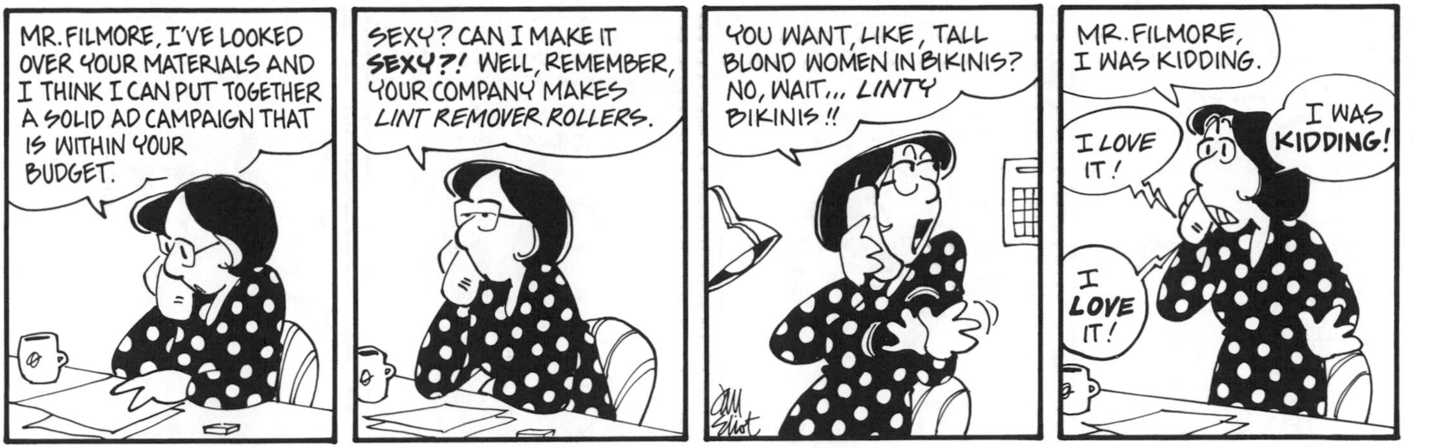
MR. FILMORE, I'VE LOOKED OVER YOUR MATERIALS AND I THINK I CAN PUT TOGETHER A SOLID AD CAMPAIGN THAT IS WITHIN YOUR BUDGET.
SEXY? CAN I MAKE IT SEXY?! WELL, REMEMBER, YOUR COMPANY MAKES LINT REMOVER ROLLERS.
YOU WANT, LIKE, TALL BLOND WOMEN IN BIKINIS? NO, WAIT... LINTY BIKINIS!!
MR. FILMORE, I WAS KIDDING.
I LOVE IT!
I WAS KIDDING!
I LOVE IT!

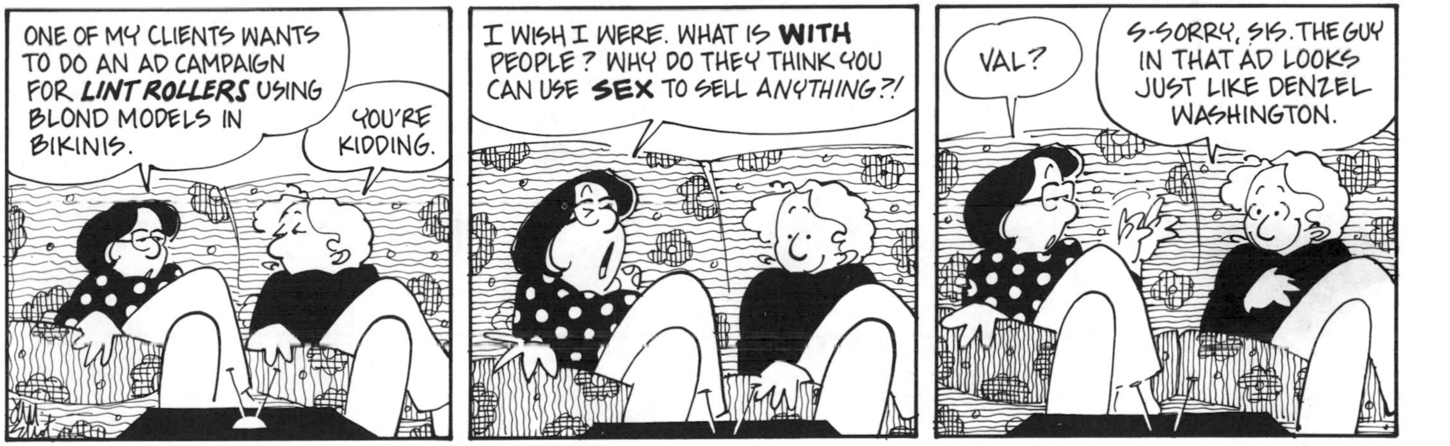
ONE OF MY CLIENTS WANTS TO DO AN AD CAMPAIGN FOR LINT ROLLERS USING BLOND MODELS IN BIKINIS.
YOU'RE KIDDING.
I WISH I WERE. WHAT IS WITH PEOPLE? WHY DO THEY THINK YOU CAN USE SEX TO SELL ANYTHING?!
VAL?
S-SORRY, SIS. THE GUY IN THAT AD LOOKS JUST LIKE DENZEL WASHINGTON.

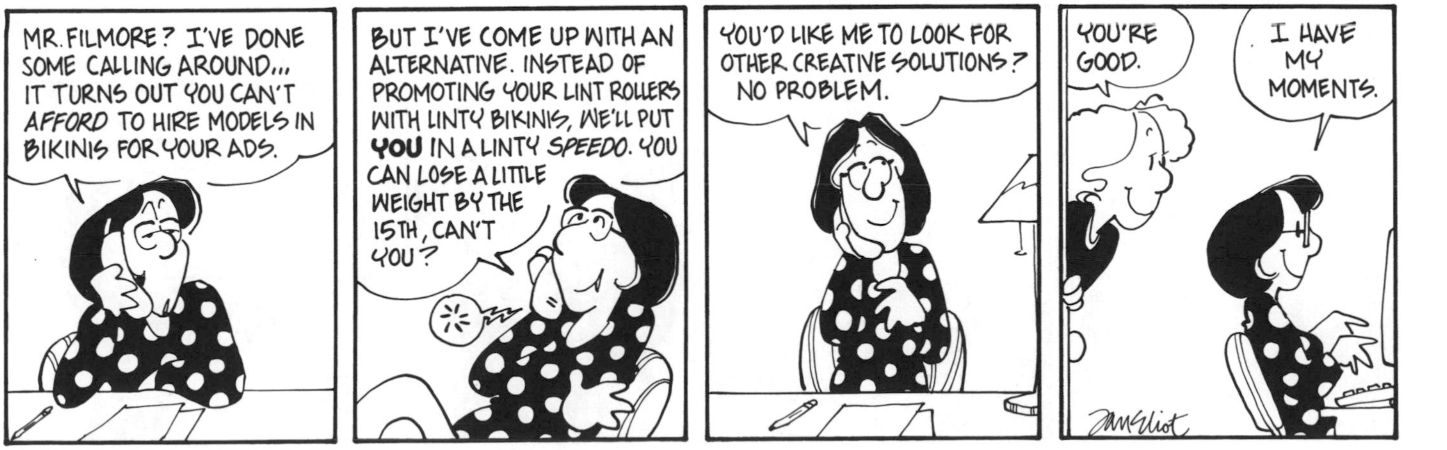
MR. FILMORE? I'VE DONE SOME CALLING AROUND... IT TURNS OUT YOU CAN'T AFFORD TO HIRE MODELS IN BIKINIS FOR YOUR ADS.
BUT I'VE COME UP WITH AN ALTERNATIVE. INSTEAD OF PROMOTING YOUR LINT ROLLERS WITH LINTY BIKINIS, WE'LL PUT YOU IN A LINTY SPEEDO. YOU CAN LOSE A LITTLE WEIGHT BY THE 15TH, CAN'T YOU?
YOU'D LIKE ME TO LOOK FOR OTHER CREATIVE SOLUTIONS? NO PROBLEM.
YOU'RE GOOD.
I HAVE MY MOMENTS.

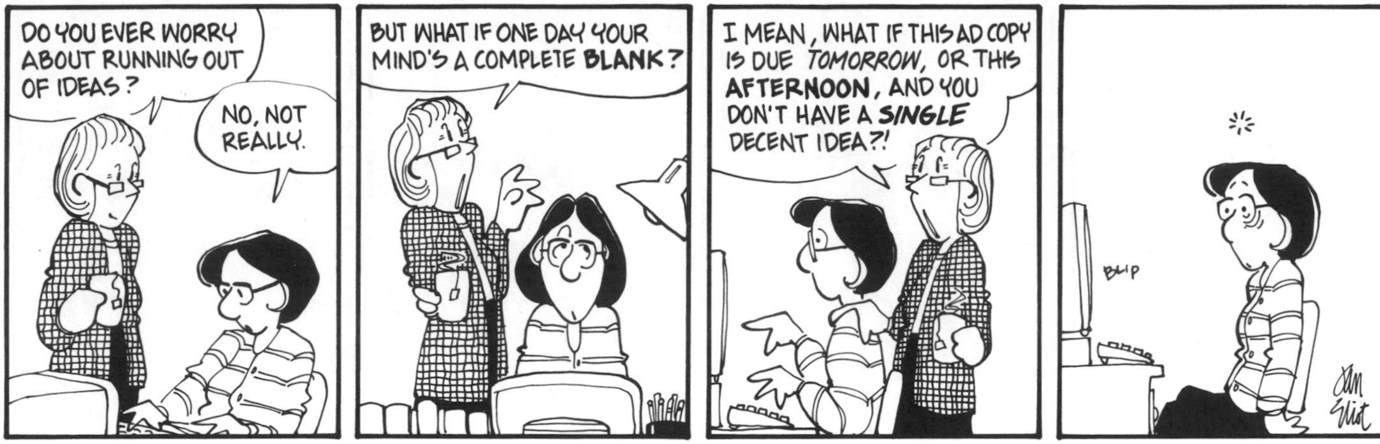
DO YOU EVER WORRY ABOUT RUNNING OUT OF IDEAS?
NO, NOT REALLY.
BUT WHAT IF ONE DAY YOUR MIND'S A COMPLETE **BLANK**?
I MEAN, WHAT IF THIS AD COPY IS DUE *TOMORROW*, OR THIS **AFTERNOON**, AND YOU DON'T HAVE A ***SINGLE*** DECENT IDEA?!
BLIP

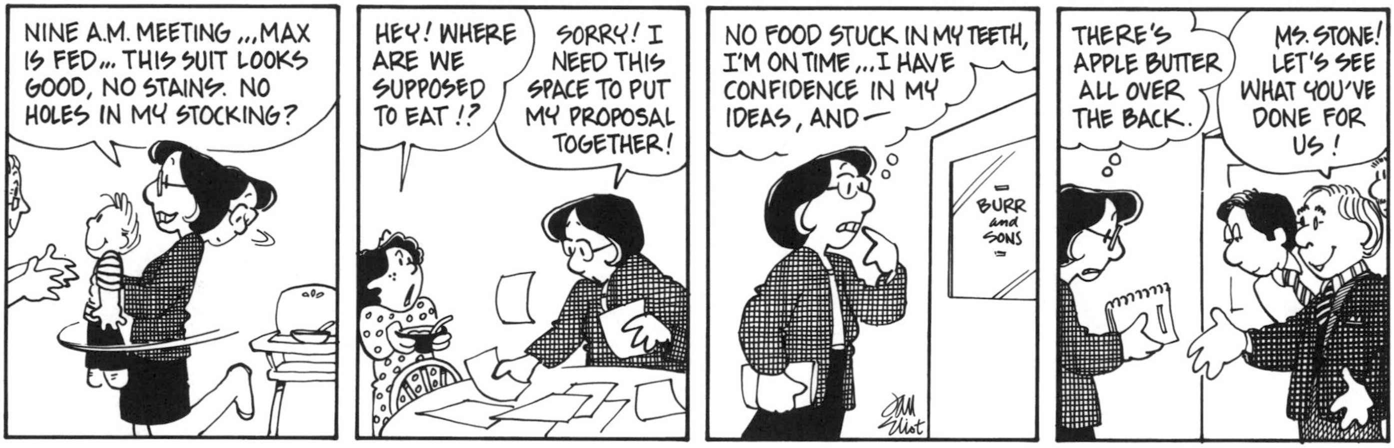
NINE A.M. MEETING ... MAX IS FED... THIS SUIT LOOKS GOOD, NO STAINS. NO HOLES IN MY STOCKING?
HEY! WHERE ARE WE SUPPOSED TO EAT!?
SORRY! I NEED THIS SPACE TO PUT MY PROPOSAL TOGETHER!
NO FOOD STUCK IN MY TEETH, I'M ON TIME ... I HAVE CONFIDENCE IN MY IDEAS, AND—
BURR and SONS
THERE'S APPLE BUTTER ALL OVER THE BACK.
MS. STONE! LET'S SEE WHAT YOU'VE DONE FOR US!

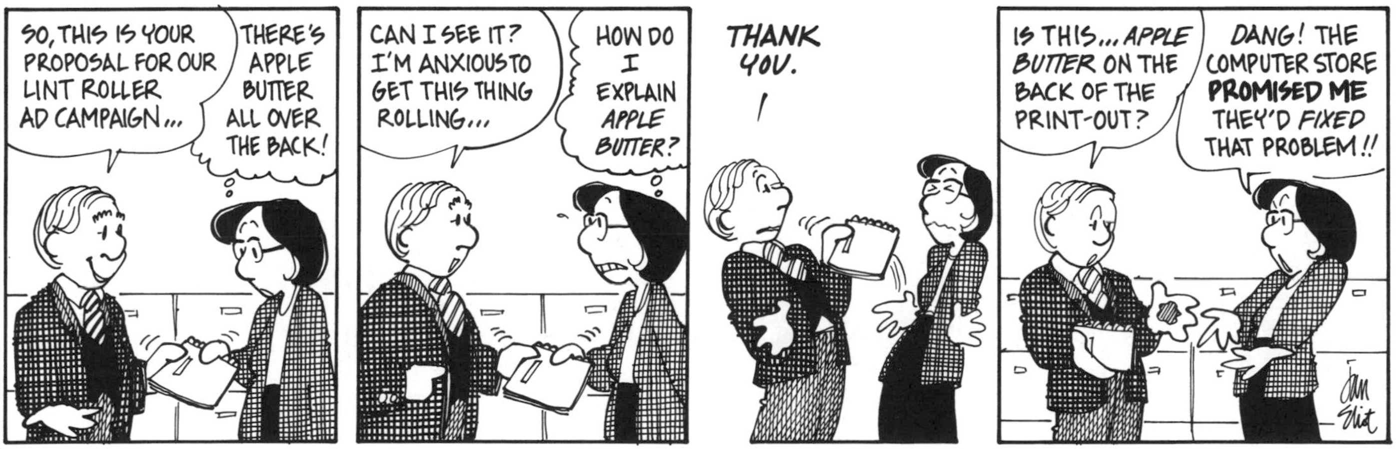
SO, THIS IS YOUR PROPOSAL FOR OUR LINT ROLLER AD CAMPAIGN...
THERE'S APPLE BUTTER ALL OVER THE BACK!
CAN I SEE IT? I'M ANXIOUS TO GET THIS THING ROLLING...
HOW DO I EXPLAIN *APPLE BUTTER*?
THANK YOU.
IS THIS... *APPLE BUTTER* ON THE BACK OF THE PRINT-OUT?
DANG! THE COMPUTER STORE **PROMISED ME** THEY'D *FIXED* THAT PROBLEM!!

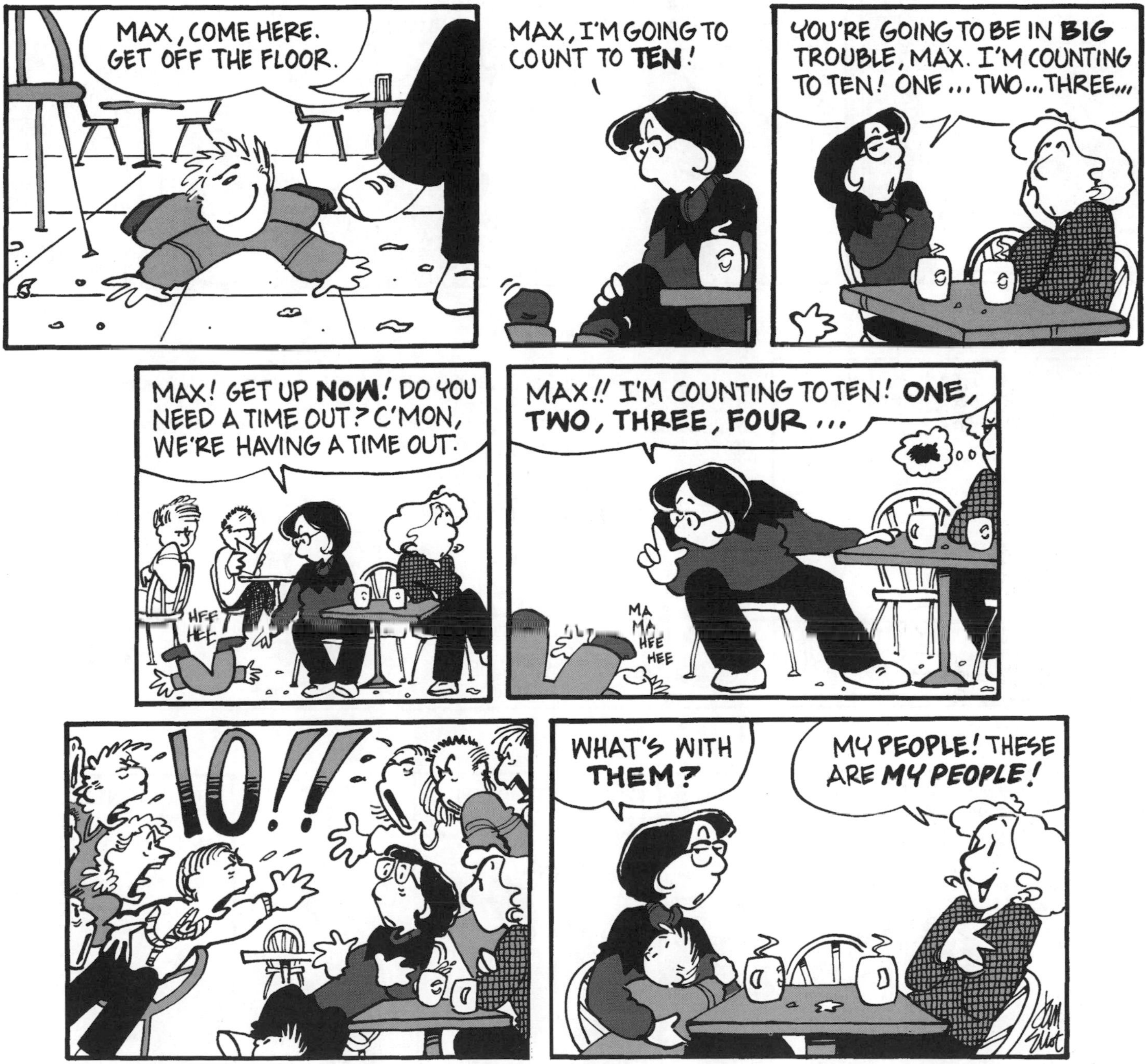
MAX, COME HERE. GET OFF THE FLOOR.
MAX, I'M GOING TO COUNT TO **TEN**!
YOU'RE GOING TO BE IN **BIG** TROUBLE, MAX. I'M COUNTING TO TEN! ONE ... TWO ... THREE ...
MAX! GET UP **NOW**! DO YOU NEED A TIME OUT? C'MON, WE'RE HAVING A TIME OUT.
HEE HEE
MAX!! I'M COUNTING TO TEN! **ONE, TWO, THREE, FOUR** ...
MA MA HEE HEE
10!!
WHAT'S WITH **THEM**?
MY **PEOPLE**! THESE ARE **MY PEOPLE**!

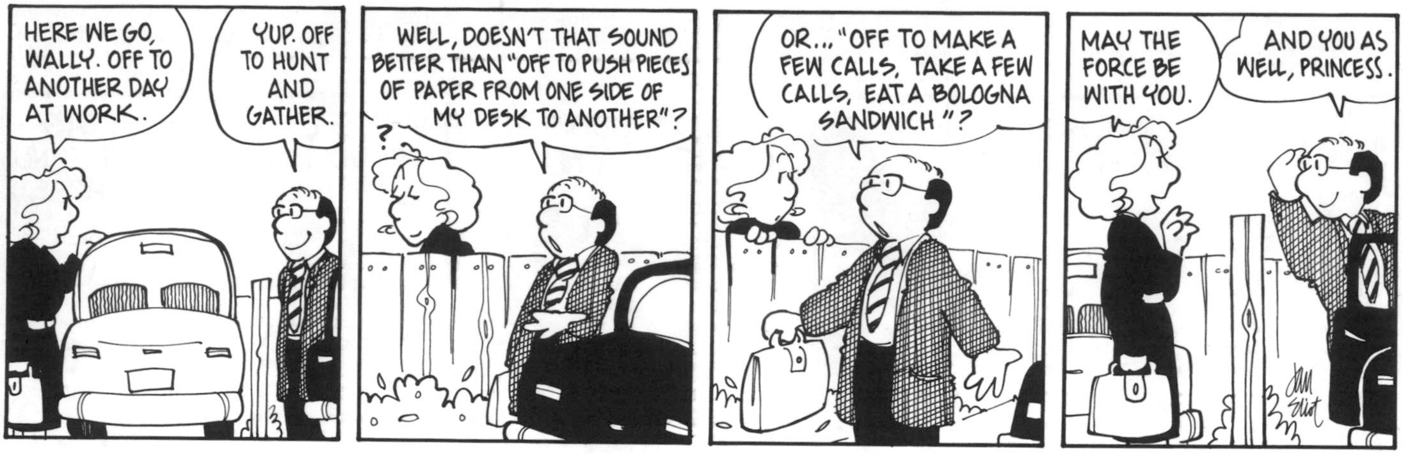
HERE WE GO, WALLY. OFF TO ANOTHER DAY AT WORK.
YUP. OFF TO HUNT AND GATHER.
WELL, DOESN'T THAT SOUND BETTER THAN "OFF TO PUSH PIECES OF PAPER FROM ONE SIDE OF MY DESK TO ANOTHER"?
?
OR... "OFF TO MAKE A FEW CALLS, TAKE A FEW CALLS, EAT A BOLOGNA SANDWICH"?
MAY THE FORCE BE WITH YOU.
AND YOU AS WELL, PRINCESS.

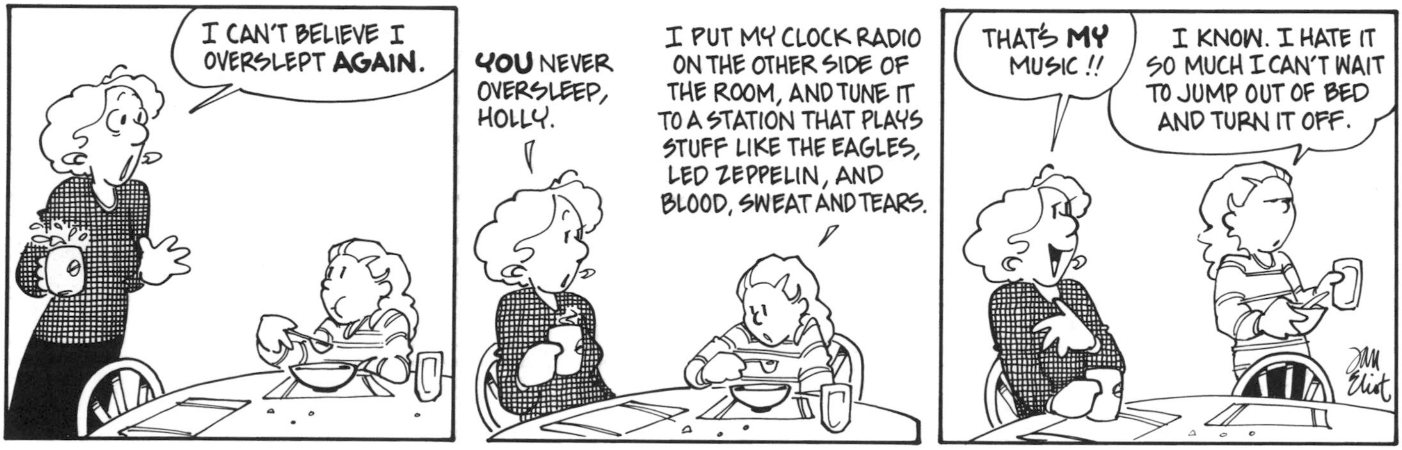
I CAN'T BELIEVE I OVERSLEPT **AGAIN**.
YOU NEVER OVERSLEEP, HOLLY.
I PUT MY CLOCK RADIO ON THE OTHER SIDE OF THE ROOM, AND TUNE IT TO A STATION THAT PLAYS STUFF LIKE THE EAGLES, LED ZEPPELIN, AND BLOOD, SWEAT AND TEARS.
THAT'S **MY** MUSIC!!
I KNOW. I HATE IT SO MUCH I CAN'T WAIT TO JUMP OUT OF BED AND TURN IT OFF.

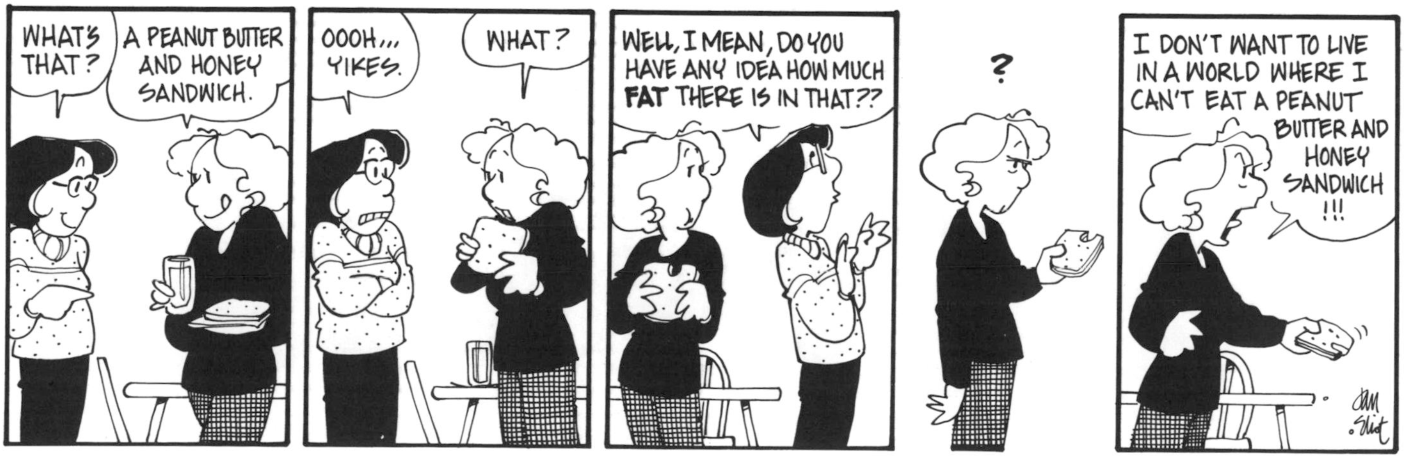
WHAT'S THAT?
A PEANUT BUTTER AND HONEY SANDWICH.
OOOH... YIKES.
WHAT?
WELL, I MEAN, DO YOU HAVE ANY IDEA HOW MUCH **FAT** THERE IS IN THAT??
?
I DON'T WANT TO LIVE IN A WORLD WHERE I CAN'T EAT A PEANUT BUTTER AND HONEY SANDWICH!!!

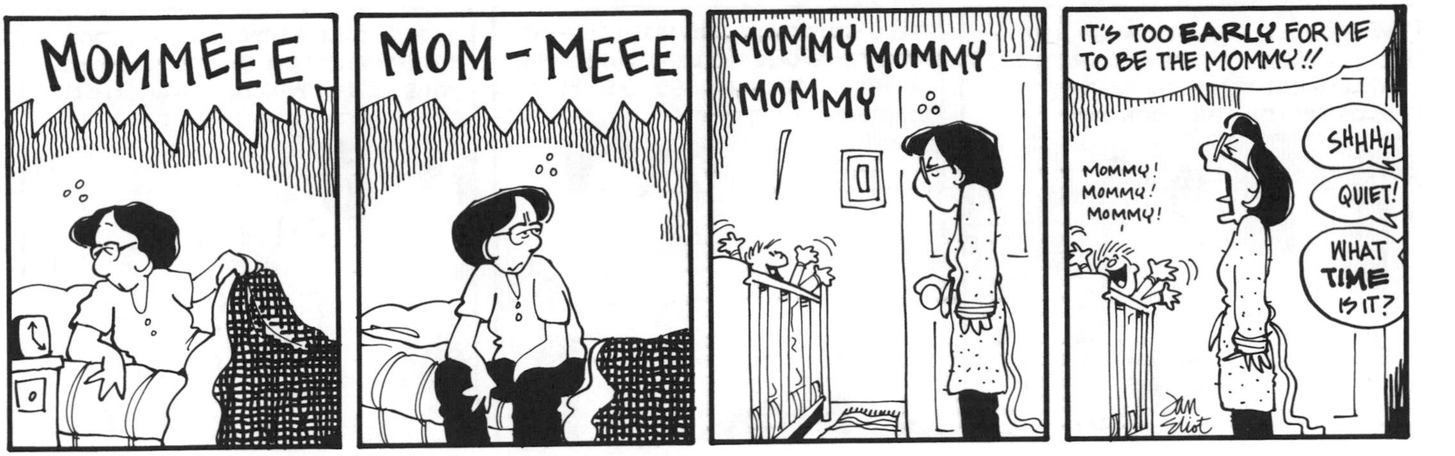
MOMMEEE
MOM-MEEE
MOMMY MOMMY
MOMMY
IT'S TOO EARLY FOR ME
TO BE THE MOMMY!!
MOMMY!
MOMMY!
MOMMY!
SHHHH
QUIET!
WHAT TIME IS IT?

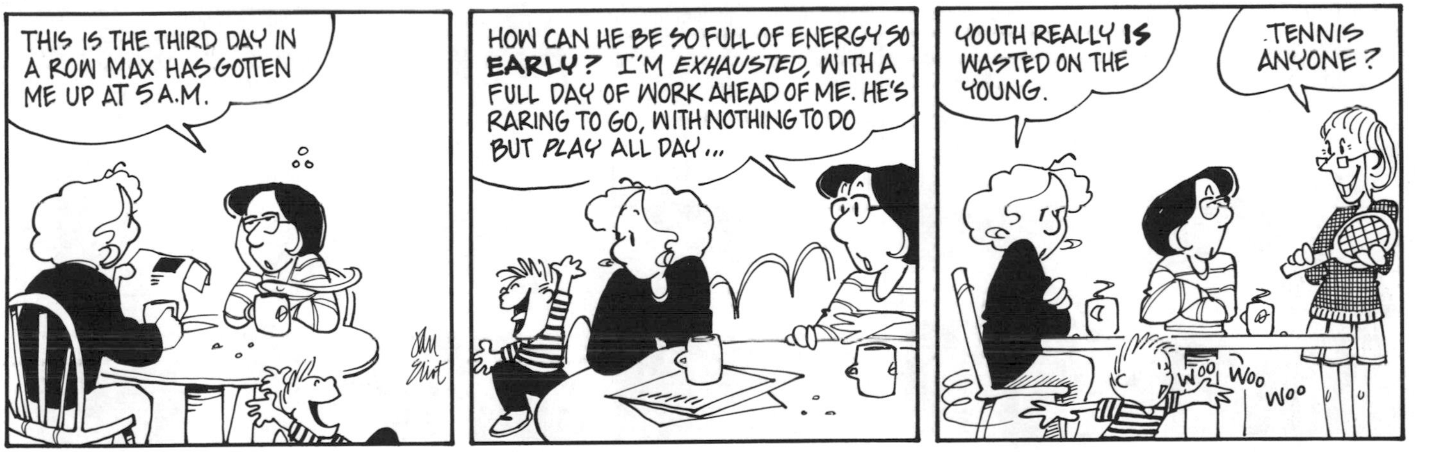
THIS IS THE THIRD DAY IN A ROW MAX HAS GOTTEN ME UP AT 5 A.M.
HOW CAN HE BE SO FULL OF ENERGY SO EARLY? I'M EXHAUSTED, WITH A FULL DAY OF WORK AHEAD OF ME. HE'S RARING TO GO, WITH NOTHING TO DO BUT PLAY ALL DAY...
YOUTH REALLY IS WASTED ON THE YOUNG.
TENNIS ANYONE?
WOO WOO WOO

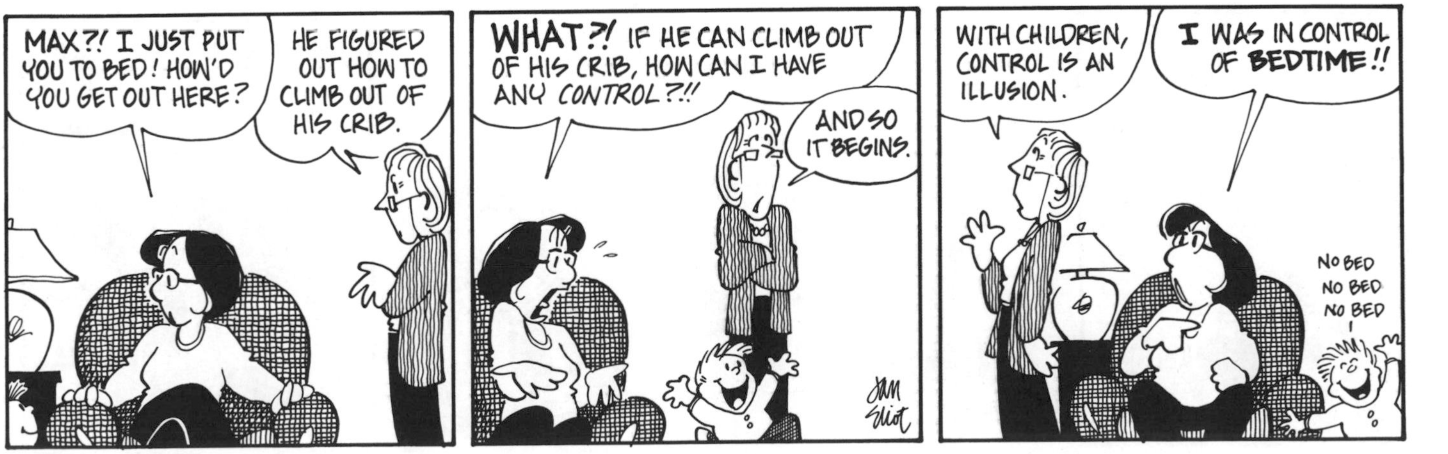
MAX?! I JUST PUT YOU TO BED! HOW'D YOU GET OUT HERE?
HE FIGURED OUT HOW TO CLIMB OUT OF HIS CRIB.
WHAT?! IF HE CAN CLIMB OUT OF HIS CRIB, HOW CAN I HAVE ANY CONTROL?!!
AND SO IT BEGINS.
WITH CHILDREN, CONTROL IS AN ILLUSION.
I WAS IN CONTROL OF BEDTIME!!
NO BED
NO BED
NO BED

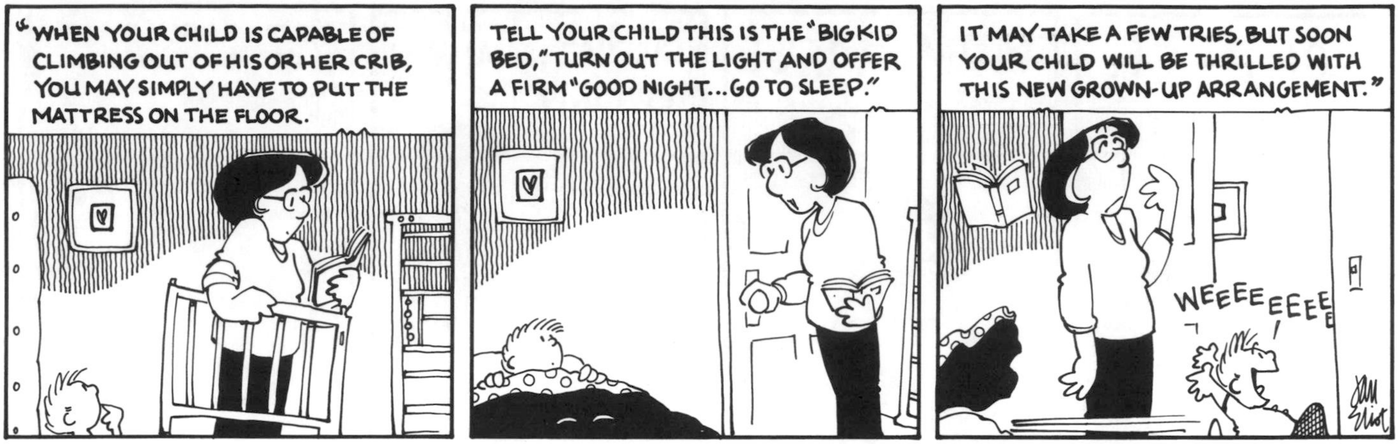
"WHEN YOUR CHILD IS CAPABLE OF CLIMBING OUT OF HIS OR HER CRIB, YOU MAY SIMPLY HAVE TO PUT THE MATTRESS ON THE FLOOR.
TELL YOUR CHILD THIS IS THE "BIG KID BED," TURN OUT THE LIGHT AND OFFER A FIRM "GOOD NIGHT... GO TO SLEEP."
IT MAY TAKE A FEW TRIES, BUT SOON YOUR CHILD WILL BE THRILLED WITH THIS NEW GROWN-UP ARRANGEMENT."
WEEEEEEEE

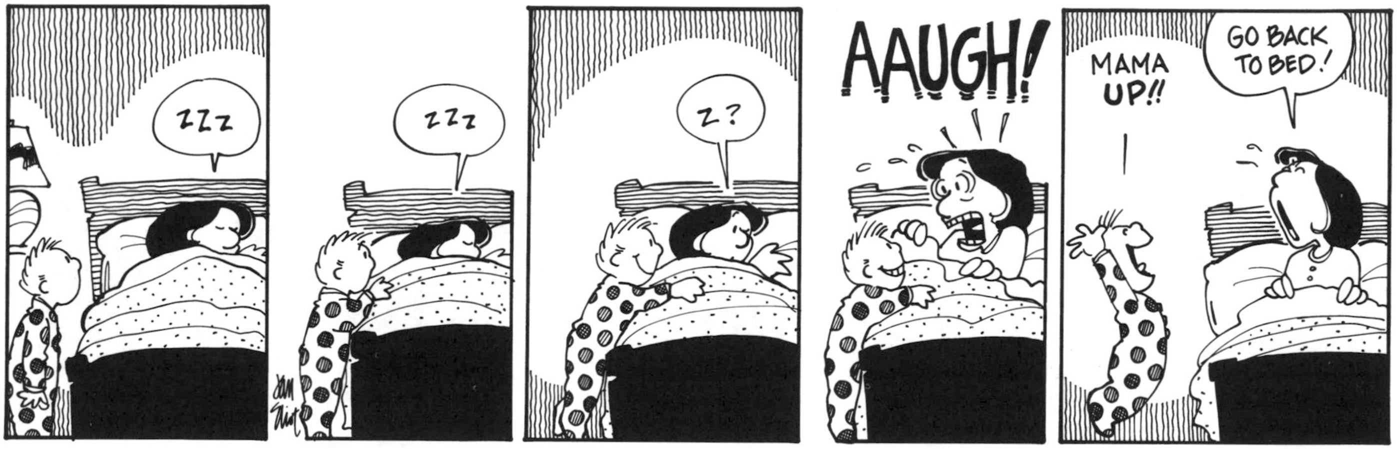
ZZZ
ZZZ
Z?
AAUGH!
MAMA UP!!
GO BACK TO BED!

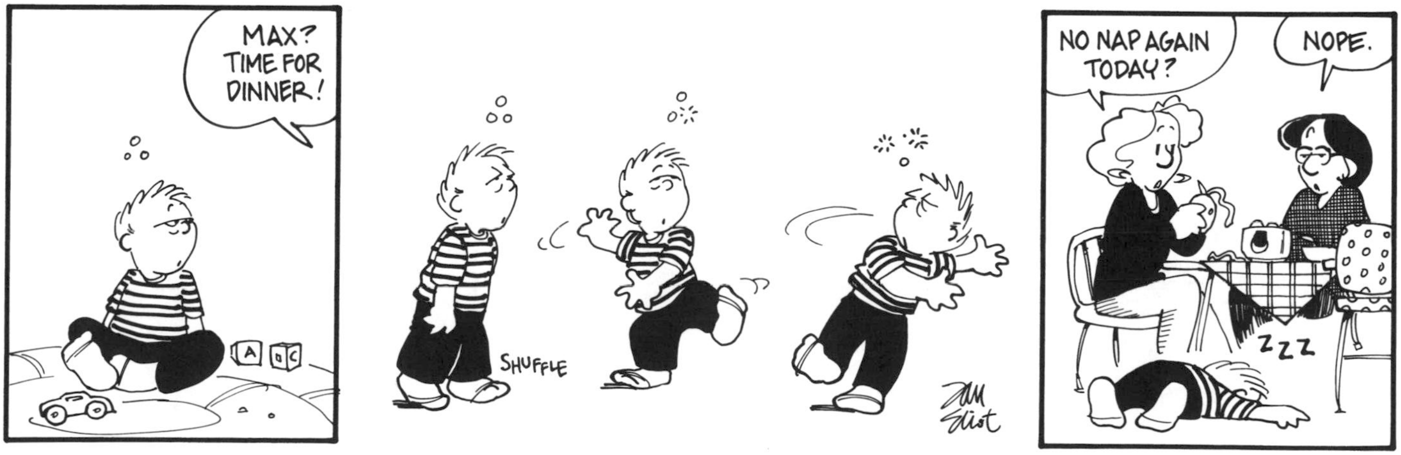
MAX? TIME FOR DINNER!
SHUFFLE
NO NAP AGAIN TODAY?
NOPE.
ZZZ

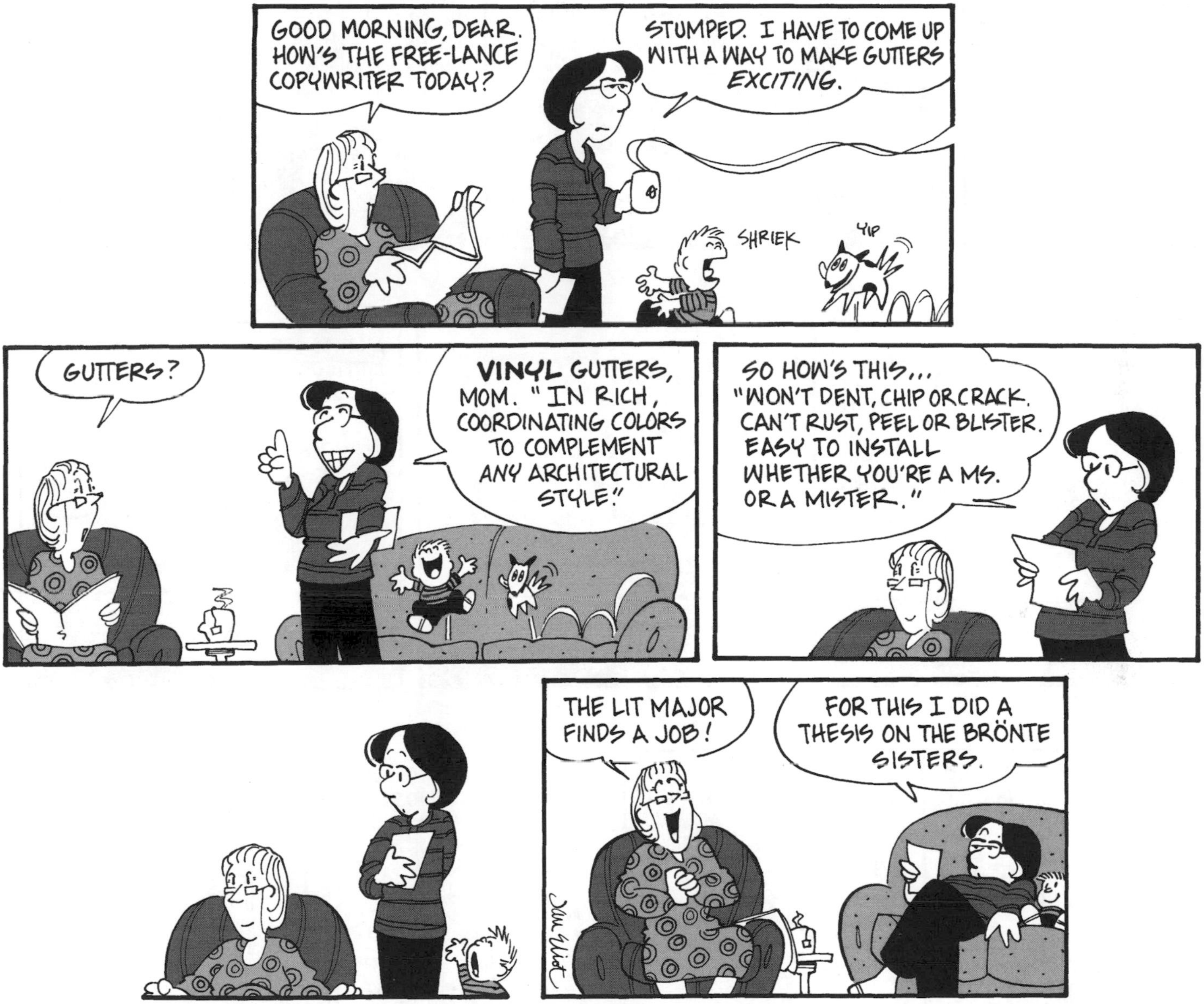
GOOD MORNING, DEAR. HOW'S THE FREE-LANCE COPYWRITER TODAY?
STUMPED. I HAVE TO COME UP WITH A WAY TO MAKE GUTTERS EXCITING.
SHRIEK
YIP
GUTTERS?
VINYL GUTTERS, MOM. "IN RICH, COORDINATING COLORS TO COMPLEMENT ANY ARCHITECTURAL STYLE."
SO HOW'S THIS... "WON'T DENT, CHIP OR CRACK. CAN'T RUST, PEEL OR BLISTER. EASY TO INSTALL WHETHER YOU'RE A MS. OR A MISTER."
THE LIT MAJOR FINDS A JOB!
FOR THIS I DID A THESIS ON THE BRÖNTE SISTERS.

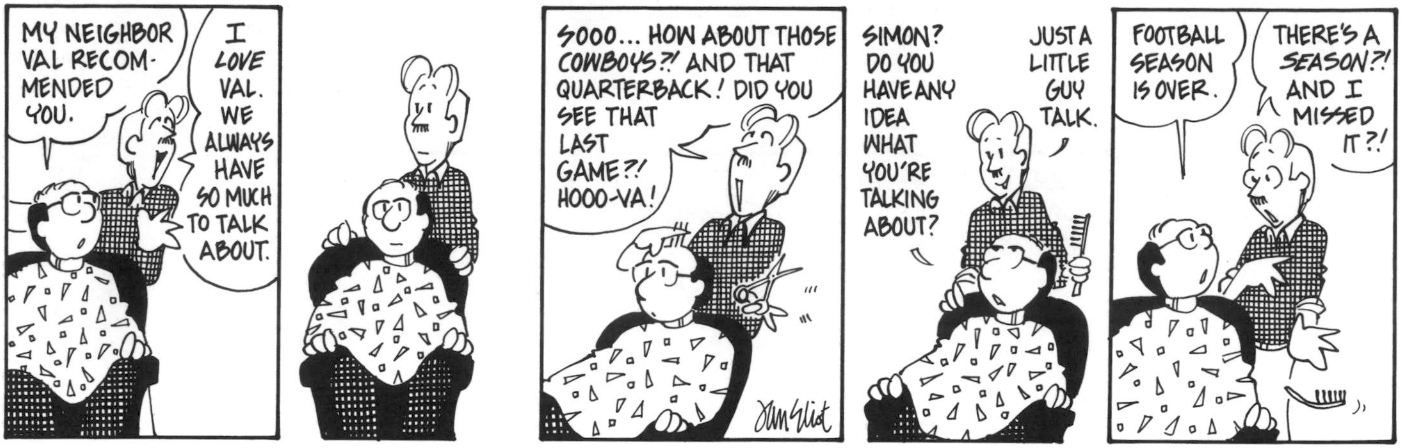
MY NEIGHBOR VAL RECOMMENDED YOU.
I LOVE VAL. WE ALWAYS HAVE SO MUCH TO TALK ABOUT.
SOOO... HOW ABOUT THOSE COWBOYS?! AND THAT QUARTERBACK! DID YOU SEE THAT LAST GAME?! HOOO-VA!
SIMON? DO YOU HAVE ANY IDEA WHAT YOU'RE TALKING ABOUT?
JUST A LITTLE GUY TALK.
FOOTBALL SEASON IS OVER.
THERE'S A SEASON?! AND I MISSED IT?!

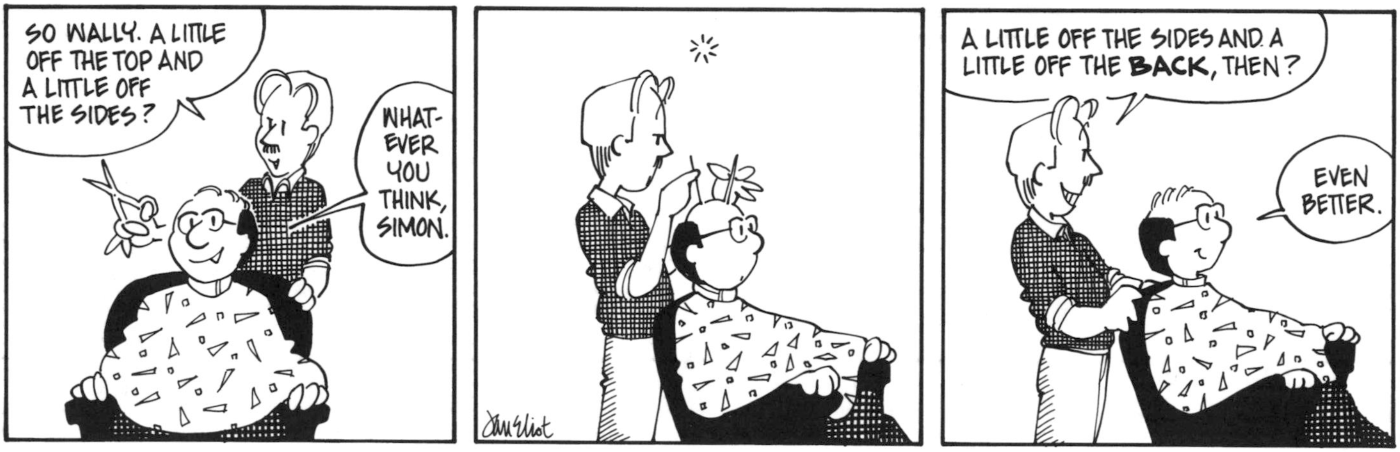
SO WALLY. A LITTLE OFF THE TOP AND A LITTLE OFF THE SIDES?
WHAT-EVER YOU THINK, SIMON.
A LITTLE OFF THE SIDES AND A LITTLE OFF THE BACK, THEN?
EVEN BETTER.

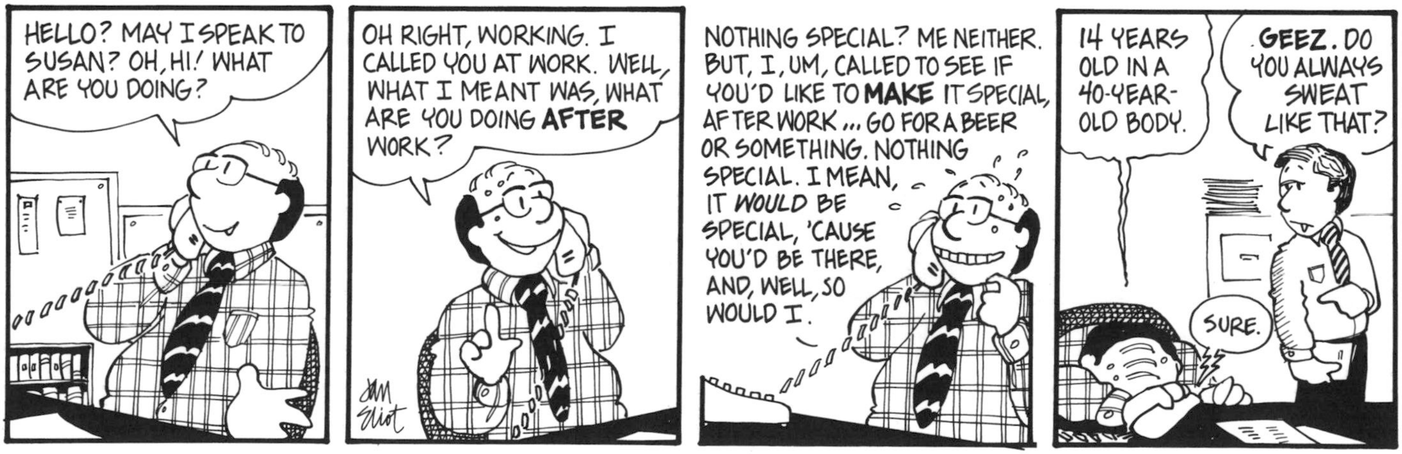
HELLO? MAY I SPEAK TO SUSAN? OH, HI! WHAT ARE YOU DOING?
OH RIGHT, WORKING. I CALLED YOU AT WORK. WELL, WHAT I MEANT WAS, WHAT ARE YOU DOING AFTER WORK?
NOTHING SPECIAL? ME NEITHER. BUT, I, UM, CALLED TO SEE IF YOU'D LIKE TO MAKE IT SPECIAL, AFTER WORK... GO FOR A BEER OR SOMETHING. NOTHING SPECIAL. I MEAN, IT WOULD BE SPECIAL, 'CAUSE YOU'D BE THERE, AND, WELL, SO WOULD I.
14 YEARS OLD IN A 40-YEAR-OLD BODY.
GEEZ. DO YOU ALWAYS SWEAT LIKE THAT?
SURE.

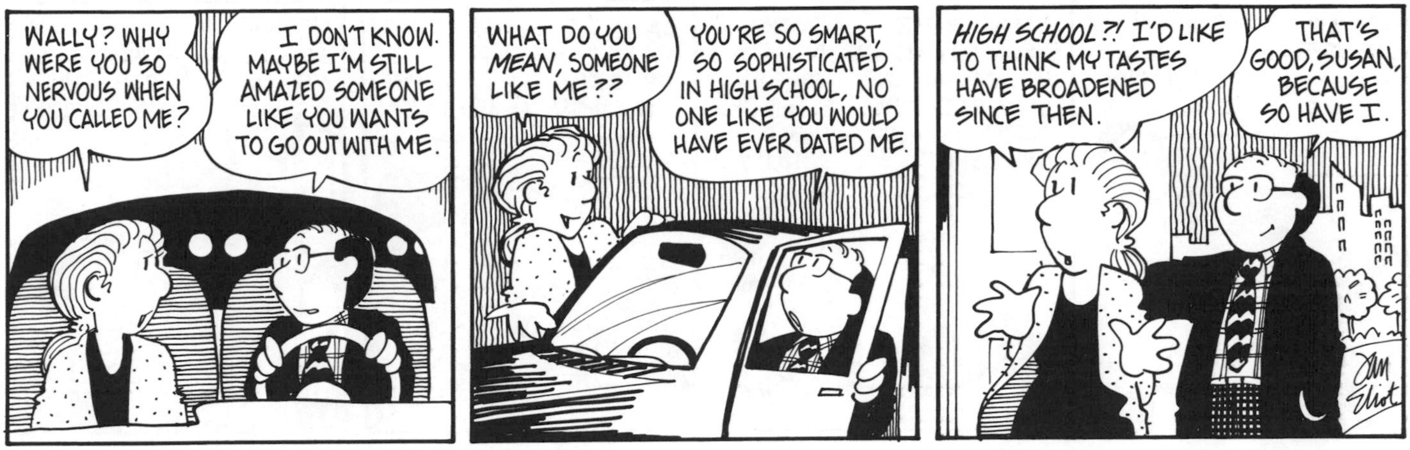
WALLY? WHY WERE YOU SO NERVOUS WHEN YOU CALLED ME?
I DON'T KNOW. MAYBE I'M STILL AMAZED SOMEONE LIKE YOU WANTS TO GO OUT WITH ME.
WHAT DO YOU *MEAN*, SOMEONE LIKE ME??
YOU'RE SO SMART, SO SOPHISTICATED. IN HIGH SCHOOL, NO ONE LIKE YOU WOULD HAVE EVER DATED ME.
HIGH SCHOOL?! I'D LIKE TO THINK MY TASTES HAVE BROADENED SINCE THEN.
THAT'S GOOD, SUSAN, BECAUSE SO HAVE I.

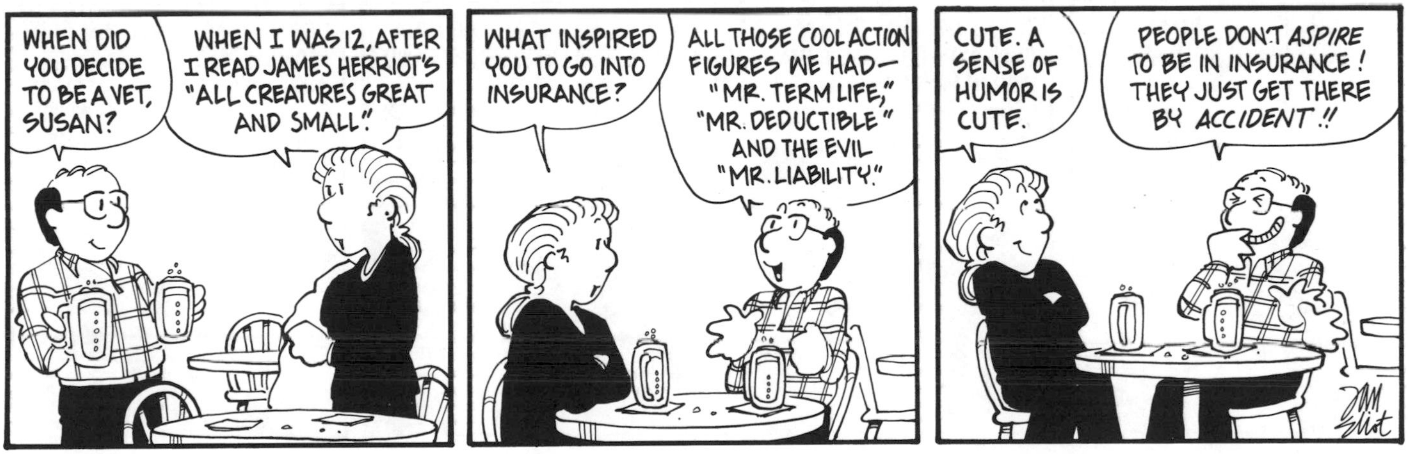
WHEN DID YOU DECIDE TO BE A VET, SUSAN?
WHEN I WAS 12, AFTER I READ JAMES HERRIOT'S "ALL CREATURES GREAT AND SMALL."
WHAT INSPIRED YOU TO GO INTO INSURANCE?
ALL THOSE COOL ACTION FIGURES WE HAD— "MR. TERM LIFE," "MR. DEDUCTIBLE" AND THE EVIL "MR. LIABILITY."
CUTE. A SENSE OF HUMOR IS CUTE.
PEOPLE DON'T *ASPIRE* TO BE IN INSURANCE! THEY JUST GET THERE BY *ACCIDENT*!!

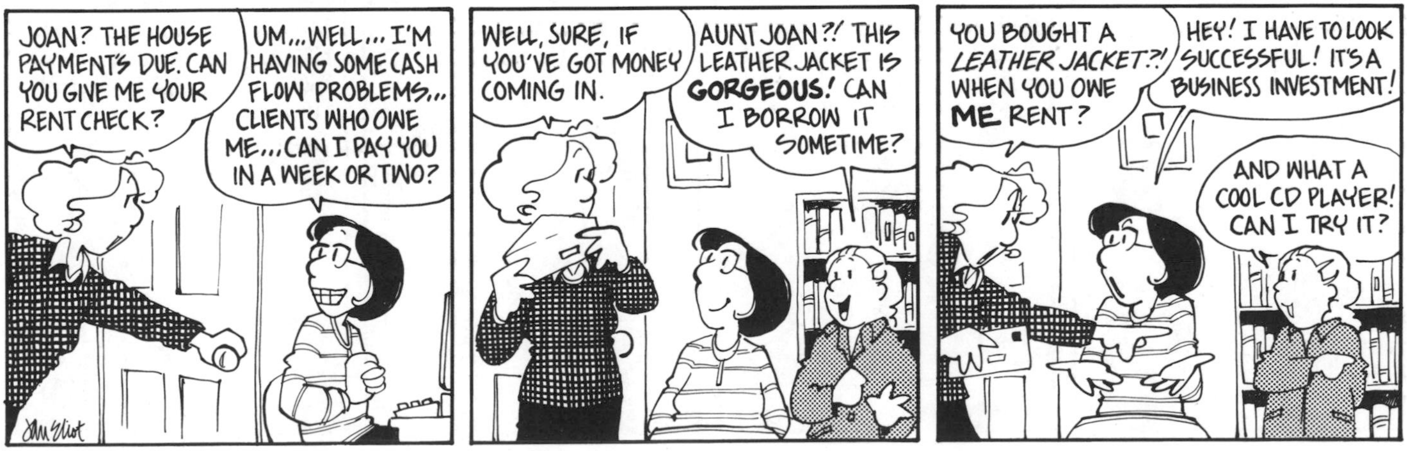
JOAN? THE HOUSE PAYMENT'S DUE. CAN YOU GIVE ME YOUR RENT CHECK?
UM... WELL... I'M HAVING SOME CASH FLOW PROBLEMS... CLIENTS WHO OWE ME... CAN I PAY YOU IN A WEEK OR TWO?
WELL, SURE, IF YOU'VE GOT MONEY COMING IN.
AUNT JOAN?! THIS LEATHER JACKET IS **GORGEOUS**! CAN I BORROW IT SOMETIME?
YOU BOUGHT A *LEATHER JACKET?!* WHEN YOU OWE **ME** RENT?
HEY! I HAVE TO LOOK SUCCESSFUL! IT'S A BUSINESS INVESTMENT!
AND WHAT A COOL CD PLAYER! CAN I TRY IT?

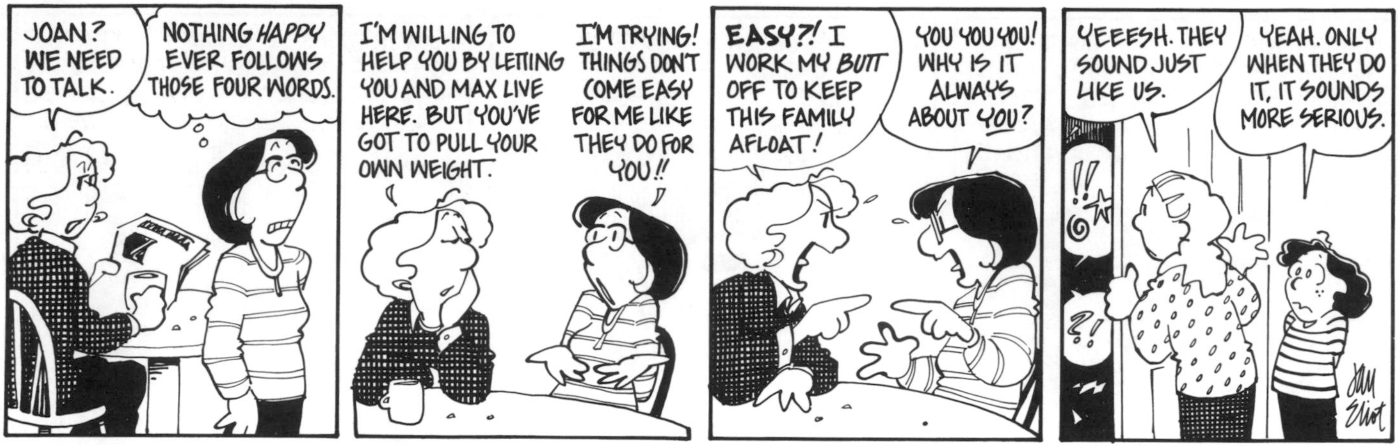
JOAN? WE NEED TO TALK.
NOTHING *HAPPY* EVER FOLLOWS THOSE FOUR WORDS.
I'M WILLING TO HELP YOU BY LETTING YOU AND MAX LIVE HERE. BUT YOU'VE GOT TO PULL YOUR OWN WEIGHT.
I'M TRYING! THINGS DON'T COME EASY FOR ME LIKE THEY DO FOR YOU!!
EASY?! I WORK MY *BUTT* OFF TO KEEP THIS FAMILY AFLOAT!
YOU YOU YOU! WHY IS IT ALWAYS ABOUT YOU?
!!
?!
YEEESH. THEY SOUND JUST LIKE US.
YEAH. ONLY WHEN THEY DO IT, IT SOUNDS MORE SERIOUS.

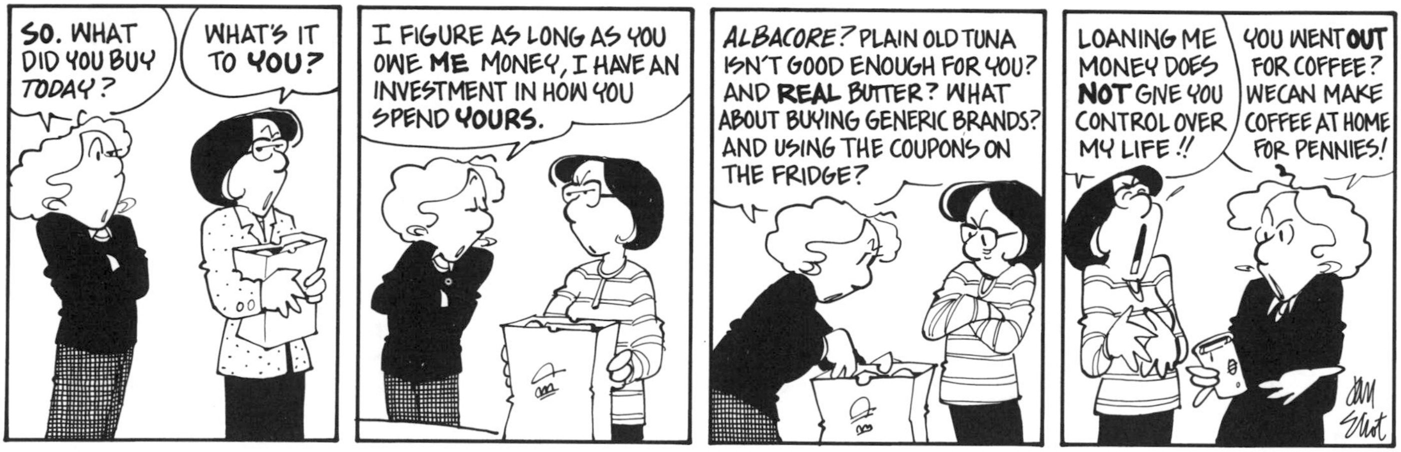
SO. WHAT DID YOU BUY *TODAY*?
WHAT'S IT TO **YOU?**
I FIGURE AS LONG AS YOU OWE **ME** MONEY, I HAVE AN INVESTMENT IN HOW YOU SPEND **YOURS.**
ALBACORE? PLAIN OLD TUNA ISN'T GOOD ENOUGH FOR YOU? AND **REAL** BUTTER? WHAT ABOUT BUYING GENERIC BRANDS? AND USING THE COUPONS ON THE FRIDGE?
LOANING ME MONEY DOES **NOT** GIVE YOU CONTROL OVER MY LIFE!!
YOU WENT **OUT** FOR COFFEE? WE CAN MAKE COFFEE AT HOME FOR PENNIES!

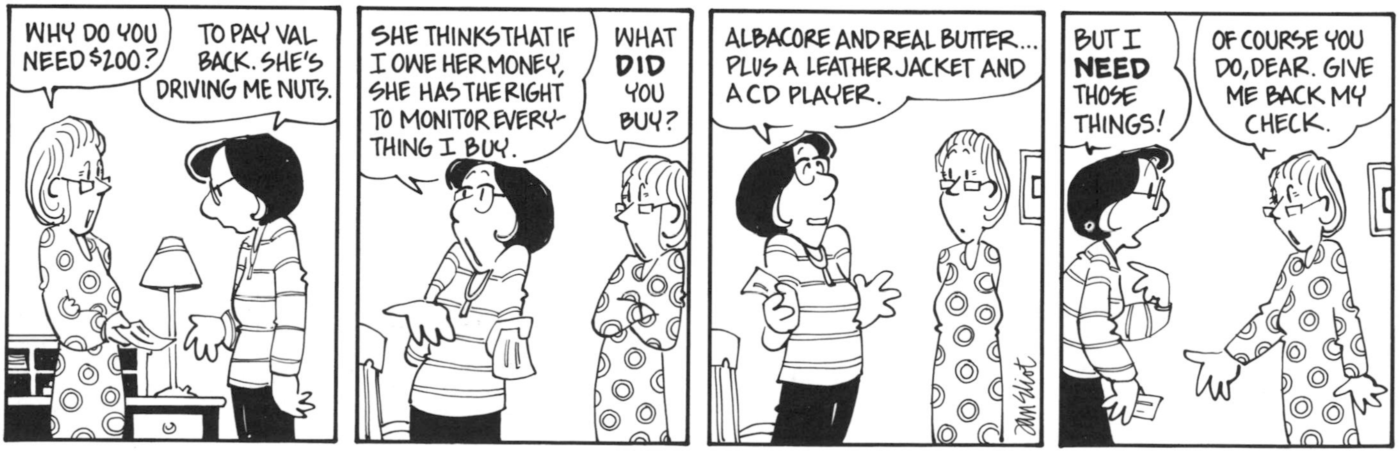
WHY DO YOU NEED $200?
TO PAY VAL BACK. SHE'S DRIVING ME NUTS.
SHE THINKS THAT IF I OWE HER MONEY, SHE HAS THE RIGHT TO MONITOR EVERYTHING I BUY.
WHAT **DID** YOU BUY?
ALBACORE AND REAL BUTTER... PLUS A LEATHER JACKET AND A CD PLAYER.
BUT I **NEED** THOSE THINGS!
OF COURSE YOU DO, DEAR. GIVE ME BACK MY CHECK.

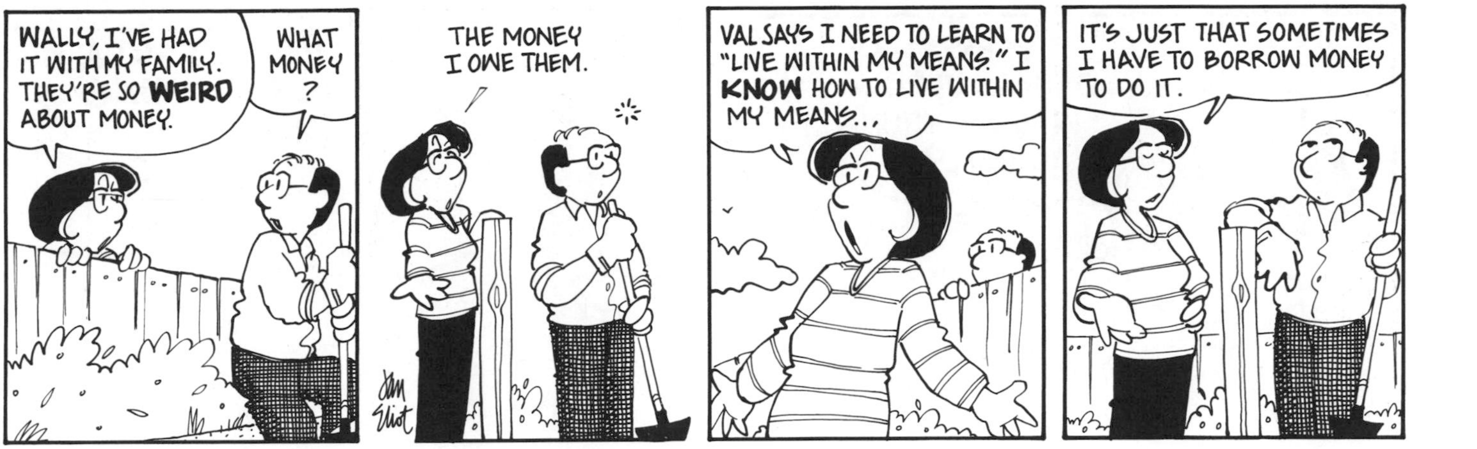
WALLY, I'VE HAD IT WITH MY FAMILY. THEY'RE SO **WEIRD** ABOUT MONEY.
WHAT MONEY?
THE MONEY I OWE THEM.
VAL SAYS I NEED TO LEARN TO "LIVE WITHIN MY MEANS." I **KNOW** HOW TO LIVE WITHIN MY MEANS...
IT'S JUST THAT SOMETIMES I HAVE TO BORROW MONEY TO DO IT.

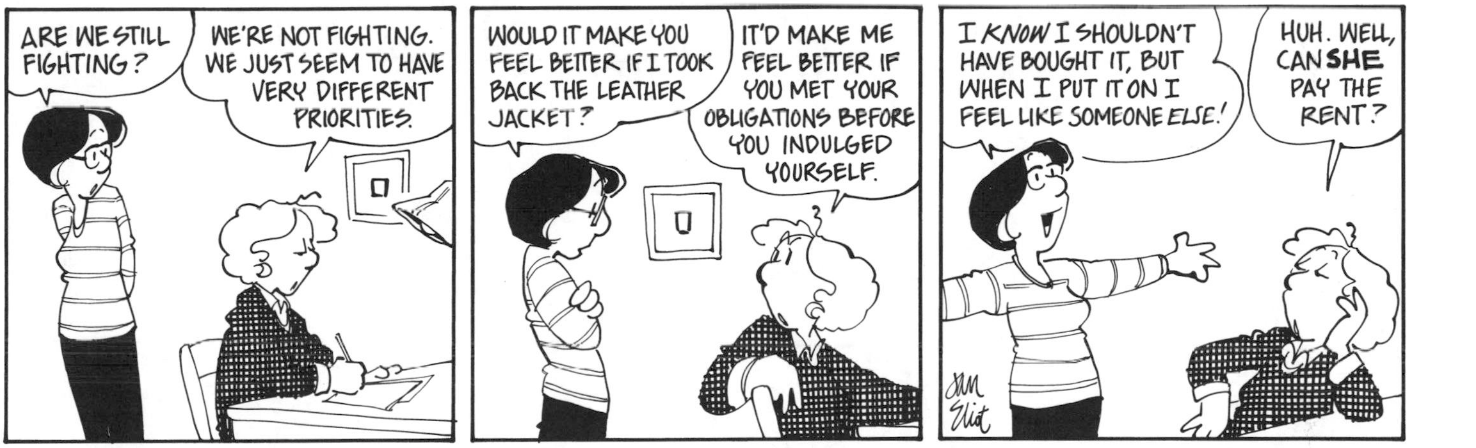
ARE WE STILL FIGHTING?
WE'RE NOT FIGHTING. WE JUST SEEM TO HAVE VERY DIFFERENT PRIORITIES.
WOULD IT MAKE YOU FEEL BETTER IF I TOOK BACK THE LEATHER JACKET?
IT'D MAKE ME FEEL BETTER IF YOU MET YOUR OBLIGATIONS BEFORE YOU INDULGED YOURSELF.
I *KNOW* I SHOULDN'T HAVE BOUGHT IT, BUT WHEN I PUT IT ON I FEEL LIKE SOMEONE *ELSE*!
HUH. WELL, CAN **SHE** PAY THE RENT?

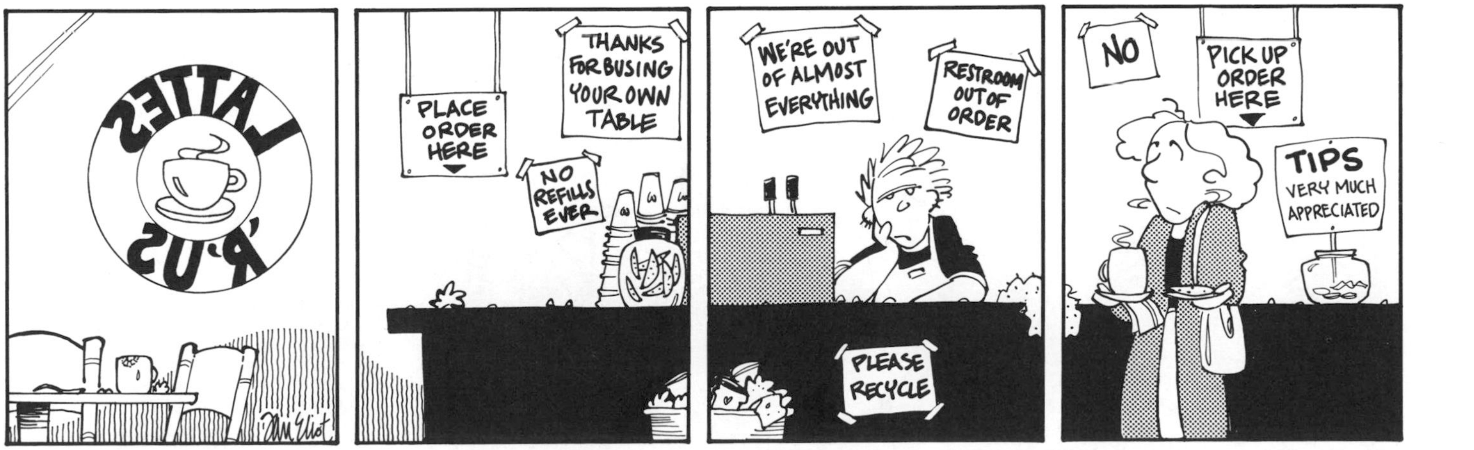
LATTES 'R' US
PLACE ORDER HERE
THANKS FOR BUSING YOUR OWN TABLE
NO REFILLS EVER
WE'RE OUT OF ALMOST EVERYTHING
RESTROOM OUT OF ORDER
PLEASE RECYCLE
NO
PICK UP ORDER HERE
TIPS VERY MUCH APPRECIATED

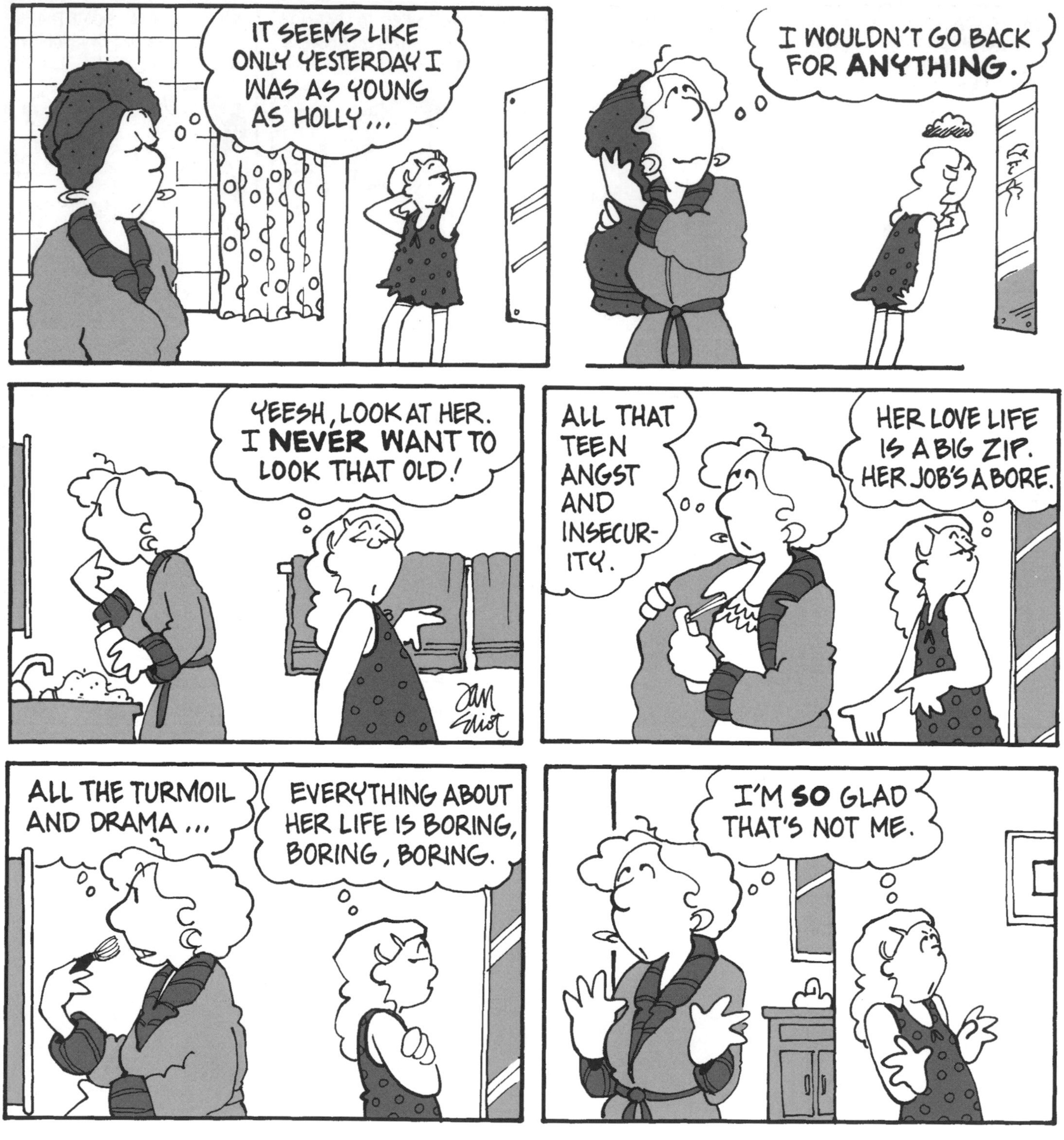
IT SEEMS LIKE ONLY YESTERDAY I WAS AS YOUNG AS HOLLY...
I WOULDN'T GO BACK FOR **ANYTHING**.
YEESH, LOOK AT HER. I **NEVER** WANT TO LOOK THAT OLD!
ALL THAT TEEN ANGST AND INSECUR-ITY.
HER LOVE LIFE IS A BIG ZIP. HER JOB'S A BORE.
ALL THE TURMOIL AND DRAMA...
EVERYTHING ABOUT HER LIFE IS BORING, BORING, BORING.
I'M **SO** GLAD THAT'S NOT ME.

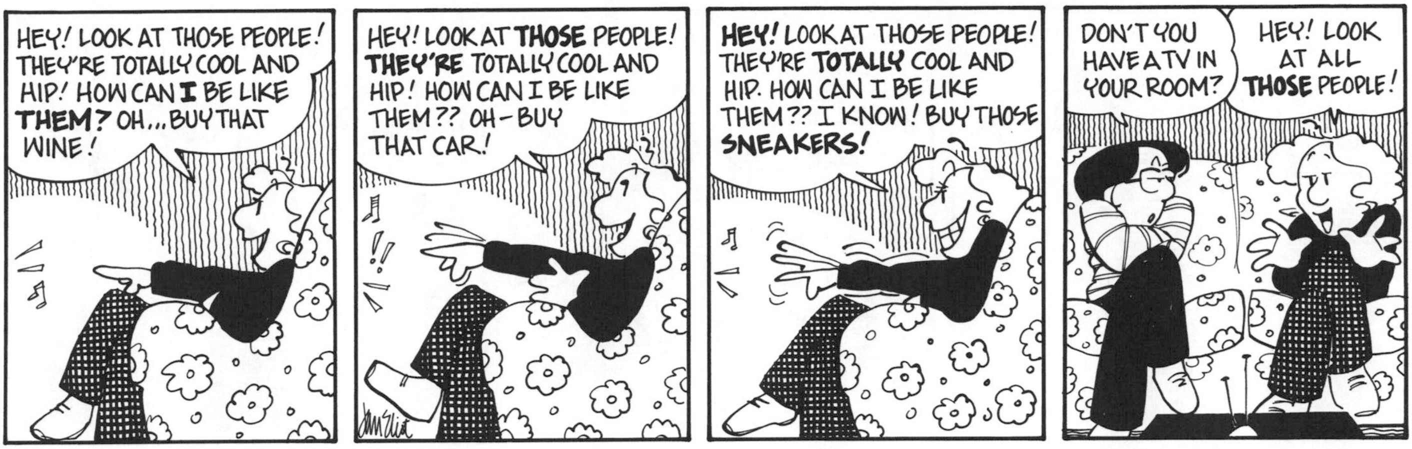
HEY! LOOK AT THOSE PEOPLE! THEY'RE TOTALLY COOL AND HIP! HOW CAN **I** BE LIKE **THEM?** OH... BUY THAT WINE!
HEY! LOOK AT **THOSE** PEOPLE! **THEY'RE** TOTALLY COOL AND HIP! HOW CAN I BE LIKE THEM?? OH-BUY THAT CAR!
HEY! LOOK AT THOSE PEOPLE! THEY'RE **TOTALLY** COOL AND HIP. HOW CAN I BE LIKE THEM?? I KNOW! BUY THOSE **SNEAKERS!**
DON'T YOU HAVE A TV IN YOUR ROOM?
HEY! LOOK AT ALL **THOSE** PEOPLE!

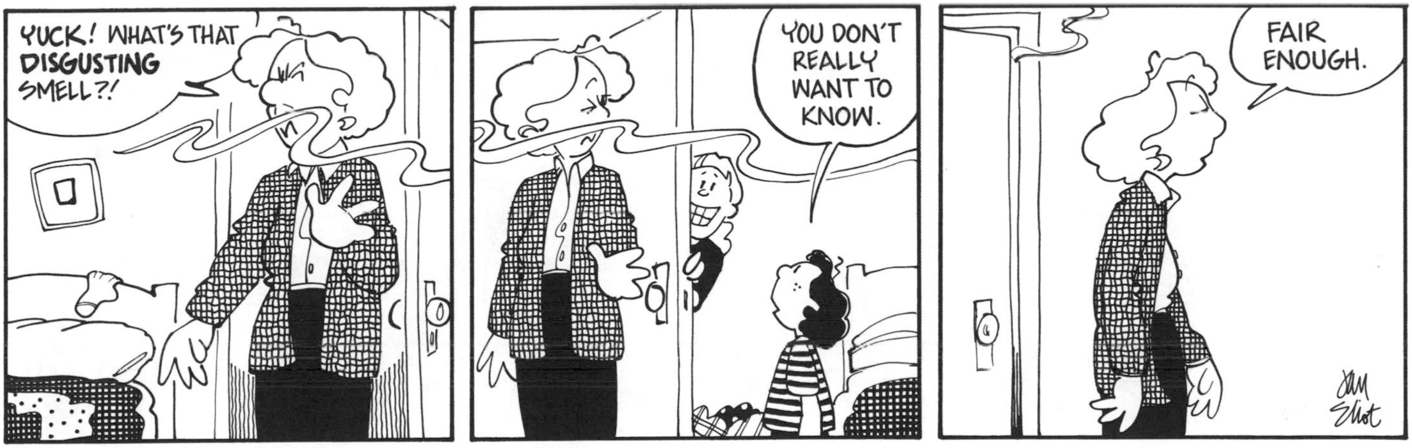
YUCK! WHAT'S THAT **DISGUSTING** SMELL?!
YOU DON'T REALLY WANT TO KNOW.
FAIR ENOUGH.

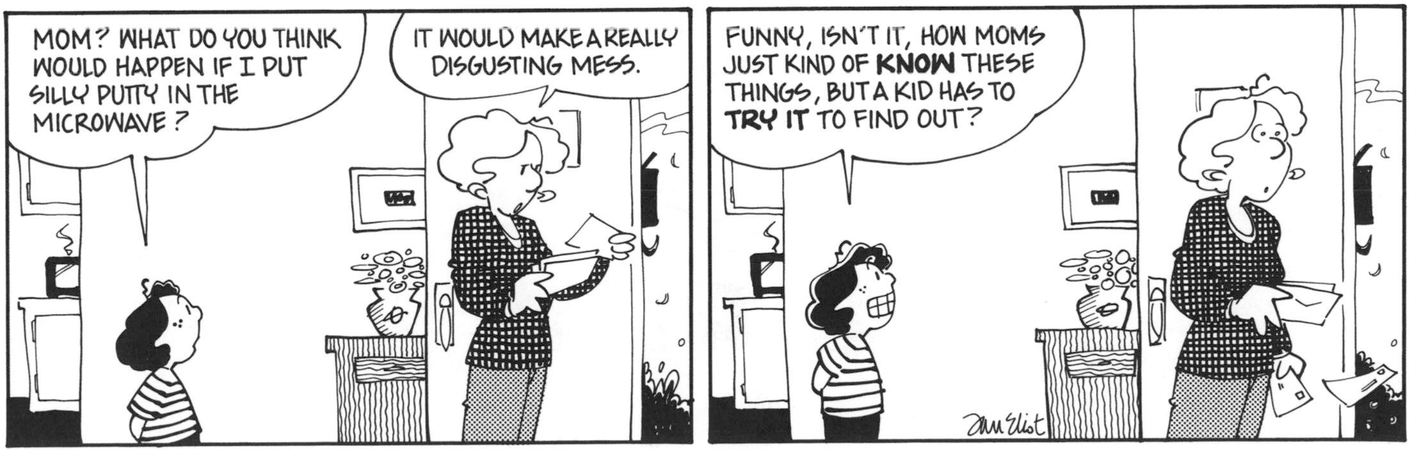
MOM? WHAT DO YOU THINK WOULD HAPPEN IF I PUT SILLY PUTTY IN THE MICROWAVE?
IT WOULD MAKE A REALLY DISGUSTING MESS.
FUNNY, ISN'T IT, HOW MOMS JUST KIND OF **KNOW** THESE THINGS, BUT A KID HAS TO **TRY IT** TO FIND OUT?

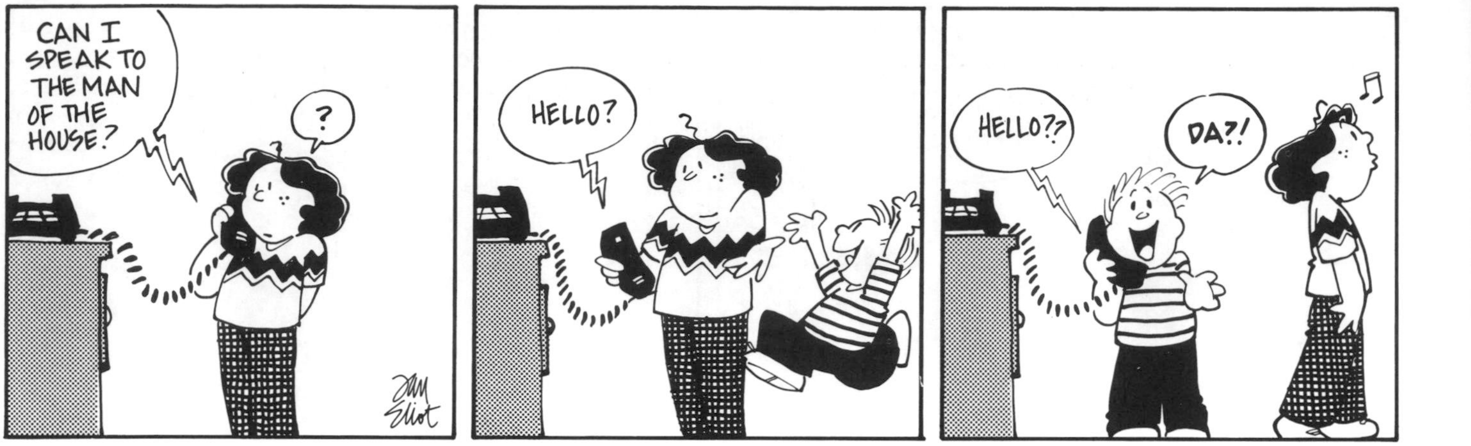
CAN I SPEAK TO THE MAN OF THE HOUSE?
?
HELLO?
HELLO??
DA?!

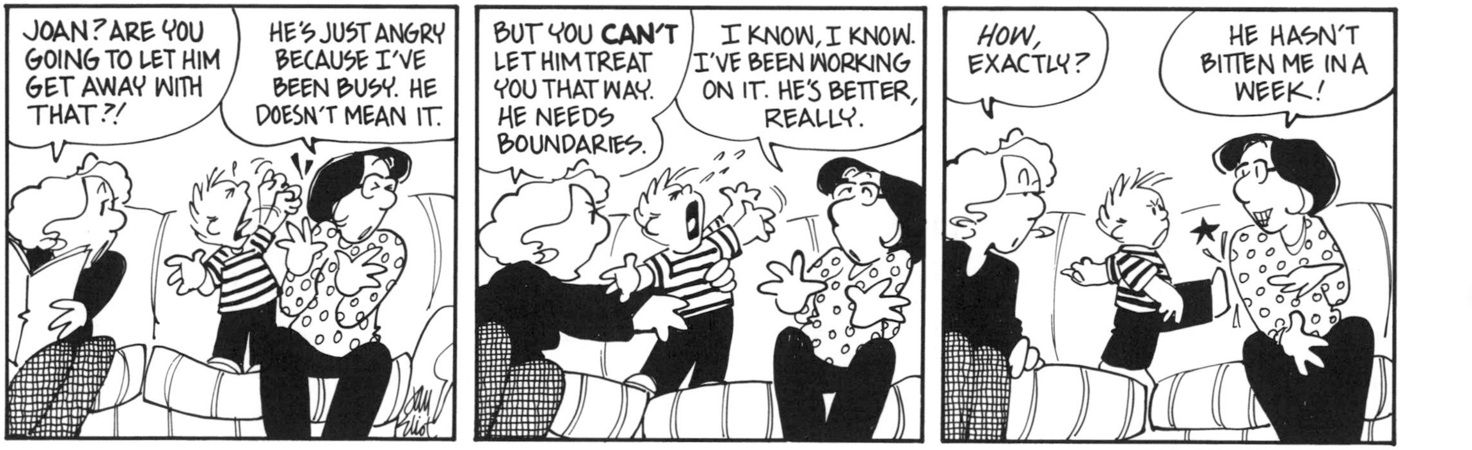
JOAN? ARE YOU GOING TO LET HIM GET AWAY WITH THAT?!
HE'S JUST ANGRY BECAUSE I'VE BEEN BUSY. HE DOESN'T MEAN IT.
BUT YOU **CAN'T** LET HIM TREAT YOU THAT WAY. HE NEEDS BOUNDARIES.
I KNOW, I KNOW. I'VE BEEN WORKING ON IT. HE'S BETTER, REALLY.
HOW, EXACTLY?
HE HASN'T BITTEN ME IN A WEEK!

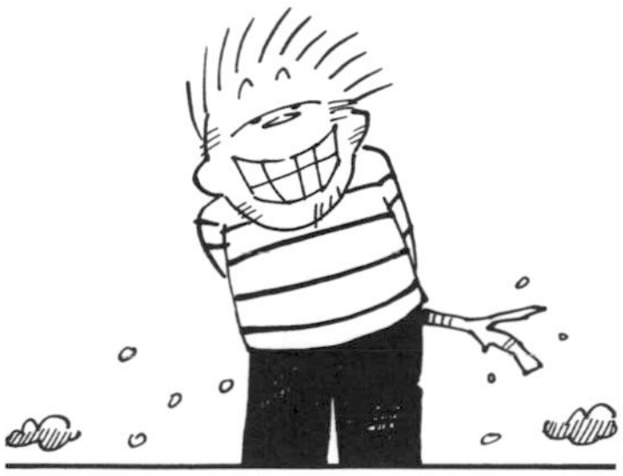

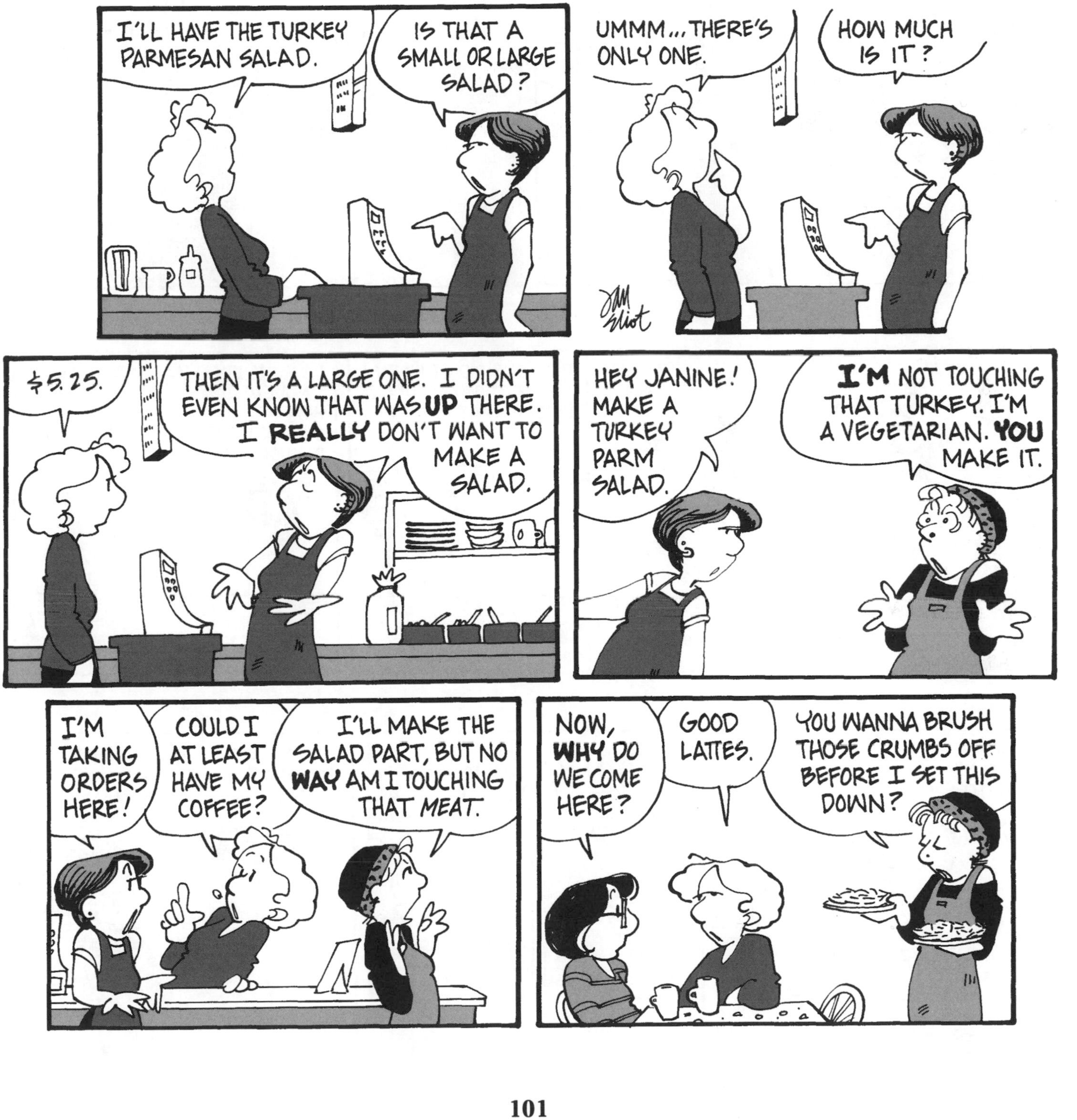

I'LL HAVE THE TURKEY PARMESAN SALAD.
IS THAT A SMALL OR LARGE SALAD?
UMMM... THERE'S ONLY ONE.
HOW MUCH IS IT?
$5.25.
THEN IT'S A LARGE ONE. I DIDN'T EVEN KNOW THAT WAS UP THERE. I REALLY DON'T WANT TO MAKE A SALAD.
HEY JANINE! MAKE A TURKEY PARM SALAD.
I'M NOT TOUCHING THAT TURKEY. I'M A VEGETARIAN. YOU MAKE IT.
I'M TAKING ORDERS HERE!
COULD I AT LEAST HAVE MY COFFEE?
I'LL MAKE THE SALAD PART, BUT NO WAY AM I TOUCHING THAT MEAT.
NOW, WHY DO WE COME HERE?
GOOD LATTES.
YOU WANNA BRUSH THOSE CRUMBS OFF BEFORE I SET THIS DOWN?

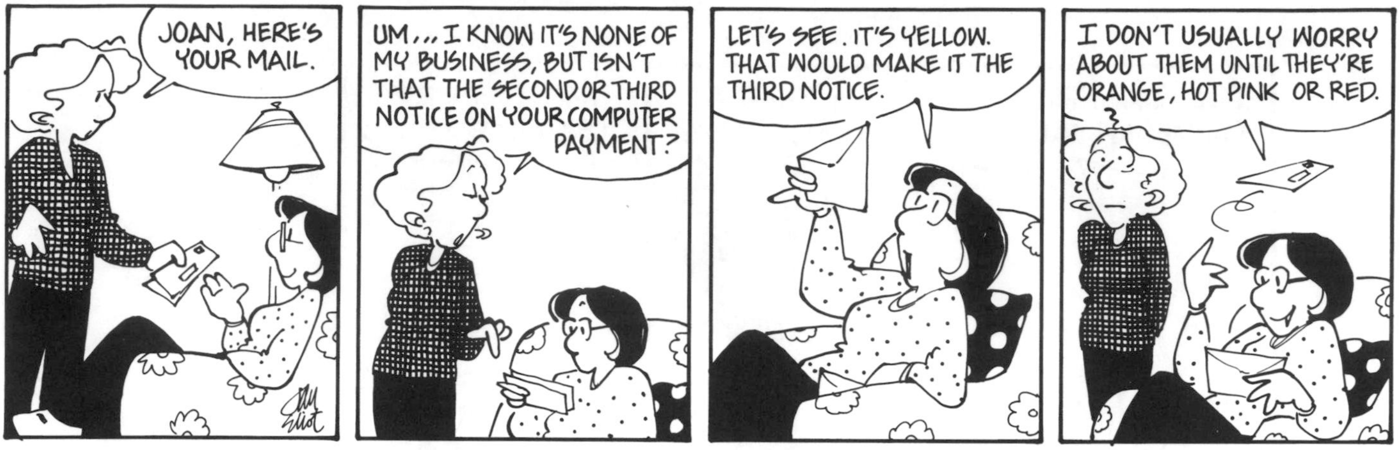

JOAN, HERE'S YOUR MAIL.
UM... I KNOW IT'S NONE OF MY BUSINESS, BUT ISN'T THAT THE SECOND OR THIRD NOTICE ON YOUR COMPUTER PAYMENT?
LET'S SEE. IT'S YELLOW. THAT WOULD MAKE IT THE THIRD NOTICE.
I DON'T USUALLY WORRY ABOUT THEM UNTIL THEY'RE ORANGE, HOT PINK OR RED.
Jan Eliot

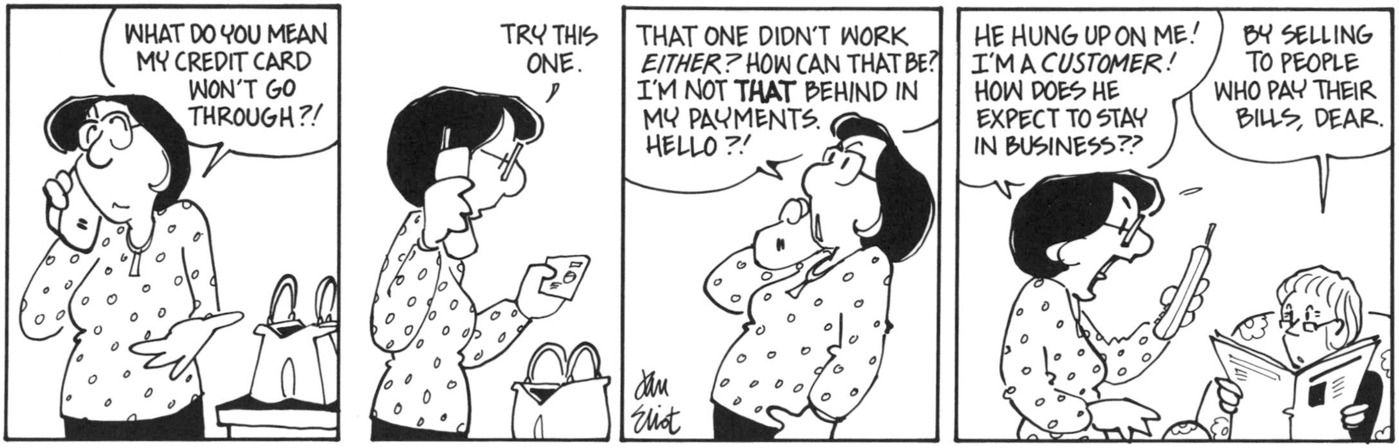

WHAT DO YOU MEAN MY CREDIT CARD WON'T GO THROUGH?!
TRY THIS ONE.
THAT ONE DIDN'T WORK *EITHER*? HOW CAN THAT BE? I'M NOT **THAT** BEHIND IN MY PAYMENTS. HELLO?!
HE HUNG UP ON ME! I'M A *CUSTOMER*! HOW DOES HE EXPECT TO STAY IN BUSINESS??
BY SELLING TO PEOPLE WHO PAY THEIR BILLS, DEAR.
Jan Eliot

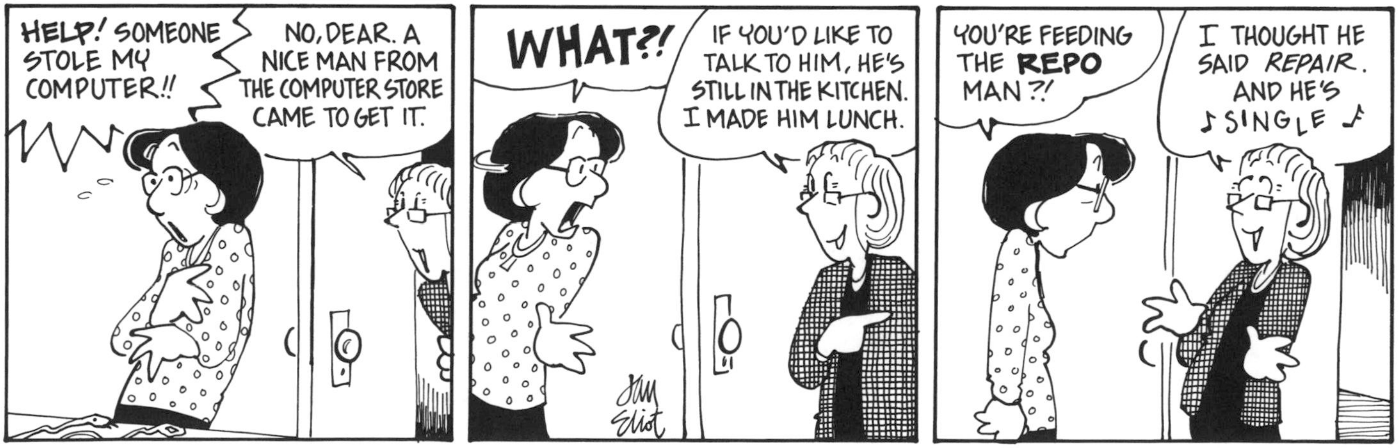

HELP! SOMEONE STOLE MY COMPUTER!!
NO, DEAR. A NICE MAN FROM THE COMPUTER STORE CAME TO GET IT.
WHAT?!
IF YOU'D LIKE TO TALK TO HIM, HE'S STILL IN THE KITCHEN. I MADE HIM LUNCH.
YOU'RE FEEDING THE **REPO** MAN?!
I THOUGHT HE SAID *REPAIR*. AND HE'S ♪ SINGLE ♪
Jan Eliot

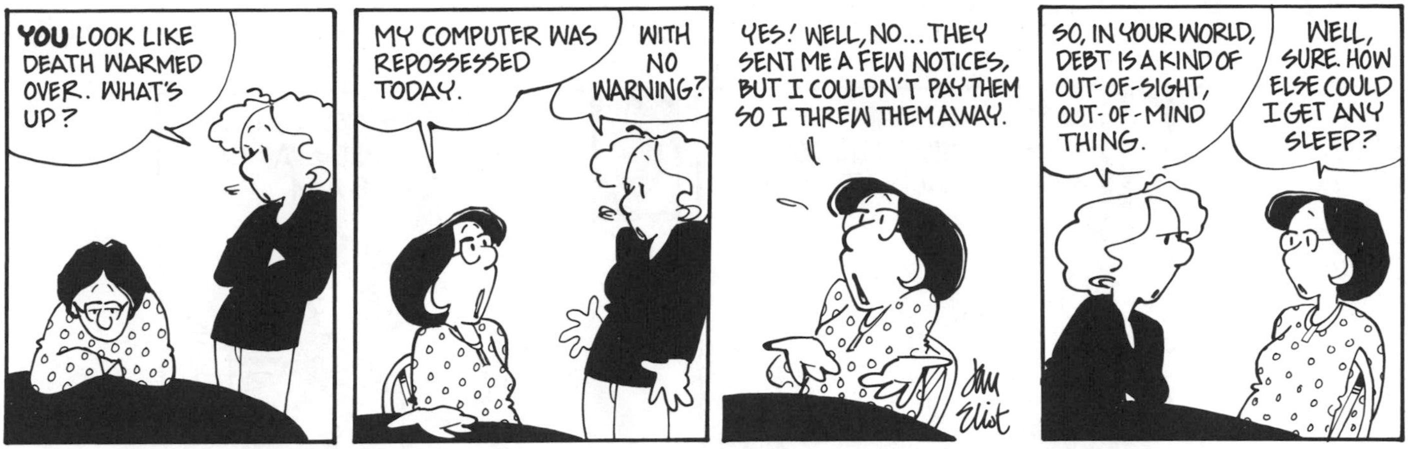

YOU LOOK LIKE DEATH WARMED OVER. WHAT'S UP?
MY COMPUTER WAS REPOSSESSED TODAY.
WITH NO WARNING?
YES! WELL, NO... THEY SENT ME A FEW NOTICES, BUT I COULDN'T PAY THEM SO I THREW THEM AWAY.
SO, IN YOUR WORLD, DEBT IS A KIND OF OUT-OF-SIGHT, OUT-OF-MIND THING.
WELL, SURE. HOW ELSE COULD I GET ANY SLEEP?

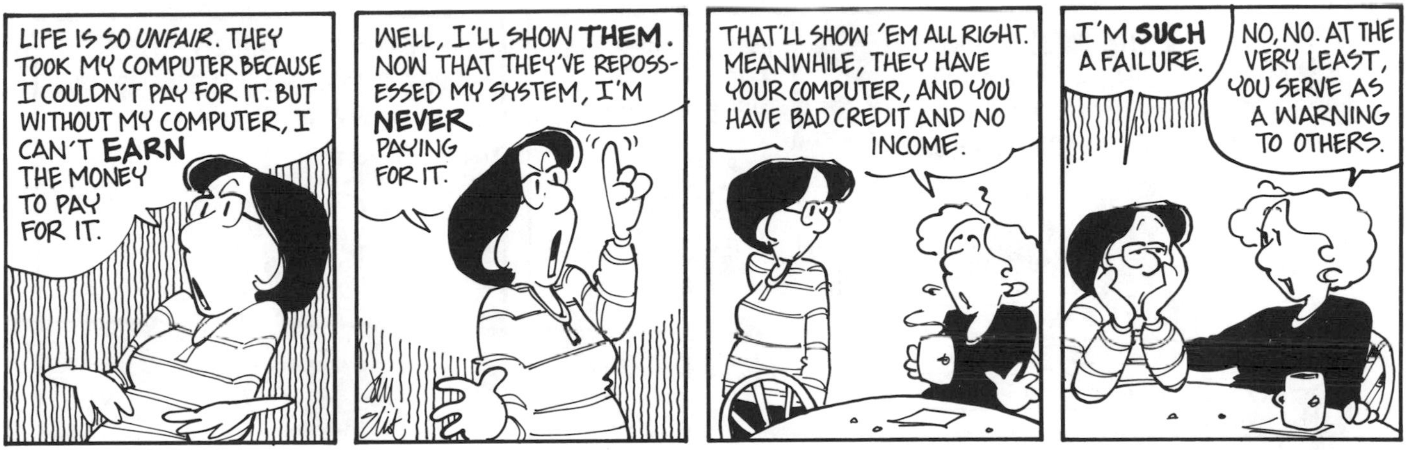

LIFE IS SO *UNFAIR*. THEY TOOK MY COMPUTER BECAUSE I COULDN'T PAY FOR IT. BUT WITHOUT MY COMPUTER, I CAN'T **EARN** THE MONEY TO PAY FOR IT.
WELL, I'LL SHOW **THEM.** NOW THAT THEY'VE REPOSSESSED MY SYSTEM, I'M **NEVER** PAYING FOR IT.
THAT'LL SHOW 'EM ALL RIGHT. MEANWHILE, THEY HAVE YOUR COMPUTER, AND YOU HAVE BAD CREDIT AND NO INCOME.
I'M **SUCH** A FAILURE.
NO, NO. AT THE VERY LEAST, YOU SERVE AS A WARNING TO OTHERS.

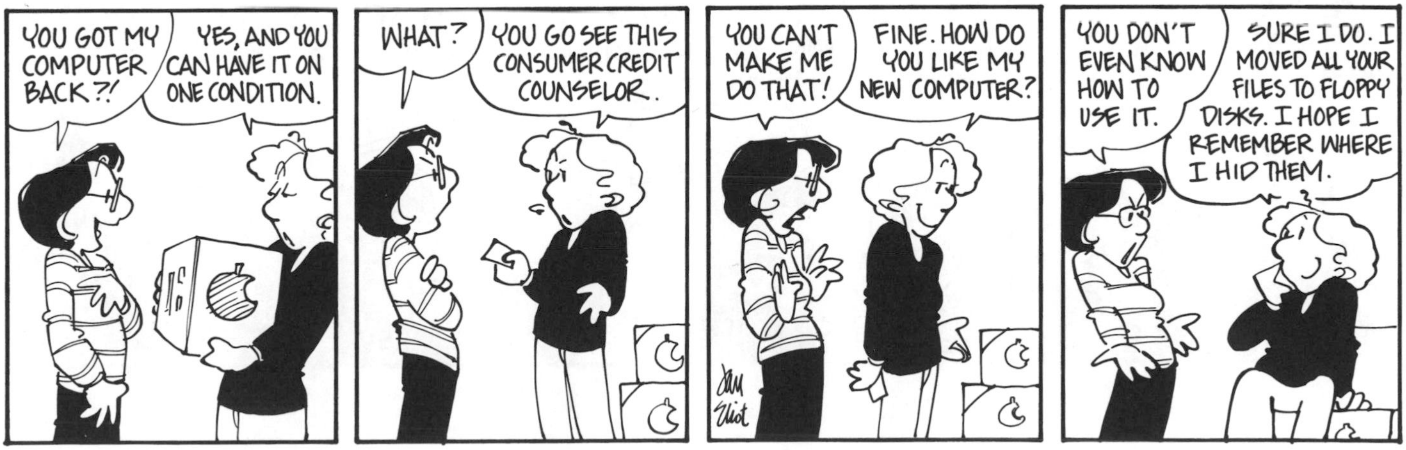

YOU GOT MY COMPUTER BACK?!
YES, AND YOU CAN HAVE IT ON ONE CONDITION.
WHAT?
YOU GO SEE THIS CONSUMER CREDIT COUNSELOR.
YOU CAN'T MAKE ME DO THAT!
FINE. HOW DO YOU LIKE MY NEW COMPUTER?
YOU DON'T EVEN KNOW HOW TO USE IT.
SURE I DO. I MOVED ALL YOUR FILES TO FLOPPY DISKS. I HOPE I REMEMBER WHERE I HID THEM.

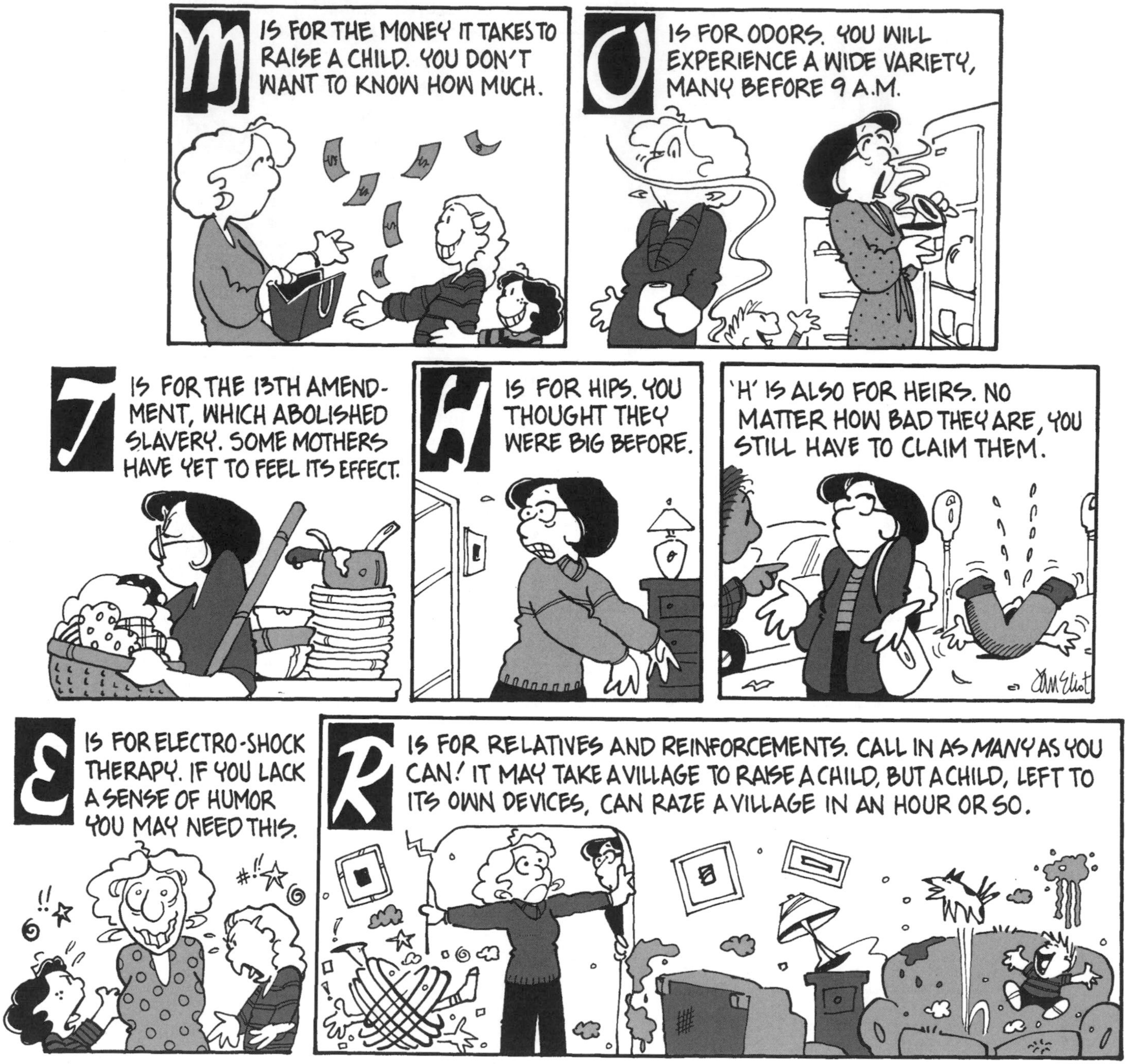
M
IS FOR THE MONEY IT TAKES TO RAISE A CHILD. YOU DON'T WANT TO KNOW HOW MUCH.
O
IS FOR ODORS. YOU WILL EXPERIENCE A WIDE VARIETY, MANY BEFORE 9 A.M.
T
IS FOR THE 13TH AMENDMENT, WHICH ABOLISHED SLAVERY. SOME MOTHERS HAVE YET TO FEEL ITS EFFECT.
H
IS FOR HIPS. YOU THOUGHT THEY WERE BIG BEFORE.
'H' IS ALSO FOR HEIRS. NO MATTER HOW BAD THEY ARE, YOU STILL HAVE TO CLAIM THEM.
E
IS FOR ELECTRO-SHOCK THERAPY. IF YOU LACK A SENSE OF HUMOR YOU MAY NEED THIS.
R
IS FOR RELATIVES AND REINFORCEMENTS. CALL IN AS MANY AS YOU CAN! IT MAY TAKE A VILLAGE TO RAISE A CHILD, BUT A CHILD, LEFT TO ITS OWN DEVICES, CAN RAZE A VILLAGE IN AN HOUR OR SO.

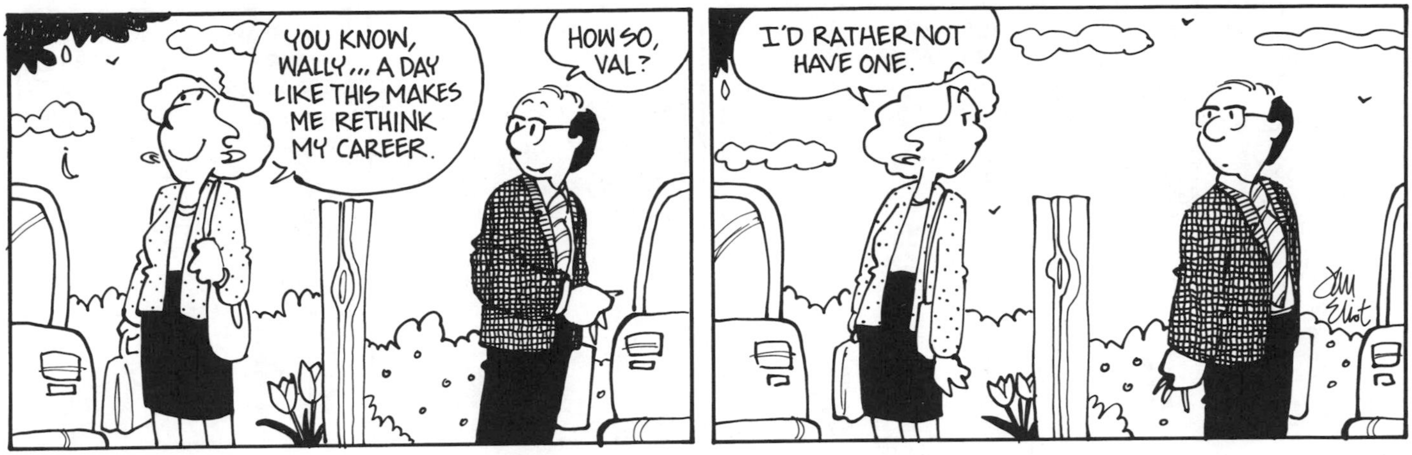
YOU KNOW, WALLY,,, A DAY LIKE THIS MAKES ME RETHINK MY CAREER.
HOW SO, VAL?
I'D RATHER NOT HAVE ONE.

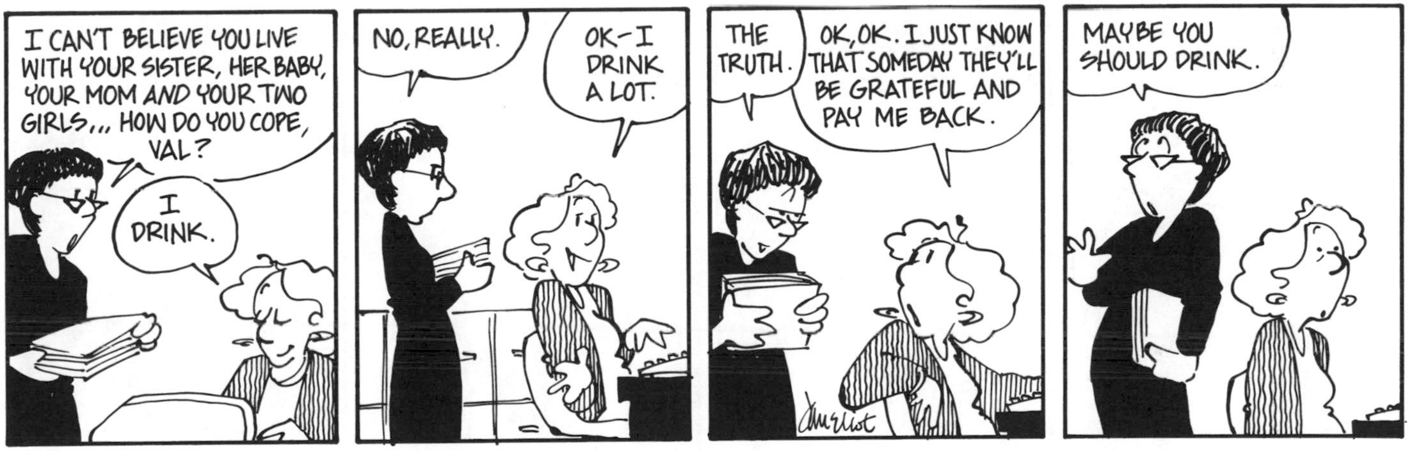
I CAN'T BELIEVE YOU LIVE WITH YOUR SISTER, HER BABY, YOUR MOM AND YOUR TWO GIRLS,,, HOW DO YOU COPE, VAL?
I DRINK.
NO, REALLY.
OK–I DRINK A LOT.
THE TRUTH.
OK, OK. I JUST KNOW THAT SOMEDAY THEY'LL BE GRATEFUL AND PAY ME BACK.
MAYBE YOU SHOULD DRINK.

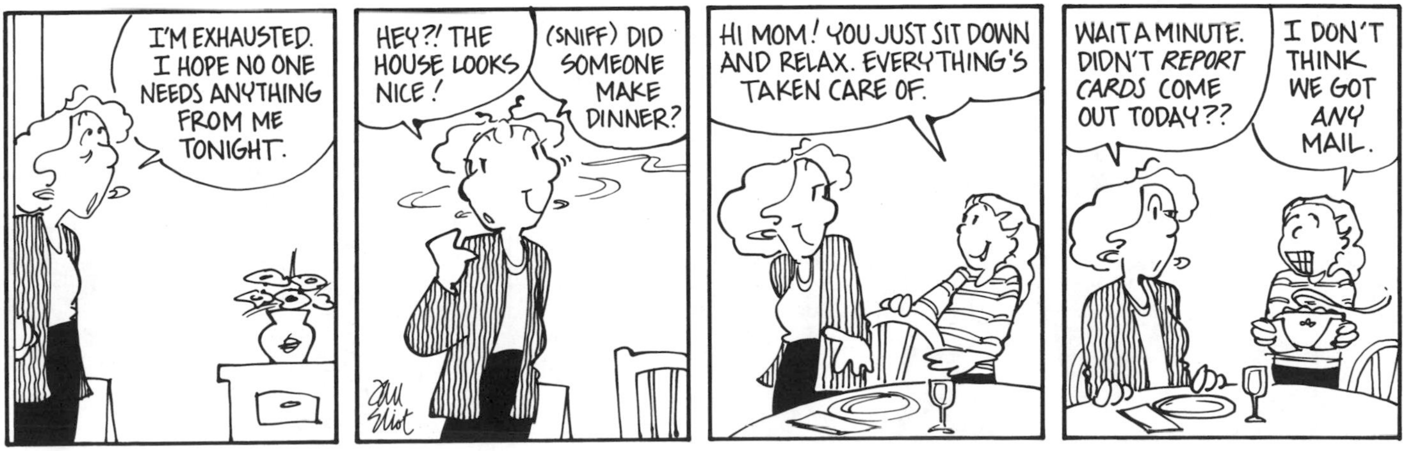
I'M EXHAUSTED. I HOPE NO ONE NEEDS ANYTHING FROM ME TONIGHT.
HEY?! THE HOUSE LOOKS NICE!
(SNIFF) DID SOMEONE MAKE DINNER?
HI MOM! YOU JUST SIT DOWN AND RELAX. EVERYTHING'S TAKEN CARE OF.
WAIT A MINUTE. DIDN'T REPORT CARDS COME OUT TODAY??
I DON'T THINK WE GOT ANY MAIL.

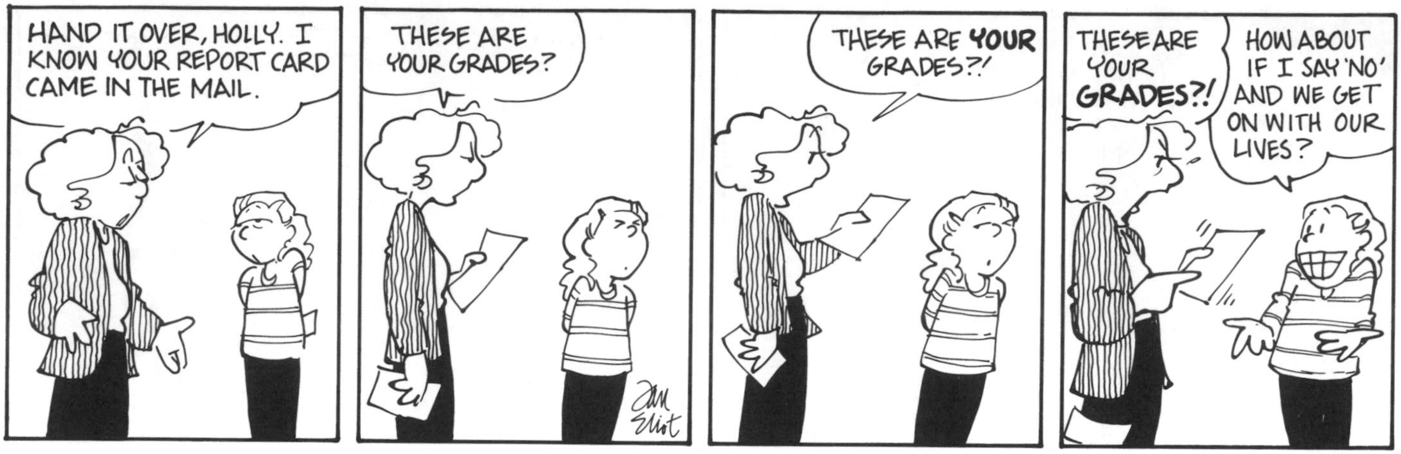
HAND IT OVER, HOLLY. I KNOW YOUR REPORT CARD CAME IN THE MAIL.
THESE ARE YOUR GRADES?
THESE ARE **YOUR** GRADES?!
THESE ARE YOUR **GRADES?!**
HOW ABOUT IF I SAY 'NO' AND WE GET ON WITH OUR LIVES?

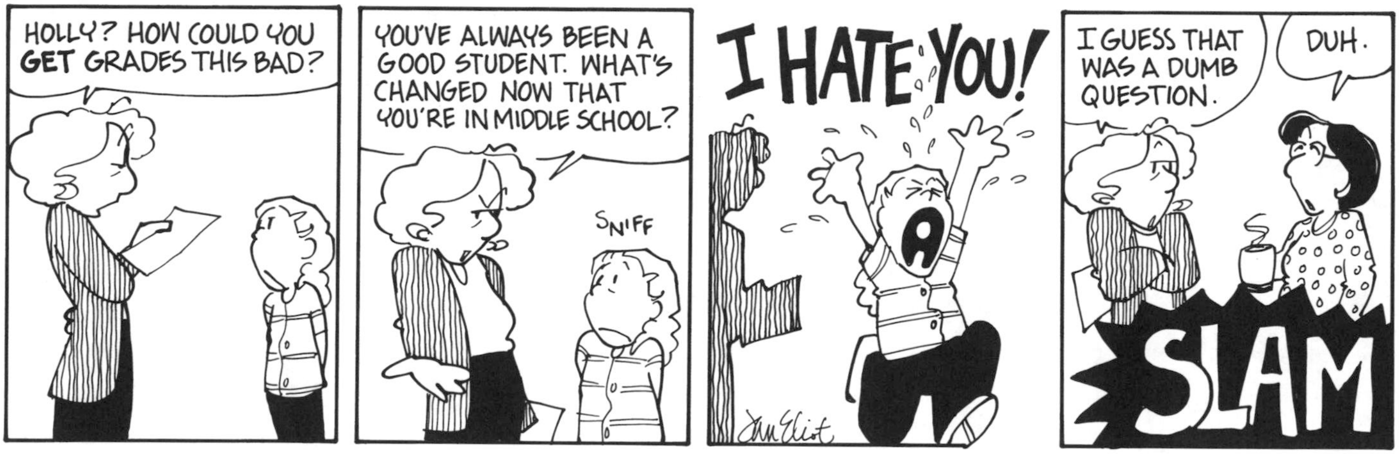
HOLLY? HOW COULD YOU **GET** GRADES THIS BAD?
YOU'VE ALWAYS BEEN A GOOD STUDENT. WHAT'S CHANGED NOW THAT YOU'RE IN MIDDLE SCHOOL?
SNIFF
I HATE YOU!
I GUESS THAT WAS A DUMB QUESTION.
DUH.
SLAM

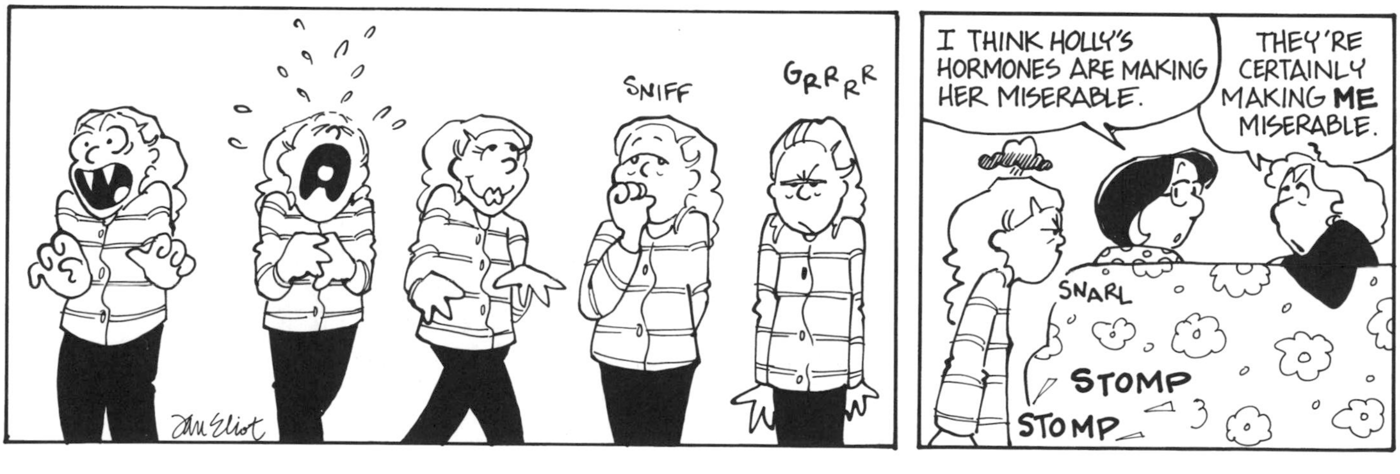
SNIFF
GRRRR
I THINK HOLLY'S HORMONES ARE MAKING HER MISERABLE.
THEY'RE CERTAINLY MAKING **ME** MISERABLE.
SNARL
STOMP
STOMP

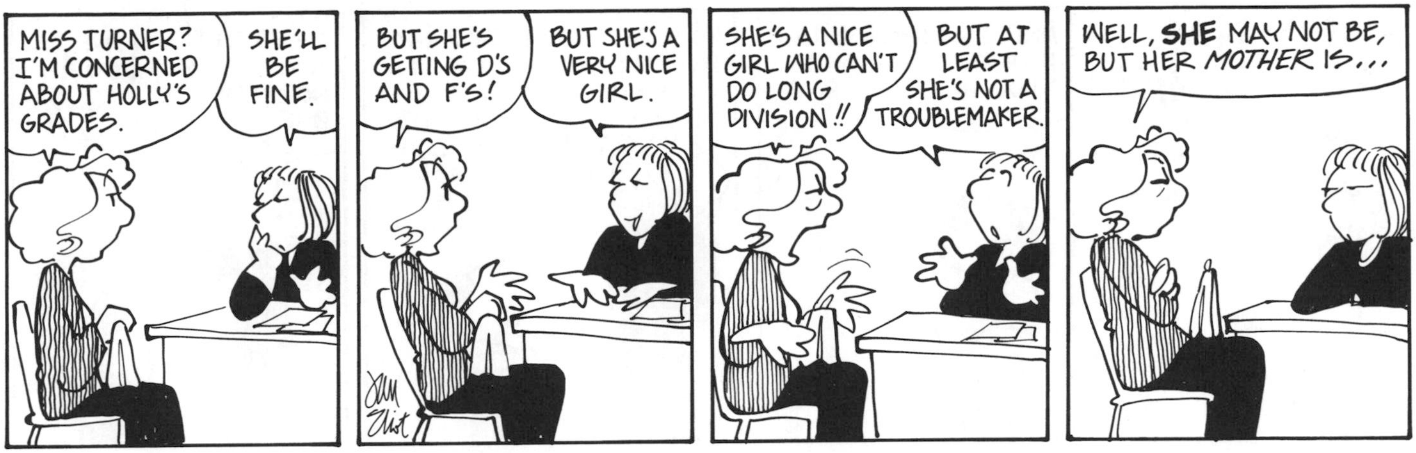
MISS TURNER? I'M CONCERNED ABOUT HOLLY'S GRADES.
SHE'LL BE FINE.
BUT SHE'S GETTING D'S AND F'S!
BUT SHE'S A VERY NICE GIRL.
SHE'S A NICE GIRL WHO CAN'T DO LONG DIVISION!!
BUT AT LEAST SHE'S NOT A TROUBLEMAKER.
WELL, **SHE** MAY NOT BE, BUT HER *MOTHER* IS...

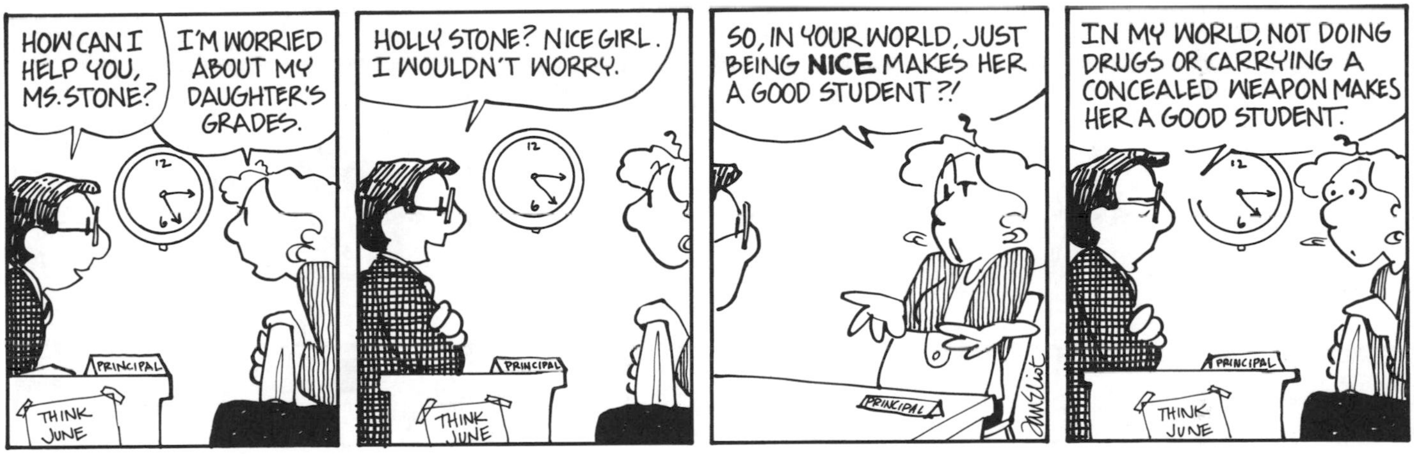
HOW CAN I HELP YOU, MS. STONE?
I'M WORRIED ABOUT MY DAUGHTER'S GRADES.
PRINCIPAL
THINK JUNE
HOLLY STONE? NICE GIRL. I WOULDN'T WORRY.
SO, IN YOUR WORLD, JUST BEING **NICE** MAKES HER A GOOD STUDENT?!
IN MY WORLD, NOT DOING DRUGS OR CARRYING A CONCEALED WEAPON MAKES HER A GOOD STUDENT.

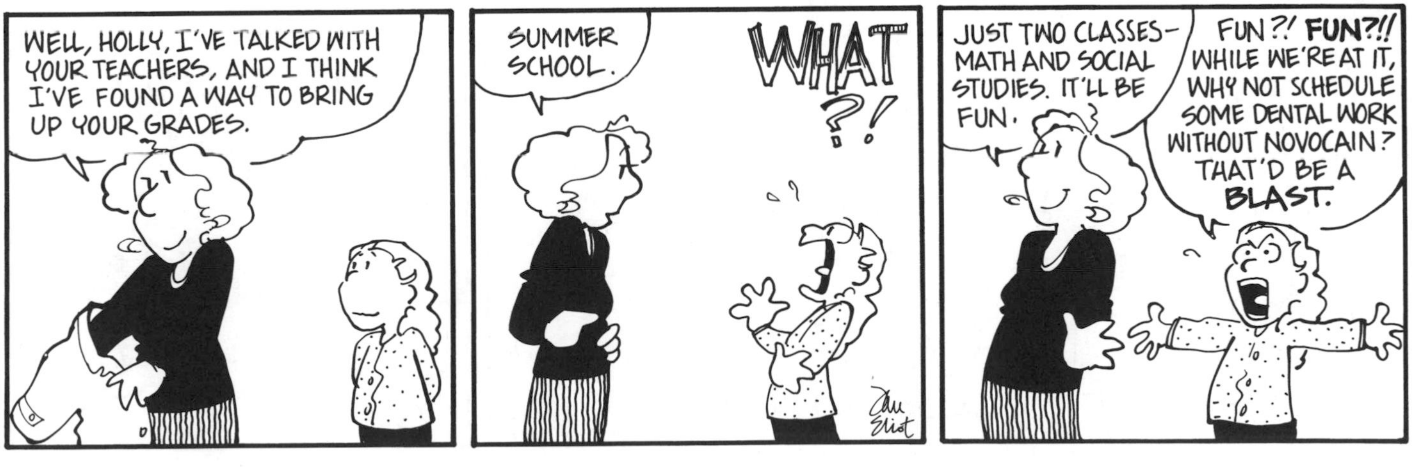
WELL, HOLLY, I'VE TALKED WITH YOUR TEACHERS, AND I THINK I'VE FOUND A WAY TO BRING UP YOUR GRADES.
SUMMER SCHOOL.
WHAT?!
JUST TWO CLASSES- MATH AND SOCIAL STUDIES. IT'LL BE FUN.
FUN?! **FUN?!!** WHILE WE'RE AT IT, WHY NOT SCHEDULE SOME DENTAL WORK WITHOUT NOVOCAIN? THAT'D BE A **BLAST.**

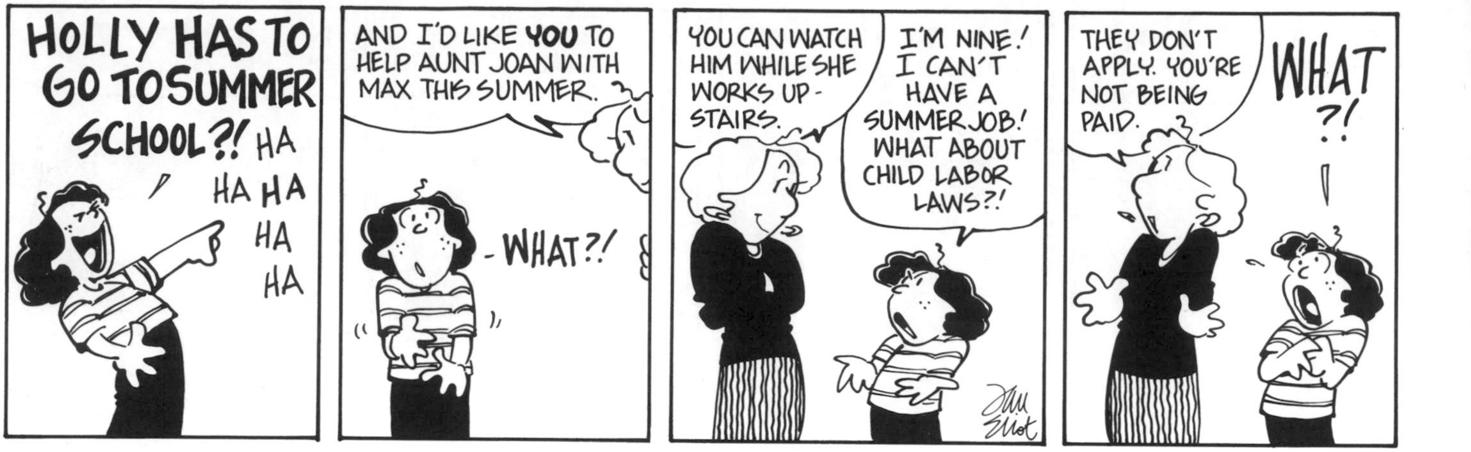
HOLLY HAS TO GO TO SUMMER SCHOOL?! HA HA HA HA HA HA
AND I'D LIKE YOU TO HELP AUNT JOAN WITH MAX THIS SUMMER.
-WHAT?!
YOU CAN WATCH HIM WHILE SHE WORKS UP-STAIRS.
I'M NINE! I CAN'T HAVE A SUMMER JOB! WHAT ABOUT CHILD LABOR LAWS?!
THEY DON'T APPLY. YOU'RE NOT BEING PAID.
WHAT ?! !

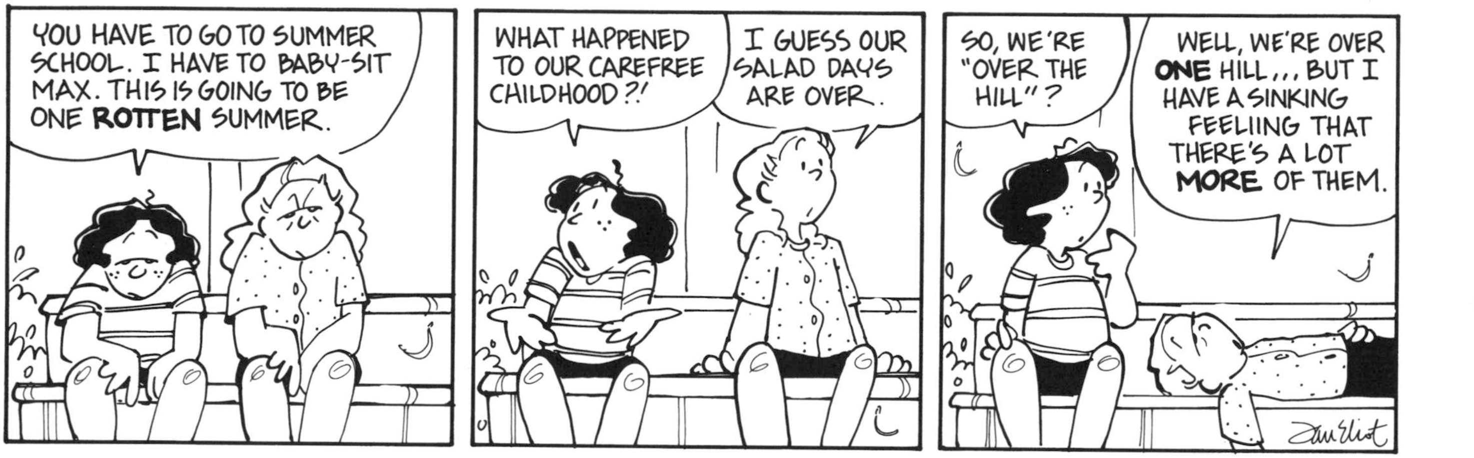
YOU HAVE TO GO TO SUMMER SCHOOL. I HAVE TO BABY-SIT MAX. THIS IS GOING TO BE ONE ROTTEN SUMMER.
WHAT HAPPENED TO OUR CAREFREE CHILDHOOD?!
I GUESS OUR SALAD DAYS ARE OVER.
SO, WE'RE "OVER THE HILL"?
WELL, WE'RE OVER ONE HILL,,, BUT I HAVE A SINKING FEELIING THAT THERE'S A LOT MORE OF THEM.

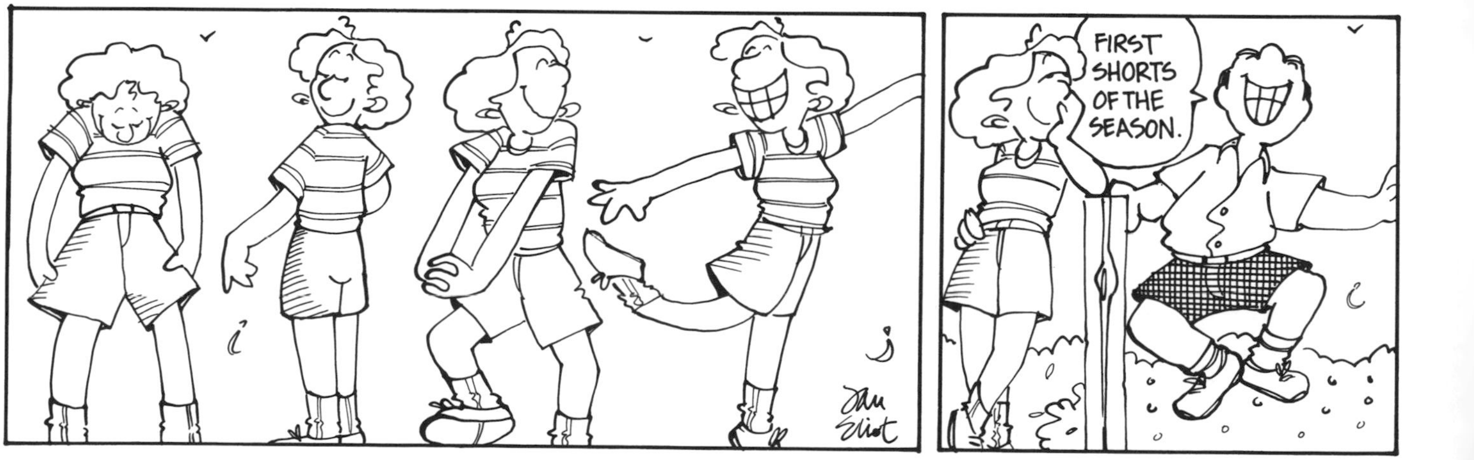
FIRST SHORTS OF THE SEASON.

MAX, NO! WHY DO KIDS LOVE PUDDLES?
SPLISH SPLISH
SPLOOSH
SPLOSH
HEE HEE
HEE
HEE
REALLY, EVIE ... MY DAUGHTERS COULD BOTH REMARRY IN A MINUTE. BUT FOR NOW, THEY'RE SIMPLY —
HOO
HOO HEE
— CHOOSING TO STAY SINGLE.
YOU TWO DO THIS JUST TO SPITE ME, DON'T YOU?
WHATEVER YOU SAY, DEAR.
PAT PAT

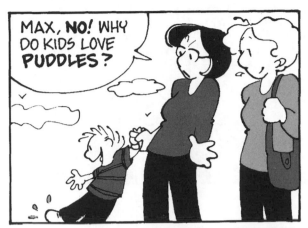

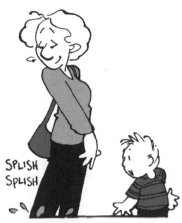

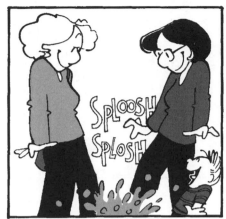

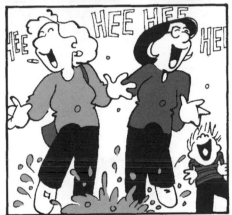

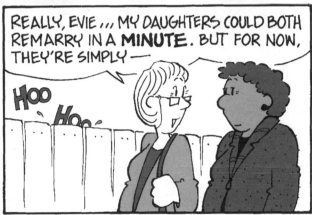

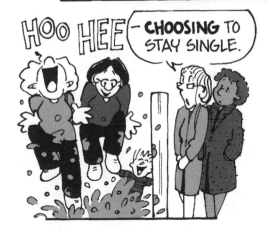

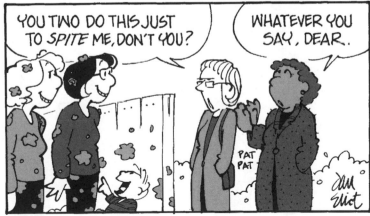

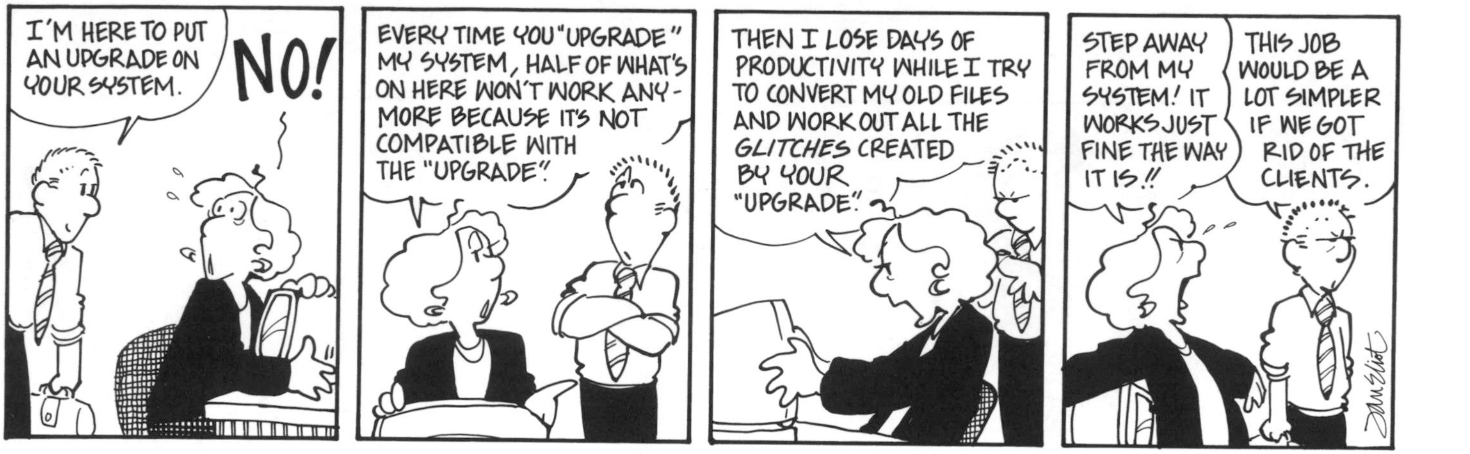
I'M HERE TO PUT AN UPGRADE ON YOUR SYSTEM.
NO!
EVERY TIME YOU "UPGRADE" MY SYSTEM, HALF OF WHAT'S ON HERE WON'T WORK ANY-MORE BECAUSE IT'S NOT COMPATIBLE WITH THE "UPGRADE".
THEN I LOSE DAYS OF PRODUCTIVITY WHILE I TRY TO CONVERT MY OLD FILES AND WORK OUT ALL THE *GLITCHES* CREATED BY YOUR "UPGRADE".
STEP AWAY FROM MY SYSTEM! IT WORKS JUST FINE THE WAY IT IS!!
THIS JOB WOULD BE A LOT SIMPLER IF WE GOT RID OF THE CLIENTS.

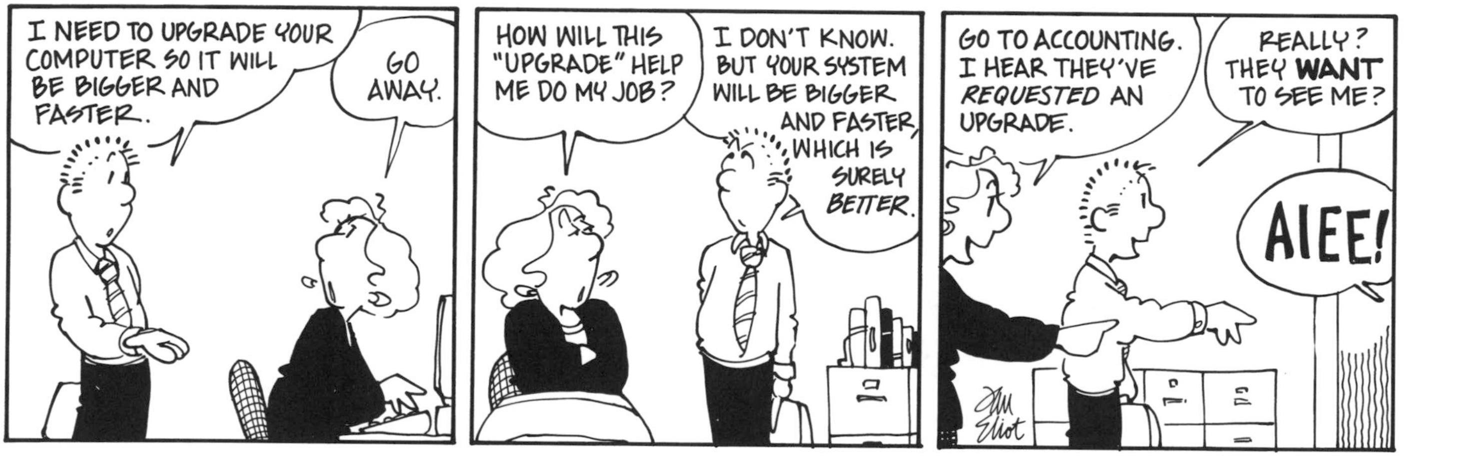
I NEED TO UPGRADE YOUR COMPUTER SO IT WILL BE BIGGER AND FASTER.
GO AWAY.
HOW WILL THIS "UPGRADE" HELP ME DO MY JOB?
I DON'T KNOW. BUT YOUR SYSTEM WILL BE BIGGER AND FASTER, WHICH IS SURELY *BETTER*.
GO TO ACCOUNTING. I HEAR THEY'VE *REQUESTED* AN UPGRADE.
REALLY? THEY **WANT** TO SEE ME?
AIEE!

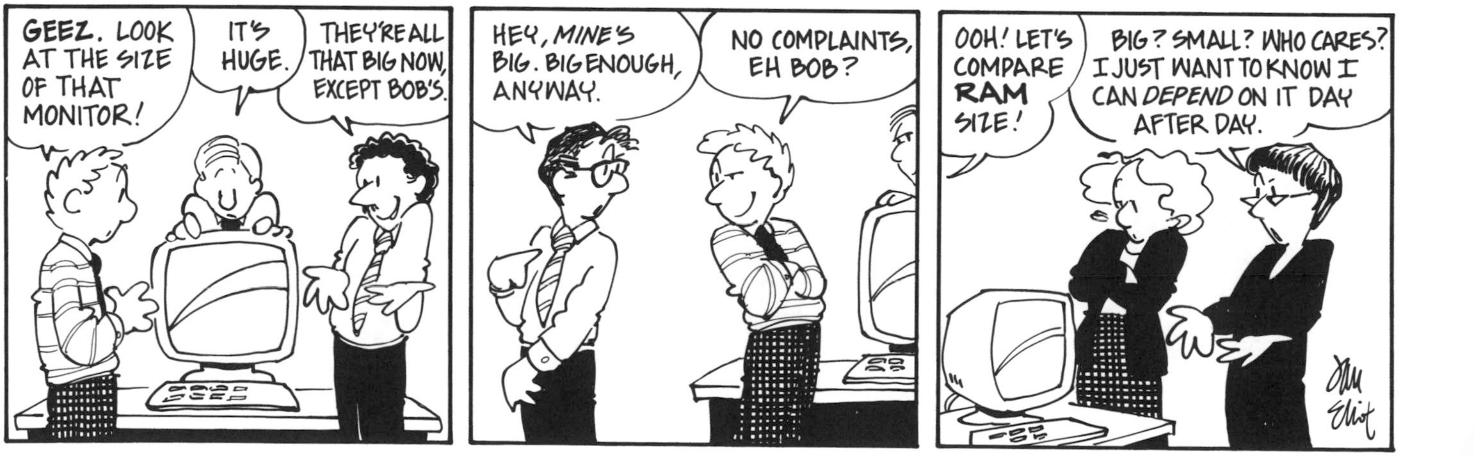
GEEZ. LOOK AT THE SIZE OF THAT MONITOR!
IT'S HUGE.
THEY'RE ALL THAT BIG NOW, EXCEPT BOB'S.
HEY, *MINE'S* BIG. BIG ENOUGH, ANYWAY.
NO COMPLAINTS, EH BOB?
OOH! LET'S COMPARE **RAM** SIZE!
BIG? SMALL? WHO CARES? I JUST WANT TO KNOW I CAN *DEPEND* ON IT DAY AFTER DAY.

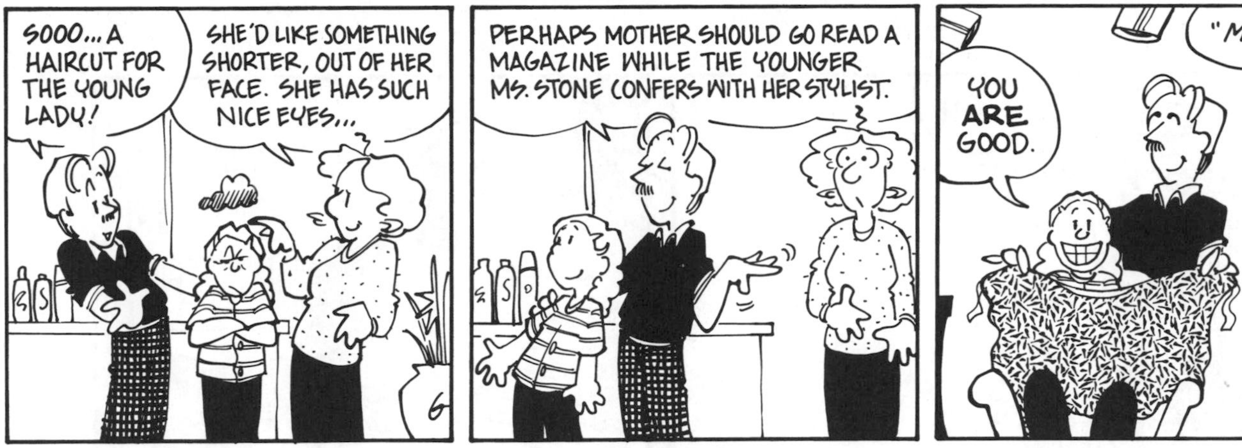
SOOO... A HAIRCUT FOR THE YOUNG LADY!
SHE'D LIKE SOMETHING SHORTER, OUT OF HER FACE. SHE HAS SUCH NICE EYES,...
PERHAPS MOTHER SHOULD GO READ A MAGAZINE WHILE THE YOUNGER MS. STONE CONFERS WITH HER STYLIST.
"MOTHER"?!
YOU **ARE** GOOD.

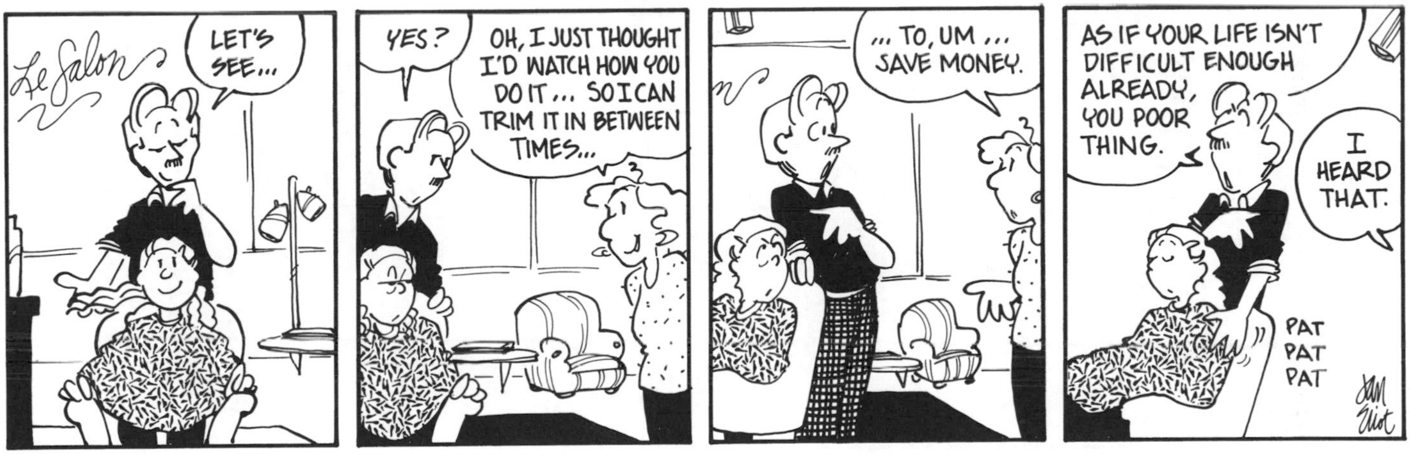
Le Salon
LET'S SEE...
YES?
OH, I JUST THOUGHT I'D WATCH HOW YOU DO IT... SO I CAN TRIM IT IN BETWEEN TIMES...
... TO, UM ... SAVE MONEY.
AS IF YOUR LIFE ISN'T DIFFICULT ENOUGH ALREADY, YOU POOR THING.
I HEARD THAT.
PAT PAT PAT

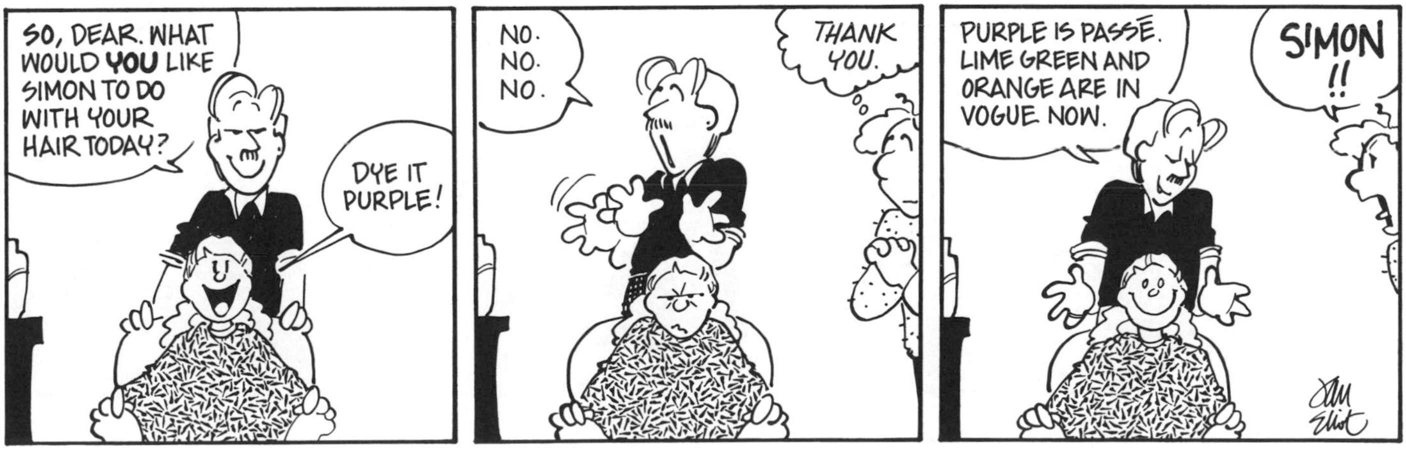
SO, DEAR. WHAT WOULD **YOU** LIKE SIMON TO DO WITH YOUR HAIR TODAY?
DYE IT PURPLE!
NO. NO. NO.
THANK YOU.
PURPLE IS PASSÉ. LIME GREEN AND ORANGE ARE IN VOGUE NOW.
SIMON !!

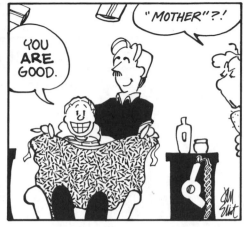

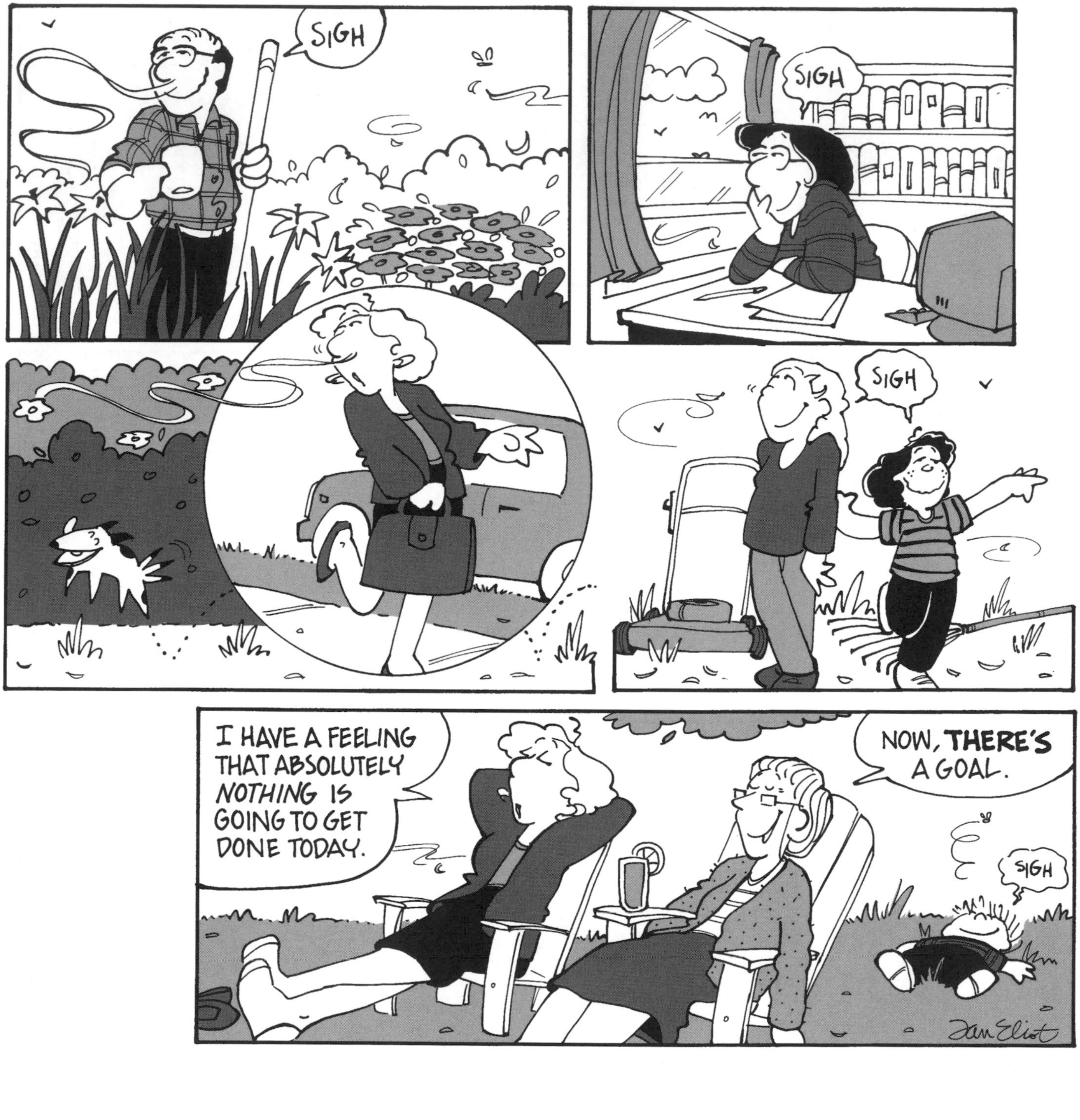
SIGH
SIGH
SIGH
I HAVE A FEELING THAT ABSOLUTELY *NOTHING* IS GOING TO GET DONE TODAY.
NOW, **THERE'S** A GOAL.
SIGH
Jan Eliot

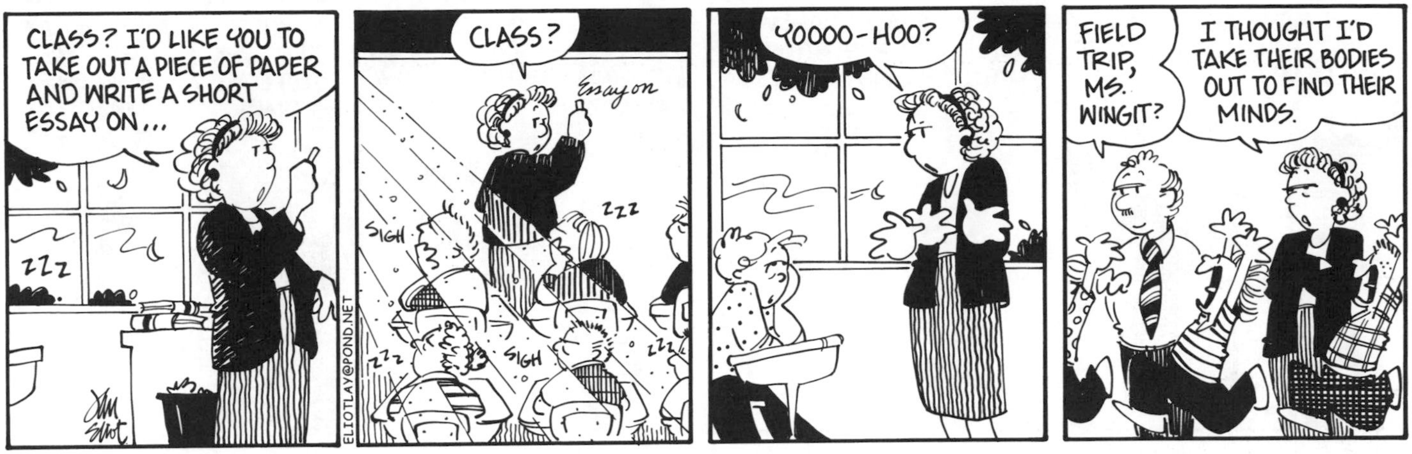
CLASS? I'D LIKE YOU TO TAKE OUT A PIECE OF PAPER AND WRITE A SHORT ESSAY ON...
ZZZ
CLASS?
Essay on
SIGH
ZZZ
SIGH
ZZZ
ELIOTLAY@POND.NET
YOOOO-HOO?
FIELD TRIP, MS. WINGIT?
I THOUGHT I'D TAKE THEIR BODIES OUT TO FIND THEIR MINDS.

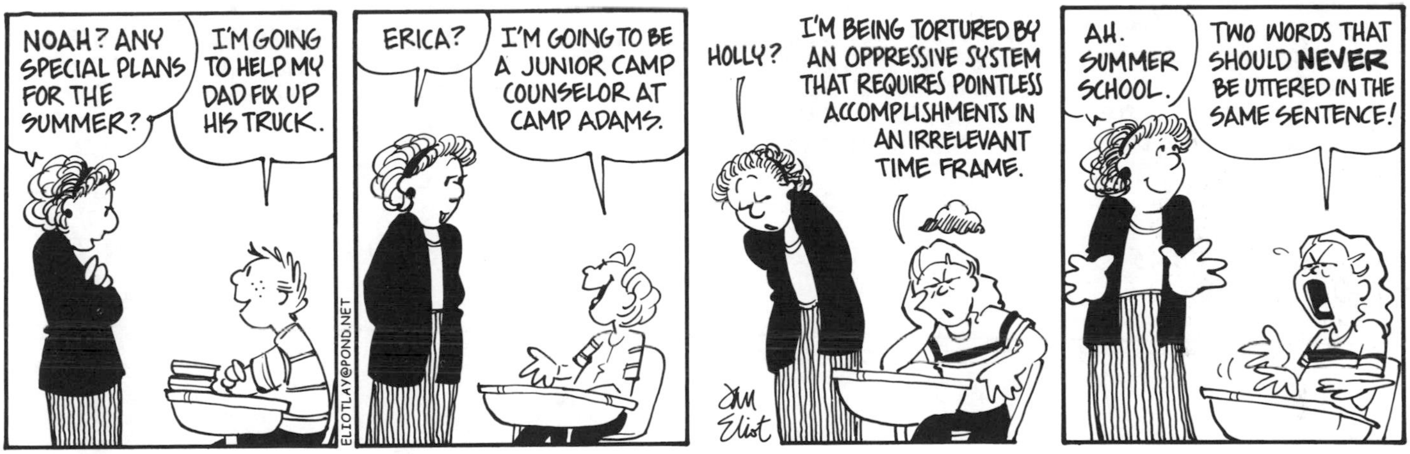
NOAH? ANY SPECIAL PLANS FOR THE SUMMER?
I'M GOING TO HELP MY DAD FIX UP HIS TRUCK.
ELIOTLAY@POND.NET
ERICA?
I'M GOING TO BE A JUNIOR CAMP COUNSELOR AT CAMP ADAMS.
HOLLY?
I'M BEING TORTURED BY AN OPPRESSIVE SYSTEM THAT REQUIRES POINTLESS ACCOMPLISHMENTS IN AN IRRELEVANT TIME FRAME.
AH. SUMMER SCHOOL.
TWO WORDS THAT SHOULD NEVER BE UTTERED IN THE SAME SENTENCE!

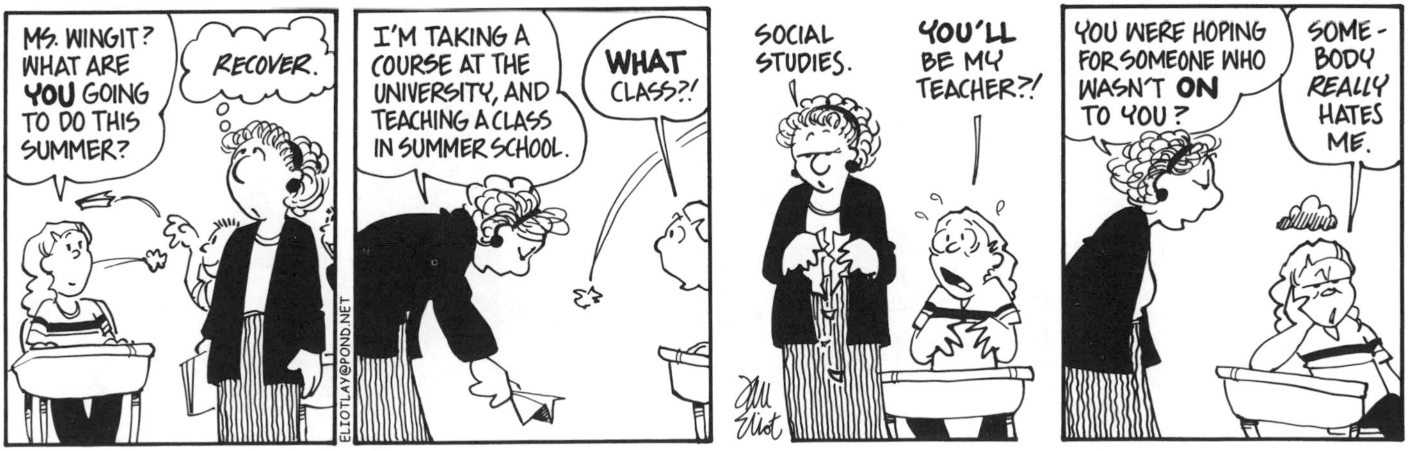
MS. WINGIT? WHAT ARE YOU GOING TO DO THIS SUMMER?
RECOVER.
ELIOTLAY@POND.NET
I'M TAKING A COURSE AT THE UNIVERSITY, AND TEACHING A CLASS IN SUMMER SCHOOL.
WHAT CLASS?!
SOCIAL STUDIES.
YOU'LL BE MY TEACHER?!
YOU WERE HOPING FOR SOMEONE WHO WASN'T ON TO YOU?
SOME-BODY REALLY HATES ME.

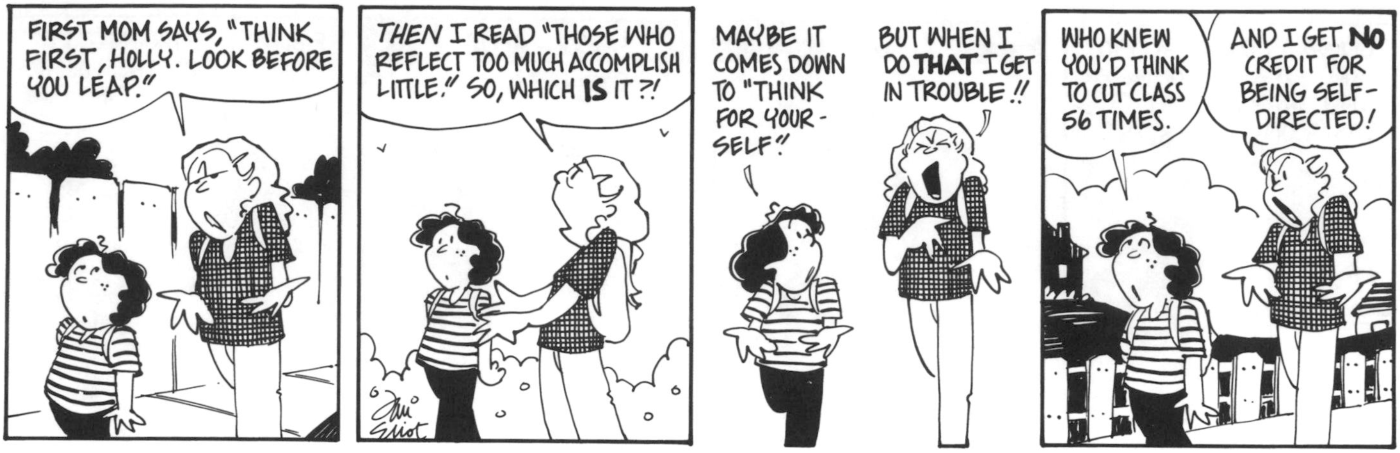
FIRST MOM SAYS, "THINK FIRST, HOLLY. LOOK BEFORE YOU LEAP."
THEN I READ "THOSE WHO REFLECT TOO MUCH ACCOMPLISH LITTLE." SO, WHICH **IS** IT ?!
MAYBE IT COMES DOWN TO "THINK FOR YOUR-SELF."
BUT WHEN I DO **THAT** I GET IN TROUBLE !!
WHO KNEW YOU'D THINK TO CUT CLASS 56 TIMES.
AND I GET **NO** CREDIT FOR BEING SELF-DIRECTED!

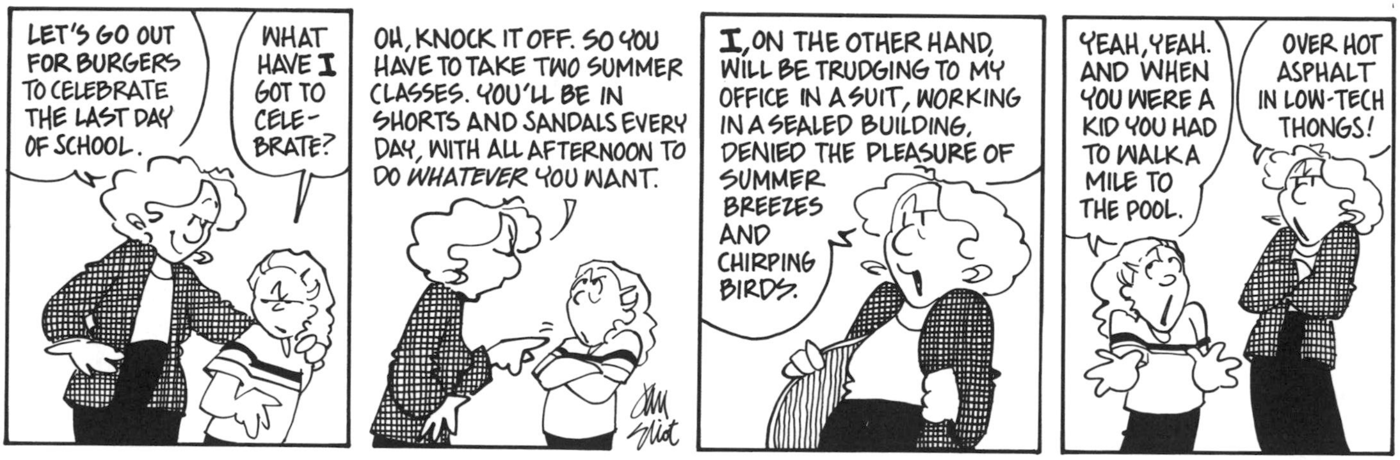
LET'S GO OUT FOR BURGERS TO CELEBRATE THE LAST DAY OF SCHOOL.
WHAT HAVE **I** GOT TO CELE-BRATE?
OH, KNOCK IT OFF. SO YOU HAVE TO TAKE TWO SUMMER CLASSES. YOU'LL BE IN SHORTS AND SANDALS EVERY DAY, WITH ALL AFTERNOON TO DO *WHATEVER* YOU WANT.
I, ON THE OTHER HAND, WILL BE TRUDGING TO MY OFFICE IN A SUIT, WORKING IN A SEALED BUILDING, DENIED THE PLEASURE OF SUMMER BREEZES AND CHIRPING BIRDS.
YEAH, YEAH. AND WHEN YOU WERE A KID YOU HAD TO WALK A MILE TO THE POOL.
OVER HOT ASPHALT IN LOW-TECH THONGS!

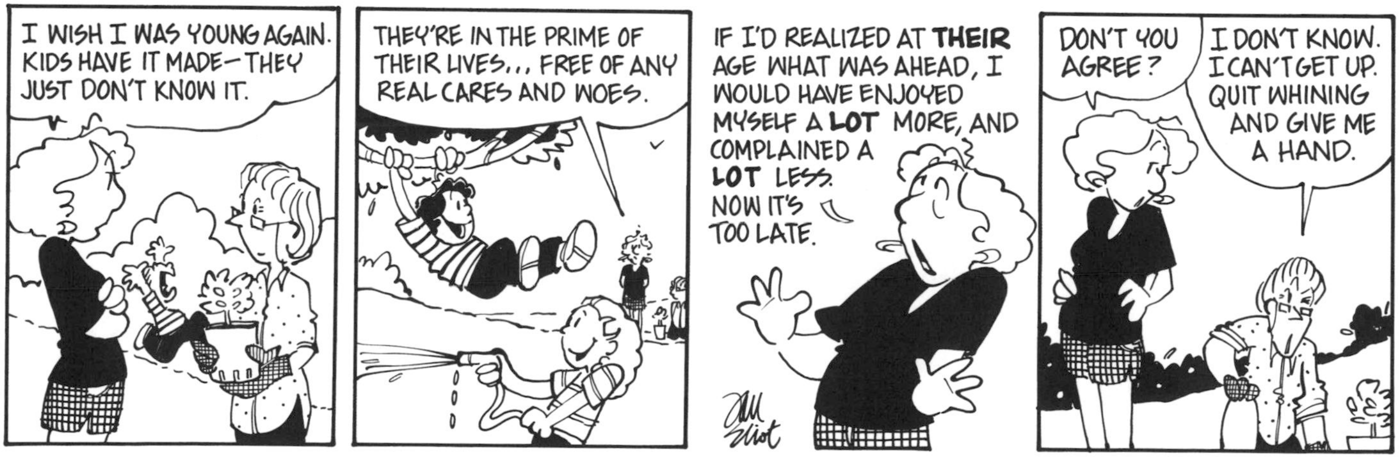
I WISH I WAS YOUNG AGAIN. KIDS HAVE IT MADE—THEY JUST DON'T KNOW IT.
THEY'RE IN THE PRIME OF THEIR LIVES... FREE OF ANY REAL CARES AND WOES.
IF I'D REALIZED AT **THEIR** AGE WHAT WAS AHEAD, I WOULD HAVE ENJOYED MYSELF A **LOT** MORE, AND COMPLAINED A **LOT** LESS. NOW IT'S TOO LATE.
DON'T YOU AGREE?
I DON'T KNOW. I CAN'T GET UP. QUIT WHINING AND GIVE ME A HAND.

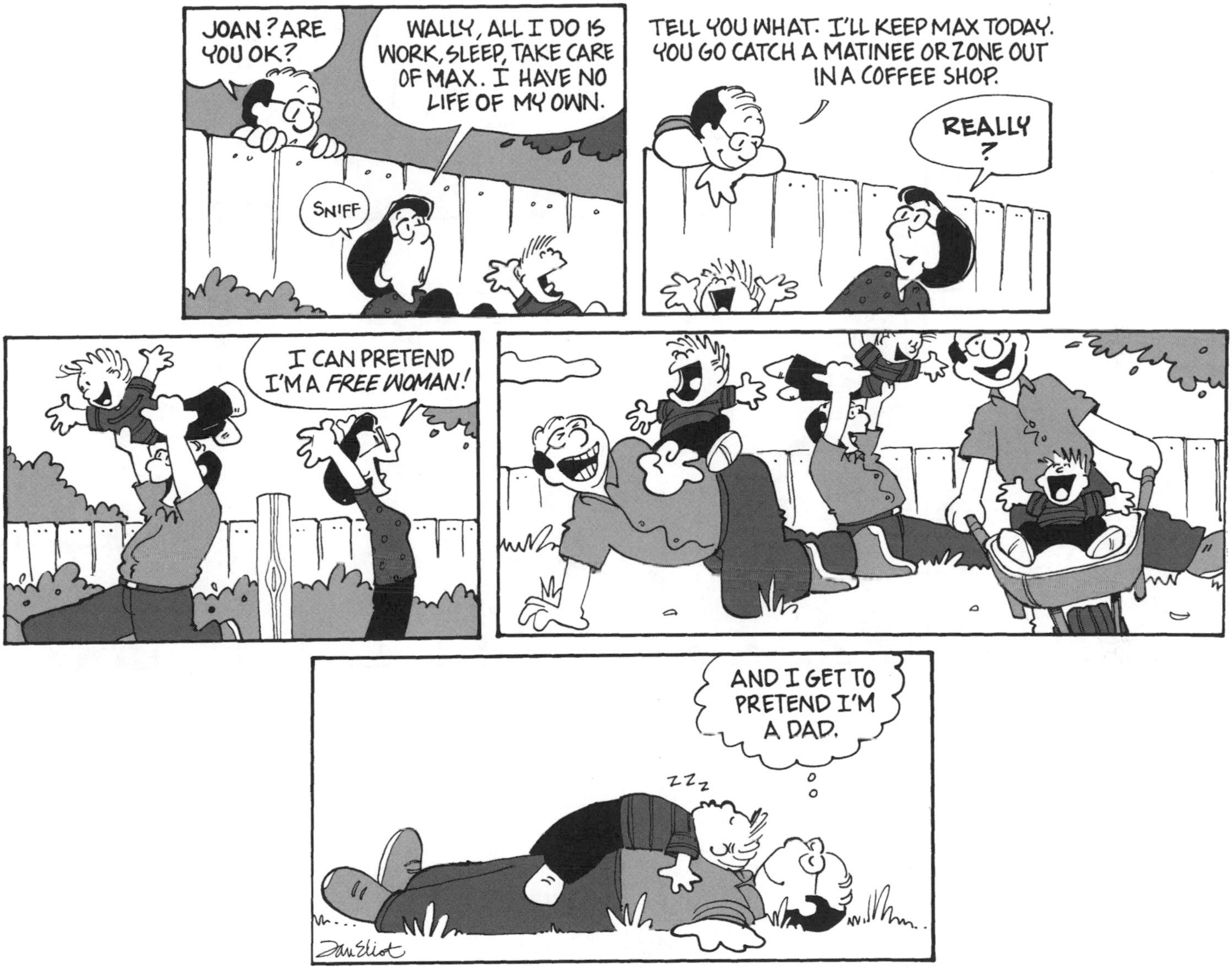
JOAN? ARE YOU OK?
WALLY, ALL I DO IS WORK, SLEEP, TAKE CARE OF MAX. I HAVE NO LIFE OF MY OWN.
SNIFF
TELL YOU WHAT: I'LL KEEP MAX TODAY. YOU GO CATCH A MATINEE OR ZONE OUT IN A COFFEE SHOP.
REALLY?
I CAN PRETEND I'M A FREE WOMAN!
AND I GET TO PRETEND I'M A DAD.
ZZZ
Dan Eliot

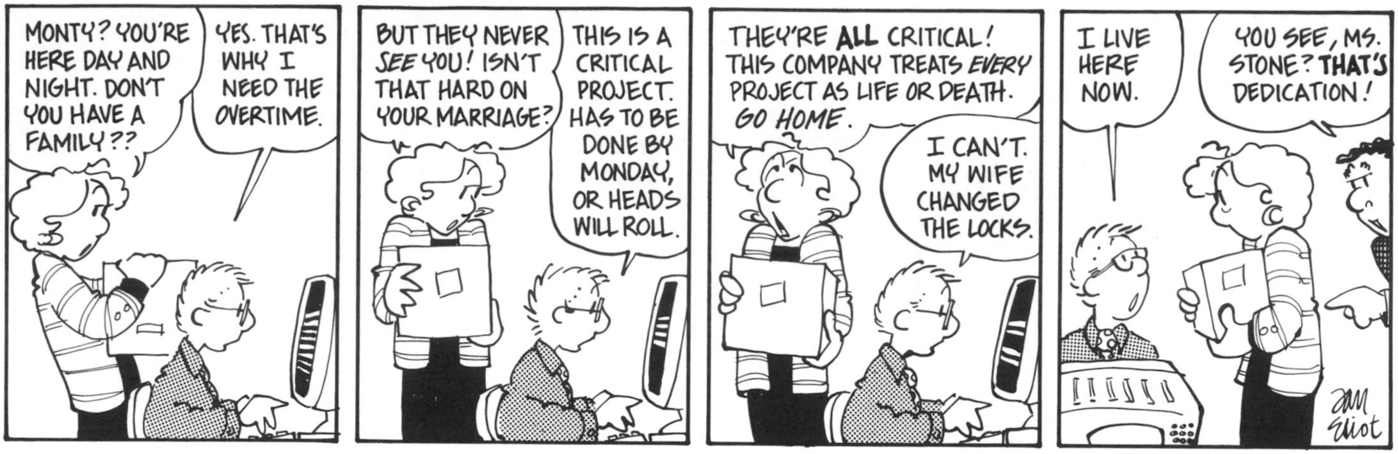
MONTY? YOU'RE HERE DAY AND NIGHT. DON'T YOU HAVE A FAMILY??
YES. THAT'S WHY I NEED THE OVERTIME.
BUT THEY NEVER *SEE* YOU! ISN'T THAT HARD ON YOUR MARRIAGE?
THIS IS A CRITICAL PROJECT. HAS TO BE DONE BY MONDAY, OR HEADS WILL ROLL.
THEY'RE **ALL** CRITICAL! THIS COMPANY TREATS *EVERY* PROJECT AS LIFE OR DEATH. *GO HOME*.
I CAN'T. MY WIFE CHANGED THE LOCKS.
I LIVE HERE NOW.
YOU SEE, MS. STONE? **THAT'S** DEDICATION!
JAN Eliot

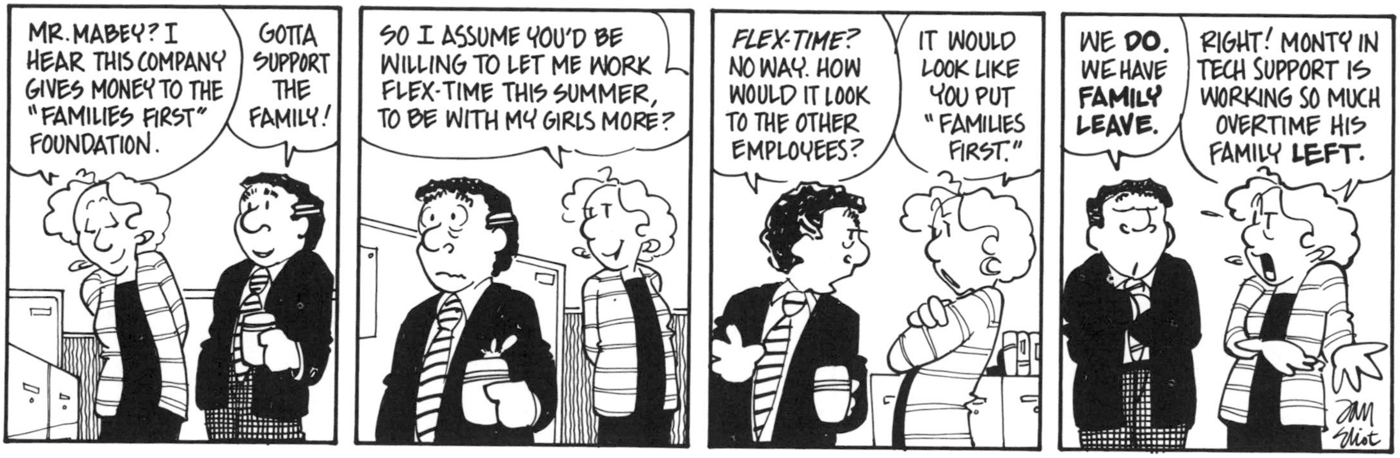
MR. MABEY? I HEAR THIS COMPANY GIVES MONEY TO THE "FAMILIES FIRST" FOUNDATION.
GOTTA SUPPORT THE FAMILY!
SO I ASSUME YOU'D BE WILLING TO LET ME WORK FLEX-TIME THIS SUMMER, TO BE WITH MY GIRLS MORE?
FLEX-TIME? NO WAY. HOW WOULD IT LOOK TO THE OTHER EMPLOYEES?
IT WOULD LOOK LIKE YOU PUT "FAMILIES FIRST."
WE **DO.** WE HAVE **FAMILY LEAVE.**
RIGHT! MONTY IN TECH SUPPORT IS WORKING SO MUCH OVERTIME HIS FAMILY **LEFT**.
JAN Eliot

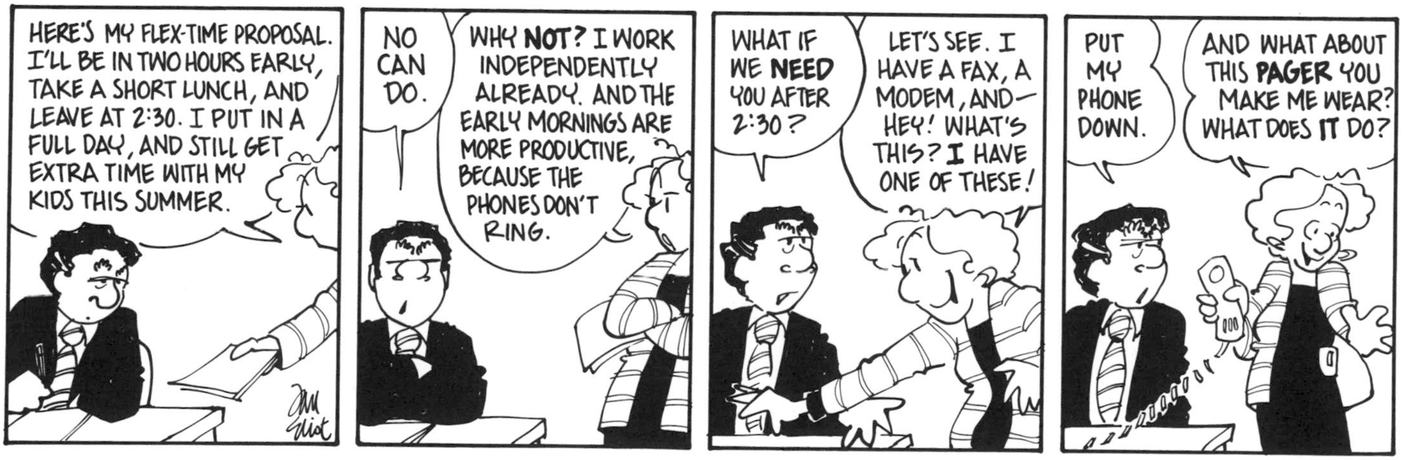
HERE'S MY FLEX-TIME PROPOSAL. I'LL BE IN TWO HOURS EARLY, TAKE A SHORT LUNCH, AND LEAVE AT 2:30. I PUT IN A FULL DAY, AND STILL GET EXTRA TIME WITH MY KIDS THIS SUMMER.
JAN Eliot
NO CAN DO.
WHY **NOT?** I WORK INDEPENDENTLY ALREADY. AND THE EARLY MORNINGS ARE MORE PRODUCTIVE, BECAUSE THE PHONES DON'T RING.
WHAT IF WE **NEED** YOU AFTER 2:30?
LET'S SEE. I HAVE A FAX, A MODEM, AND— HEY! WHAT'S THIS? **I** HAVE ONE OF THESE!
PUT MY PHONE DOWN.
AND WHAT ABOUT THIS **PAGER** YOU MAKE ME WEAR? WHAT DOES **IT** DO?

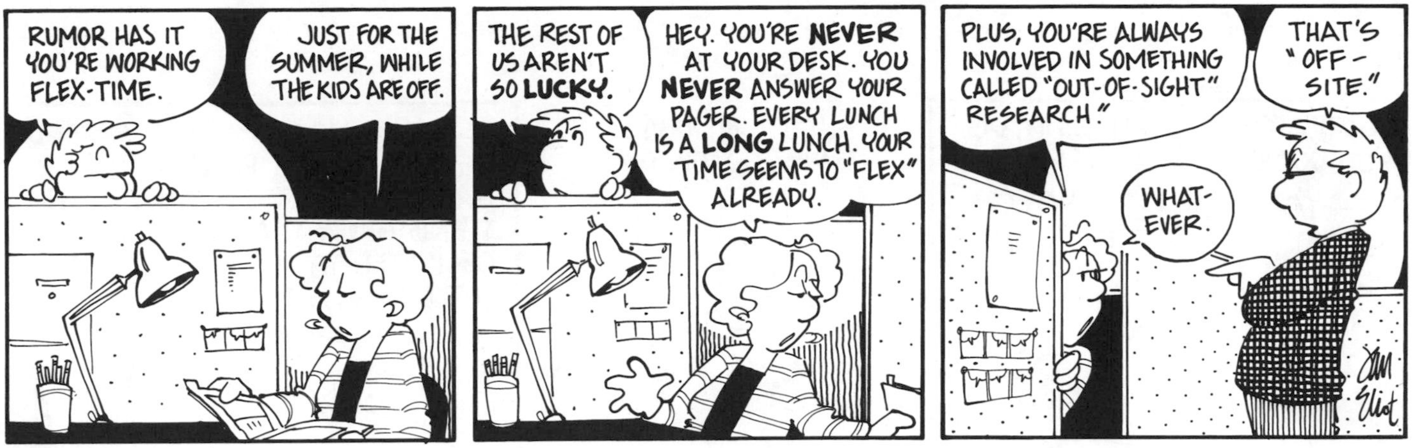
RUMOR HAS IT YOU'RE WORKING FLEX-TIME.
JUST FOR THE SUMMER, WHILE THE KIDS ARE OFF.
THE REST OF US AREN'T SO LUCKY.
HEY. YOU'RE NEVER AT YOUR DESK. YOU NEVER ANSWER YOUR PAGER. EVERY LUNCH IS A LONG LUNCH. YOUR TIME SEEMS TO "FLEX" ALREADY.
PLUS, YOU'RE ALWAYS INVOLVED IN SOMETHING CALLED "OUT-OF-SIGHT" RESEARCH."
THAT'S "OFF-SITE."
WHAT-EVER.

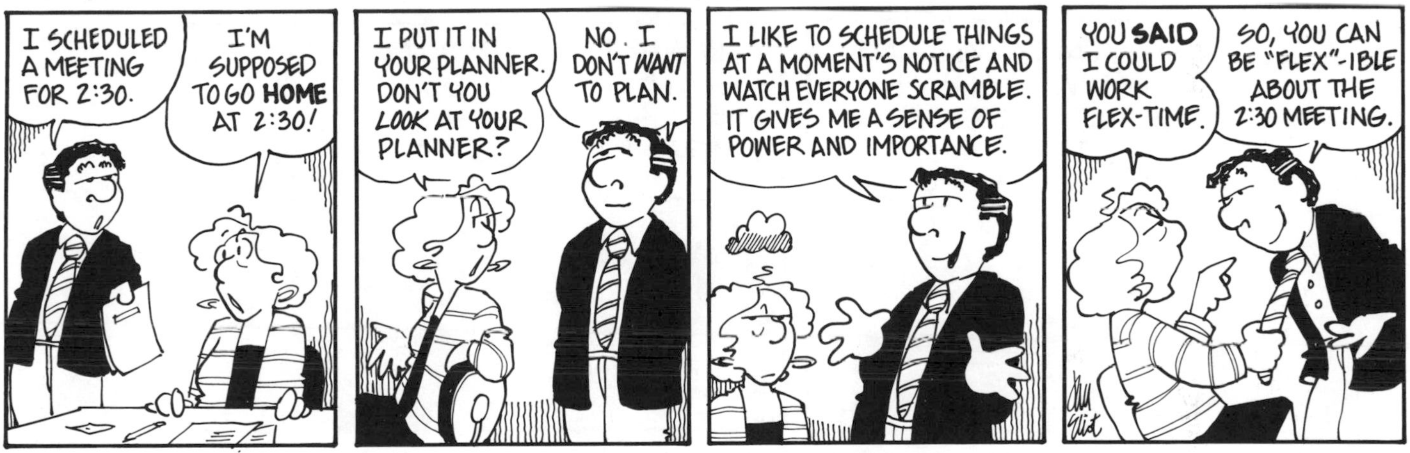
I SCHEDULED A MEETING FOR 2:30.
I'M SUPPOSED TO GO HOME AT 2:30!
I PUT IT IN YOUR PLANNER. DON'T YOU LOOK AT YOUR PLANNER?
NO. I DON'T WANT TO PLAN.
I LIKE TO SCHEDULE THINGS AT A MOMENT'S NOTICE AND WATCH EVERYONE SCRAMBLE. IT GIVES ME A SENSE OF POWER AND IMPORTANCE.
YOU SAID I COULD WORK FLEX-TIME.
SO, YOU CAN BE "FLEX"-IBLE ABOUT THE 2:30 MEETING.

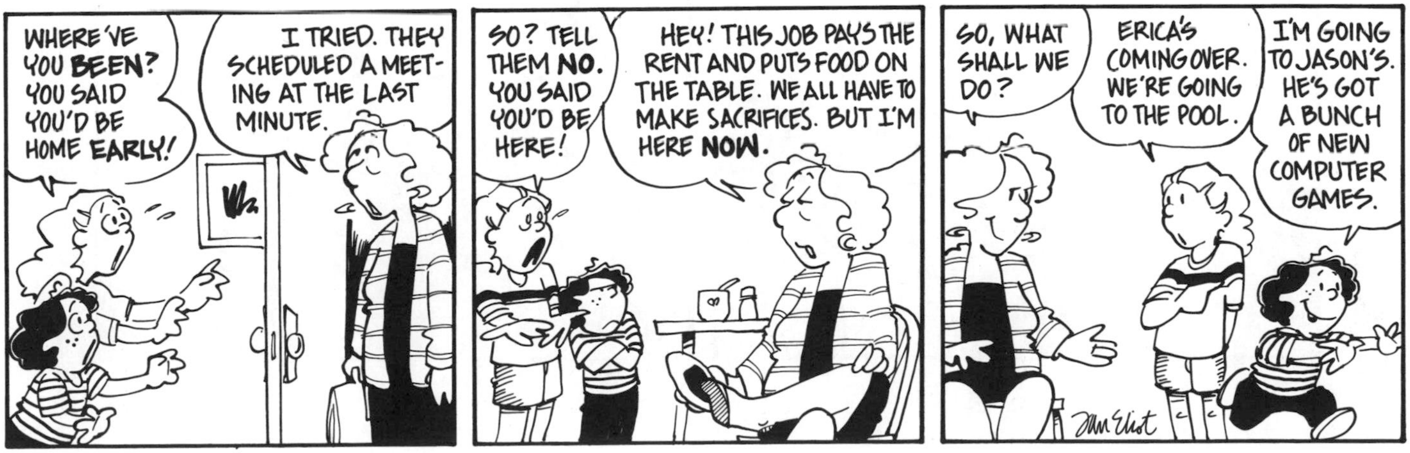
WHERE'VE YOU BEEN? YOU SAID YOU'D BE HOME EARLY!
I TRIED. THEY SCHEDULED A MEETING AT THE LAST MINUTE.
SO? TELL THEM NO. YOU SAID YOU'D BE HERE!
HEY! THIS JOB PAYS THE RENT AND PUTS FOOD ON THE TABLE. WE ALL HAVE TO MAKE SACRIFICES. BUT I'M HERE NOW.
SO, WHAT SHALL WE DO?
ERICA'S COMING OVER. WE'RE GOING TO THE POOL.
I'M GOING TO JASON'S. HE'S GOT A BUNCH OF NEW COMPUTER GAMES.

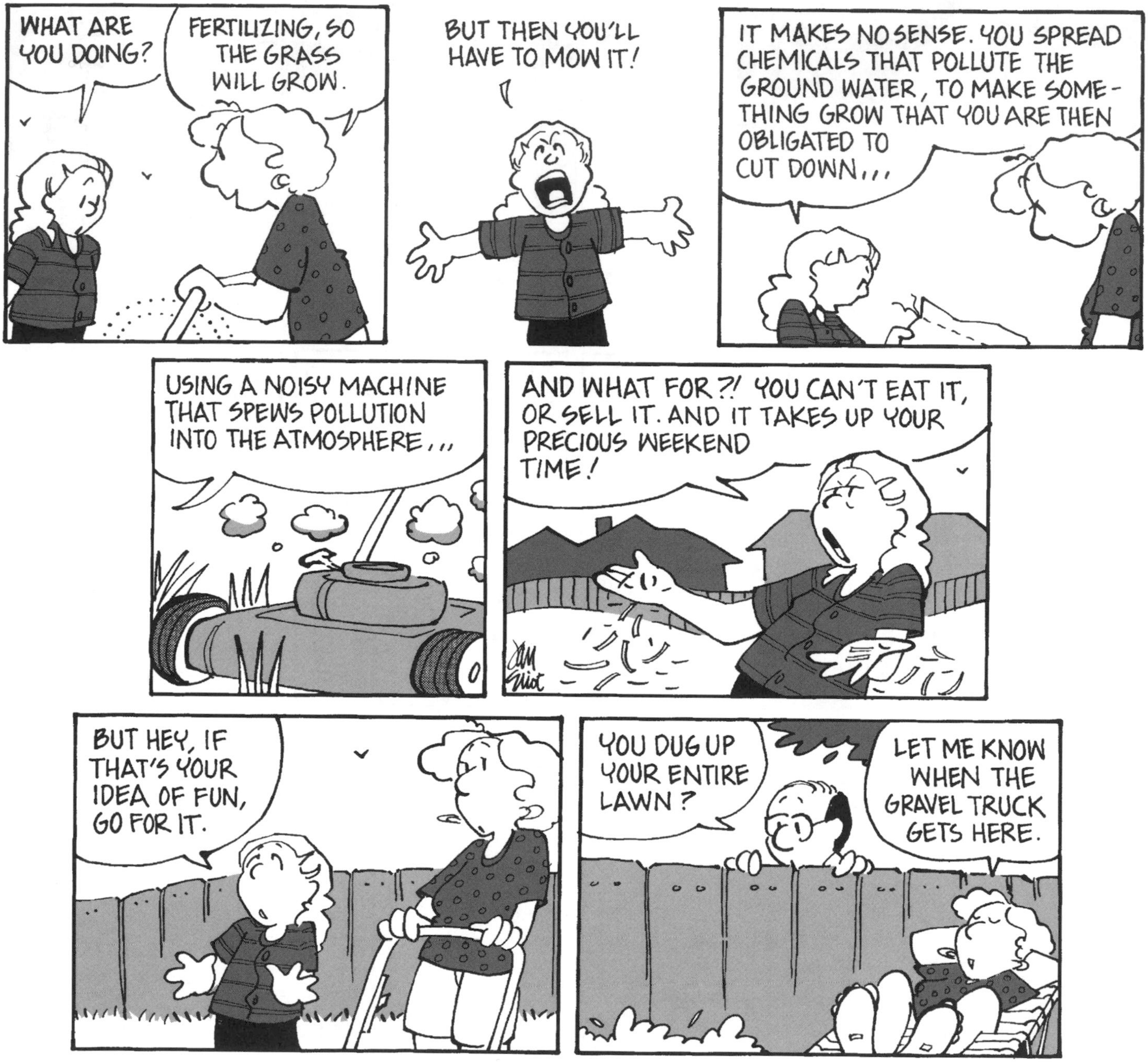
WHAT ARE YOU DOING?
FERTILIZING, SO THE GRASS WILL GROW.
BUT THEN YOU'LL HAVE TO MOW IT!
IT MAKES NO SENSE. YOU SPREAD CHEMICALS THAT POLLUTE THE GROUND WATER, TO MAKE SOME-THING GROW THAT YOU ARE THEN OBLIGATED TO CUT DOWN...
USING A NOISY MACHINE THAT SPEWS POLLUTION INTO THE ATMOSPHERE...
AND WHAT FOR?! YOU CAN'T EAT IT, OR SELL IT. AND IT TAKES UP YOUR PRECIOUS WEEKEND TIME!
BUT HEY, IF THAT'S YOUR IDEA OF FUN, GO FOR IT.
YOU DUG UP YOUR ENTIRE LAWN?
LET ME KNOW WHEN THE GRAVEL TRUCK GETS HERE.

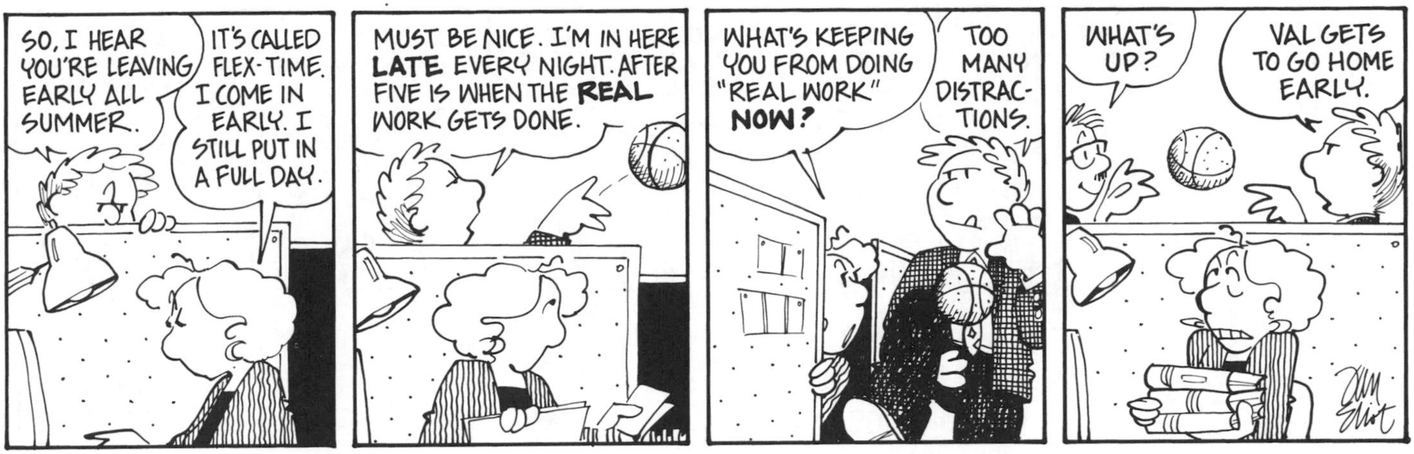
SO, I HEAR YOU'RE LEAVING EARLY ALL SUMMER.
IT'S CALLED FLEX-TIME. I COME IN EARLY. I STILL PUT IN A FULL DAY.
MUST BE NICE. I'M IN HERE LATE EVERY NIGHT. AFTER FIVE IS WHEN THE REAL WORK GETS DONE.
WHAT'S KEEPING YOU FROM DOING "REAL WORK" NOW?
TOO MANY DISTRACTIONS.
WHAT'S UP?
VAL GETS TO GO HOME EARLY.

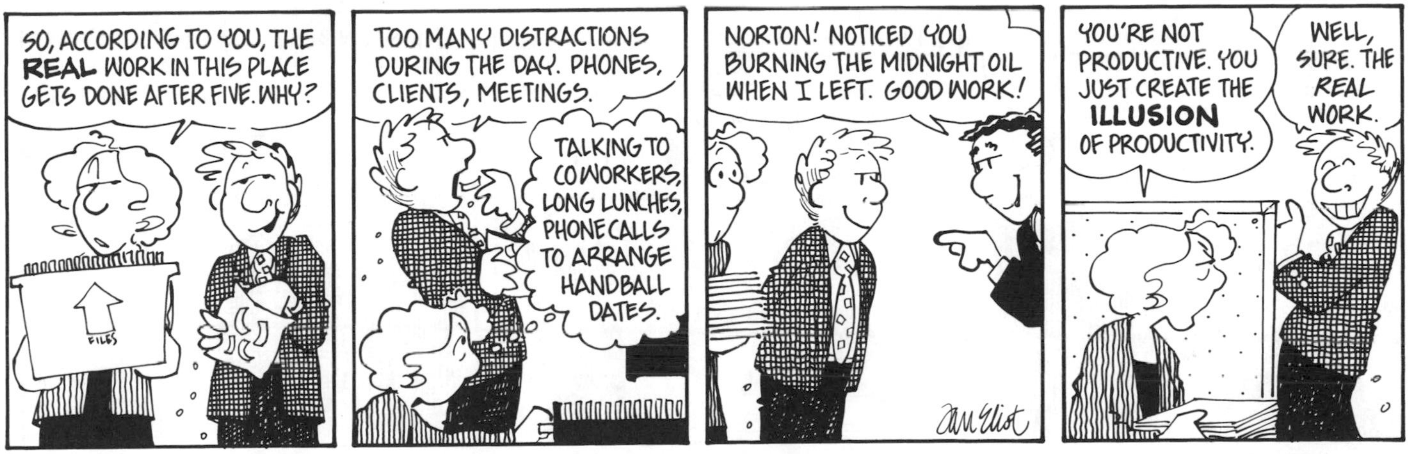
SO, ACCORDING TO YOU, THE REAL WORK IN THIS PLACE GETS DONE AFTER FIVE. WHY?
FILES
TOO MANY DISTRACTIONS DURING THE DAY. PHONES, CLIENTS, MEETINGS.
TALKING TO COWORKERS, LONG LUNCHES, PHONE CALLS TO ARRANGE HANDBALL DATES.
NORTON! NOTICED YOU BURNING THE MIDNIGHT OIL WHEN I LEFT. GOOD WORK!
YOU'RE NOT PRODUCTIVE. YOU JUST CREATE THE ILLUSION OF PRODUCTIVITY.
WELL, SURE. THE REAL WORK.

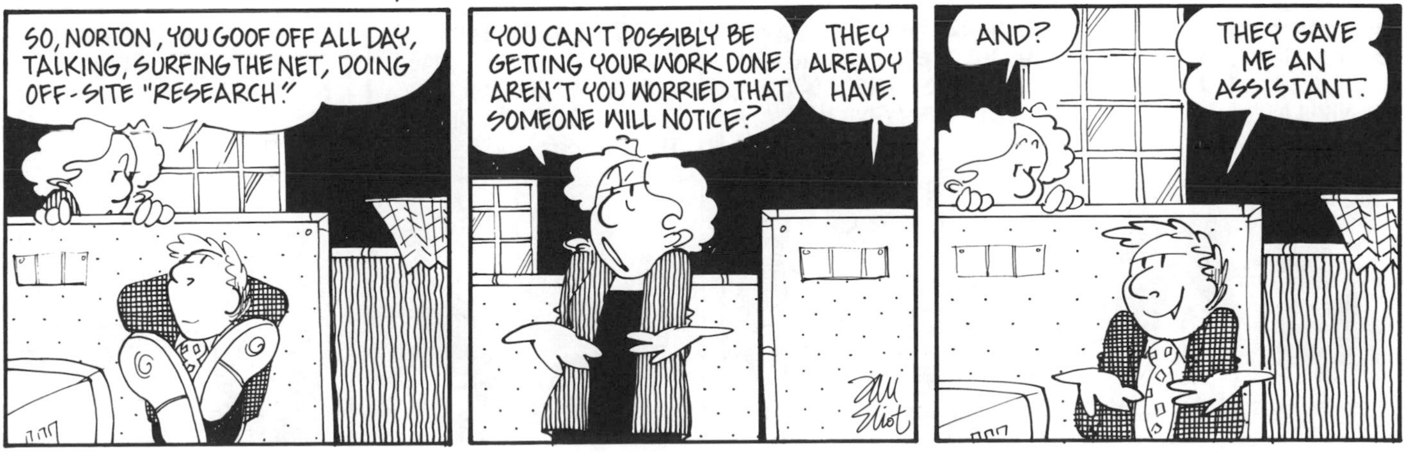
SO, NORTON, YOU GOOF OFF ALL DAY, TALKING, SURFING THE NET, DOING OFF-SITE "RESEARCH."
YOU CAN'T POSSIBLY BE GETTING YOUR WORK DONE. AREN'T YOU WORRIED THAT SOMEONE WILL NOTICE?
THEY ALREADY HAVE.
AND?
THEY GAVE ME AN ASSISTANT.

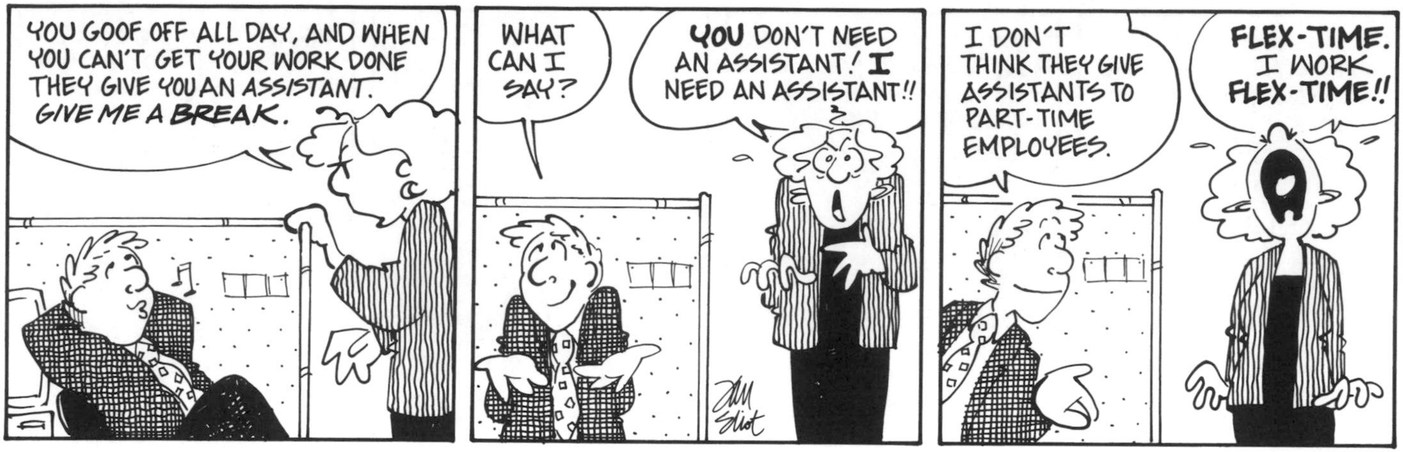
YOU GOOF OFF ALL DAY, AND WHEN YOU CAN'T GET YOUR WORK DONE THEY GIVE YOU AN ASSISTANT. GIVE ME A BREAK.
WHAT CAN I SAY?
YOU DON'T NEED AN ASSISTANT! I NEED AN ASSISTANT!!
I DON'T THINK THEY GIVE ASSISTANTS TO PART-TIME EMPLOYEES.
FLEX-TIME. I WORK FLEX-TIME!!

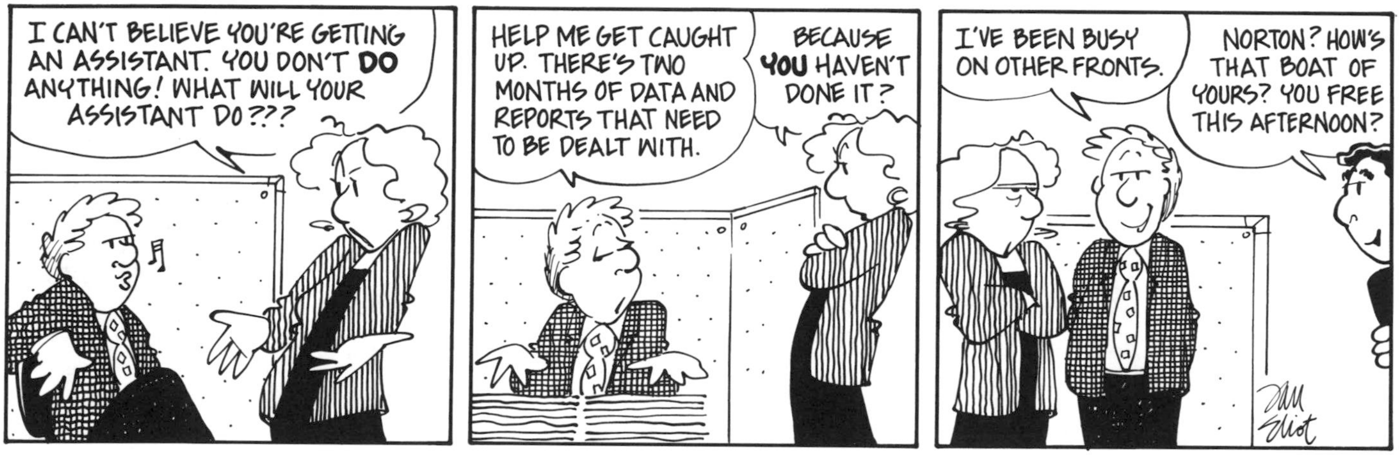
I CAN'T BELIEVE YOU'RE GETTING AN ASSISTANT. YOU DON'T DO ANYTHING! WHAT WILL YOUR ASSISTANT DO???
HELP ME GET CAUGHT UP. THERE'S TWO MONTHS OF DATA AND REPORTS THAT NEED TO BE DEALT WITH.
BECAUSE YOU HAVEN'T DONE IT?
I'VE BEEN BUSY ON OTHER FRONTS.
NORTON? HOW'S THAT BOAT OF YOURS? YOU FREE THIS AFTERNOON?

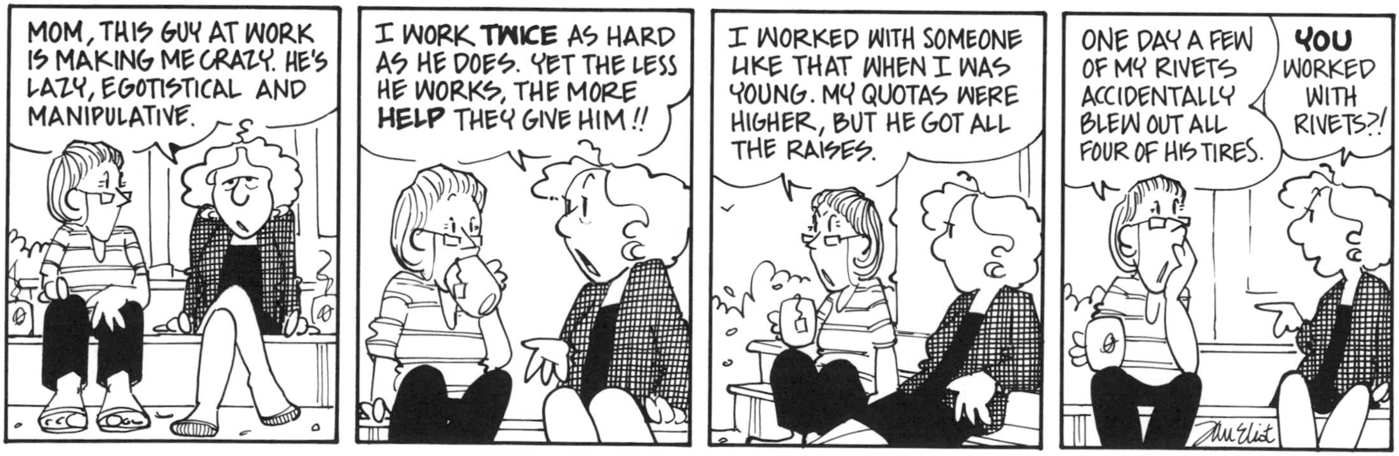
MOM, THIS GUY AT WORK IS MAKING ME CRAZY. HE'S LAZY, EGOTISTICAL AND MANIPULATIVE.
I WORK TWICE AS HARD AS HE DOES. YET THE LESS HE WORKS, THE MORE HELP THEY GIVE HIM!!
I WORKED WITH SOMEONE LIKE THAT WHEN I WAS YOUNG. MY QUOTAS WERE HIGHER, BUT HE GOT ALL THE RAISES.
ONE DAY A FEW OF MY RIVETS ACCIDENTALLY BLEW OUT ALL FOUR OF HIS TIRES.
YOU WORKED WITH RIVETS?!

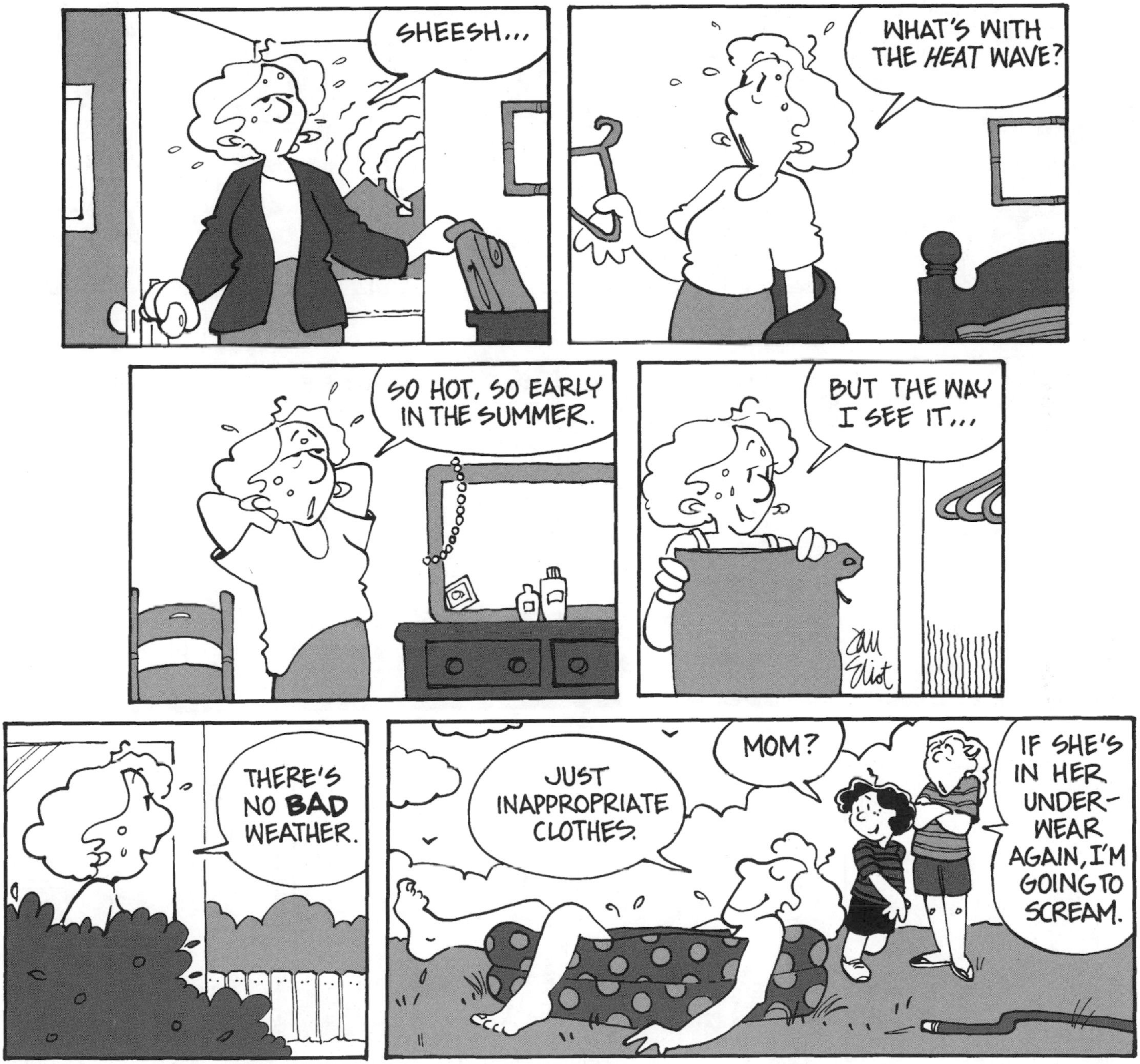
SHEESH...
WHAT'S WITH THE HEAT WAVE?
SO HOT, SO EARLY IN THE SUMMER.
BUT THE WAY I SEE IT...
Jan Eliot
THERE'S NO BAD WEATHER.
JUST INAPPROPRIATE CLOTHES.
MOM?
IF SHE'S IN HER UNDER-WEAR AGAIN, I'M GOING TO SCREAM.

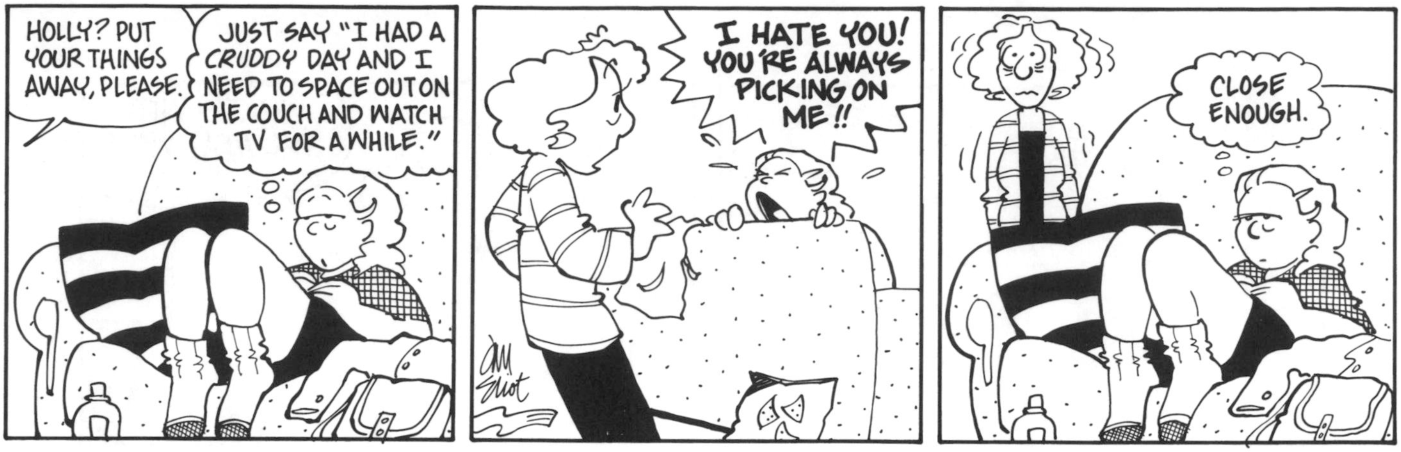
HOLLY? PUT YOUR THINGS AWAY, PLEASE.
JUST SAY "I HAD A CRUDDY DAY AND I NEED TO SPACE OUT ON THE COUCH AND WATCH TV FOR A WHILE."
I HATE YOU! YOU'RE ALWAYS PICKING ON ME!!
CLOSE ENOUGH.

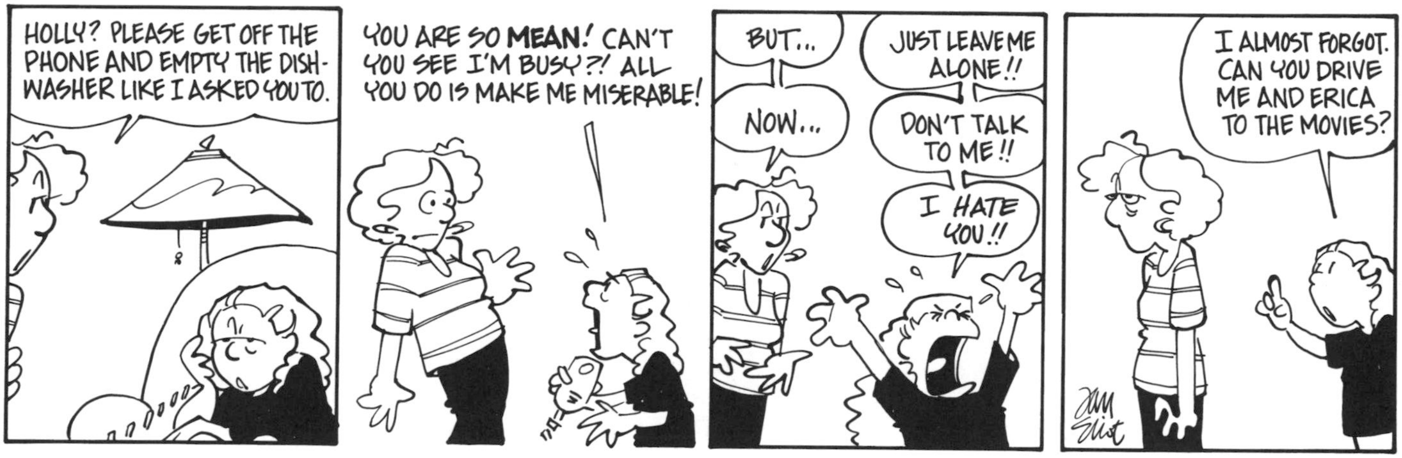
HOLLY? PLEASE GET OFF THE PHONE AND EMPTY THE DISHWASHER LIKE I ASKED YOU TO.
YOU ARE SO MEAN! CAN'T YOU SEE I'M BUSY?! ALL YOU DO IS MAKE ME MISERABLE!
BUT...
NOW...
JUST LEAVE ME ALONE!!
DON'T TALK TO ME!!
I HATE YOU!!
I ALMOST FORGOT. CAN YOU DRIVE ME AND ERICA TO THE MOVIES?

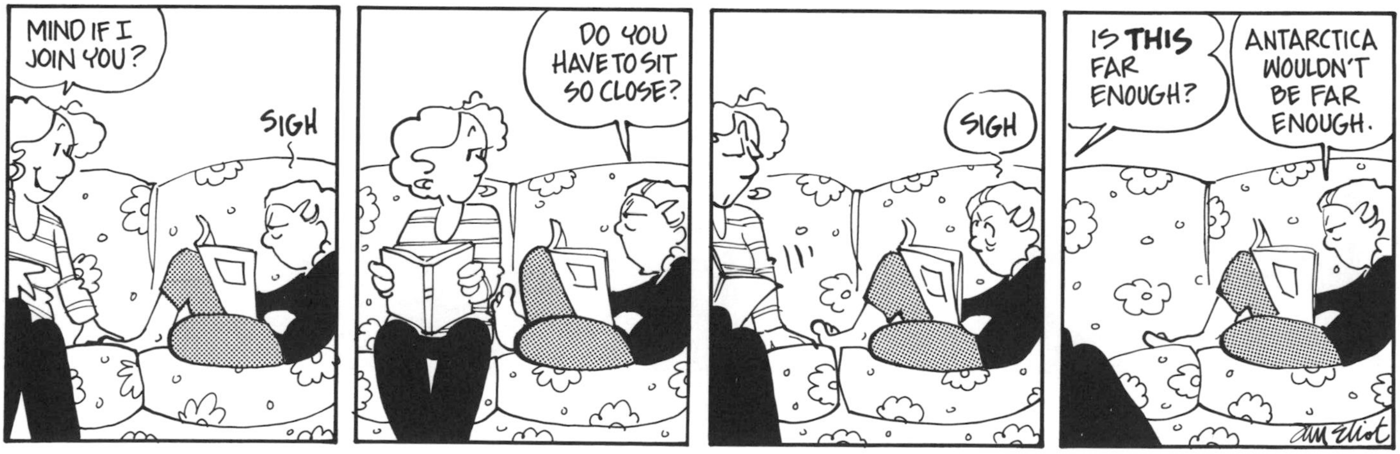
MIND IF I JOIN YOU?
SIGH
DO YOU HAVE TO SIT SO CLOSE?
SIGH
IS THIS FAR ENOUGH?
ANTARCTICA WOULDN'T BE FAR ENOUGH.

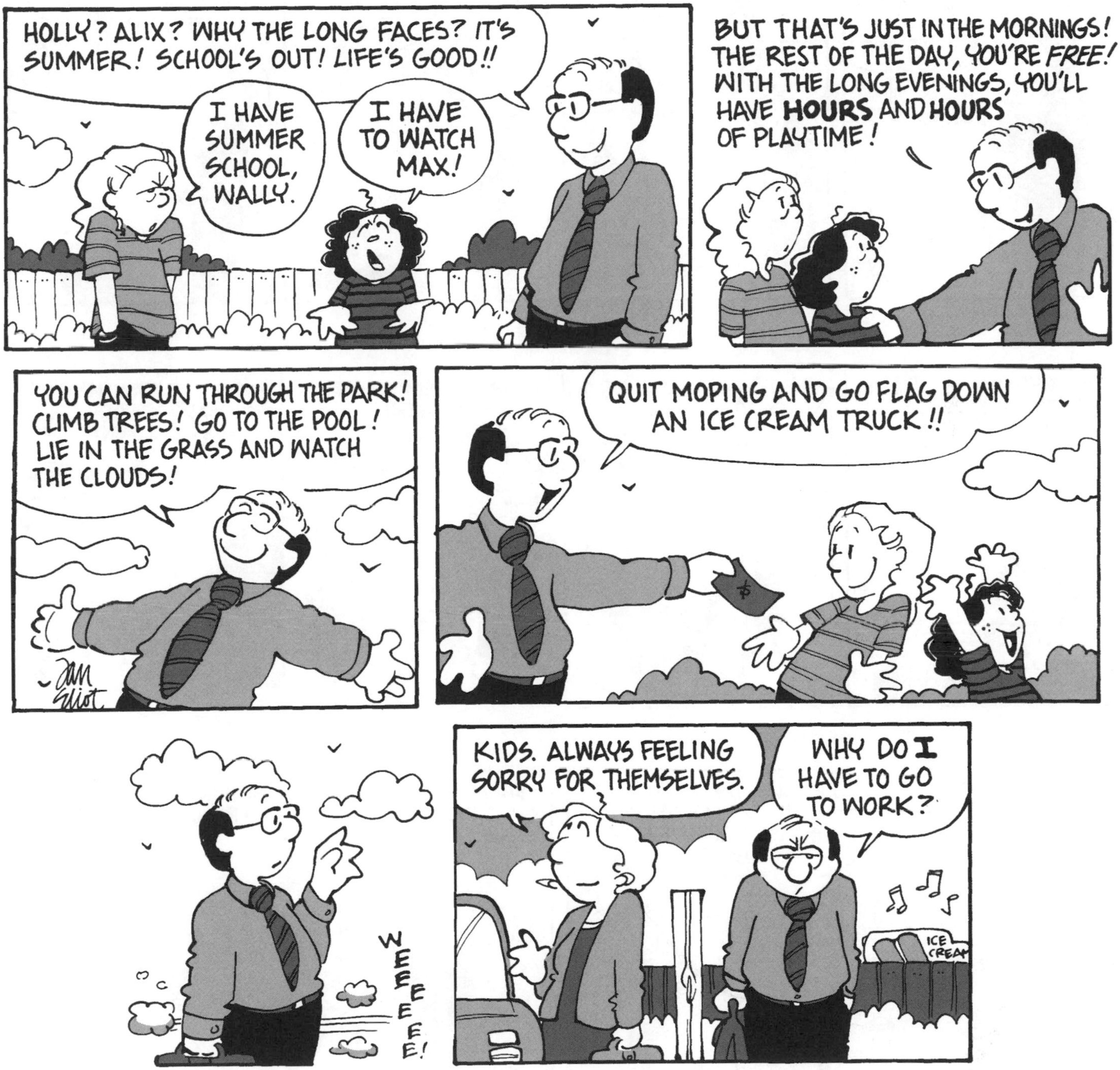
HOLLY? ALIX? WHY THE LONG FACES? IT'S SUMMER! SCHOOL'S OUT! LIFE'S GOOD!!
I HAVE SUMMER SCHOOL, WALLY.
I HAVE TO WATCH MAX!
BUT THAT'S JUST IN THE MORNINGS! THE REST OF THE DAY, YOU'RE FREE! WITH THE LONG EVENINGS, YOU'LL HAVE HOURS AND HOURS OF PLAYTIME!
YOU CAN RUN THROUGH THE PARK! CLIMB TREES! GO TO THE POOL! LIE IN THE GRASS AND WATCH THE CLOUDS!
QUIT MOPING AND GO FLAG DOWN AN ICE CREAM TRUCK!!
WEEEEEEE!
KIDS. ALWAYS FEELING SORRY FOR THEMSELVES.
WHY DO I HAVE TO GO TO WORK?
ICE CREAM

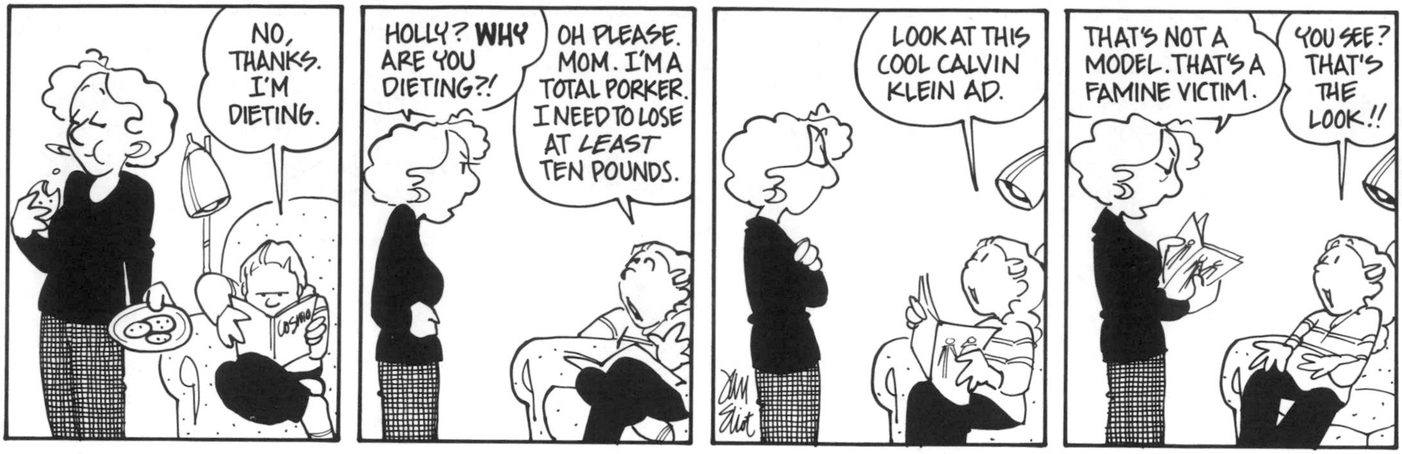
NO, THANKS. I'M DIETING.
HOLLY? **WHY** ARE YOU DIETING?!
OH PLEASE. MOM. I'M A TOTAL PORKER. I NEED TO LOSE AT *LEAST* TEN POUNDS.
LOOK AT THIS COOL CALVIN KLEIN AD.
THAT'S NOT A MODEL. THAT'S A FAMINE VICTIM.
YOU SEE? THAT'S THE LOOK!!

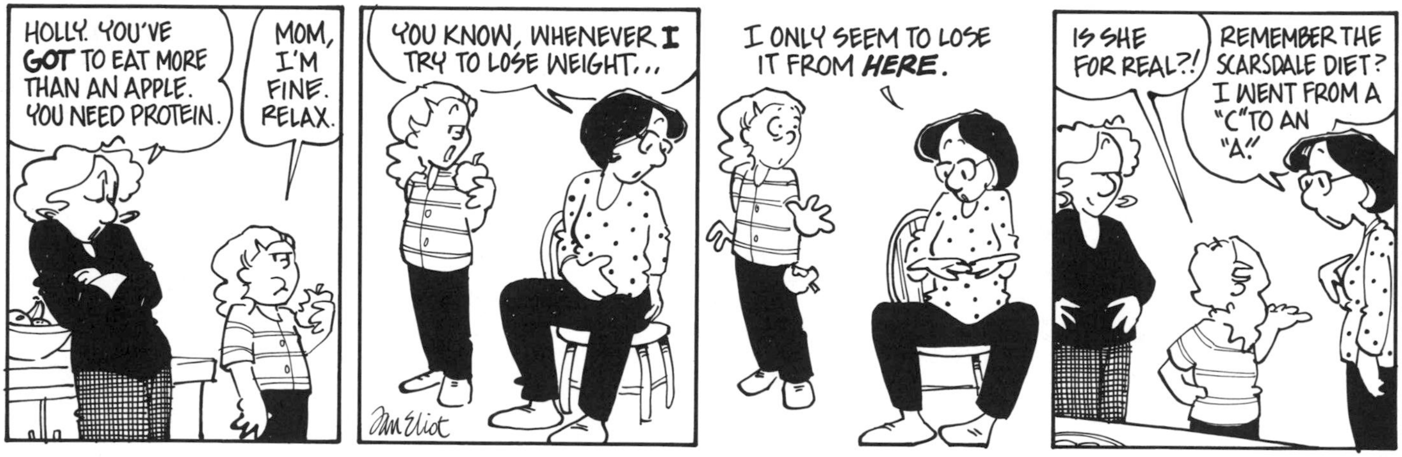
HOLLY. YOU'VE **GOT** TO EAT MORE THAN AN APPLE. YOU NEED PROTEIN.
MOM, I'M FINE. RELAX.
YOU KNOW, WHENEVER **I** TRY TO LOSE WEIGHT...
I ONLY SEEM TO LOSE IT FROM ***HERE***.
IS SHE FOR REAL?!
REMEMBER THE SCARSDALE DIET? I WENT FROM A "C" TO AN "A".

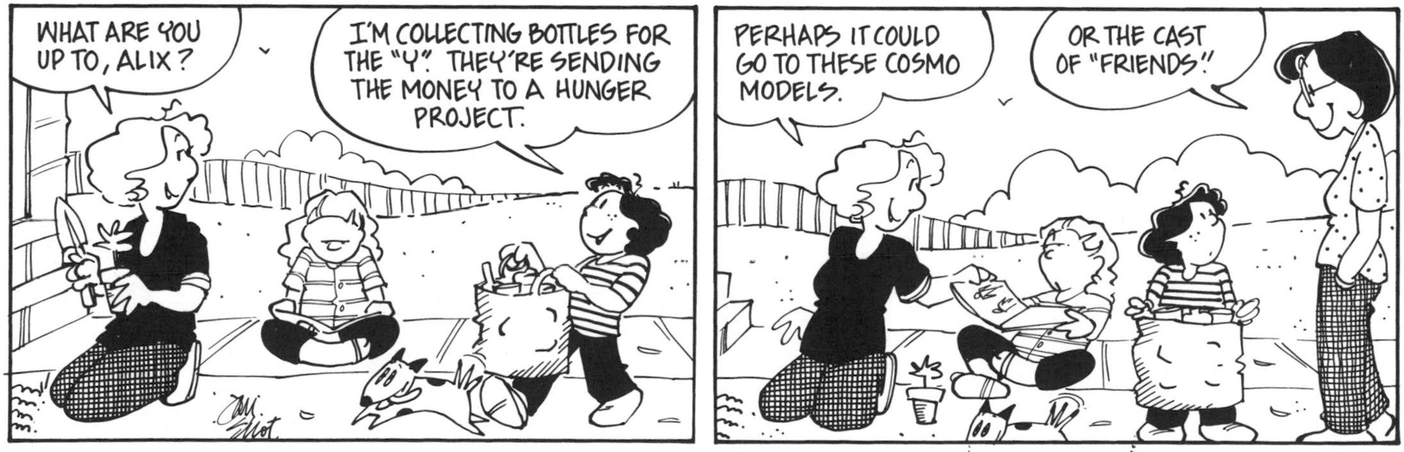
WHAT ARE YOU UP TO, ALIX?
I'M COLLECTING BOTTLES FOR THE "Y". THEY'RE SENDING THE MONEY TO A HUNGER PROJECT.
PERHAPS IT COULD GO TO THESE COSMO MODELS.
OR THE CAST OF "FRIENDS".

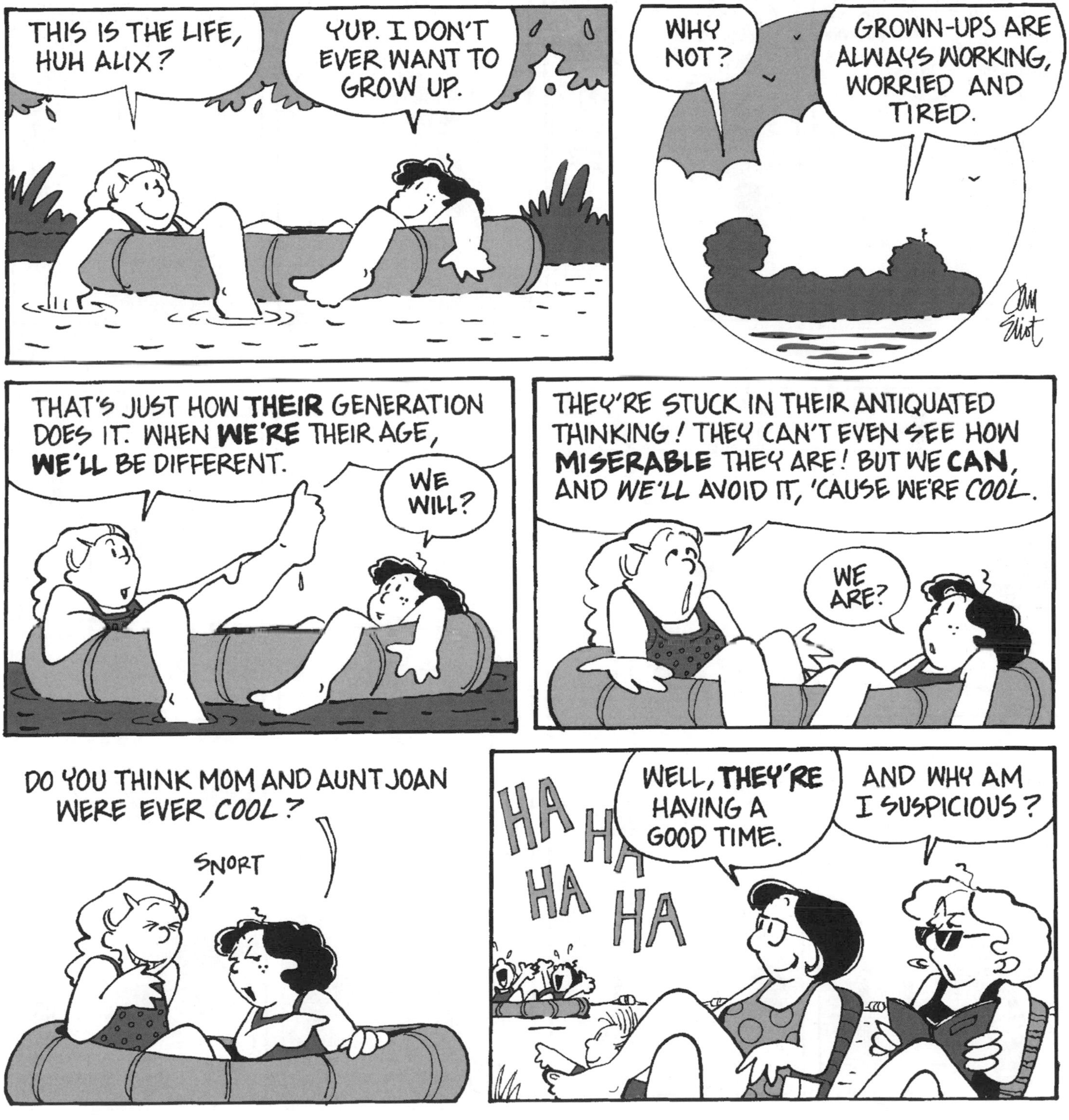

THIS IS THE LIFE, HUH ALIX?
YUP. I DON'T EVER WANT TO GROW UP.
WHY NOT?
GROWN-UPS ARE ALWAYS WORKING, WORRIED AND TIRED.
THAT'S JUST HOW THEIR GENERATION DOES IT. WHEN WE'RE THEIR AGE, WE'LL BE DIFFERENT.
WE WILL?
THEY'RE STUCK IN THEIR ANTIQUATED THINKING! THEY CAN'T EVEN SEE HOW MISERABLE THEY ARE! BUT WE CAN, AND WE'LL AVOID IT, 'CAUSE WE'RE COOL.
WE ARE?
DO YOU THINK MOM AND AUNT JOAN WERE EVER COOL?
SNORT
HA HA HA HA
WELL, THEY'RE HAVING A GOOD TIME.
AND WHY AM I SUSPICIOUS?

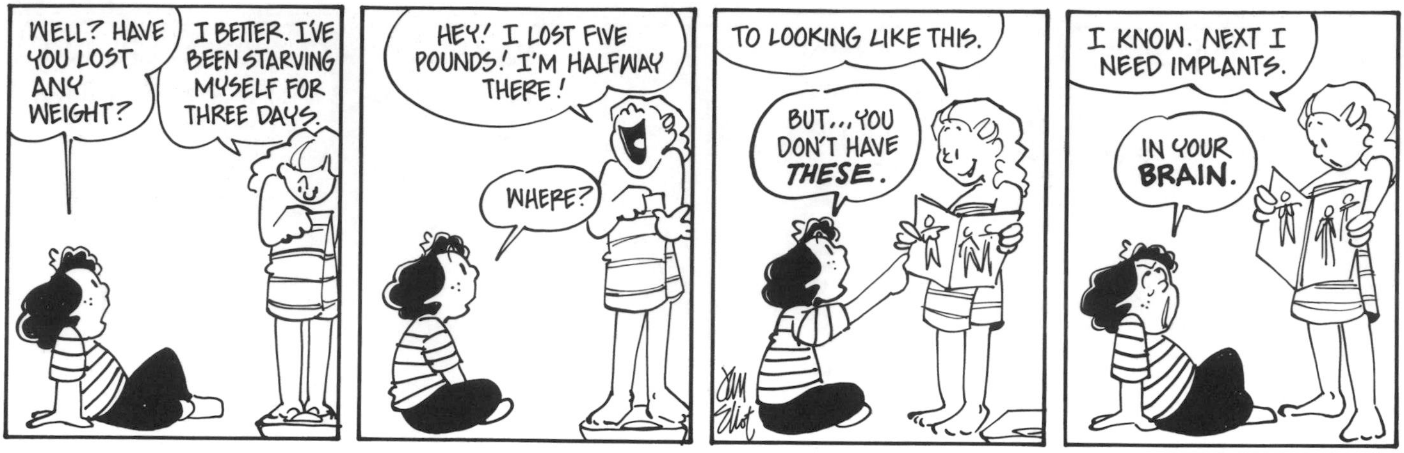
WELL? HAVE YOU LOST ANY WEIGHT?
I BETTER. I'VE BEEN STARVING MYSELF FOR THREE DAYS.
HEY! I LOST FIVE POUNDS! I'M HALFWAY THERE!
WHERE?
TO LOOKING LIKE THIS.
BUT... YOU DON'T HAVE THESE.
I KNOW. NEXT I NEED IMPLANTS.
IN YOUR BRAIN.

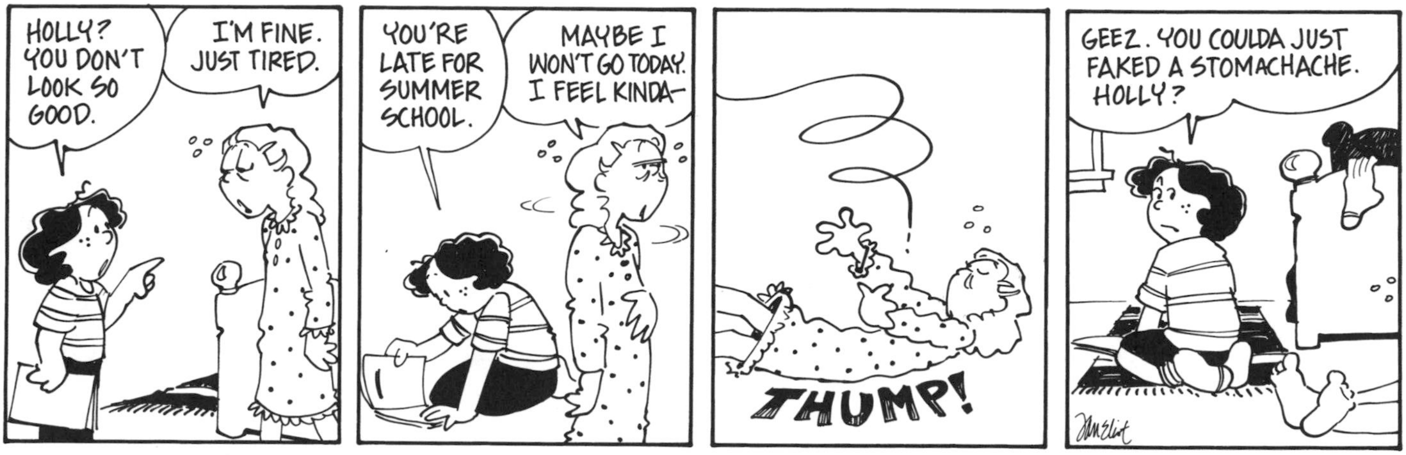
HOLLY? YOU DON'T LOOK SO GOOD.
I'M FINE. JUST TIRED.
YOU'RE LATE FOR SUMMER SCHOOL.
MAYBE I WON'T GO TODAY. I FEEL KINDA-
THUMP!
GEEZ. YOU COULDA JUST FAKED A STOMACHACHE. HOLLY?

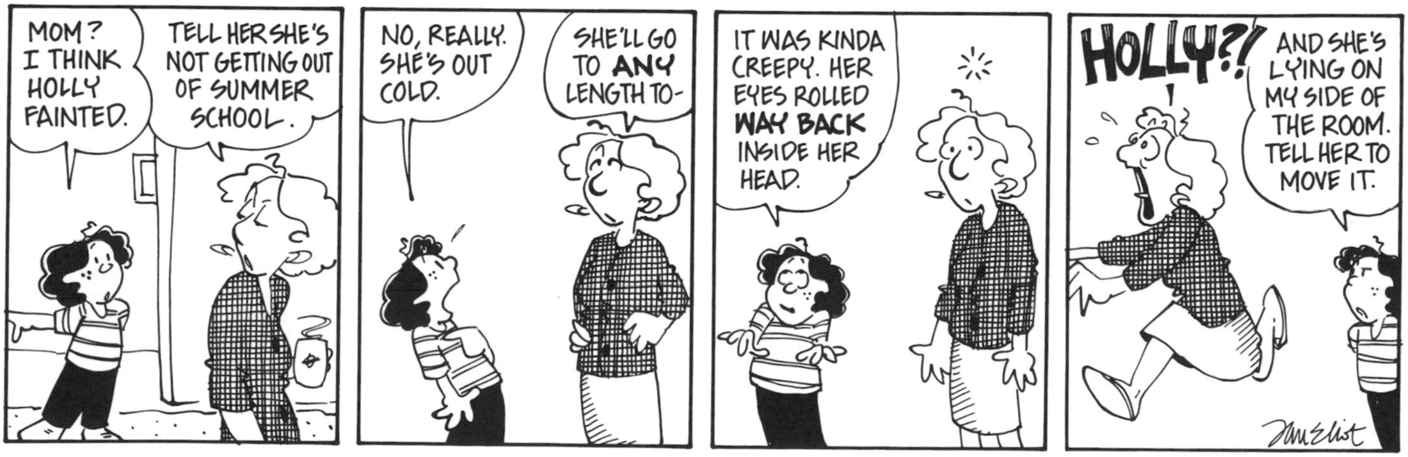
MOM? I THINK HOLLY FAINTED.
TELL HER SHE'S NOT GETTING OUT OF SUMMER SCHOOL.
NO, REALLY. SHE'S OUT COLD.
SHE'LL GO TO ANY LENGTH TO-
IT WAS KINDA CREEPY. HER EYES ROLLED WAY BACK INSIDE HER HEAD.
HOLLY?!
AND SHE'S LYING ON MY SIDE OF THE ROOM. TELL HER TO MOVE IT.

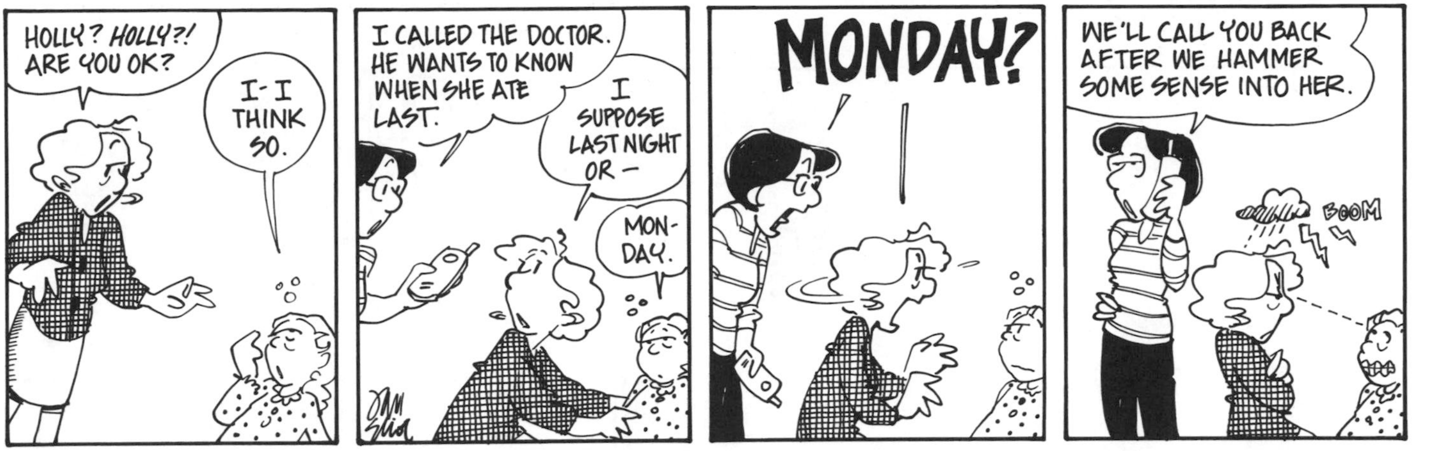
HOLLY? HOLLY?! ARE YOU OK?
I- I THINK SO.
I CALLED THE DOCTOR. HE WANTS TO KNOW WHEN SHE ATE LAST.
I SUPPOSE LAST NIGHT OR –
MON- DAY.
MONDAY?
WE'LL CALL YOU BACK AFTER WE HAMMER SOME SENSE INTO HER.
BOOM

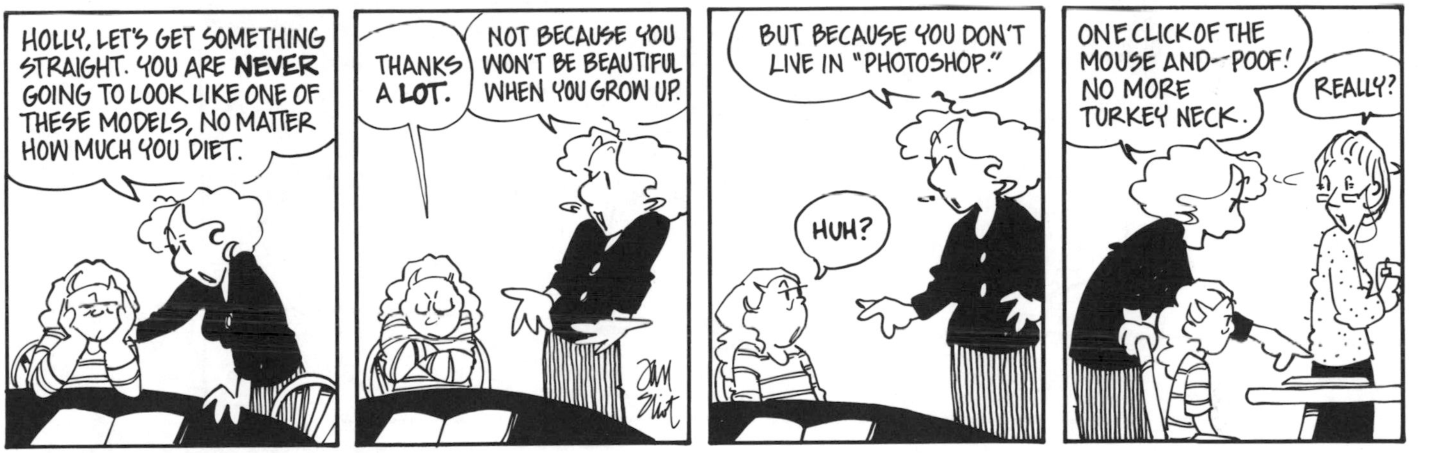
HOLLY, LET'S GET SOMETHING STRAIGHT. YOU ARE NEVER GOING TO LOOK LIKE ONE OF THESE MODELS, NO MATTER HOW MUCH YOU DIET.
THANKS A LOT.
NOT BECAUSE YOU WON'T BE BEAUTIFUL WHEN YOU GROW UP.
BUT BECAUSE YOU DON'T LIVE IN "PHOTOSHOP."
HUH?
ONE CLICK OF THE MOUSE AND—POOF! NO MORE TURKEY NECK.
REALLY?

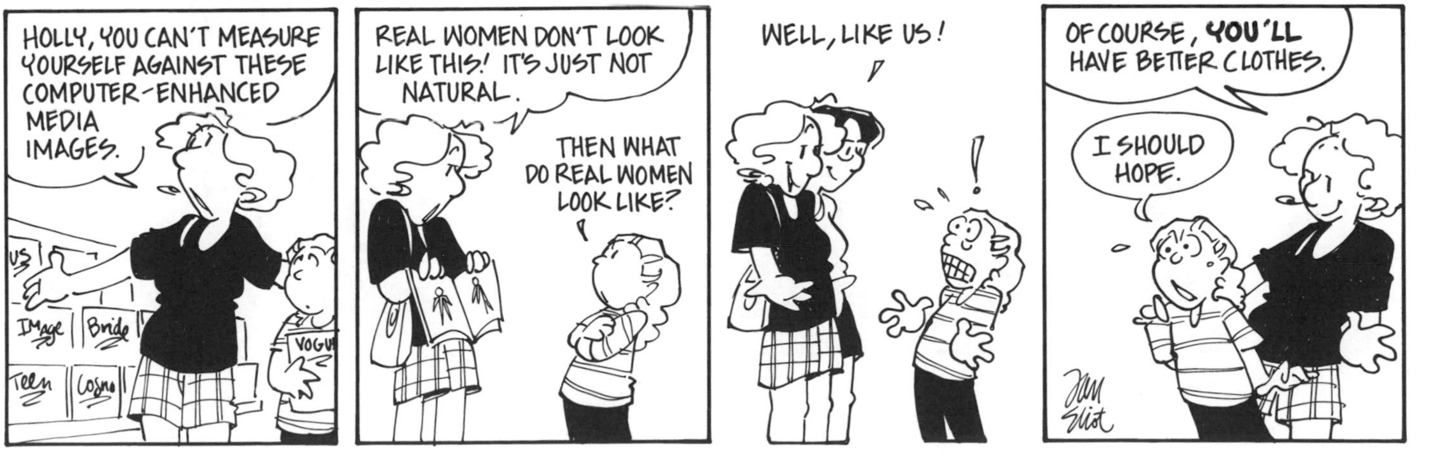
HOLLY, YOU CAN'T MEASURE YOURSELF AGAINST THESE COMPUTER-ENHANCED MEDIA IMAGES.
US
IMage
Bride
VOGU
Teen
Cosmo
REAL WOMEN DON'T LOOK LIKE THIS! IT'S JUST NOT NATURAL.
THEN WHAT DO REAL WOMEN LOOK LIKE?
WELL, LIKE US!
!
OF COURSE, YOU'LL HAVE BETTER CLOTHES.
I SHOULD HOPE.

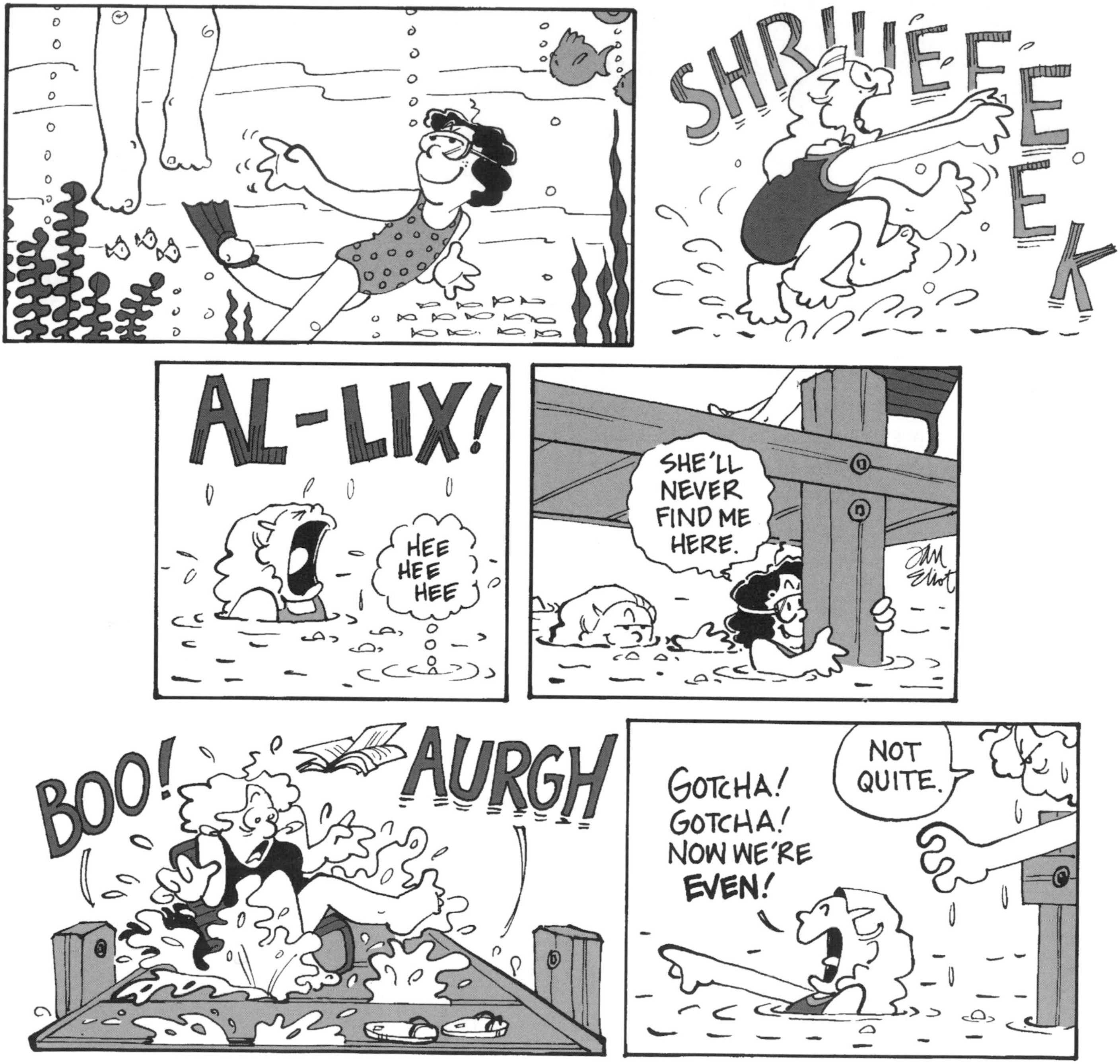
SHRIIEEEEK
AL-LIX!
HEE HEE HEE
SHE'LL NEVER FIND ME HERE.
BOO!
AURGH
GOTCHA! GOTCHA! NOW WE'RE EVEN!
NOT QUITE.

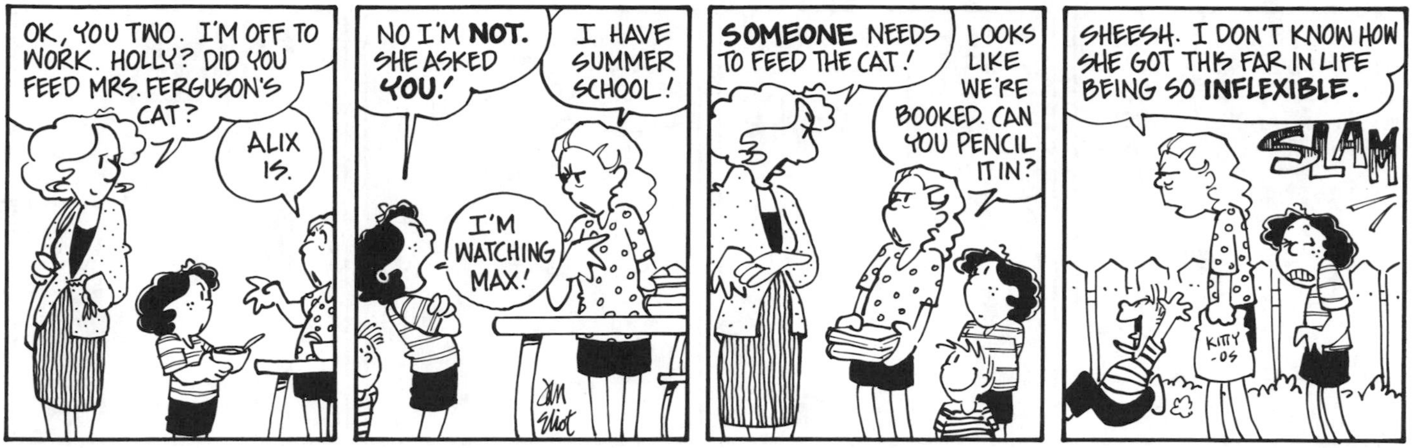
OK, YOU TWO. I'M OFF TO WORK. HOLLY? DID YOU FEED MRS. FERGUSON'S CAT?
ALIX IS.
NO I'M **NOT.** SHE ASKED **YOU**!
I HAVE SUMMER SCHOOL!
I'M WATCHING MAX!
SOMEONE NEEDS TO FEED THE CAT!
LOOKS LIKE WE'RE BOOKED. CAN YOU PENCIL IT IN?
SHEESH. I DON'T KNOW HOW SHE GOT THIS FAR IN LIFE BEING SO **INFLEXIBLE.**
SLAM
KITTY-OS

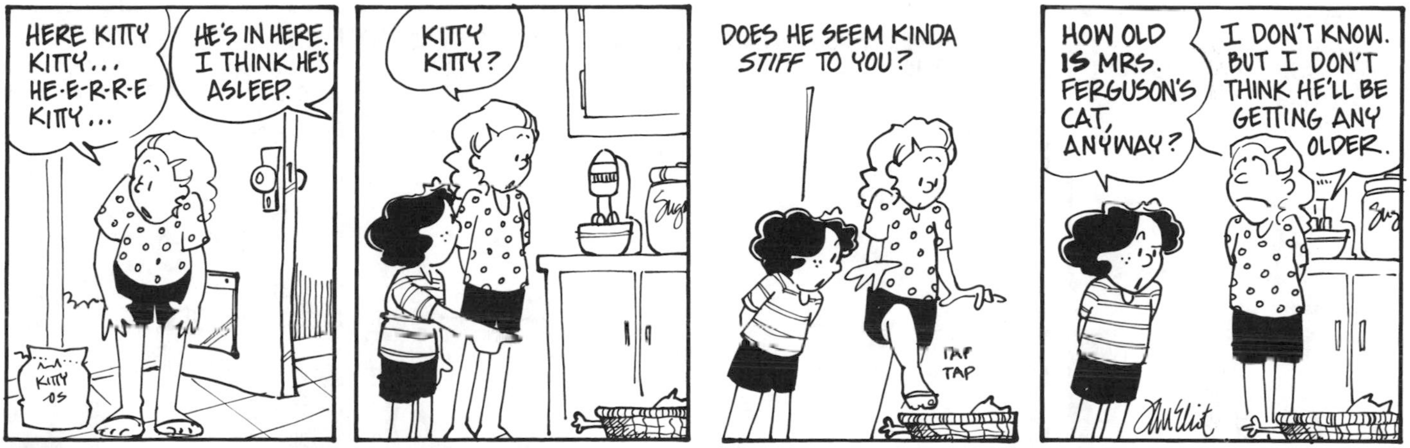
HERE KITTY KITTY... HE-E-R-R-E KITTY...
HE'S IN HERE. I THINK HE'S ASLEEP.
KITTY-OS
KITTY KITTY?
DOES HE SEEM KINDA *STIFF* TO YOU?
TAP TAP
HOW OLD **IS** MRS. FERGUSON'S CAT, ANYWAY?
I DON'T KNOW. BUT I DON'T THINK HE'LL BE GETTING ANY OLDER.

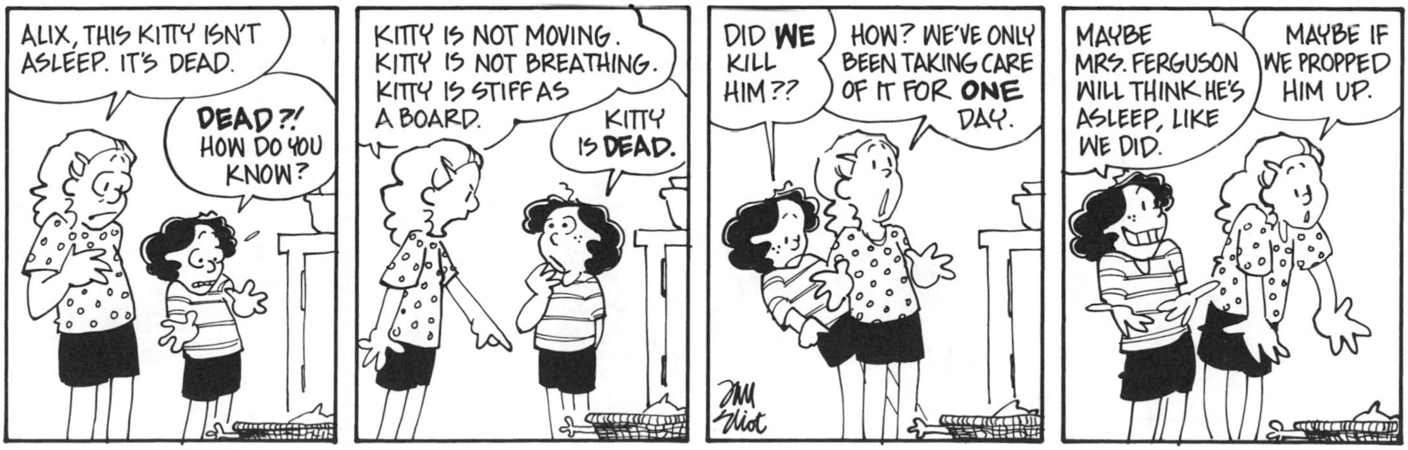
ALIX, THIS KITTY ISN'T ASLEEP. IT'S DEAD.
DEAD?! HOW DO YOU KNOW?
KITTY IS NOT MOVING. KITTY IS NOT BREATHING. KITTY IS STIFF AS A BOARD.
KITTY IS **DEAD.**
DID **WE** KILL HIM??
HOW? WE'VE ONLY BEEN TAKING CARE OF IT FOR **ONE** DAY.
MAYBE MRS. FERGUSON WILL THINK HE'S ASLEEP, LIKE WE DID.
MAYBE IF WE PROPPED HIM UP.

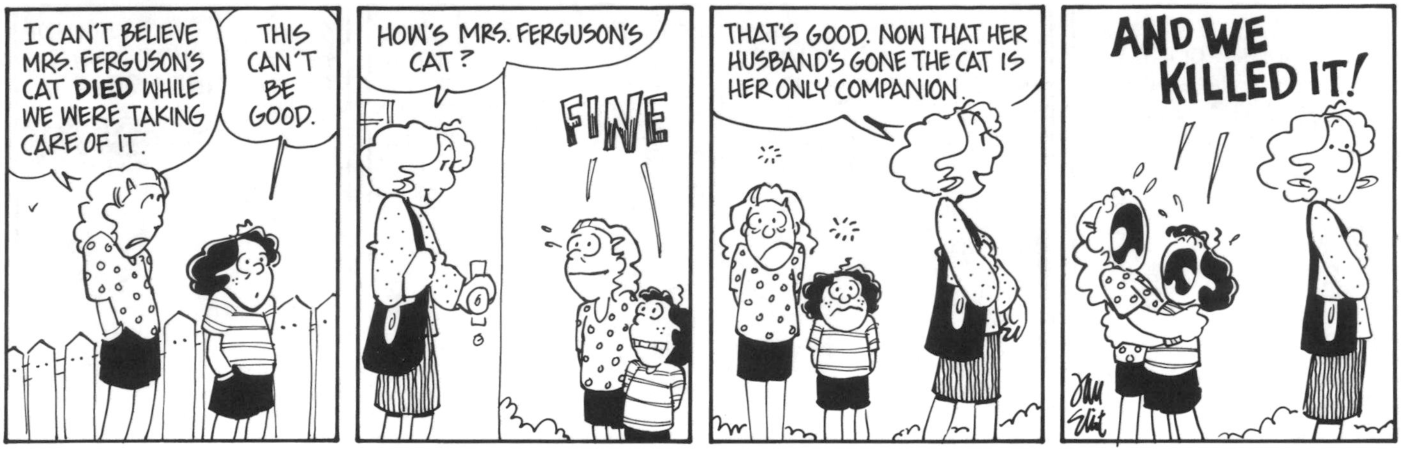
I CAN'T BELIEVE MRS. FERGUSON'S CAT **DIED** WHILE WE WERE TAKING CARE OF IT.
THIS CAN'T BE GOOD.
HOW'S MRS. FERGUSON'S CAT?
FINE
THAT'S GOOD. NOW THAT HER HUSBAND'S GONE THE CAT IS HER ONLY COMPANION.
AND WE KILLED IT!

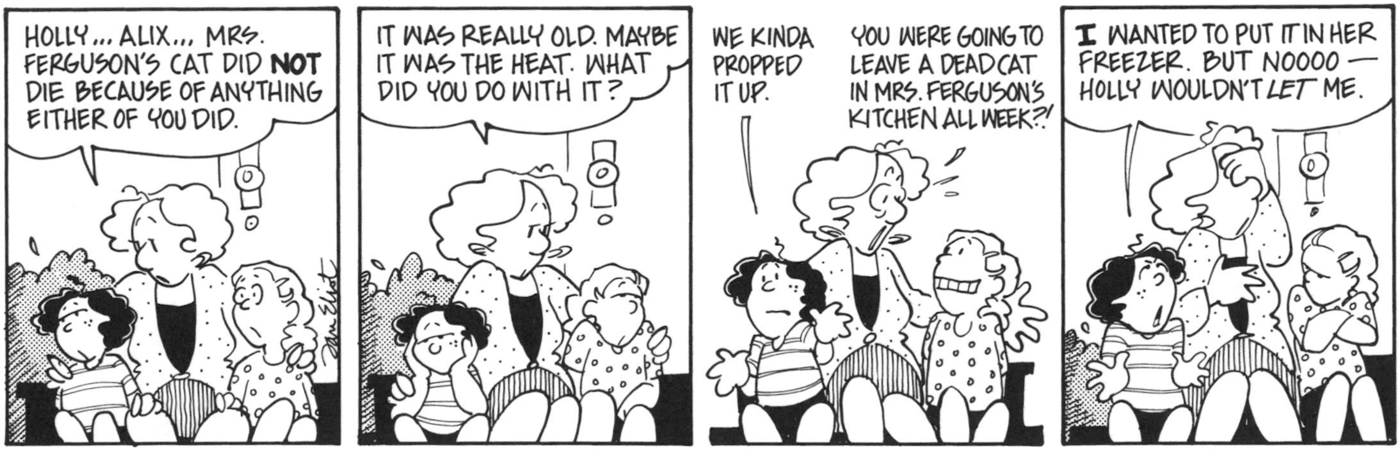
HOLLY... ALIX... MRS. FERGUSON'S CAT DID **NOT** DIE BECAUSE OF ANYTHING EITHER OF YOU DID.
IT WAS REALLY OLD. MAYBE IT WAS THE HEAT. WHAT DID YOU DO WITH IT?
WE KINDA PROPPED IT UP.
YOU WERE GOING TO LEAVE A DEAD CAT IN MRS. FERGUSON'S KITCHEN ALL WEEK?!
I WANTED TO PUT IT IN HER FREEZER. BUT NOOOO — HOLLY WOULDN'T *LET* ME.

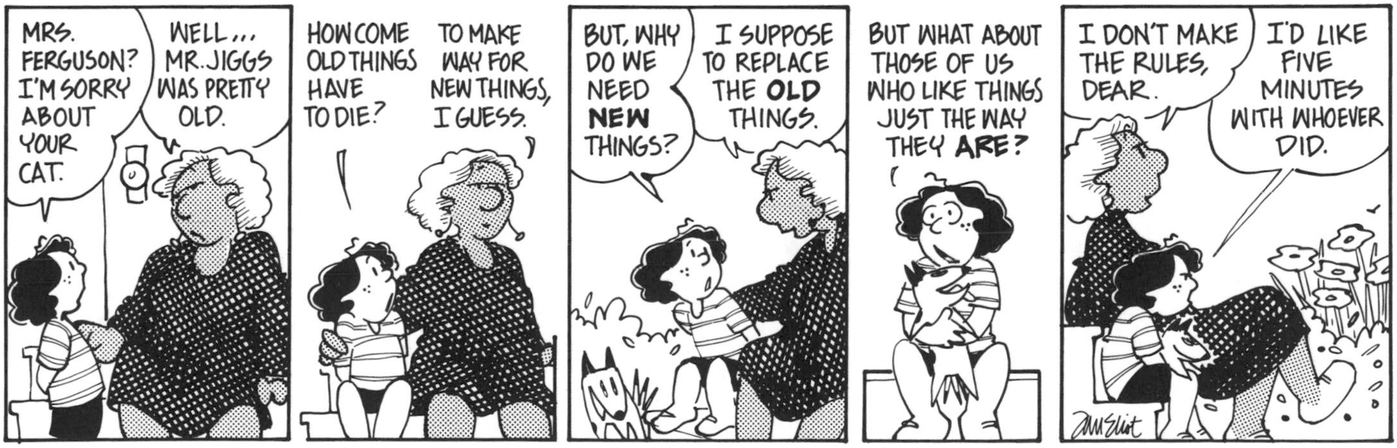
MRS. FERGUSON? I'M SORRY ABOUT YOUR CAT.
WELL... MR. JIGGS WAS PRETTY OLD.
HOW COME OLD THINGS HAVE TO DIE?
TO MAKE WAY FOR NEW THINGS, I GUESS.
BUT, WHY DO WE NEED **NEW** THINGS?
I SUPPOSE TO REPLACE THE **OLD** THINGS.
BUT WHAT ABOUT THOSE OF US WHO LIKE THINGS JUST THE WAY THEY **ARE**?
I DON'T MAKE THE RULES, DEAR.
I'D LIKE FIVE MINUTES WITH WHOEVER DID.

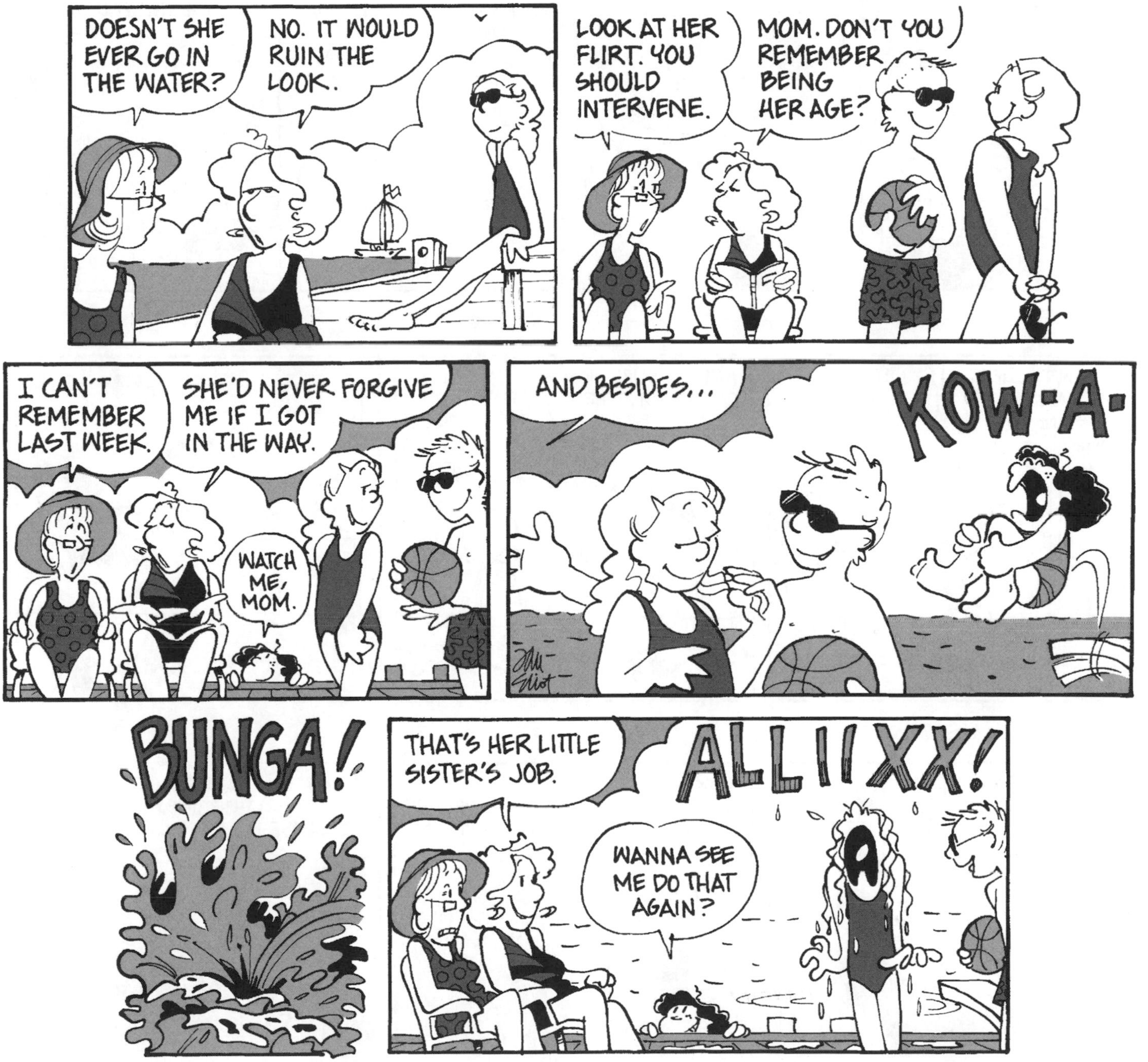
DOESN'T SHE EVER GO IN THE WATER?
NO. IT WOULD RUIN THE LOOK.
LOOK AT HER FLIRT. YOU SHOULD INTERVENE.
MOM. DON'T YOU REMEMBER BEING HER AGE?
I CAN'T REMEMBER LAST WEEK.
SHE'D NEVER FORGIVE ME IF I GOT IN THE WAY.
WATCH ME, MOM.
AND BESIDES...
KOW-A-
BUNGA!
THAT'S HER LITTLE SISTER'S JOB.
ALLIIXX!
WANNA SEE ME DO THAT AGAIN?

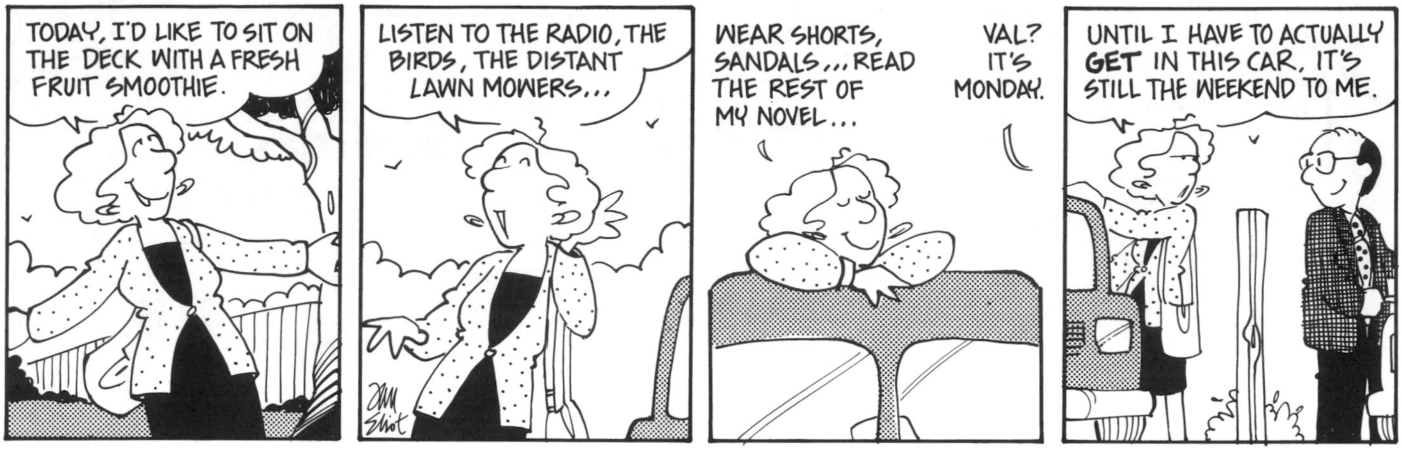
TODAY, I'D LIKE TO SIT ON THE DECK WITH A FRESH FRUIT SMOOTHIE.
LISTEN TO THE RADIO, THE BIRDS, THE DISTANT LAWN MOWERS...
WEAR SHORTS, SANDALS,... READ THE REST OF MY NOVEL...
VAL? IT'S MONDAY.
UNTIL I HAVE TO ACTUALLY GET IN THIS CAR, IT'S STILL THE WEEKEND TO ME.

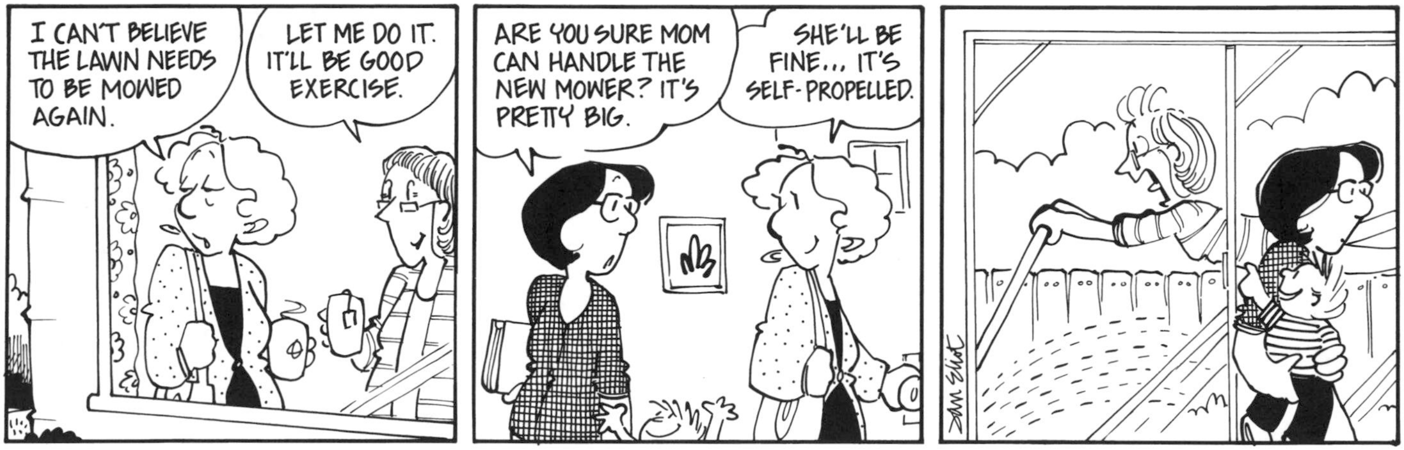
I CAN'T BELIEVE THE LAWN NEEDS TO BE MOWED AGAIN.
LET ME DO IT. IT'LL BE GOOD EXERCISE.
ARE YOU SURE MOM CAN HANDLE THE NEW MOWER? IT'S PRETTY BIG.
SHE'LL BE FINE... IT'S SELF-PROPELLED.

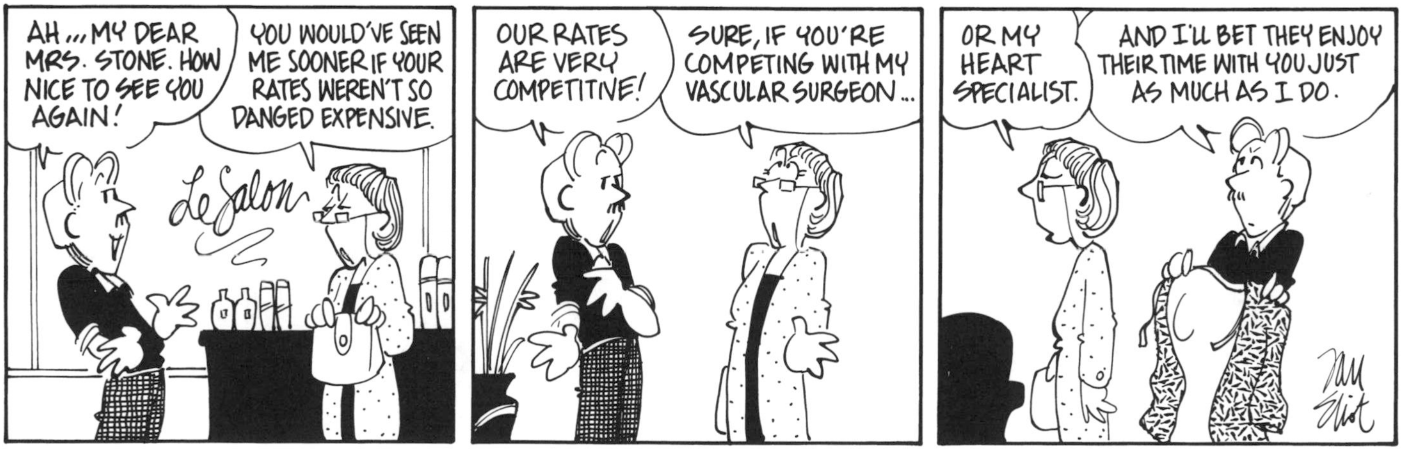
AH... MY DEAR MRS. STONE. HOW NICE TO SEE YOU AGAIN!
YOU WOULD'VE SEEN ME SOONER IF YOUR RATES WEREN'T SO DANGED EXPENSIVE.
Le Salon
OUR RATES ARE VERY COMPETITIVE!
SURE, IF YOU'RE COMPETING WITH MY VASCULAR SURGEON...
OR MY HEART SPECIALIST.
AND I'LL BET THEY ENJOY THEIR TIME WITH YOU JUST AS MUCH AS I DO.

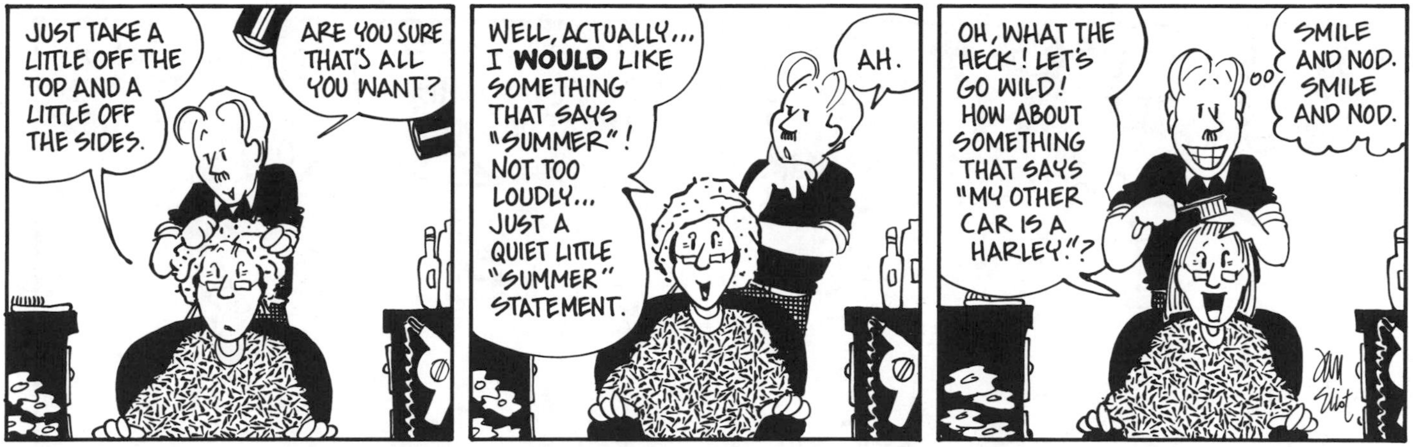
JUST TAKE A LITTLE OFF THE TOP AND A LITTLE OFF THE SIDES.
ARE YOU SURE THAT'S ALL YOU WANT?
WELL, ACTUALLY... I **WOULD** LIKE SOMETHING THAT SAYS "SUMMER"! NOT TOO LOUDLY... JUST A QUIET LITTLE "SUMMER" STATEMENT.
AH.
OH, WHAT THE HECK! LET'S GO WILD! HOW ABOUT SOMETHING THAT SAYS "MY OTHER CAR IS A HARLEY"?
SMILE AND NOD. SMILE AND NOD.

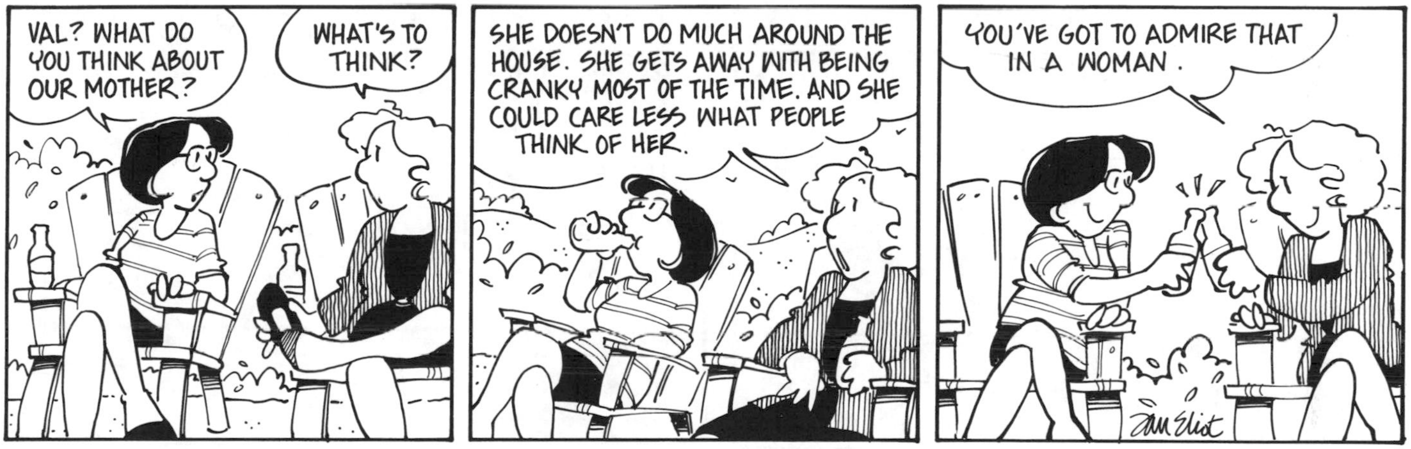
VAL? WHAT DO YOU THINK ABOUT OUR MOTHER?
WHAT'S TO THINK?
SHE DOESN'T DO MUCH AROUND THE HOUSE. SHE GETS AWAY WITH BEING CRANKY MOST OF THE TIME. AND SHE COULD CARE LESS WHAT PEOPLE THINK OF HER.
YOU'VE GOT TO ADMIRE THAT IN A WOMAN.
Jan Eliot

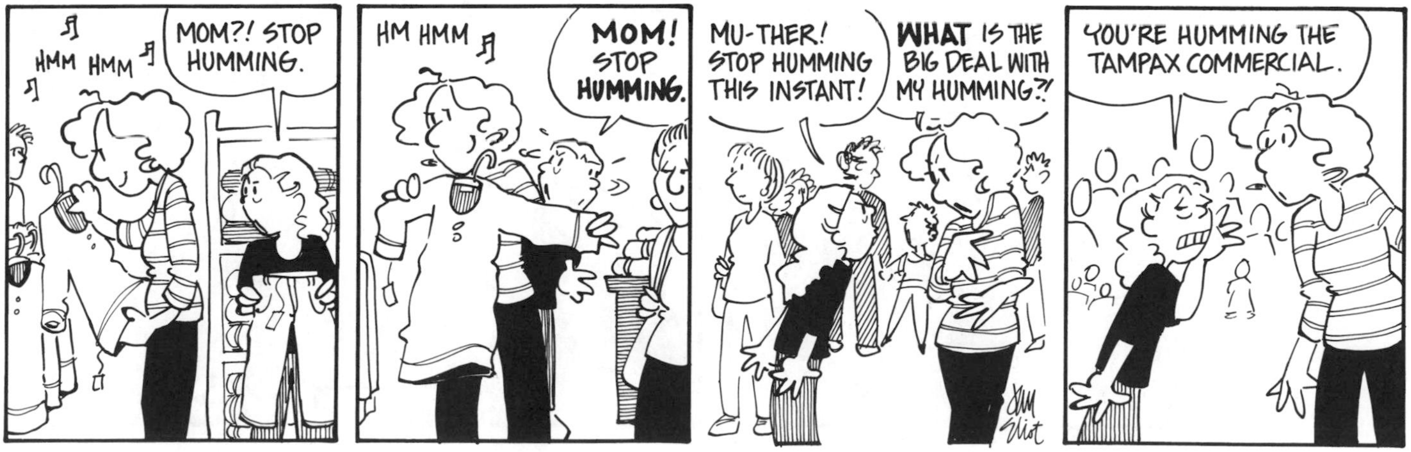
HMM HMM
MOM?! STOP HUMMING.
HM HMM
MOM! STOP **HUMMING.**
MU-THER! STOP HUMMING THIS INSTANT!
WHAT IS THE BIG DEAL WITH MY HUMMING?!
YOU'RE HUMMING THE TAMPAX COMMERCIAL.

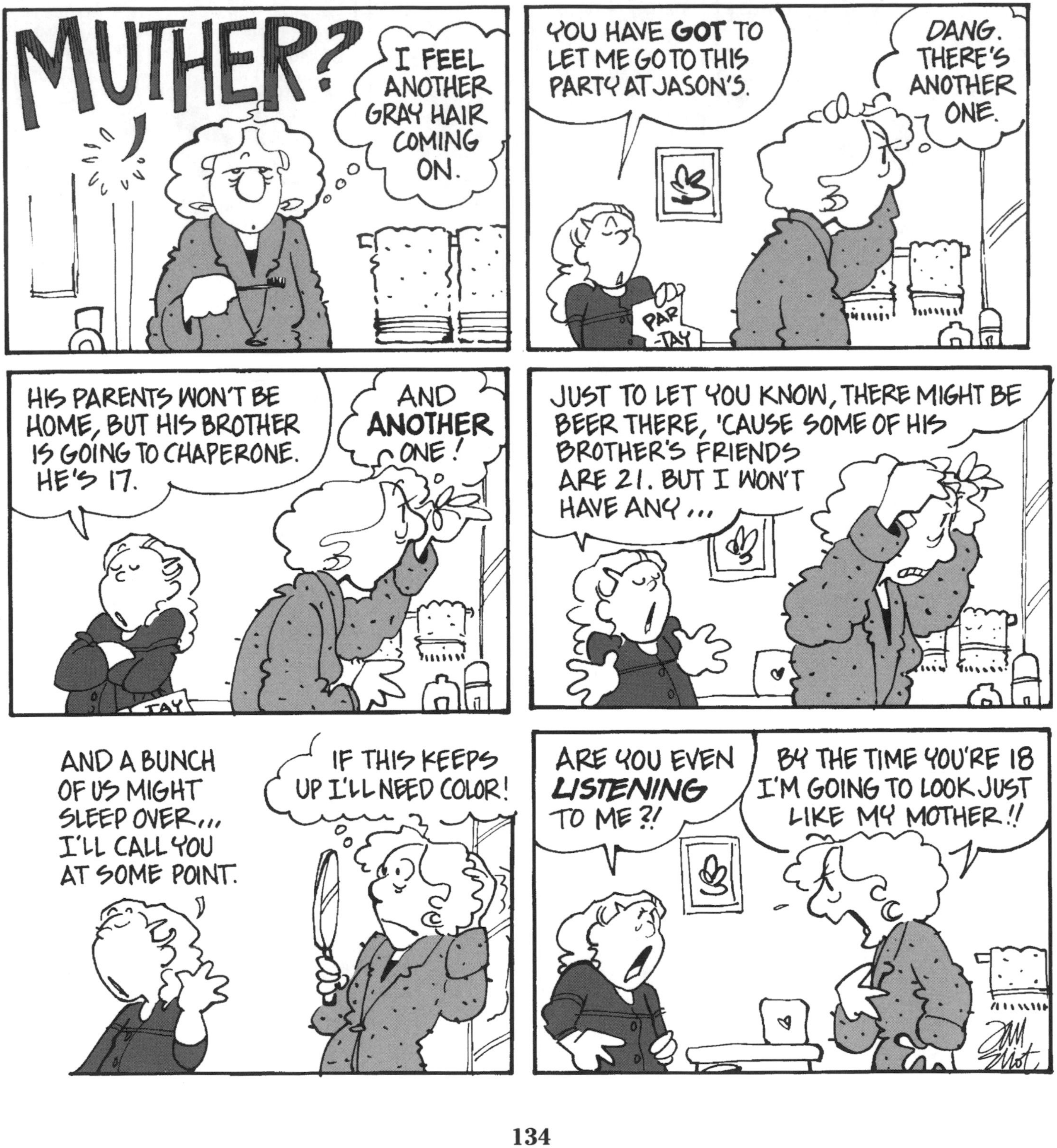
MUTHER?
I FEEL ANOTHER GRAY HAIR COMING ON.
YOU HAVE **GOT** TO LET ME GO TO THIS PARTY AT JASON'S.
DANG. THERE'S ANOTHER ONE.
PAR-TAY
HIS PARENTS WON'T BE HOME, BUT HIS BROTHER IS GOING TO CHAPERONE. HE'S 17.
AND **ANOTHER** ONE!
JUST TO LET YOU KNOW, THERE MIGHT BE BEER THERE, 'CAUSE SOME OF HIS BROTHER'S FRIENDS ARE 21. BUT I WON'T HAVE ANY...
AND A BUNCH OF US MIGHT SLEEP OVER... I'LL CALL YOU AT SOME POINT.
IF THIS KEEPS UP I'LL NEED COLOR!
ARE YOU EVEN ***LISTENING*** TO ME?!
BY THE TIME YOU'RE 18 I'M GOING TO LOOK JUST LIKE MY MOTHER!!

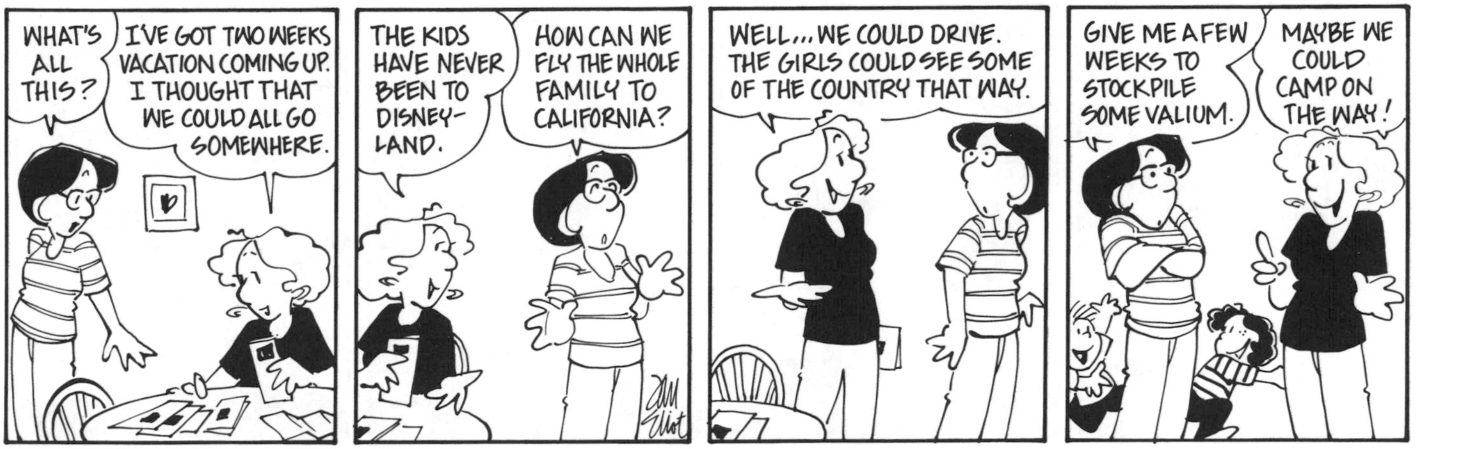
WHAT'S ALL THIS?
I'VE GOT TWO WEEKS VACATION COMING UP. I THOUGHT THAT WE COULD ALL GO SOMEWHERE.
THE KIDS HAVE NEVER BEEN TO DISNEY-LAND.
HOW CAN WE FLY THE WHOLE FAMILY TO CALIFORNIA?
WELL,... WE COULD DRIVE. THE GIRLS COULD SEE SOME OF THE COUNTRY THAT WAY.
GIVE ME A FEW WEEKS TO STOCKPILE SOME VALIUM.
MAYBE WE COULD CAMP ON THE WAY!

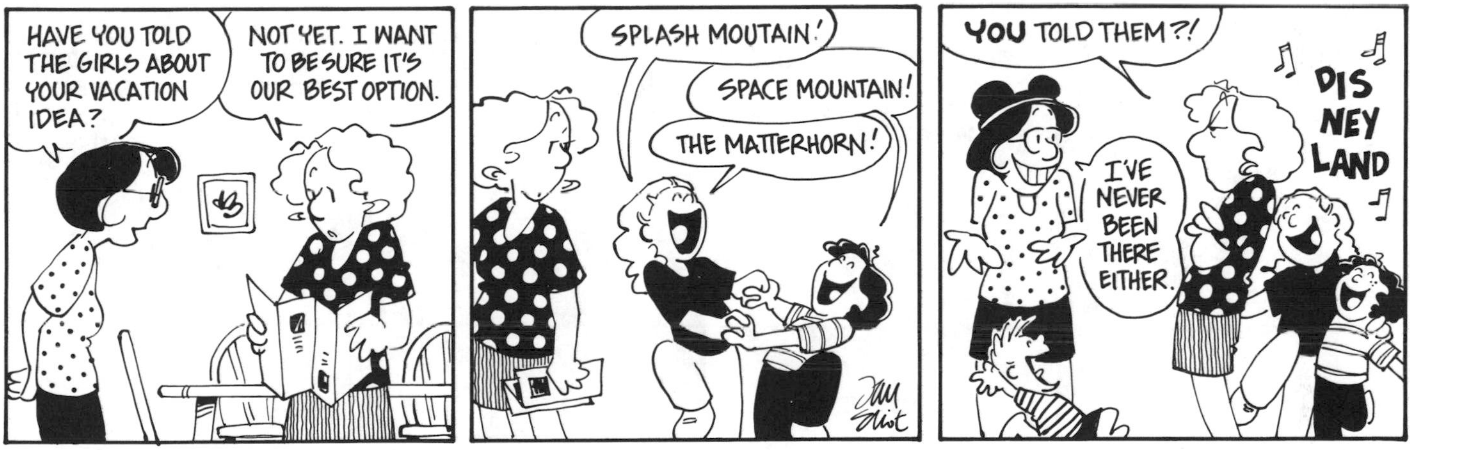
HAVE YOU TOLD THE GIRLS ABOUT YOUR VACATION IDEA?
NOT YET. I WANT TO BE SURE IT'S OUR BEST OPTION.
SPLASH MOUTAIN!
SPACE MOUNTAIN!
THE MATTERHORN!
YOU TOLD THEM?!
I'VE NEVER BEEN THERE EITHER.
DIS NEY LAND

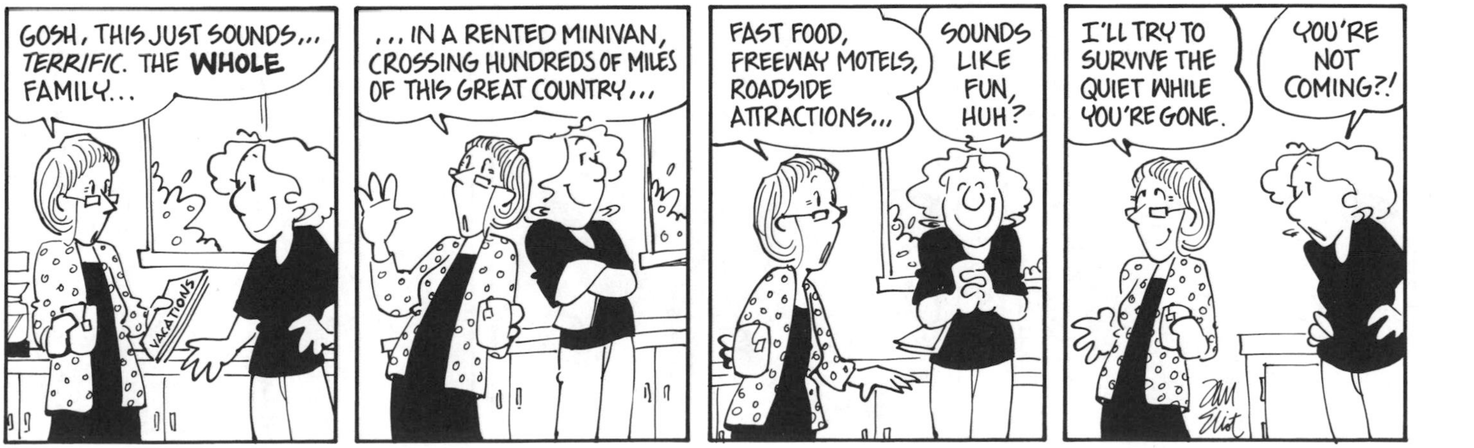
GOSH, THIS JUST SOUNDS... TERRIFIC. THE WHOLE FAMILY...
VACATIONS
... IN A RENTED MINIVAN, CROSSING HUNDREDS OF MILES OF THIS GREAT COUNTRY...
FAST FOOD, FREEWAY MOTELS, ROADSIDE ATTRACTIONS...
SOUNDS LIKE FUN, HUH?
I'LL TRY TO SURVIVE THE QUIET WHILE YOU'RE GONE.
YOU'RE NOT COMING?!

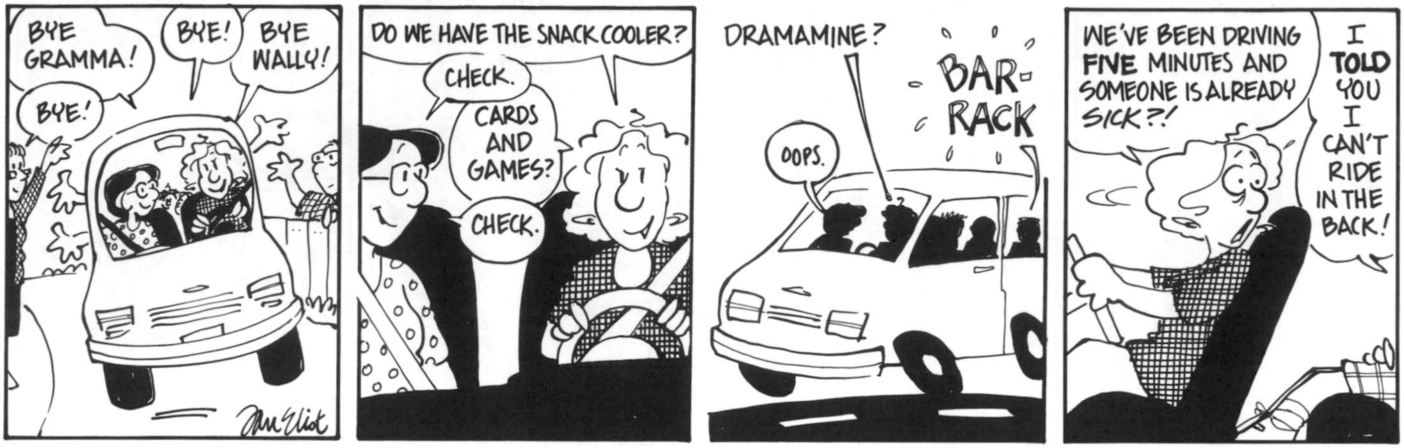
BYE GRAMMA!
BYE!
BYE!
BYE WALLY!
DO WE HAVE THE SNACK COOLER?
CHECK.
CARDS AND GAMES?
CHECK.
DRAMAMINE?
OOPS.
BAR RACK
WE'VE BEEN DRIVING FIVE MINUTES AND SOMEONE IS ALREADY SICK?!
I TOLD YOU I CAN'T RIDE IN THE BACK!

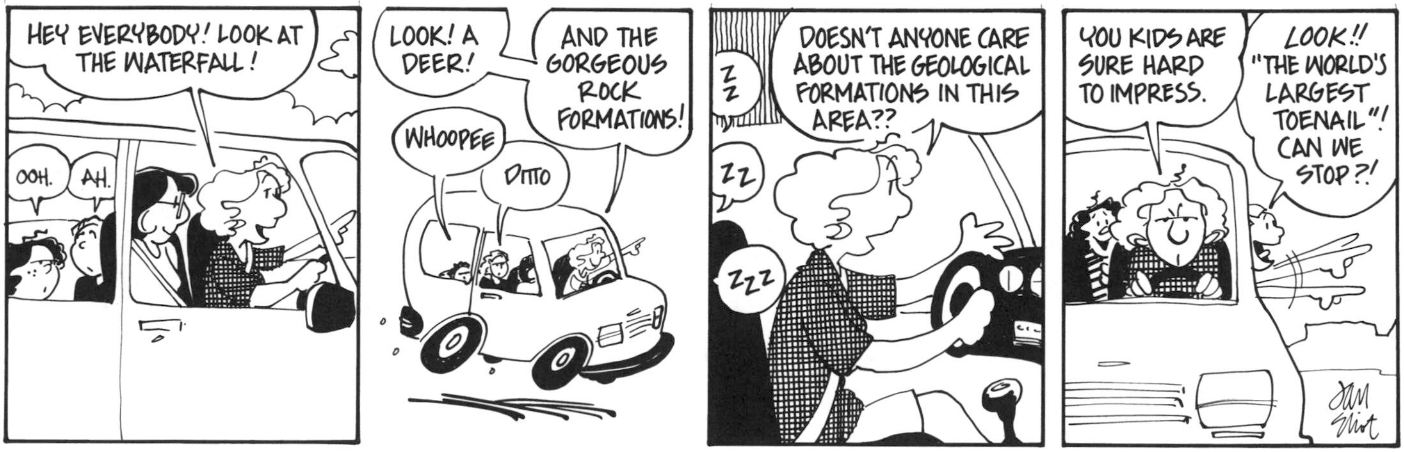
HEY EVERYBODY! LOOK AT THE WATERFALL!
OOH.
AH.
LOOK! A DEER!
AND THE GORGEOUS ROCK FORMATIONS!
WHOOPEE
DITTO
DOESN'T ANYONE CARE ABOUT THE GEOLOGICAL FORMATIONS IN THIS AREA??
Z Z
ZZ
ZZZ
YOU KIDS ARE SURE HARD TO IMPRESS.
LOOK!! "THE WORLD'S LARGEST TOENAIL"! CAN WE STOP?!

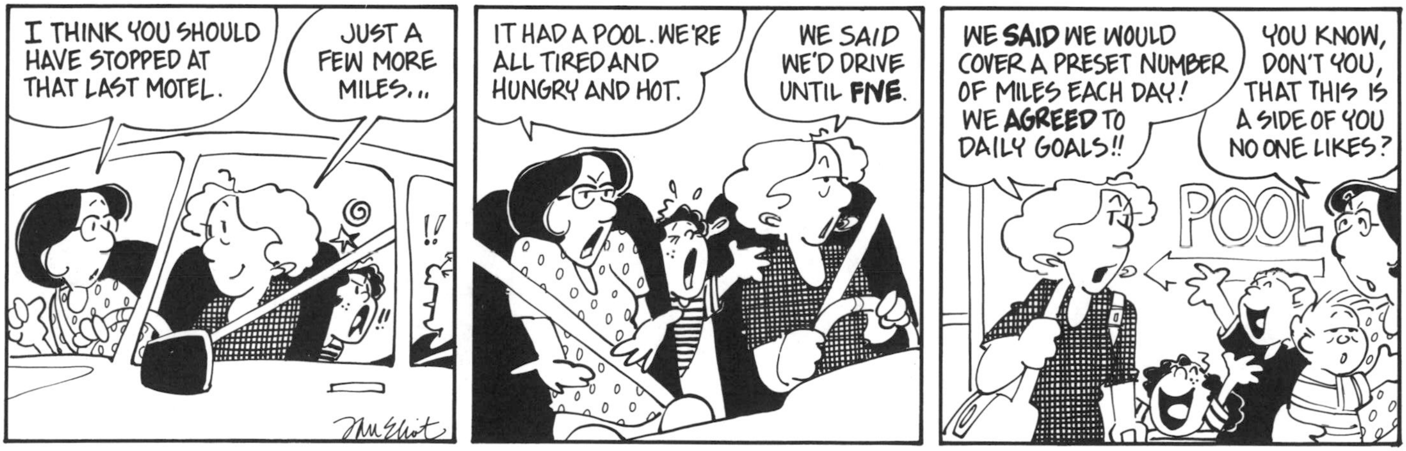
I THINK YOU SHOULD HAVE STOPPED AT THAT LAST MOTEL.
JUST A FEW MORE MILES...
!!
IT HAD A POOL. WE'RE ALL TIRED AND HUNGRY AND HOT.
WE SAID WE'D DRIVE UNTIL FIVE.
WE SAID WE WOULD COVER A PRESET NUMBER OF MILES EACH DAY! WE AGREED TO DAILY GOALS!!
YOU KNOW, DON'T YOU, THAT THIS IS A SIDE OF YOU NO ONE LIKES?
POOL

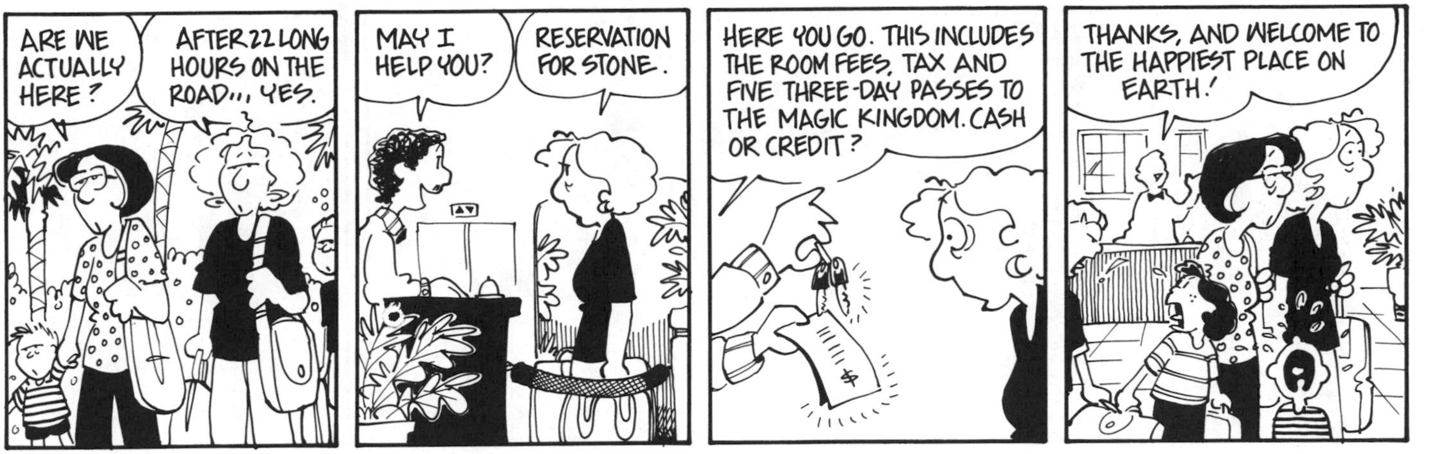
ARE WE ACTUALLY HERE?
AFTER 22 LONG HOURS ON THE ROAD... YES.
MAY I HELP YOU?
RESERVATION FOR STONE.
HERE YOU GO. THIS INCLUDES THE ROOM FEES, TAX AND FIVE THREE-DAY PASSES TO THE MAGIC KINGDOM. CASH OR CREDIT?
THANKS, AND WELCOME TO THE HAPPIEST PLACE ON EARTH!

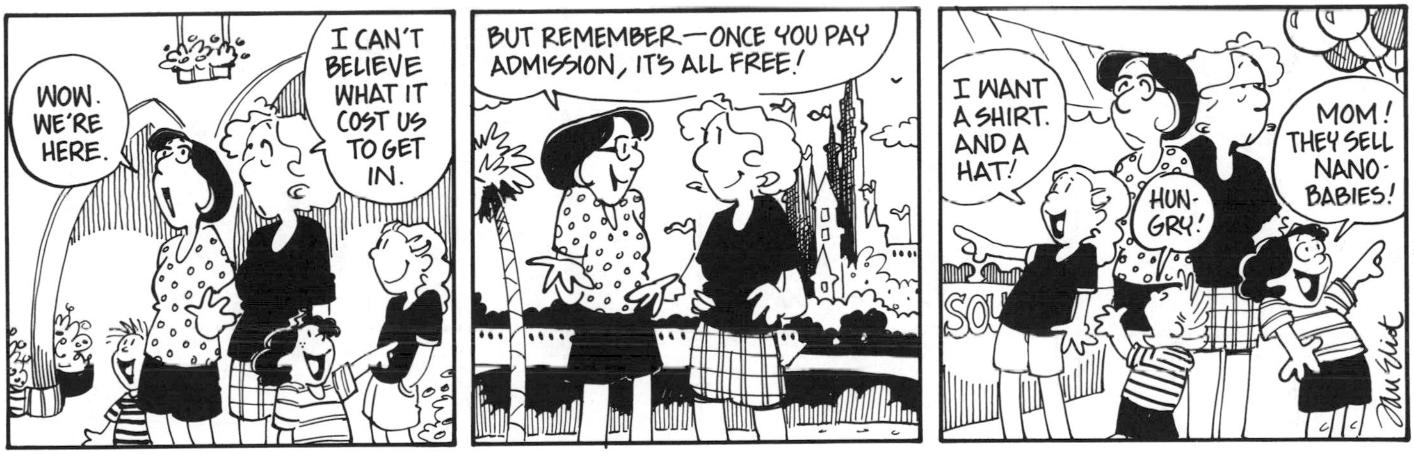
WOW. WE'RE HERE.
I CAN'T BELIEVE WHAT IT COST US TO GET IN.
BUT REMEMBER—ONCE YOU PAY ADMISSION, IT'S ALL FREE!
I WANT A SHIRT. AND A HAT!
HUN-GRY!
MOM! THEY SELL NANO-BABIES!

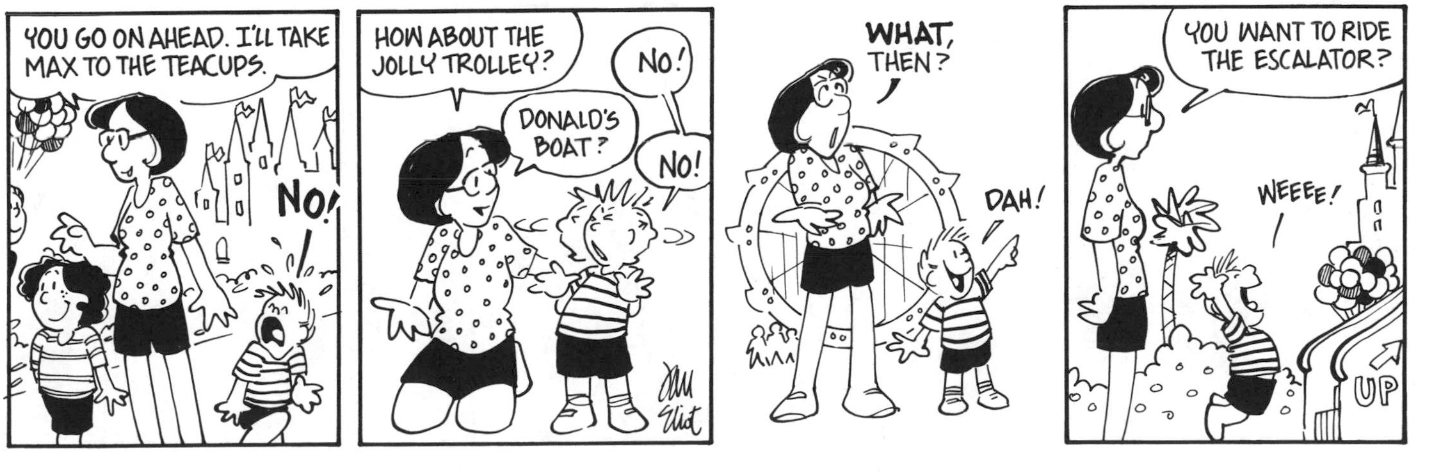
YOU GO ON AHEAD. I'LL TAKE MAX TO THE TEACUPS.
NO!
HOW ABOUT THE JOLLY TROLLEY?
NO!
DONALD'S BOAT?
NO!
WHAT, THEN?
DAH!
YOU WANT TO RIDE THE ESCALATOR?
WEEEE!
UP

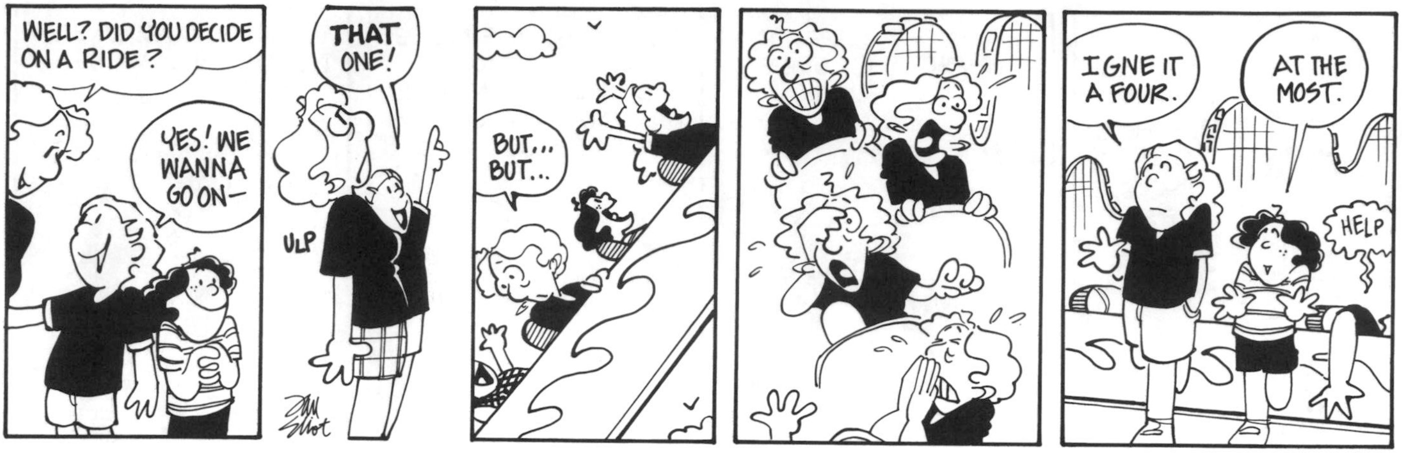

WELL? DID YOU DECIDE ON A RIDE?
YES! WE WANNA GO ON–
THAT ONE!
ULP
BUT... BUT...
I GAVE IT A FOUR.
AT THE MOST.
HELP

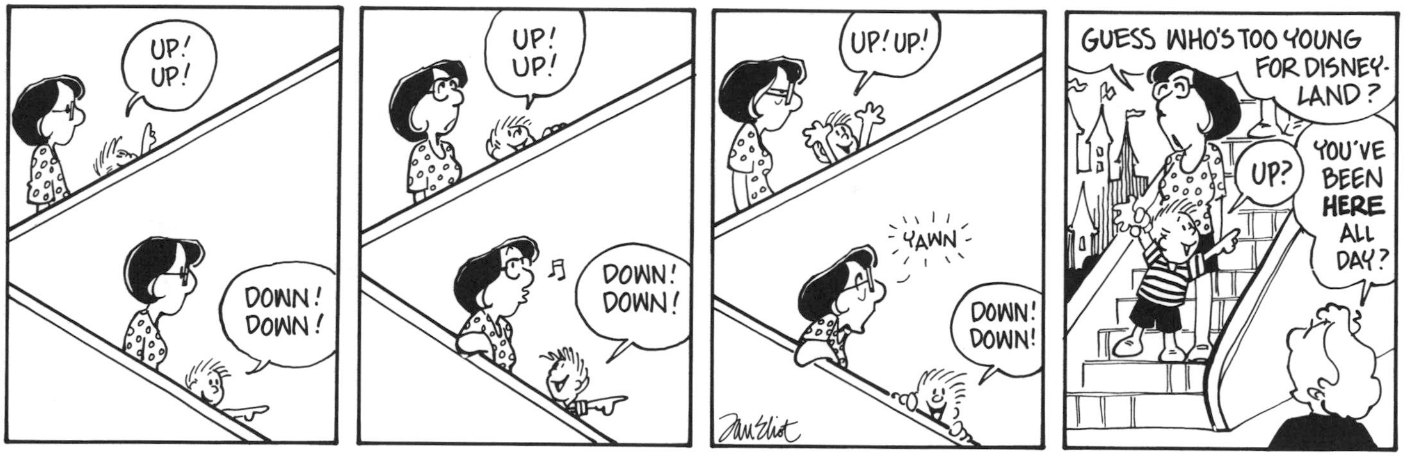

UP! UP!
DOWN! DOWN!
UP! UP!
DOWN! DOWN!
UP! UP!
YAWN
DOWN! DOWN!
GUESS WHO'S TOO YOUNG FOR DISNEY-LAND?
UP?
YOU'VE BEEN HERE ALL DAY?

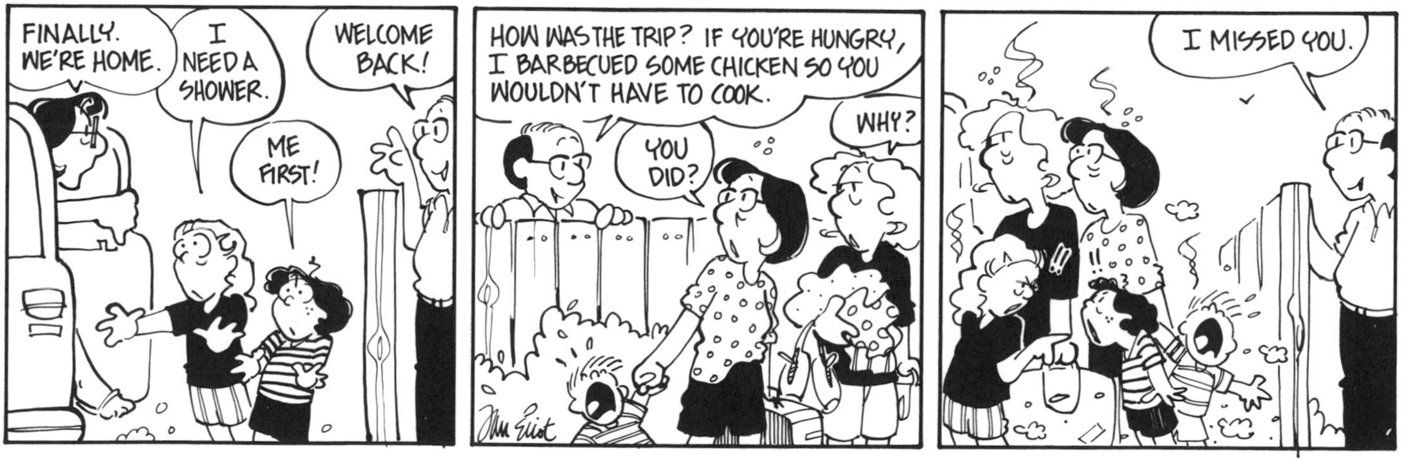

FINALLY. WE'RE HOME.
I NEED A SHOWER.
WELCOME BACK!
ME FIRST!
HOW WAS THE TRIP? IF YOU'RE HUNGRY, I BARBECUED SOME CHICKEN SO YOU WOULDN'T HAVE TO COOK.
YOU DID?
WHY?
I MISSED YOU.

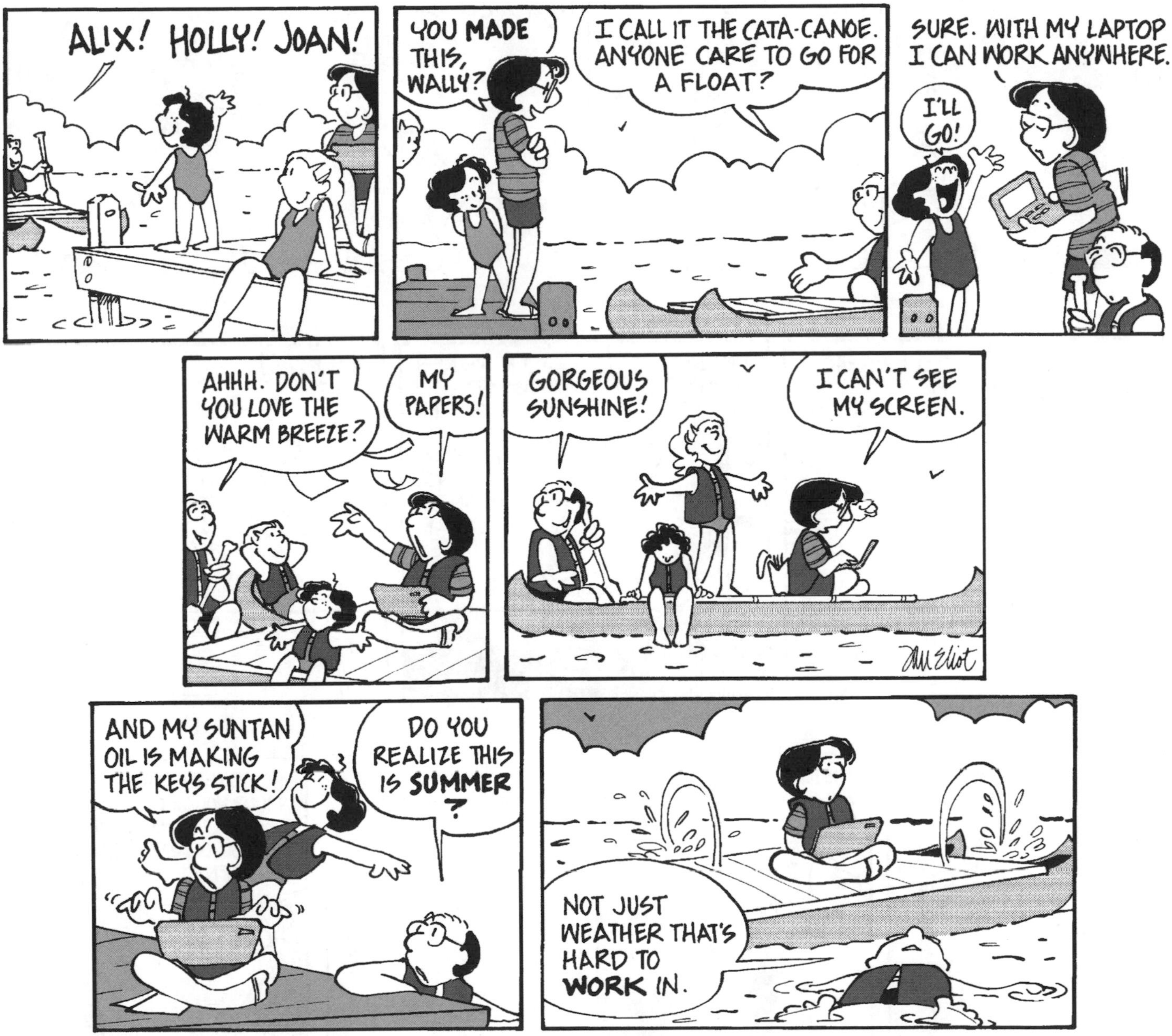
ALIX! HOLLY! JOAN!
YOU MADE THIS, WALLY?
I CALL IT THE CATA-CANOE. ANYONE CARE TO GO FOR A FLOAT?
I'LL GO!
SURE. WITH MY LAPTOP I CAN WORK ANYWHERE.
AHHH. DON'T YOU LOVE THE WARM BREEZE?
MY PAPERS!
GORGEOUS SUNSHINE!
I CAN'T SEE MY SCREEN.
AND MY SUNTAN OIL IS MAKING THE KEYS STICK!
DO YOU REALIZE THIS IS SUMMER?
NOT JUST WEATHER THAT'S HARD TO WORK IN.

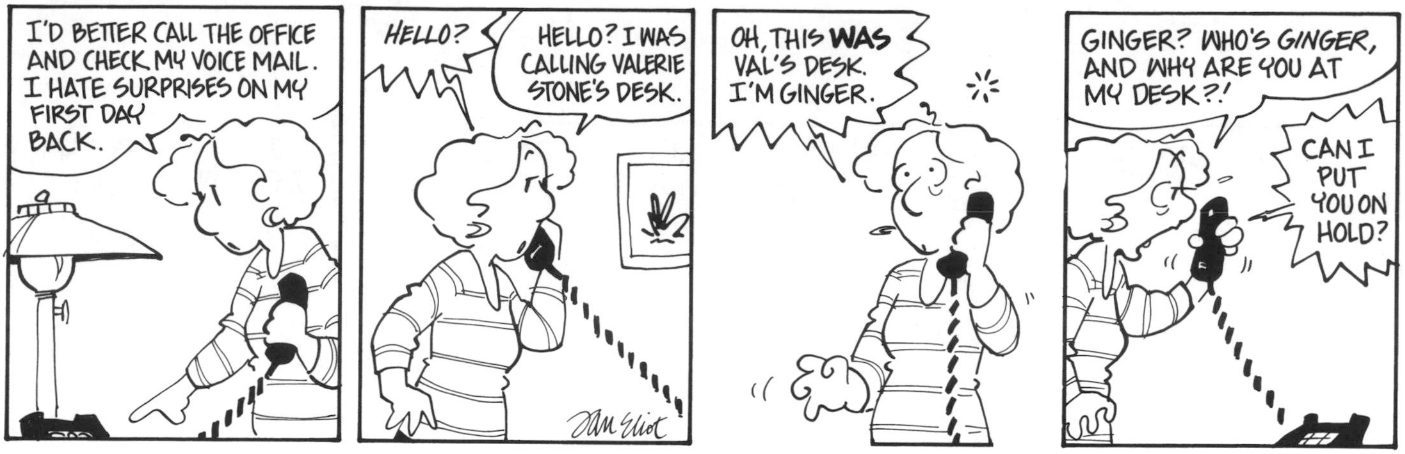

I'D BETTER CALL THE OFFICE AND CHECK MY VOICE MAIL. I HATE SURPRISES ON MY FIRST DAY BACK.
HELLO?
HELLO? I WAS CALLING VALERIE STONE'S DESK.
OH, THIS **WAS** VAL'S DESK. I'M GINGER.
GINGER? WHO'S *GINGER*, AND WHY ARE YOU AT MY DESK?!
CAN I PUT YOU ON HOLD?

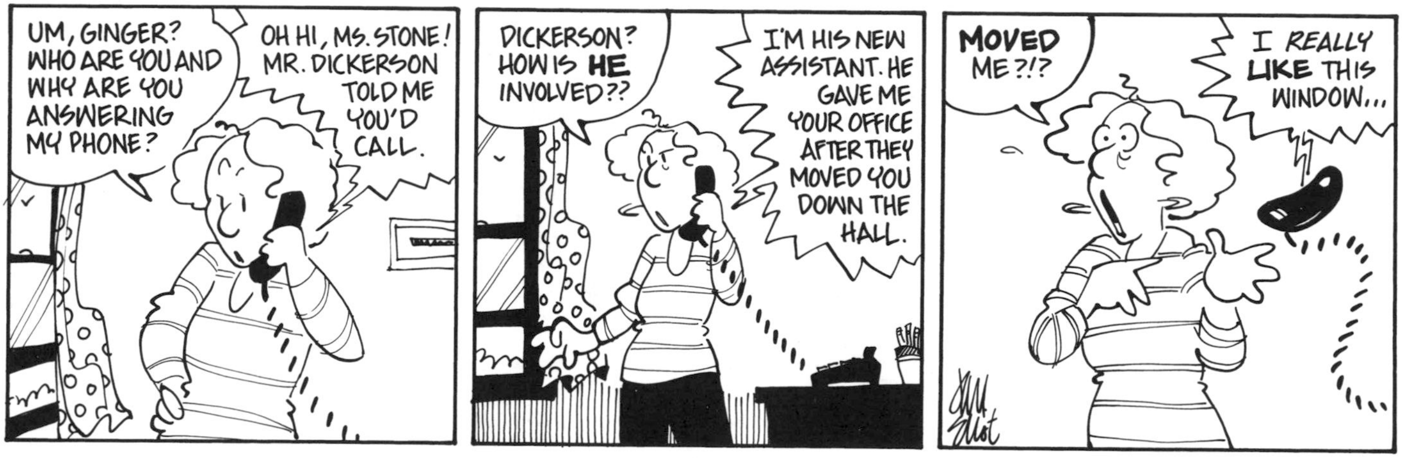

UM, GINGER? WHO ARE YOU AND WHY ARE YOU ANSWERING MY PHONE?
OH HI, MS. STONE! MR. DICKERSON TOLD ME YOU'D CALL.
DICKERSON? HOW IS **HE** INVOLVED??
I'M HIS NEW ASSISTANT. HE GAVE ME YOUR OFFICE AFTER THEY MOVED YOU DOWN THE HALL.
MOVED ME?!?
I *REALLY* **LIKE** THIS WINDOW...

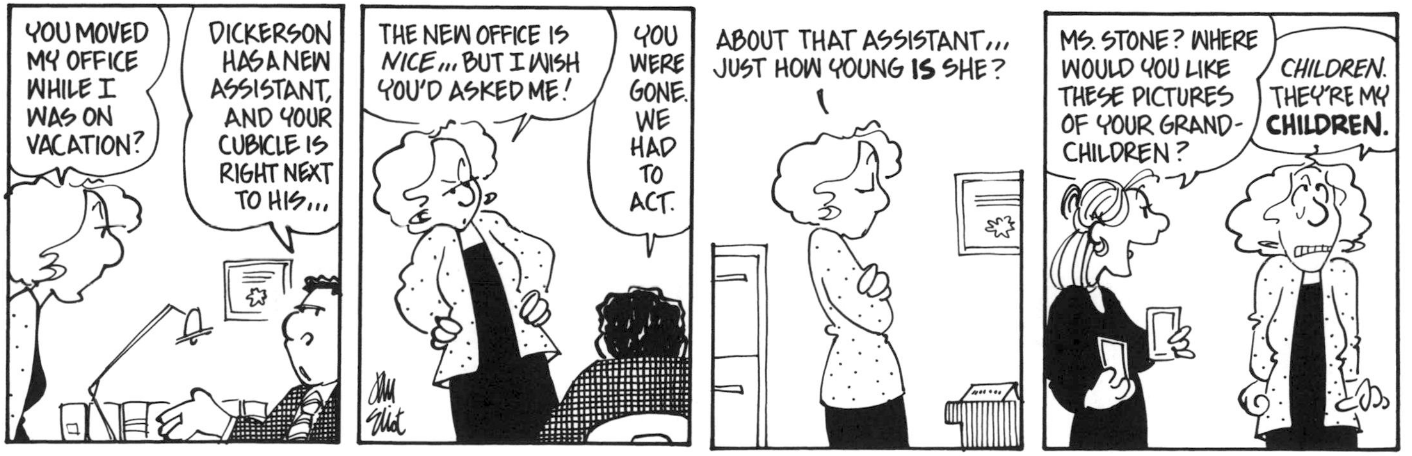

YOU MOVED MY OFFICE WHILE I WAS ON VACATION?
DICKERSON HAS A NEW ASSISTANT, AND YOUR CUBICLE IS RIGHT NEXT TO HIS...
THE NEW OFFICE IS *NICE*... BUT I WISH YOU'D ASKED ME!
YOU WERE GONE. WE HAD TO ACT.
ABOUT THAT ASSISTANT... JUST HOW YOUNG **IS** SHE?
MS. STONE? WHERE WOULD YOU LIKE THESE PICTURES OF YOUR GRAND-CHILDREN?
CHILDREN. THEY'RE MY **CHILDREN.**

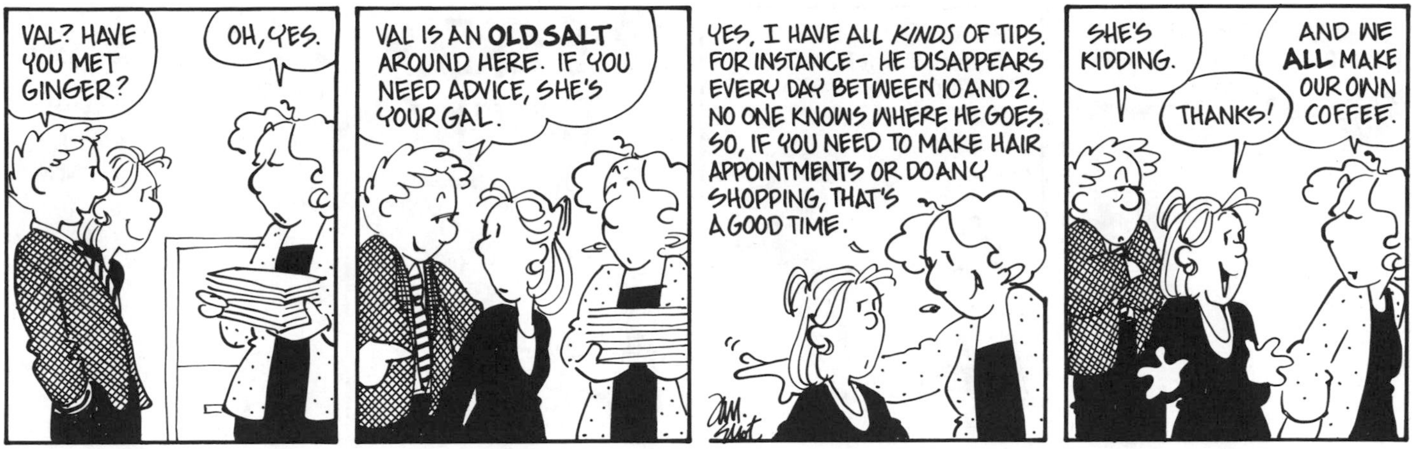
VAL? HAVE YOU MET GINGER?
OH, YES.
VAL IS AN **OLD SALT** AROUND HERE. IF YOU NEED ADVICE, SHE'S YOUR GAL.
YES, I HAVE ALL *KINDS* OF TIPS. FOR INSTANCE - HE DISAPPEARS EVERY DAY BETWEEN 10 AND 2. NO ONE KNOWS WHERE HE GOES. SO, IF YOU NEED TO MAKE HAIR APPOINTMENTS OR DO ANY SHOPPING, THAT'S A GOOD TIME.
SHE'S KIDDING.
THANKS!
AND WE **ALL** MAKE OUR OWN COFFEE.

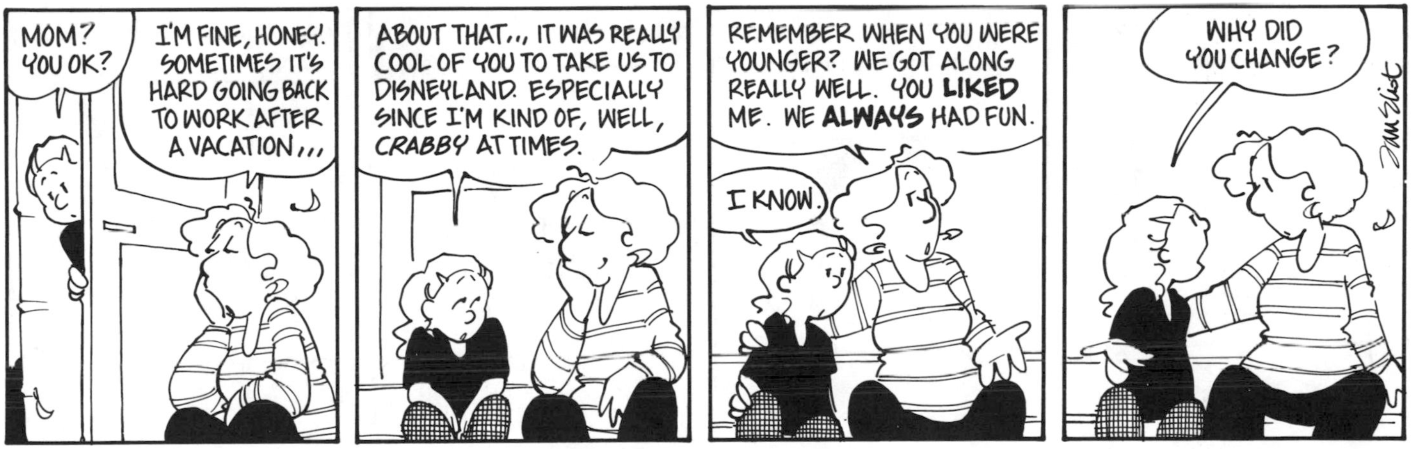
MOM? YOU OK?
I'M FINE, HONEY. SOMETIMES IT'S HARD GOING BACK TO WORK AFTER A VACATION...
ABOUT THAT... IT WAS REALLY COOL OF YOU TO TAKE US TO DISNEYLAND. ESPECIALLY SINCE I'M KIND OF, WELL, *CRABBY* AT TIMES.
REMEMBER WHEN YOU WERE YOUNGER? WE GOT ALONG REALLY WELL. YOU **LIKED** ME. WE **ALWAYS** HAD FUN.
I KNOW.
WHY DID YOU CHANGE?

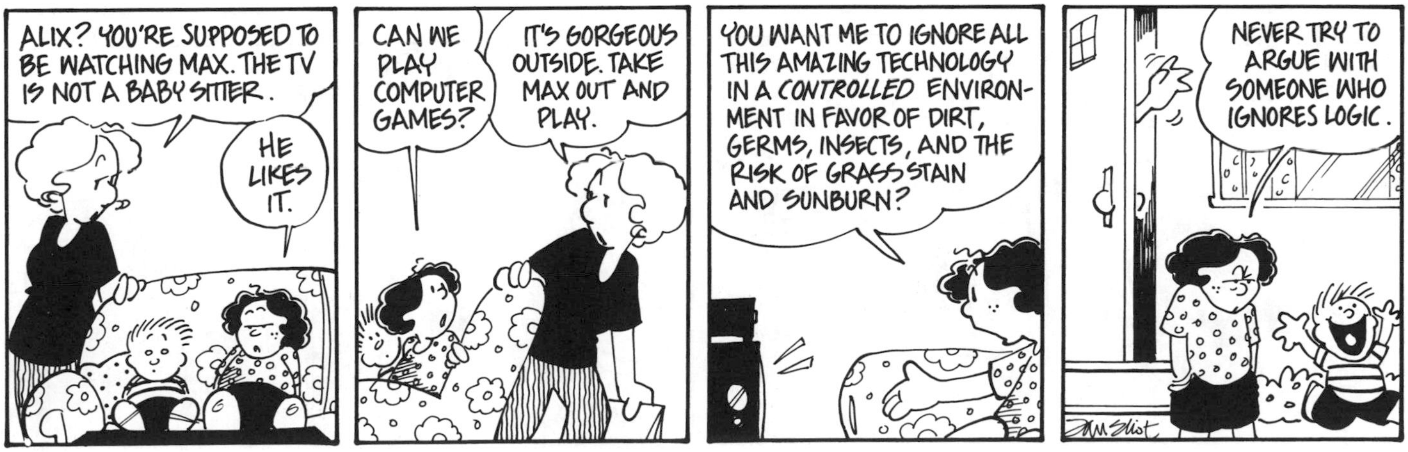
ALIX? YOU'RE SUPPOSED TO BE WATCHING MAX. THE TV IS NOT A BABY SITTER.
HE LIKES IT.
CAN WE PLAY COMPUTER GAMES?
IT'S GORGEOUS OUTSIDE. TAKE MAX OUT AND PLAY.
YOU WANT ME TO IGNORE ALL THIS AMAZING TECHNOLOGY IN A *CONTROLLED* ENVIRONMENT IN FAVOR OF DIRT, GERMS, INSECTS, AND THE RISK OF GRASS STAIN AND SUNBURN?
NEVER TRY TO ARGUE WITH SOMEONE WHO IGNORES LOGIC.

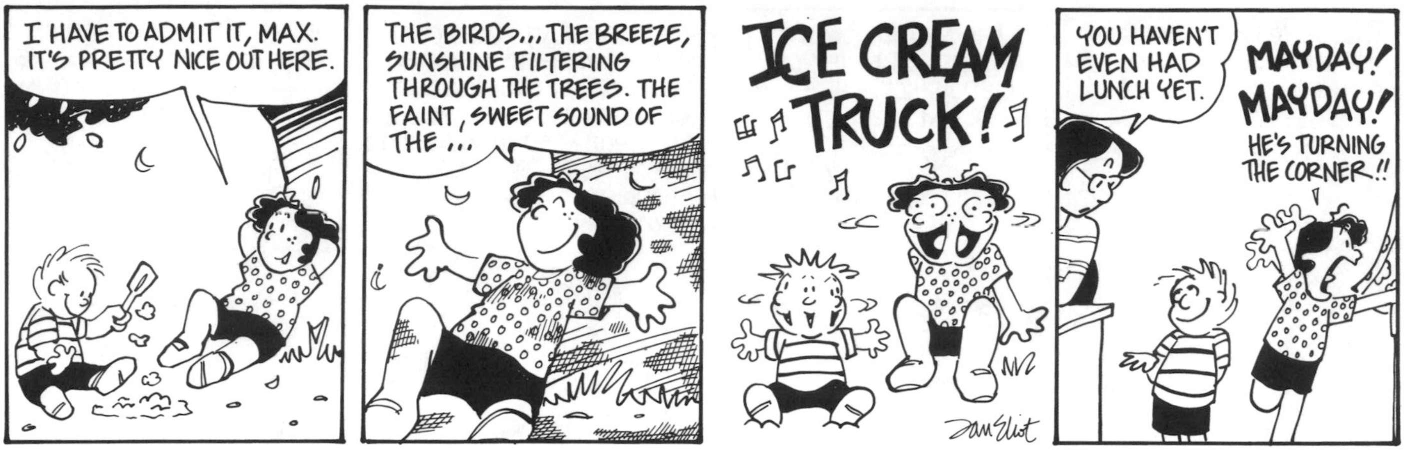
I HAVE TO ADMIT IT, MAX. IT'S PRETTY NICE OUT HERE.
THE BIRDS... THE BREEZE, SUNSHINE FILTERING THROUGH THE TREES. THE FAINT, SWEET SOUND OF THE ...
ICE CREAM TRUCK!
YOU HAVEN'T EVEN HAD LUNCH YET.
MAYDAY! MAYDAY!
HE'S TURNING THE CORNER!!

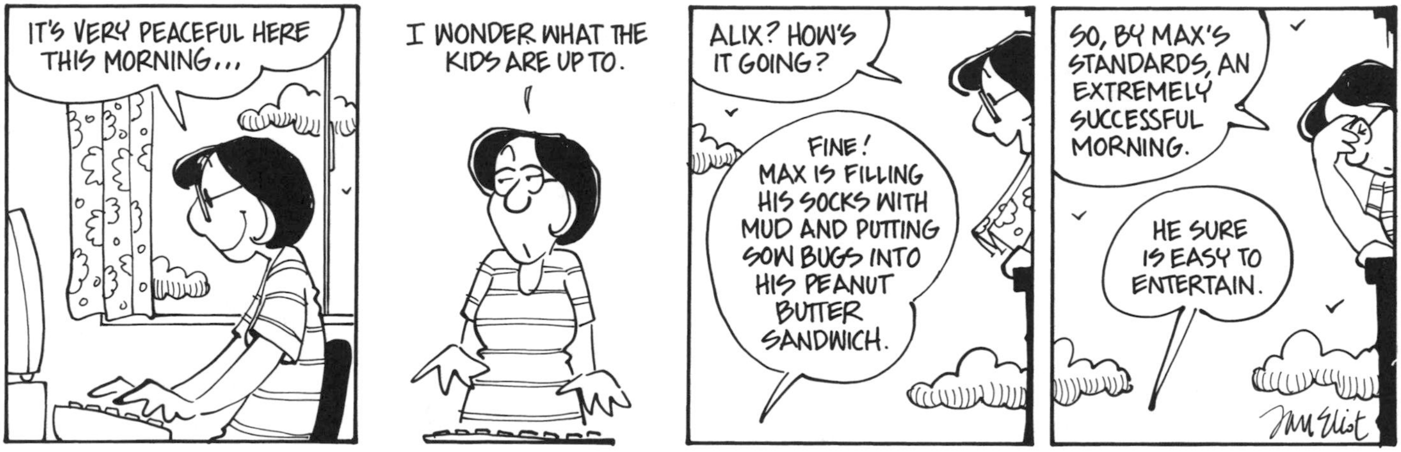
IT'S VERY PEACEFUL HERE THIS MORNING...
I WONDER WHAT THE KIDS ARE UP TO.
ALIX? HOW'S IT GOING?
FINE! MAX IS FILLING HIS SOCKS WITH MUD AND PUTTING SOW BUGS INTO HIS PEANUT BUTTER SANDWICH.
SO, BY MAX'S STANDARDS, AN EXTREMELY SUCCESSFUL MORNING.
HE SURE IS EASY TO ENTERTAIN.

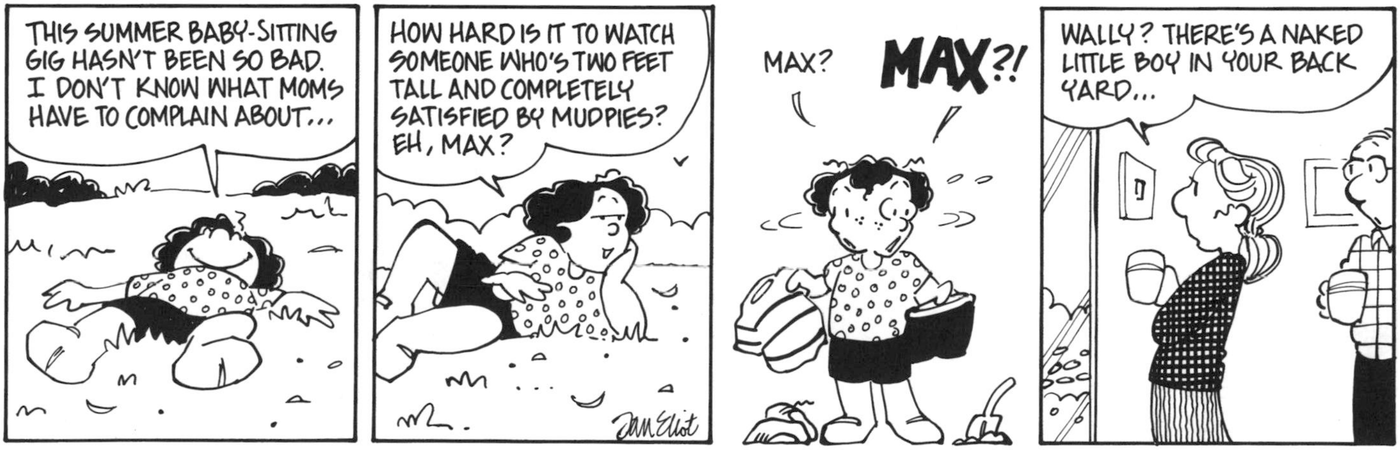
THIS SUMMER BABY-SITTING GIG HASN'T BEEN SO BAD. I DON'T KNOW WHAT MOMS HAVE TO COMPLAIN ABOUT...
HOW HARD IS IT TO WATCH SOMEONE WHO'S TWO FEET TALL AND COMPLETELY SATISFIED BY MUDPIES? EH, MAX?
MAX?
MAX?!
WALLY? THERE'S A NAKED LITTLE BOY IN YOUR BACK YARD...

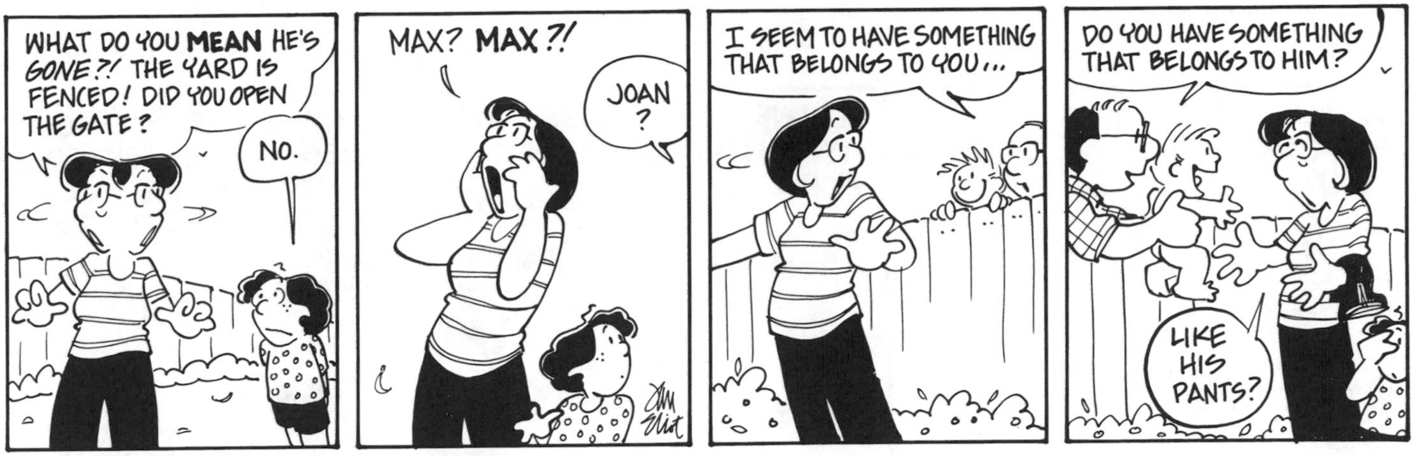
WHAT DO YOU MEAN HE'S GONE?! THE YARD IS FENCED! DID YOU OPEN THE GATE?
NO.
MAX? MAX?!
JOAN?
I SEEM TO HAVE SOMETHING THAT BELONGS TO YOU...
DO YOU HAVE SOMETHING THAT BELONGS TO HIM?
LIKE HIS PANTS?

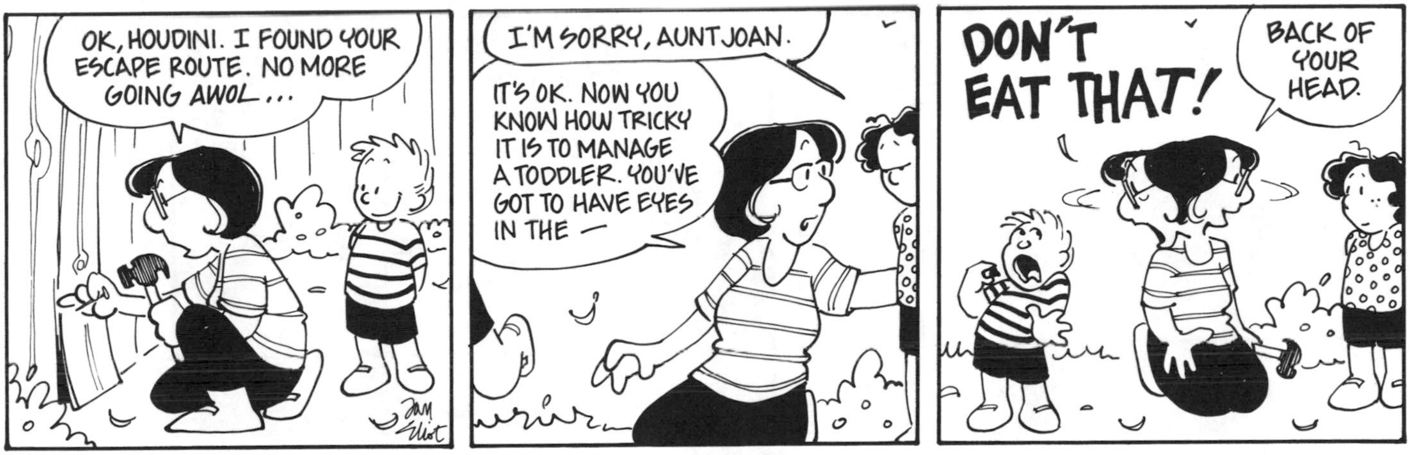
OK, HOUDINI. I FOUND YOUR ESCAPE ROUTE. NO MORE GOING AWOL...
I'M SORRY, AUNT JOAN.
IT'S OK. NOW YOU KNOW HOW TRICKY IT IS TO MANAGE A TODDLER. YOU'VE GOT TO HAVE EYES IN THE —
DON'T EAT THAT!
BACK OF YOUR HEAD.

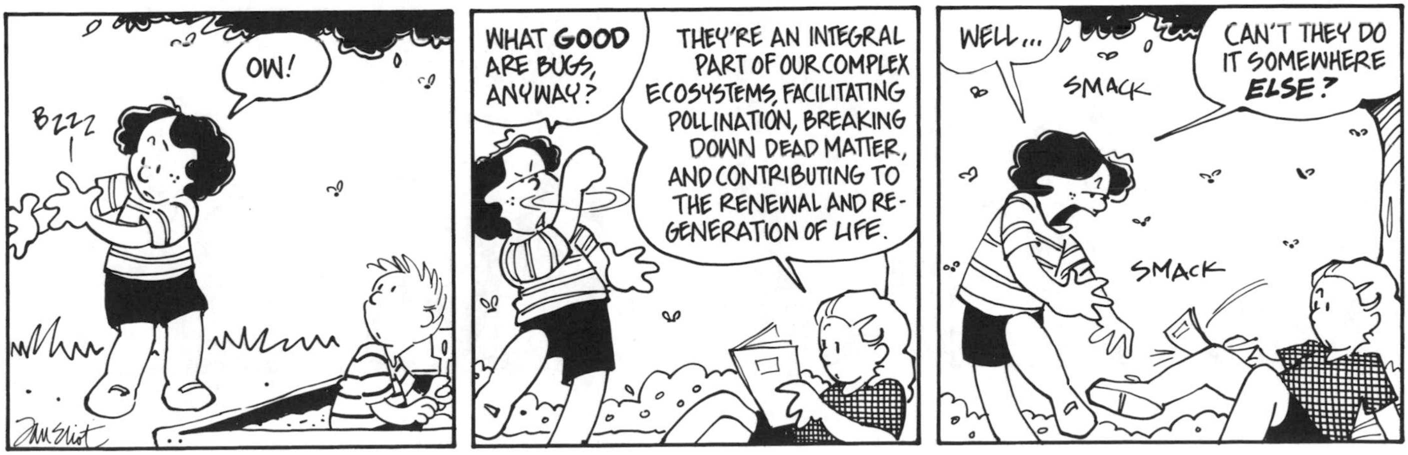
BZZZ
OW!
WHAT GOOD ARE BUGS, ANYWAY?
THEY'RE AN INTEGRAL PART OF OUR COMPLEX ECOSYSTEMS, FACILITATING POLLINATION, BREAKING DOWN DEAD MATTER, AND CONTRIBUTING TO THE RENEWAL AND RE-GENERATION OF LIFE.
WELL...
SMACK
CAN'T THEY DO IT SOMEWHERE ELSE?
SMACK

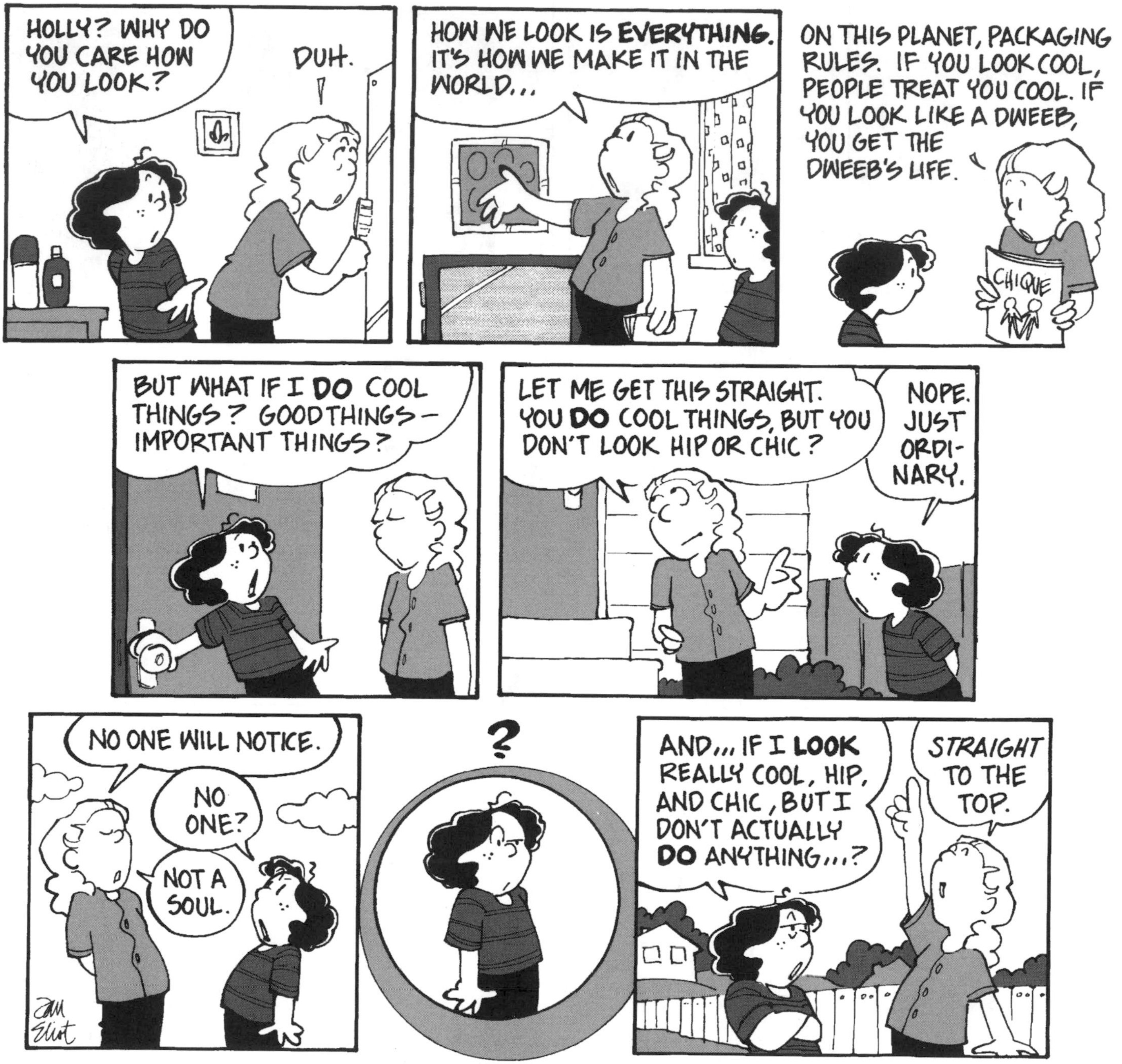
HOLLY? WHY DO YOU CARE HOW YOU LOOK?
DUH.
HOW WE LOOK IS **EVERYTHING.** IT'S HOW WE MAKE IT IN THE WORLD...
ON THIS PLANET, PACKAGING RULES. IF YOU LOOK COOL, PEOPLE TREAT YOU COOL. IF YOU LOOK LIKE A DWEEB, YOU GET THE DWEEB'S LIFE.
CHIQUE
BUT WHAT IF I **DO** COOL THINGS? GOOD THINGS– IMPORTANT THINGS?
LET ME GET THIS STRAIGHT. YOU **DO** COOL THINGS, BUT YOU DON'T LOOK HIP OR CHIC?
NOPE. JUST ORDI- NARY.
NO ONE WILL NOTICE.
NO ONE?
NOT A SOUL.
Jan Eliot
?
AND... IF I **LOOK** REALLY COOL, HIP, AND CHIC, BUT I DON'T ACTUALLY **DO** ANYTHING...?
STRAIGHT TO THE TOP.

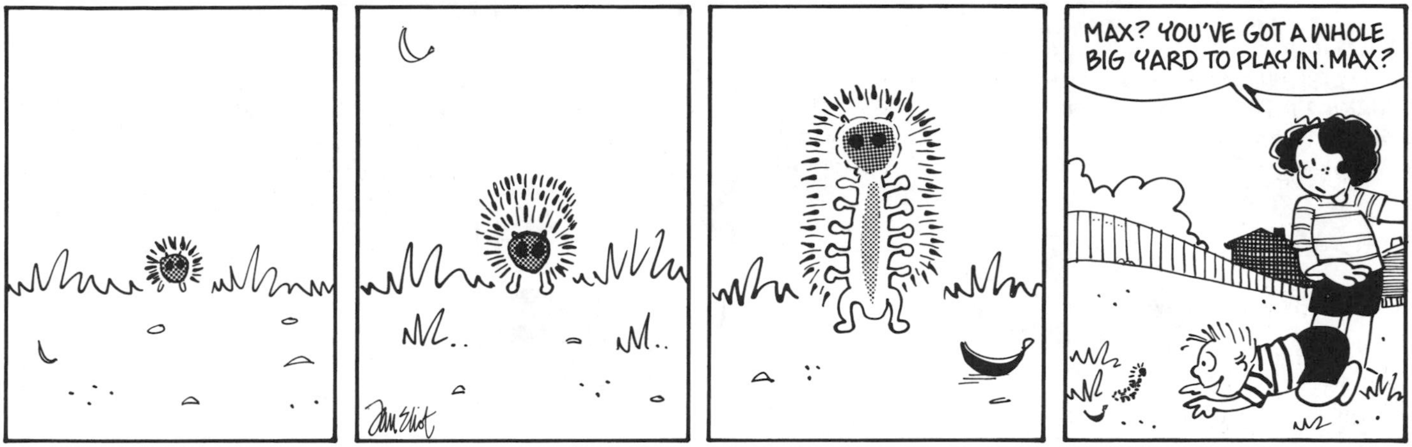
MAX? YOU'VE GOT A WHOLE BIG YARD TO PLAY IN. MAX?

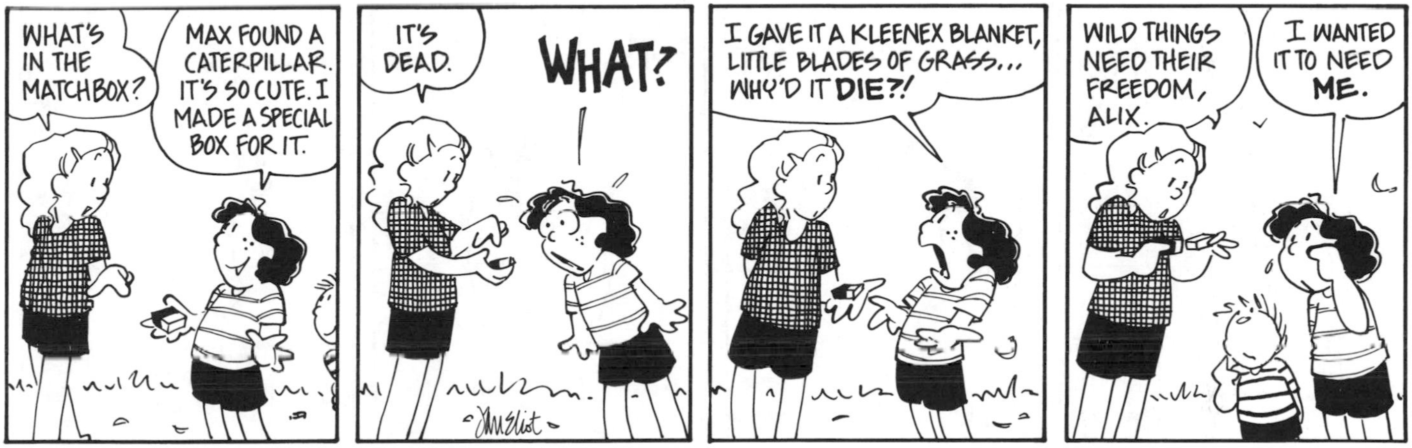
WHAT'S IN THE MATCHBOX?
MAX FOUND A CATERPILLAR. IT'S SO CUTE. I MADE A SPECIAL BOX FOR IT.
IT'S DEAD.
WHAT?
I GAVE IT A KLEENEX BLANKET, LITTLE BLADES OF GRASS... WHY'D IT DIE?!
WILD THINGS NEED THEIR FREEDOM, ALIX.
I WANTED IT TO NEED ME.

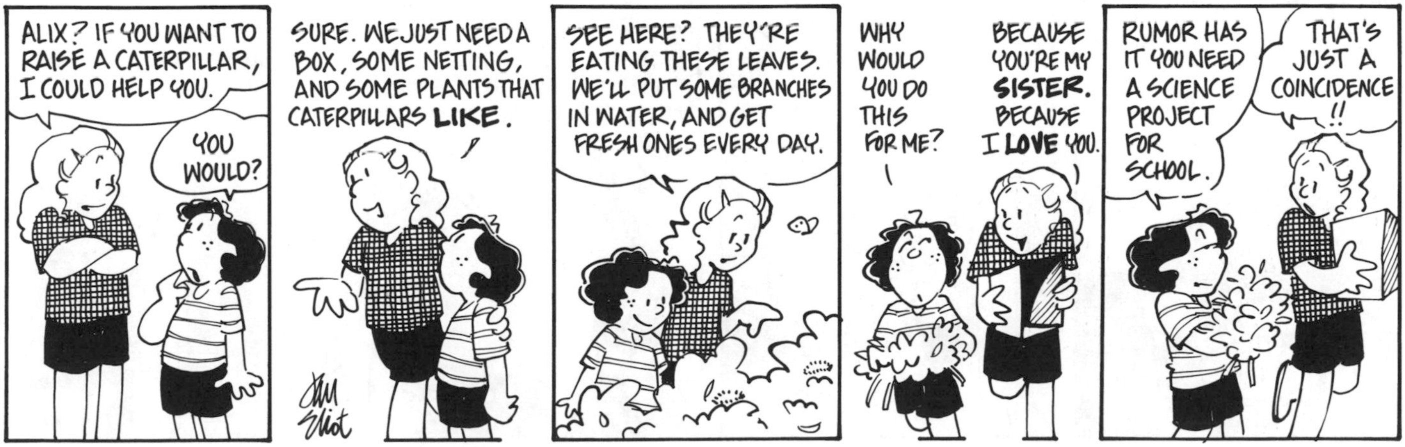
ALIX? IF YOU WANT TO RAISE A CATERPILLAR, I COULD HELP YOU.
YOU WOULD?
SURE. WE JUST NEED A BOX, SOME NETTING, AND SOME PLANTS THAT CATERPILLARS LIKE.
SEE HERE? THEY'RE EATING THESE LEAVES. WE'LL PUT SOME BRANCHES IN WATER, AND GET FRESH ONES EVERY DAY.
WHY WOULD YOU DO THIS FOR ME?
BECAUSE YOU'RE MY SISTER. BECAUSE I LOVE YOU.
RUMOR HAS IT YOU NEED A SCIENCE PROJECT FOR SCHOOL.
THAT'S JUST A COINCIDENCE!!

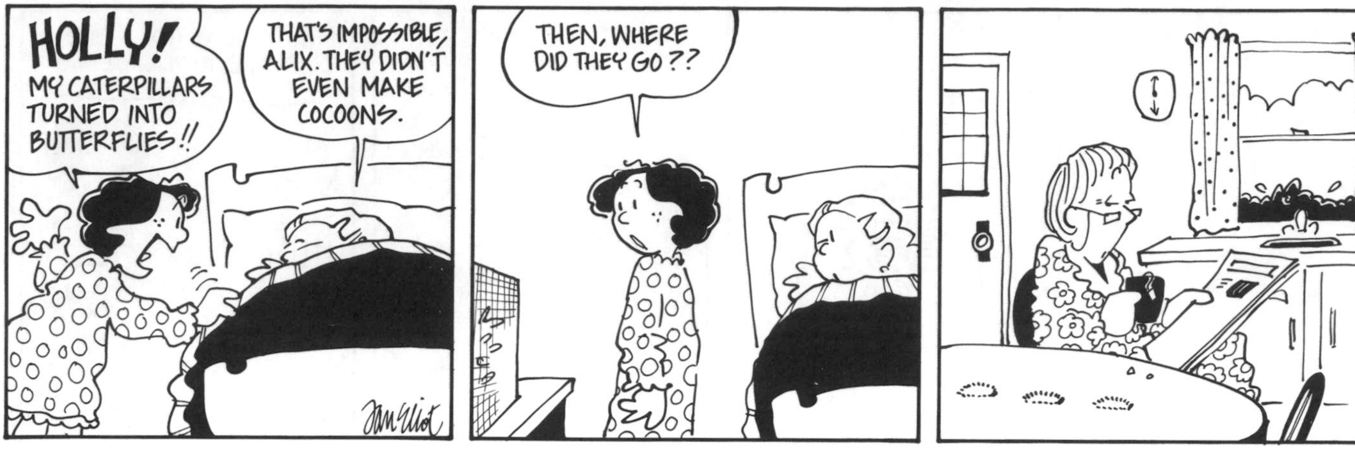

HOLLY! MY CATERPILLARS TURNED INTO BUTTERFLIES!!
THAT'S IMPOSSIBLE, ALIX. THEY DIDN'T EVEN MAKE COCOONS.
THEN, WHERE DID THEY GO??

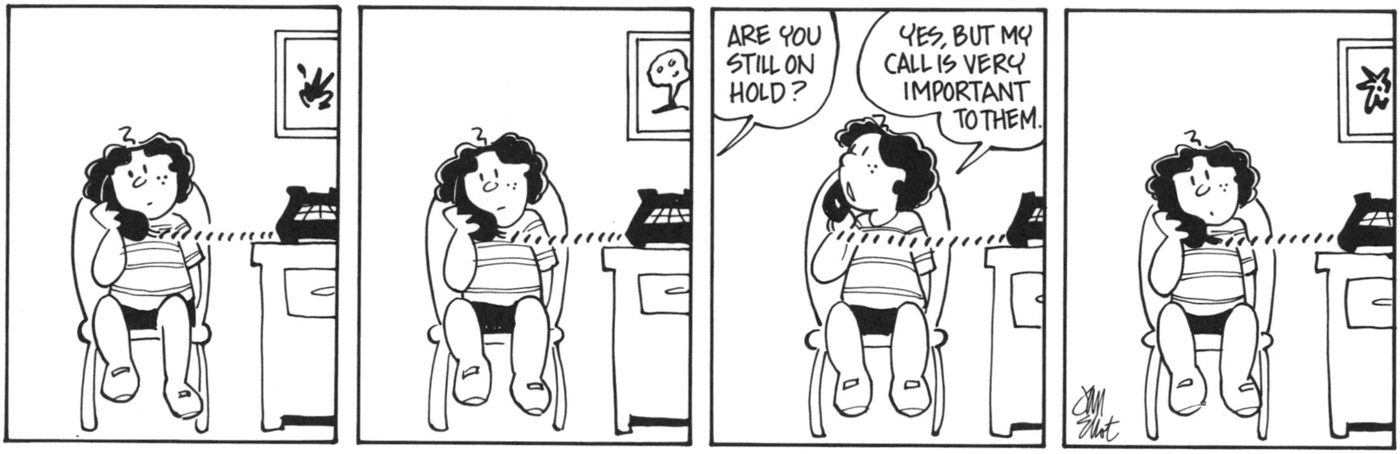

ARE YOU STILL ON HOLD?
YES, BUT MY CALL IS VERY IMPORTANT TO THEM.

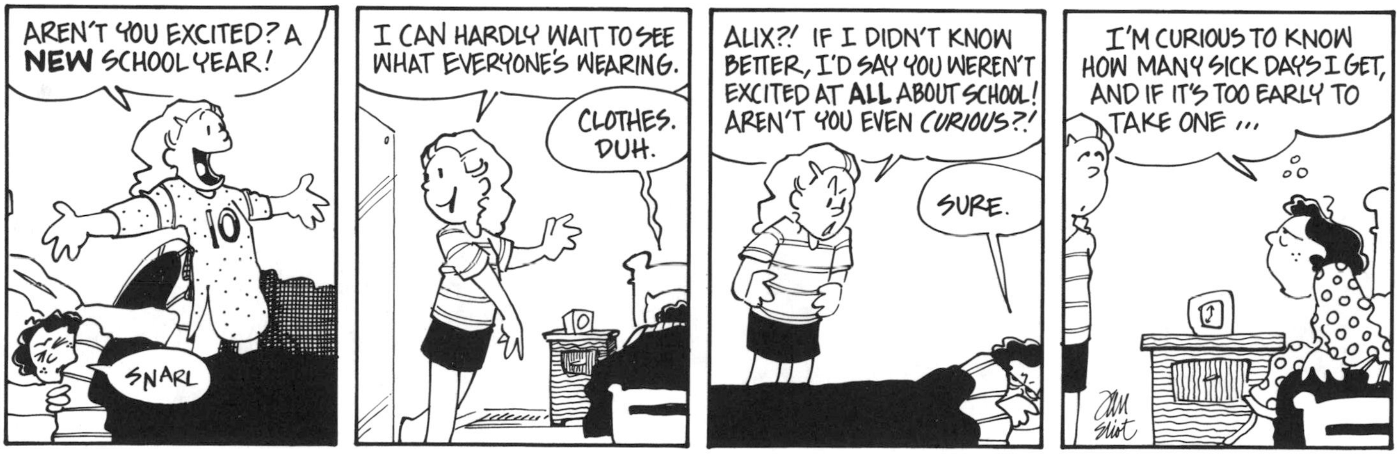

AREN'T YOU EXCITED? A NEW SCHOOL YEAR!
SNARL
I CAN HARDLY WAIT TO SEE WHAT EVERYONE'S WEARING.
CLOTHES. DUH.
ALIX?! IF I DIDN'T KNOW BETTER, I'D SAY YOU WEREN'T EXCITED AT ALL ABOUT SCHOOL! AREN'T YOU EVEN CURIOUS?!
SURE.
I'M CURIOUS TO KNOW HOW MANY SICK DAYS I GET, AND IF IT'S TOO EARLY TO TAKE ONE ...

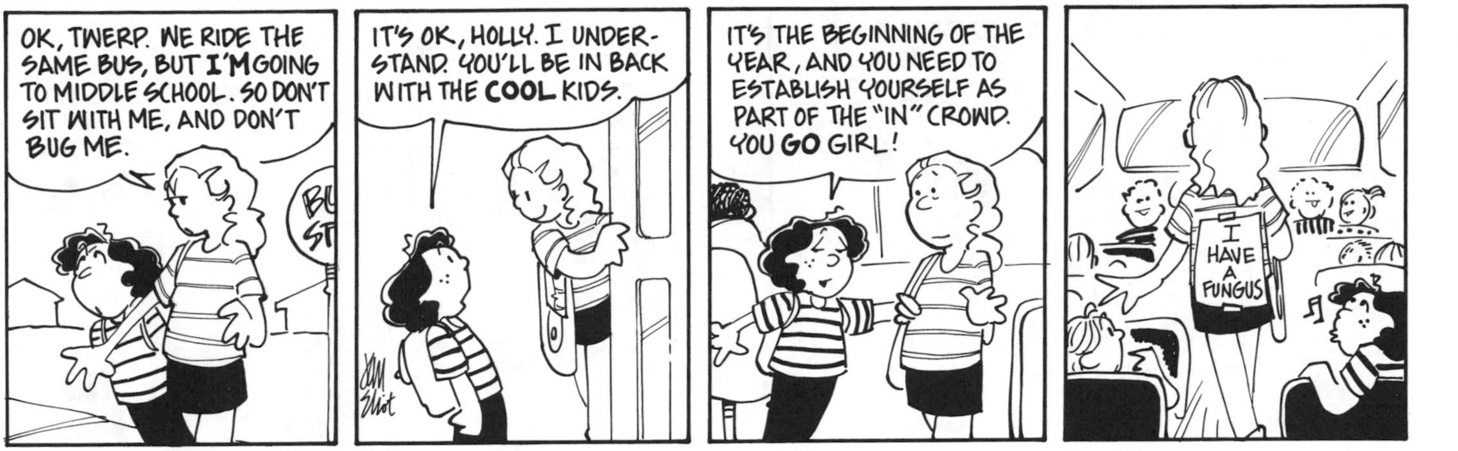
OK, TWERP. WE RIDE THE SAME BUS, BUT I'M GOING TO MIDDLE SCHOOL. SO DON'T SIT WITH ME, AND DON'T BUG ME.
IT'S OK, HOLLY. I UNDERSTAND. YOU'LL BE IN BACK WITH THE COOL KIDS.
IT'S THE BEGINNING OF THE YEAR, AND YOU NEED TO ESTABLISH YOURSELF AS PART OF THE "IN" CROWD. YOU GO GIRL!
I HAVE A FUNGUS

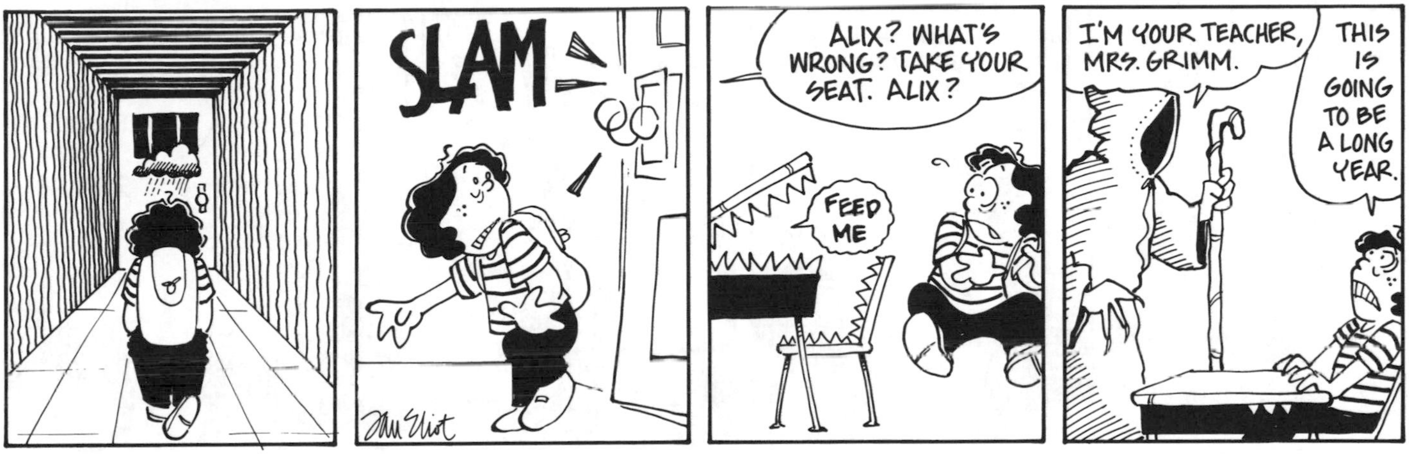
SLAM
ALIX? WHAT'S WRONG? TAKE YOUR SEAT. ALIX?
FEED ME
I'M YOUR TEACHER, MRS. GRIMM.
THIS IS GOING TO BE A LONG YEAR.

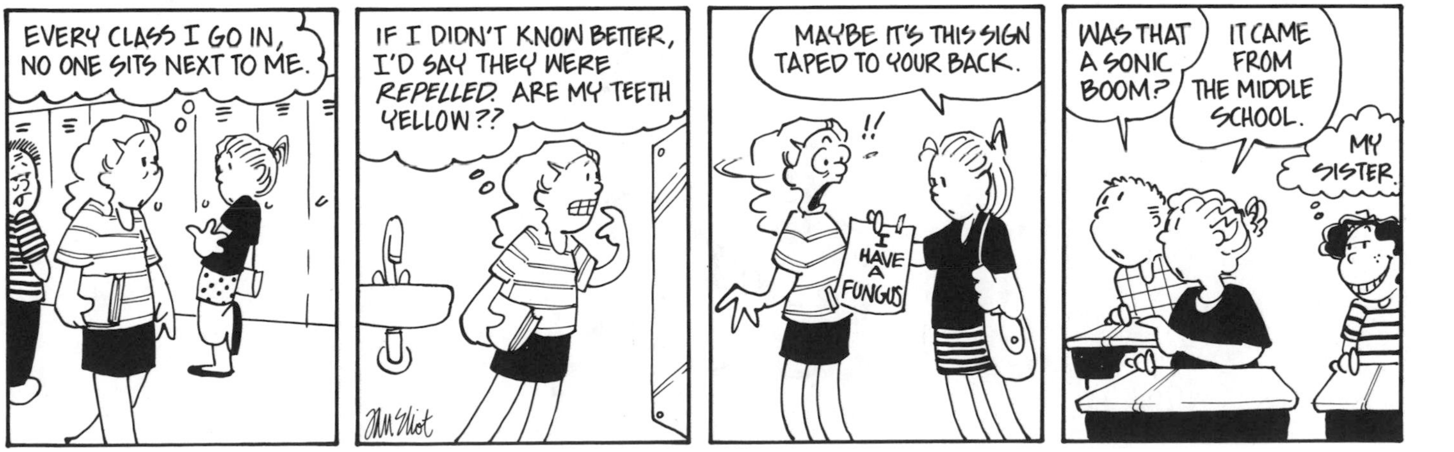
EVERY CLASS I GO IN, NO ONE SITS NEXT TO ME.
IF I DIDN'T KNOW BETTER, I'D SAY THEY WERE REPELLED. ARE MY TEETH YELLOW??
MAYBE IT'S THIS SIGN TAPED TO YOUR BACK.
!!
I HAVE A FUNGUS
WAS THAT A SONIC BOOM?
IT CAME FROM THE MIDDLE SCHOOL.
MY SISTER.

 HERE COMES HOLLY...

 I'D BETTER TAKE COVER.

 SLAM

 WHATEVER YOU DID, ALIX, YOU CAN'T HIDE FOREVER.

COULD SOMEBODY COME WITH ME TO THE BATHROOM?

 VERY ORIGINAL, PUTTING A SIGN ON MY BACK THAT SAID "I HAVE A FUNGUS." AND ON THE FIRST DAY OF SCHOOL.

 UM, THANKS.... HEH HEH.... YOU'RE CERTAINLY BEING A GOOD SPORT ABOUT IT.

 YOW!!

 THERE SEEM TO BE ICE CUBES MELTING INTO MY SHEETS.

AND YOU'RE GOING TO BE SUCH A GOOD SPORT ABOUT IT.

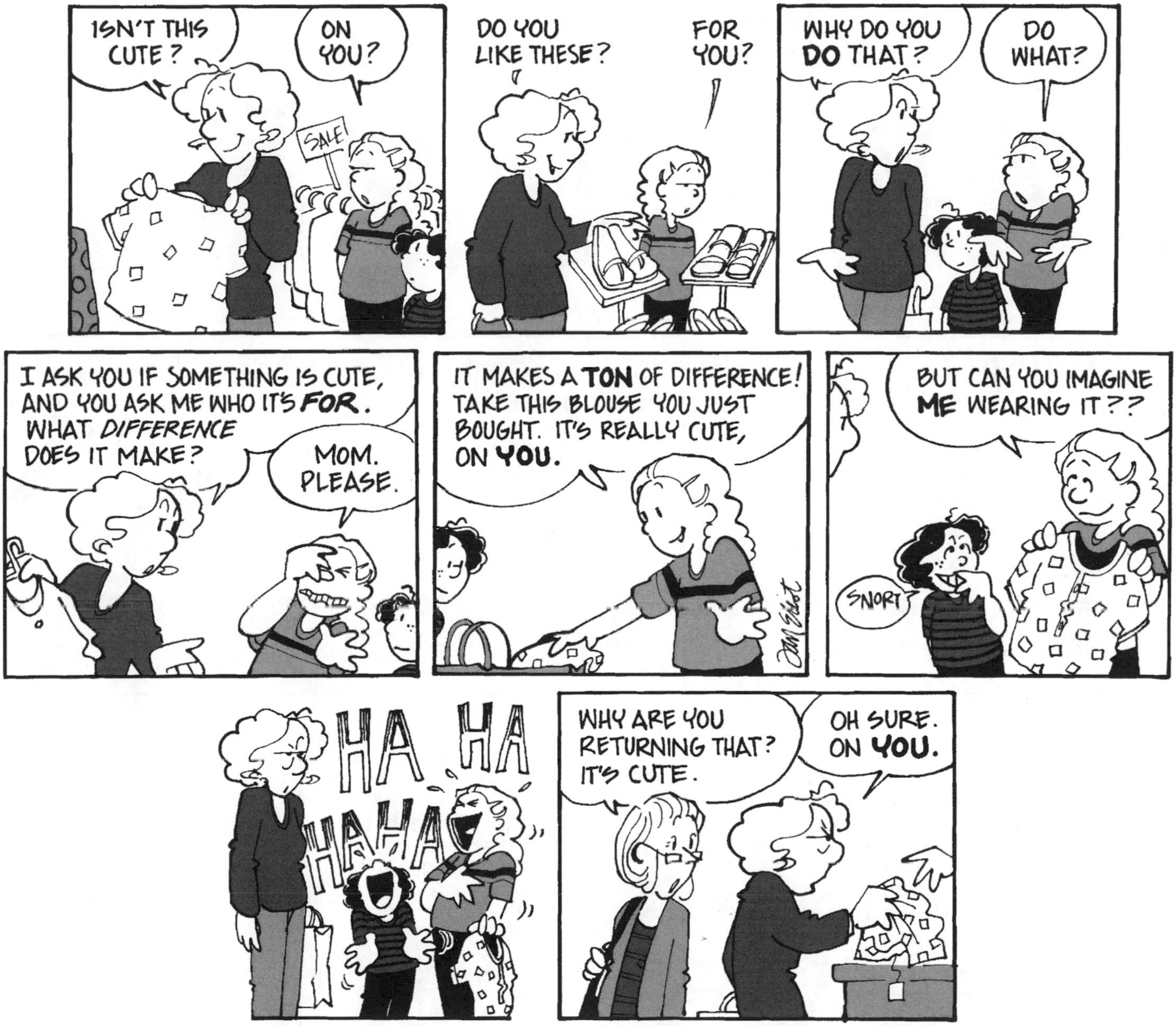
ISN'T THIS CUTE?
ON YOU?
SALE
DO YOU LIKE THESE?
FOR YOU?
WHY DO YOU DO THAT?
DO WHAT?
I ASK YOU IF SOMETHING IS CUTE, AND YOU ASK ME WHO IT'S FOR. WHAT DIFFERENCE DOES IT MAKE?
MOM. PLEASE.
IT MAKES A TON OF DIFFERENCE! TAKE THIS BLOUSE YOU JUST BOUGHT. IT'S REALLY CUTE, ON YOU.
BUT CAN YOU IMAGINE ME WEARING IT??
SNORT
HA HA
HAHAHA
WHY ARE YOU RETURNING THAT? IT'S CUTE.
OH SURE. ON YOU.

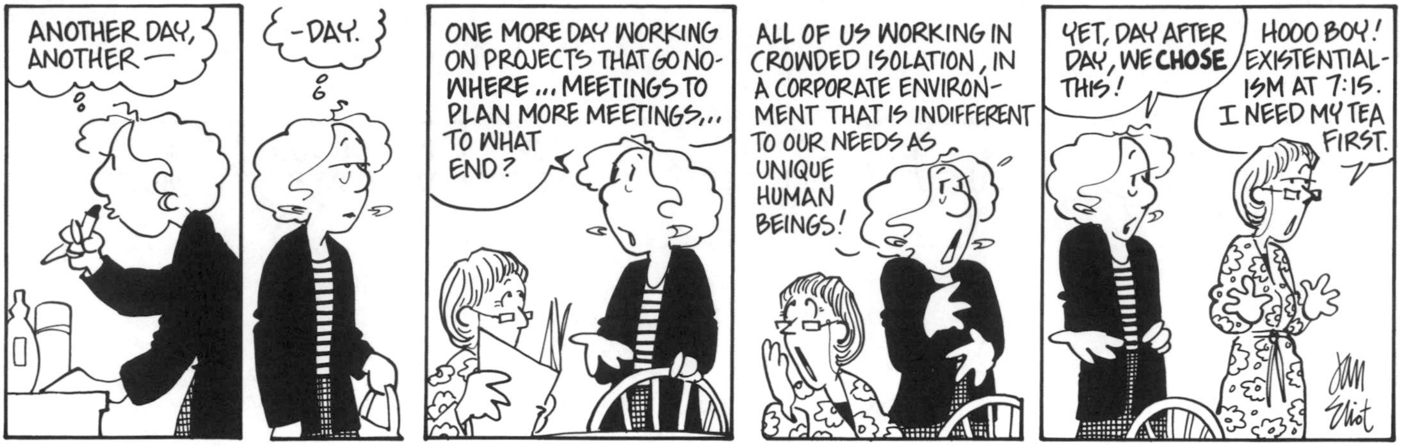
ANOTHER DAY, ANOTHER —
-DAY.
ONE MORE DAY WORKING ON PROJECTS THAT GO NOWHERE ... MEETINGS TO PLAN MORE MEETINGS,... TO WHAT END?
ALL OF US WORKING IN CROWDED ISOLATION, IN A CORPORATE ENVIRONMENT THAT IS INDIFFERENT TO OUR NEEDS AS UNIQUE HUMAN BEINGS!
YET, DAY AFTER DAY, WE **CHOSE** THIS!
HOOO BOY! EXISTENTIALISM AT 7:15. I NEED MY TEA FIRST.
JAN ELIOT

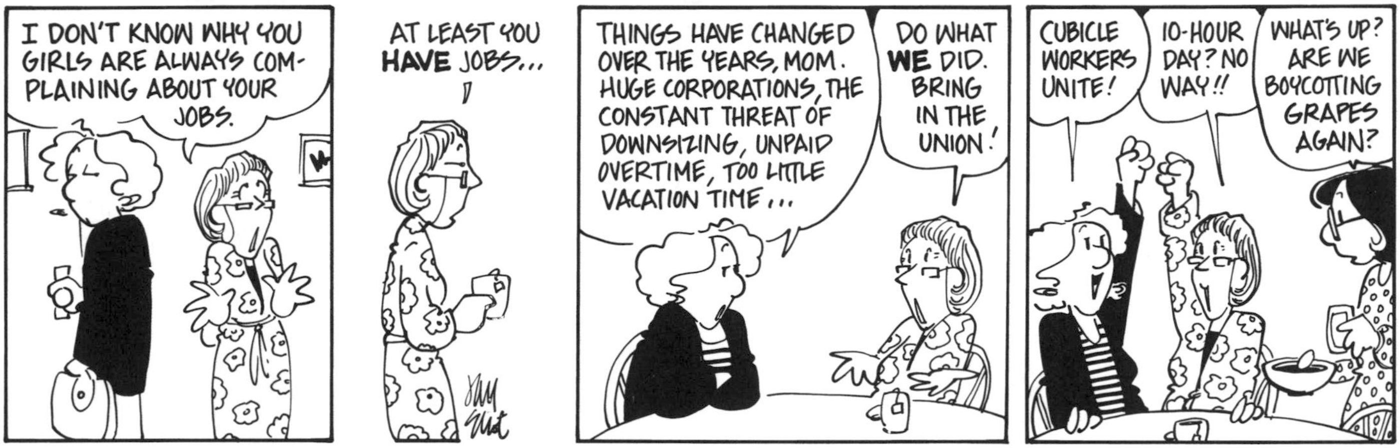
I DON'T KNOW WHY YOU GIRLS ARE ALWAYS COMPLAINING ABOUT YOUR JOBS.
AT LEAST YOU **HAVE** JOBS...
JAN ELIOT
THINGS HAVE CHANGED OVER THE YEARS, MOM. HUGE CORPORATIONS, THE CONSTANT THREAT OF DOWNSIZING, UNPAID OVERTIME, TOO LITTLE VACATION TIME...
DO WHAT **WE** DID. BRING IN THE UNION!
CUBICLE WORKERS UNITE!
10-HOUR DAY? NO WAY!!
WHAT'S UP? ARE WE BOYCOTTING GRAPES AGAIN?

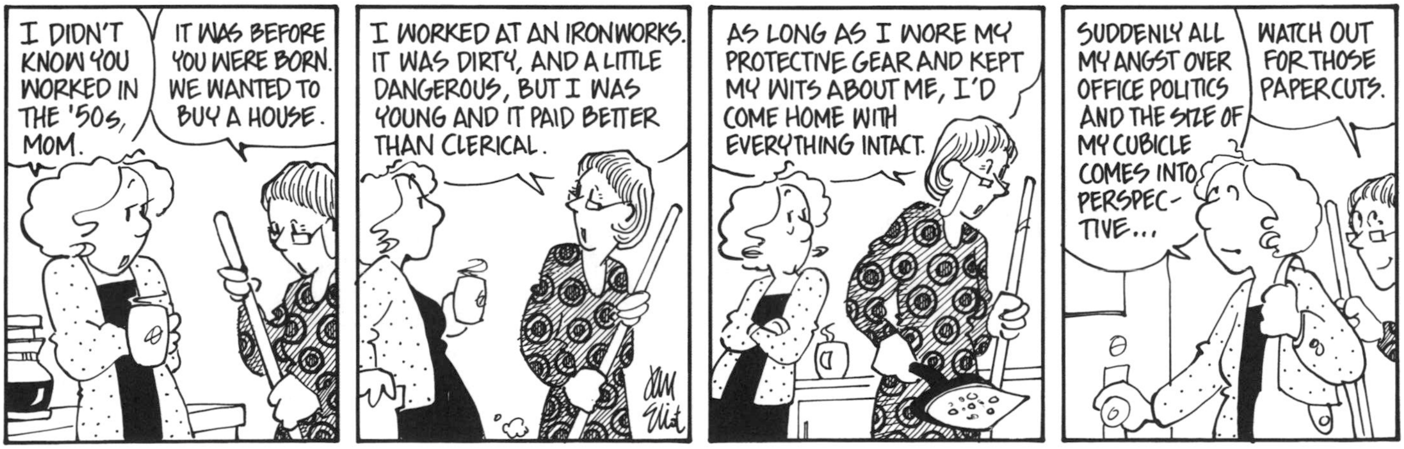
I DIDN'T KNOW YOU WORKED IN THE '50s, MOM.
IT WAS BEFORE YOU WERE BORN. WE WANTED TO BUY A HOUSE.
I WORKED AT AN IRONWORKS. IT WAS DIRTY, AND A LITTLE DANGEROUS, BUT I WAS YOUNG AND IT PAID BETTER THAN CLERICAL.
JAN ELIOT
AS LONG AS I WORE MY PROTECTIVE GEAR AND KEPT MY WITS ABOUT ME, I'D COME HOME WITH EVERYTHING INTACT.
SUDDENLY ALL MY ANGST OVER OFFICE POLITICS AND THE SIZE OF MY CUBICLE COMES INTO PERSPECTIVE...
WATCH OUT FOR THOSE PAPER CUTS.

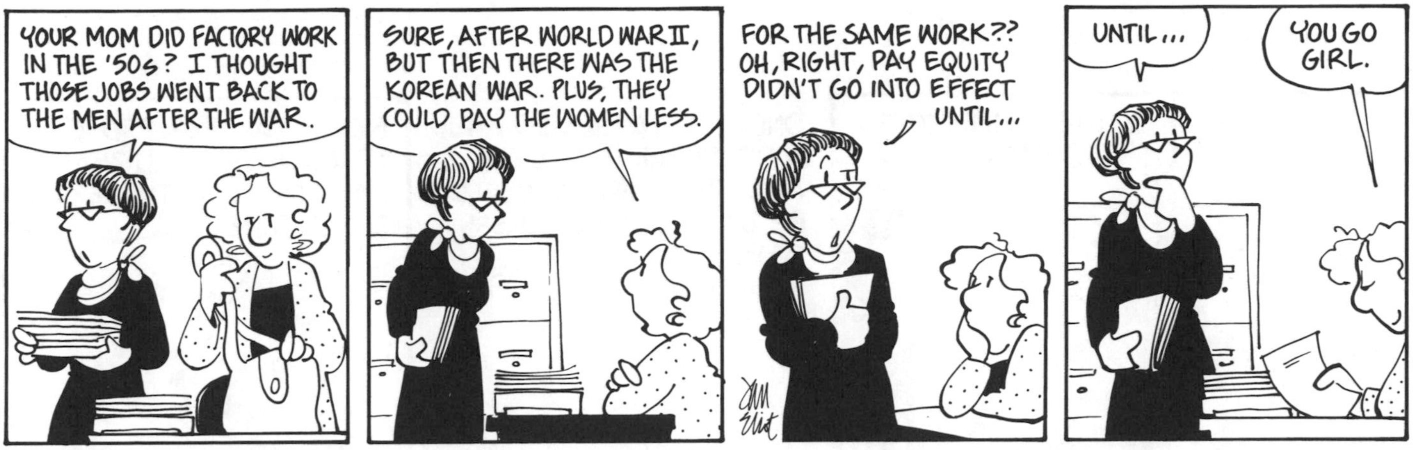
YOUR MOM DID FACTORY WORK IN THE '50s? I THOUGHT THOSE JOBS WENT BACK TO THE MEN AFTER THE WAR.
SURE, AFTER WORLD WAR II, BUT THEN THERE WAS THE KOREAN WAR. PLUS, THEY COULD PAY THE WOMEN LESS.
FOR THE SAME WORK?? OH, RIGHT, PAY EQUITY DIDN'T GO INTO EFFECT UNTIL...
UNTIL...
YOU GO GIRL.

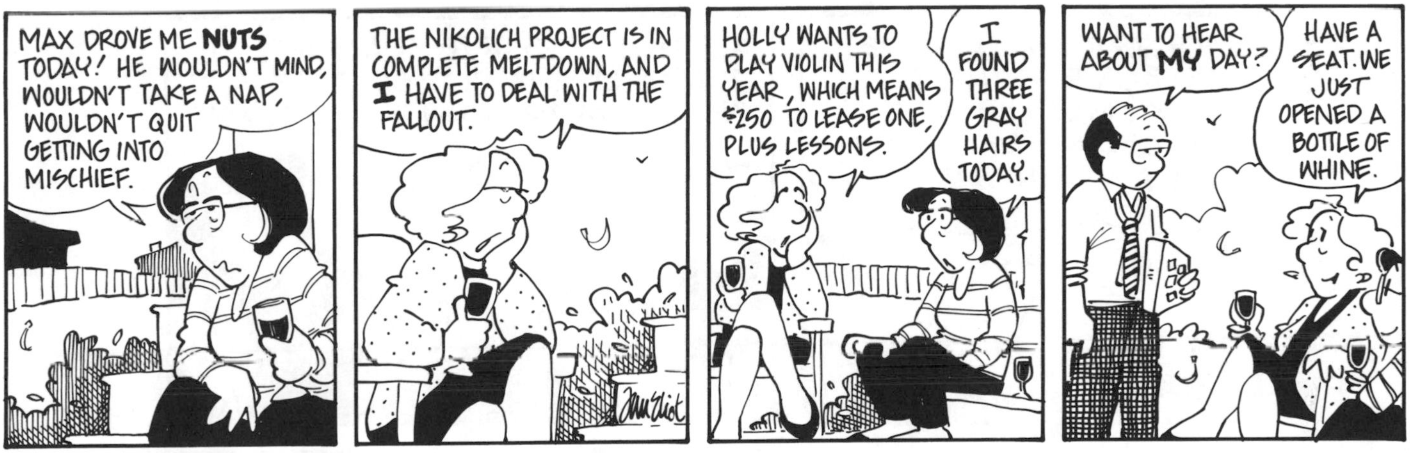
MAX DROVE ME NUTS TODAY! HE WOULDN'T MIND, WOULDN'T TAKE A NAP, WOULDN'T QUIT GETTING INTO MISCHIEF.
THE NIKOLICH PROJECT IS IN COMPLETE MELTDOWN, AND I HAVE TO DEAL WITH THE FALLOUT.
HOLLY WANTS TO PLAY VIOLIN THIS YEAR, WHICH MEANS $250 TO LEASE ONE, PLUS LESSONS.
I FOUND THREE GRAY HAIRS TODAY.
WANT TO HEAR ABOUT MY DAY?
HAVE A SEAT. WE JUST OPENED A BOTTLE OF WHINE.

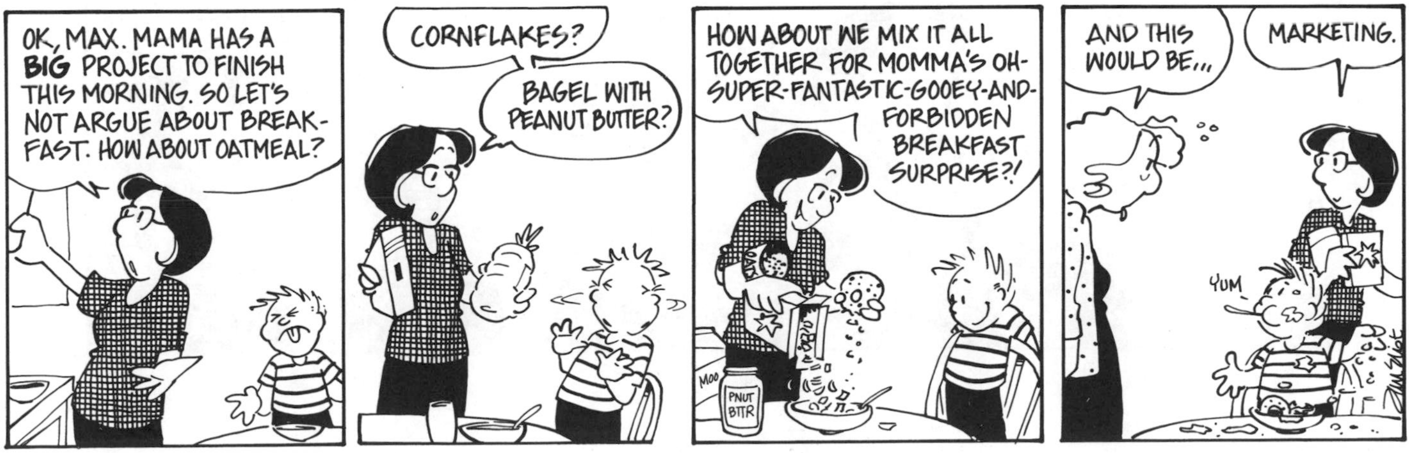
OK, MAX. MAMA HAS A BIG PROJECT TO FINISH THIS MORNING. SO LET'S NOT ARGUE ABOUT BREAKFAST. HOW ABOUT OATMEAL?
CORNFLAKES?
BAGEL WITH PEANUT BUTTER?
HOW ABOUT WE MIX IT ALL TOGETHER FOR MOMMA'S OH-SUPER-FANTASTIC-GOOEY-AND-FORBIDDEN BREAKFAST SURPRISE?!
MOO
PNUT BTTR
AND THIS WOULD BE...
MARKETING.
YUM

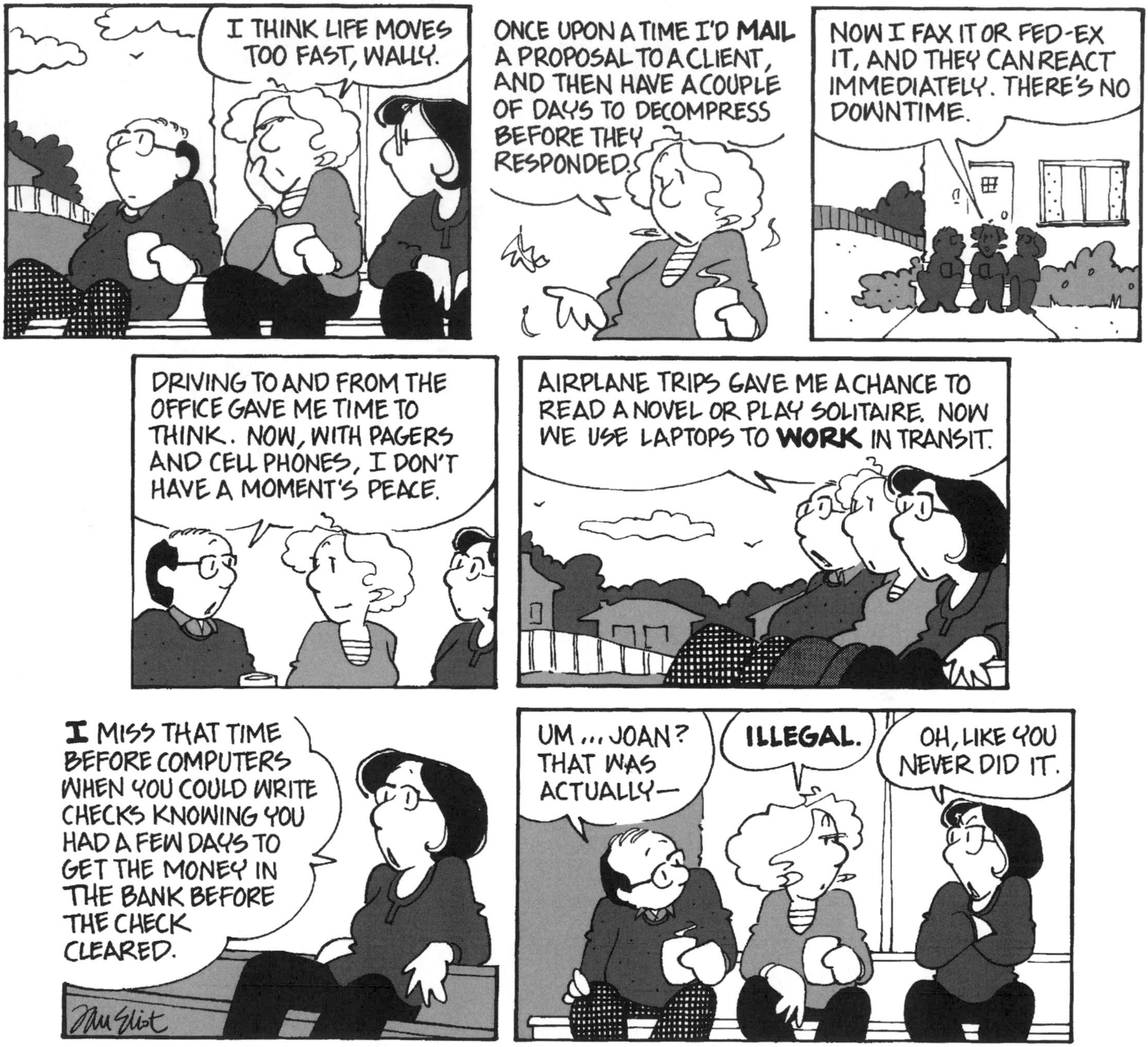
I THINK LIFE MOVES TOO FAST, WALLY.
ONCE UPON A TIME I'D MAIL A PROPOSAL TO A CLIENT, AND THEN HAVE A COUPLE OF DAYS TO DECOMPRESS BEFORE THEY RESPONDED.
NOW I FAX IT OR FED-EX IT, AND THEY CAN REACT IMMEDIATELY. THERE'S NO DOWNTIME.
DRIVING TO AND FROM THE OFFICE GAVE ME TIME TO THINK. NOW, WITH PAGERS AND CELL PHONES, I DON'T HAVE A MOMENT'S PEACE.
AIRPLANE TRIPS GAVE ME A CHANCE TO READ A NOVEL OR PLAY SOLITAIRE. NOW WE USE LAPTOPS TO WORK IN TRANSIT.
I MISS THAT TIME BEFORE COMPUTERS WHEN YOU COULD WRITE CHECKS KNOWING YOU HAD A FEW DAYS TO GET THE MONEY IN THE BANK BEFORE THE CHECK CLEARED.
UM ... JOAN? THAT WAS ACTUALLY—
ILLEGAL.
OH, LIKE YOU NEVER DID IT.

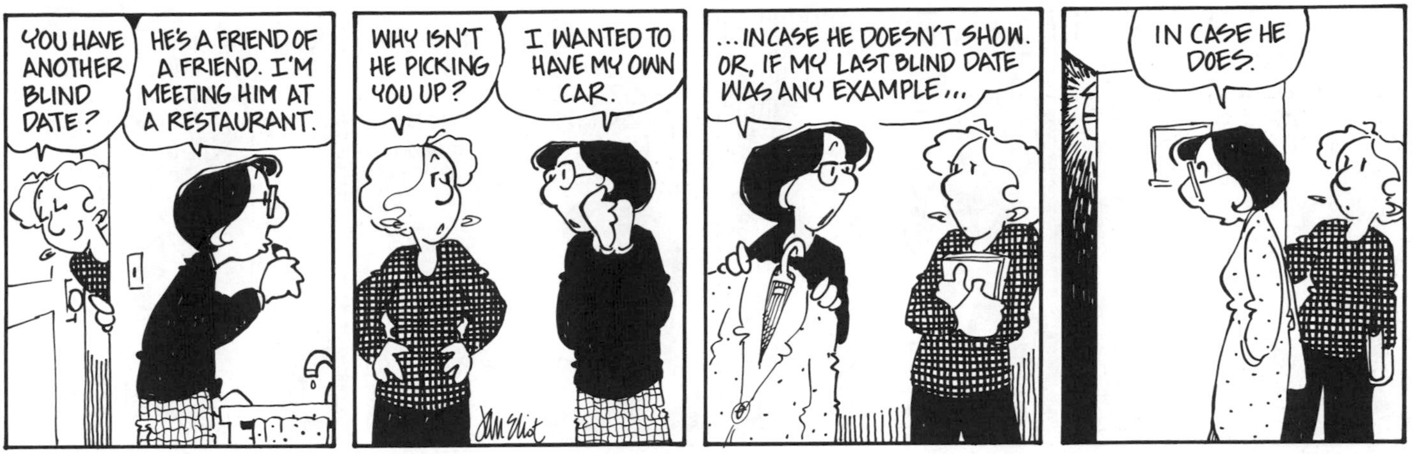
YOU HAVE ANOTHER BLIND DATE?
HE'S A FRIEND OF A FRIEND. I'M MEETING HIM AT A RESTAURANT.
WHY ISN'T HE PICKING YOU UP?
I WANTED TO HAVE MY OWN CAR.
...IN CASE HE DOESN'T SHOW. OR, IF MY LAST BLIND DATE WAS ANY EXAMPLE...
IN CASE HE DOES.

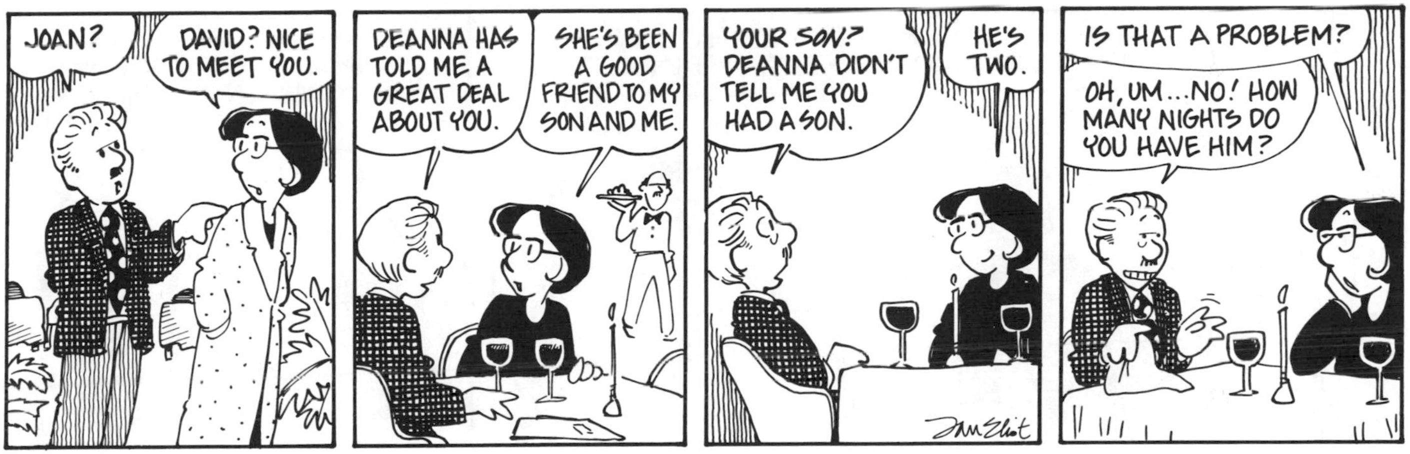
JOAN?
DAVID? NICE TO MEET YOU.
DEANNA HAS TOLD ME A GREAT DEAL ABOUT YOU.
SHE'S BEEN A GOOD FRIEND TO MY SON AND ME.
YOUR *SON?* DEANNA DIDN'T TELL ME YOU HAD A SON.
HE'S TWO.
IS THAT A PROBLEM?
OH, UM...NO! HOW MANY NIGHTS DO YOU HAVE HIM?

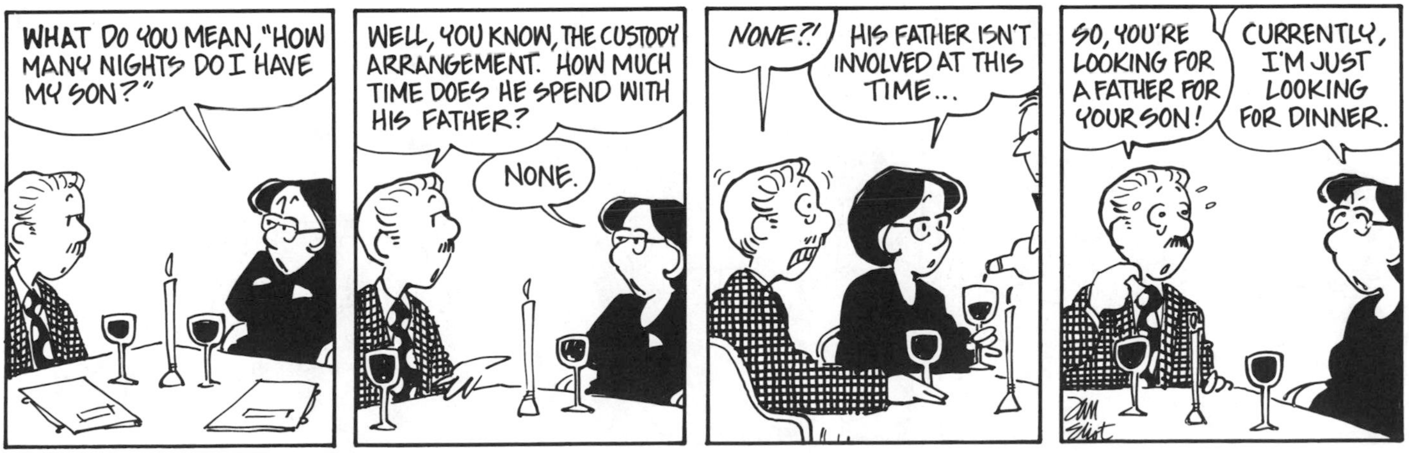
WHAT DO YOU MEAN, "HOW MANY NIGHTS DO I HAVE MY SON?"
WELL, YOU KNOW, THE CUSTODY ARRANGEMENT. HOW MUCH TIME DOES HE SPEND WITH HIS FATHER?
NONE.
NONE?!
HIS FATHER ISN'T INVOLVED AT THIS TIME...
SO, YOU'RE LOOKING FOR A FATHER FOR YOUR SON!
CURRENTLY, I'M JUST LOOKING FOR DINNER.

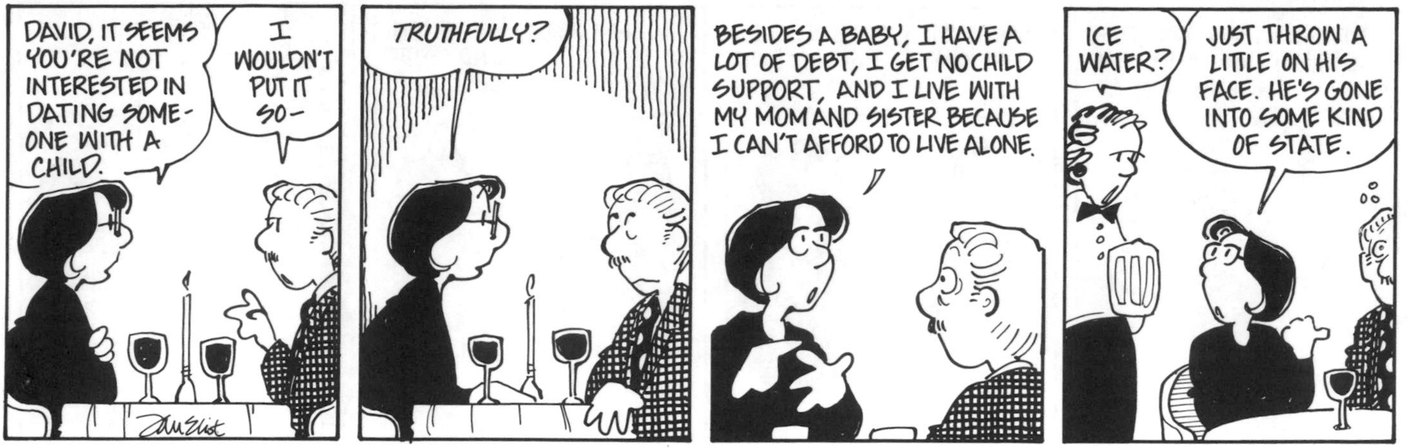
DAVID, IT SEEMS YOU'RE NOT INTERESTED IN DATING SOMEONE WITH A CHILD.
I WOULDN'T PUT IT SO–
TRUTHFULLY?
BESIDES A BABY, I HAVE A LOT OF DEBT, I GET NO CHILD SUPPORT, AND I LIVE WITH MY MOM AND SISTER BECAUSE I CAN'T AFFORD TO LIVE ALONE.
ICE WATER?
JUST THROW A LITTLE ON HIS FACE. HE'S GONE INTO SOME KIND OF STATE.

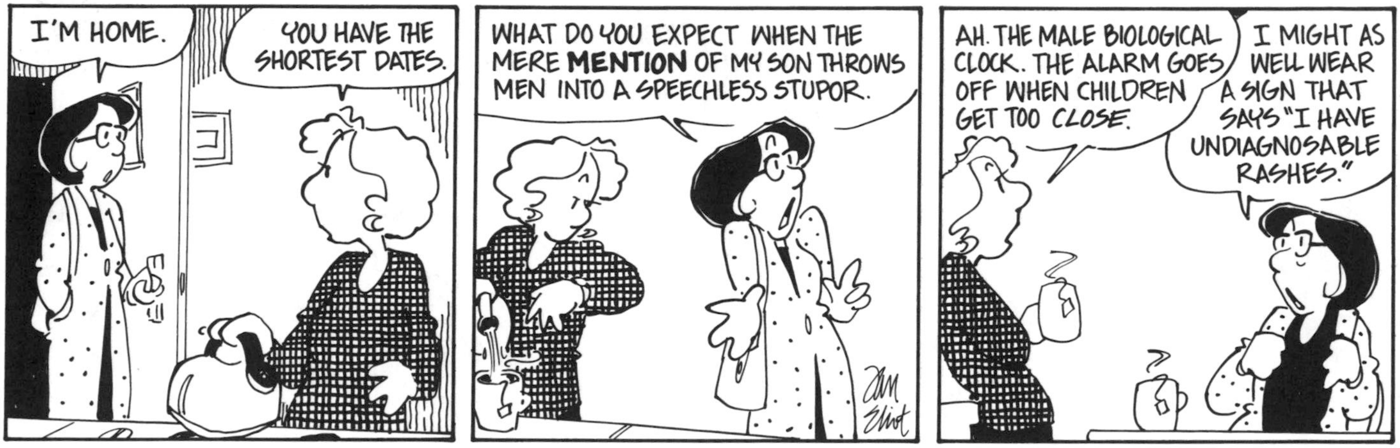
I'M HOME.
YOU HAVE THE SHORTEST DATES.
WHAT DO YOU EXPECT WHEN THE MERE **MENTION** OF MY SON THROWS MEN INTO A SPEECHLESS STUPOR.
AH. THE MALE BIOLOGICAL CLOCK. THE ALARM GOES OFF WHEN CHILDREN GET TOO *CLOSE*.
I MIGHT AS WELL WEAR A SIGN THAT SAYS "I HAVE UNDIAGNOSABLE RASHES."

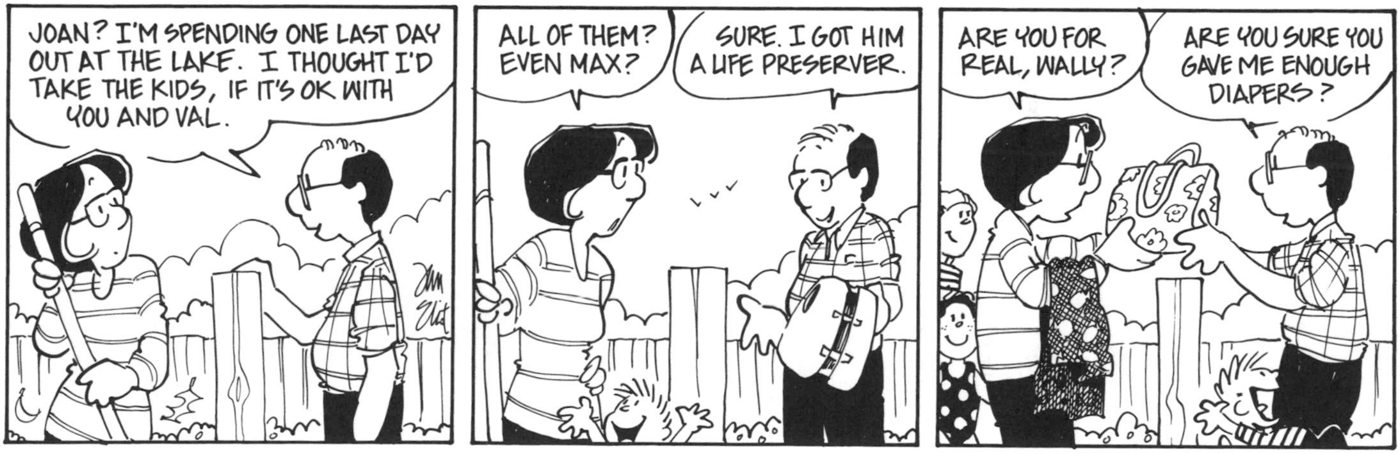
JOAN? I'M SPENDING ONE LAST DAY OUT AT THE LAKE. I THOUGHT I'D TAKE THE KIDS, IF IT'S OK WITH YOU AND VAL.
ALL OF THEM? EVEN MAX?
SURE. I GOT HIM A LIFE PRESERVER.
ARE YOU FOR REAL, WALLY?
ARE YOU SURE YOU GAVE ME ENOUGH DIAPERS?

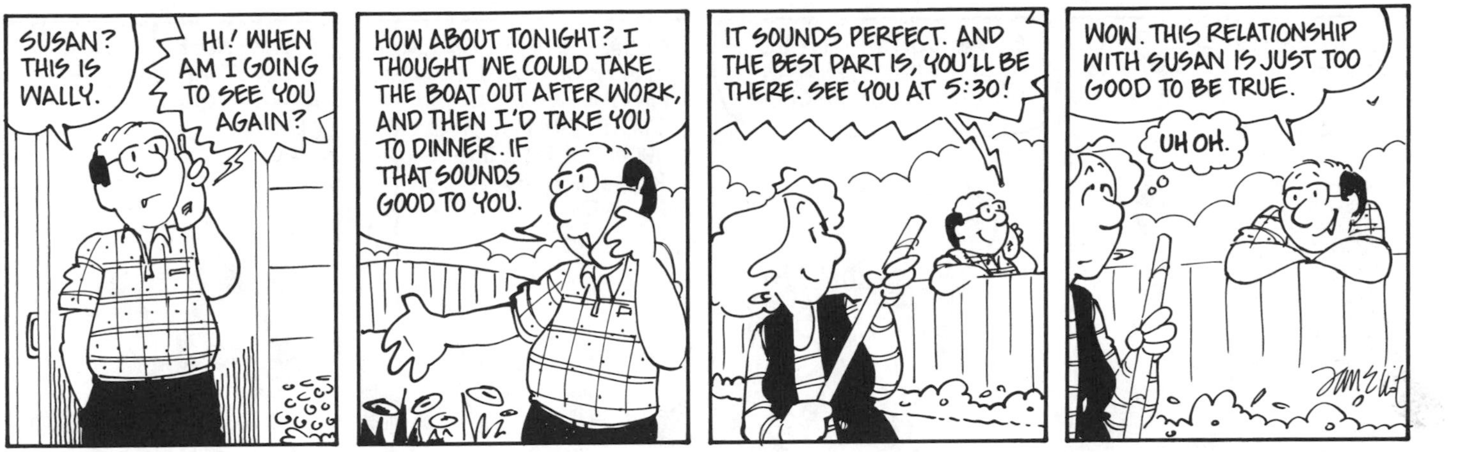
SUSAN? THIS IS WALLY.
HI! WHEN AM I GOING TO SEE YOU AGAIN?
HOW ABOUT TONIGHT? I THOUGHT WE COULD TAKE THE BOAT OUT AFTER WORK, AND THEN I'D TAKE YOU TO DINNER. IF THAT SOUNDS GOOD TO YOU.
IT SOUNDS PERFECT. AND THE BEST PART IS, YOU'LL BE THERE. SEE YOU AT 5:30!
WOW. THIS RELATIONSHIP WITH SUSAN IS JUST TOO GOOD TO BE TRUE.
UH OH.

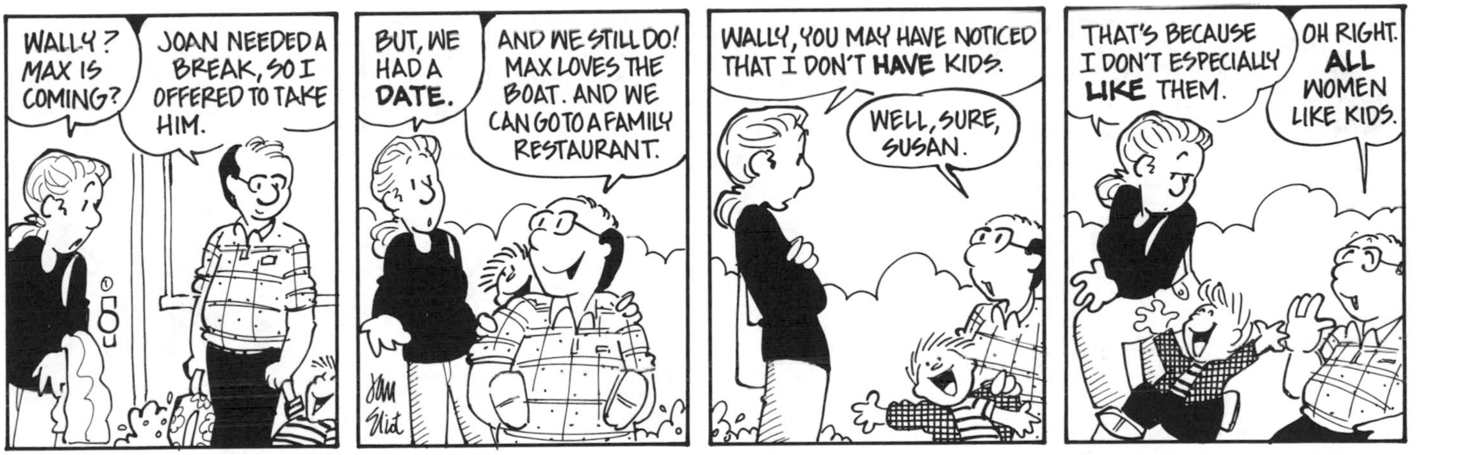
WALLY? MAX IS COMING?
JOAN NEEDED A BREAK, SO I OFFERED TO TAKE HIM.
BUT, WE HAD A **DATE.**
AND WE STILL DO! MAX LOVES THE BOAT. AND WE CAN GO TO A FAMILY RESTAURANT.
WALLY, YOU MAY HAVE NOTICED THAT I DON'T **HAVE** KIDS.
WELL, SURE, SUSAN.
THAT'S BECAUSE I DON'T ESPECIALLY **LIKE** THEM.
OH RIGHT. **ALL** WOMEN LIKE KIDS.

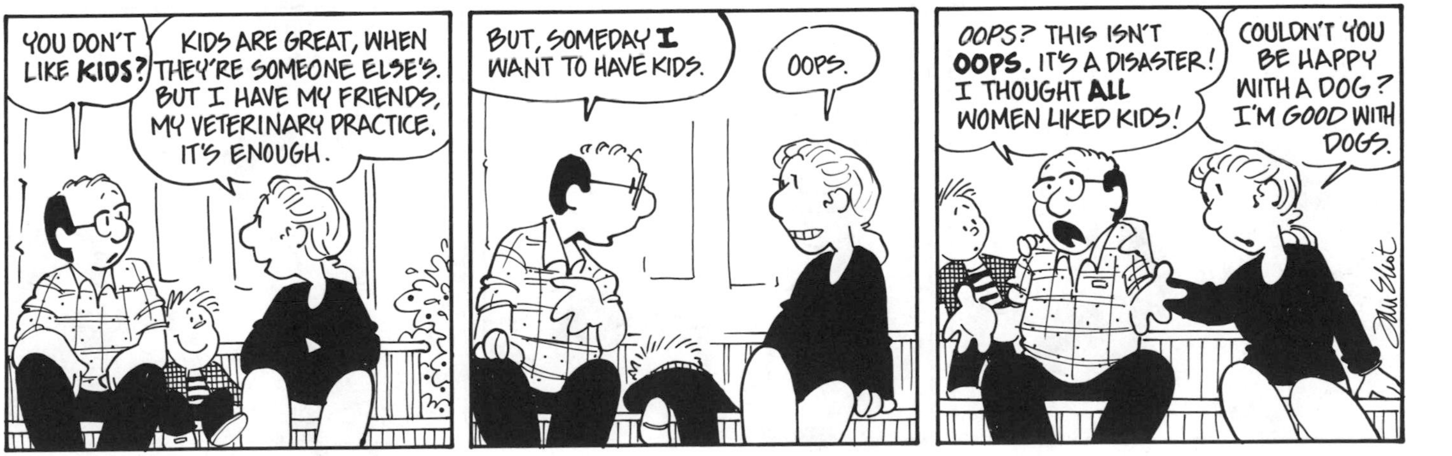
YOU DON'T LIKE **KIDS?**
KIDS ARE GREAT, WHEN THEY'RE SOMEONE ELSE'S. BUT I HAVE MY FRIENDS, MY VETERINARY PRACTICE. IT'S ENOUGH.
BUT, SOMEDAY **I** WANT TO HAVE KIDS.
OOPS.
OOPS? THIS ISN'T **OOPS.** IT'S A DISASTER! I THOUGHT **ALL** WOMEN LIKED KIDS!
COULDN'T YOU BE HAPPY WITH A DOG? I'M *GOOD* WITH DOGS.

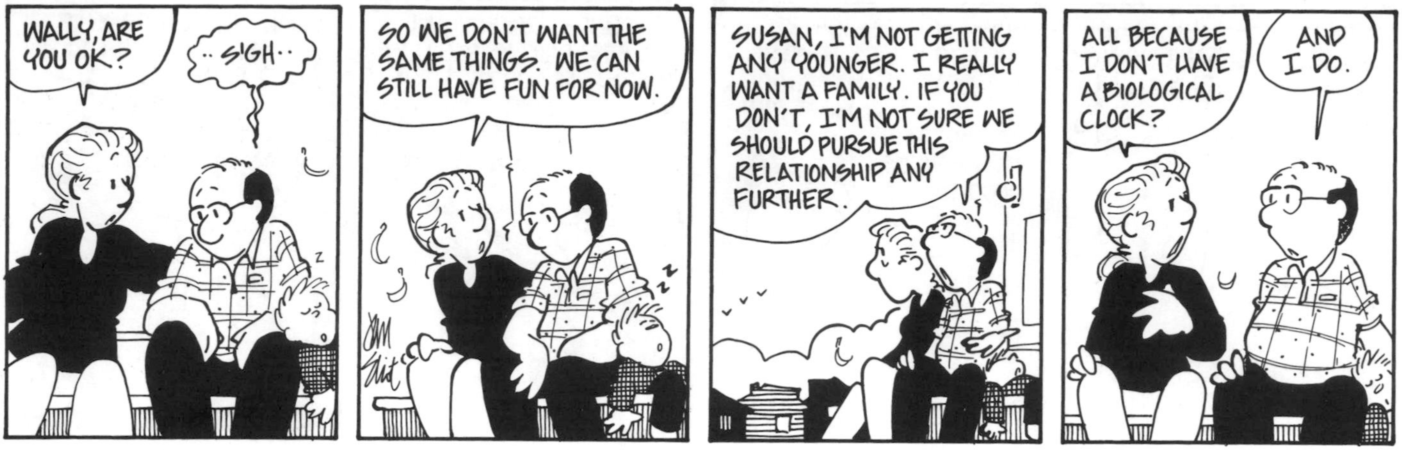
WALLY, ARE YOU OK?
.. SIGH ..
SO WE DON'T WANT THE SAME THINGS. WE CAN STILL HAVE FUN FOR NOW.
SUSAN, I'M NOT GETTING ANY YOUNGER. I REALLY WANT A FAMILY. IF YOU DON'T, I'M NOT SURE WE SHOULD PURSUE THIS RELATIONSHIP ANY FURTHER.
ALL BECAUSE I DON'T HAVE A BIOLOGICAL CLOCK?
AND I DO.

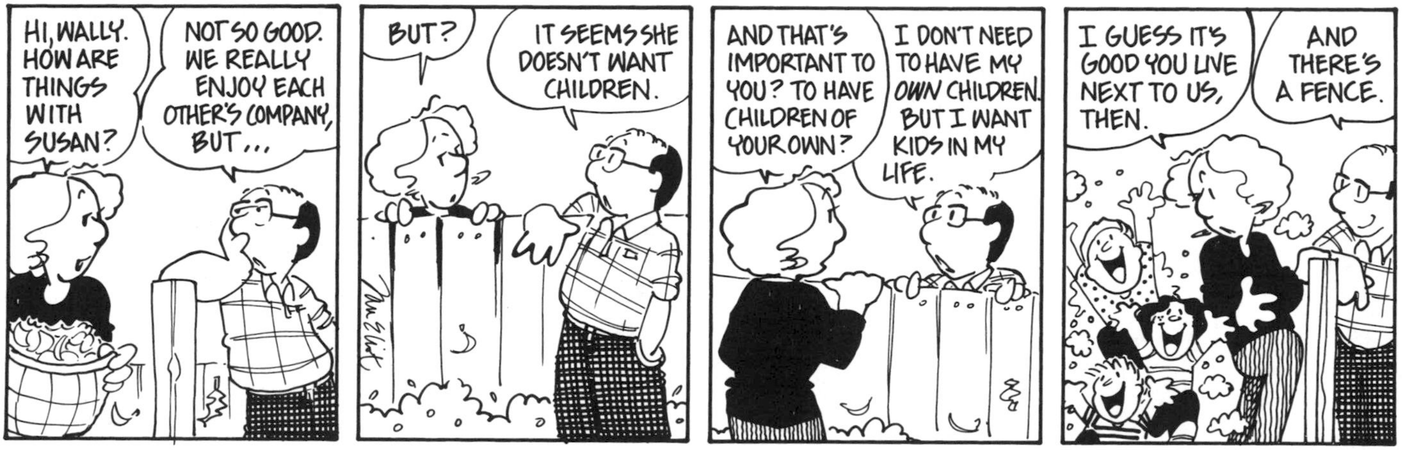
HI, WALLY. HOW ARE THINGS WITH SUSAN?
NOT SO GOOD. WE REALLY ENJOY EACH OTHER'S COMPANY, BUT ...
BUT?
IT SEEMS SHE DOESN'T WANT CHILDREN.
AND THAT'S IMPORTANT TO YOU? TO HAVE CHILDREN OF YOUR OWN?
I DON'T NEED TO HAVE MY OWN CHILDREN. BUT I WANT KIDS IN MY LIFE.
I GUESS IT'S GOOD YOU LIVE NEXT TO US, THEN.
AND THERE'S A FENCE.

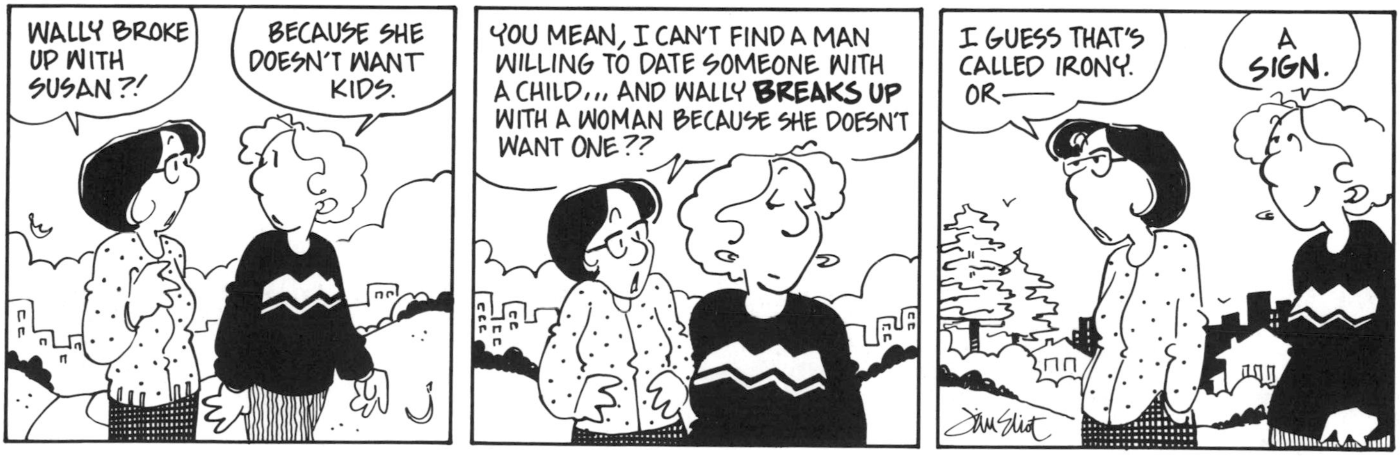
WALLY BROKE UP WITH SUSAN?!
BECAUSE SHE DOESN'T WANT KIDS.
YOU MEAN, I CAN'T FIND A MAN WILLING TO DATE SOMEONE WITH A CHILD,,, AND WALLY BREAKS UP WITH A WOMAN BECAUSE SHE DOESN'T WANT ONE??
I GUESS THAT'S CALLED IRONY. OR—
A SIGN.

HERE'S A STORY ABOUT A GUY WHO FIRED 11,500 PEOPLE FROM ONE CORPORATION.

AFTER THAT, HIS COMPANY'S STOCK INCREASED BY 40%, HE GOT A BIG BONUS, AND WAS HIRED BY ANOTHER COMPANY TO DO THE SAME THING. APPARENTLY FIRING PEOPLE IS GOOD FOR BUSINESS.

COULD MOM LOSE **HER** JOB?

MAYBE. BUT THEY SAY THERE'LL BE NEW JOBS TO REPLACE THE OLD ONES...

EXCEPT THEY'LL PAY LESS. SO, SOME PEOPLE MIGHT MAKE LESS AT RETIREMENT THAN THEY DID IN THEIR 20s.

BUT ACCORDING TO THIS, THAT'S OK, BECAUSE IT'S GOOD FOR BUSINESS, AND WHAT'S GOOD FOR BUSINESS IS GOOD FOR THE REST OF US. MOSTLY.

EVEN ALL THOSE PEOPLE WHO GOT FIRED?

NO. THEY'RE TOAST. BUT BUSINESS LOOKS AT THE **BIG** PICTURE.

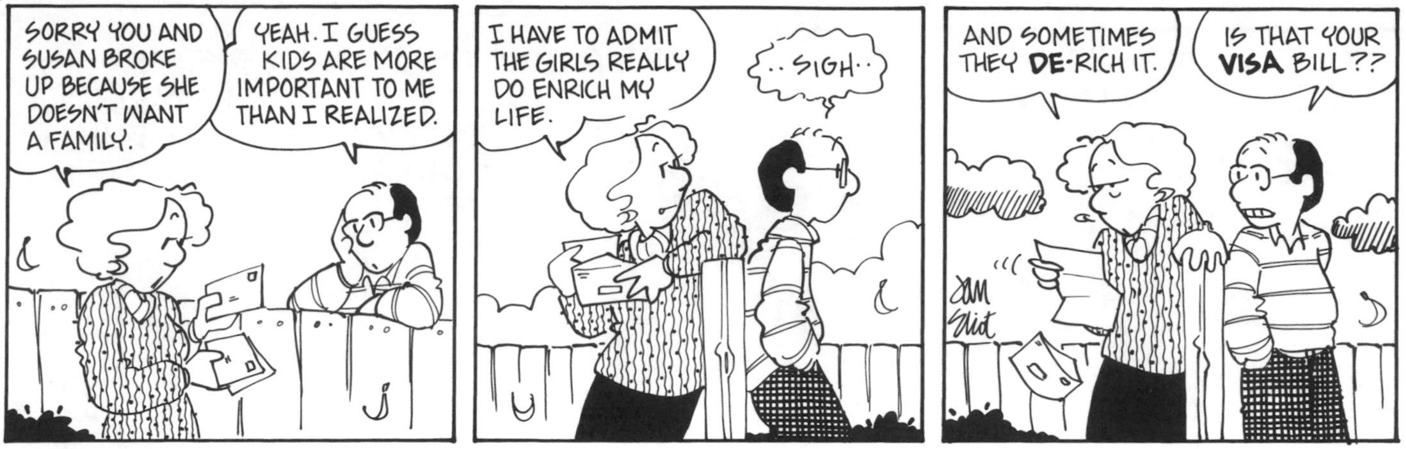
SORRY YOU AND SUSAN BROKE UP BECAUSE SHE DOESN'T WANT A FAMILY.
YEAH. I GUESS KIDS ARE MORE IMPORTANT TO ME THAN I REALIZED.
I HAVE TO ADMIT THE GIRLS REALLY DO ENRICH MY LIFE.
..SIGH..
AND SOMETIMES THEY DE-RICH IT.
IS THAT YOUR VISA BILL??

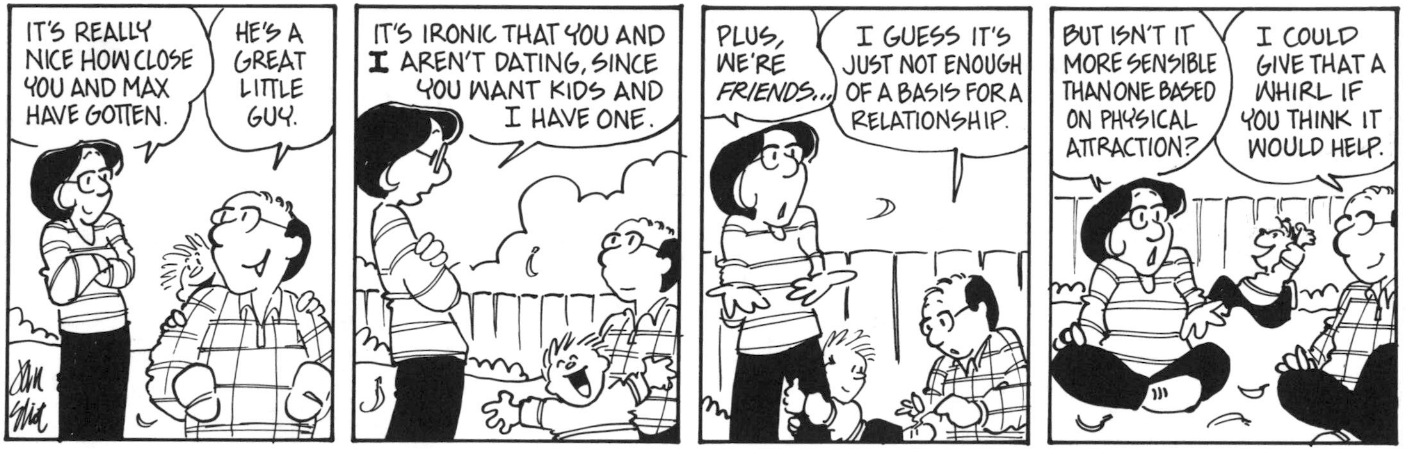
IT'S REALLY NICE HOW CLOSE YOU AND MAX HAVE GOTTEN.
HE'S A GREAT LITTLE GUY.
IT'S IRONIC THAT YOU AND I AREN'T DATING, SINCE YOU WANT KIDS AND I HAVE ONE.
PLUS, WE'RE FRIENDS...
I GUESS IT'S JUST NOT ENOUGH OF A BASIS FOR A RELATIONSHIP.
BUT ISN'T IT MORE SENSIBLE THAN ONE BASED ON PHYSICAL ATTRACTION?
I COULD GIVE THAT A WHIRL IF YOU THINK IT WOULD HELP.

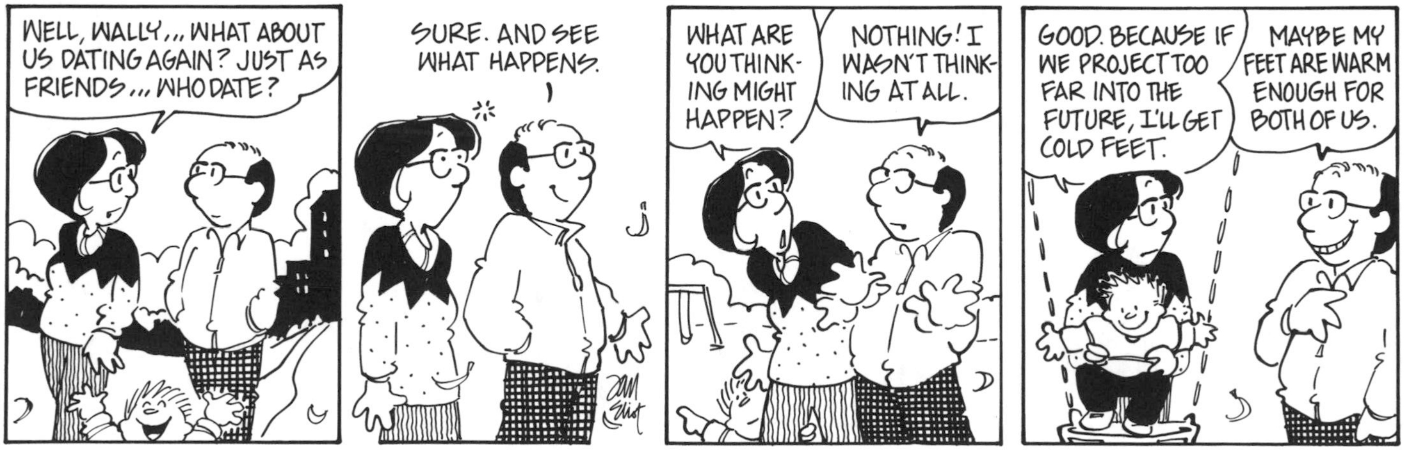
WELL, WALLY... WHAT ABOUT US DATING AGAIN? JUST AS FRIENDS... WHO DATE?
SURE. AND SEE WHAT HAPPENS.
WHAT ARE YOU THINKING MIGHT HAPPEN?
NOTHING! I WASN'T THINKING AT ALL.
GOOD. BECAUSE IF WE PROJECT TOO FAR INTO THE FUTURE, I'LL GET COLD FEET.
MAYBE MY FEET ARE WARM ENOUGH FOR BOTH OF US.

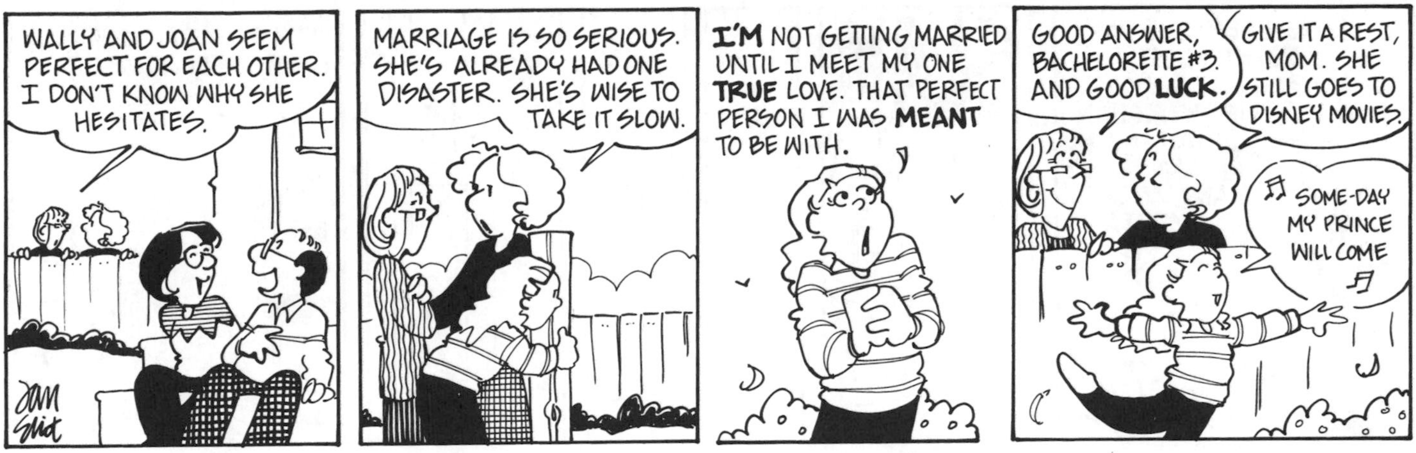
WALLY AND JOAN SEEM PERFECT FOR EACH OTHER. I DON'T KNOW WHY SHE HESITATES.
MARRIAGE IS SO SERIOUS. SHE'S ALREADY HAD ONE DISASTER. SHE'S WISE TO TAKE IT SLOW.
I'M NOT GETTING MARRIED UNTIL I MEET MY ONE TRUE LOVE. THAT PERFECT PERSON I WAS MEANT TO BE WITH.
GOOD ANSWER, BACHELORETTE #3. AND GOOD LUCK.
GIVE IT A REST, MOM. SHE STILL GOES TO DISNEY MOVIES.
SOME-DAY MY PRINCE WILL COME

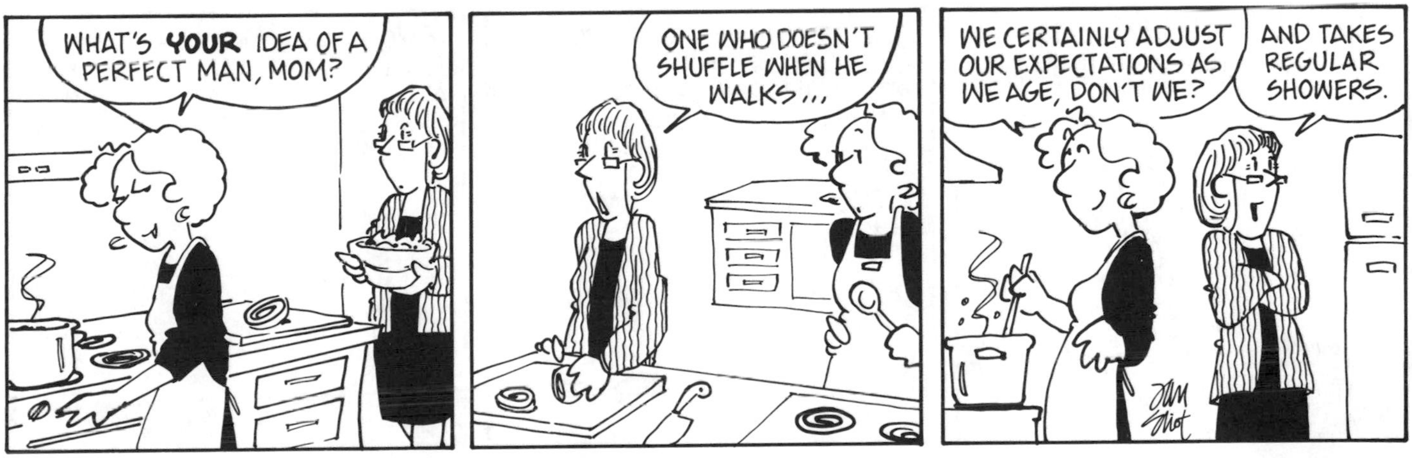
WHAT'S YOUR IDEA OF A PERFECT MAN, MOM?
ONE WHO DOESN'T SHUFFLE WHEN HE WALKS...
WE CERTAINLY ADJUST OUR EXPECTATIONS AS WE AGE, DON'T WE?
AND TAKES REGULAR SHOWERS.

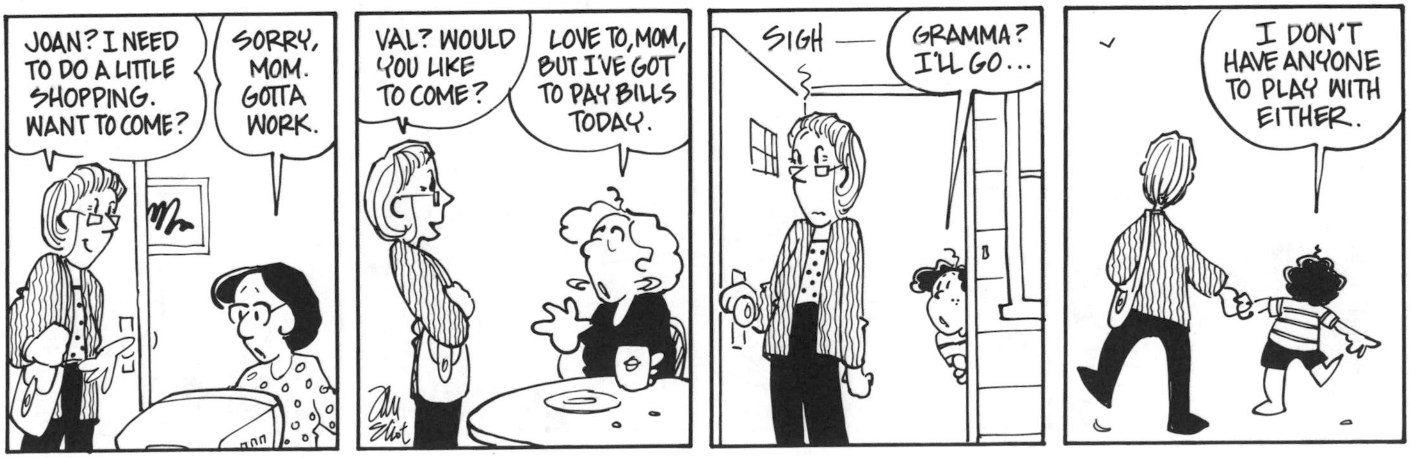
JOAN? I NEED TO DO A LITTLE SHOPPING. WANT TO COME?
SORRY, MOM. GOTTA WORK.
VAL? WOULD YOU LIKE TO COME?
LOVE TO, MOM, BUT I'VE GOT TO PAY BILLS TODAY.
SIGH —
GRAMMA? I'LL GO...
I DON'T HAVE ANYONE TO PLAY WITH EITHER.

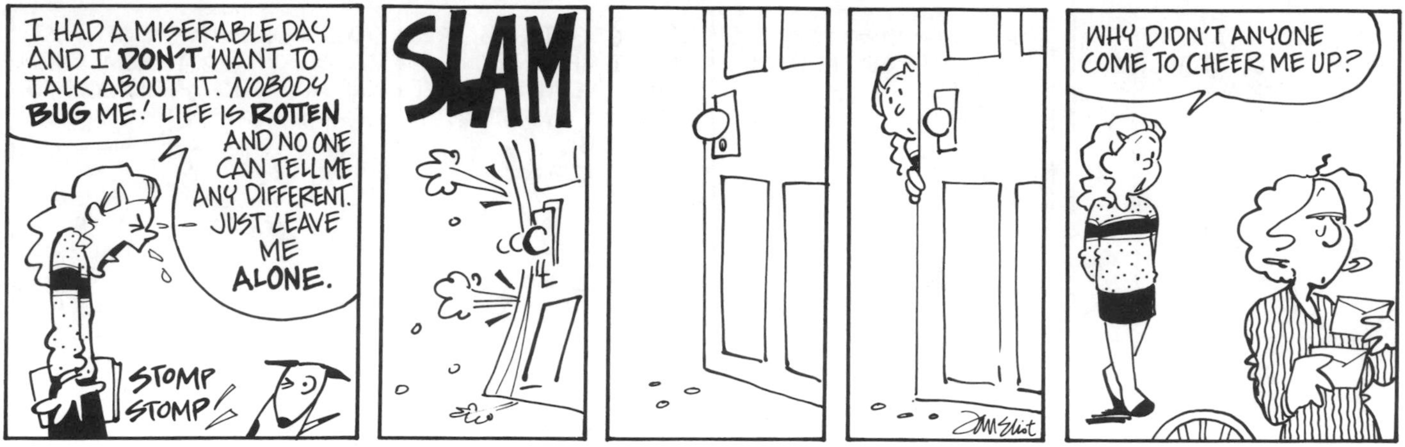
I HAD A MISERABLE DAY AND I **DON'T** WANT TO TALK ABOUT IT. *NOBODY* **BUG** ME! LIFE IS **ROTTEN** AND NO ONE CAN TELL ME ANY DIFFERENT. JUST LEAVE ME **ALONE**.
STOMP STOMP
SLAM
WHY DIDN'T ANYONE COME TO CHEER ME UP?

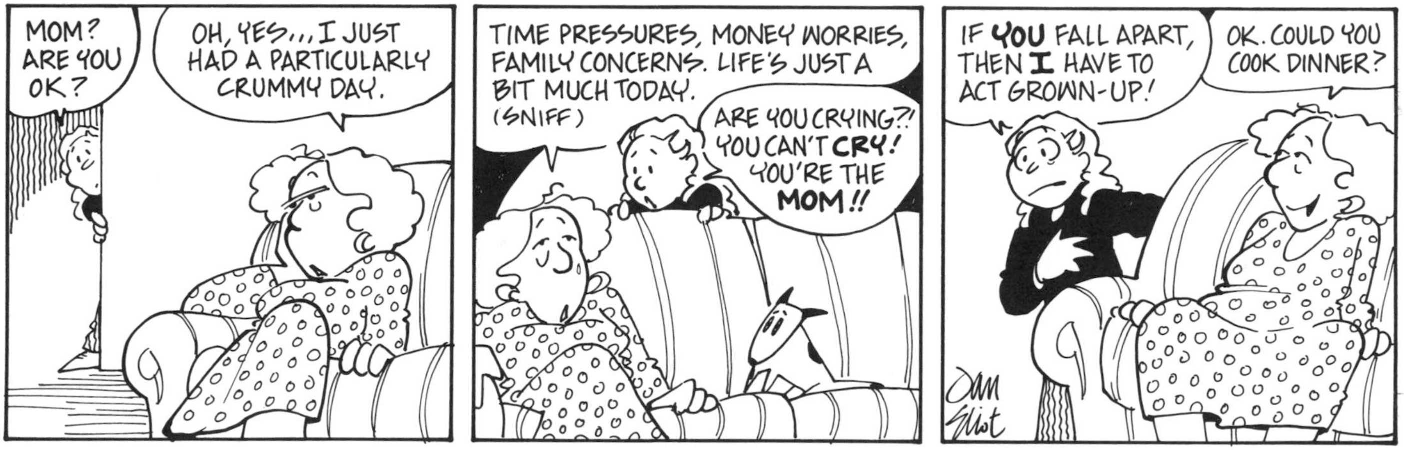
MOM? ARE YOU OK?
OH, YES... I JUST HAD A PARTICULARLY CRUMMY DAY.
TIME PRESSURES, MONEY WORRIES, FAMILY CONCERNS. LIFE'S JUST A BIT MUCH TODAY. (SNIFF)
ARE YOU CRYING?! YOU CAN'T **CRY**! YOU'RE THE **MOM**!!
IF **YOU** FALL APART, THEN **I** HAVE TO ACT GROWN-UP!
OK. COULD YOU COOK DINNER?

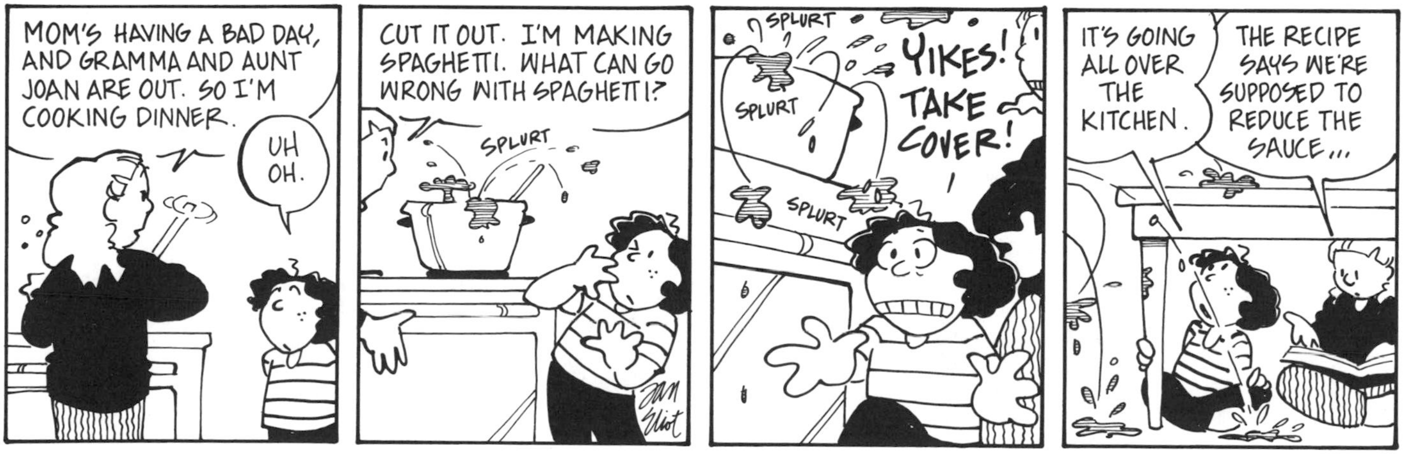
MOM'S HAVING A BAD DAY, AND GRAMMA AND AUNT JOAN ARE OUT. SO I'M COOKING DINNER.
UH OH.
CUT IT OUT. I'M MAKING SPAGHETTI. WHAT CAN GO WRONG WITH SPAGHETTI?
SPLURT
SPLURT
SPLURT
SPLURT
YIKES! TAKE COVER!
IT'S GOING ALL OVER THE KITCHEN.
THE RECIPE SAYS WE'RE SUPPOSED TO REDUCE THE SAUCE...

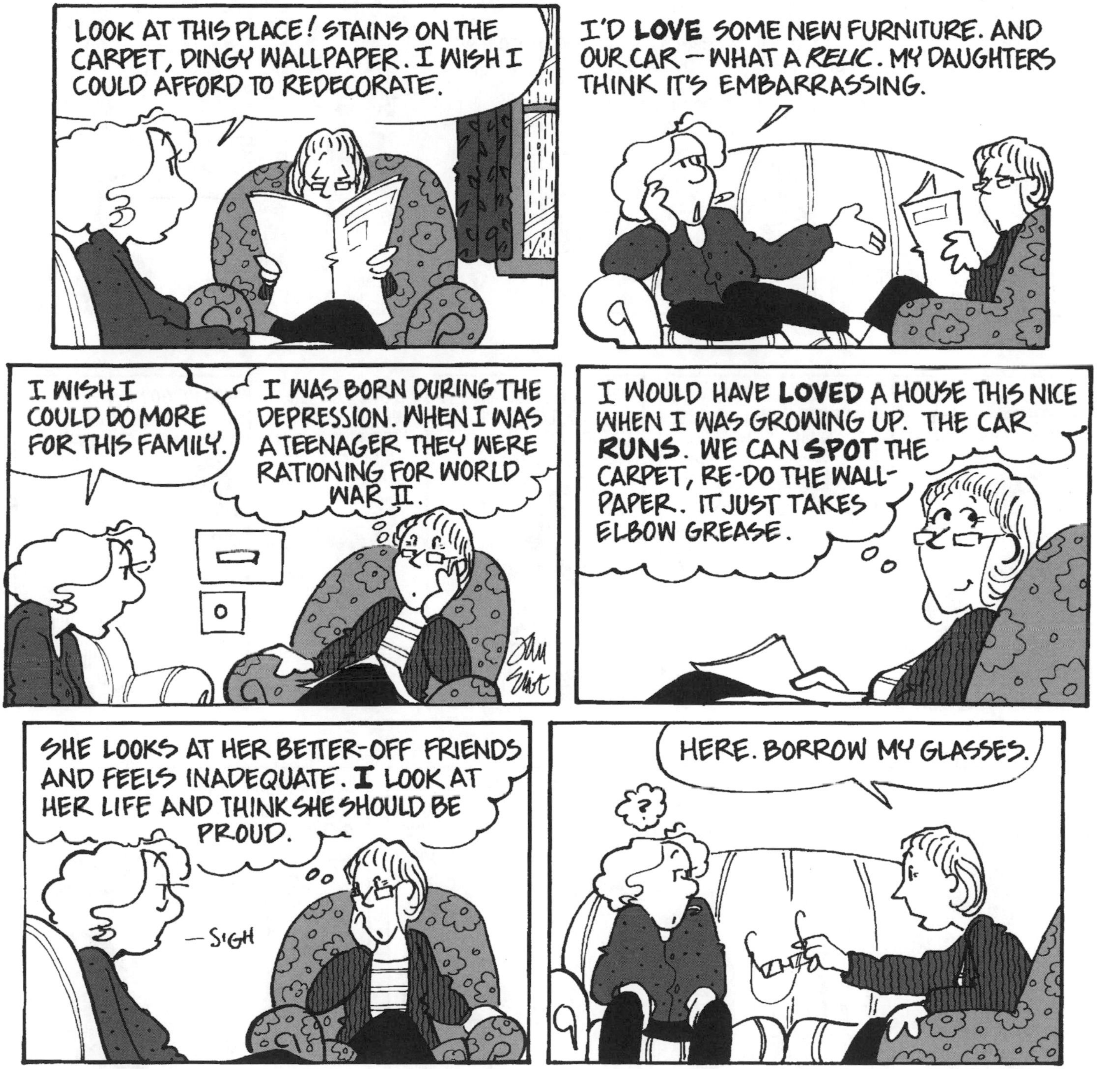
LOOK AT THIS PLACE! STAINS ON THE CARPET, DINGY WALLPAPER. I WISH I COULD AFFORD TO REDECORATE.
I'D **LOVE** SOME NEW FURNITURE. AND OUR CAR — WHAT A *RELIC*. MY DAUGHTERS THINK IT'S EMBARRASSING.
I WISH I COULD DO MORE FOR THIS FAMILY.
I WAS BORN DURING THE DEPRESSION. WHEN I WAS A TEENAGER THEY WERE RATIONING FOR WORLD WAR II.
I WOULD HAVE **LOVED** A HOUSE THIS NICE WHEN I WAS GROWING UP. THE CAR **RUNS**. WE CAN **SPOT** THE CARPET, RE-DO THE WALL-PAPER. IT JUST TAKES ELBOW GREASE.
SHE LOOKS AT HER BETTER-OFF FRIENDS AND FEELS INADEQUATE. **I** LOOK AT HER LIFE AND THINK SHE SHOULD BE PROUD.
— SIGH
?
HERE. BORROW MY GLASSES.

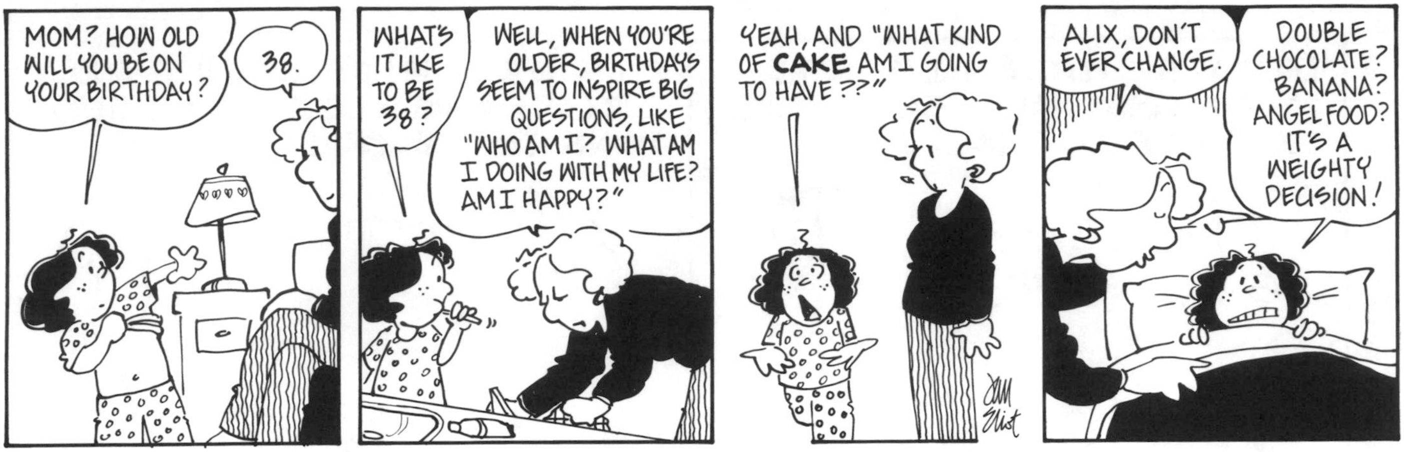
MOM? HOW OLD WILL YOU BE ON YOUR BIRTHDAY?
38.
WHAT'S IT LIKE TO BE 38?
WELL, WHEN YOU'RE OLDER, BIRTHDAYS SEEM TO INSPIRE BIG QUESTIONS, LIKE "WHO AM I? WHAT AM I DOING WITH MY LIFE? AM I HAPPY?"
YEAH, AND "WHAT KIND OF **CAKE** AM I GOING TO HAVE??"
ALIX, DON'T EVER CHANGE.
DOUBLE CHOCOLATE? BANANA? ANGEL FOOD? IT'S A WEIGHTY DECISION!

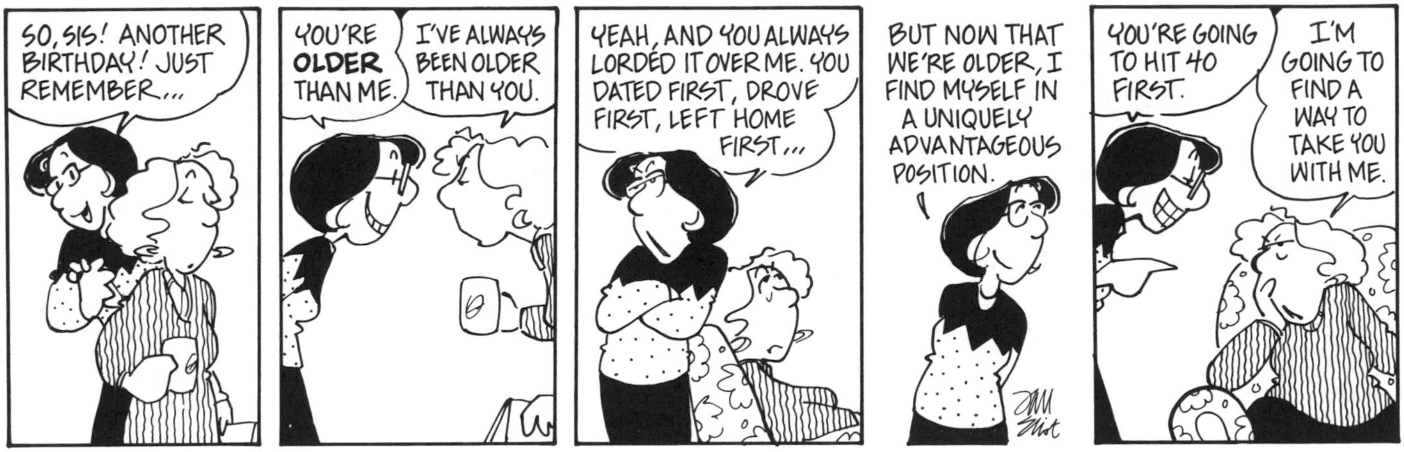
SO, SIS! ANOTHER BIRTHDAY! JUST REMEMBER...
YOU'RE **OLDER** THAN ME.
I'VE ALWAYS BEEN OLDER THAN YOU.
YEAH, AND YOU ALWAYS LORDED IT OVER ME. YOU DATED FIRST, DROVE FIRST, LEFT HOME FIRST...
BUT NOW THAT WE'RE OLDER, I FIND MYSELF IN A UNIQUELY ADVANTAGEOUS POSITION.
YOU'RE GOING TO HIT 40 FIRST.
I'M GOING TO FIND A WAY TO TAKE YOU WITH ME.

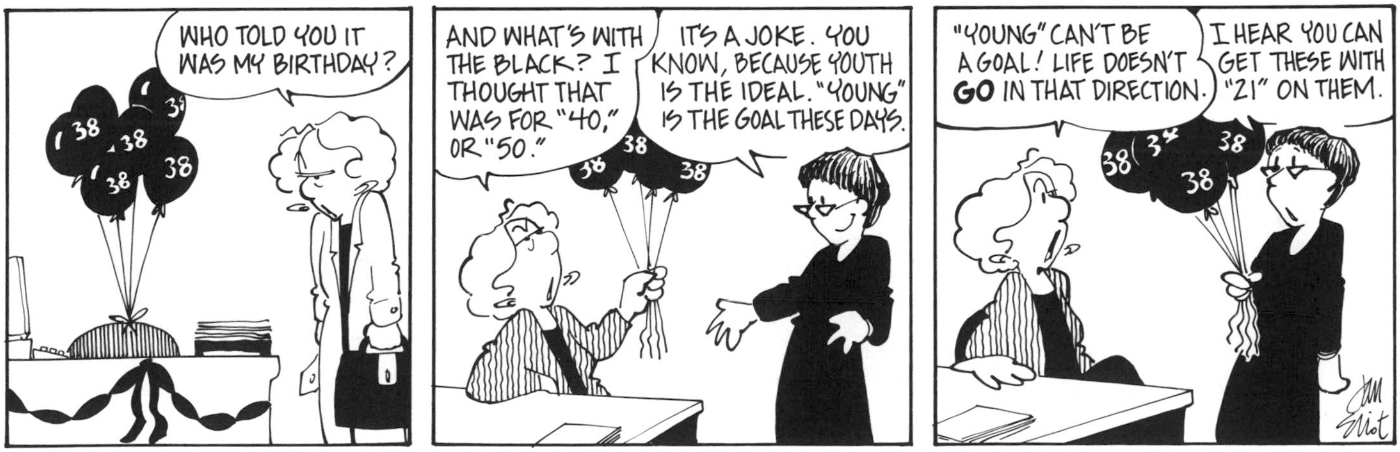
WHO TOLD YOU IT WAS MY BIRTHDAY?
AND WHAT'S WITH THE BLACK? I THOUGHT THAT WAS FOR "40," OR "50."
IT'S A JOKE. YOU KNOW, BECAUSE YOUTH IS THE IDEAL. "YOUNG" IS THE GOAL THESE DAYS.
"YOUNG" CAN'T BE A GOAL! LIFE DOESN'T **GO** IN THAT DIRECTION.
I HEAR YOU CAN GET THESE WITH "21" ON THEM.

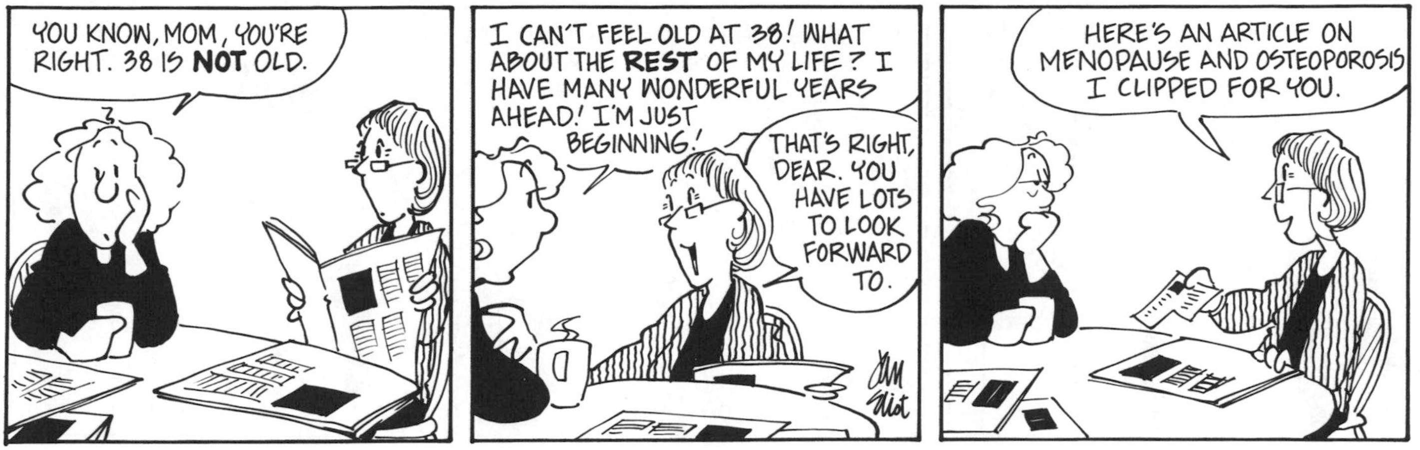
YOU KNOW, MOM, YOU'RE RIGHT. 38 IS **NOT** OLD.
I CAN'T FEEL OLD AT 38! WHAT ABOUT THE **REST** OF MY LIFE? I HAVE MANY WONDERFUL YEARS AHEAD! I'M JUST BEGINNING!
THAT'S RIGHT, DEAR. YOU HAVE LOTS TO LOOK FORWARD TO.
HERE'S AN ARTICLE ON MENOPAUSE AND OSTEOPOROSIS I CLIPPED FOR YOU.

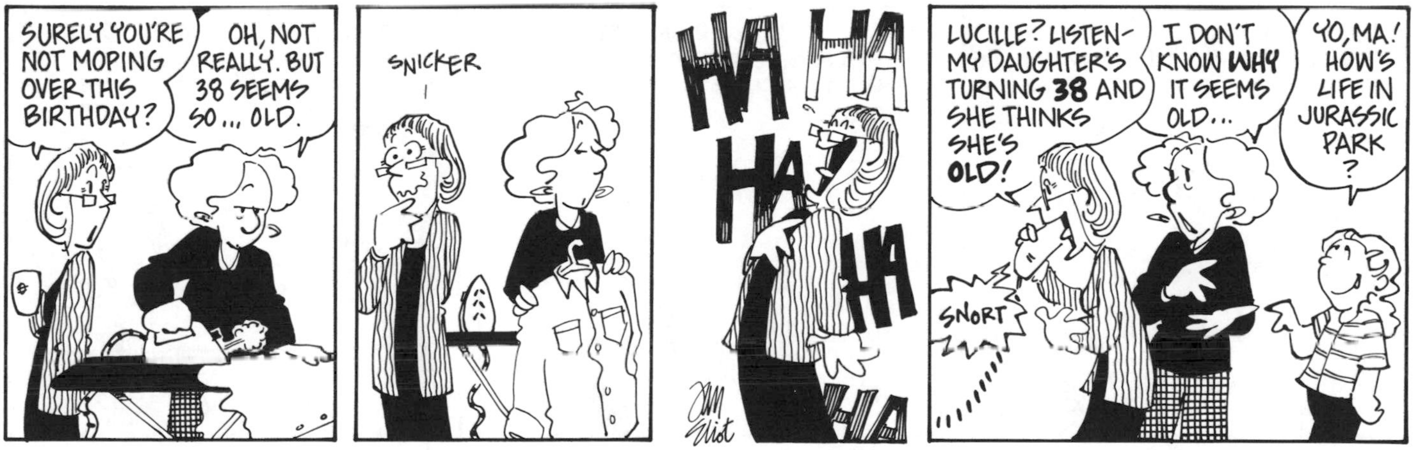
SURELY YOU'RE NOT MOPING OVER THIS BIRTHDAY?
OH, NOT REALLY. BUT 38 SEEMS SO... OLD.
SNICKER
HA HA HA HA HA
LUCILLE? LISTEN- MY DAUGHTER'S TURNING **38** AND SHE THINKS SHE'S **OLD**!
SNORT
I DON'T KNOW **WHY** IT SEEMS OLD...
YO, MA! HOW'S LIFE IN JURASSIC PARK?

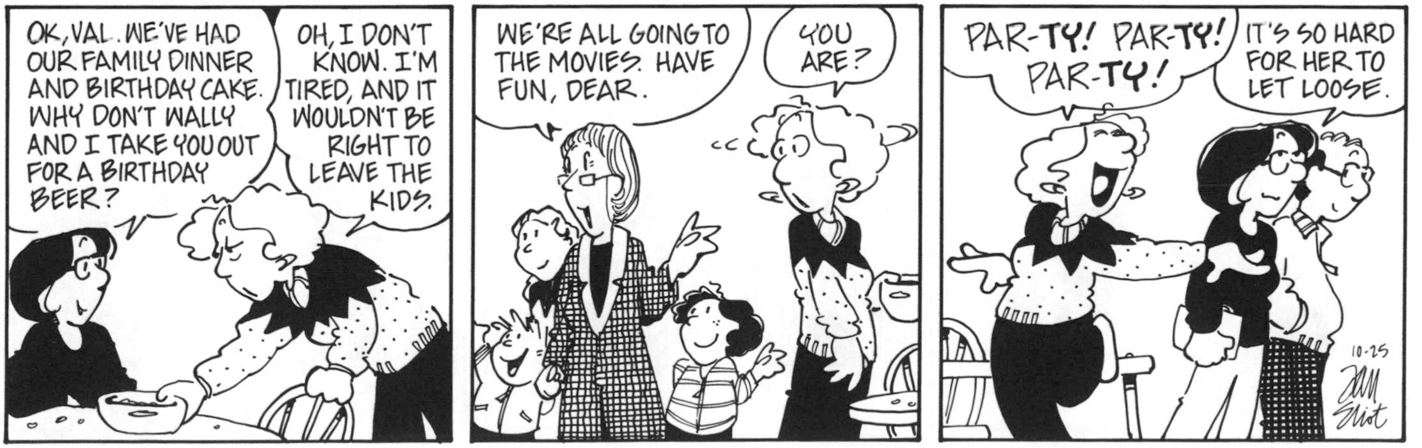
OK, VAL. WE'VE HAD OUR FAMILY DINNER AND BIRTHDAY CAKE. WHY DON'T WALLY AND I TAKE YOU OUT FOR A BIRTHDAY BEER?
OH, I DON'T KNOW. I'M TIRED, AND IT WOULDN'T BE RIGHT TO LEAVE THE KIDS.
WE'RE ALL GOING TO THE MOVIES. HAVE FUN, DEAR.
YOU ARE?
PAR-**TY**! PAR-**TY**! PAR-**TY**!
IT'S SO HARD FOR HER TO LET LOOSE.
10-25

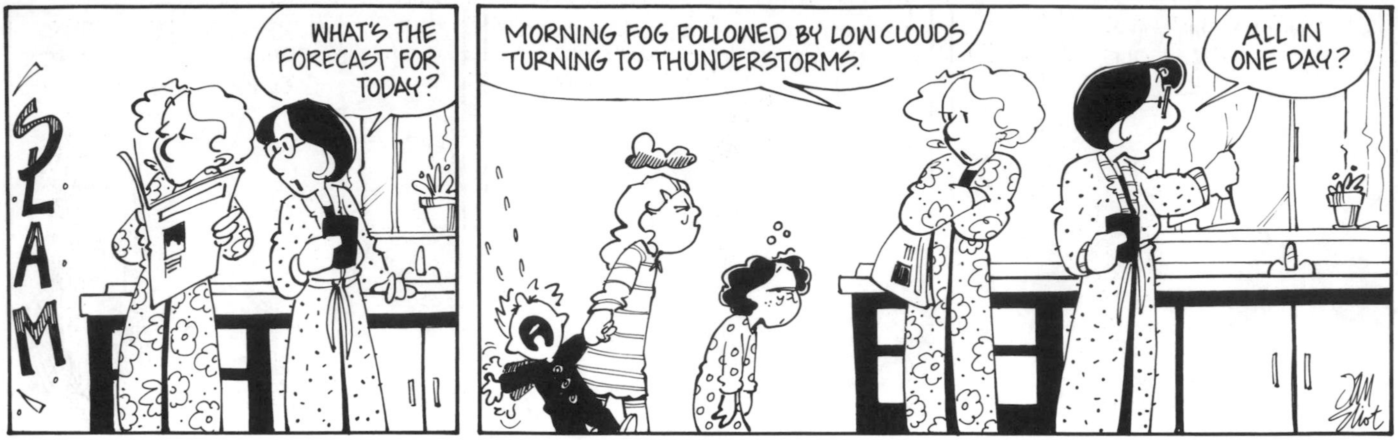
SLAM
WHAT'S THE FORECAST FOR TODAY?
MORNING FOG FOLLOWED BY LOW CLOUDS TURNING TO THUNDERSTORMS.
ALL IN ONE DAY?

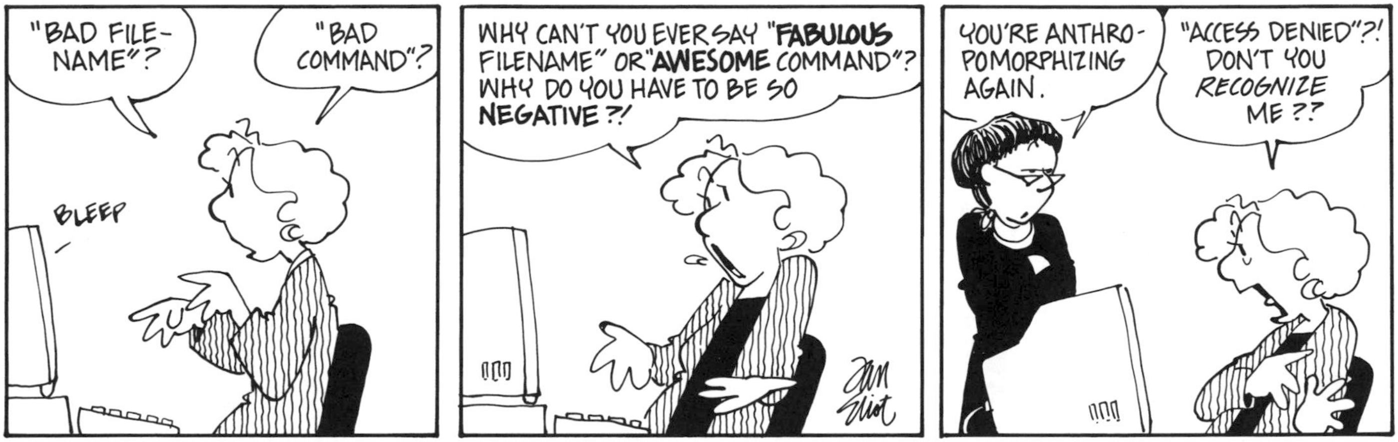
"BAD FILE-NAME"?
"BAD COMMAND"?
BLEEP
WHY CAN'T YOU EVER SAY "FABULOUS FILENAME" OR "AWESOME COMMAND"? WHY DO YOU HAVE TO BE SO NEGATIVE?!
YOU'RE ANTHRO-POMORPHIZING AGAIN.
"ACCESS DENIED"?! DON'T YOU RECOGNIZE ME??

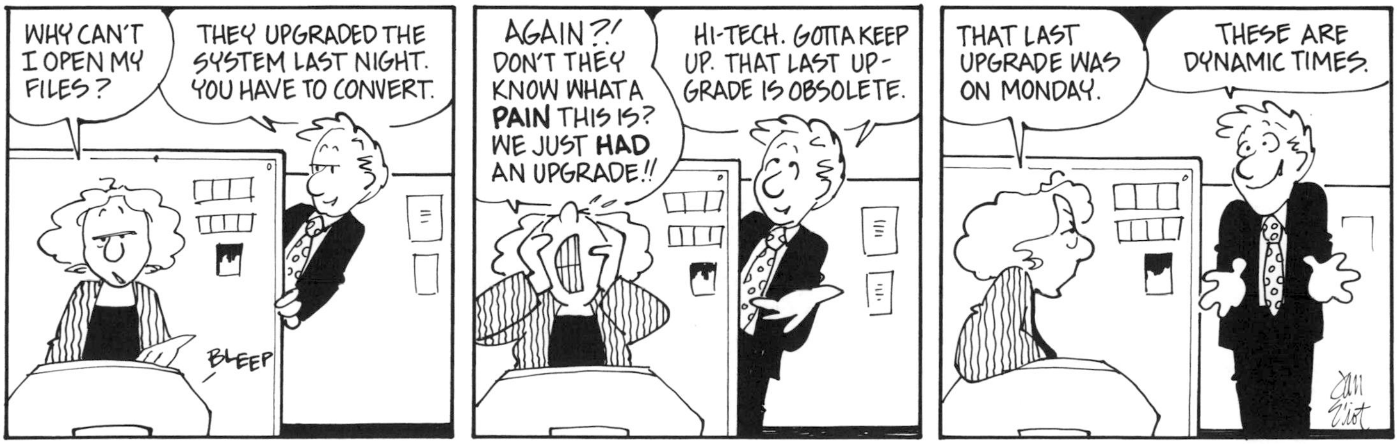
WHY CAN'T I OPEN MY FILES?
THEY UPGRADED THE SYSTEM LAST NIGHT. YOU HAVE TO CONVERT.
BLEEP
AGAIN?! DON'T THEY KNOW WHAT A PAIN THIS IS? WE JUST HAD AN UPGRADE!!
HI-TECH. GOTTA KEEP UP. THAT LAST UP-GRADE IS OBSOLETE.
THAT LAST UPGRADE WAS ON MONDAY.
THESE ARE DYNAMIC TIMES.

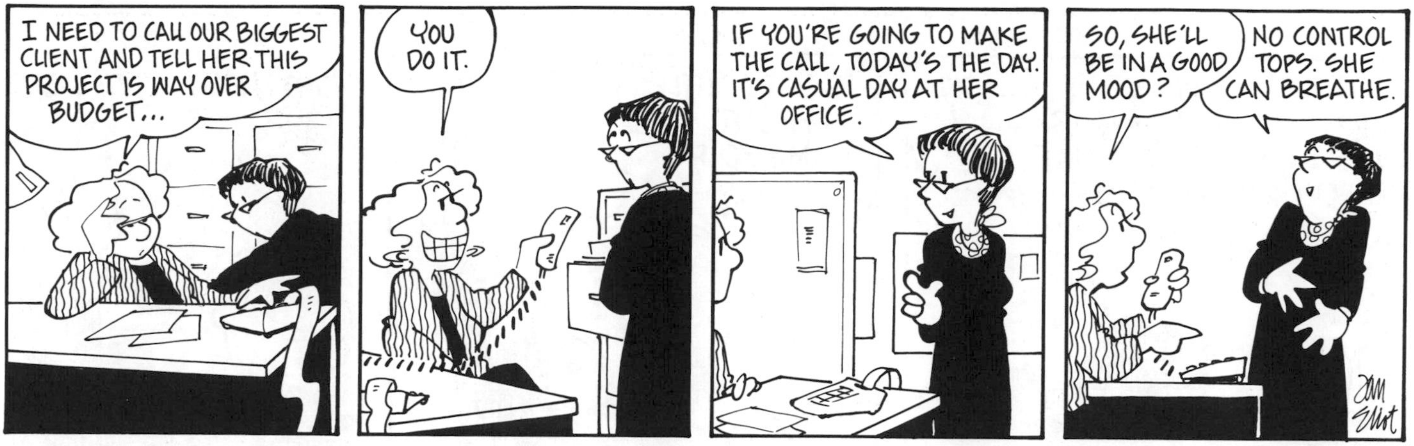
I NEED TO CALL OUR BIGGEST CLIENT AND TELL HER THIS PROJECT IS WAY OVER BUDGET...
YOU DO IT.
IF YOU'RE GOING TO MAKE THE CALL, TODAY'S THE DAY. IT'S CASUAL DAY AT HER OFFICE.
SO, SHE'LL BE IN A GOOD MOOD?
NO CONTROL TOPS. SHE CAN BREATHE.
JAN Eliot

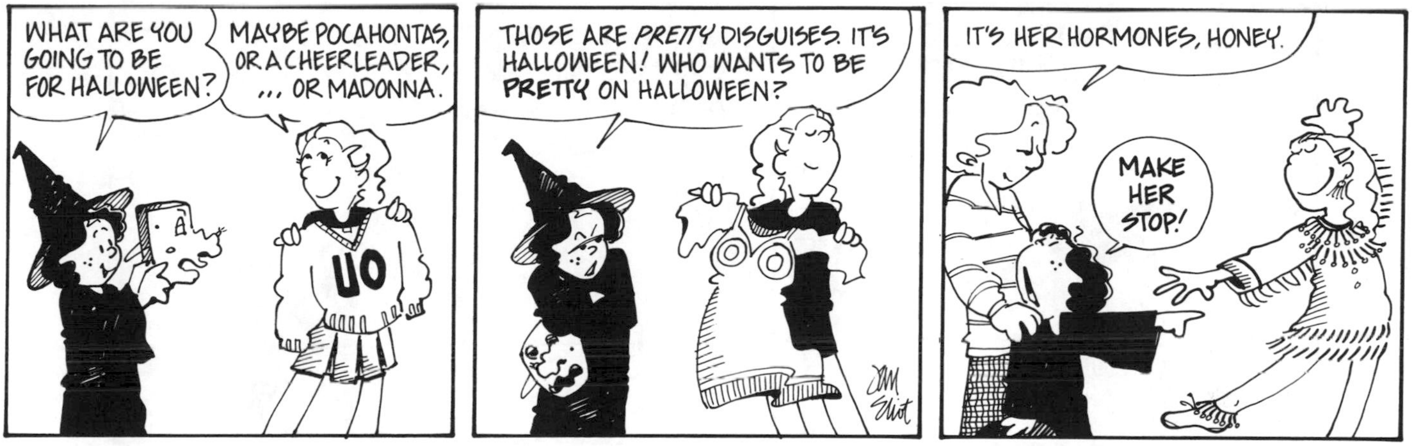
WHAT ARE YOU GOING TO BE FOR HALLOWEEN?
MAYBE POCAHONTAS, OR A CHEERLEADER, ... OR MADONNA.
UO
THOSE ARE PRETTY DISGUISES. IT'S HALLOWEEN! WHO WANTS TO BE PRETTY ON HALLOWEEN?
JAN Eliot
IT'S HER HORMONES, HONEY.
MAKE HER STOP!

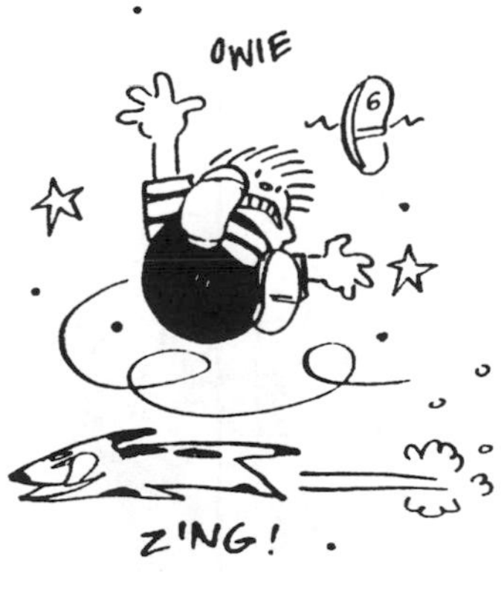
OWIE
Z'NG!

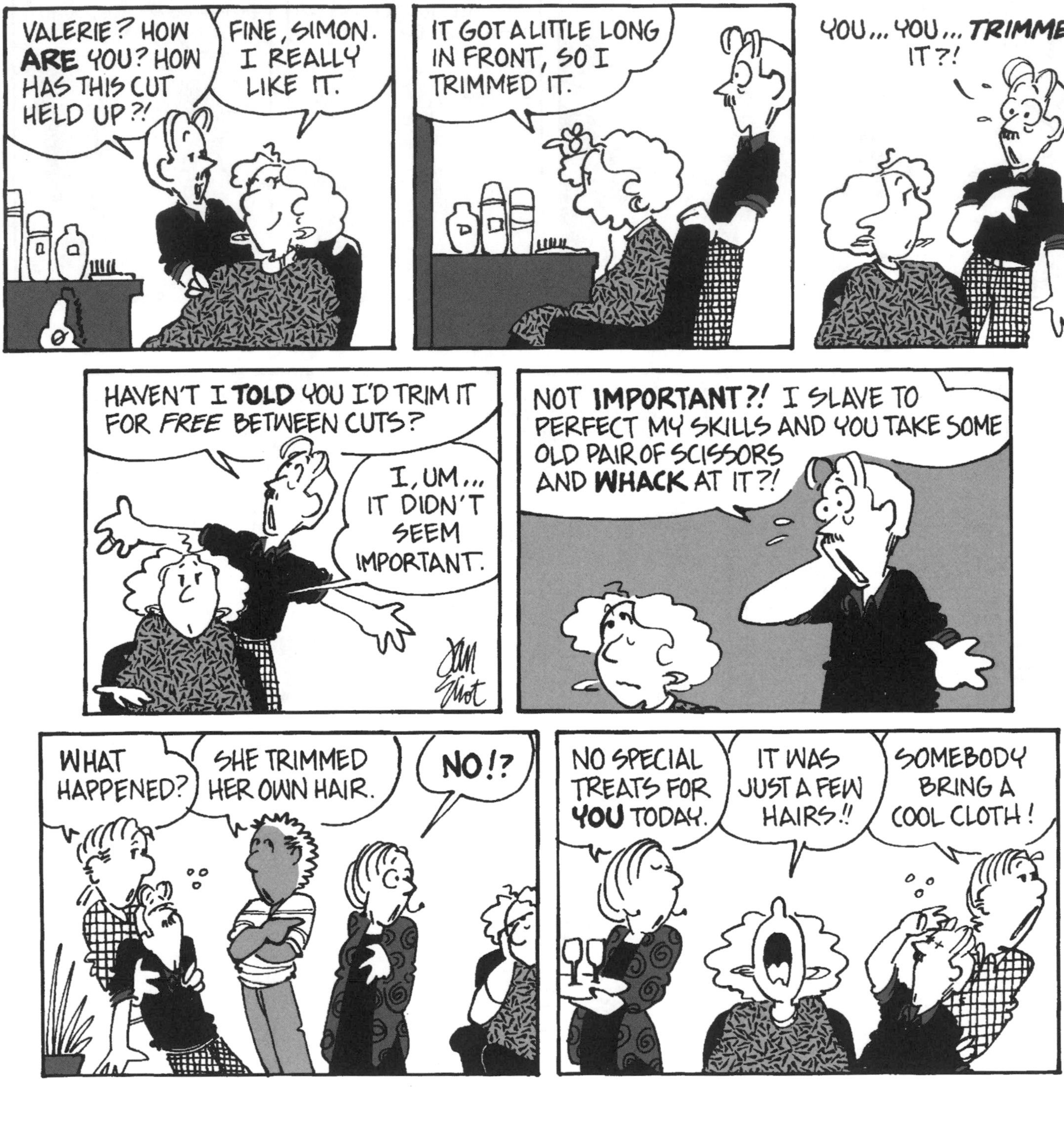
VALERIE? HOW ARE YOU? HOW HAS THIS CUT HELD UP?!
FINE, SIMON. I REALLY LIKE IT.
IT GOT A LITTLE LONG IN FRONT, SO I TRIMMED IT.
YOU... YOU... TRIMMED IT?!
HAVEN'T I TOLD YOU I'D TRIM IT FOR FREE BETWEEN CUTS?
I, UM... IT DIDN'T SEEM IMPORTANT.
NOT IMPORTANT?! I SLAVE TO PERFECT MY SKILLS AND YOU TAKE SOME OLD PAIR OF SCISSORS AND WHACK AT IT?!
WHAT HAPPENED?
SHE TRIMMED HER OWN HAIR.
NO!?
NO SPECIAL TREATS FOR YOU TODAY.
IT WAS JUST A FEW HAIRS!!
SOMEBODY BRING A COOL CLOTH!

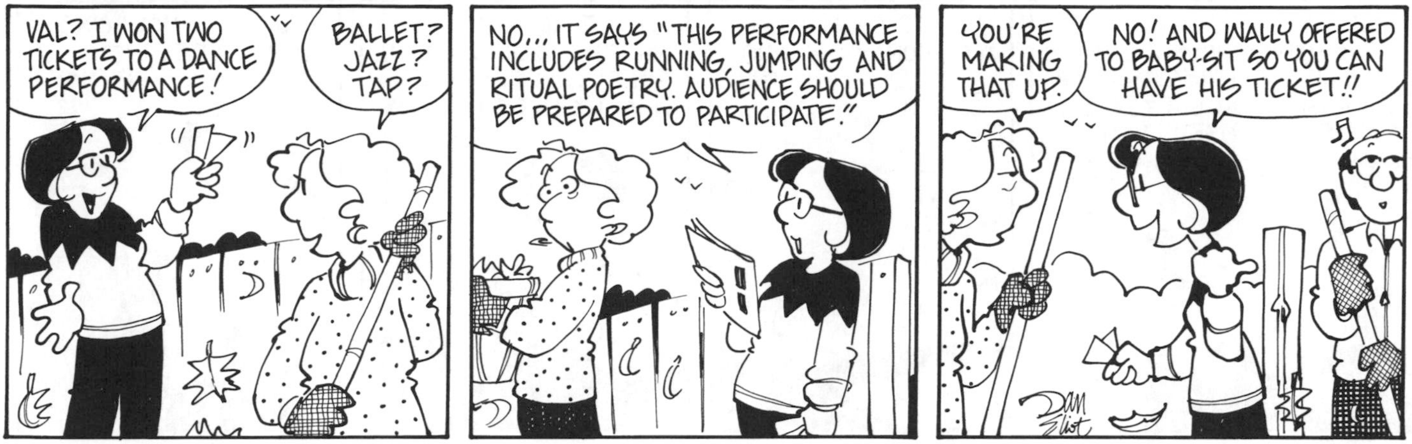
VAL? I WON TWO TICKETS TO A DANCE PERFORMANCE!
BALLET? JAZZ? TAP?
NO... IT SAYS "THIS PERFORMANCE INCLUDES RUNNING, JUMPING AND RITUAL POETRY. AUDIENCE SHOULD BE PREPARED TO PARTICIPATE."
YOU'RE MAKING THAT UP.
NO! AND WALLY OFFERED TO BABY-SIT SO YOU CAN HAVE HIS TICKET!!

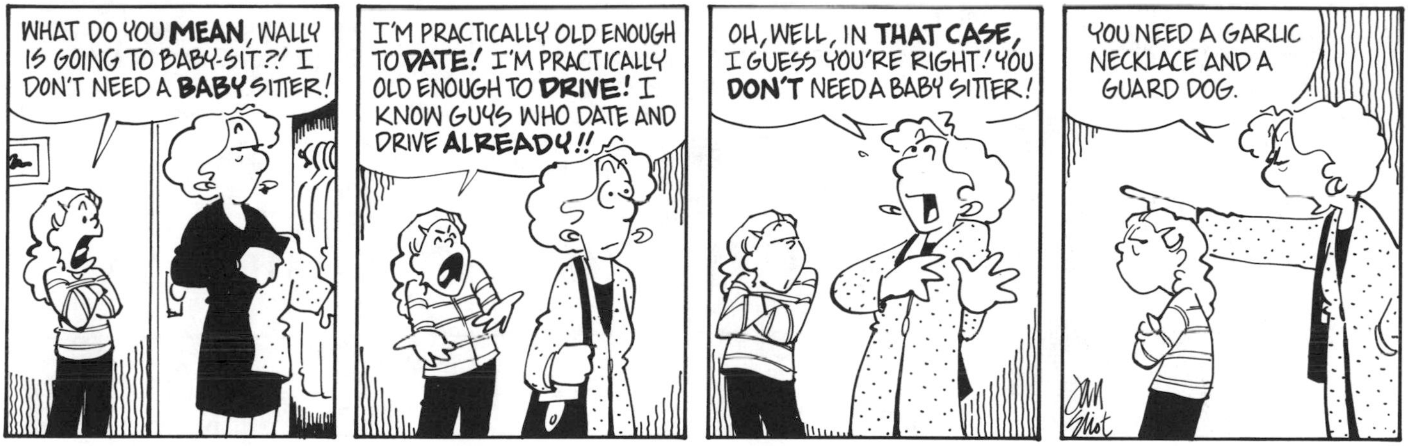
WHAT DO YOU **MEAN**, WALLY IS GOING TO BABY-SIT?! I DON'T NEED A **BABY** SITTER!
I'M PRACTICALLY OLD ENOUGH TO **DATE!** I'M PRACTICALLY OLD ENOUGH TO **DRIVE!** I KNOW GUYS WHO DATE AND DRIVE **ALREADY!!**
OH, WELL, IN **THAT CASE,** I GUESS YOU'RE RIGHT! YOU **DON'T** NEED A BABY SITTER!
YOU NEED A GARLIC NECKLACE AND A GUARD DOG.

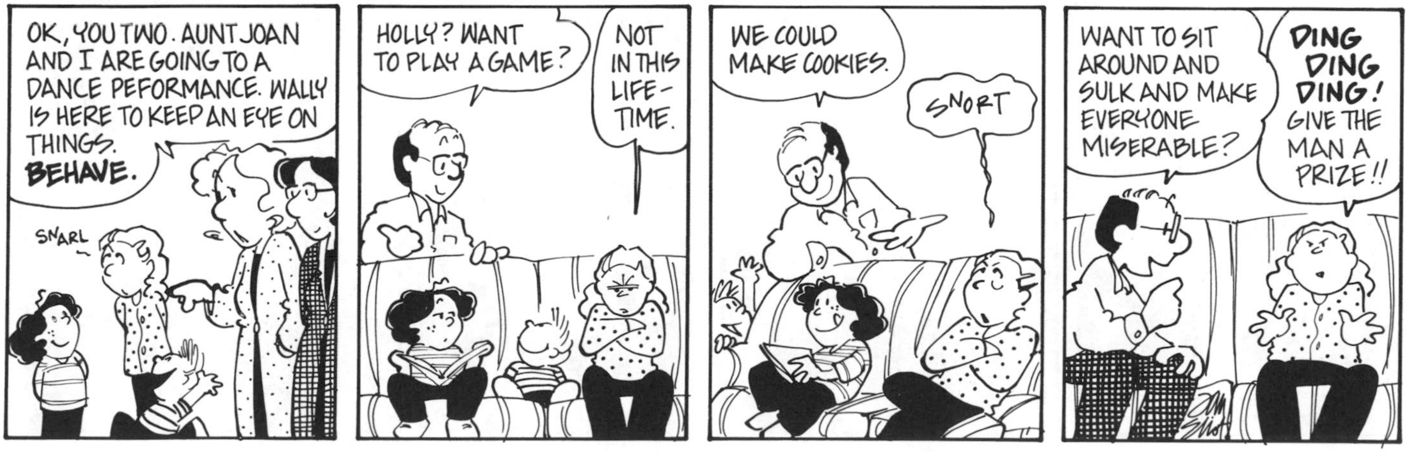
OK, YOU TWO. AUNT JOAN AND I ARE GOING TO A DANCE PEFORMANCE. WALLY IS HERE TO KEEP AN EYE ON THINGS. **BEHAVE.**
SNARL
HOLLY? WANT TO PLAY A GAME?
NOT IN THIS LIFE-TIME.
WE COULD MAKE COOKIES.
SNORT
WANT TO SIT AROUND AND SULK AND MAKE EVERYONE MISERABLE?
DING DING DING! GIVE THE MAN A PRIZE!!

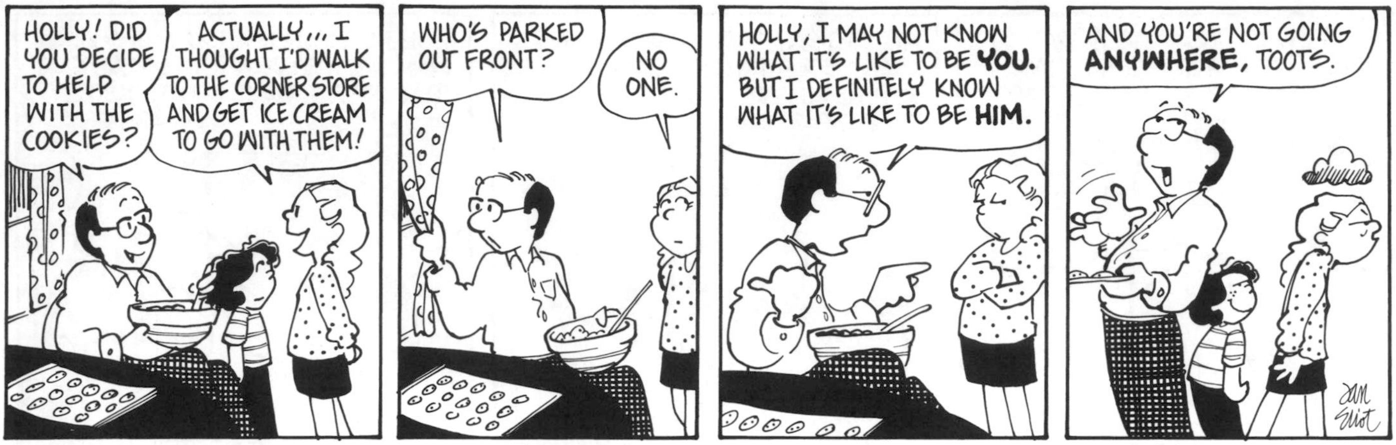
HOLLY! DID YOU DECIDE TO HELP WITH THE COOKIES?
ACTUALLY... I THOUGHT I'D WALK TO THE CORNER STORE AND GET ICE CREAM TO GO WITH THEM!
WHO'S PARKED OUT FRONT?
NO ONE.
HOLLY, I MAY NOT KNOW WHAT IT'S LIKE TO BE **YOU.** BUT I DEFINITELY KNOW WHAT IT'S LIKE TO BE **HIM.**
AND YOU'RE NOT GOING **ANYWHERE,** TOOTS.

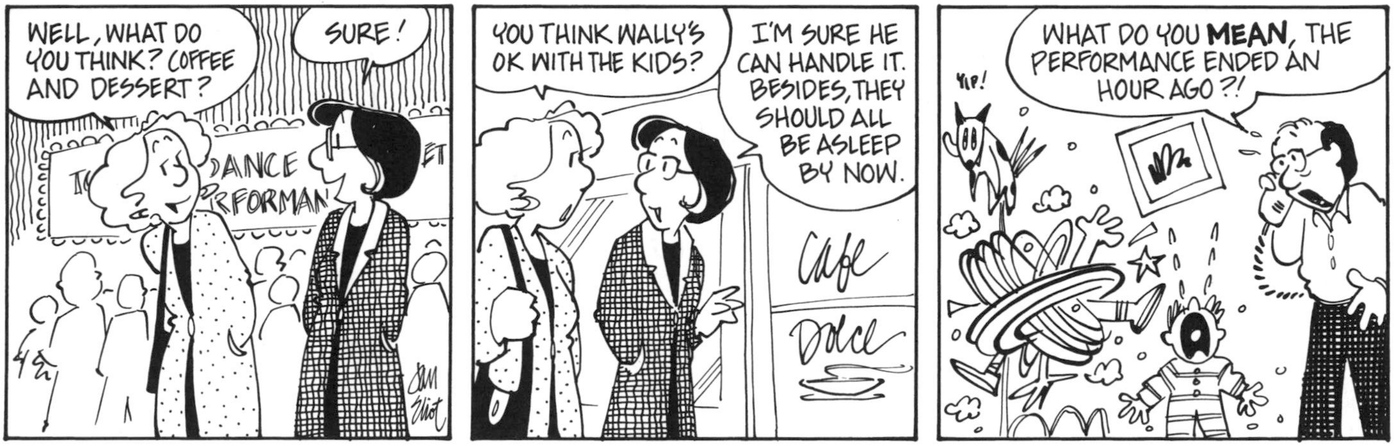
WELL, WHAT DO YOU THINK? COFFEE AND DESSERT?
SURE!
YOU THINK WALLY'S OK WITH THE KIDS?
I'M SURE HE CAN HANDLE IT. BESIDES, THEY SHOULD ALL BE ASLEEP BY NOW.
Cafe Dolce
YIP!
WHAT DO YOU **MEAN,** THE PERFORMANCE ENDED AN HOUR AGO?!

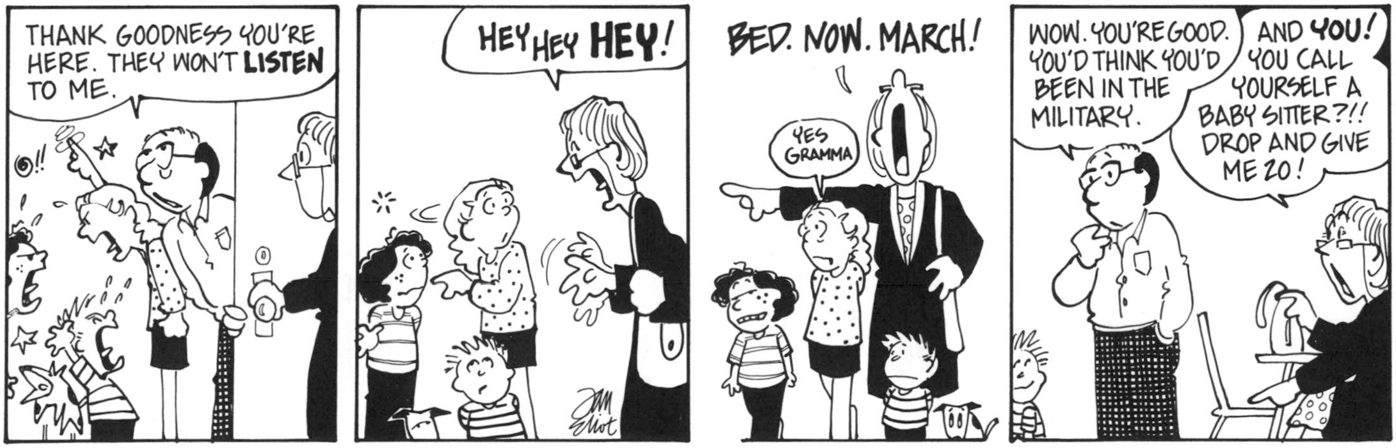
THANK GOODNESS YOU'RE HERE. THEY WON'T **LISTEN** TO ME.
HEY HEY **HEY**!
BED. NOW. MARCH!
YES GRAMMA
WOW. YOU'RE GOOD. YOU'D THINK YOU'D BEEN IN THE MILITARY.
AND **YOU**! YOU CALL YOURSELF A BABY SITTER?!! DROP AND GIVE ME 20!

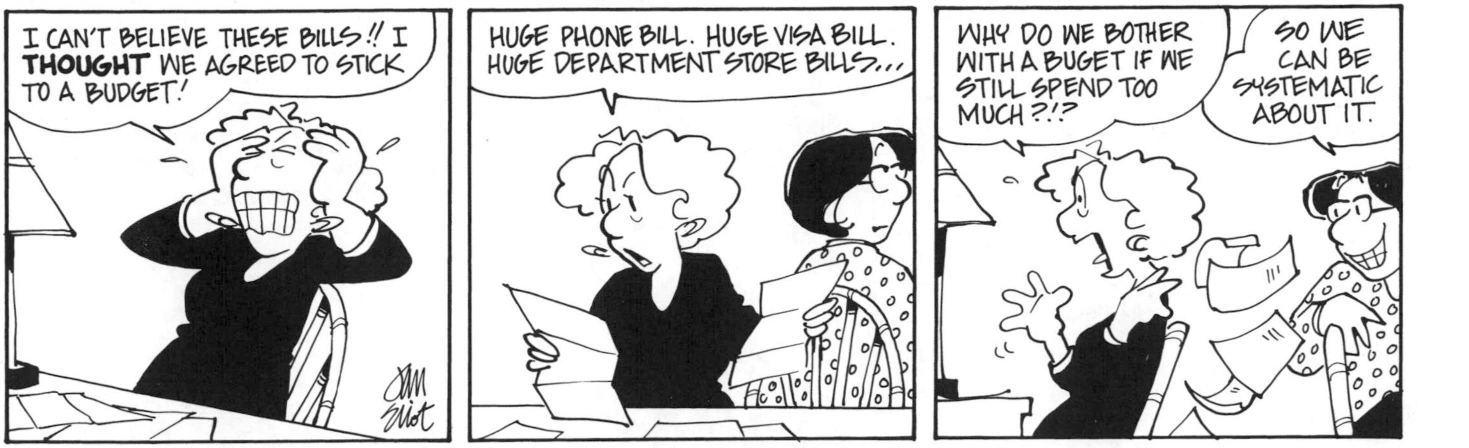
I CAN'T BELIEVE THESE BILLS!! I **THOUGHT** WE AGREED TO STICK TO A BUDGET!
HUGE PHONE BILL. HUGE VISA BILL. HUGE DEPARTMENT STORE BILLS...
WHY DO WE BOTHER WITH A BUGET IF WE STILL SPEND TOO MUCH?!?
SO WE CAN BE SYSTEMATIC ABOUT IT.

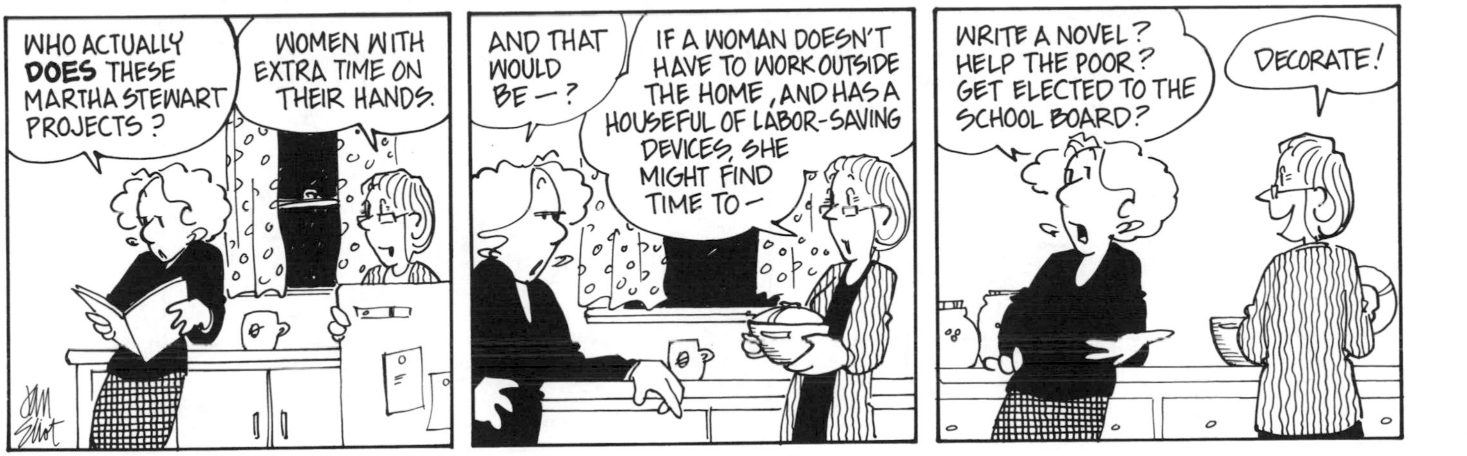
WHO ACTUALLY **DOES** THESE MARTHA STEWART PROJECTS?
WOMEN WITH EXTRA TIME ON THEIR HANDS.
AND THAT WOULD BE —?
IF A WOMAN DOESN'T HAVE TO WORK OUTSIDE THE HOME, AND HAS A HOUSEFUL OF LABOR-SAVING DEVICES, SHE MIGHT FIND TIME TO—
WRITE A NOVEL? HELP THE POOR? GET ELECTED TO THE SCHOOL BOARD?
DECORATE!

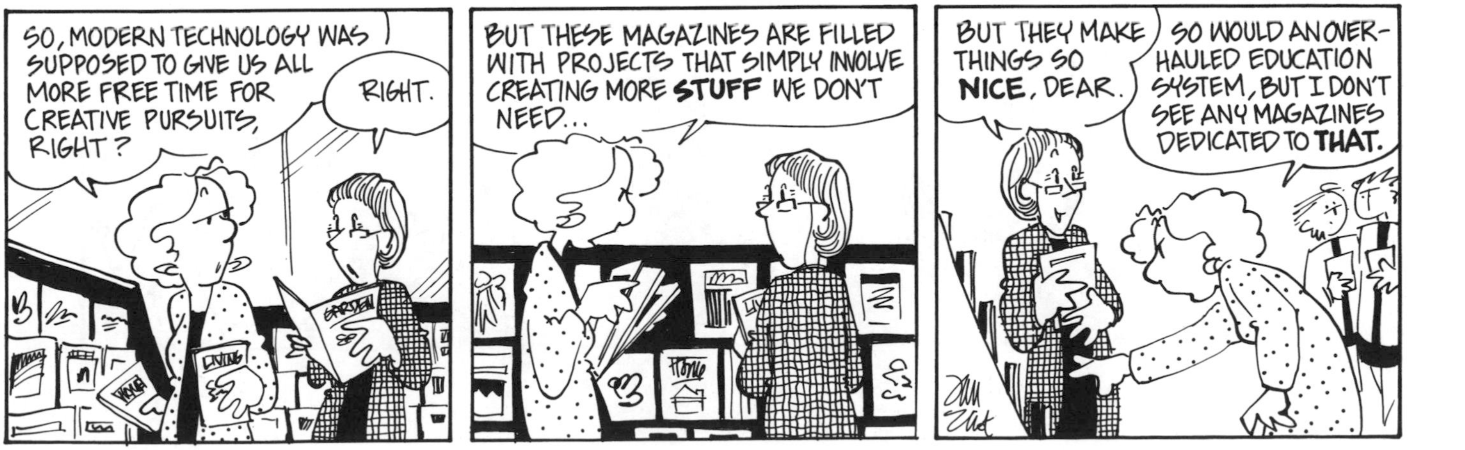
SO, MODERN TECHNOLOGY WAS SUPPOSED TO GIVE US ALL MORE FREE TIME FOR CREATIVE PURSUITS, RIGHT?
RIGHT.
BUT THESE MAGAZINES ARE FILLED WITH PROJECTS THAT SIMPLY INVOLVE CREATING MORE **STUFF** WE DON'T NEED...
BUT THEY MAKE THINGS SO **NICE**, DEAR.
SO WOULD AN OVER-HAULED EDUCATION SYSTEM, BUT I DON'T SEE ANY MAGAZINES DEDICATED TO **THAT**.

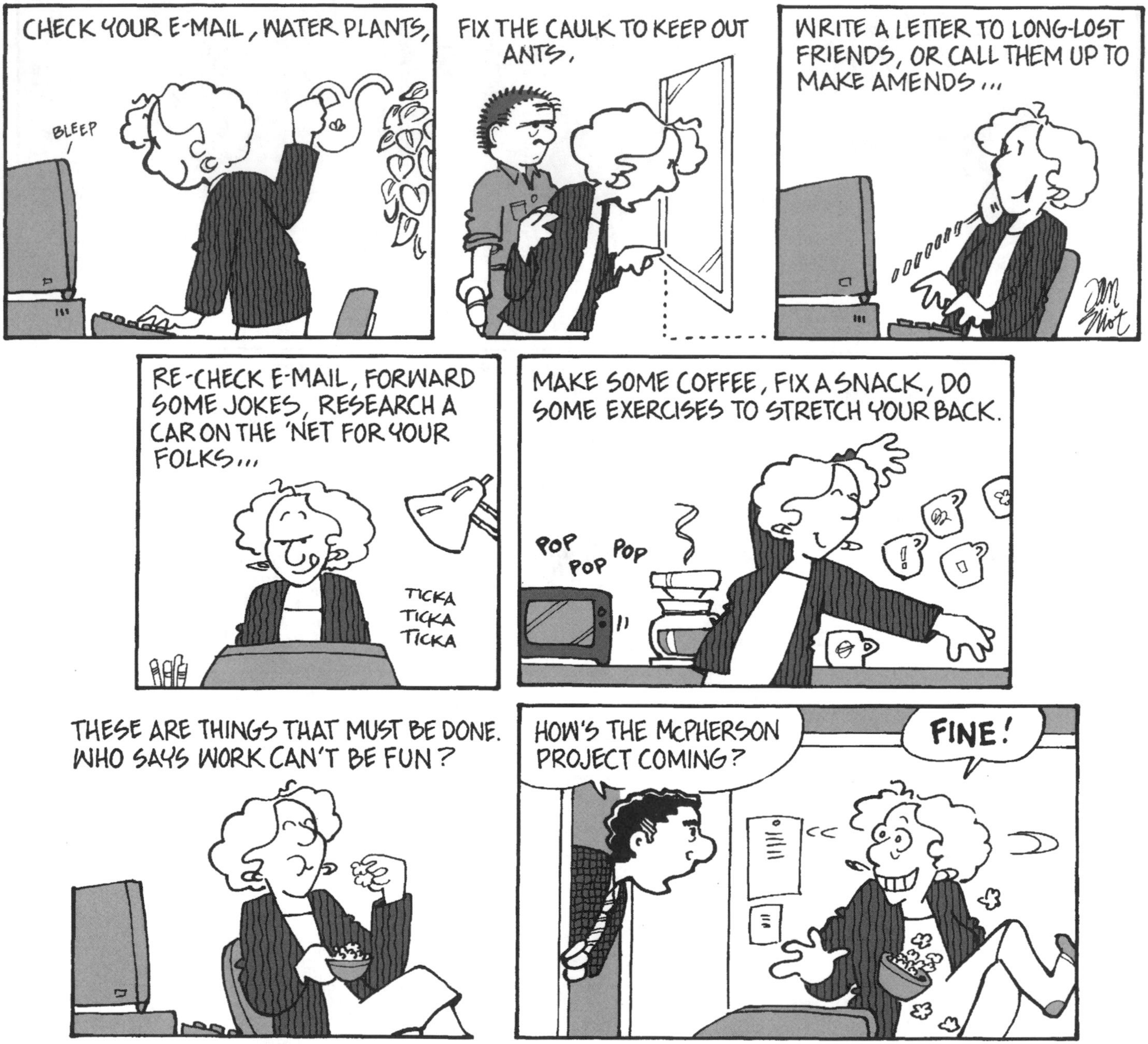
CHECK YOUR E-MAIL, WATER PLANTS,
BLEEP
FIX THE CAULK TO KEEP OUT ANTS,
WRITE A LETTER TO LONG-LOST FRIENDS, OR CALL THEM UP TO MAKE AMENDS...
RE-CHECK E-MAIL, FORWARD SOME JOKES, RESEARCH A CAR ON THE 'NET FOR YOUR FOLKS...
TICKA TICKA TICKA
MAKE SOME COFFEE, FIX A SNACK, DO SOME EXERCISES TO STRETCH YOUR BACK.
POP POP POP
THESE ARE THINGS THAT MUST BE DONE. WHO SAYS WORK CAN'T BE FUN?
HOW'S THE McPHERSON PROJECT COMING?
FINE!

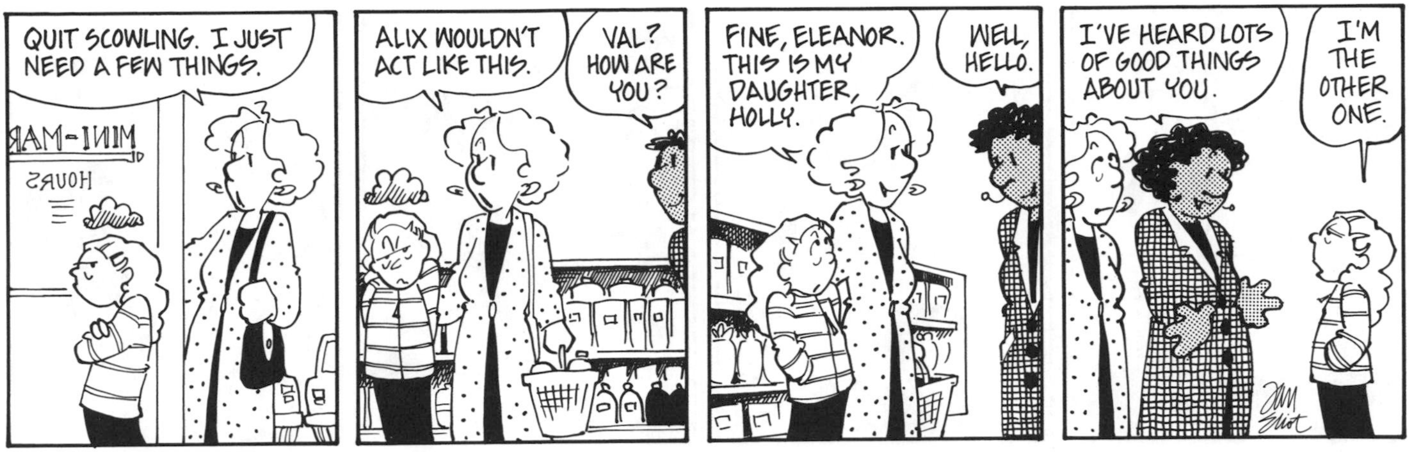
QUIT SCOWLING. I JUST NEED A FEW THINGS.
ALIX WOULDN'T ACT LIKE THIS.
VAL? HOW ARE YOU?
FINE, ELEANOR. THIS IS MY DAUGHTER, HOLLY.
WELL, HELLO.
I'VE HEARD LOTS OF GOOD THINGS ABOUT YOU.
I'M THE OTHER ONE.

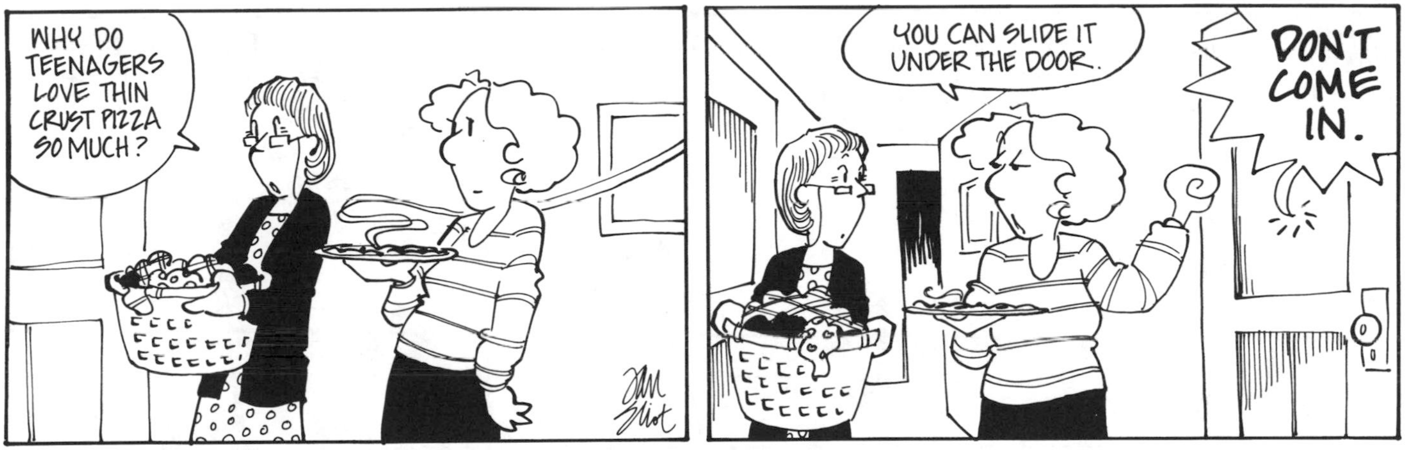
WHY DO TEENAGERS LOVE THIN CRUST PIZZA SO MUCH?
YOU CAN SLIDE IT UNDER THE DOOR.
DON'T COME IN.

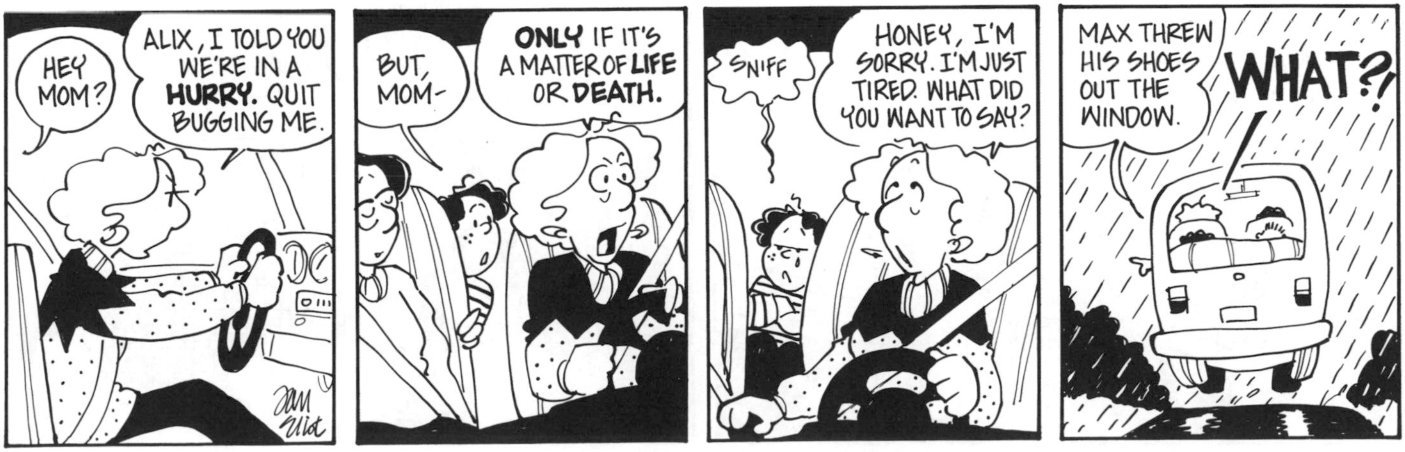
HEY MOM?
ALIX, I TOLD YOU WE'RE IN A HURRY. QUIT BUGGING ME.
BUT, MOM-
ONLY IF IT'S A MATTER OF LIFE OR DEATH.
SNIFF
HONEY, I'M SORRY. I'M JUST TIRED. WHAT DID YOU WANT TO SAY?
MAX THREW HIS SHOES OUT THE WINDOW.
WHAT?!

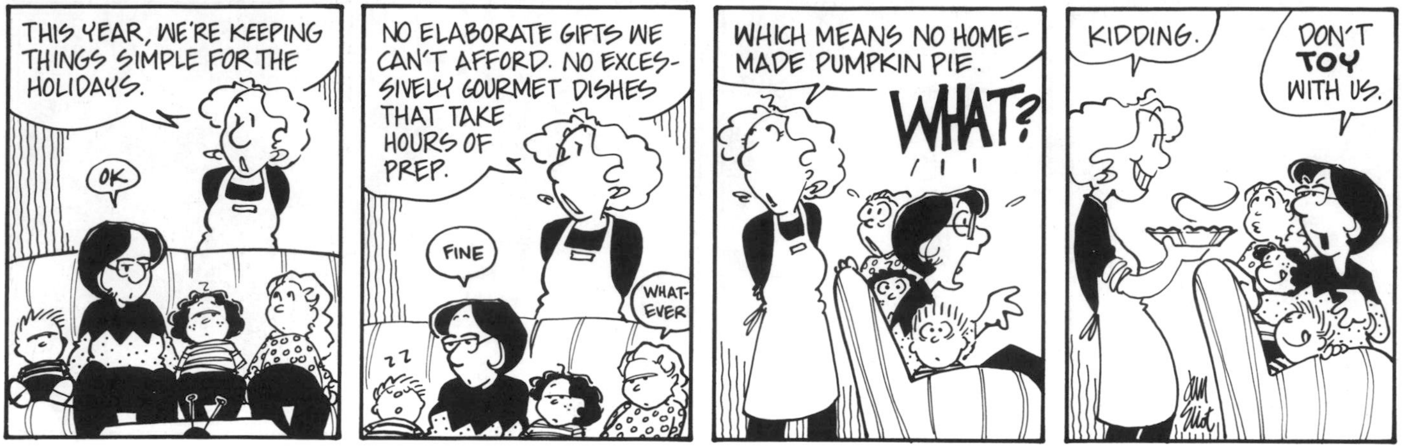
THIS YEAR, WE'RE KEEPING THINGS SIMPLE FOR THE HOLIDAYS.
OK
NO ELABORATE GIFTS WE CAN'T AFFORD. NO EXCESSIVELY GOURMET DISHES THAT TAKE HOURS OF PREP.
FINE
WHATEVER
Z Z
WHICH MEANS NO HOME-MADE PUMPKIN PIE.
WHAT?
KIDDING.
DON'T TOY WITH US.

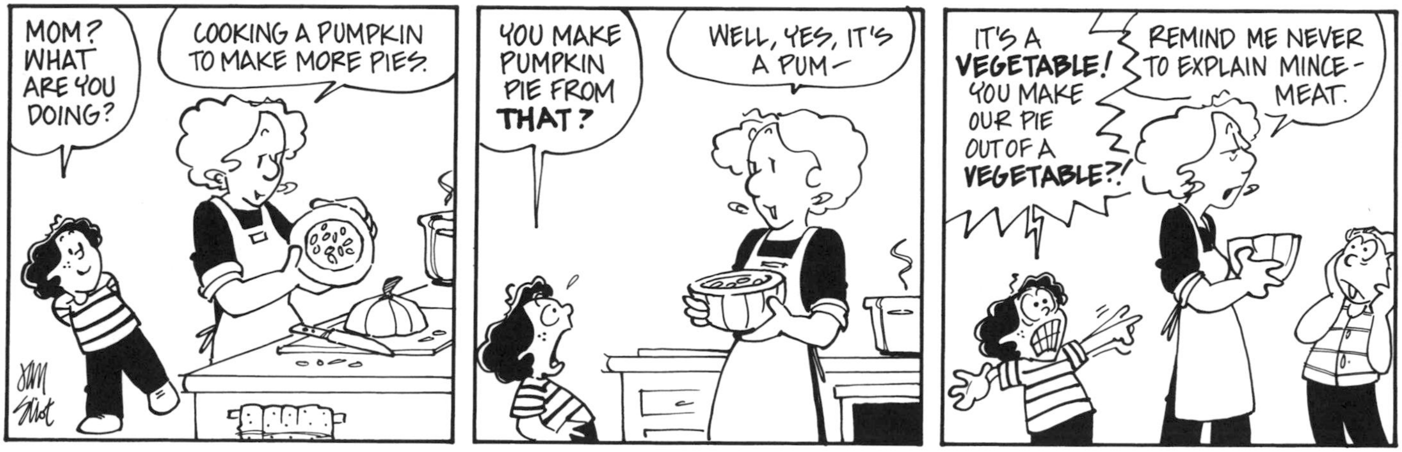
MOM? WHAT ARE YOU DOING?
COOKING A PUMPKIN TO MAKE MORE PIES.
YOU MAKE PUMPKIN PIE FROM THAT?
WELL, YES, IT'S A PUM-
IT'S A VEGETABLE! YOU MAKE OUR PIE OUT OF A VEGETABLE?!
REMIND ME NEVER TO EXPLAIN MINCE-MEAT.

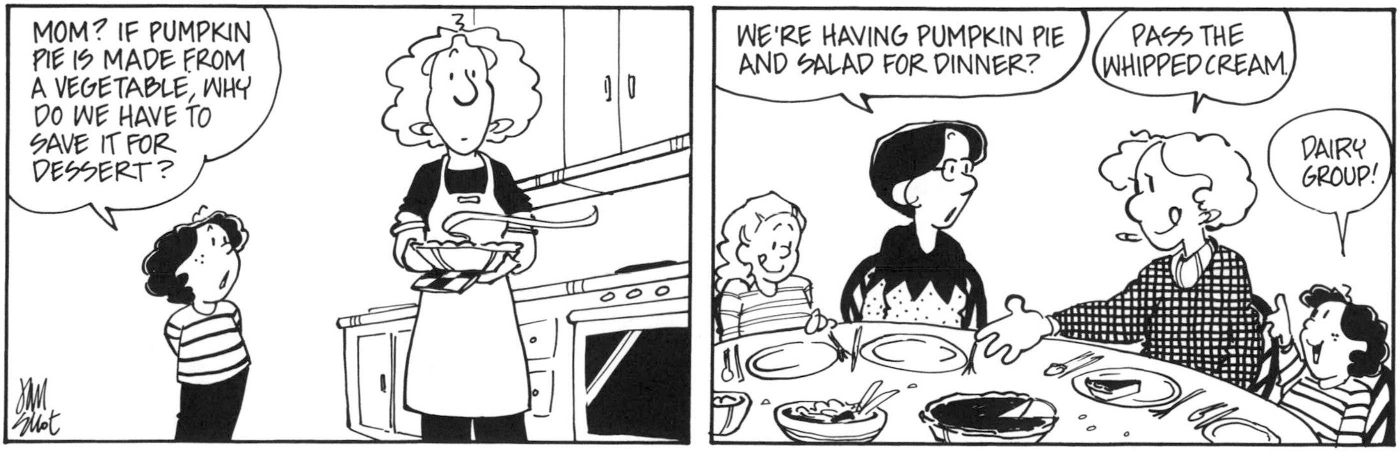
MOM? IF PUMPKIN PIE IS MADE FROM A VEGETABLE, WHY DO WE HAVE TO SAVE IT FOR DESSERT?
WE'RE HAVING PUMPKIN PIE AND SALAD FOR DINNER?
PASS THE WHIPPED CREAM.
DAIRY GROUP!

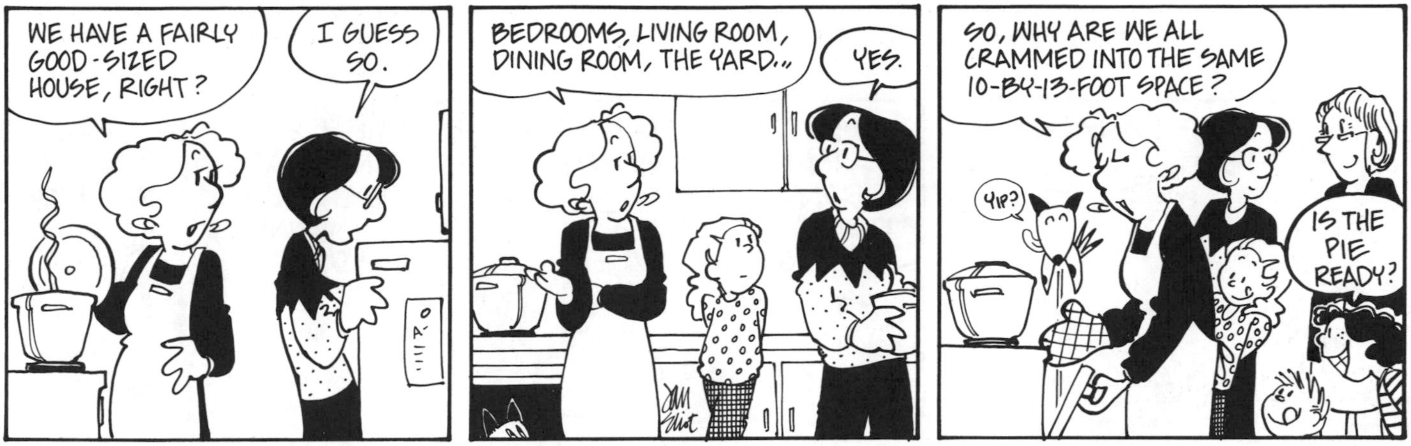
WE HAVE A FAIRLY GOOD-SIZED HOUSE, RIGHT?
I GUESS SO.
BEDROOMS, LIVING ROOM, DINING ROOM, THE YARD...
YES.
SO, WHY ARE WE ALL CRAMMED INTO THE SAME 10-BY-13-FOOT SPACE?
YIP?
IS THE PIE READY?

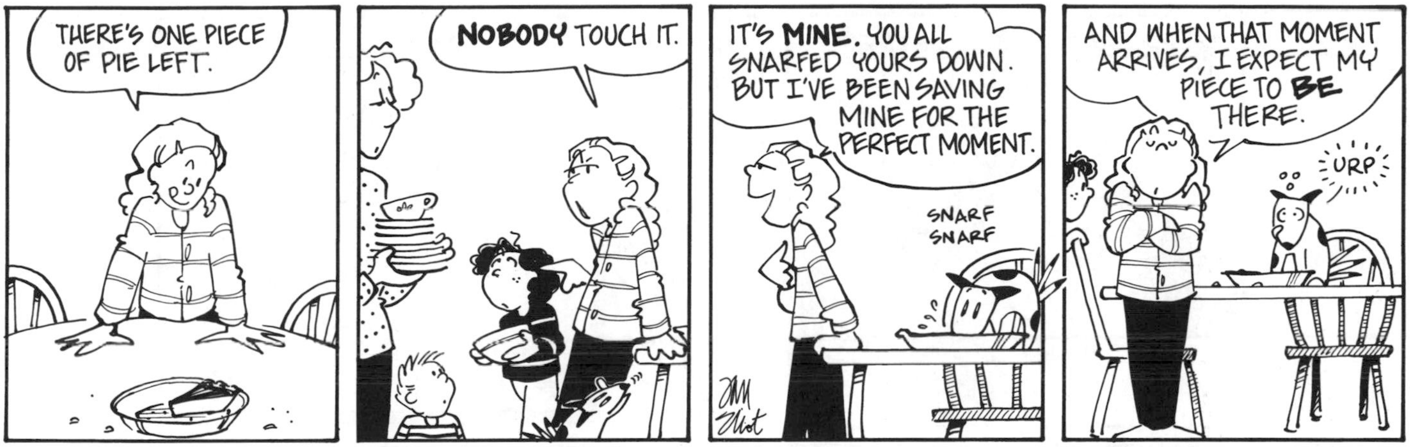
THERE'S ONE PIECE OF PIE LEFT.
NOBODY TOUCH IT.
IT'S MINE. YOU ALL SNARFED YOURS DOWN. BUT I'VE BEEN SAVING MINE FOR THE PERFECT MOMENT.
SNARF SNARF
AND WHEN THAT MOMENT ARRIVES, I EXPECT MY PIECE TO BE THERE.
URP

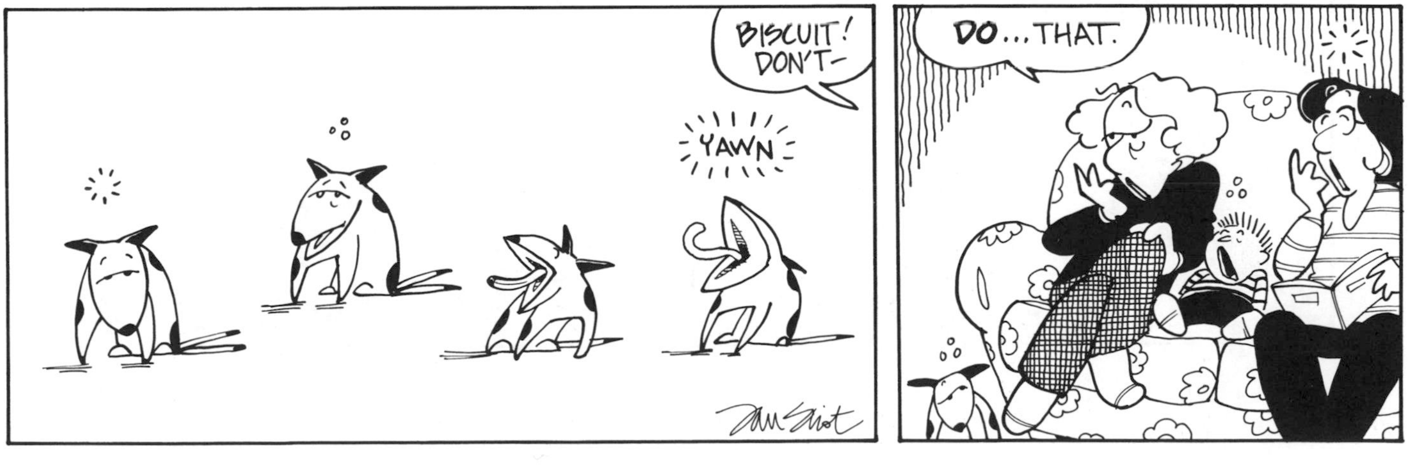
BISCUIT! DON'T-
YAWN
DO... THAT.

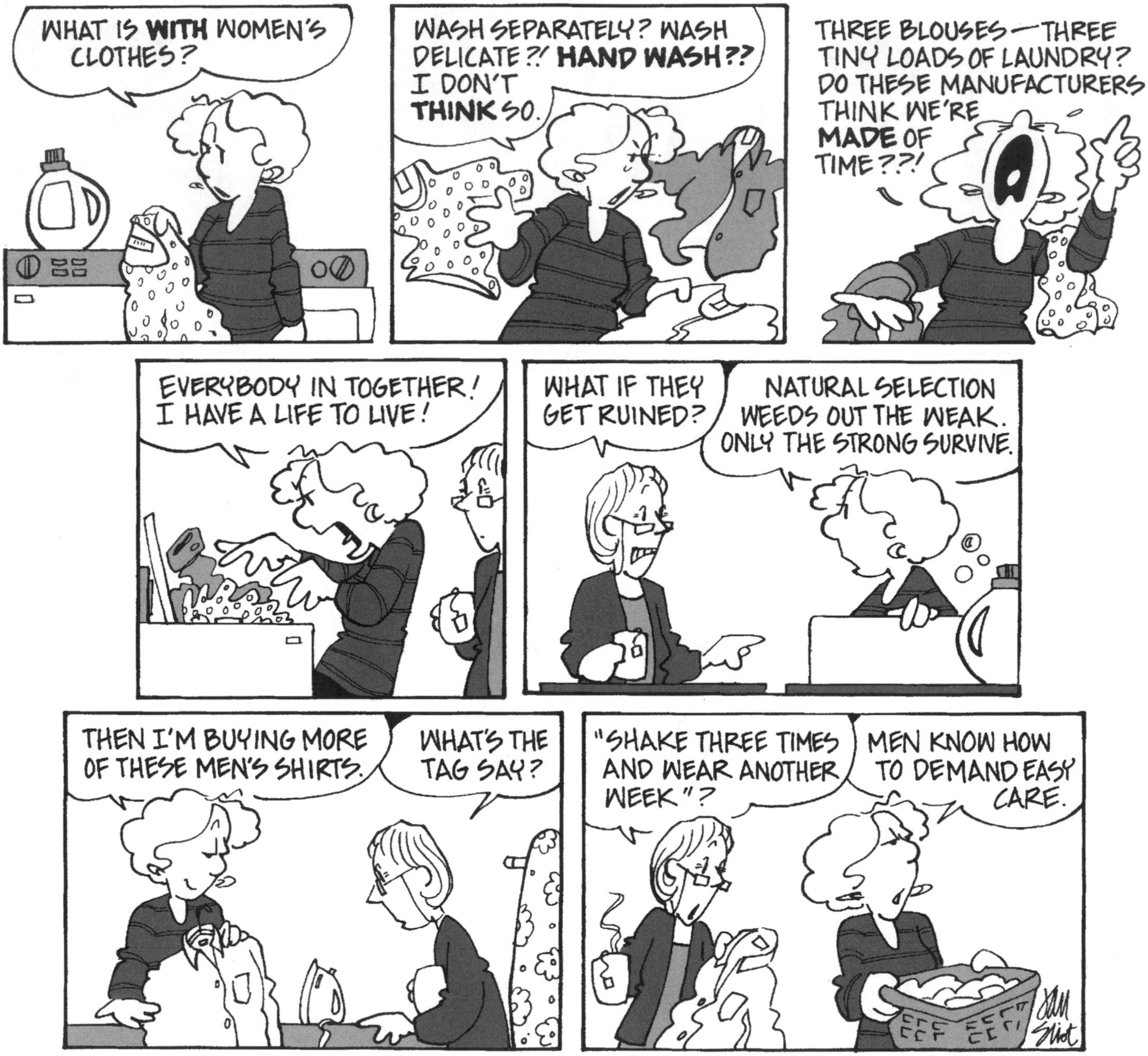
WHAT IS **WITH** WOMEN'S CLOTHES?
WASH SEPARATELY? WASH DELICATE?! **HAND WASH??** I DON'T **THINK** SO.
THREE BLOUSES — THREE TINY LOADS OF LAUNDRY? DO THESE MANUFACTURERS THINK WE'RE **MADE** OF TIME??!
EVERYBODY IN TOGETHER! I HAVE A LIFE TO LIVE!
WHAT IF THEY GET RUINED?
NATURAL SELECTION WEEDS OUT THE WEAK. ONLY THE STRONG SURVIVE.
THEN I'M BUYING MORE OF THESE MEN'S SHIRTS.
WHAT'S THE TAG SAY?
"SHAKE THREE TIMES AND WEAR ANOTHER WEEK"?
MEN KNOW HOW TO DEMAND EASY CARE.

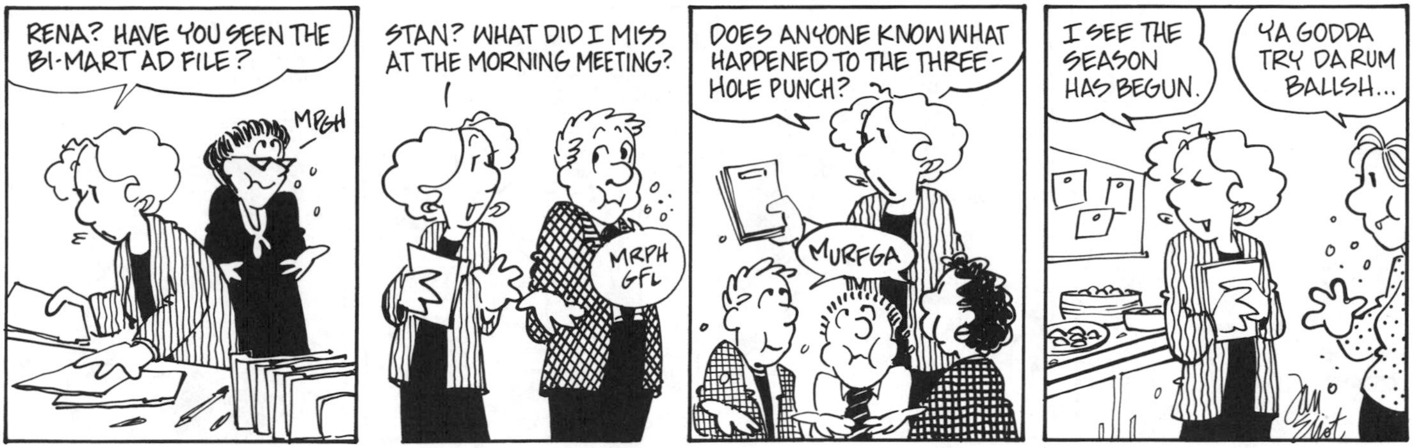
RENA? HAVE YOU SEEN THE BI-MART AD FILE?
MPGH
STAN? WHAT DID I MISS AT THE MORNING MEETING?
MRPH GFL
DOES ANYONE KNOW WHAT HAPPENED TO THE THREE-HOLE PUNCH?
MURFGA
I SEE THE SEASON HAS BEGUN.
YA GODDA TRY DA RUM BALLSH...

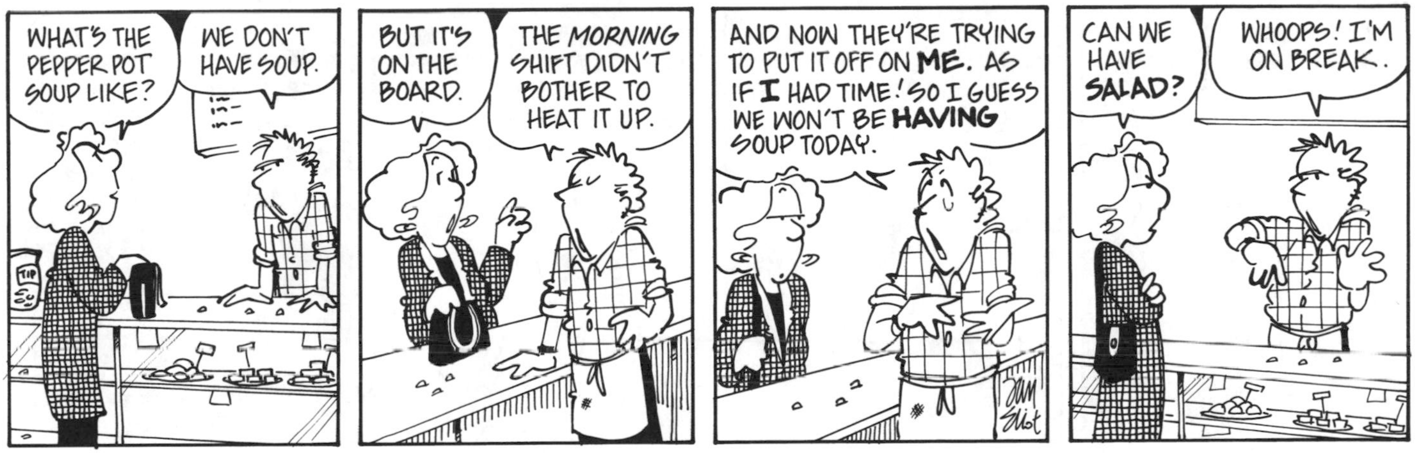
WHAT'S THE PEPPER POT SOUP LIKE?
WE DON'T HAVE SOUP.
BUT IT'S ON THE BOARD.
THE MORNING SHIFT DIDN'T BOTHER TO HEAT IT UP.
AND NOW THEY'RE TRYING TO PUT IT OFF ON ME. AS IF I HAD TIME! SO I GUESS WE WON'T BE HAVING SOUP TODAY.
CAN WE HAVE SALAD?
WHOOPS! I'M ON BREAK.

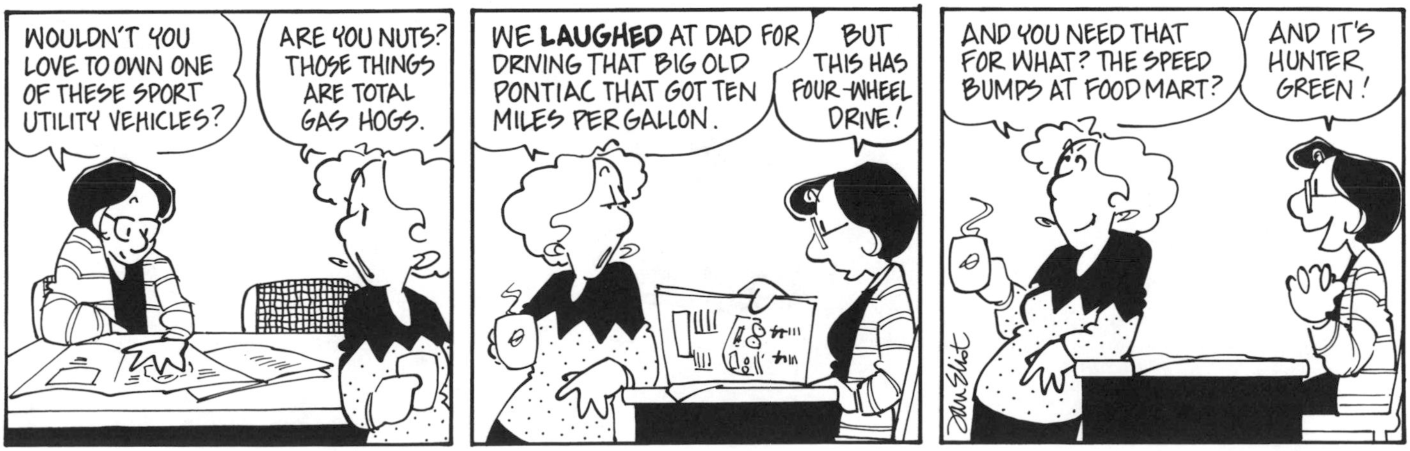
WOULDN'T YOU LOVE TO OWN ONE OF THESE SPORT UTILITY VEHICLES?
ARE YOU NUTS? THOSE THINGS ARE TOTAL GAS HOGS.
WE LAUGHED AT DAD FOR DRIVING THAT BIG OLD PONTIAC THAT GOT TEN MILES PER GALLON.
BUT THIS HAS FOUR-WHEEL DRIVE!
AND YOU NEED THAT FOR WHAT? THE SPEED BUMPS AT FOOD MART?
AND IT'S HUNTER GREEN!

WHAT DO YOU THINK ABOUT THIS MIDDLE SCHOOL TEACHER?

HM?

SOME OF THE PARENTS THINK HIS LIFESTYLE IS TOO "ALTERNATIVE." THEY DON'T THINK HE SHOULD BE AROUND THEIR CHILDREN.

SLAM @ ☆ ! # ☆ !

I THINK THEY SHOULD KISS THE FEET OF ANYONE WHO'S WILLING....

STOMP STOMP

I'LL PICK YOU UP RIGHT HERE AFTER THE MOVIE.

I'M SORRY, MA'AM. THEY CAN'T SEE THIS ONE.

NOW SHOWING

WHY NOT?

IT HAS ...NUDITY. THEY CAN SEE THE MOVIE IN THEATER TWO.

HOW CAN **THAT** MOVIE HAVE A LOWER RATING?! IT HAS VIOLENCE, CRUELTY, GUNS, BOMBS, DISMEMBERMENT....

BUT NO *NUDITY.* WE HAVE TO PROTECT THEM.

TWO TICKETS TO SEE THE GUY GET HIS HEAD BLOWN OFF, PLEASE.

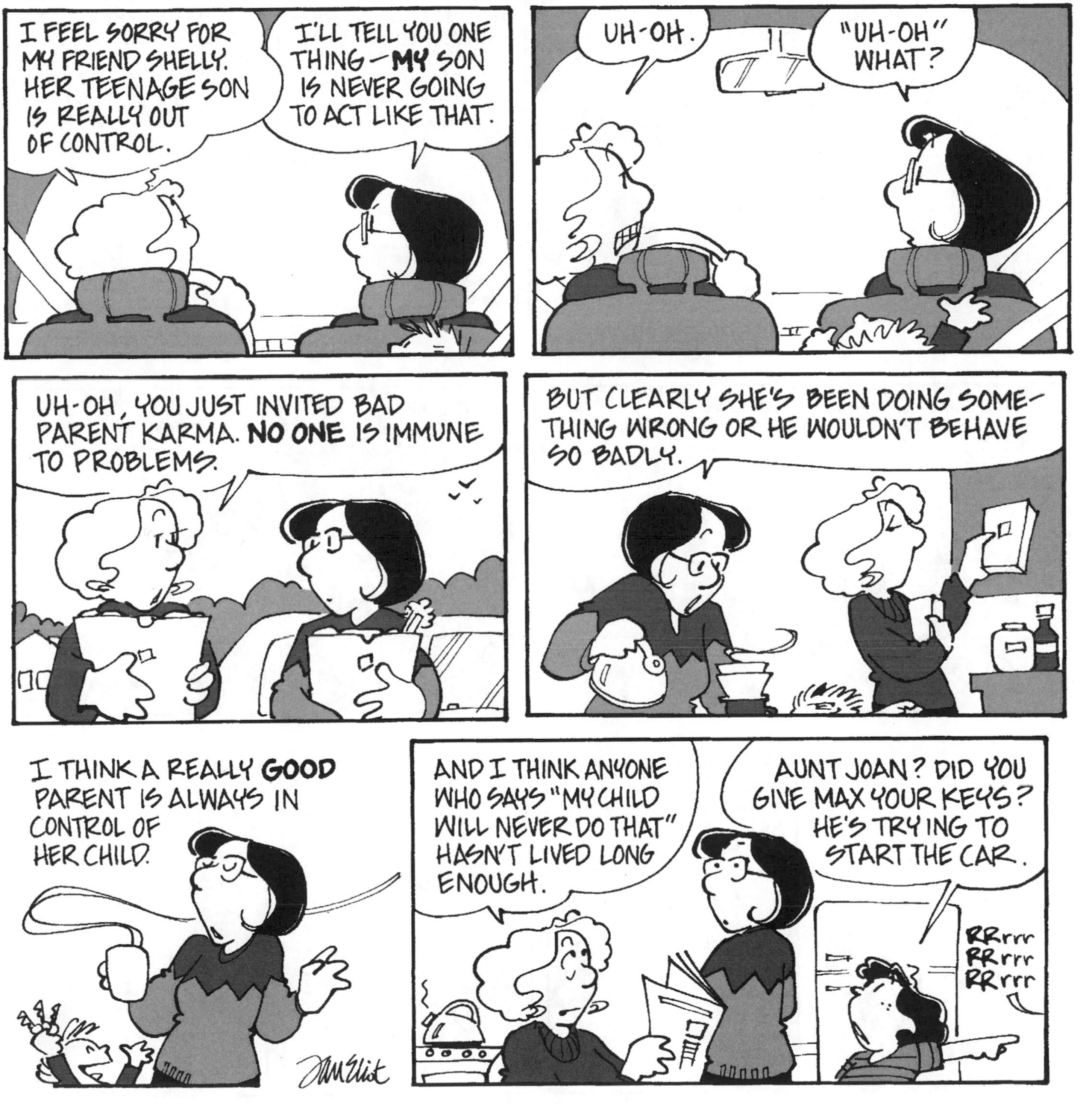
I FEEL SORRY FOR MY FRIEND SHELLY. HER TEENAGE SON IS REALLY OUT OF CONTROL.
I'LL TELL YOU ONE THING—**MY** SON IS NEVER GOING TO ACT LIKE THAT.
UH-OH.
"UH-OH" WHAT?
UH-OH, YOU JUST INVITED BAD PARENT KARMA. **NO ONE** IS IMMUNE TO PROBLEMS.
BUT CLEARLY SHE'S BEEN DOING SOMETHING WRONG OR HE WOULDN'T BEHAVE SO BADLY.
I THINK A REALLY **GOOD** PARENT IS ALWAYS IN CONTROL OF HER CHILD.
AND I THINK ANYONE WHO SAYS "MY CHILD WILL NEVER DO THAT" HASN'T LIVED LONG ENOUGH.
AUNT JOAN? DID YOU GIVE MAX YOUR KEYS? HE'S TRYING TO START THE CAR.
RRrrr RRrrr RRrrr

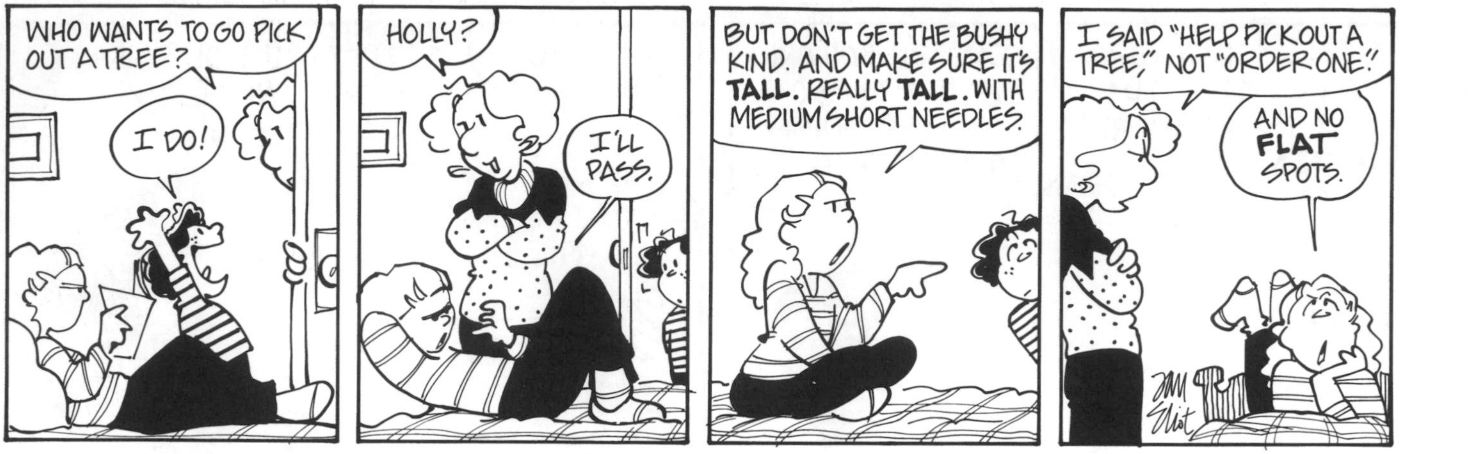
WHO WANTS TO GO PICK OUT A TREE?
I DO!
HOLLY?
I'LL PASS.
BUT DON'T GET THE BUSHY KIND. AND MAKE SURE IT'S **TALL.** REALLY **TALL.** WITH MEDIUM SHORT NEEDLES.
I SAID "HELP PICK OUT A TREE," NOT "ORDER ONE."
AND NO **FLAT** SPOTS.

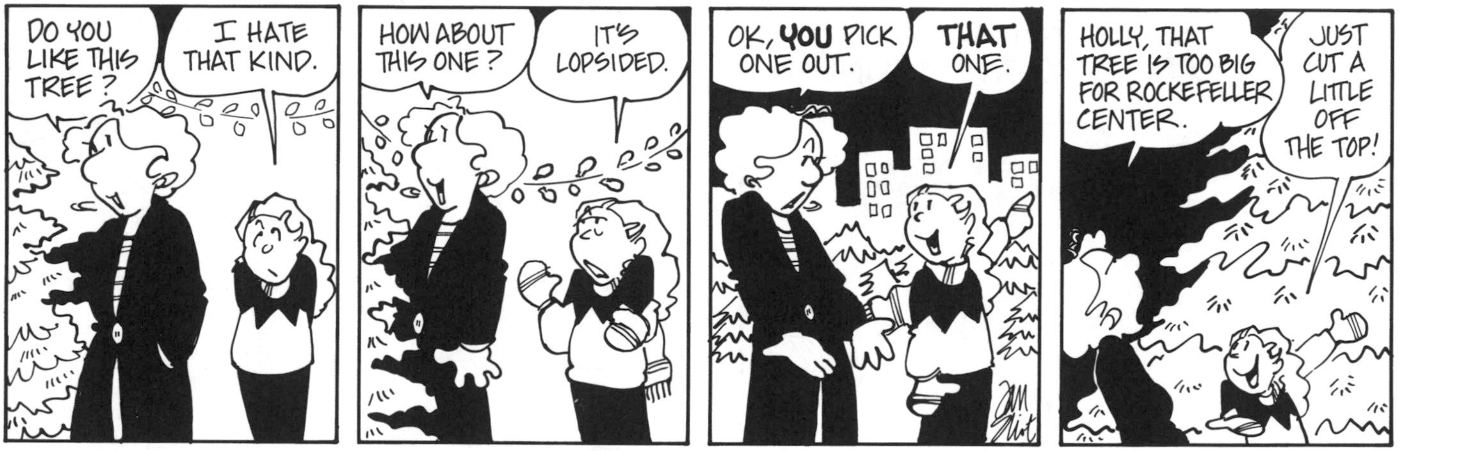
DO YOU LIKE THIS TREE?
I HATE THAT KIND.
HOW ABOUT THIS ONE?
IT'S LOPSIDED.
OK, **YOU** PICK ONE OUT.
THAT ONE.
HOLLY, THAT TREE IS TOO BIG FOR ROCKEFELLER CENTER.
JUST CUT A LITTLE OFF THE TOP!

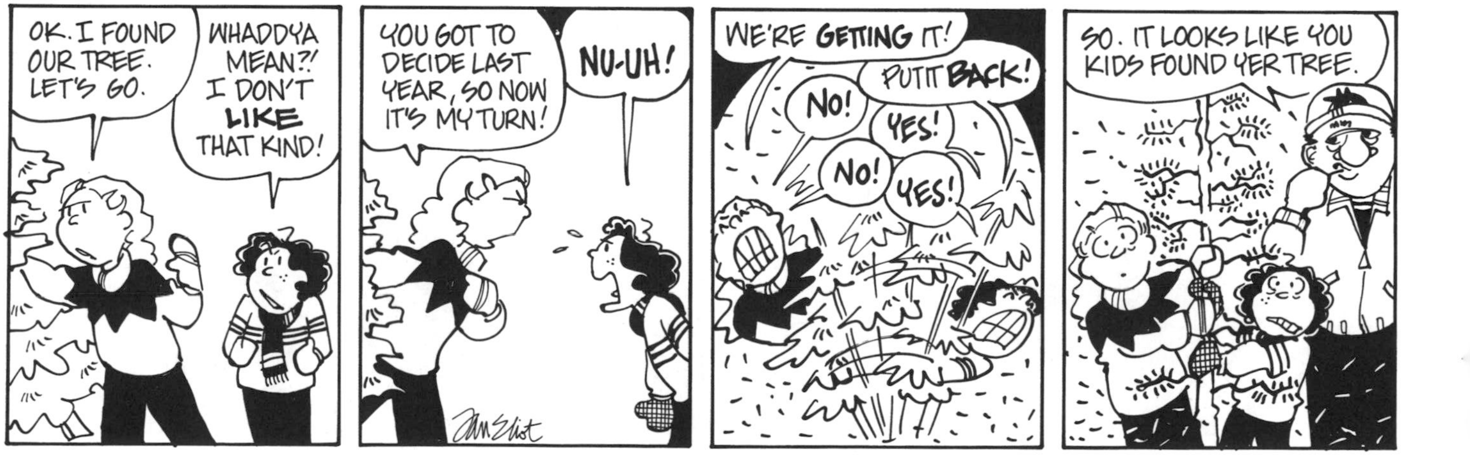
OK. I FOUND OUR TREE. LET'S GO.
WHADDYA MEAN?! I DON'T **LIKE** THAT KIND!
YOU GOT TO DECIDE LAST YEAR, SO NOW IT'S MY TURN!
NU-UH!
WE'RE **GETTING** IT!
PUT IT **BACK**!
NO!
YES!
NO!
YES!
SO. IT LOOKS LIKE YOU KIDS FOUND YER TREE.

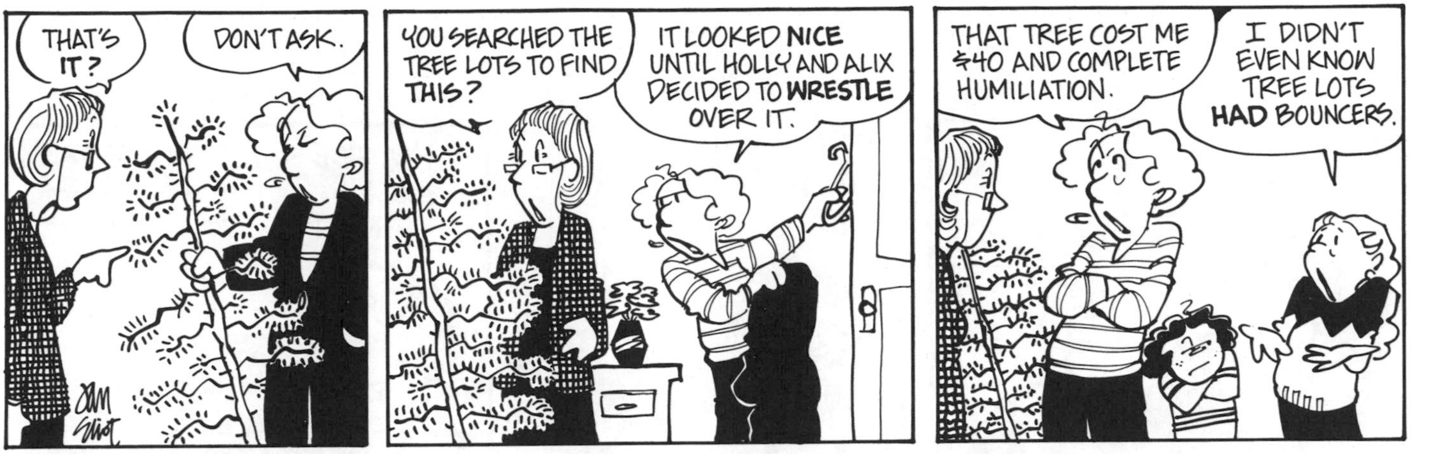
THAT'S IT?
DON'T ASK.
YOU SEARCHED THE TREE LOTS TO FIND THIS?
IT LOOKED NICE UNTIL HOLLY AND ALIX DECIDED TO WRESTLE OVER IT.
THAT TREE COST ME $40 AND COMPLETE HUMILIATION.
I DIDN'T EVEN KNOW TREE LOTS HAD BOUNCERS.

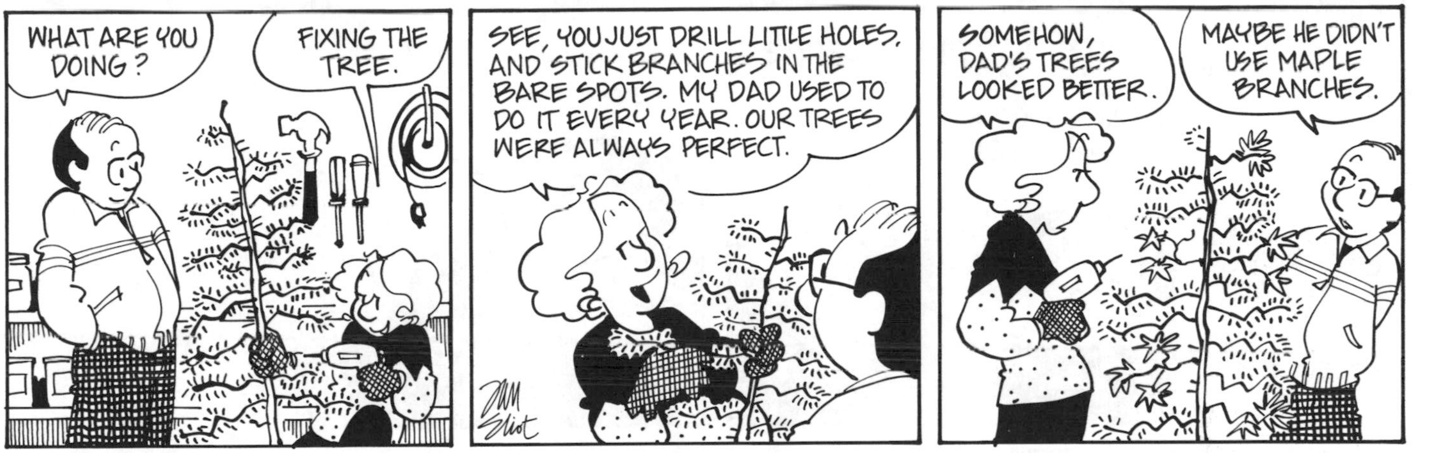
WHAT ARE YOU DOING?
FIXING THE TREE.
SEE, YOU JUST DRILL LITTLE HOLES, AND STICK BRANCHES IN THE BARE SPOTS. MY DAD USED TO DO IT EVERY YEAR. OUR TREES WERE ALWAYS PERFECT.
SOMEHOW, DAD'S TREES LOOKED BETTER.
MAYBE HE DIDN'T USE MAPLE BRANCHES.

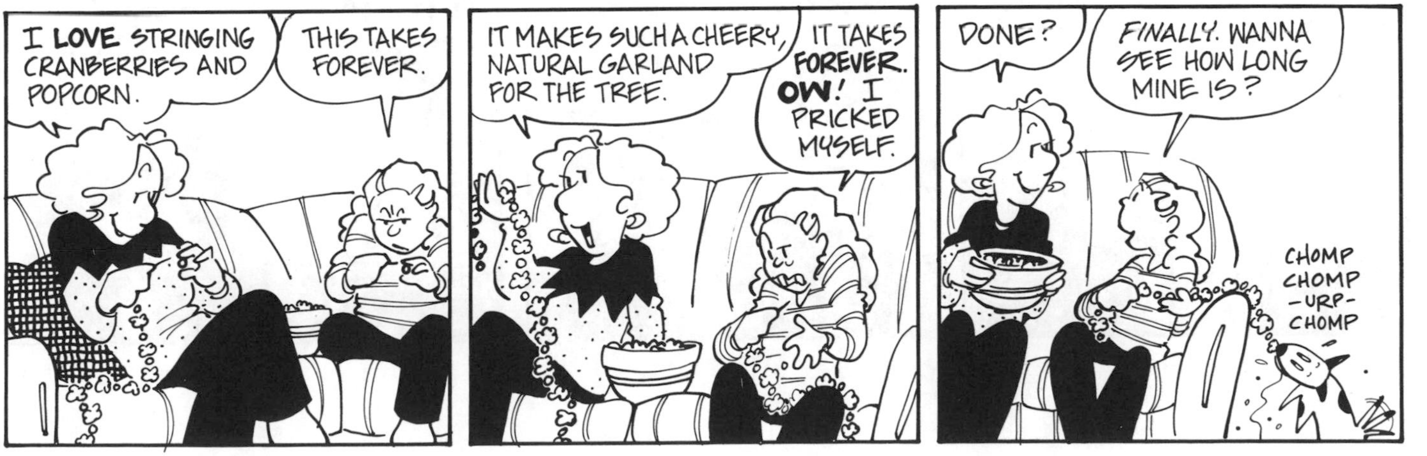
I LOVE STRINGING CRANBERRIES AND POPCORN.
THIS TAKES FOREVER.
IT MAKES SUCH A CHEERY, NATURAL GARLAND FOR THE TREE.
IT TAKES FOREVER. OW! I PRICKED MYSELF.
DONE?
FINALLY. WANNA SEE HOW LONG MINE IS?
CHOMP
CHOMP
-URP-
CHOMP

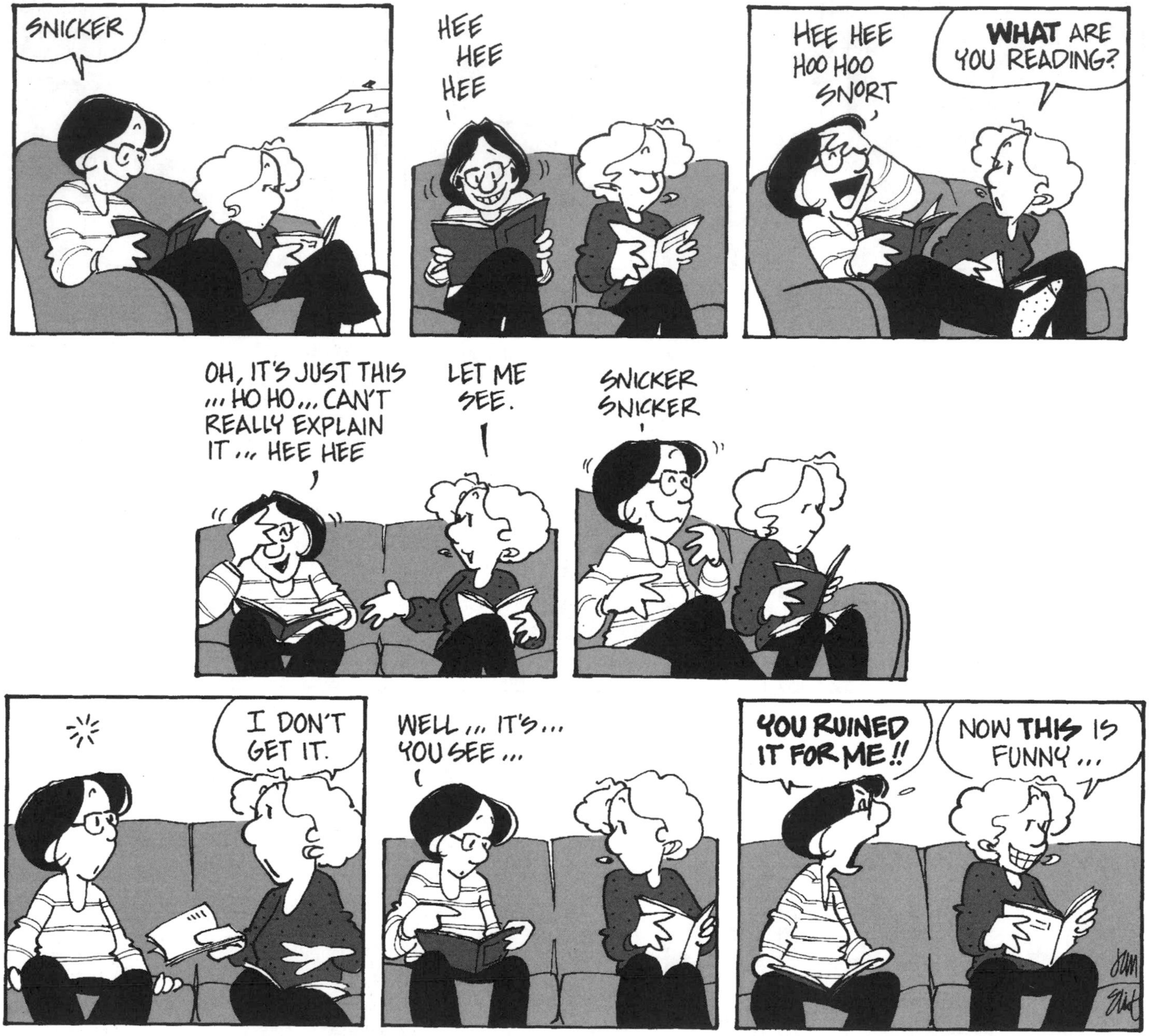
SNICKER
HEE HEE HEE
HEE HEE HOO HOO SNORT
WHAT ARE YOU READING?
OH, IT'S JUST THIS ... HO HO ... CAN'T REALLY EXPLAIN IT ... HEE HEE
LET ME SEE.
SNICKER SNICKER
I DON'T GET IT.
WELL ... IT'S ... YOU SEE ...
YOU RUINED IT FOR ME!!
NOW THIS IS FUNNY ...

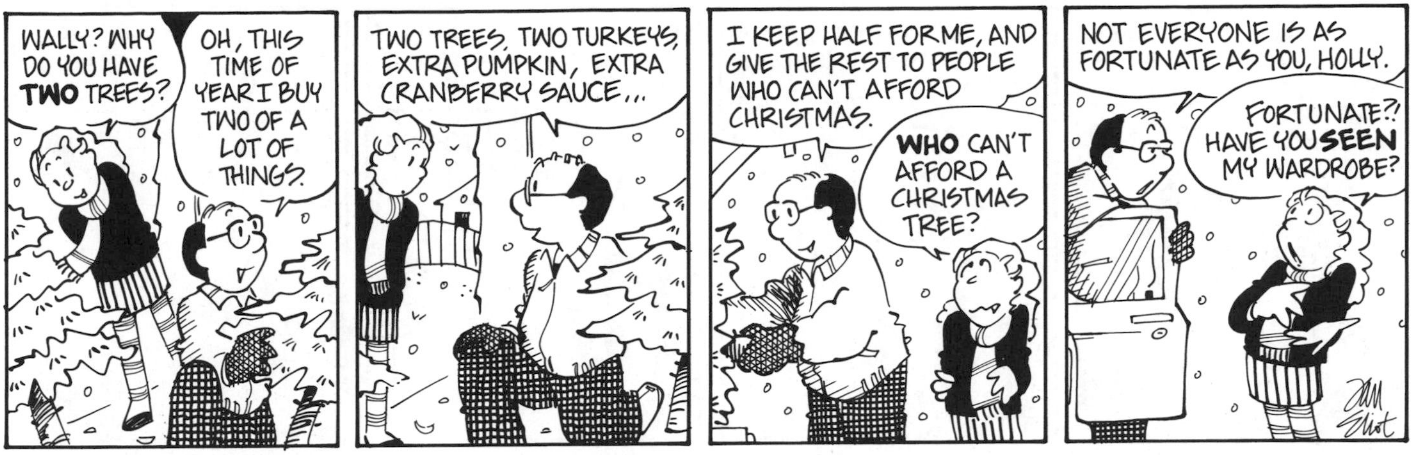
WALLY? WHY DO YOU HAVE **TWO** TREES?
OH, THIS TIME OF YEAR I BUY TWO OF A LOT OF THINGS.
TWO TREES, TWO TURKEYS, EXTRA PUMPKIN, EXTRA CRANBERRY SAUCE...
I KEEP HALF FOR ME, AND GIVE THE REST TO PEOPLE WHO CAN'T AFFORD CHRISTMAS.
WHO CAN'T AFFORD A CHRISTMAS TREE?
NOT EVERYONE IS AS FORTUNATE AS YOU, HOLLY.
FORTUNATE?! HAVE YOU **SEEN** MY WARDROBE?

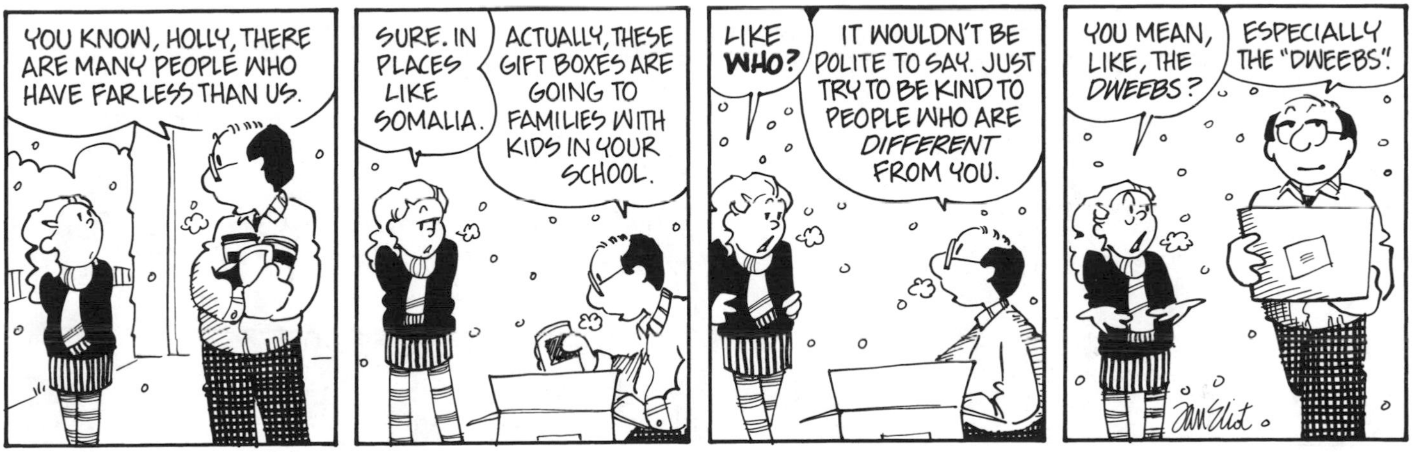
YOU KNOW, HOLLY, THERE ARE MANY PEOPLE WHO HAVE FAR LESS THAN US.
SURE. IN PLACES LIKE SOMALIA.
ACTUALLY, THESE GIFT BOXES ARE GOING TO FAMILIES WITH KIDS IN YOUR SCHOOL.
LIKE **WHO?**
IT WOULDN'T BE POLITE TO SAY. JUST TRY TO BE KIND TO PEOPLE WHO ARE *DIFFERENT* FROM YOU.
YOU MEAN, LIKE, THE *DWEEBS*?
ESPECIALLY THE "DWEEBS".

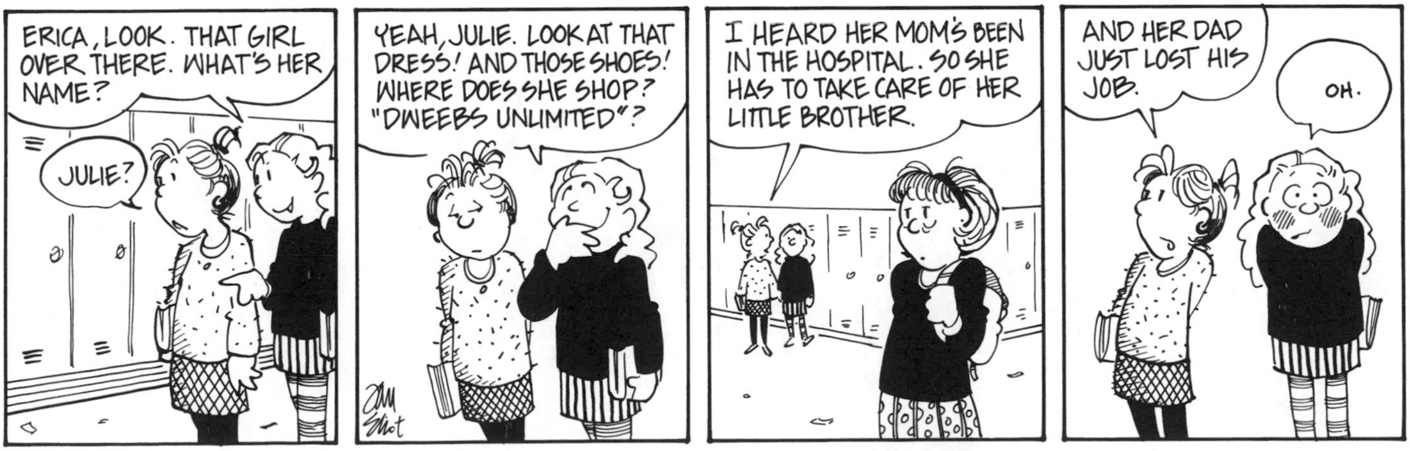
ERICA, LOOK. THAT GIRL OVER THERE. WHAT'S HER NAME?
JULIE?
YEAH, JULIE. LOOK AT THAT DRESS! AND THOSE SHOES! WHERE DOES SHE SHOP? "DWEEBS UNLIMITED"?
I HEARD HER MOM'S BEEN IN THE HOSPITAL. SO SHE HAS TO TAKE CARE OF HER LITTLE BROTHER.
AND HER DAD JUST LOST HIS JOB.
OH.

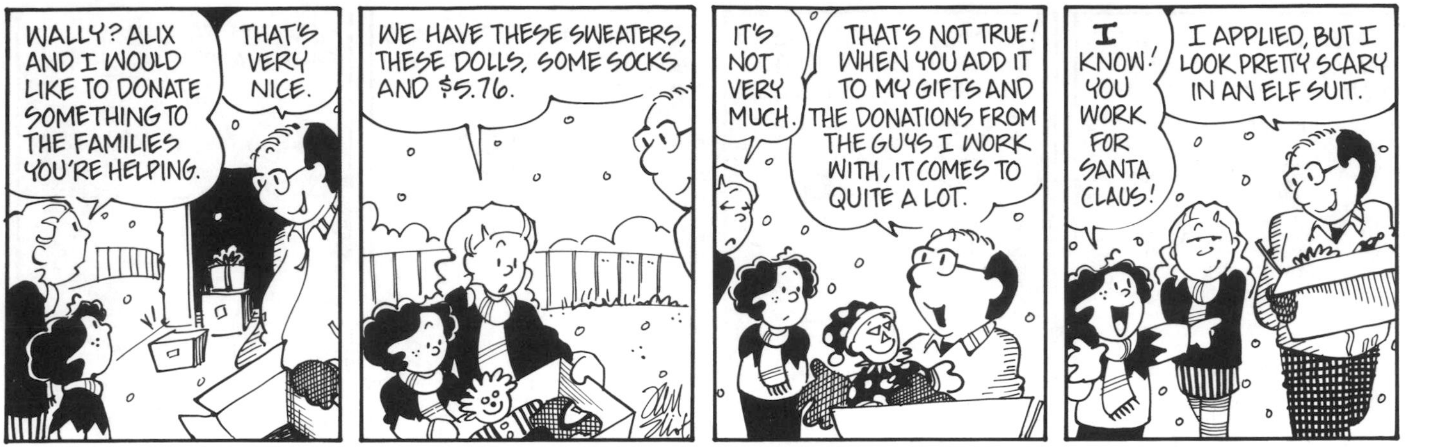
WALLY? ALIX AND I WOULD LIKE TO DONATE SOMETHING TO THE FAMILIES YOU'RE HELPING.
THAT'S VERY NICE.
WE HAVE THESE SWEATERS, THESE DOLLS, SOME SOCKS AND $5.76.
IT'S NOT VERY MUCH.
THAT'S NOT TRUE! WHEN YOU ADD IT TO MY GIFTS AND THE DONATIONS FROM THE GUYS I WORK WITH, IT COMES TO QUITE A LOT.
I KNOW! YOU WORK FOR SANTA CLAUS!
I APPLIED, BUT I LOOK PRETTY SCARY IN AN ELF SUIT.

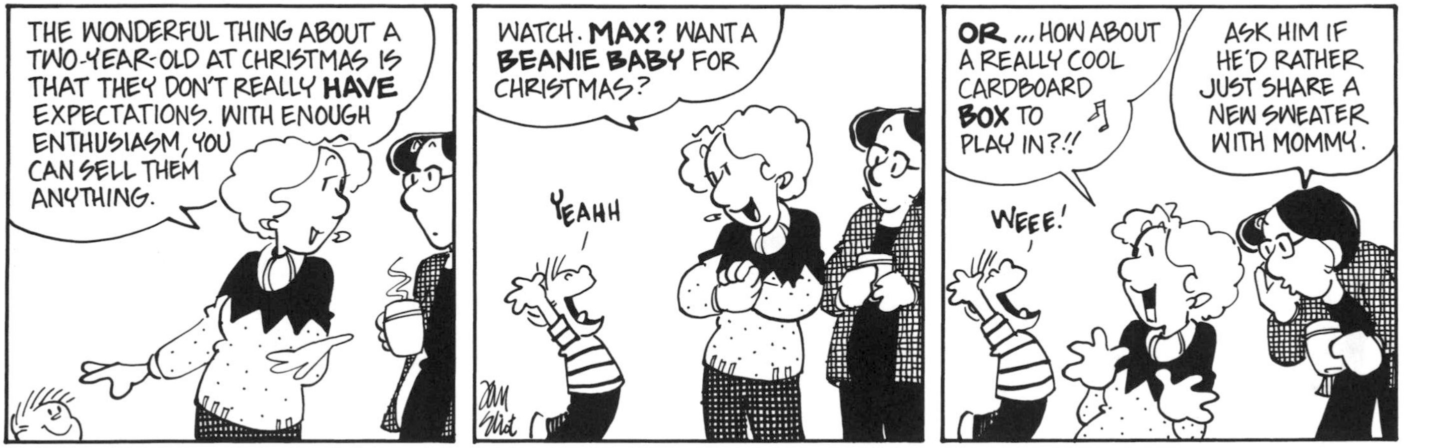
THE WONDERFUL THING ABOUT A TWO-YEAR-OLD AT CHRISTMAS IS THAT THEY DON'T REALLY HAVE EXPECTATIONS. WITH ENOUGH ENTHUSIASM, YOU CAN SELL THEM ANYTHING.
WATCH. MAX? WANT A BEANIE BABY FOR CHRISTMAS?
YEAHH
OR ... HOW ABOUT A REALLY COOL CARDBOARD BOX TO PLAY IN?!!
WEEE!
ASK HIM IF HE'D RATHER JUST SHARE A NEW SWEATER WITH MOMMY.

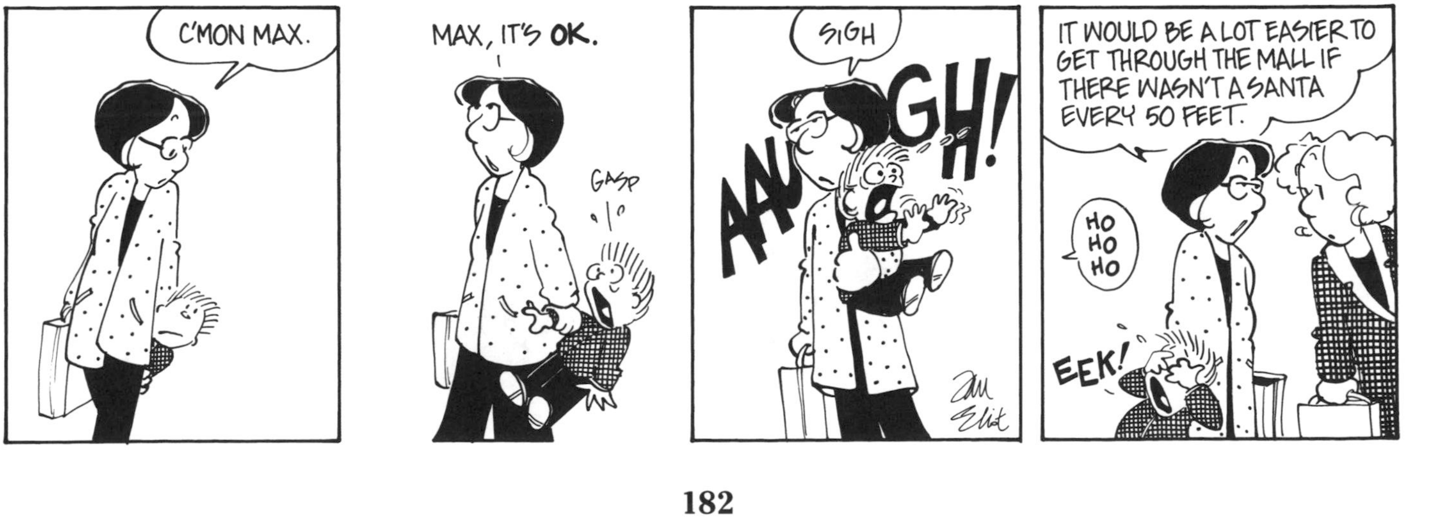
C'MON MAX.
MAX, IT'S OK.
GASP
SIGH
AAUGH!
IT WOULD BE A LOT EASIER TO GET THROUGH THE MALL IF THERE WASN'T A SANTA EVERY 50 FEET.
HO HO HO
EEK!

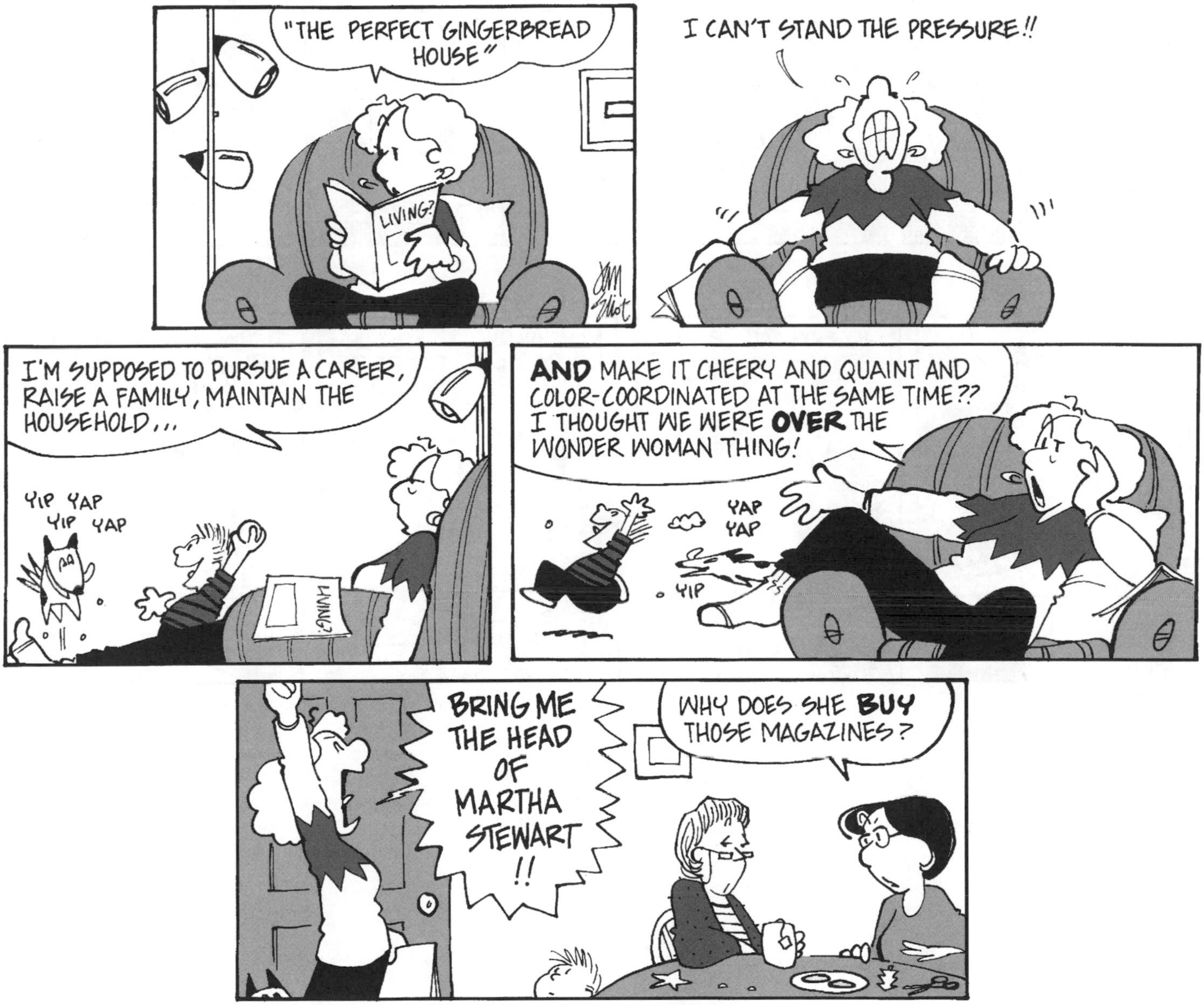
"THE PERFECT GINGERBREAD HOUSE"
LIVING?
I CAN'T STAND THE PRESSURE!!
I'M SUPPOSED TO PURSUE A CAREER, RAISE A FAMILY, MAINTAIN THE HOUSEHOLD...
YIP YAP YIP YAP
LIVING?
AND MAKE IT CHEERY AND QUAINT AND COLOR-COORDINATED AT THE SAME TIME?? I THOUGHT WE WERE OVER THE WONDER WOMAN THING!
YAP YAP
YIP
BRING ME THE HEAD OF MARTHA STEWART!!
WHY DOES SHE BUY THOSE MAGAZINES?

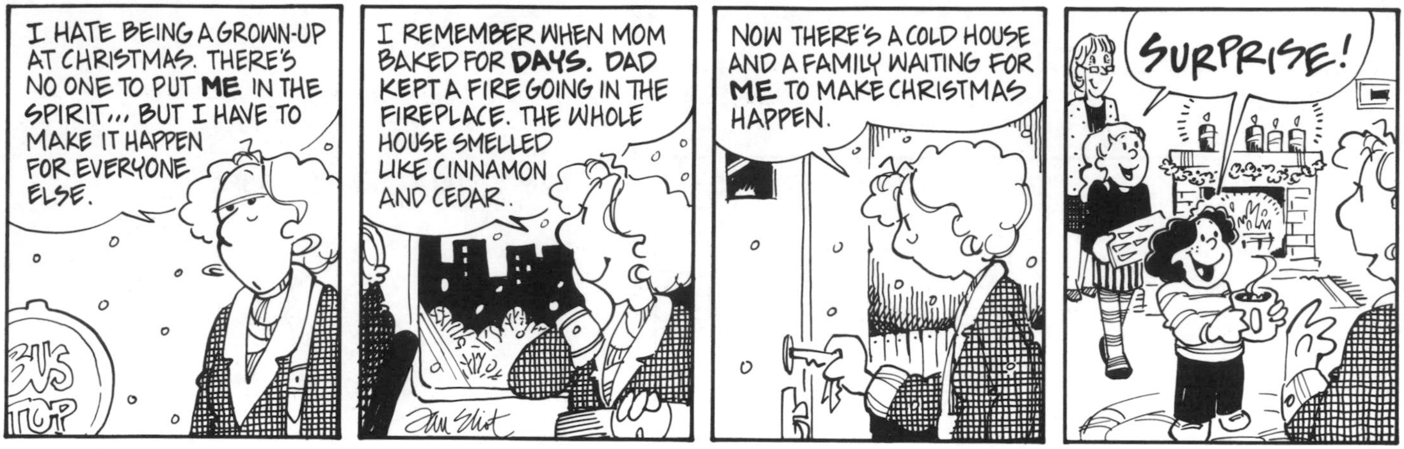
I HATE BEING A GROWN-UP AT CHRISTMAS. THERE'S NO ONE TO PUT **ME** IN THE SPIRIT... BUT I HAVE TO MAKE IT HAPPEN FOR EVERYONE ELSE.
BUS STOP
I REMEMBER WHEN MOM BAKED FOR **DAYS.** DAD KEPT A FIRE GOING IN THE FIREPLACE. THE WHOLE HOUSE SMELLED LIKE CINNAMON AND CEDAR.
NOW THERE'S A COLD HOUSE AND A FAMILY WAITING FOR **ME** TO MAKE CHRISTMAS HAPPEN.
SURPRISE!

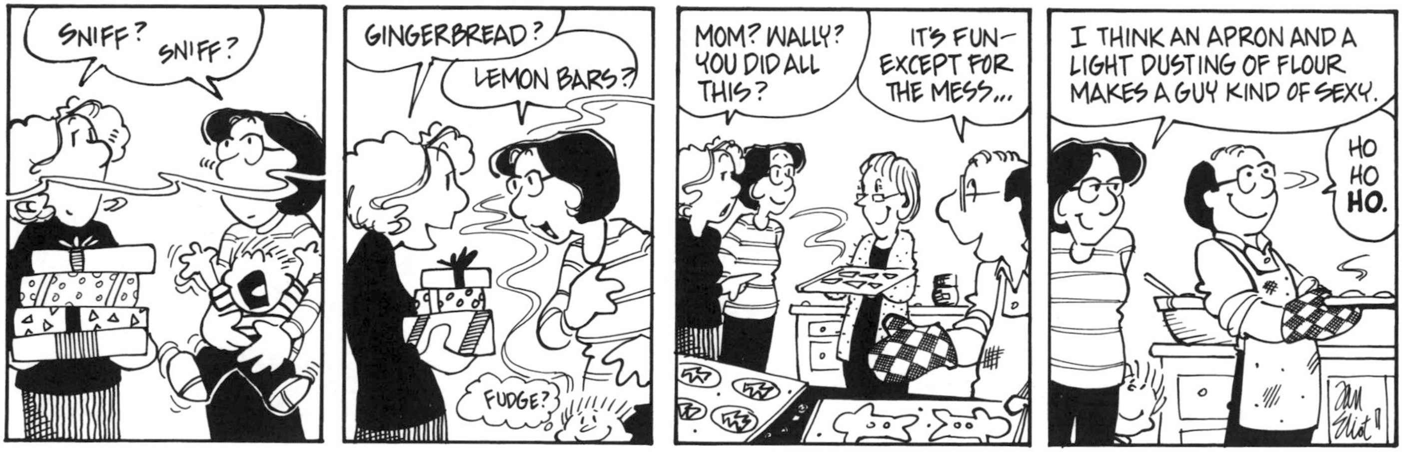
SNIFF? SNIFF?
GINGERBREAD?
LEMON BARS?
FUDGE?
MOM? WALLY? YOU DID ALL THIS?
IT'S FUN-EXCEPT FOR THE MESS...
I THINK AN APRON AND A LIGHT DUSTING OF FLOUR MAKES A GUY KIND OF SEXY.
HO HO **HO.**

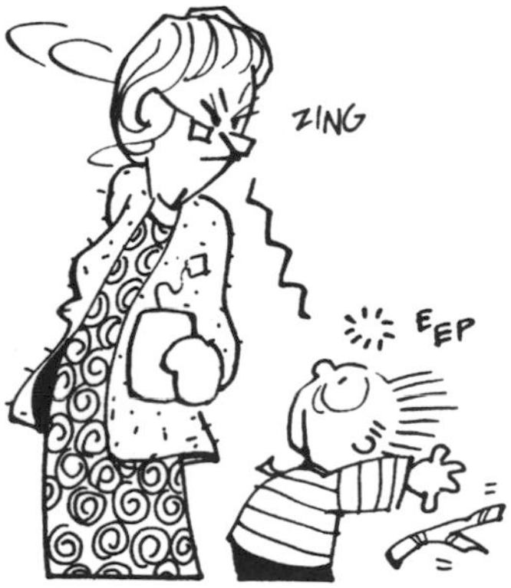
ZING
EEP

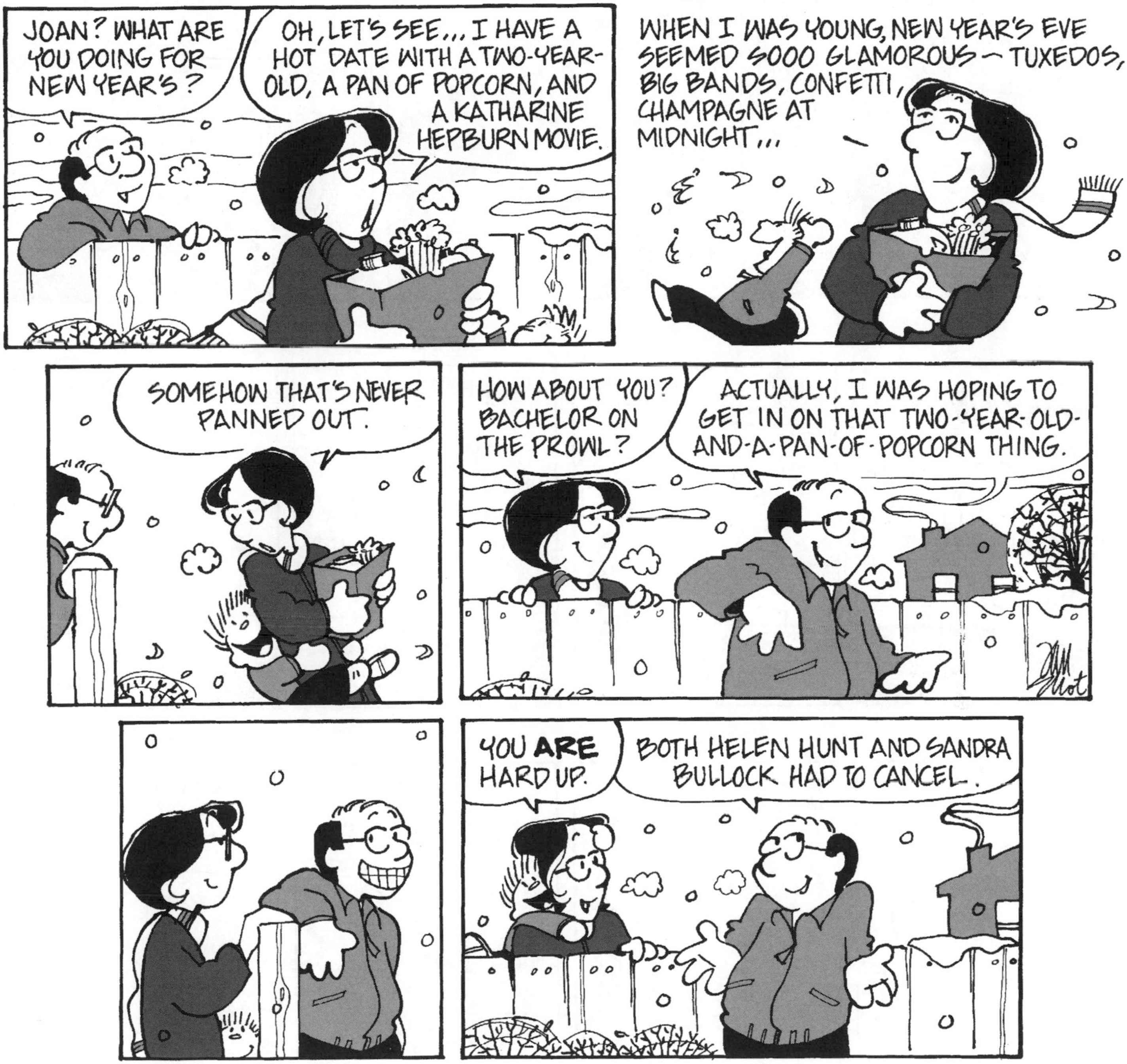
JOAN? WHAT ARE YOU DOING FOR NEW YEAR'S?
OH, LET'S SEE... I HAVE A HOT DATE WITH A TWO-YEAR-OLD, A PAN OF POPCORN, AND A KATHARINE HEPBURN MOVIE.
WHEN I WAS YOUNG, NEW YEAR'S EVE SEEMED SOOO GLAMOROUS — TUXEDOS, BIG BANDS, CONFETTI, CHAMPAGNE AT MIDNIGHT...
SOMEHOW THAT'S NEVER PANNED OUT.
HOW ABOUT YOU? BACHELOR ON THE PROWL?
ACTUALLY, I WAS HOPING TO GET IN ON THAT TWO-YEAR-OLD-AND-A-PAN-OF-POPCORN THING.
YOU **ARE** HARD UP.
BOTH HELEN HUNT AND SANDRA BULLOCK HAD TO CANCEL.

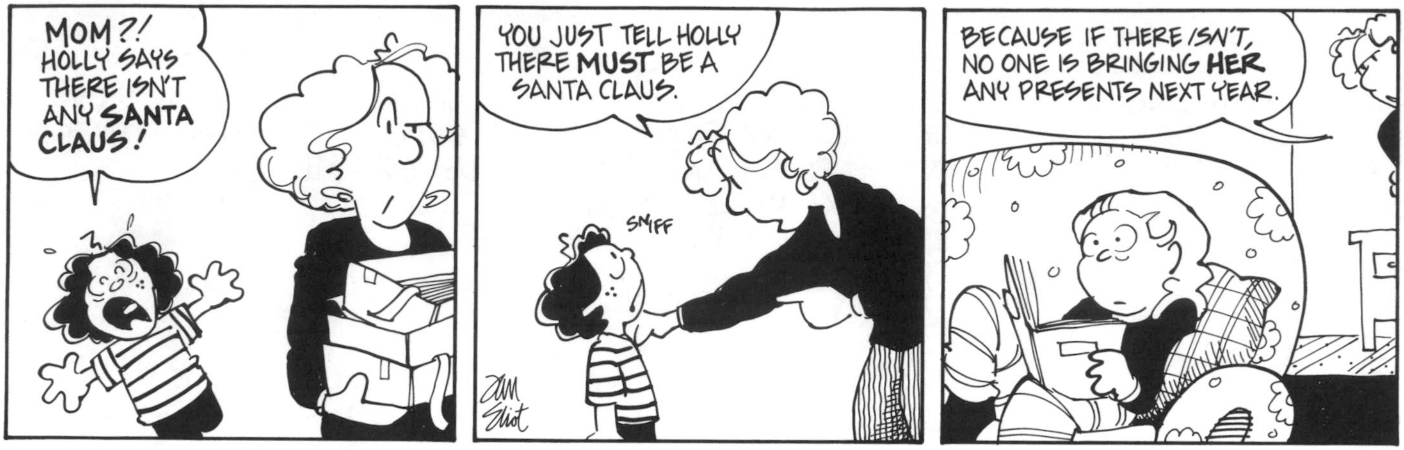
MOM?! HOLLY SAYS THERE ISN'T ANY SANTA CLAUS!
YOU JUST TELL HOLLY THERE MUST BE A SANTA CLAUS.
SNIFF
BECAUSE IF THERE ISN'T, NO ONE IS BRINGING HER ANY PRESENTS NEXT YEAR.

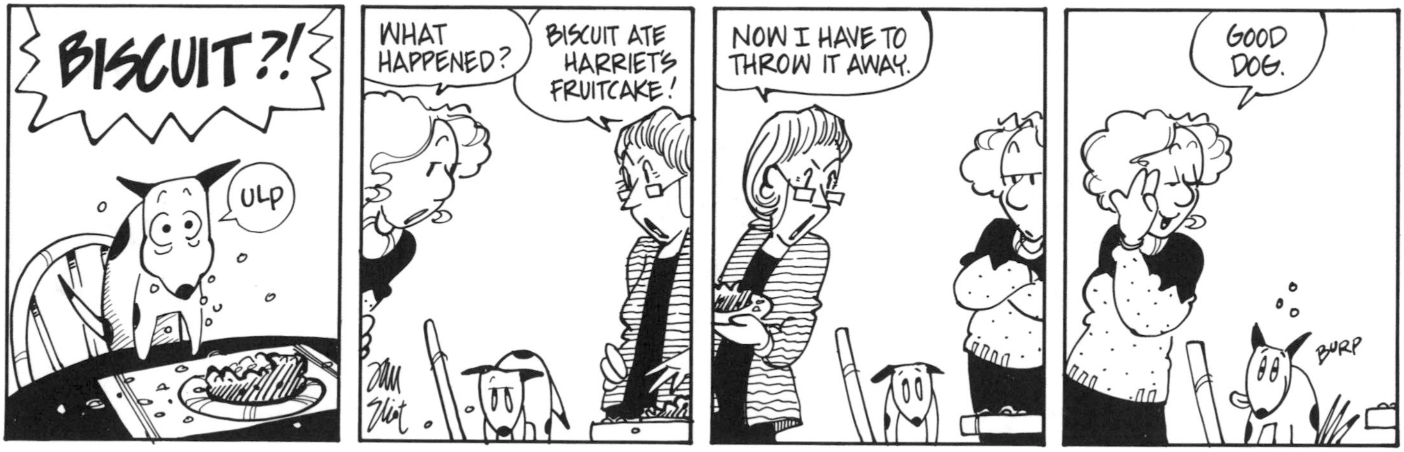
BISCUIT?!
ULP
WHAT HAPPENED?
BISCUIT ATE HARRIET'S FRUITCAKE!
NOW I HAVE TO THROW IT AWAY.
GOOD DOG.
BURP

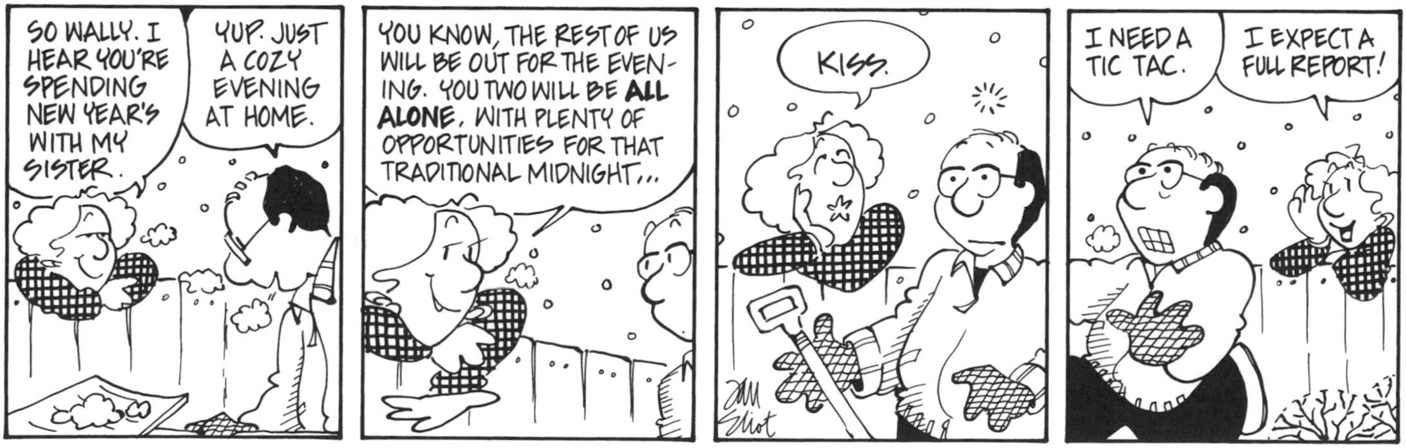
SO WALLY. I HEAR YOU'RE SPENDING NEW YEAR'S WITH MY SISTER.
YUP. JUST A COZY EVENING AT HOME.
YOU KNOW, THE REST OF US WILL BE OUT FOR THE EVENING. YOU TWO WILL BE ALL ALONE, WITH PLENTY OF OPPORTUNITIES FOR THAT TRADITIONAL MIDNIGHT...
KISS.
I NEED A TIC TAC.
I EXPECT A FULL REPORT!

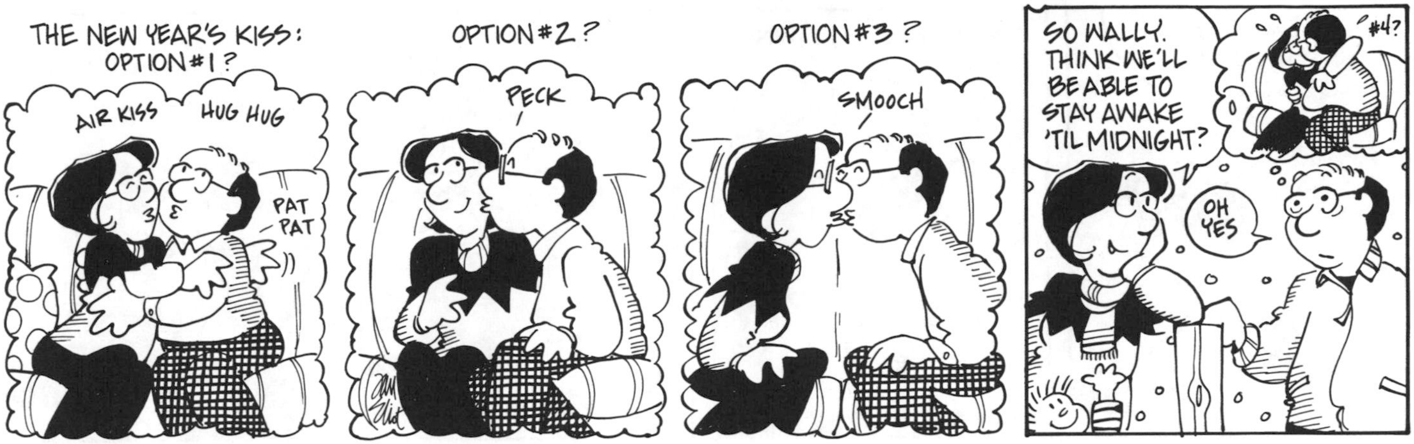
THE NEW YEAR'S KISS: OPTION #1?
AIR KISS
HUG HUG
PAT PAT
OPTION #2?
PECK
OPTION #3?
SMOOCH
SO WALLY. THINK WE'LL BE ABLE TO STAY AWAKE 'TIL MIDNIGHT?
#4?
OH YES

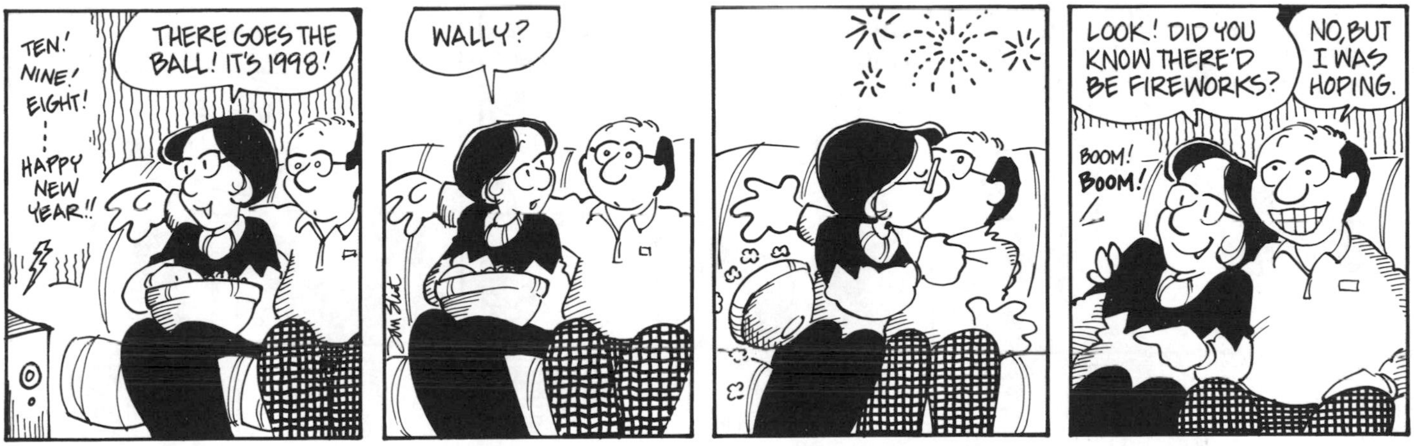
TEN! NINE! EIGHT! HAPPY NEW YEAR!!
THERE GOES THE BALL! IT'S 1998!
WALLY?
LOOK! DID YOU KNOW THERE'D BE FIREWORKS?
NO, BUT I WAS HOPING.
BOOM! BOOM!

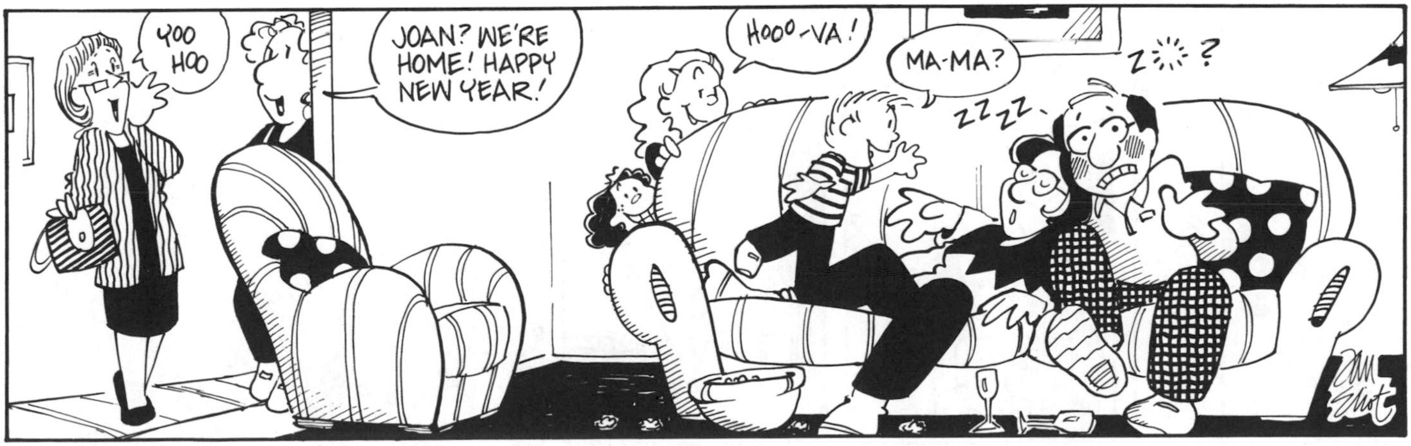
YOO HOO
JOAN? WE'RE HOME! HAPPY NEW YEAR!
HOOO-VA!
MA-MA?
ZZZZ
Z ?

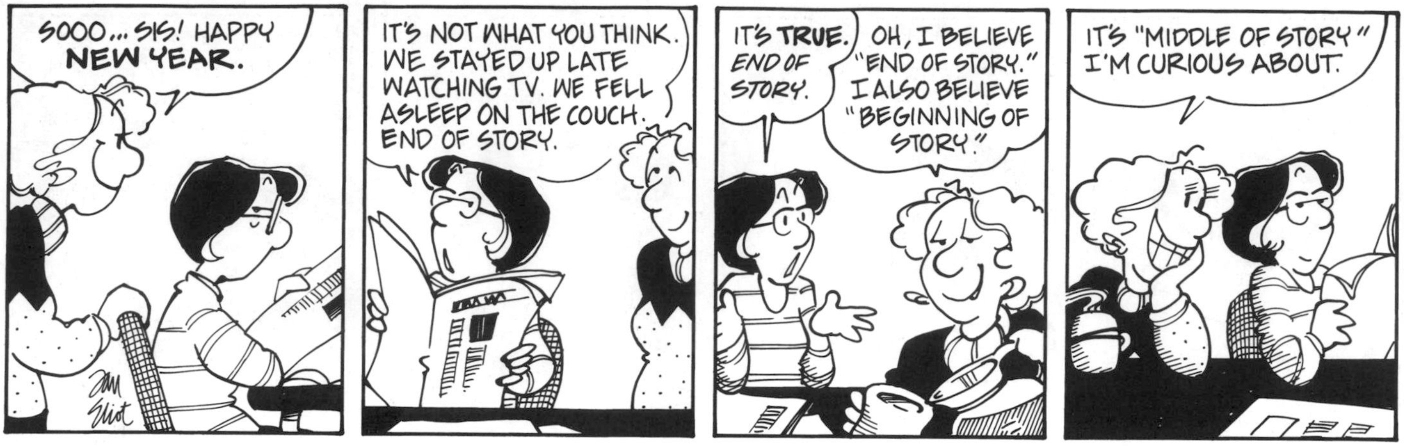
SOOO... SIS! HAPPY NEW YEAR.
IT'S NOT WHAT YOU THINK. WE STAYED UP LATE WATCHING TV. WE FELL ASLEEP ON THE COUCH. END OF STORY.
IT'S TRUE. END OF STORY.
OH, I BELIEVE "END OF STORY." I ALSO BELIEVE "BEGINNING OF STORY."
IT'S "MIDDLE OF STORY" I'M CURIOUS ABOUT.

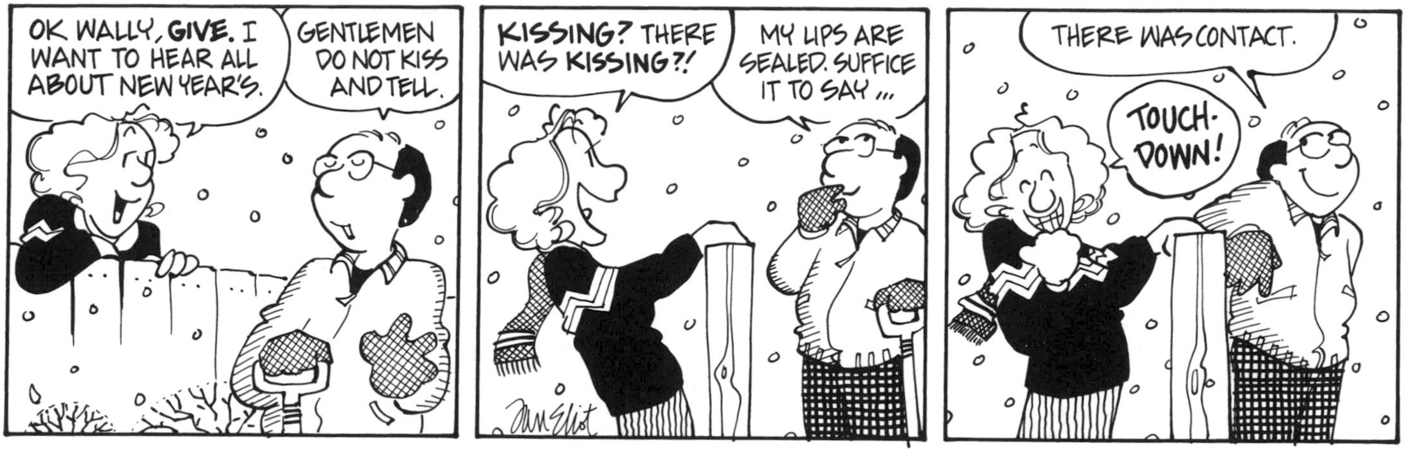
OK WALLY, GIVE. I WANT TO HEAR ALL ABOUT NEW YEAR'S.
GENTLEMEN DO NOT KISS AND TELL.
KISSING? THERE WAS KISSING?!
MY LIPS ARE SEALED. SUFFICE IT TO SAY ...
THERE WAS CONTACT.
TOUCH-DOWN!

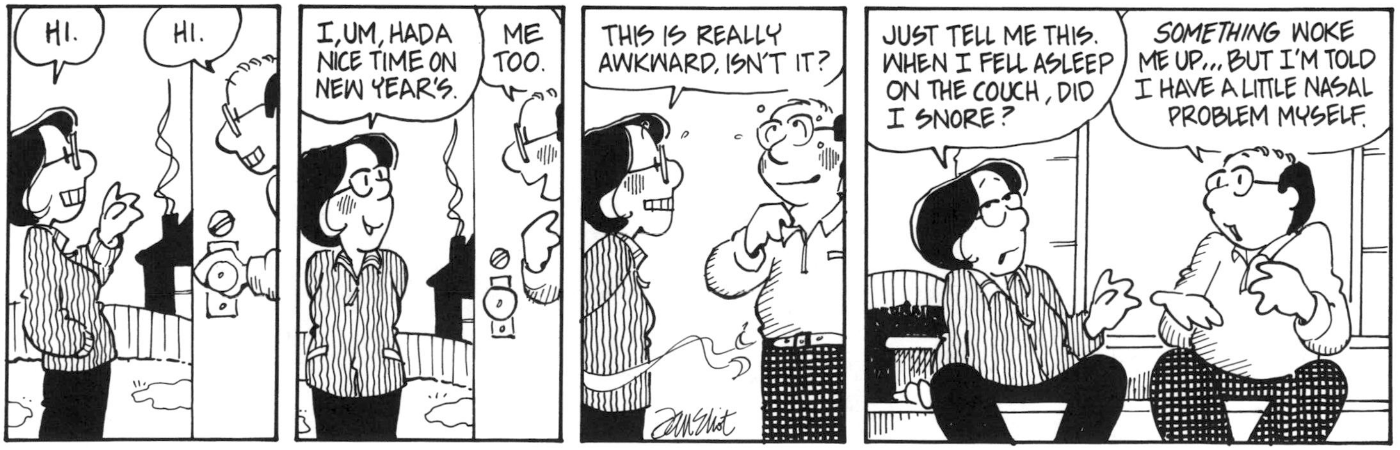
HI.
HI.
I, UM, HAD A NICE TIME ON NEW YEAR'S.
ME TOO.
THIS IS REALLY AWKWARD, ISN'T IT?
JUST TELL ME THIS. WHEN I FELL ASLEEP ON THE COUCH, DID I SNORE?
SOMETHING WOKE ME UP... BUT I'M TOLD I HAVE A LITTLE NASAL PROBLEM MYSELF.

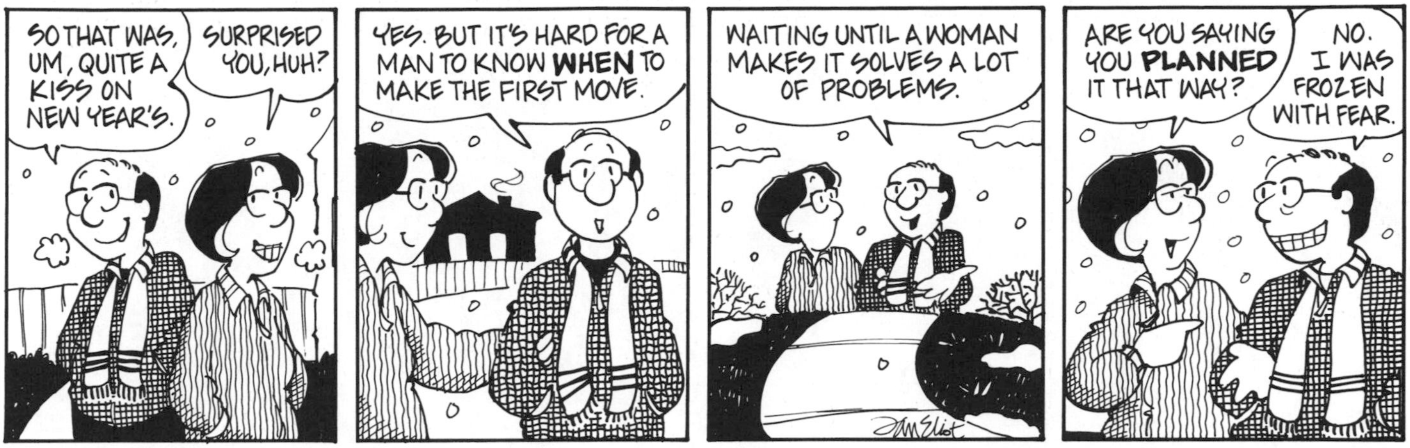
SO THAT WAS, UM, QUITE A KISS ON NEW YEAR'S.
SURPRISED YOU, HUH?
YES. BUT IT'S HARD FOR A MAN TO KNOW **WHEN** TO MAKE THE FIRST MOVE.
WAITING UNTIL A WOMAN MAKES IT SOLVES A LOT OF PROBLEMS.
ARE YOU SAYING YOU **PLANNED** IT THAT WAY?
NO. I WAS FROZEN WITH FEAR.

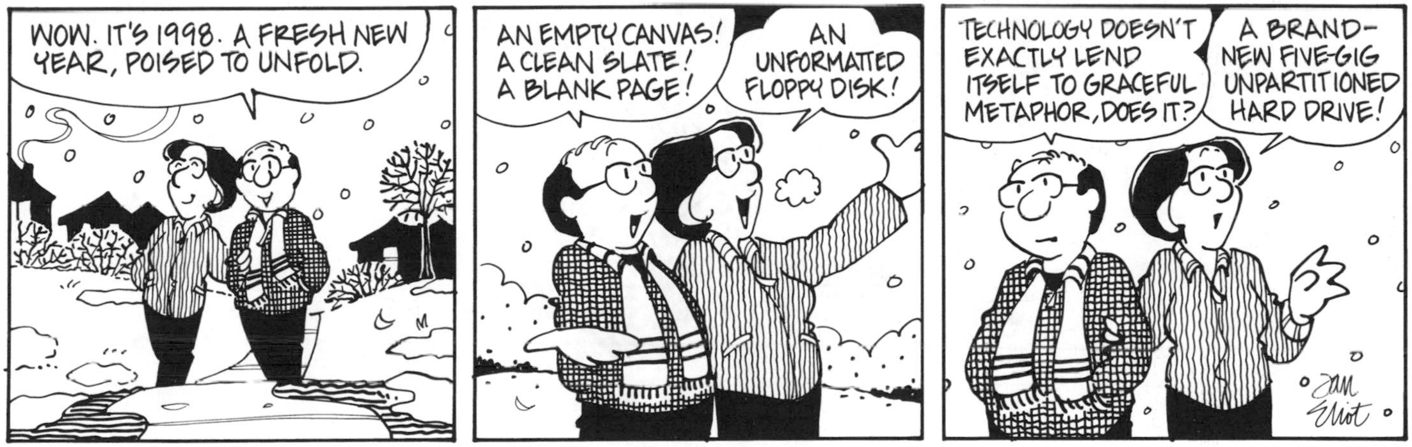
WOW. IT'S 1998. A FRESH NEW YEAR, POISED TO UNFOLD.
AN EMPTY CANVAS! A CLEAN SLATE! A BLANK PAGE!
AN UNFORMATTED FLOPPY DISK!
TECHNOLOGY DOESN'T EXACTLY LEND ITSELF TO GRACEFUL METAPHOR, DOES IT?
A BRAND-NEW FIVE-GIG UNPARTITIONED HARD DRIVE!

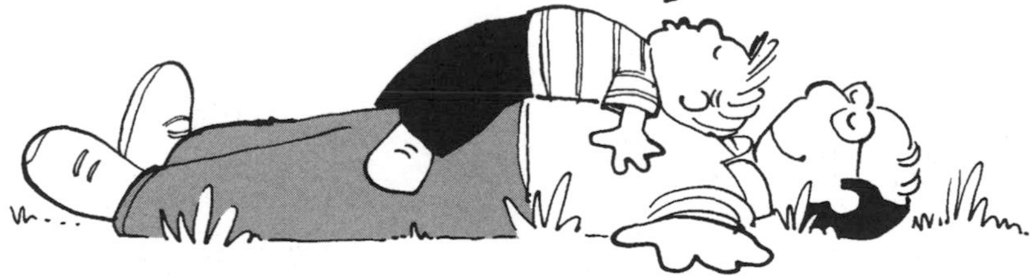
ZZZ

Also by Jan Eliot:

Stone Soup *The First Collection of the Syndicated Cartoon*
from Andrews McMeel Publishing

Both books are available through your local bookstore, or online at www.uexpress.com.

To date, the comic strip *Stone Soup* has been syndicated to newspapers in the U.S., Canada, England, Finland, India, and Micronesia. If your local paper does not carry *Stone Soup*, you can contact the managing editor and tell him or her that you'd like to be able to read *Stone Soup* every day.

Stone Soup can also be read daily online at www.uexpress.com, as well as at the Web sites of subscribing newspapers.